DATE DUE

NO 27 '91			

DEMCO 38-296

Edward R. Ford

The Details of Modern Architecture

Volume 2

1928 to 1988

The MIT Press

Cambridge, Massachusetts

London, England

This book was set in Univers and Trump Mediaeval by Graphic Composition, Inc.
Printed and bound in the United States of America.

Library of Congress Cataloging-in-Publication Data

Ford, Edward R.
  The details of modern architecture, volume 2 : 1928 to 1988 / Edward R. Ford.
    p. cm.
  Bibliography : p.
  Includes index.
  ISBN 0-262-06185-6
  1. Architecture—Details. 2. Architecture, Modern—19th century.
3. Architecture, Modern—20th century. I. Title.
NA2840.F67 1996
724′.5—dc20   89-31772
                                                      CIP

To Presley and Jeanette

Contents

Preface   ix

Abbreviations and Sources   xv

1   **Introduction: The Artifacts of Industrialization**   1

2   **Eliel Saarinen in Detroit: 1926–1940**   23

3   **The Conversion of Erik Gunnar Asplund: 1930–1940**   51

4   **Richard Neutra and the Architecture of Surface: 1933–1952**   87

5   **Alvar Aalto and Marcel Breuer: Light, Industrialization, and the Vernacular, 1928–1963**   117

6   **Le Corbusier after 1928: 1928–1965**   165

7   **Saarinen, Eames, Fuller, and the Case Study Houses: 1940–1959**   217

8   **Eero Saarinen after 1945: 1945–1962**   265

9   **Louis Kahn, Sigurd Lewerentz, and the New Brutalism: 1954–1974**   305

10   **The Venturis, Graves, Scarpa, and the Layers of History: 1963–1984**   349

11   **High Tech, Deconstruction, and the Present Day: 1972–1988**   379

12   **Conclusion**   421

Notes   431

Bibliography   437

Index   441

Preface

An author who works as slowly as myself runs the risk of being overtaken, if not overrun, by history, as seems now to be the case. Much has changed since I began work on the first volume of this series in 1985. The nostalgia for the lost qualities of traditional construction that characterized Postmodernism has been replaced by the more technologically sophisticated and evocative images of Deconstructivism. In 1985 there was a scarcity of books that dealt with constructional properties of major buildings of the twentieth century. Today there are a large number of excellent ones and more on the way.

Much has remained the same. The simplistic notions of good construction that the first book attempted to revise are very much with us. If contemporary architecture has adapted a radically different set of images in the last ten years, it has brought with it the same old prejudices regarding construction: that monolithic construction is good, that layered construction is bad, that anything that is revealed is virtuous, that anything that is concealed is wrong, that good building consists of massive solid load-bearing concrete walls, that bad construction consists of masonry-clad steel frames.

Nevertheless, there seems to be little point in recapitulating the arguments of the first book accompanied by another massive body of evidence. There are as many examples in this volume to illustrate these points as in the last for anyone who wishes to see them, and I have discussed the issue, but for the most part I have focused on a different set of ideas and paradigms, ideas whose formal aspirations may ultimately be for us as inaccessible and remote as those of the Greek temple: those concepts of structural correctness exemplified by the Gothic cathedral, industrialization and its products, and vernacular objects, whether rustic or machine-made.

The focus of this volume is one of structural expression, the mechanisms for achieving it, and the models that exemplified, to Modern architects, its correct application. Much of the Modernist constructional debate has centered around this issue in its various manifestations. Does good construction employ the adequate or the minimal quantity of material? Does good construction manifest substantial or minimal weight? Does good construction seek a perfect level of craftsmanship, or something more rude, vital, rugged, and immediate? International Style and High Tech Modernists were more likely to minimize material and weight while maximizing precision craftsmanship. Those architects who were the adversaries of the International Stylists—the architects of the late Arts and Crafts movement, the New Brutalists, and the other movements that saw virtue in traditional building—were far more likely to reverse this, idealizing maximum material and weight while celebrating a less demanding level of execution. For both schools of thought, paradigms were often more important than the axioms they illustrated, and this story is less a history of ideas than a history of the interpretation of forms, the models whose perfection these architects sought to equal: the twelfth-century Gothic cathedral; its nineteenth-century equivalents, the suspension bridge and the clipper ship; and most importantly those of the twentieth century, the airplane and the automobile.

While I characterized Modernism's idealization of monolithic construction as largely problematic in the first volume, I have to admit a more equivocal assessment of Modernism's obsession with weight, industrialization, and craft. On the one hand it has given us an idealized version of good building that emphasizes certain characteristics—economy of material, minimal weight, and dynamic equilibrium—as virtuous, despite the fact that these characteristics only rarely translate into an economy of capital. On the other hand it is an attitude that has provided Modernism's finest moments. It has provided, as was its intention, a Modern style; it has not provided, as was its intention, a world in which this style could comfortably live.

I have tried to let the designers speak for themselves, in their own words, and to let them defend themselves as well when criticized. Nevertheless I have, perhaps too frequently, injected my own comments and evaluations of the works discussed here, on the theory that it is better to declare one's prejudices outright than to project a nonexistent objectivity. While a theory as to what constitutes good building may be essential to a theory of what constitutes good architecture, it is not sufficient. The validity or invalidity of any system of structural or constructional expression cannot exist in isolation, and one may judge a work to be in some ways constructionally deficient while admiring the whole. I hope it is apparent how much I admire all of the work here presented, that some of those buildings of which I am most critical are among those that I find the most moving, and that some of those architects with whom I most disagree are among those that I most respect. It was not the intent of this book or its predecessor simply to expose the ways in which the construction of Modern architecture has been misrepresented or misunderstood, but rather to get beyond shallow, oversimplified ideas of good building to a deeper understanding of those buildings we admire, which must include a recognition of their shortcomings and failures.

A study of detail is by definition a study in depth, which precludes, to a point, a study in breadth. This is not a comprehensive history of construction or detailing in Modern architecture; it is rather a history of the way fifteen architects dealt with the problem. Particularly when one is dealing with the subject of detail, there is often more to be learned in the study of the development of individuals than in the study of movements whose unity is more stylistic than constructional. I know that some readers will be frustrated that some key Modern buildings have not been included, and will disagree with my choice of others that were. In general I have included those works and the parts of those works that were relevant to the issue at hand, rather than striving for an unobtainable comprehensiveness. At the same time I have included some buildings that fall wide of this mark simply because I felt that they could not be ignored.

Thus I have included Erik Gunnar Asplund's and Eliel Saarinen's post-1930 work, for example, in part because it is far more relevant than their earlier work to the idea of Modernism's response to industrialization, but also because of the scarcity of technological information on their earlier buildings. I have not included some material relevant to the themes of the book as a whole, such as the curtain wall designs of Gordon Bunshaft or what few details exist of Pierre Chareau's Maison de Verre, since they have been so extensively and completely published elsewhere and I have little to add, and because their omission made room for previously unpublished materials of a similar nature, i.e., Asplund and Aalto's similar experiments with light and Eero Saarinen's curtain walls. Some key buildings were omitted because the documentation has been lost or is inaccessible. Other buildings are missing or less comprehensively presented because their authors or the heirs of those authors did not wish them to be included, or placed restrictions on the number of illustrations or the manner in which the work could be discussed. I regret those omissions, those of Mies van der Rohe in particular. I had hoped to include a chapter on his American work, but this had to be withdrawn at the last minute because I could not meet the restrictions placed on the reproduction of his work by the Museum of Modern Art without compromising the quality of the book as a whole.

The original drawings included here are based in every case on the actual working drawings, the numbers and archival locations of which are keyed in the captions. Where possible this information has been confirmed by survey, or if that was impossible by photographs. The drawings are nevertheless subject to uncertainty, which is noted on the drawings or shown with dotted lines. If I was hampered by a scarcity of technical information in the first volume, I have been inundated with massive quantities in the second, which has necessitated some editing. Needless to say a great deal of technical information had to be omitted for editorial reasons or because it could not be graphically described at the scale in question. In these cases I have generally included the technical information relevant to the issue under discussion, while omitting most of the remainder.

While I realize that there are problems resulting from the redrawing of construction drawings in axonometric or other form, I hope that the advantages of doing so are equally apparent. The argument against this practice is that the originals are a better source, that reproduction invites error, and that the artist's vision is in some way being distorted by this process. These points have some validity, but the simple fact remains that the best way to communicate an architectural thought is an architectural drawing, not a paragraph, and that this process has corrected a far greater number of misconceptions than it is likely to have created. Most of the original drawings in question would be only partially legible to the professional in published form and incomprehensible to the novice in any form. It may be that the drawing showing the layout of ductwork at Sigurd Lewerentz's church at Klippan is a work of art, but it is not one that suffers by the process of making it comprehensible to the layman through redrawing.

The first volume left a number of readers with the impression that it was an apology for Classicism and an attack on Modernism. To a degree it was. Classicism was not so indifferent to construction as Modernists would like us to suppose, nor was Modernism so religiously indebted to construction as to have a solely rational reason for its existence. But constructional realities will not align themselves so readily with stylistic prejudices. There is much that is rational about Modernism, and there is certainly much that is constructionally irrational about Classicism and Postmodernism. I should state for the record that, if it is necessary for me to adopt a stylistic label, I am neither Classicist, Postmodernist, nor Deconstructivist, but a Modern architect. Not because I find any of these labels more deficient than the others (and they are all deficient in some way), but because I find the language of Modernism to rich in unexplored possibilities and profound insights to be abandoned due to its numerous failures and difficulties.

There are literally hundreds of employees, consultants, architects, engineers, associated architects, and others who made significant contributions to the buildings presented here. I deeply regret that I am unable to credit them all, for I am sure that in some cases they not only developed but initiated some of the ideas under discussion. Nevertheless an architect, like a film director, bears the ultimate responsibility for the totality of his or her work, and rather than trying to name the individual contributions piecemeal I have in most cases emphasized the principal author. I was unable to interview many of those who worked on the buildings presented here, but I am grateful to the few whom I did. A list of these people is included in the bibliography under the relevant chapters.

The following institutions not only granted me access to their archives and permission to reproduce material in their collections, but provided much guidance as well. The illustrations appear courtesy of: the Alvar Aalto Foundation and Alvar Aalto, Architects, Helsinki; the Archives of American Art of the Smithsonian Institution; the Avery Library, Columbia University, New York; the Buckminster Fuller Institute, Santa Barbara, and Allegra Fuller Snyder; the Busch-Reisinger Museum, Harvard University Art Museums, Cambridge; the Caproni Archive, Rome; the Cranbrook Archives and Historical Collections of the Cranbrook Educational Community, Bloomfield Hills, Michigan; the Museum of Finnish Architecture, Helsinki; the Finnish State Railways, Helsinki; the Fiske Kimball Fine Arts Library of the University of Virginia, Charlottesville; the Fondation Le Corbusier, Paris; the General Motors Corporation, Detroit; the Getty Foundation, Santa Monica; the Henry Ford Museum & Greenfield Village, Dearborn, Michigan; the Hart/Herreshoff Nautical Collections at the MIT Museum, Cambridge; Kevin Roche John Dinkeloo and Associates, Hamden, Connecticut; the Library of Congress, Prints and Photographs Division; the Louis I. Kahn Archive at the University of Pennsylvania and the Pennsylvania Historical and Museum Commission, Philadelphia; the Massachusetts Institute of Technology, Cambridge; the Musée d'Art Moderne de la Ville de Paris; the Musée de l'Air et de l'Espace, Le Bourget; the Museum of the City of New York; the National Air and Space Museum of the Smithsonian Institution; the Rosenfeld Collection of the Mystic Seaport Museum, Inc., Mystic, Connecticut; the Salk Institute for Biological Studies, La Jolla, California; Smith, Hinchman & Grylls, Inc., Detroit; the Swedish Architecture Museum, Stockholm; the George Arents Research Library for Special Collections at Syracuse University; the Neutra Papers at the UCLA Library, Department of Special Collections, Los Angeles, and Dion Neutra, architect; and Yale University, New Haven.

I would like to thank Elissa Aalto, Herbert Beckhard, Constance Breuer, Lucia Eames Demetrios, Dion Neutra, Kevin Roche, and Allegra Fuller Snyder who allowed me to reproduce material to which they hold the copyrights, and the following offices who donated photographs, drawings, information, and time: Coop Himmelblau; Ray Eames and the Eames Office; Sir Norman Foster and Partners; Frank O. Gehry & Associates; Michael Graves, Architect; Josef Paul Kleihues, Architect; Pierre Koenig, Architect; Morphosis Architects; Glenn Murcutt & Associates; Jean Nouvel, Architect; the Renzo Piano Building Workshop; the Richard Rogers Partnership; Paul Rudolph, Architect; Bernard Tschumi, Architect; James Stirling, Michael Wilford and Associates; Venturi, Scott Brown and Associates; and Vilhelm Wohlert, Architect.

A number of individuals provided advice, guidance, information, and photographs, including: Gregg Bleam, Mark Coir, Jonathan Fabian, Mitch Glass, Peter MacKeith, George Moon, Richard Murphy, Christian Overland, Peter Papademetriou, Terry Smith, Max Underwood, Robert Vickery, Andrew Watts, William Wischmeyer, and all my colleagues at the University of Virginia. Kirk Martini and Lotta Löfgren helped with the translations; Eric White, Erich Wefing, and Maureen Zell assisted with the drawings. I must also thank my wife Jane, my son James, and Schaeffer Somers for help with the manuscript, in addition to their patience with this long enterprise. I would also like to thank all of the staff at the MIT Press for their contributions, support, assistance, and perseverance.

I have received major financial help from:

The National Endowment for the Arts,
The Graham Foundation for Advanced Studies in the Fine Arts, and
The Dean's Forum of The University of Virginia,

whose assistance not only made the book possible but greatly enhanced the quality and quantity of material presented.

Charlottesville, Virginia
March 1995

A NOTE REGARDING THE DRAWINGS

I am happy that the first volume has appeared as often in architectural offices as in academic libraries, but I must remind the reader that neither that book nor this one is a pattern book or a comprehensive technical guide for architectural practice. A great deal of technical information on the details illustrated has not been described or has been only partially described. Many of the details conform to practices no longer followed and to standards that today are considered inadequate. The aim is to inspire, not to facilitate imitation, and the wholesale lifting of details from this book unaltered is an invitation to technical difficulty.

Abbreviations and Sources

BN	Box number
DN	Drawing number, used with uncatalogued drawings
UND	Unnumbered drawing
UCM	Uncatalogued material
oc	On center
2 × 4	Nominal size of wood structural member in inches (the actual size is usually a fraction of an inch smaller)
4″ brick	The nominal size of a masonry unit in inches (in American common brick the actual size is ⅜ inch smaller)
	When all the dimensions of an element are in the same units, the unit designation is omitted from all but the last number. Hence 3 × 8″ is the equivalent of 3″ × 8.″

ARCHIVES

AAA	Alvar Aalto Foundation and Archive
ARL/SU	Arents Research Library, Syracuse University
BFI/AF	Buckminster Fuller Institute/Allegra Fuller Snyder
CBA	Cranbook Archives
FLC	Fondation Le Corbusier
KRJD&A	Kevin Roche John Dinkeloo and Associates (Eero Saarinen Archive)
LK/UP	Louis I. Kahn Collection, University of Pennsylvania and Pennsylvania Historical Museum Commission
LOC	Library of Congress, Prints and Photographs Division
NASM	National Air and Space Museum, Smithsonian Institution
SAM	Swedish Architecture Museum
UCLA/DN	UCLA Special Collections/Dion Neutra
YU	Yale University

OFFICES

BT	Bernard Tschumi, Architect
CH	Coop Himmelblau
FG	Frank O. Gehry & Associates
GMA	Glenn Murcutt & Associates
MG	Michael Graves, Architect
NF	Sir Norman Foster and Partners
PK	Pierre Koenig, Architect
PR	Paul Rudolph, Architect
RP	Renzo Piano Building Workshop
RR	Richard Rogers Partnership
SHG	Smith Hinchman & Grylls, Inc.
SW	James Stirling and Michael Wilford
VSBA	Venturi, Scott Brown and Associates

PERIODICALS

AAR	Arts and Architecture
AF	Architectural Forum
AJ	Architects Journal
AMA	American Architect and Architecture
AR	Architectural Record
B+W	Bauen + Wohnen
JA	Japan Architect
LAV	L'Architecture Vivante
LHA	L'Homme et Architecture

Periodical titles are followed by month, month plus day, or issue number and year.

BOOKS

CSH	Esther McCoy, *The Case Study Houses: 1945–1962* (Los Angeles: Hennessey & Ingalls, 1977)
NA	Alfred Roth, *The New Architecture* (Zurich: Artemis, 1975)
OC	Le Corbusier, *Oeuvre complète*, 8 vols. (Zurich: Girsberger, 1930–1970)

The Details of Modern Architecture

1   Introduction: The Artifacts of Industrialization

THE CATHEDRAL

On a Saturday evening in 1887 the study class of the All Souls Unitarian Church of Chicago presented a costume ball featuring characters from Victor Hugo's *Les Misérables*. Appearing in the minor role of a French army officer was a new member of the congregation, Frank Lloyd Wright, age twenty. The event is significant for what happened that evening—Wright met Catherine Tobin, who would become his first wife—and for what happened the next day. Wright, with Victor Hugo on his mind, stopped by the church library on his way to the service and picked up a copy of *Notre-Dame de Paris*, and, rather than attending the service, read chapter 2 of book V, "The Book Will Kill the Edifice."

Wright called this chapter "one of the truly great things written on architecture" and said, "It taught me the difference between romanticism and sentimentality." Wright's first reading of *Notre-Dame* had been as a boy of sixteen in Spring Green, Wisconsin. Not long after, as a student at the University of Wisconsin, he first encountered the work of Eugène-Emmanuel Viollet-le-Duc, the restorer of Notre-Dame, but more importantly the author of the *Entretiens sur l'architecture*. Wright later said of this book: "Here you find everything you need to know of architecture." [1]

Although there is nothing in Wright's work stylistically, structurally, or programmatically resembling Notre-Dame or any other Gothic building, the Gothic cathedral, particularly the classic French cathedrals of the twelfth century, embodied for him the principles of what good architecture and building ought to be, and Viollet-le-Duc was the guide to what these principles were.

In 1884 Auguste Perret, age ten, browsing in his father's library, discovered Viollet-le-Duc's *Dictionnaire raisonné*. As with Wright, the decision to become an architect had already been made for him, and although he was to go on to study at the Neoclassical École des Beaux-Arts and then on to a successful career as a Classical Modernist, he retained throughout his life a reverence for the Gothic cathedral and for Viollet-le-Duc. He said later: "Viollet-le-Duc was my real master . . . it was he who enabled me to resist the influence of the École des Beaux-Arts." [2]

On August 1, 1908, Charles Jeanneret (later to become Le Corbusier) received his first paycheck from his first employer in Paris, Auguste Perret, with which he purchased the ten volumes of Viollet-le-Duc's *Dictionnaire*, probably at Perret's suggestion. Unlike Wright or Perret, Le Corbusier left no testimonial to Viollet-le-Duc in later life, but his copy, particularly the section on the construction of Gothic cathedrals, is marked with his comments.[3]

As with Wright, there is little in Le Corbusier that can be directly associated with the Gothic cathedral, and only one or two buildings in all of Perret's work. Clearly for all three men the cathedral illustrated not a style that ought to be imitated but principles that ought to be observed.

If Notre-Dame was a model not of forms but of principles, what were the principles? To Victor Hugo the cathedral was "a gigantic book in stone . . . speaking of liberty, the people, man," but to the professional critics there was no real consensus of what the building meant. Take for example the views of Perret's intellectual master, Viollet-le-Duc, and those of Perret's academic master at the École, Julien Guadet. To Guadet the west front represented the model of good composition and construction: "no accident, no inclemency, no passage of time seems to destroy or compromise this ensemble so well planted, so strong in its proportions."[4] Viollet-le-Duc by contrast thought the front too heavy without its planned but unbuilt towers: "While the front of Notre Dame de Paris in its present condition is very beautiful, it must nevertheless be admitted that everything has been so admirably arranged for carrying the eye up to the stone spires, that their absence is to be regretted. There is a superfluous strength in the construction of the towers, since they support nothing."[5]

But the disagreement went beyond the issue of whether the building contained the appropriate or excessive quantity of material. To Viollet-le-Duc the lessons of Notre-Dame were to be seen in its sides and rear, in the assembly of vaults and flying buttresses, for this demonstrated the chief virtues of the Gothic. First of all, economy: "Today we have gotten into the habit of using hulking, enormous masses of stone in constructions that are themselves of minor importance; we have gotten into the habit, in other words, of putting in place structures with ten times the resistance that is necessary. . . . We would expend fabulous sums in order to equal what in the twelfth century builders were able to accomplish with comparatively minimal resources."[6] Secondly, the means by which this was accomplished, equilibrium: "These structures were subject to oblique pressures, and hence the law of the equilibrium of forces is what governed them, in place of the old Roman law of inert stability; it was also essential that all their members enjoy a certain elasticity. . . . They had adopted a system of construction where every force in play was an active force; where inert resistances acting through compact masses were simply nonexistent."[7]

These virtues were not self-evident to a Classicist like Guadet, who, by contrast, found the rear of Notre-Dame admirable but disturbing. However clever and well engineered, it did not and could not represent good building, precisely because of its state of precarious equilibrium: "The mind wonders what would occur if a shock, a crushed stone, should jeopardize this astonishing equilibrium; astonishing, but one ought to say artificial and precarious in comparison with the marvelous main facade."[8]

These two issues—what constituted an appropriate economy of material and the importance of achieving a stability that was not only real but perceptible—transcended the Classic-Gothic stylistic debate.

To Viollet-le-Duc the best building was that which accomplished the most with the least. The structure of a cathedral utilized the structural capacity of stone, in fact its inability to take tensile stresses, to enclose the largest space and attain the greatest height with the minimum quantity of material. The means for doing so were to transcend the simple post and lintel system of the Greeks and the massive castings of the Romans to achieve a delicate equilibrium in which every thrust was met with a counter thrust, in which every stone played a critical part, so that its removal would threaten the stability of the whole.

To Guadet architecture was the construction of institutions. Its aim was not only to achieve but to convey stability, the solidity and permanence of the bank, the city hall, or the church. Architecture should communicate permanence and repose. If this required more material, this was a small price to pay. The precarious assembly of vault and flying buttress of the Gothic cathedral, however clever, not only lacked repose but, by its very nature, lacked the reassurance that architecture should possess. Although the cathedral evoked wonder at its dynamic equilibrium, this was not a quality that good architecture ought to overtly display. The assembly of vaults, buttresses, and piers may inspire astonishment and admiration, but not confidence and serenity. William Morris wrote of Amiens:

There is no mystery here, and indeed no repose. Like the age which projected it, like the impulsive communal movement which was here its motive, the Pointed style at Amiens is full of excitement. Go, for repose, to classic work, with the simple vertical law of pressure downwards, or to its Lombard, Rhenish, or Norman derivatives. Here, rather, you are conscious restlessly of that sustained equilibrium of oblique pressure on all sides, which is the essence of the hazardous Gothic construction, a construction of which the "flying buttress" is the most significant feature.[9]

The cathedral achieved style through economy of means, through the nature of the material, but it was an unsettling nature that was thus revealed. If the vault emphasized the unique structural nature of the stone, it did so by endowing the stone with precisely those visual qualities that it did not inherently possess: lightness and thinness. The nineteenth-century observer (and the twentieth as well) would have no difficulty drawing a line between the Gothic sculptor and the Gothic architect. The sculptor's task was to make stone appear as flowers or as human flesh, to make stone suggest those qualities—softness, lightness, warmth— that it does not possess. It was the Gothic architect's job to do the opposite, to look deep into the nature of stone and bring out its inherent qualities, but the results were not dissimilar; making manifest the structural properties of the stone resulted in forms that denied rather than affirmed its mass and brittleness. One might convincingly argue that the Great Pyramid is a more accurate architectural rendering of the nature of stone, but the exemplary status of the Gothic cathedral persisted, and the cathedral came to illustrate another principle: that the correct architectural form was inherent "in the nature of the material."

Ultimately of course it was Viollet-le-Duc's ideas that were to prevail in Modernism, not those of Guadet (it should be pointed out that both Viollet-le-Duc's theories and his restorations of Gothic buildings have since been shown to be wildly inaccurate, but this is something of which Wright, Perret, and Le Corbusier were unaware at the time), and the principles of economy of material and equilibrium became primary tenets of Modernism. But there were other, more subtle lessons to be found in the cathedral that were equally important to Modernism: firstly the perception of buildings as composed of a frame or skeleton and skin and secondly the idea that, despite the interdependence of parts, the function of each should be clearly expressed. Viollet-le-Duc wrote in the *Entretiens*:

If the vaults are divided by ribs, it is because these ribs are so many sinews performing a function. Each vertical support depends for its stability on being stayed and weighted; every arch-thrust meets another which counteracts it. Walls, as supports, no longer appear: they have become mere enclosures. The entire system consists of a framework which maintains itself, not by its mass, but by the combination of oblique forces neutralising each other. The vault ceases to be a crust— a shell in one piece; it is an ingenious combination of pressures which are really in action and are directed on certain points of support disposed so as to receive them and transmit them to the ground.[10]

These are principles that might as easily have been articulated by a Classicist, but Viollet-le-Duc's reason for stating them were clear, for the idea of the frame and the idea of articulating the function and identity of each member of the frame were the key to translating twelfth-century principles into nineteenth-century construction, and it was obvious, even in 1872 when the second volume of the *Entretiens* was published, that the mechanism for doing this was iron.

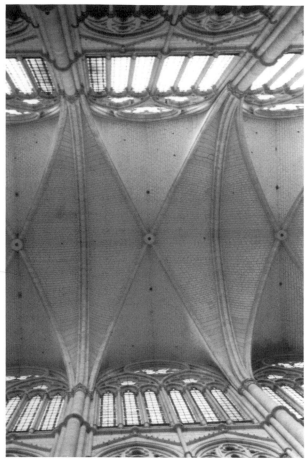

1.1

1.2

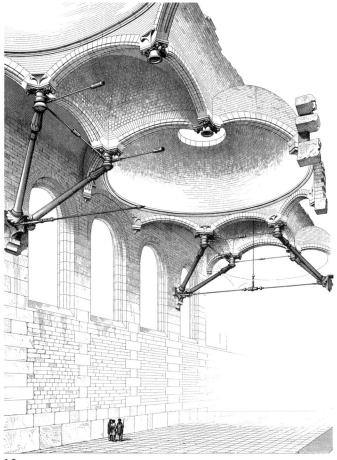

1.3

1.4

Amiens Cathedral
Amiens, France, 1222–1288

1.1   **Vault.**

1.2   **Flying buttresses.**

1.3   **Eugène-Emmanuel Viollet-le-Duc,**
masonry and iron construction,
from *Entretiens sur l'architecture.*

1.4   **John and Washington Roebling,**
Brooklyn Bridge under construction,
1881.
*(Museum of the City of New York, Gift of
the Essex Institute)*

In that book Viollet-le-Duc presented a series of projects for buildings that incorporated iron and stone into hybrid structures. They are notable in that they take pains to avoid the most typical method of using iron or steel, as a frame encased in another material, usually masonry, in part because of his erroneous belief that trouble would arise from the different coefficients of thermal expansion of iron and the surrounding material: "When, therefore, we would build masonry vaulting on iron, the latter should retain its liberty of movement and be able to expand without rending the concrete envelope which it supports. The fastenings should remain visible—clearly seen—so that, should any part give way, it may be promptly repaired." [11] The technical correctness of this solution was born out by analogy with the skeletal nature of Gothic construction: "Whenever an attempt has been made to mingle the two systems, mischief has resulted in the shape of dislocations and unequal settlements. In this particular, a close examination of our great medieval French buildings will supply us with a useful precedent, for in these edifices the frame (that is, the piers, arches, vaulting, buttresses, and flying-buttresses) is independent of the enclosure." [12]

While the problems of buildings such as Soufflot's Panthéon confirm this analysis, it is an idea that, if carried to its logical conclusion, would have precluded the use of reinforced concrete. But Viollet-le-Duc's reason for maintaining iron and stone as independent entities went well beyond technical expediency and a conceptual resemblance to twelfth-century Gothic. It was a method that allowed the iron to seek its own form, to find its own nature. He wrote of one of his own designs: "Objection might be made to the thinness of the forms proper to metal. This aspect of meagerness is in fact very unpleasing when the iron-work is placed in a position of competition,—when it is mixed up, as it were, with architectural stone-work. No such effect is produced when the iron is not put in competition with the architectural forms proper to stone-work." [13]

If the key to architectural character lay in the nature of materials, each material must have its own form, and if equilibrium was the highest form of architectural structure then it must consist of different forms of different materials, set in structural opposition to one another. This would be the key to the new architecture:

If, as remarked before, iron is destined in our modern buildings only to serve as a security for imperfect masonry, or to disguise its presence beneath parasitical castings, it would be as well for us to let it alone, and to build as they used to build in the time of Louis the Fourteenth, taking forms borrowed from a doubtful antiquity and overloading them with a hybrid ornamentation. But if iron is prescribed, *not* proscribed, *be it understood,—we should try to find forms suitable to its properties and manufacture; we ought not to disguise it, but seek for those forms until we have found them.* [14]

THE BRIDGE

Viollet-le-Duc had no more dedicated a reader than the American critic Montgomery Schuyler, and this is perhaps why Schuyler found the completion of the bridge built to connect Brooklyn and Manhattan in 1883 to be the answer to the question "What is the Modern style?" He wrote in *Harper's Weekly* the same year:

It is not unimaginable that [a] future archaeologist, looking from one of these towers upon the solitude of a mastless river and a dispeopled land, may have no other means of reconstructing our civilization than that which is furnished him by the tower on which he stands. What will his judgment of us be?

The most strictly scientific of constructors would scarcely take the ground that he did not care how his work looked, when his work was so conspicuous and so durable as the Brooklyn Bridge. . . . Architecture is to him the unintelligent use of building material. Assuredly this view is born out by a majority of the "architecturesque" buildings that he sees, and he does not lack express authority for it. Whereas the engineer's definition of good masony is "the least material to perform a certain duty," Mr. Fergusson declares that "an architect ought always to allow himself such a margin of strength that he may disregard or play with his construction;" and Mr. Ruskin defines architecture to be the addition to a building of unnecessary features. An engineer has, therefore, some warrant for considering that he is sacrificing to the graces and doing all that can be reasonably expected of him to produce an architectural monument, if in designing the piers of a chain-bridge he employs an unnecessary amount of material and adds unnecessary features. But if we go back to the time when engineers were artists, and study what a modern scientific writer had described as "that paragon of constructive skill, a Pointed cathedral," we shall find that the architecture and the construction cannot be disjointed.[15]

It is easy to see why Schuyler found the bridge so appealing and so like a cathedral, as it met so many of Viollet-le-Duc's criteria. The maximum span is achieved with the minimum of materials. The masonry and the steel structures were separated; each took the form appropriate to its structural nature, creating an assembly in which the compressive stresses in the masonry counteracted the tensile stresses in the steel. It achieved the same kind of equilibrium as a cathedral, one that did not rely on inherent mass but on the appropriate arrangement of forces, and of course it achieved a maximum economy of material.

The connection that Schuyler saw between the cathedral and the bridge goes beyond principle to formal similarities, and he takes Roebling to task for the weak design of the towers, suggesting that he should look to Amiens or Rhiems for guidance, and adding: "What can we say but that the designer of the cathedral began where the designer of the bridge left off?"[16] To many architects, of course, style was not the result of the economical use of material, whether stone or steel. Schuyler mentions Fergusson and Ruskin as dissenters; he could have thrown in Julien Guadet and Geoffrey Scott, but the group included a number of "Modern" architects as well. Charles Rennie Mackintosh wrote:

Iron & glass though eminently suitable for many purposes will never worthily take the place of stone, because of this defect the want of mass. . . . Now we can pile up the hugest buildings with the least possible means of support, and that on most economical principles as design can be turned out of the foundry by repetition without limit, to the minimising of intellectual labor and so also to the payment of it. But time has passed, and practical experience has shown that apart altogether from any defect in stability or actual comfort the want of appearance of stability is fatal to the introduction of such a style for either domestic, civil or ecclesiastical buildings. These demand actual mass even if of a weaker material taking bulk for bulk.[17]

Nevertheless the suspension bridge became, along with the cathedral, a model for many artists and architects of what the Modern style ought to be. The Russian Constructivist Vladimir Mayakovsky wrote in 1925:

the masts
            passing under the bridge
looked
       no larger than pins.
I am proud
          of just this
                    mile of steel;
upon it,
         my visions come to life, erect—
here's a fight
             for construction
                             instead of style,
an austere disposition
                  of bolts
                          and steel.

. . . .

This rib
      reminds us
                  of a machine—
just imagine,
            would there be hands enough,
after planting
            a steel foot
                  in Manhattan,
to yank
      Brooklyn to oneself
                  by the lip?
By the cables
            of electric strands,
I recognize
         the era succeeding
                  the steam age—
here
   men
         had ranted
                  on radio.
Here
   men
         had ascended
                  in planes.[18]

Erik Gunnar Asplund said that the bridge was "a work of engineering which—in my opinion—stands on a pinnacle with the best works of architecture. Static clarity, rhythm, beauty of line." Le Corbusier, in contrast to Schuyler, liked the towers, saying that they were "very handsome because they are *American* and not 'Beaux-Arts.' They are full of native sap and they are not graceful, but strong."[19]

The suspension bridge was to many Modernists an answer to a seemingly unanswerable question. What is the proper style of the nineteenth century? The way to escape from the styles was to achieve style, the way to style was through character, the way to character was through economy, and the way to economy was through truth: through the nature of the material. The bridge was, however, only the first of many such models.

THE SHIP
While Schuyler kept his eye on the bridge, Mayakovsky (and Hart Crane as well) could not talk about the bridge without talking about the ships passing below. There was for them a natural formal affinity between the cable and tower structure of the bridge and the rope and mast construction of the ship. To the colder eye the ship revealed the same principles at work. Rope in tension, mast in compression, along with the contrasting beauty of the sail, resisting the pressure of air while the hull resisted the pressure of water. Horatio Greenough had written:

Observe a ship at sea! Mark the majestic form of her hull as she rushes through the water, observe the graceful bend of her body, the gentle transition from round to flat, the grasp of her keel, the leap of her bows, the symmetry and rich tracery of her spars and rigging, and those grand wind muscles, her sails. Behold an organization second only to that of an animal, obedient as the horse, swift as the stag, and bearing the burden of a thousand camels from pole to pole! . . . Could we carry into our civil architecture the responsibilities that weigh upon our shipbuilding, we should ere long have edifices as superior to the parthenon, for the purposes that we require, as the Constitution *or the* Pennsylvania *is to the galley of the Argonauts. Could our blunders on terra firma be put to the same dread test that those of shipbuilders are, little would be now left to say on this subject.*[20]

If Greenough could see the principles of good building within the ship, many of his contemporaries could just as easily see the converse, the principle of the ship in the cathedral. William Morris wrote: "From the flagstone at one's foot to the dis-

1.5

1.6

Farman Goliath, F-60

Henri Farman

1919

1.5 **View.**
(National Air and Space Museum, Smithsonian Institution, SI Neg. No. 86-13488)

1.6 **Tail section under construction.**
(National Air and Space Museum, Smithsonian Institution, SI Neg. No. 87-11274)

tant keystone of the *chevet*, noblest of its species—reminding you of how many largely graceful things, sails of a ship in the wind, and the like! . . . The astonishing boldness of the vault, the astonishing lightness of what keeps it above one; . . . Those who built it might have had for their one and only purpose to enclose as large a space as possible with the given material."[21] And his disciple, William Lethaby, wrote in *Architecture:* "From another point of view a Gothic cathedral may be compared to a great cargo-ship which has to attain a balance between speed and safety. The church and the ship were both designed in the same way by a slow perfecting of parts; all was effort acting on custom, beauty was mastery, fitness, size with economy of material. Originality was insight for the essential and the inevitable."[22]

If the ship and the bridge were designed on the same principles as the cathedral, then they must necessarily manifest the same dynamic equilibrium while also lacking repose. Lethaby wrote:

Yet, as the ship beneath the bunting was a balanced structure of wood, and as the effort was always to get the utmost result from given means, so the great cathedral was a balanced structure of stone which found its perfected form at the limits where men could do no more. Thus it was that a cathedral was not designed, but discovered, or "revealed." Indeed building has been found out—like speech, writing, the use of metals—hence a noble structure is not a thing of will, of design, of scholarship. A true architecture is the discovery of the nature of things in building, a continuous development along some line of direction imposed by needs, desires, and traditions.[23]

Many Modernists were not comfortable even discussing this issue. The idea that different structural techniques could lead to certain compositional techniques and thus evoke different reactions seemed to suggest that stylistic prejudice was at work rather than cool reason. Many, while acknowledging that modern artifacts obeyed different compositional rules, insisted that these were unique to the modern era, and unrelated to twelfth-century problems in statics.

THE PLANE

The cathedral and the bridge may have given Modern architecture its philosophy, but it was the airplane that gave it poetry. The former may have provided its logic, but its forms came from elsewhere—from the Farman Goliath, the Caproni triplane, the Junkers F-13. Le Corbusier wrote: "The airplane is the symbol of the new age. At the apex of the immense pyramid of mechanical progress it opens the *New Age*, it wings its way into it."[24]

Being poetic, the lessons of the airplane were more elusive than those of the cathedral. It was not that the model of the airplane did not yield up principles and forms (it did in abundance); it was that the model under analysis continued to evolve.

All the planes illustrated in Le Corbusier's *Vers une architecture*, like most pre-1920 planes, are not sheet metal but canvas, wood, and wire. They not only use materials similar to those of the suspension bridge and the clipper ship, but use them in the same way—the canvas as a suspended membrane, the wood as compressive struts, and the wire cables in tension. They conform to the same concept of material. Each material has its own unique form, each form utilizes that material in its best and highest structural capacity, and each is set in formal opposition to other dissimilar materials. Perhaps this type of plane was the image in Le Corbusier's mind while he wrote in *Aircraft:*

The aluminum framework of an airplane—search for economy of material, for lightness, always the fundamental, the essential law of nature.

Similarly the marrow of our bones, the same fibers "of equal resistance" exist. . . .

The schools of the 19th century destroyed the "human scale" and destroyed "respect for material."

The airplane, on the other hand, embodies the purest expression of the human scale and a miraculous exploitation of material. . . .

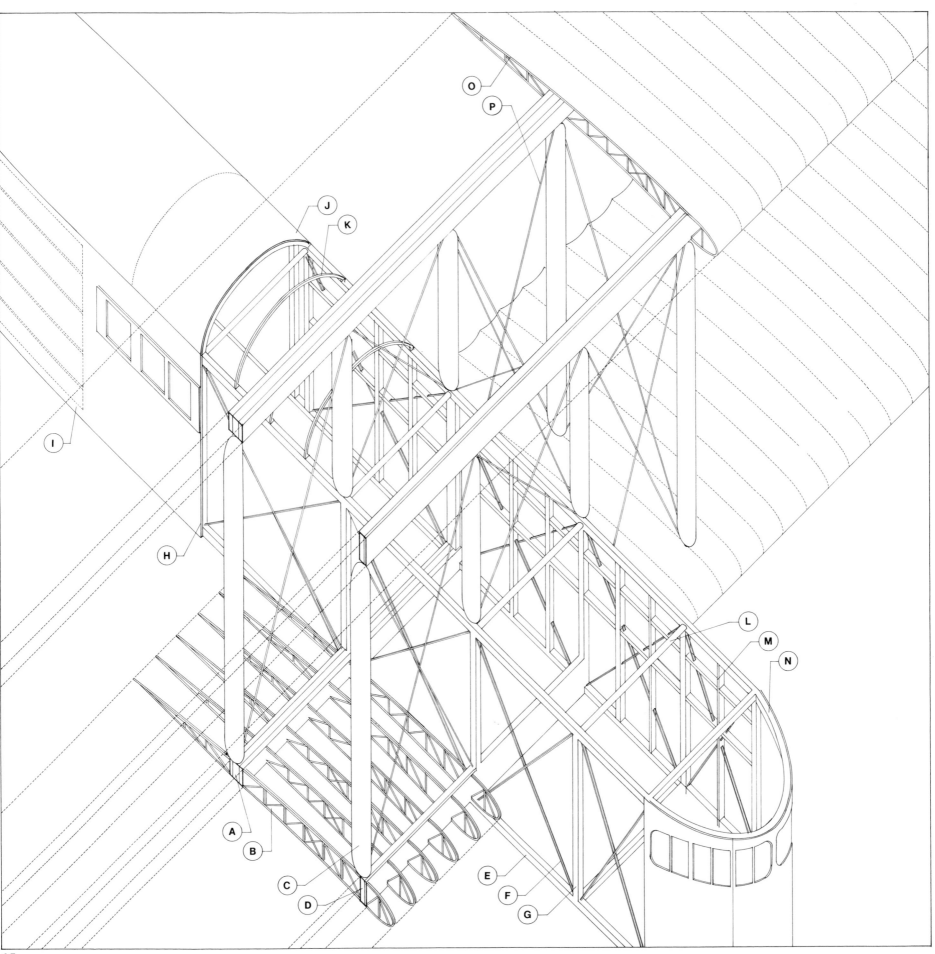

1.7

Farman Goliath, F-60

Henri Farman

1919

1.7   **Structure** (canvas and wood covering partially shown).

A   Wood spar.

B   Trussed rib airfoil sections to support canvas covering. Unlike in most planes of the time, these have an identical cross section.

C   Wing struts. Since these are exposed, they are aerodynamically shaped. This strut in reality is interrupted by the engine, but is shown complete for clarity.

D   Wood spar structurally connecting wing and fuselage.

E   Wood longerons.

F   Steel cables diagonally bracing the fuselage so that it behaves like a truss. The two wings are also tied together to form a truss.

G   Vertical truss member connecting top and bottom wing spars.

H   Plywood covering the cabin and cockpit. Earlier models covered this portion with canvas.

I   Canvas on wood strips on rear portion of fuselage. Unlike in later planes, the structural frame is self-supporting without the covering.

J   Roof.

K   Curved wood ribs to support roof.

L   Steel pipe brace.

M   Intermediate supports for plywood facing.

N   Nose framing.

O   Truss rib of upper wing.

P   Steel cable wing bracing.
(NASM, based on the Air Union F-HMFU
Île-de-France in the Musée de l'Air et de
l'Espace)

The head of the workshop is in touch with life, in the middle of his machines and materials. The materials are around him, under his hand—hard or soft, brittle or elastic, fibrous or crystalline, thick or thin, heavy or light, their characteristic properties constantly demonstrated by the way in which they repel or combine.

The workmen are constantly thinking about materials. The drawing and the plan by which these materials will be set to work is only a shorthand note of their intrinsic character.[25]

This early skin and bones type of airplane reinforced all the Gothic Revival concepts of building in the same way as did the bridge, car, and clipper ship, as well as giving it an anthropomorphic connection. As bones are in compression, as muscles are in tension, so are the mast of a ship and its ropes, so are the tower of the bridge and its cables, so are the struts of the plane and its guy wires. It sealed the superiority of the principle of lightness and material economy over stability and firmness. A passenger afraid of flying will not be reassured by a heavier airplane.

THE CAR

If there was any resistance in hard-core Modernism to the doctrine of economy of material, it was swept away by the other objects that joined the bridge and the ship as paragons of Modern design: the automobile and the airplane. Economy of materials is also minimum weight, and strength per unit weight is the primary design characteristic of any vehicle. The appearance of permanence and stability is rarely a criterion in automobile design, and if buildings were to be designed and built like cars, it would not be a criterion in architecture. This philosophy was articulated in 1922 by an unlikely theoretician of Modern architecture, Henry Ford:

For some clumsy reason we have come to confuse strength with weight. The crude methods of early building undoubtedly had something to do with this. The old ox-cart weighed a ton—and it had so much excess weight that it was weak! To carry a few tons of humanity from New York to Chicago, the railroad builds a train that weighs many hundred tons, and the result is an absolute loss of real strength and the extravagant waste of untold millions in the form of power. The law of diminishing returns begins to operate at the point where strength becomes weight. Weight may be desirable in a steam roller but nowhere else. Strength has nothing to do with weight. The mentality of the man who does things in the world is agile, light and strong. The most beautiful things in the world are those from which all excess weight has been eliminated. Strength is never just weight—either in men or things.[26]

Material efficiency played its part in this philosophy, but more important was standardization. Ford said in 1903: "The way to make automobiles is to make one automobile like another automobile, to make them all alike, to make them come through the factory just alike; just as one pin is like another pin when it comes from a pin factory, or one match is like another match when it comes from a match factory."[27]

Figure 1.12, a publicity photograph taken in August 1913 outside the plant in Highland Park designed for Ford by Albert Kahn, shows over 1,000 cars, one-third of one day's production of Model Ts. Like pins and matches, they are all alike. All are black, all have brass radiators, all have identical engines, transmissions, and brakes. This was the end product of the principle of mass production that Charles Sorensen, Ford's engineer, described as "machine-produced interchangeable parts and orderly flow of those parts first to subassembly, then to final assembly,"[28] a single, standardized, typological product—not a luxury car, not an economy car, not a sports car, a subcompact or compact, but a single simple car, perfected over time, serving the needs of all, free of stylistic convention and at the lowest possible cost due to production in quantity.

To an influential group of architects these principles seemed a magical answer to a stylistic dilemma. The Modernist architect, preparing to discard the types and standards of old—the orders of Vignola and Palladio, the types of Durand—could readily find comfort in presuming to discover the modern equivalents of orders and types through the science of mass production. Walter Gropius wrote in 1935:

1.8

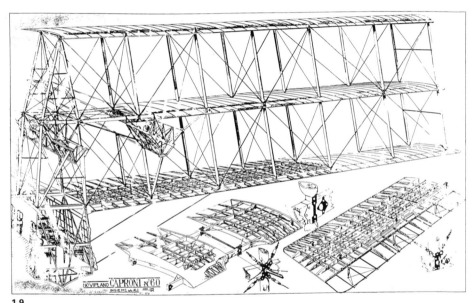

1.9

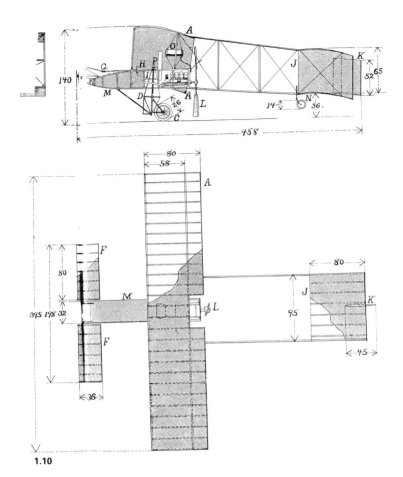

1.10

1.11

Gianni Caproni

Caproni Hydroplane CA-60

1921

1.8 **View.** This is the photo used in Le Corbusier's *Vers une architecture.* (National Air and Space Museum, Smithsonian Institution, SI Neg. No. A 1017)

1.9 **Construction.** The plane made one unsuccessful flight before crashing into Lago Maggiore. (Caproni Archive)

1.10 **Henri Farman's Voisin.** (Victor Lougheed, Vehicles of the Air)

1.11 **Robert Delaunay,** L'Équipe de Cardiff, third representation, 1912-1913. Farman's Voisin is visible at top center, with the Eiffel Tower behind. (Musée de la Ville de Paris, © SPADEM)

"Standardization is not an impediment to the development of civilization, but, on the contrary one of its immediate prerequisites. A standard may be defined as that simplified practical exemplar of anything in general use which embodies a fusion of the best of its anterior forms—a fusion preceded by the elimination of the personal content of their designers and all otherwise ungeneric or non-essential features."[29]

The model of the car explains some of Modernism's technical obsessions, particularly "dry" construction and precision construction, as these were the techniques of automobile production. Gropius wrote:

Dry assembly offers the best prospects because (to take only one of its advantages) moisture in one form or another is the principal obstacle to economy in masonry or brick construction (mortar joints). Moisture is the direct cause of most of the weaknesses of the old methods of building. It leads to badly fitting joints, warping and staining, unforeseen piecework and serious loss of time and money through delays in drying. By eliminating this factor, and so assuring the perfect interlocking of all component parts, the pre-fabricated house makes it possible to guarantee a fixed price and a definite period of construction. Moreover the use of reliable modern materials enables the stability and insulation of a building to be increased and its weight and bulk decreased.[30]

Le Corbusier was a better known if ultimately less dogmatic convert to standardization than Gropius, and he became for a time its primary apostle. Le Corbusier was not to visit a Ford factory until 1935, when he toured the plant at River Rouge. It was not a voyage of discovery but of confirmation:

I come out of the Ford factories at Detroit. As an architect, I am plunged into a kind of stupor. When I take less than a thousand dollars to a building lot I cannot get even a single room built! Here, for the same money, you can buy a Ford car. The Ford of today combines the most useful automotive developments. All of those mechanical marvels are yours for less than a thousand dollars! On a building lot men work with axes, picks, hammers; they saw, they plane, they work things out well or badly. On one side barbarism, on the other—here at the Ford plant—modern times. . . .

That evening I speak at Cranbrook Academy.

—"This is the dramatic conflict which is strangling architecture, which causes 'building' to remain off the roads of progress. In the Ford factory, everything is collaboration, unity of views, unity of purpose, a perfect convergence of the totality of gestures and ideas. With us, in building, there is nothing but contradictions, hostilities, dispersion, divergence of views, affirmation of opposed purposes, pawing the ground."[31]

That Le Corbusier saw the Rouge Plant as a demonstration of "unity of views, unity of purpose" is a testament to the power of preconceived opinion to shape perception, or the power of the translation of language to distort facts. In 1932, three years before Le Corbusier's visit, four people had been killed in a labor dispute outside the Rouge Plant. In 1937, two years after his visit, Ford security guards attacked UAW pickets in the "battle of the overpass."

If Le Corbusier did not see this atmosphere of tension, or saw it and did not wish to acknowledge it, he missed something else even more important. If he found in Detroit confirmation of his idea of standards and types it was through carefully selected evidence. Had he chosen to visit the Chevrolet factory in Flint, sixty miles away, he would have seen it flatly contradicted. In 1924, one year after *Vers une architecture* was published, Model T sales began to decline. 1926 this model ceased production, despite the addition of optional colors. By the time of Le Corbusier's visit it was dead. The new apostle of mass production was Alfred P. Sloan, Jr., president of General Motors. If he sold fewer books than Ford, he was selling as many or more cars per year by 1930, and for a simple reason: the public rejection of the idea of a single model. Sloan wrote: "It is perfectly possible from the engineering and manufacturing standpoint to make two cars at not a great difference in price and weight, but considerably different in appearance."[32]

1.12

1.13

Highland Park Ford Plant

Albert Kahn

Highland Park, Michigan, 1909–1914

1.12 **View showing 1,000 Model Ts,** one-third of one day's production in August 1913.

(Henry Ford Museum & Greenfield Village, PO.716)

1.13 **Assembly line,** showing final chassis assembly in 1914.

(Henry Ford Museum & Greenfield Village, PO.883.859)

Sloan's method was to maximize variety without losing the economic advantages of mass production. Major structural components were standardized, but different chassis types were combined with different body types and other options to create five different models. The models ranged from cheap and small to expensive and large, with Chevrolet at the bottom and Cadillac at the top. More than this, models were eventually changed on a yearly basis. (This was in part illusory, as major changes were made on a two-to-three-year cycle.) The object was to keep the customer buying cars. The prototypical Ford client bought one Model T and drove it until it wore out, then bought another. The GM client was continually buying cars, moving upward from Chevrolet to Buick to Oldsmobile, moving forward from the 1936 model to the 1937 model to the 1938 model. By 1926 when the Model T ceased production, there were more GM than Ford buyers.

Architects, needless to say, found the General Motors philosophy of mass production as horrifying as they found the Ford philosophy appealing. It was not just that Sloanism separated engineering from design, or that it held form hostage to marketing, or that it accentuated rather than resolved class differences, or that it implied a constantly changing but never evolving product whose object was never to achieve perfection but to continue to change. Sloanism did all these things, but the key was again the problem of style. Ford's standards seemed an escape from the endless parade of stylistic alternatives that had been run through in the nineteenth century. The new architecture was to transcend fashion and achieve an ideal "typical" of the twentieth century. Sloanism implied not only that stylistic change would continue, but that it would be accelerated and encouraged, that it would be deliberately cut off from technology, and that architectural forms, motifs, and ornaments would be appropriated and discarded in the manner of chrome trim and tail fins, being altered for the sake of alteration.

This explains why the idea of standardization, specifically the Ford idea of rigid types, survived as an architectural idea into the 1960s while dying in the automotive industry after ten years. It was Ford who gave Modernism its idea of mass production via Le Corbusier and Gropius, not Sloan.

Standardization had as many Modernist critics as adherents. Wright called it "a form of dying of which to beware." Asplund wrote: "Endless repetition of a standardized element, mass production without the expression of the individual life is dangerous."[33] Alvar Aalto, in his later years, rarely missed an opportunity to ridicule it, and Mies along with many others viewed it with intense skepticism, but none were willing to adopt Sloan's philosophy of industrialization in its place.

THE PHYSICS OF THE NEW PAINTING

The admiration for and analysis of industrial objects was not confined to poets and architects, and if architects such as Le Corbusier were able to discover something profound in a Farman Goliath or Blériot monoplane, it was often because painters had seen it first. Yet the painter's understanding was first graphic and only later (if at all) tectonic. Paradoxically while Modern painting acted to heighten the awareness of the material qualities of objects, it often acted at the same time to call these objects into question. If it appreciated the minimal quality of the products of industrialization, it was often because this also seemed to be directed toward the realization of objects that were in a sense nonexistent. For the painter's primary concern was not with matter but light.

Umberto Boccioni, one of the primary Futurist painters, was one of the first to appreciate and depict the locomotive and the automobile, but his style was not to describe their real forms but the imaginary virtual forms they defined in movement. He rendered air, smoke, and light itself with the same solidity as stone and metal, and in his writings described what he called "physical transparency:"

Areas between one object and another are not merely empty spaces but continuing materials of different intensities, which we reveal with visible lines which do not correspond to any photographic truth. This is why in our paintings we do not have objects and empty spaces but only a greater or lesser intensity and solidity of space. . . .

This measuring of objects, and of the atmospheric forms which they create and in which they are contained, forms the quantitative *value of an object.*[34]

Like many of his day, Boccioni was influenced by the popular, if not entirely accurate, scientific ideas of Henri Bergson, whom Boccioni quoted in the same manifesto: "Bergson said: 'Any division of matter into autonomous bodies with absolutely defined contours is artificial division,' and elsewhere: 'Any movement, viewed as a transition from one state of rest to another, is absolutely indivisible.'"[35]

The French Cubist Robert Delaunay was perhaps less articulate than Boccioni, but his paintings illustrate these same paradoxes. His *Équipe de Cardiff* (1912–1913) is primarily a depiction of football players, but in the background are three objects that reappear in much of Delaunay's work of the period: the Eiffel Tower, a Ferris wheel, and a biplane. These are precisely the type of objects that Le Corbusier and Gropius were to depict several years later as the superior products of an industrial culture, those the architect ought to study and emulate in building design. Yet Delaunay's rendering of these objects systematically eliminates any useful information the architect might want to know, all tectonic qualities being absent. The plane, for example, is clearly a Voisin Biplane (figure 1.10), and while Delaunay depicts its form fairly accurately, the struts, guy wires, ribs, engines, and landing gear have all been eliminated. As Delaunay made clear in "Light" (1913), he was less interested in matter than light, less interested in the way these objects were the result of properties of materials than in the way they refracted and reflected light. For Delaunay and for many Modern artists, the minimal products of industrialization were admirable not because they illustrated the nature of the material, but because they implied its absence altogether in the definition of form.

The Russian Futurist (or Constructivist) movement, like its Italian counterpart, was often more concerned with the appearance than with the mechanics of the machinery it admired. Vladimir Tatlin epitomized the more material and utilitarian aspect of Russian Constructivism, while the aesthetic or spiritual wing was centered on Kazimir Malevich. But if Malevich was not interested, like Tatlin, in the machine as the ultimate product of art, he was no less interested in machinery as a source of art, and what he admired in machinery was again the minimal quantity of weight and material. He wrote: "Statics, speed, dynamics are the new expressions in power of new artistic creation and of all life. All forms live by them and all power forms rest on the economy that depends on statics, speed and dynamism. In comprehending the highest tension of speed, we receive as the result the real image of a machine which will be built on the economic principle of attaining an object as fast as possible."[36]

Malevich's attitude was less mechanical than it was spiritual, and he carried the idea of material minimalism to its perhaps illogical conclusion. If an object was more virtuous for having less weight and using less material, was not the ideal object that which had no material reality? He wrote:

God, feeling the weight in himself, dispersed it in his system, and the weight became light and relieved him, placing man in a weightless system; and man, not feeling it, lived like an engine driver who does not feel the weight of his locomotive in motion, but had only to remove one part from the system for its weight to come down and crush him. Likewise Adam transgressed the limits of the system and its weight collapsed onto him. As a result the whole of humanity is laboring in sweat and sufferings to free itself from beneath the weight of the collapsed system, is striving to distribute the weight in systems, wishing to repair the mistake— hence his culture consists of distributing weight in systems of weightlessness. . . .

God relieved himself of weight or, as weight, dispersed himself in weightlessness but, dispensing thought in weightlessness, himself remained free. Man too in all three points strives for the same thing—to disperse weight and himself become weightless, i.e. enter God.[37]

Malevich's assertion that the visible world is an imperfect realization of an ideal world, that material forms are inexact models of ideal immaterial forms, is a common one in Western thought, particularly in Christianity. It is not surprising that

Malevich saw Modern design in its minimal realizations of form as bringing us closer to this spiritual reality. It is rather surprising that more artists did not make the same connection.

If mysticism is common in Modern art (and in Expressionist architecture), it is rare if not totally absent from International Style Modernism. Yet this view of the world as caught between the poles of pure spirit and pure material is not uncommon in the agnostic rationalism of the 1920s. Implicit in the work of Boccioni, Delaunay, Malevich, and many other painters of the 1910s is a formal hierarchy in which purely illusionistic forms are superior or equal to real ones and in which those that are composed of minimal ethereal materials are valued because they appear to be composed of no material at all but of pure light. If this credo is not overtly stated in the writings of any of these three, it is spelled out precisely in the writings of an artist much more directly involved in Modern architecture, László Moholy-Nagy.

Moholy-Nagy's importance to architecture began when he was brought to the Bauhaus in the 1920s by Walter Gropius to direct the metal workshop and to revise the foundation course, whose aim was to acquaint beginning students of all design disciplines with the properties of materials. These were two tasks for which he had little experience and perhaps even less interest. While his interest in the objects of industrialization is clear, it is not their material but rather their immaterial qualities that fascinated him. In his autobiographical notes, written in 1938, he said:

Many of my paintings of that period show the influence of the industrial "landscape" of Berlin. They were not projections of reality rendered with photographic eyes, but rather new structures, built up as my own version of machine technology, reassembled from the dismantled parts. Soon these dismantled parts appeared in my montage pictures. On my walks I found scrap machine parts, screws, bolts, mechanical devices. I fastened, glued, and nailed them on wooden boards, combined with drawings and paintings. It seemed to me that in this way I could produce real spatial articulation, frontally and in profile, as well as more intense color effects. Light falling on the actual objects in the constructions made the colors appear more alive than any painted combination. I planned three-dimensional assemblages, constructions, executed in glass and metal. Flooded with light, I thought they would bring to the fore the most powerful color harmonies. In trying to sketch this type of "glass architecture," I hit upon the idea of transparency. This problem has occupied me for a long time.

The capacities of one man seldom allow the handling of more than one problem area, I suspect this is why my work since those days has been only a paraphrase of the original problem, light. I became interested in painting-with-light, not on the surface of the canvas, but directly in space.[38]

All of the media in which Moholy-Nagy worked—photography, photomontage, motion pictures, kinetic sculpture, and painting—relate in some way to light, more specifically to its relationship to industrial objects and the ability of light to dematerialize through reflection, transparency, and penetration.

Moholy-Nagy's photographs, similar to that of the airship frame in figure 1.14, although rendered in different style and media than the paintings of Delaunay and Malevich, show much the same paradox. What he finds valuable in the constructions he photographs is not the meticulous engineering that minimized the quantity of materials required to construct them, but the way in which they serve as diffusers of light, the way in which they are transparent, the way in which they are delaminated and dematerialized by the action of light. Many of his photographs of the period, particularly those that use reversed negatives and his photograms (prints made without a camera), resemble X rays, probably deliberately so. Like Boccioni's work they imply a kind of Bergsonian physics, in which matter, however opaque in reality, is penetrated by light, in which light is conceived as extending beyond the visible spectrum, and in which matter may not exist at all but everything is light and energy.

Even if material objects do exist, they are less important than "virtual" ones. Moholy-Nagy wrote in 1922: "We must therefore put into the place of the static

1.14

1.15

1.14 **Barnes Wallis,** *R-100* airship under
construction, 1924–1930.
*(National Air and Space Museum, Smith-
sonian Institution, SI Neg. No. A 94-7910)*

1.15 **László Moholy-Nagy,** *Light-Space
Modulator*, 1922–1930.
*(Courtesy of the Busch-Reisinger Mu-
seum, Harvard University Art Museums,
Gift of Sibyl Moholy-Nagy)*

principle of classical art the dynamic principle of universal life. Stated practically: instead of static material construction (material and form relations) dynamic construction (vital construction and force relations) must be evolved in which the material is employed only as the carrier of forces."[39] His *Von Material zu Architektur (From Material to Architecture)*, written in 1929 as an explanation of his Bauhaus work, contains little real information on material or architecture, but rather sings the praises of forms defined solely by light. In the sections that deal with sculpture, he sets up hierarchies of formal development over time. At the low, primitive end of the scale is blocked-out form, exemplified by the Great Pyramid. In its highest developmental form sculpture achieved kinetic form, in which virtual forms are defined only by movement and are without corresponding physical reality. In between are various other perforated forms and forms that defy gravity, with the implication that those having the least mass are of the greatest value.

Moholy-Nagy developed a similar hierarchy of architectural forms, progressing from closed forms through perforated and suspended forms to forms perforated in all three dimensions. He also described these stages as progressing from single cells to multiple cells, adding a biomorphic dimension to the hierarchy. In any case material was not of primary importance. He wrote: "Space creation is not primarily a question of building material."[40]

Despite his apparent lack of interest in materials as generators of form, Moholy-Nagy attacked his assignments at the Bauhaus with vigor, and along with Josef Albers created the series of exercises in material exploration in the foundation course that were to be one of the primary educational legacies of the Bauhaus. These exercises, although not purely structural in nature, emphasized ideas about formal development already articulated by architects and engineers—that the best form uses the least material to enclose the most space, and that it does so by exploiting the primary structural strength or sometimes weakness of that material. But the implication here went further; according to Moholy-Nagy, the better form required a minimal amount of material, but the best might have no mass at all but be composed of pure light.

Moholy-Nagy's architectural influence perhaps ultimately lay not at so theoretical a level, but in his use of sculptural devices with architectural implications. His *Light-Space Modulator* is composed entirely of perforated and louvered screens that reflect light while allowing it to penetrate. Both of these elements were to become components of a number of subsequent Modernist works.

In their 1963 essay "Transparency: Literal and Phenomenal," Colin Rowe and Robert Slutzky, perhaps unintentionally, implied that the effects of the Cubist phenomenal transparency of Gris and Le Corbusier were superior to the machine-inspired literal transparency of Moholy-Nagy and Gropius. Whatever the merits of their argument, it is misleading to suppose that the effects of literal transparency are confined to glass boxes and glazed corners.

VERNACULAR BUILDINGS AND VERNACULAR OBJECTS

Industrialization and its products, of course, produced as many critics as admirers both in society and in architecture and brought with them a heightened awareness of those things perceived as its antithesis—the vernacular, the regional, the handcrafted. But this was really only new fuel thrown on an old fire. The idea that the untrained innocent builder had vision beyond the trained and educated architect long predates industrialization and continues in strength today. Laugier's primitive hut, Gottfried Semper's Caribbean dwelling, Claude Lévi-Strauss's bricoleur are all manifestations of the same "primitive man" and his buildings.

In this view the primitive and the vernacular are seen as without style, for primitive-vernacular man could see truth. He had no cultural baggage, no awareness of Classic or Gothic or Modern, no academies, no treatises, no history. Thus unencumbered, he could see the issues clearly and build accordingly. The principal difficulty with drawing on vernacular sources as models of good building was that, by definition, they often had no universally applicable forms and fewer universally applicable principles. William Morris was, along with John Ruskin, the chief spokesman for this point of view in the nineteenth century. But while constantly lauding vernacular building, Morris is a bit unclear as to what lessons modern architects should draw from it, particularly in terms of building.

One might assume that the appeal of the vernacular was incompatible with that of industrialism, but such was not the case. Le Corbusier, Gropius, and Mies often noted the superior qualities of vernacular building, even during the heyday of International Style Modernism. In 1911 Le Corbusier, while visiting a folk museum in Germany, did study sketches of what he called the "hut of the savage" and the "primitive tent." He was to continue to sketch and comment on these images throughout his career. He wrote in *Précisions* in 1929:

I have drawn the hut of the savage, the primitive temple, the house of the peasant, and I have said: these organisms created with the authenticity that nature itself places in its works—economy, purity, intensity—it is they that, one day of sunshine and clear-sightedness, became palaces. I have shown the house of the fisherman built with a clear-cut truth, indisputable; my eyes, diving one day into architecture, into the eternal facts of architecture, suddenly discovered it. "This house," I cried out to myself, "is a palace!" [41]

Ironically, this was written in 1928, while he was designing the Villa Savoye, but the industrial and the vernacular did not present to Le Corbusier irreconcilable alternatives. He wrote of vernacular builders: "They realize a program that is at no point encumbered by pretensions to history, to culture, to the taste of the day. They build a home, a shelter, from day to day with humble materials found locally. They make this with their hands and without a great professional knowledge, here they are attentive to the smallest gesture, economical of their smallest effort, sensible to every ingenuity, willing to attain the maximum with a minimum." [42]

Nor was he alone. In a 1923 lecture Mies van der Rohe presented, as instances of exemplary building, an Indian tent, a "leaf" hut, various Eskimo dwellings, and German farm buildings. He said of the leaf hut: "This is the leaf hut of an Indian. Have you ever seen anything more perfect in terms of function and use of material? Is that not the best possible use of the jungle shadow?" [43] He ends, however, with what he calls a contemporary suitable dwelling, the liner *Imperator*. Like Le Corbusier, he was untroubled by any inconsistencies between the industrial and the vernacular.

Forty years later this idea had lost little of its power. In 1968 Louis Kahn wrote in an introduction to a book on vernacular buildings in Texas:

The stone and wood, not bought but found, are used true to the rights one dares to take in gratitude for the gifts of nature. These noble and most ancient materials which in all ages inspired numerous and beautiful variations in the expressions of their orders here were used true to their nature with clarity and economy.

Later, the Architect appears, admiring the work of the unschooled men, sensing in their work their integrity and psychological validity. [44]

If most of the canons of Modernism—mass production, structural rationalism, and material efficiency—have fallen by the wayside, this one has not; but equally important was another aspect of the vernacular, the vernacular mass-produced object. Just as primitive buildings were seen as the superior creations of anonymous, unbiased, and uneducated minds, so to many Modernists were the creations of industry and engineers. The designer of the grain elevator or the factory was thought to succeed because of his lack of architectural training. Smaller-scale objects were perceived in a similar way. Le Corbusier was constantly singing the praise of everyday "object types": bottles, pipes, file cabinets, and bowler hats, objects perhaps deliberately chosen for being mundane. Asplund wrote in "Art and Technology" of the virtues of a mechanical bearing bracket: "One such example is the bearing bracket pictured below, which has undergone a delicate formal reworking with a very refined result without any apparent change in the economics and technical qualities. An anonymous work of art." [45] This idea was given considerable impetus by Modern artists, particularly Marcel Duchamp, whose readymades, industrial objects displayed as works of art, were not totally tongue-in-cheek. Upon seeing an airplane propeller he is reported to have said: "Art is dead. How can painting compete with that?"[46]

The architect most closely associated with this idea, and with the identification of this idea with America, was Adolf Loos. His friend Richard Neutra recalled:

Loos was at heart interested in handicraft, and one of his ideals in this field was the well-finished Viennese cabinetwork which, even before this period, had been obliterated by gaudy Victorianism and threatened by Art Nouveau *fashions. Smiling, he would say that the most beautiful piece of cabinetwork was the American oak toilet seat. It was wonderful! Today plastic is used, but in those days there were well-curved and shaped oak seats. Loos became dithyrambic about this graceful but matter-of-fact article, how it was fitted on the china fixture, how neatly it was joined, and how well it would withstand all abuse. He always gave this as an example of American cabinetwork, and his eyes shone with the enthusiasm of a craftsman or a man whose life's work is to hand-shape boomerangs or tobacco pipes or well-finished unique Cremona violins.*

Perhaps it strangely sparked my admiration for the United States' precise though repetitive industrialized *technology. It became clear to me that for economic and political reasons it comprised almost a whole continent without tariff boundaries and a terrifically expanded continent-wide market for toilet seats, doorknobs, appliances, tools, and devices—not to mention the export possibilities.*[47]

This idea gave rise to another idealized form of building. Not the standardized building, but the building made of standard parts—the building that could be ordered out of catalogues, a building that, like Duchamps' readymades, made the mundane virtuous, that isolated the apparently ordinary in order to display its inherent beauty. Thus the best building material might be the least expensive and the most ordinary, and the best design might be one that was selected and assembled rather than fabricated.

CONCLUSION

If there is a radical difference between the forms of nineteenth-century architecture and the forms of twentieth-century architecture, there is not quite so radical a difference between the theories. If architects admired the suspension bridge, the clipper ship, the Farman Goliath, or the Model T (or the Japanese temple or the pueblos of the American Southwest), it was because they found there a confirmation of their analysis of the Doric temple and the Gothic cathedral. There were, to be sure, some discrepancies, but for the most part the ideal constructional principles of the twentieth century conform to the idealized theories of the nineteenth. In summary these were:

The doctrine of material efficiency. The best structure is that which uses the minimum material to enclose the maximum space no matter how complex the resulting system, how complicated the process of assembly, or how precious the materials required.

The doctrine that structure equals architecture. If form was the result of structure and if that structure must be made clear and if all that hid the structure was bad, there was no alternative but to make what was not structure invisible, i.e., glass, as it was in the cathedral.

The doctrine of transparency. If architecture was thus reduced to skin and bones, the frame plus its cover of glass or other curtain walls, it was imperative that the curtain wall appear just that, a curtain; it could have no structural characteristics. So if great lengths were traversed to express the structure, the bones, equally great lengths were gone to suppress the structure of the skin.

The doctrine of monolithic construction. Monolithic construction was a feature that the plane and the automobile decidedly did not have in common with the cathedral. The car from the beginning, and the airplane as it developed from the beginning, concealed most or all of their structural frame, nor did the enclosing envelopes reveal much about what was below. While recognizing this, most architects were unwilling to let go of the ideal of the wall of the cathedral where all was visible.

The doctrine of standardization. In order to be appropriate to its time, architecture must be industrialized, and in order to be industrialized its components must be reduced to a limited number of standard parts.

The cult of the everyday. If the custom-made industrial prototype represented one idea, bricolage represented another, the building constructed from everyday found objects.

If Detroit was the Jerusalem of Modernism, it was so only to the pilgrims who came there like Le Corbusier. It did not seem so to its residents, who, if they found answers there, found them not at Highland Park or Dearborn but at Cranbrook, where Eliel Saarinen came to work in the 1920s.

2   Eliel Saarinen in Detroit: 1926–1940

Lily Swann Saarinen takes me one afternoon to see Cranbrook. . . . Cranbrook is beautifully done—too beautifully. As though it were wished there. The elaborate romantic-modern Egyptian of the Girls' school. The Gothic modern of the Boys'. The clean functional modern of the museum. The Swedish modern art buildings, all cloistered, all set apart, all precious—the Ivory Tower sitting on the outside of the volcano of Detroit.

Diary of Anne Morrow Lindbergh, October 24, 1942

How is one to understand the "nature of materials," through history or through experiment? Is it to be discovered in tradition, particularly vernacular tradition, or is it more correctly manifested in the products of the machine age? Many Modernists would shrug off this question. To Le Corbusier or Alvar Aalto, the answer was that it could be found in both.

This was less likely to be the case in early Modernism, and to those involved in the Helsinki Railway Station competition of 1904, it was the crucial question. Eliel Saarinen's winning entry, in the Finnish National Romantic style, made extensive use of boulders and picturesque compositional devices, and was in Saarinen's mind, and perhaps in reality, based on Finnish vernacular forms. To the critics of the winning entry, particularly Sigurd Frosterus (who was also a competitor), the proper relationship of form and material was found not in traditional forms, Finnish or otherwise, but in the products of industrialization. To Saarinen, however, truth to material was manifested in the old, not the new, in tradition, particularly Finnish tradition. He wrote in 1948:

My colleagues [Herman Gesellius and Armas Lindgren] and I in Finland adhered to the theory that function and material decide the nature of form. This was by no means an original thought; rather, it was a fundamental one. But because this fundamental thought had for so long been buried beneath all kinds of accumulated stylistic nonsense, it was necessary to dig it out from its ornamental grave and to reinstate it in its place of honesty. To do this, however, meant that one had to go backward in time to a period when the employment of material was honest.[1]

Saarinen was not content with a symbolic cladding that described the construction, nor did he feel that tradition could take precedent over honesty:

Some critics with "sharp appraising eyes" have discovered that none of the styles, old or new, are truthful—neither in their means of expression, nor in their methods of construction. No matter what style-period the critics study, they are always able to find fallacies of one kind or another. Consoles do not support cornices as their shapes indicate, but are hung as mere decorations from the cornices themselves. The real construction is often concealed behind fake forms, indicating another construction. The facade is often only a decorative mask having little in common with inner space-organization and mode of construction. The critics discover all this and many other kinds of untruth throughout the various styles. And

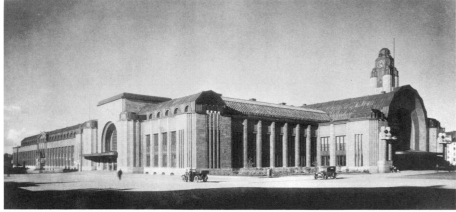

2.1

2.2

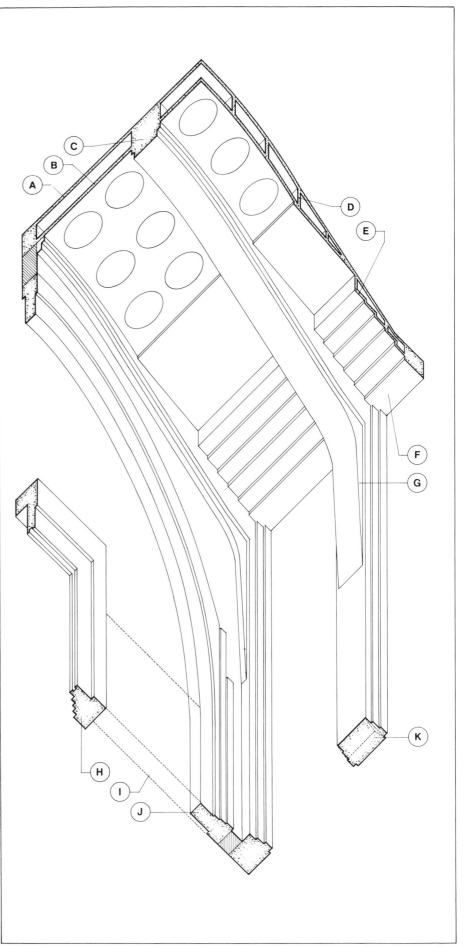

2.3

Helsinki Railway Station

Eliel Saarinen

Helsinki, Finland, 1904–1914

2.1 **View.**
(Courtesy of Cranbrook Archives)

2.2 **Interior, showing vaults.**

2.3 **Wall section at vault, showing structure only.**

A 6 cm upper concrete slab. Unlike some of Saarinen's later vaults, this one is structural and self-supporting.

B 4 cm lower concrete slab. The double slab construction gives increased stiffness through greater depth while reducing the weight that a solid slab would produce.

C Rigid concrete frame. Like a table leg, the upper beam and column joint are rigid while the base is free to rotate when the frame is loaded.

D 8 cm ribs.

E 6 cm and 4 cm concrete slabs.

F Concrete edge beam.

G The tapered form characteristic of the rigid frame is concealed by finish materials.

H Concrete portal.

I Masonry with windows above (not shown).

J Concrete arch.

K Base of frame set in asphalt with crossed rebars so that only compressive loads are transferred to grade.

(Finnish State Railways, DN 70, 71)

as their "sharp appraising eyes" are eager to trace this trend to untruth even in the genuine styles, they then arrive at the conclusion that truth and form do not have much to do with one another. Things being so, they say, criticism has to be based on other virtues than truthfulness and honesty in the treatment of form. According to their opinion, therefore, ethics is not essential in art, whereas the decorative side is of prime importance.[2]

Whether the boulders of Saarinen's competition design for the Helsinki Station were to be real or ornamental was not for its critics the question; the forms themselves were the issue. To Frosterus, new materials dictated the abandonment of traditional forms. He wrote of Saarinen's design:

Geologically speaking, stones are unchanged, but science has given us the means to exploit them to an extent quite different from what was possible in prehistoric times and the Middle Ages. The mechanics of materials and statics allow us to express daring new proportions. And we in Finland really have the opportunity to cultivate something of our own. From the proud, solid granite, with its unique durability, assured and deliberate architecture could be conjured up, light and airy, daring and buoyant. But where do we see anything like this? Where? Cumbersome blocks of stones heaped together, dead material; dormant power which will never be roused; an extravagant misinterpretation of the nature of stones which can no longer be branded as thoughtlessness since we HAVE the science.[3]

To Frosterus the key to rational building lay not in tradition, local or otherwise, but in the study of industrialization and its products: "We have more to learn about form from the construction of machinery, bicycles, cars, from battleships and railway bridges, than from historical styles. Such knowledge may seem imported, but the fact that this country is not a leading centre of civilization should not discourage us from profiting by the gains of culture."[4]

An aspect of Saarinen's design equally offensive to Frosterus was the vaults of the main waiting rooms. To Saarinen, with his background in the Arts and Crafts movement, the use of plaster vaults would have been a falsehood, a sham, but concrete vaults were acceptable since they would in fact be structural. To Frosterus, concrete vaults might be consistent with the structural properties of the material, but they were not its true expression. Frosterus wrote in the same article:

The new materials call for new forms—a simple, acknowledged fact. And yet it is still not perceived that to make cross-vaults, barrel-vaults and stellar-vaults (shapes borrowed from the stone mason) from concrete—in which fantasy, freed of all tradition, has unlimited play—is as unpardonable as making Gothic forms from iron—not to mention the axiom on the unsuitability of stone shapes for plaster or wood, truths that have penetrated the public consciousness so much that offenses on this account only occasionally occur.[5]

Although Saarinen never fully embraced the doctrines of Modernist rationalism, his executed version of the Helsinki Station is radically altered from the competition design, and in ways that minimize or eliminate those elements Frosterus found objectionable. The granite of the exterior, although massive, is smooth, faced with geometric ornamentation and with none of the pseudonaturalistic boulders of the original proposal. Gone also are many of the picturesque elements and asymmetrical massing of the early design. The concrete vaults remain, however, although in modified form.

The vaults and frames of the executed design are based on modern structural principles, but are heavily modified for sculptural, even ornamental, purposes. The vault of the waiting room, for example, is actually a double concrete shell composed of two thin layers of concrete separated by concrete purlins of the same thickness (figure 2.3). These "vaults" are supported by a series of rigid concrete frames with pinned connections at their bases.

It is a characteristic of this type of frame that the column-beam connection transfers bending moments and therefore must be rigid, while the column-ground connection does not transfer moments and is therefore free to rotate, i.e., pinned. The typical form of the rigid frame is thick at its upper corners and thin at its base,

2.4

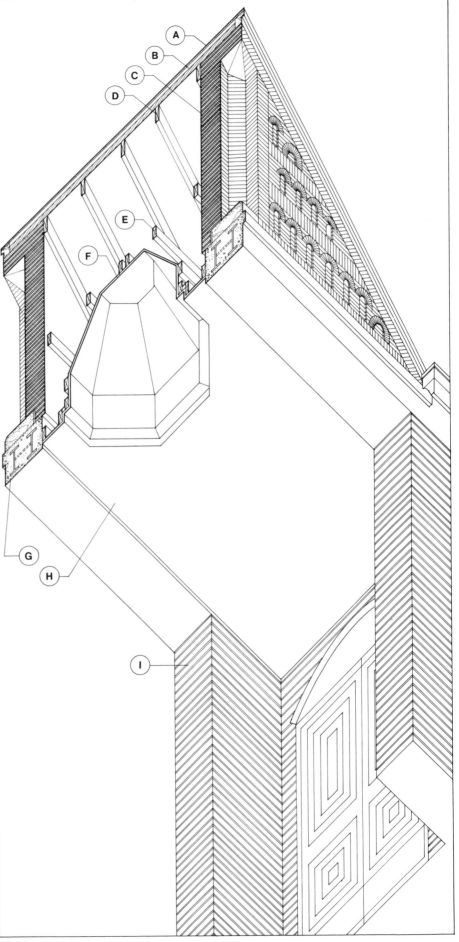

2.5

Cranbrook School

Eliel Saarinen

Bloomfield Hills, Michigan, 1925–1930

Main gate

2.4   **View.**

2.5   **Section.**
A   Tile roof with cement fill at edge.
B   Roof board to support tile.
C   Tile wall with recessed niches.
D   2 × 4 roof rafters.
E   2 × 4 rafter ties. The load on the rafters and roof pushes the lower ends apart; these members tie those ends together.
F   Light fixture (not shown).
G   Concrete lintel with two 8 I 18.4 steel beams bearing on brick pier beyond to support masonry over opening. Like many Arts and Crafts architects, Saarinen was not averse to using exposed concrete but used it as a kind of artificial stone.
H   Plaster ceiling supported by 2 × 4 wood joists.
I   Dutch brick and stone wall.
    (CBA AD 07.143)

tapering toward the ground like the legs of a table. The frames of the waiting room follow this configuration, but the angle of the column is hidden by a wall of ornamental tiles, giving it a more traditional appearance. The vault itself is heavily configured in a pattern that recalls traditional construction while articulating, at least in part, the structure behind. The egg-shaped coffers align with the hollows between beams above, but the slab itself is not coffered, only ribbed.

Despite the rigor of the revised design of the station, how consistently Saarinen and his partners adhered to even the traditionalist principles of rational building is open to question, as their early work abounds in what in the nineteenth century were called falsehoods. Their pavilion for the 1900 world's fair in Paris, although resembling a Finnish vernacular stone church, was neither stone nor a church. The vaults were canvas-covered wood framing given a coating of "cocolit." The stone walls were plaster except for the portals, and while it had the plan of a church, this had little to do with its internal function. A world's fair pavilion is arguably more a model of a building than a building proper, but there were other examples: the false log facings in some of their early apartment buildings, and the steel column of the Pohjola Building, which is given an elaborate wood encrustation. These were precisely the practices that Saarinen condemned in his later career.

While his work following the Helsinki station is not without falsehoods, it is not without constructional rigor as well, but it was a rigor based on tradition rather than "economy of material" or "equilibrium." Saarinen was willing to use new materials—concrete—and new forms—the rigid frame—but he sought to bring them into alignment with traditional forms (the coffered vault, for example), and he did not subscribe to many of the Modernist doctrines that accompanied industrialization and its forms. If he felt that new materials would generate new forms, he felt that they would do so by growing out of the old.

Few Modernists were less interested in industrialization and standardization than Eliel Saarinen, and it is more than ironic that fate was eventually to place him at its heart, Detroit, and that he was to spend the second half of his career, the "Modern" half, at Cranbrook, fifteen miles from Highland Park and twenty miles from River Rouge, designing schools for the children of auto executives.

THE CRANBROOK SCHOOL

If it is true, as Victor Hugo predicted, that the printing press has destroyed architecture, no blame can be assigned to George Booth, founder of the Detroit Evening News and of Booth Newspapers, Inc., but also the founder of the Cranbrook Educational Community, an institution that began as an arts and crafts community but grew to include the Brookside Preschool, the Cranbrook School for Boys, the Kingswood School for Girls, the Cranbrook Academy of Art, as well as a library, a museum, an academy of science, and a church that rivals in size and opulence some smaller cathedrals. Booth's institution has done as much as any to advance the cause of architecture in the United States.

The association of Cranbrook with Eliel Saarinen has obscured the role of George Booth, who was far more than the school's founder and chief patron. Booth provided sketches for, and closely supervised the building of, Cranbrook School (originally the Cranbrook Boy's School), Saarinen's first built American work. Two other architects and former Saarinen students were involved as well: Henry Booth, George's son, and Robert Swanson, Saarinen's future partner and son-in-law. This helps explain in part some of the oddities of Cranbrook School. While it is usually attributed to Saarinen, it shows the influence of other hands. It is far more a doctrinaire Arts and Crafts work than any of Saarinen's previous work in Finland and is certainly old-fashioned for its date (1925); but none of this should obscure the value of the work.

Like many of Saarinen's building complexes it seems modeled on his ideal, the Piazza San Marco, being composed of a trapezoidal space with an offset (and largely useless) observatory tower surrounded by buildings in slightly varied styles. The San Marco analogy, which implied a variety of architectural styles, and the un-

2.6

2.7

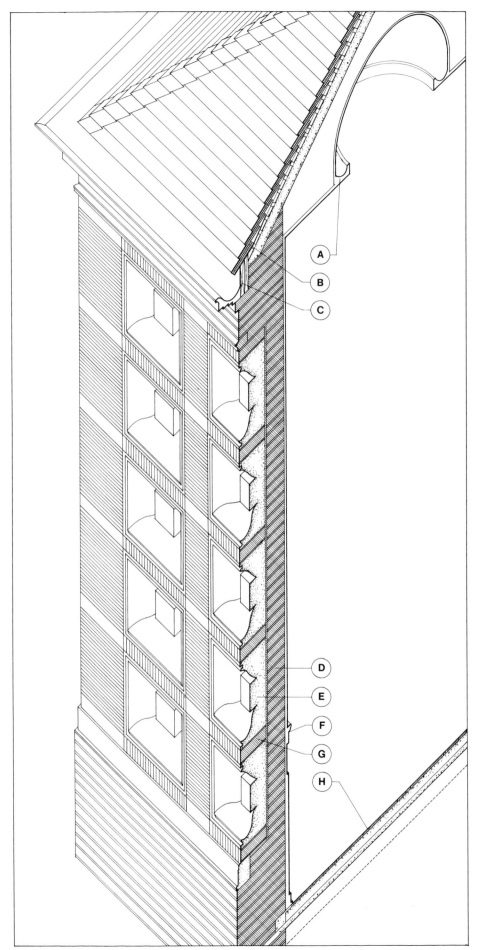

2.8

Cranbrook School

Eliel Saarinen

Bloomfield Hills, Michigan, 1925–1930

Vestibule at dining hall

2.6 **View.**

2.7 **Detail.**

2.8 **Wall section.**
- A Plaster ceiling with cove for recessed lights.
- B Roof construction of tile nailed to wood screeds set on a gypsum structural deck, with a layer of felt to intercept any water that penetrates the tiles.
- C Copper gutter with two 2 × 10 supports.
- D Brick with interior plaster. Like most walls at Cranbrook, it is built without cavities or insulation.
- E Stone.
- F Wood wainscot.
- G Tile. The bands run vertically and horizontally in a nonstructural manner.
- H Tile on ribbed concrete slab.
  (CBA AD 07.528)

wieldy design team perhaps explain the complex and fascinating group of parts that made up the structural systems of the school. Most of the buildings are structured of load-bearing masonry walls supporting one-way concrete ribbed slabs. Concrete, being fireproof, had come to replace wood in this type of building after the turn of the century. What is unusual is the array of substructures set into this concrete frame.

Take for example the L-shaped building that makes up the northwest corner of the main quadrangle. The room at the angle of the L is the North Hall. It has all the elements of the hall of the late nineteenth-century country house: fireplace, inglenook, meandering stair, wood paneling, and heavy exposed timber beams. The beams are solid 10 × 12 timbers and are structural, but in an odd way, in that they support primarily themselves. The adjacent floors are concrete; the roof above is supported by steel trusses, semi-independent of the structure below. The timber beams in effect support only the ceiling and interior of the hall, which is thus structurally a building within a building. The problem created by these wood beams is one of perception, for there is little in the space to indicate the presence of the adjacent steel and concrete.

The adjacent one-story study hall has a similar mixture of exposed traditional materials and concealed modern ones. Its roof is supported by timber trusses, and, as in the North Hall, the timbers are solid and are structural, but in this case they actually support the roof. Yet the true structure and the perceived structure again diverge. The purlins of the roof hidden by the plaster ceiling are not wood but steel. Although there is exposed steel in the structure (the center tie rod), the general impression given is that the building is timber frame.

In the original plans the exposed timber in these two rooms, along with the adjacent common room, constituted the only exposed structure (or apparent structure) in the building. The ribbed concrete slabs that made up the typical floors were to be completely covered below with plaster. This would have been a clear deception, implying that the entire roof and floor structure was wood. However, at some point after the completion of contract drawings the plaster ceiling was eliminated in the main lobby. The true concrete structure was thus exposed, at least in a small part of the building, and was covered with a stencil pattern. This partially clarifies the expression of the building's true structure: the wood beams and trusses were not false, only atypical.

More explicitly false is the structure used in the last room of the wing, the library, which is covered by a shallow vault apparently supported by a series of elongated wood columns. Only about half of these columns are structural, and those are steel sections encased in wood. The actual roof structure is of steel trusses, but the trusses are concealed by a false plaster vault. This was a construction used by many in practice but generally condemned by rationalists of every persuasion. The vaulted form was associated with masonry or at least concrete, in which the curved form configured the material in a way that minimized tensile stresses, that masonry cannot withstand. Here the plaster vault is nonstructural and is carried by the trusses, which are distorted into an illogical shape to allow for the rise of the vault.

The false vault cannot be blamed on Booth or Swanson, as there are many false vaults in Saarinen's work (as there are many real vaults as well). The plaster was undoubtedly chosen over stone or concrete because it was less expensive, but it also shows Saarinen's lack of interest in a rigorous structural expression. Like many of his Arts and Crafts contemporaries, Saarinen placed the rigor in the craft of building rather than in the structure. In practice this translated into considerable attention given to walls often at the expense of floors and roofs. Typically the means of articulating the wall was the motif. Saarinen's design strategies invariably revolved around motifs; though not as rigidly applied in the Cranbrook School as in later projects, they are nevertheless there.

The most common motifs employed at the school are concentric squares, octagons, and hexagons, but the most important is the elongated vertical opening with a

2.9

2.10

Cranbrook School
Eliel Saarinen
Bloomfield Hills, Michigan, 1925–1930
Academic buildings

2.9 **View.**
(Courtesy of Cranbrook Archives)

2.10 **Main lobby ceiling.** Here the concrete is exposed and decorated.

2.11 **Partial framing plan at northwest corner.**
A Concrete observatory tower.
B Masonry bearing walls.
C One-way concrete slab with ribs 25½″ oc. These are exposed only in one location, the entry lobby and corridor.
D Concrete column. The structure is of exterior bearing walls with an interior frame.
E One-way concrete slab with ribs 25½″ oc; depth varies. This makes up most of the structure and is concealed by a flat plaster ceiling.
F North Hall. Solid timber beams and columns. See figure 2.13. Most of the exposed structures are wood while all of the concealed ones are steel or concrete.
G Study hall. Exposed wood truss with concealed steel channel purlins.
H Common room framing of 10 × 12 wood beams partially hung by steel cables and angles from steel truss above.
I Library. Steel columns encased in wood. This was a commonly condemned but frequently practiced deception.
J Steel truss and purlins of library roof.
K Wood ornamental column.
(CBA AD 07.110, AD 07.126, AD 07.122)

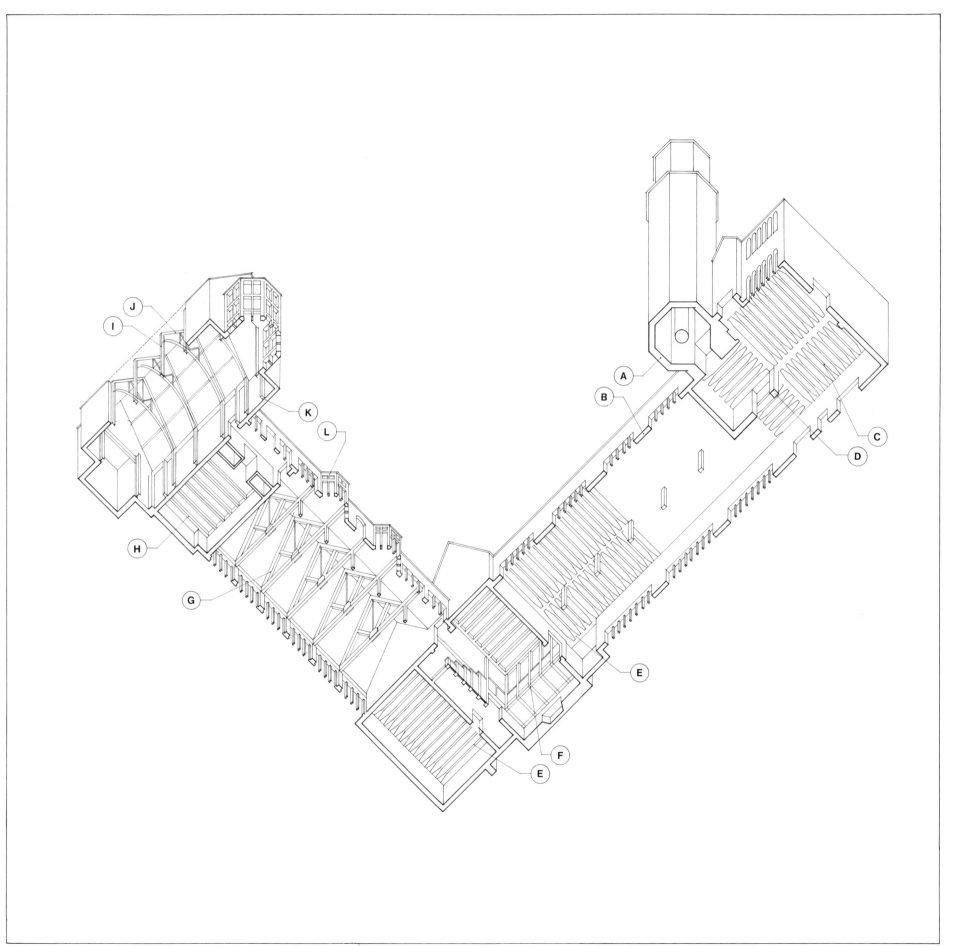

A

B

C

D

E

F

G

H

I

J

K

L

E

2.11

2.12

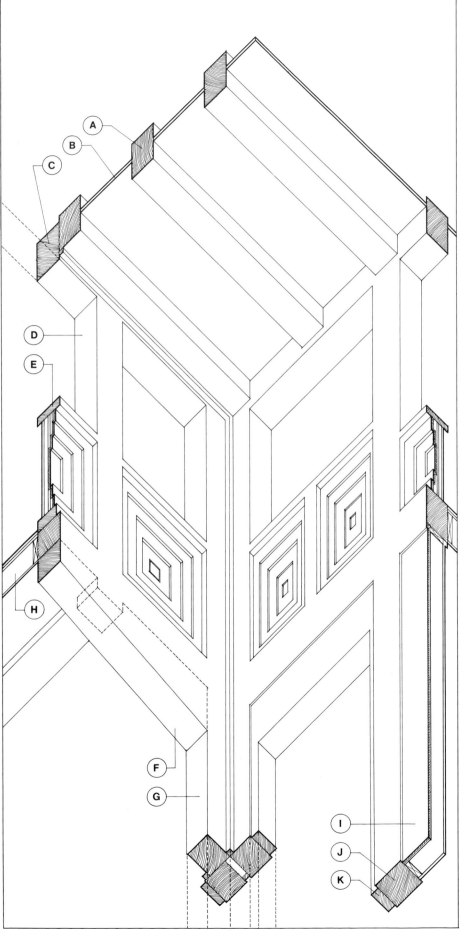

2.13

Cranbrook School

Eliel Saarinen

Bloomfield Hills, Michigan, 1925–1930

North Hall

2.12   Detail.

2.13   Interior wall section.

A   10 × 12 wood beams. The wood structure forms a solid subbuilding within the concrete and steel structure of the building as a whole.

B   Plaster ceiling.

C   10 × 12 edge beams.

D   10 × 12 wood posts. These stop at the second floor.

E   Solid wood paneling. The later Cranbrook buildings use almost exclusively wood-veneered paneling, while the earlier ones use almost exclusively solid wood.

F   Tapered wood beam. This forms an "arched" opening over the inglenook.

G   10 × 12 wood post.

H   2 × 8 wood joists and floor.

I   Wood paneling on wood stud and plaster wall.

J   10 × 12 stair column. Although all the wood posts are the same size, many do not extend up to the roof or down to the floor.

K   Solid wood trim.

(CBA AD 07.109)

shallow relieving arch at the top. Saarinen manipulates the motif by changing its size and scale. In the main entry gate the pediment is filled with these elements (figure 2.4). They are only 4 to 6 inches across; being executed in thin tiles rather than larger bricks, they have a miniature quality and seem almost to be representational rather than real arches. Of course used in this way they serve no functional purpose. The lintel supporting them is not stone but concrete. Saarinen, like many of his contemporaries, gladly explored new materials, but usually in traditional ways.

The arch motif occurs throughout the complex, often in ways that are largely decorative, used for niches without sculptures or relieving arches where none are required. Yet this has a structural logic. What connects this motif to the material is the relieving arch. There are few lintels, concealed or exposed, in the older parts of the Cranbrook School. The openings are spanned with brick in a way that demonstrates through necessity the nature of brick.

The dining hall and dormitory, built one year after the northwest corner of the quadrangle, are considerably more original and less old-fashioned, but one should not forget that they are contemporary with Le Corbusier's villa at Garches (1927). Despite the greater formal unity of these two buildings and despite their lack of traditional references, they contain many of the same characteristics of detail and the same perplexing contradictions as the first part of the school: a rigid adherence to the structural qualities of materials in the wall combined with a lackadaisical attitude toward the materials of the roof, a general interest in expressing the smaller structural forces at work while ignoring the larger, and the repetition of he same motifs in different material and scales. Most problematical is the dining hall roof, which, like that of the library, is not a true or at least a pure vault, in that its concrete shell is dependent on the steel trusses for support; the trusses are designed not with a sense of structural efficiency but to accommodate the curved form of the vault. It may be argued that the wide, flat soffits on either side of the curve clarify the structural nature of the vault, but the best one can say of this is that it is devoid of structural expression. It is at best a hybrid, built more out of a desire for solidity than structural logic. In the debate between those who sought a logical economy of material and those who sought a not always logical demonstration of solidity, Saarinen tended to side with the latter.

The five years from 1925 to 1930 that marked the building of Cranbrook School were some of the most productive of Saarinen's career, and by their end his style had undergone a number of changes and absorbed a number of influences: the Art Deco movement, the work of Frank Lloyd Wright, and that of German Expressionists such as Hans Poelzig. The last phases of the Cranbrook School, which overlap with his work on the Kingswood School, show the effect of these influences on the exteriors.

This accounts in part for the complexity of the fenestration systems at the Cranbrook School. The varieties of window types that are used would seem to defy analysis (figure 2.14), the main quadrangle alone containing seemingly every variety of lintel, sash, operating type, and configuration imaginable within traditional architectural languages. One of the more charming but questionable practices of the Arts and Crafts movement was to vary the fenestration in this manner, implying a building that had evolved over time by agglomeration. This was hardly the case at the Cranbrook School, as the oldest and newest buildings are only separated by several years, but there were changes over these years that reflect Saarinen's changing attitudes toward structural expression.

However arbitrary the fenestration may appear, there is nonetheless an order to its variation, albeit a complex one, that demonstrates both the properties of the materials and the nature of the spaces served by the windows. There is a tendency to use the material surrounding the window to describe the function of the room behind, and to use the type of elements spanning openings to explain the structural forces at work in the wall, though there are exceptions in both cases.

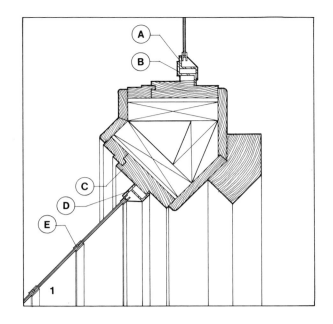

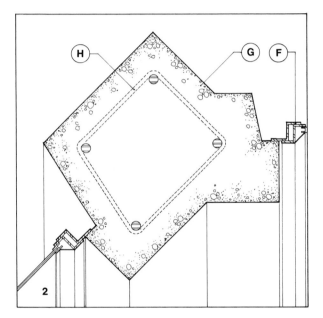

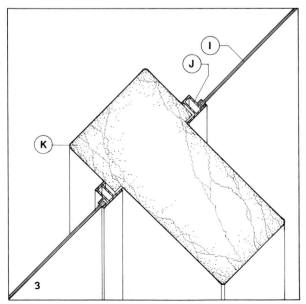

2.14

Cranbrook School

Eliel Saarinen

Bloomfield Hills, Michigan, 1925–1930

2.14   Window types.

1   Dormitory wood windows:

A   Operable steel section.

B   Fixed steel section.

C   Wood jamb.

D   Fixed steel window.

E   Leaded glass inserts. These serve no functional purpose but give the window a medieval appearance.

2   Corner detail of bay window at study hall:

F   Steel casement window similar to type 1, with glass with leaded inserts.

G   Concrete mullions. The entire bay is concrete.

H   ¾" vertical reinforcing bars with ⁵⁄₁₆" ties 10" oc.

3   Window at museum:

I   Glass.

J   Aluminum window.

K   Mankato stone mullion. Although greatly simplified, the detail is similar to those used in the older Cranbrook buildings.

(CBA AD 07.526, AD 07.110, AF, 12.1943)

2.15   Roof structure of study hall. The concealed portions of the structure are steel while the exposed parts are wood. While it contains no false structure, its appearance is deceptive in implying that the entire structure is wood.

A   18.4 I ridge beam.

B   9½ × 11½" solid Douglas fir wood beam forming top chord of truss.

C   1⅛" tension rod. Since this member of the truss is in pure tension, it can be a thin steel rod.

D   9½ × 9½" solid Douglas fir wood beam forming bottom chord of truss, notched to receive intermediates.

E   1⅛" gusset plates. These act to connect the two wood members of the truss.

F   7½ × 9½" solid Douglas fir truss intermediate bolted to top chord with ¾" drift bolt. All of the wood structure is exposed.

G   6 C 3.7 channel purlin bolted to timber with ¾" bolts and 6 × 4 × 12" angles. All of the steel structure is concealed except for the tie rod.

H   Plaster ceiling and finish (partially shown).

I   Concrete seat to transfer the truss load to the wall in a uniform manner.

J   Wood bracket. This serves no functional purpose but hides the bolt end.

(CBA AD 07.754)

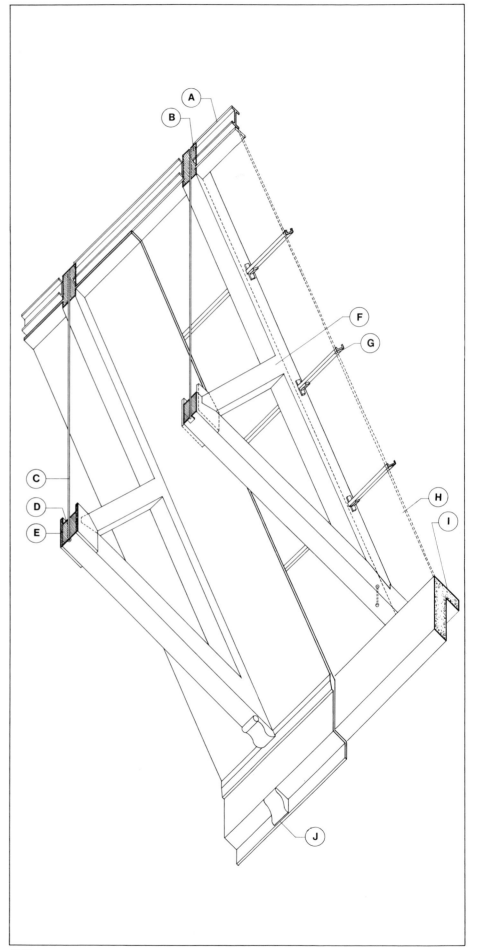

2.15

2.16

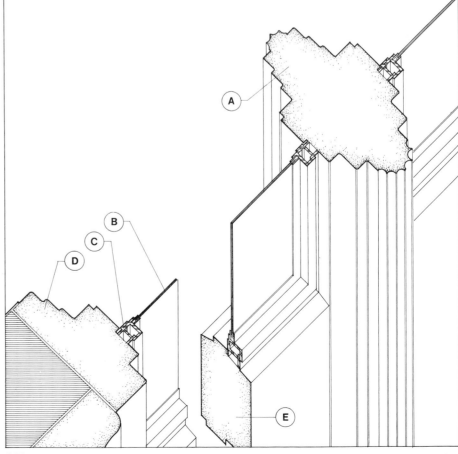

2.17

Cranbrook School

Eliel Saarinen

Bloomfield Hills, Michigan, 1925–1930

Dining hall

2.16 **View.**

2.17 **Limestone window mullion.**

A   Limestone center mullion. The stepped profile motif used throughout the building is an example of Saarinen's idea of correlation.

B   Glass.

C   Outswinging steel casement windows with leaded inserts.

D   Limestone trim at masonry wall with ³/₁₆″ joints.

E   Intermediate limestone horizontal.
(CBA AD 07.516)

2.18 **Wall section.**

A   Plaster ceiling with roof truss and vault beyond.

B   Tile roof nailed to lath supports on 1 × 2 wood screeds 19″ oc embedded in gypsum block, with felt to intercept any water that penetrates the tiles.

C   Double-shelled copper gutter.

D   Small masonry vault over window.

E   Masonry wall with plaster on interior and tile cornice. Almost all the openings in the dining hall are spanned with arches.

F   Stone mullions and trim with ³/₁₆″ joints. See figure 2.17.

G   Steel window with leaded inserts.

H   Wood wainscot on masonry wall. See figure 2.20.

I   Wood floor on ribbed concrete slab.
(CBA AD 07.526)

2.18

2.19

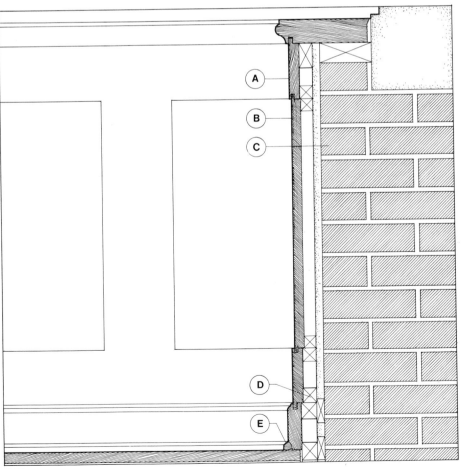

2.20

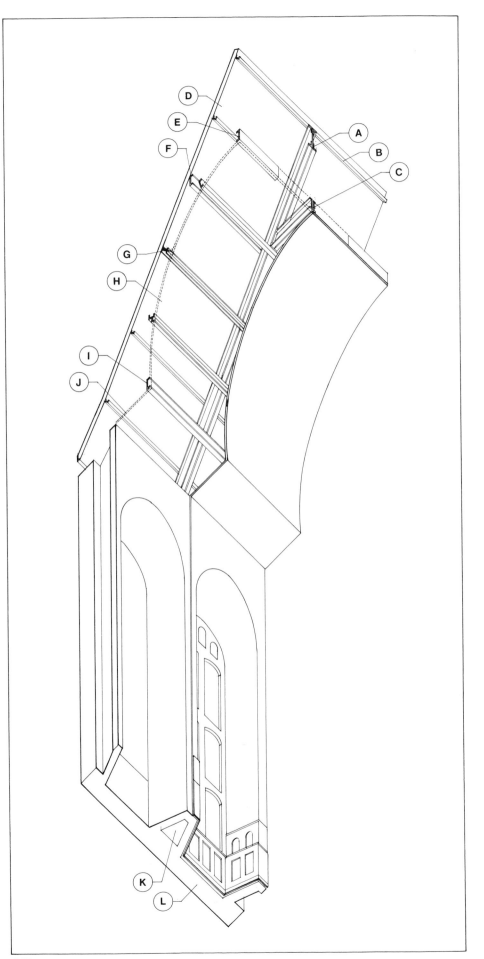

2.21

Cranbrook School

Eliel Saarinen

Bloomfield Hills, Michigan, 1925–1930

Dining hall

2.19 Interior.
(Courtesy of Cranbrook Archives)

2.20 Paneling.

A Solid rail. Unlike the later paneling at Cranbrook which is veneered, this is made mostly of solid pieces.

B Panel. Solid pieces of wood are difficult to obtain in this size, and some of the panels are plywood.

C Plaster on masonry wall.

D Blocking. The wood paneling is held free of the wall to ensure evenness and to provide an air space for ventilation to keep the wood dry.

E Base molding and wood base. This covers the joint between wood floor and wall to accommodate expansion of the wood floor.
(CBA AD 07.544)

2.21 Interior wall section.

A Top chord of truss from four 6 × 4 × ⅝″ steel angles and ½ × 16″ web. There is a truss only at every other pier.

B 12 C 20.7 steel channel purlin to transfer the load of the concrete deck to the trusses.

C Two 12 C 20.2 steel channel collar beams to tie the two top chords of the trusses together at their bases.

D 2½″ concrete on hyrib lath to structurally support the roof tiles.

E 8 C 11.5 steel channel radials to support concrete slab and plaster ceiling.

F 12 C 20.7 steel channel collar beam.

G Two 8 C 11.5 steel channels with tie plates to ceiling below.

H 2½″ cement on hyrib slab with plaster finish, partially shown. While the vault is relatively solid, it is not self-supporting as a true vault would be but is structurally dependent on the truss.

I 8 C 11.5 steel channel to support plaster soffit (bridging not shown).

J Plaster soffit.

K Masonry piers with voids for ventilation and heating. Although using extensive steel, it is a load-bearing masonry building.

L Masonry bearing wall.
(CBA AD 07.248)

The most important building, the dining hall, has arched openings with limestone infill and steel windows set into the stone. The academic buildings, such as the study hall, also have stone or concrete mullions with steel windows inserted into the openings. The less important rooms have similar wood windows with leaded glass or wood frames with steel casements. Some of the common room windows also have stone surrounds, but in smaller sizes. Rooms of intermediate importance, such as entry halls or stairways, have large-scale wood bay windows with inset steel casements. (All of these systems were commonly used by Gothic and Queen Anne Revival architects to imitate medieval styles and materials, and Saarinen perhaps altered the profiles to avoid any overt stylistic references.) In this aspect the window types express room function rather than structural logic: the arched openings are far more prevalent, for example, in the dining hall, not out of structural necessity, as the openings are the same size as many others with flat lintels, but to demonstrate the importance of the building.

Conversely, in a typical dormitory wall one can find three different window types, one an arch, one a segmented arch, and one a square opening (accomplished with a concealed steel lintel), all superimposed in ascending order. The rooms they serve are identical; the different openings serve only to demonstrate the increased load on the wall toward the ground and the increasing lightness of the wall toward the top. Many traditionalists eschewed the use of concealed steel lintels since they hid the means of support and thus did not express the nature of the material. Saarinen mixed all types—arches and lintels, concealed or exposed—to suit his purpose.

Another trend is also apparent in the development of Cranbrook, a move away from structural expression altogether. Just as Saarinen tended not to expose or define structure on the exterior, in his later buildings he used more and more concealed lintels and fewer arches. The first building, the academic building, has massive brick buttresses, not unfunctional but hardly structurally necessary, as demonstrated by their absence in later buildings with identical structural requirements. The outside of Page Hall, for example, is designed in a way sympathetic to the older buildings and in a manner almost as traditional, but not in the same style. The common room is the outstanding example of this juxtaposition—Art Deco inside, stripped down medieval outside. Structurally it is perhaps the penultimate Saarinen building, neither structurally dishonest nor structurally expressive. The actual structure consists of concrete floors and beams on masonry bearing walls, the ribbed slab and beams of the concrete covered with plaster. The only modification to the flat ceiling is the octagonal openings for a light fixture. There is nothing to indicate what the structure is or is not.

Whatever the reason for the idiosyncrasies of the Cranbrook School—Saarinen's stylistic development or his evolving relationship with his patron and associates—one should not assume that he was unhappy with the results. The variety of details and the apparent stylistic evolution yielded precisely the type of urban space that Saarinen idealized in his book *The City*, as exemplified by the Piazza San Marco.

THE KINGSWOOD SCHOOL

It is hard to believe that the first buildings of the Cranbrook School of 1925 and the Kingswood School of 1929, also at Cranbrook, are the work of the same architect, but the same could be said of Saarinen's work in Finland in contrast to the Cranbrook Art Academy. The reason for the formal difference between the two schools is Frank Lloyd Wright, whose influence is visible in the latter.

Wright's importance for Saarinen went beyond form to ideas. In Saarinen's later career the ideal of tradition as the source of the material-form relationship is replaced by another, the Wrightian idea of "organic order." Saarinen wrote:

In her material use nature is thoroughly true—just as she is thoroughly true in her whole organic structure. We know that any cell in a living organism has its specific assignment to perform and that to that end there is no material waste. We know that the cellular construction of the beehive is perfect engineering from the point of view of efficient use of material. And so, no matter how deeply one might delve into nature's structural form-shaping in order to find evidence of untruth, all the more would one be convinced of the lack of such evidence.[6]

2.22

2.23

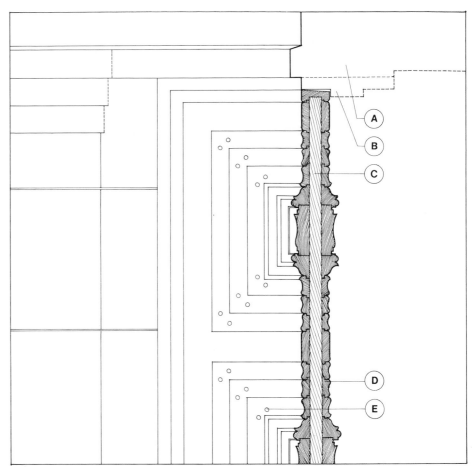

2.24

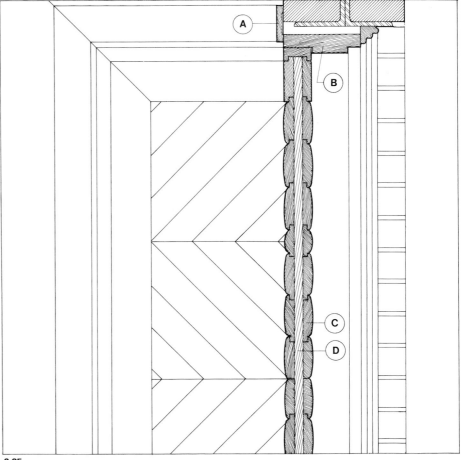

2.25

2.22   **Door at Cranbrook School.**

2.23   **Door detail.**

2.24   **Section of door at Cranbrook School dining hall, 1925.**
- A Limestone facing and/or lintel.
- B Wood door frame and stop.
- C Wood boards. A less expensive wood is used to provide a structural core.
- D Tongue and groove oak boards with oak end cap. This type of joint allows the wood to move with changes in humidity while remaining structurally attached. The concentric square motif is used throughout Cranbrook in a variety of materials.
- E Pegs.
  (CBA AD 07.643)

2.25   **Section at door of Art Academy, 1932.**
- A Oak molding to cover joint between wood frame and the concrete and steel lintel.
- B Frame and door stop.
- C Milled tongue and groove oak boards. While the concentric square motif is similar to that in figure 2.24, the profile of the boards has been greatly simplified.
- D Wood core. A lower-quality wood is used where it is not visible. The ends are capped with finish wood.
  (CBA AD 11.132)

Organic order can mean many things, of course: the geometric grids of Louis Sullivan, the geometric motifs of Frank Lloyd Wright, or the irregular curves of Alvar Aalto. Saarinen saw organic order as a combination of the first two, as can be seen in his example of the honeycomb. He distinguished between the expression and the modes of correlation of organic order. Correlation represented a type of repeated motif, invariably a geometric one: "A healthy organism, through an orderly set of vibrations, always has rhythmic configuration of cell-pattern; whereas an unhealthy organism, through its disorderly set of vibrations, shows a distinct leaning to disintegration."[7]

Wright's influence pervades many aspects of Kingswood, the plan, the elevations, and the roof in particular; but not, interestingly enough, the structure. The structure of Kingswood is generally the same as that of the Cranbrook School, brick bearing walls supporting concrete floors or roofs with the occasional use of steel trusses, and here too the concrete is used in a way that sometimes conforms to and sometimes conflicts with Modernist notions of truth to materials. There are a variety of ceiling types in Kingswood—flat with recessed lighting in corridors and small classrooms, shallow curved vaults in the crafts room and study hall, a series of saucer domes in the dance space, and highly configured vaults in the dining room and auditorium. The flat ceilings are plaster applied to the underside of a one-way concrete ribbed slab, a system that is neither structurally dishonest nor structurally expressive. The smaller vaults are cast-in-place concrete, are structural, and are structurally expressive in a literal way. The vaults of the dining room and auditorium are by the same conventional wisdom structurally expressive, but in a dishonest way. The former is of plaster hung from steel trusses. The auditorium ceiling is a grid of hemispherical domes with a light at the center of each; it appears to be a type of two-way ribbed slab, but as in the dining hall it is imply a plaster ceiling hung from steel trusses. (The auditorium ceiling closely resembles Eero Saarinen's Irwin Union Bank and Trust in Columbus, Indiana, except that Eero's is at a larger scale with domes of concrete.) Perhaps the most precise thing one can say about these contradictions between form and structure is that Saarinen saw the ceiling more as a mechanism for distributing light than as an opportunity for structural expression, which, if it occurred at all, was confined to columns and walls. One might be tempted to say that he was simply indifferent to any kind of structural expression, but this is not the case either, particularly in the columns of the Kingswood School.

Many architects of the 1920s and 1930s were dealing with "dishonest" forms of architecture that resulted when steel and concrete frames were clad in traditional styles that had originated in masonry wall construction. Saarinen avoided this problem by building traditionally. New materials are used at Kingswood—concrete, steel windows, steel trusses—but they are used in traditional configurations. The building structure is a tightly interconnected mixture of brick bearing walls, concrete vaults and slabs, stone columns, and steel trusses. They were all of necessity built simultaneously, and probably with some difficulty. A typical contemporary builder would try to minimize the structural dependency of so many materials on one another in order to allow the construction of each component to proceed unhindered.

The columns must have been a particular problem. The normal procedure in 1929 or today would be to use a concrete column clad in stone veneer. Besides minimizing the quantity of an expensive material, stone veneering simplifies the problem of sequencing. The concrete, being the structure on which all other materials are supported, must be erected first. Stone, by contrast, requires shop drawings, approval of shop drawings, ordering from the quarry, delivery, and perhaps pre-cutting, and is thus one of the last materials to arrive at the building site. If the stone is given a structural role the remainder of the structure must await its arrival. At Kingswood, however, the stone columns are solid and they are structural. Each section of the shaft is in two to four solid pieces with concealed vertical joints, but except for cavities for the roof drains the columns are solid (figure 2.28). There are two types of columns, one floral, one geometric. Both are examples of Saarinen's

2.26

2.27

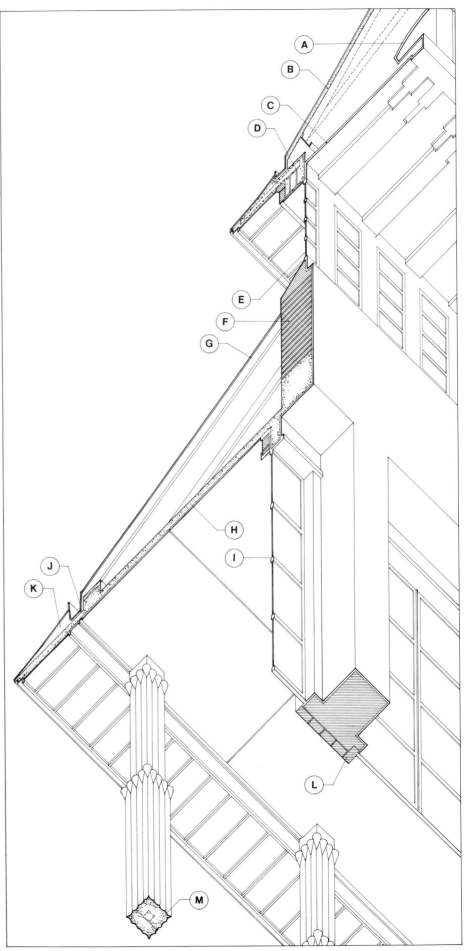

2.28

Kingswood School

Eliel Saarinen

Bloomfield Hills, Michigan, 1929–1931

2.26 **View.**

(Courtesy of Cranbrook Archives)

2.27 **Dining hall interior.**

2.28 **Interior wall section at dining hall.**

A Plaster ceiling. Although the curved shape implies that this is a vault, it is only partially structural and depends on the trusses for support. Most of Saarinen's vaults, including many of the smaller ones at Kingswood, were real concrete vaults.

B Standing seam copper roof on cement tile roof slab on steel truss (not shown).

C Ornamental plaster soffit.

D Two 9 I 21.8 steel beams and ¼ × 15″ plate with 3 C 4.1 channel lookouts 4′ 0″ oc to support cornice. Unlike in the early Cranbrook buildings, these openings are spanned with steel lintels rather than exposed stone lintels or arches.

E Steel window with leaded glass.

F Solid brick wall supported by concrete beam.

G Lower copper roof on wood joists.

H Concrete slab and soffit.

I Steel window with rowlock course over window.

J Copper gutter.

K Concrete poured using copper soffitt as form.

L Load-bearing brick pier.

M Mankato stone column from four solid pieces of stone in a pinwheel.

(CBA AD 08.396, AD 08.427)

idea of organic form, and both are cellular in the organic sense of the repetition of a clear unit, a system that recalls Alvar Aalto's work. More Wrightian are the geometric columns, which are obviously a conventionalized natural form.

The stone details have little formal similarity to those of the Cranbrook School, particularly in that the role of stone is reversed in the two schools. The Cranbrook School has few stone columns, with stone used rather for trim: lintels, mullions, sills, stringcourses. Although Kingswood has stone columns, it has little stone trim. This is only one of the many differences in the wall details. The Cranbrook School used slate roofs that flared out at the wall (figure 2.18), a detail used by many Arts and Crafts architects. At Kingswood the gently sloping copper roof is cantilevered, but the gutter is recessed to allow the drain to be concealed in the wall. The copper gutter was used to form the edge of the concrete slab (another example of the difficult-to-sequence interdependence of materials). The window openings show the greatest change from the details of the Cranbrook School. The stone sills are gone, replaced by brick. The relieving arches and stone lintels are gone, replaced by concealed steel angles, resulting in square and rectilinear openings without trim. At the Cranbrook School the numerous relieving arches were one of the few elements that expressed the structural qualities of the brick. Here the brick is given a kind of membrane treatment.

The window openings are surrounded by concentric rectangles of brick that ignore the structural difference between the vertical and the horizontal, but this again is one of the motifs that gives the school, in Saarinen's terms, its formal correlation. The motif of concentric rectangles occurs throughout the school in two and three dimensions, applied to brick, stone, wood, carpets, tile, walls, and ceilings. As with some of Wright's motifs, it is difficult to follow the logic. If these motifs grow out of the nature of the material, how can they be applied to so many materials of such different structural properties? Unlike with the early windows of the Cranbrook School there is little interest in explaining this quality of the material, i.e., its structural limitations. And if the early walls of the Cranbrook School are remarkable for the complete absence of concealed lintels, the Kingswood School is remarkable for the absence of exposed ones. One of the more elegant applications of the concentric square motif is in the movable partition between the dining room and auditorium (figure 2.31). It contains a complex set of concealed hinges that allow either a simple set of swinging doors or a sliding door of the entire panel. (Some of the panels are fixed, but it is impossible to tell this from the surface detail.) The motif itself is achieved through thin sheets of oak applied to a wood core.

The details of this door and the wood paneling show how far Saarinen had come since the first parts of the Cranbrook School were finished. The wood paneling of the two dining halls serves the same functional purpose but is fabricated according to two entirely different sets of rules. In the older dining hall the pieces, insofar as possible, are solid wood, with some of the larger panels of veneered plywood. Each piece is rabbited into the adjacent piece so that movement in the wood due to change in humidity will not open the joints. Moldings are used to cover the joints between wood and plaster and between wood panel and wood floor. Alternating pieces have their rectilinear profiles altered in some way by curved moldings, in part to visually soften the profiles, in part as a kind of visual code long established to structurally explain the transitions, to demonstrate support at a projection, to demonstrate stability at a base. The only thing unusual in these profiles is deliberate crudeness and naiveté. They are single curves as opposed to the more standard large and small contrasting curves (figure 2.20), but this is standard Arts and Crafts practice in imitation of vernacular prototypes.

All of these elements are absent from the Kingswood paneling and doors. The wood is completely veneered; the surface, except for incisions, is completely flat. There are few rabbets and no moldings. The details rely on the dimensional stability that is a characteristics of plywood. Nor is there any demonstration of structural loads. The panels with their concentric motifs seem to defy rather than explain gravity, and the ornament, such as it is, is unrelated to joints, most of which are uncovered butt joints.

2.29

2.30

Kingswood School

Eliel Saarinen

Bloomfield Hills, Michigan, 1929–1931

2.29   **Geometric Mankato stone columns.**

2.30   **Floral Mankato stone columns.**

The vocabulary of materials and details developed for Kingswood is the most refined and formally coherent of any at Cranbrook, and it seems odd that Saarinen rarely chose to use it elsewhere. Except for the Institute of Science (1936), however, few of the subsequent or even contemporary buildings share much of the Kingswood vocabulary. Perhaps because Saarinen felt it inappropriate or perhaps out of sheer restlessness, he pursued decidedly different ends in his subsequent work.

THE CRANBROOK ART ACADEMY, MUSEUM AND LIBRARY

Simultaneously with the construction of the Cranbrook and Kingswood schools, Saarinen had been working on buildings for the art academy. The best known of the early buildings were the houses Saarinen built for himself and the sculptor Carl Milles (1928) and the Milles studio (1931). Although the motifs are similar to those used at Kingswood, the larger formal arrangements are quite different. The difference in scale and program between the Academy buildings and Kingswood accounts for some of the architectural differences, and in the late buildings the economic effects of the Depression perhaps played a part in determining their simplicity. Many of the studios are detailed with a utilitarian attitude, with few finishes and little trim or ornament, but continue the trends toward absence of structural expression in joinery and visual unity through the use of nonstructural motifs.

The large steel windows are squares set in concentric brick squares, and as at Kingswood they ignore the environmental and structural differences among head, jamb, and sill in favor of a uniform detail. The concentric square or hexagon motif appears also in the doors, as it does in most of the doors at Cranbrook, but like other details it had evolved. In the Cranbrook School the door was made in three layers: an inner core of 1-inch construction-grade wood, covered inside and out with finish tongue and groove boards set in concentric figures. The tongue and groove boards are complex compound curves, and are held in place with exposed fasteners. In the Kingswood doors only the two-dimensional shapes remain in the flat veneer arrangement described above. In the Milles studio Saarinen returns to the older construction system with three layers of solid wood, but the boards are given only a simple, flat curvature.

Saarinen's last buildings at Cranbrook were the library and museum, begun in 1939 and finished in 1942. They were meant to be Cranbrook's centerpiece, and they have provided its most familiar image along with the adjacent sculpture group by Milles. These buildings enjoy a certain popularity, particularly with contemporary Classicists, but most contemporary critics prefer the picturesque surprises and finer detail of the older work. This is particularly true of the detailing of the library and museum, which is ponderous and lacks the subtle refinements and delicacy of Kingswood or the Cranbrook School.

As in Saarinen's earlier work, a desire for solidity outweighs any concern for economy of material, particularly in the industrial sense, a concept that was much in vogue by 1940. He could not have been farther from the International Style Modernists in this regard, and his appreciation of Gothic architecture did not extend to an appreciation of its economy of material. He shared with many Classicists a belief that the expression of structural stability outweighs any concern for minimalism:

It is said—for example—that the reinforced concrete column, to be truthful in construction, must be dimensioned according to the load to be carried. This, of course, is a perfectly logical thought, and as such it must be highly recommended. On the other hand, if this perfectly logical and highly recommendable thought is brought to its extreme consequence, so that we are led to consider any form *untrue where more material had been used than utmost economy requires, there soon are controversies in sight. According to this, for example, the exquisite Doric column must be considered false in construction, since there is more material used than is needed for the load it has to carry.*

2.31

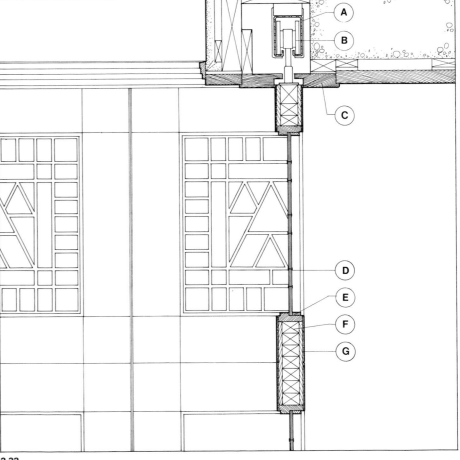

2.32

Kingswood School

Eliel Saarinen

Bloomfield Hills, Michigan, 1929–1931

Partition between dining room and auditorium

2.31 View.
(Courtesy of Cranbrook Archives)

2.32 Section.

A Steel track to support sliding door anchored to concrete lintel.

B Wheels allowing for the partition to slide horizontally into a pocket in the wall.

C Wood trim and blocking to cover concrete lintel. This section is removable so that the door track can be adjusted.

D ¼" glass with leaded inserts.

E Finish wood oak end piece and glass stop. This covers the end of the veneer and the wood core.

F Wood core.

G ⅛" oak veneer with grooves. This allows for use of a smaller quantity of the more expensive finish wood.

(CBA AD 08.412)

Well, if this point holds, then there is much untruth in nature's form-shaping too. Such would be the case with the dimensioning of the human body, for example. Please compare the human legs with the legs of a flamingo, and you have a good starting point for an argument. The legs of a flamingo are slender indeed, yet they seem to carry the body quite satisfactorily.[8]

Despite the modernist imagery of the Cranbrook Museum and Library (figure 2.33), and despite considerable use of modern materials, the structure and constructional systems are traditional in configuration. The two solid blocks of the library and museum are load-bearing masonry walls supporting one-way concrete slab floors and roofs of steel beams. There is considerable Mankato stone used here, for the most part in a structural role.

The portico is the most complex piece, and like much of Saarinen's work it seems contradictory in its intentions. It is supported by stone columns and a composite roof in which steel trusses have their bottom chords embedded in a concrete slab that forms the roof of the portico. The ceiling is the one piece of exposed concrete structure in the building. It is not, as it appears, a flat slab but an inverted one-way slab. The columns supporting the slab are solid Mankato stone, and while there is a difference in style between these columns and those of the Kingswood School, the construction is the same, solid stone rather than a nonstructural veneer on top of a concrete column.

The portico has a scaleless quality due to its minimal detailing. Its only modification is the three faint recessions recalling the concentric rectangle motif of other Saarinen work. In this minimalist aspect, it has a strong resemblance to the portico of Erik Gunnar Asplund's Woodland Crematorium in Stockholm, which was under construction at the same time. The stone mullions of the adjacent buildings, although simple rectilinear profiles, recall by contrast the hierarchies set up in the older Cranbrook buildings. Just as Saarinen used steel windows set in stone trim in the Cranbrook School to locate the dining hall and common room, he made a similar distinction here as the windows of the studio are steel with brick jambs, while those of the more important library are aluminum set in stone.

The library and museum ended Saarinen's work at Cranbrook but by no means ended the work of the firm Saarinen, Swanson, and Saarinen, which enjoyed considerable success during and after the Second World War. And if Saarinen was content to ignore the industrial images that surrounded him in Detroit, those who had produced those images were not content to ignore him, and it was perhaps inevitable that in postwar Detroit he would have to come to terms with the technology of the automobile and airplane. The first challenge came in 1942 when he was asked to design the master plan for Willow Run, a new town adjacent to Ford's B-24 plant. The second came in 1945 when he was chosen by Harley Earl to design the General Motors Technical Center.

He was far from the obvious choice, if GM's goal was an architecture that was not only compatible with the technology of automobile design but expressive of that technology. While Eliel Saarinen did not disdain the machine, he was more interested in its techniques than its aesthetics. He wrote in 1948:

Our time is beginning to understand the beauty of forms expressing contemporary functional demands. One learns to understand the beauty of a functionally designed airplane, a railroad car, an automobile, a motorship, et cetera. . . . But even if the non-functional course of imitative decoration is abandoned, and the machine-inspired functional course is accepted, there still are two different ways to go. In the first place, there is the way leading toward the enthronement of the spirit of the machine. And in the second place, there is the way leading toward the enthronement of the principle of the machine. . . . To accept the spirit of the machine as the basis of form-development, is equivalent to mechanization of form. This means that form-expression grows directly from machine-facilities, and that the influence of human atmosphere—human aura—within and about our homes, is bound to be affected by the spirit of these machine-facilities. Accepting such an attitude, man is forced to dwell in a coldly mechanized atmosphere. He

2.33

2.34

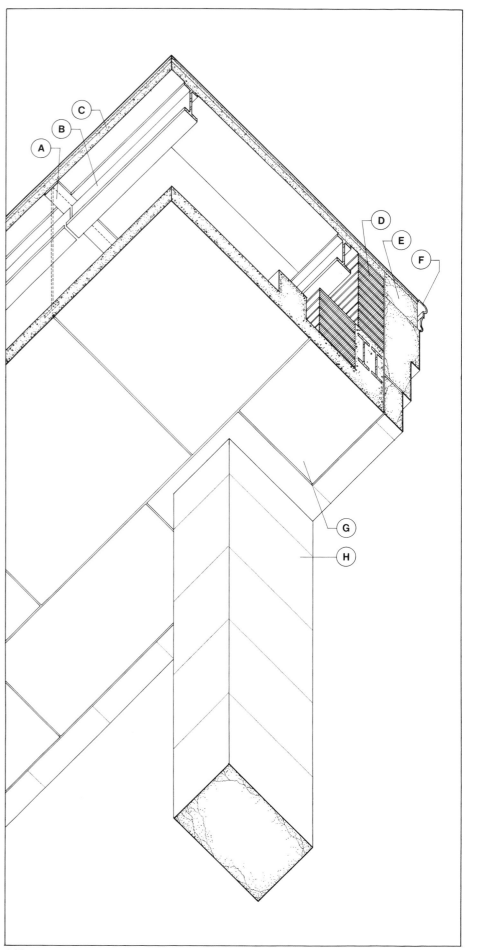

2.35

Cranbrook Museum and Library

Eliel Saarinen

Bloomfield Hills, Michigan, 1939–1942

2.33 **Portico.**

2.34 **Columns and roof of portico.**

2.35 **Wall section of portico.**
  A WF 30 steel girder.
  B Steel purlin supporting the concrete deck and carrying the loads back to the girder.
  C Composition roof on concrete deck.
  D Brick backup wall.
  E Mankato stone cornice.
  F 22 gauge aluminum trim.
  G Inverted ribbed concrete slab. Although part of the structure is exposed, it does not give a clear indication of the real nature of the structure.
  H Solid Mankato stone column. Unlike a clad stone column, this must be installed first rather than last since it is structural.
  (CBA AD 11.225, AD 11.1727)

will be surrounded by forms breathing the machine spirit, though they are machines neither by nature nor by function. Thus an art-form would come into existence which might be expressive of our mechanized age, but which might not be expressive of the human cultural aspirations of this mechanized age. Consequently, such a mechanized art-form cannot be truly genuine from a humanly acceptable point of view. It is affected. The spirit of the machine has been imposed upon form. The functional principle of the machine has been slighted.[9]

If the elder Saarinen was opposed to "imposing the spirit of the machine upon form" in print, he was not in fact, and the machine, in theory and in image, is the controlling factor in the 1945 design for the Technical Center. One should not, however, rush to accuse Eliel of yet another inconsistency, for the work is probably not his but that of his son Eero, and if the father was reluctant to adapt the imagery and ideals of industrialization, this cannot be said of the son, who could not wait to embrace them.

3   The Conversion of Erik Gunnar Asplund: 1930–1940

Of course, if a person says that spiritual light is different from the kind that the senses perceive, there is no point in arguing with him, provided he grants that in this event the light which the visual power perceives is not a spiritual nature. In fact, nothing prevents one name being applied to several things, however different they may be.

St. Thomas Aquinas, *Exposition of Aristotle on the Soul*

Asplund was a man of two careers, one Classical, one Modern, but his version of the Classical was always a light one. His Classical elements were paper-thin pilasters rather than round robust columns. His windows were seldom deep set in thick masonry, but seemed to be pasted onto membrane walls. Domes were never heavy vaults of stone but rather dissolved into an artificial sky. Even when he worked in masonry, the articulation of mass was subdued, as in the Stockholm Public Library.

This attitude was not atypical of Asplund's contemporaries among the Nordic Classicists. Nordic Classicism was a movement both vernacular and classical at the same time, but was based in either case on examples that did not lend themselves to an expression of mass. It was a style in any case that was not a promising point of departure for any type of structural expression. The aim of Nordic Classicism, as of many other movements at the turn of the century, was to transcend style, to free architecture from fashion and whim, and as with many other movements the means to accomplish this was a return to beginnings, in this case to primitive Doric buildings. The goal was to achieve the timeless, the basic, the elemental, hence the almost primitive and often incorrect use of Classical elements. Unfortunately this naiveté was often achieved at the expense of accuracy of structural expression, and Nordic Classicism is full of falsehoods—columns that do not support, pediments where there are no roofs, and vaults that are hung rather than self-supporting.

Asplund's first building at the Woodland Cemetery complex, the Woodland Chapel, shows all of the virtues and most of the problems of the style. Asplund and Sigurd Lewerentz had won the competition for the cemetery in 1914, but Lewerentz was effectively fired in the 1930s and Asplund continued alone until his death in 1940. Like many Asplund projects, it spans the length of his career and marks his career's many changes. The first buildings, Lewerentz's Chapel of the Resurrection and Asplund's Woodland Chapel, were very much in the style of Nordic Classicism.

In form, the Woodland Chapel is a steeply sloped pyramid-like roof supported by wood Doric columns, six of which form a portico and eight of which support an internal dome. The roof structure is of wood trusses supported by the walls and the wood columns, and the trusses are distorted considerably from their logical structural locations to accommodate the opening for the dome. The differences

3.1

3.2

between the chapel's real structural system and the implied structural system are considerable. The dome is a downright falsehood, being plaster suspended from wood trusses rather than a true masonry dome. The columns are real enough (although made of wood) but are topped only by a flat ceiling of wood planks; the complex structure of beams and trusses above is neither shown nor indicated. In Asplund's defense, one can argue that the columns and domes are not meant to be read as structure. Both are light and visually detached from what is around them. The columns are unfluted, incorrectly proportioned, have no entablature, and are separated from the ceiling by wood blocks. The dome has no ribs, coffers, or moldings, and could not appear lighter.

These types of elements—vestigial forms, originating in stone construction but executed in inappropriate materials, devoid of structural logic—were precisely those that Modernism wished to discard, and Asplund later did discard most of them, but he took with him certain attitudes toward structural elements and materials. The first of these was an interest in minimal mass, in lightness. Most of his Classical buildings, except for the Stockholm Public Library, deprive the Classical elements of the mass and weight originally associated with them. Secondly, Asplund uses recognizable elements, such as columns, as a kind of architectural quotation, complete with an architectural quotation mark; i.e., they are detached from the beams they support, the walls they engage, the ground on which they sit. In his Classical phase Asplund treated walls, windows, balustrades, and other elements this way, as in the doors and windows of the Villa Snellman or Lister County Courthouse or the entry to the Stockholm Library; and he continued to treat them this way after he became a Modernist.

THE STOCKHOLM EXHIBITION

Asplund entered the Modern movement in spectacular fashion with the design of the Stockholm Exhibition of the Swedish Arts and Crafts Society in 1930. This name does not begin to describe the array of industrial and commercial objects—boats, planes, gigantic electric signs—that the exhibition included, externally enclosed by thin opaque white screens or large sheets of glazing. The intention seems to have been to make the architecture almost disappear. Asplund wrote of the Entry Pavilion: "It is perhaps not a building but rather a necessary, festive advertising arrangement, dressed during the day in colorful international flags and at night in rich illumination."[1] And Asplund's friend Alvar Aalto wrote after visiting the exhibition:

Asplund's architecture explodes all the boundaries. The purpose is a celebration with no preconceived notions as to whether it should be achieved with architectural or other means. It is not a composition in stone, glass, and steel, as the functionalist hating exhibition visitor might imagine, but rather a composition in houses, flags, searchlights, flowers, fireworks, happy people and clean tablecloths.

The more the center of gravity within architecture is displaced from valuing individual synthesis, monuments, etc. toward a more organizational concept or relevant problems the more meaningful becomes what we call an "exhibition."[2]

Kenneth Frampton suggests that Asplund's Modernist influences were not so much the International Style architects as the Russian Constructivists. The first proposal for the exhibition featured airships, cables, lights, and other elements recalling the propaganda kiosks and mass demonstration designs of the Russian Constructivists, and there is a clear link between the advertising mast Asplund designed for the exhibition, with its array of electric signs, and constructivist projects such as Aleksandr Vesnin's Pravda Tower or the propaganda kiosks of Alecsandra Ekster or Gustav Klutis.

Whatever the source of these ideas, there were two key tenets of Modernism to which Asplund subscribed, however erratically. The first was material minimalism, that buildings should be designed like boats or planes to achieve maximum strength with minimum weight. The Transport Pavilion (figure 3.5) is a case in point, with its thin, light roof rising over the sailboats and planes below. The other idea is that implied by the advertising mast, suggesting an architecture that had no

3.3

3.4

3.5

Stockholm Exhibition

Erik Gunnar Asplund

Stockholm, 1930

material, of light only, of pure transparency, in which materials have not so much been minimized as transformed into energy. This is best illustrated by the columns of the Entry Pavilion, which, although made of steel, are hollowed out to contain lights and partially enclosed in glass so that at night they appear to be columns of pure light.

Ironically the steel frames that were the key to the Modernist imagery are only a small part of the whole. Only the Entry and Transport pavilions, Paradise Restaurant, and bandstand used steel extensively. The remainder of the buildings were of wood framing with Eternit (asbestos) panels. Nevertheless, the steel and stucco language of the Stockholm Exhibition was one of the International Style's purist expressions. Seldom was the structural steel so literally expressed and exposed. Never before or again were the screen walls so thin. But the exhibition was also in some ways an end. By 1930 many of the leaders of the International Style, particularly Le Corbusier, were abandoning the pure expression in favor of a richer palate of materials and structure.

But if the Stockholm Exhibition placed Asplund at the forefront of International Style Modernism, he was an unlikely candidate for the role and Scandinavia an unlikely place for it to happen. Sweden was no more in a position to implement large-scale building industrialization than Germany or France, perhaps less so. Traditional materials such as wood and brick were often more accessible and economical than steel and concrete. When Asplund and Aalto changed from traditional to "modern" forms they changed from traditional to "modern" building systems, perhaps seeing themselves as accelerating the pace of industrialization in their native countries. The climate posed another problem. Exposed structural frames, thin screenlike walls, and large areas of glazing were difficult to achieve in a climate where problems of heat loss, thermal expansion, and weathering favored layered and clad systems of construction with small openings.

If Asplund was undaunted by these problems it is perhaps because his interest in minimal construction was not altogether structural, that while he might design to achieve a minimal mass, it was in the interest of an aesthetic end. Like Moholy-Nagy, his interest was in a virtual mass, one that existed only in light. His influences here were probably less modern painting than modern philosophy. Stuart Wrede points out the connection between this Modernist idea of transparency and dematerialization and the ideas of Oswald Spengler, of whom Asplund was an admirer. In a 1931 article Asplund wrote:

Under the pressure of reality people are now beginning all over the world to turn away from the traditional conception [of enclosing space], as it works against the solution of real problems, and are beginning to arrive at the principle of dissolved space. . . .

According to this conception, architectural space attempts, in other words, not to enclose itself as an architecturally defined and independent entity, but to open itself up for sun, nature, human life, and movement.

The dissolution and transformability of space, the opening up of the building mass, the intimate connection between outside and inside all seem to indicate to me that our architectural conception of space is approaching the Spenglerian archetype: the endless space.[3]

But like Moholy-Nagy, Asplund saw the evidence of this space in both the Gothic cathedral and the creations of modern engineering. He wrote in the same article describing a cable and mast radio tower in Ankara:

I have spoken about the dissolution of architectural space and open city space. But our modern conception of space also consists of something else. . . . It also holds true for the spatial value of the buildings and objects themselves. I don't mean to suggest that our perception points to a dissolution of building solidity in the same way as that of a city space, for a house of course has to have a certain completed bodily mass, but it indicates an opening up of building solidity—a removal of material weight, massiveness, an intensification of the constructional

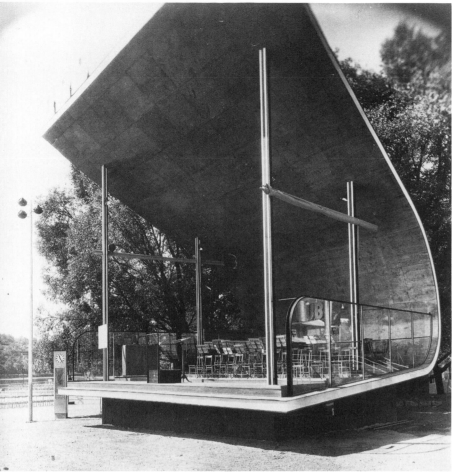

3.6

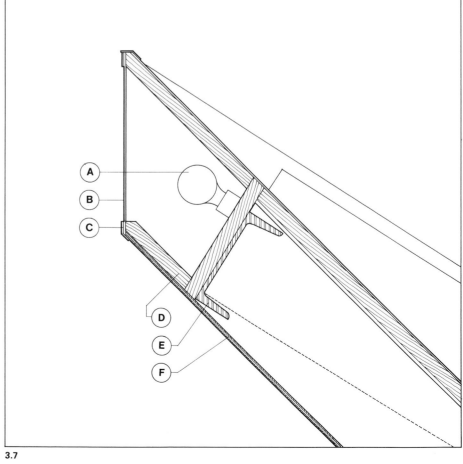

3.7

3.6   **View.**

(Kälgrens ateljé: Swedish Architecture Museum)

3.7   **Edge detail.**

A   Incandescent light. This demonstrated the hollow nature of the construction and gave the curved plane a glowing edge, creating the impression of two warped layers filled with light.

B   Translucent lens to diffuse light and illuminate edge.

C   Metal edge to hold lens and cover end of wood.

D   Wood planking.

E   Steel channel framing. The steel columns are exposed while the steel beams are concealed.

F   Plywood cladding.

(SAM AM-88-02-8705)

expression—as we can learn in principle from this beautiful engineering project, the radio station in Ankara, and from the Gothic Style.[4]

Hakon Ahlberg, Asplund's colleague, took another view, and saw Asplund as falling under the spell of Le Corbusier, abandoning the laws of architecture for those of engineering, i.e., the economical use of material:

Old time architecture's comfortable elaboration of proportions between holes and brick surfaces should—quite consistently—be replaced by a more dramatic demonstration of the play of static forces. But since materials and designs were still much the same as before, the technique itself must be brushed up. There was witnessed the paradoxical change that the architect, who shortly before had kept the engineer carefully hidden behind the scenes, now chased him out on the stage to entertain the public with his art.[5]

The engineer in this case was Stig Ödeen, who Asplund had met at the time he was working on the Stockholm Exhibition, and Ödeen was to play a major role in minimizing the structure of Asplund's next building, the Bredenberg Department Store.

Asplund never again duplicated either the formal or structural language of the Stockholm Exhibition, perhaps because of formal predilection but more likely due to functional necessity. Unlike his hybrid load-bearing wall and frame buildings of 1915 to 1930, most of Asplund's post-1930 buildings employ steel and concrete frames, but these frames are rarely literally exposed. The need for fireproofing, the need for cladding and insulation, and the complex programs of his post-1930 commissions made a direct exposure of the frame impossible. The Stockholm Exhibition buildings were temporary, had minimal, if any, environmental requirements, and were thus not subject to these limitations. Out of these conditions grew Asplund's second Modern constructional language, in which buildings are usually of composite construction (concrete and steel) but in which the frame is expressed by analogous means. The steel frames of the Gothenburg Law Courts Annex, the Bredenberg Store, and the Woodland Crematorium are never exposed, but through the manipulation of their encrustations of concrete, stone, or stucco are almost sculptural reinterpretations of the exposed steel framing of the Stockholm Exhibition.

THE BREDENBERG DEPARTMENT STORE

This was Asplund's first major completed building following the Stockholm Exhibition, and had he sought a commission to demonstrate the possibilities of his new frame and skin style, he could not have done better than this seven-story commercial building in central Stockholm.

Both ideas of the Stockholm Exhibition—the minimizing of materials and the dematerialization of the building through light—are present here. Asplund explained their use in pragmatic terms. A street widening cut the site in half, necessitating a small, narrow floor plan, and in order to maximize floor area the structure had to occupy the minimum area. Likewise the prominent electric sign and thin, transparent walls were explained as necessities of advertising.

There were a number of modern curtain wall or "skin and bones" facades built by 1930, and the typical Modernist version called for the wall to stand free in front of the columns. This maximizes the structural capacity of concrete by cantilevering the edge of the slab and makes possible the free facade, unencumbered by columns. This was the doctrinaire version established by Le Corbusier in the 1920s and used by International Style architects with few exceptions. But Asplund's attachment to the column, although muted, was still strong, and he wished to show the frame; thus he places the columns on the plane of the exterior wall. This also, of course, had the effect of the minimizing the thickness of the entire assembly.

Bredenberg was Asplund's first building with a complete steel frame; only the party wall is a bearing wall. The steel frame could not be exposed, of course, due to the fireproofing and insulation that are required in a building of this size in this climate and location. Asplund used a composite system, a mixture of concrete and steel,

3.8

3.9

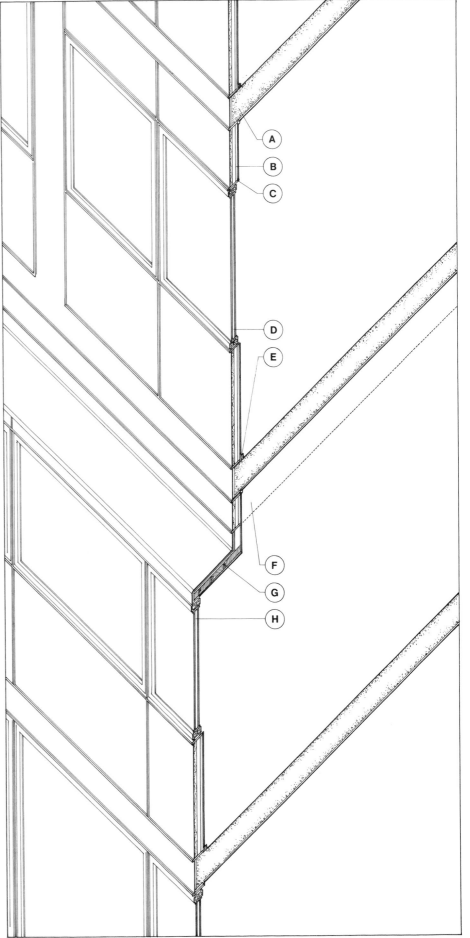

3.10

Bredenberg Department Store

Erik Gunnar Asplund

Stockholm, 1933–1935

3.8 **View.**

(Hansa Photo: Swedish Architecture Museum)

3.9 **Facade after reconstruction.**

3.10 **Wall section.**

A 18 cm cinder concrete structural slab spanning between composite beams. The structure, although only partially exposed, is expressed.

B Typical wall construction of 3 cm travertine, 4 cm thick cork with asphalt coating, air space, and 2 mm sheet metal interior finish.

C Steel plates and clips to support stone. The windows are attached to these as well.

D Double Idesta steel window with copper flashing.

E Wood trim and base.

F INF 45 steel beam at column beyond encased in concrete.

G Cover of projecting bay of lead sheet roofing supported by 12 mm porous masonite on 2 cm wood planks.

H Projecting bay. Although constructed similarly to the wall above, it is cantilevered beyond the plane of the wall so that the stone panels are continuous.

(SAM AM-88-02-9098, 9145, 9283)

in which the concrete not only fireproofs the steel but bonds with it so that both materials behave as one structure. Such a composite structure normally appears to be concrete, but Asplund sculptured the concrete of the columns to suggest the profiles of the steel sections inside, developing his own modern order of columns and entablature that he used in many buildings of the 1930s.

Unlike the typical International Style facade, Asplund's solution pushed the composite steel and concrete columns to the minimalist edge. They are not exposed but covered with a thin layer of plaster. On the interior the concrete is cut out to provide space for the heating pipes, but this also has the effect of sculpting the concrete in the shape of the wide flange inside so that it becomes a way of representing the steel structure without exposing it. The panels between columns were filled with thin travertine slabs, and it was here that Asplund applied the idea of a minimal building envelope with the most rigor and the least technical restraint, achieving aesthetic success at the expense of technical failure. The travertine panels are only a thin veneer 3 cm thick. This was not unusual in itself; buildings had been constructed of marble veneers almost as long as they had been constructed of marble. The thin slab requires additional support, traditionally provided by a thicker backup wall of brick or other masonry, so that the actual wall is often a foot or more thick. Asplund dispensed with the backup wall and hung the marble slabs between flat steel bars running between the concrete floor slabs. These steel bars were exposed on the exterior but not on the interior. A layer of cork insulation, an air space, and sheet metal internal finish were added to the wall, but the total thickness remained less than 3½ inches. The windows were steel as well and also hung from the steel bars supporting the stone, giving the facade both technical and aesthetic unity. The windows are the double-pivoting type common in Scandinavia. Asplund had used double windows before although seldom in steel, but the steel window profile is slimmer than that of wood. Again, he kept each element to its minimum dimension.

This was Asplund's great virtue as a detailer. No one else could design so taut a wall. No one could pack so much tension into so shallow a space. No one could so carefully articulate each of the parts while preserving the unity of the whole. On a conceptual level the facade is a great success, and went further than most of Asplund's contemporaries in reconciling the desires of modern construction theory with the realities of modern construction practices. It expressed the frame without exposing it. It built in an honest way but acknowledged the layered nature of modern building and the need for fireproofing and insulation. It gave an accurate description of the structural behavior of the building by exposing not only its primary but its secondary structural systems. If one judges the quality of architectural detailing by the quantity of constructional facts it reveals, Bredenberg is superior to any building by Le Corbusier. Asplund shows us major girders, internal steel, major and minor structural framing, all of which are visible from the exterior or interior. In Le Corbusier's contemporary dormitory, the Pavillon Suisse, all of these are present but not so many are visible.

All these virtues, however, cannot make up for the building's technical shortcomings. The stone facade has not weathered well. Presumably this was due to exposing the steel bars of the exterior wall to the elements, the resulting chemical reaction possibly acting to deteriorate the stone. There are many successful applications of stone veneers in Scandinavia, but there are many unsuccessful ones as well. Alvar Aalto in particular was to experience similar problems. Stone supported by metal frames is a system in common use today but the supports are placed behind the face of the stone, protected from the weather but also invisible from the exterior.

The one dramatic interruption in the rigid structural frame of Bredenberg was the stair. Since encouraging customers to go up to the upper floors of the store was an important consideration, this was a key architectural feature. The structure of the stair itself is notable for its minimalism, consisting only of a folded slab 7 cm thick with no stringers (beams) underneath for support as in conventional stair structures. In the handrail and baluster of this stair is found the germ of another Asplund detailing concept, what Alvar Aalto called the humanizing of architecture,

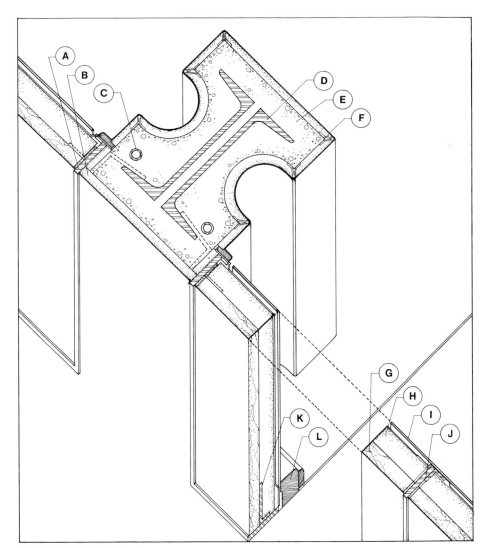

3.12

3.11

Bredenberg Department Store

Erik Gunnar Asplund

Stockholm, 1933–1935

3.11   Wall detail of rebuilt facade.

3.12   Column and wall details.

A   9 × 85 mm steel plate at column for window attachment. The wall is only 4 inches thick, less than half the thickness of a typical veneered stone wall. It has been completely rebuilt because of corrosion.

B   2 cm stucco on column.

C   Electrical conduit.

D   Two steel channels. The structure is a composite system in which a steel frame is encased in concrete to provide additional structural support and fireproofing.

E   Cinder concrete. The sides of the column are hollowed out to indicate the profile of the steel beneath and to accommodate the steam pipes (not shown).

F   Plaster with corner screeds to provide the plasterer with a guide to form the shape of the column and prevent chipping of the plaster.

G   3 cm travertine panel attached to steel bar with clip angles.

H   4 cm thick cork to insulate the wall, with asphalt coating to create a vapor barrier, preventing water vapor on the interior from reaching the cold side of the insulation where it would condense, potentially damaging the wall.

I   2 mm sheet metal interior finish and air space, probably a further defense against condensation.

J   Steel plate with 2 × 2 cm steel angle attached to stone. Placing these between rather than behind the stone slabs allowed the means of support to be shown but also exposed the steel to corrosion.

K   8 × 65 mm steel plate angle.

L   Wood trim and wood base to cover and close the joint between floor and wall.

(SAM AM-88-02-9135)

the origin of which he ascribed to Asplund. The railing support is designed in accordance with the ideas of minimal material and dematerialization through light. The supports on the stair are "industrial," consisting of round 2.5-cm metal tubes. The railing support at the well is a wood and glass display case, also framed by 2.5-cm tubes overhanging the edge of the slab. The handrail, however, is neither metallic, geometric, nor industrial, but a solid wood element of red beech curved into an organic shape. Thus where the human body, the hand, comes into contact with architecture different rules apply. The handrail is shaped to fit the hand and is formed of a material not cold to the touch. These considerations of comfort, what Asplund and Aalto both called psychological factors, outweigh any dogmas of industrialization in the determination of form.

Aalto and Asplund were in close contact during this period, with Aalto making almost monthly visits to Asplund's office, and both were fascinated with the idea of dematerialization of mass through light. In practice this translated into frequent use of louvered screens in the work of both men, and Bredenberg shows the beginning of this idea in the detailing of the cloakroom, where, rather than solid enclosing walls, the screens are made of thin, tightly spaced wood fins, supported by a tubular structure similar to that used in the stair. The louvered screen was to become almost a cliché in the work of both architects, and is used in widely different applications, such as windows, railings, skylights, and other elements.

The use of small-scale, repetitive, identical elements in their work was in part their response to the pressing issue of the day, standardization. Many architects in Scandinavia took the line of Gropius and the early Le Corbusier, that building components should be mass-produced in large-scale, Model T-like components. Asplund, while calling for standardization, wished to do so on a smaller scale. He wrote in 1936: "There should be a standardization of the parts, not of the whole. We can without sacrificing a sense of well-being have the same carpentry, sanitation equipment, the same construction of wall or stair details as a lot of other families, that does not matter. But we do not want all homes of a certain size to be identical or all details to be repeated endlessly."[6]

The frequent use of repetitive louvered screens in the work of Aalto and Asplund was a small-scale version of a cellular standardization. Both saw the true inspiration for standardization in nature. Asplund wrote: "But the standardization of parts and the variation of the whole are not incompatible. We can arrive at significantly different character with the same construction elements. There is a certain parallelism between architectural and human plasticity—the figure suggests that the same standard elements used and arranged in different ways can result in significantly different character natural both for buildings intended for disciplined work and for homes."[7]

Bredenberg is the first and perhaps only permanent expression of Asplund's pure Modern style, for in subsequent work he immediately began to introduce elements from his Classical past. The Modern elements remain, but coexist alongside yet another Asplund language, that of reinterpreted Classicism. This was a particularly useful strategy when Asplund took up a project he had begun twenty years before, the Gothenburg Law Courts.

THE GOTHENBURG LAW COURTS ANNEX

Asplund won the competition for the extension to the Gothenburg Law Courts in 1913, but for various reasons construction did not begin until 1934, and during that time the scheme went through a variety of formal and stylistic configurations. The large number of alternatives considered was in part the result of the stylistic changes of Asplund's personal development, but there was also the question of how to join the new building to the old. Should the two buildings be of equal importance? Should the two buildings be joined to form one with an unbroken if highly asymmetrical facade, or should it be an annex, a new building, subservient to the old?

3.13

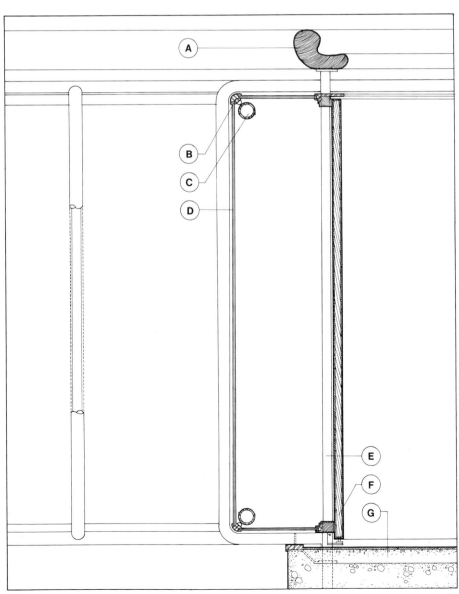

3.14

Bredenberg Department Store

Erik Gunnar Asplund

Stockholm, 1933–1935

3.13 **Stair.** Note the concrete stair constructed of 2½″ concrete slabs without supporting beams.
(C. G. Rosenberg: Swedish Architecture Museum)

3.14 **Section of casework at stair.**
A Red beech handrail. The parts that come into contact with the hand have an organic shape. Compare the Aalto handrails in figure 5.11.
B Glass frame attached to 2.5 cm tube frame beyond.
C Light fixture.
D 5 mm plate glass display case.
E 2.5 cm tube support for railing.
F Red beech doors to access display case.
G Concrete slab of stair landing.
(SAM AM-88-02-9164)

It is not easy to say which of these options Asplund chose. Internally, in lieu of two separate courtyards, he gave the new building an enclosed, glazed court with a transparent link to the old open courtyard. On the outward-facing facades he chose a frame and panel design that, although Modern, took the Neoclassical design of the older building as a point of departure.

One of his assistants, Åke Porne, recalled:

I said [to Asplund] "we thought that the best way of showing consideration for the old building was not by extending it, continuing the architecture, but by doing something new but with consideration for the old part." "I'm not at all convinced of that," said Asplund. "No, here we'll have to stick to the inside. Our contribution here will be the inside."

We were puzzled by this, because we thought that the outside and the inside were interdependent. But they weren't allowed to be that. . . . We wondered when Asplund would change his mind, because that he would have to do. And so he did eventually, but in this peculiar way that, without any intermediate stage between the new and the old, he elongated the building with its pilaster divisions and everything so that the front with the entrance came to be skewed. We thought it very curious indeed.[8]

The building thus has two distinct parts—the solid U shape of the exterior that completes the form of the old courthouse, and the new "courtyard," actually an atrium, with a glazed link to the old—and there are two languages of detail to correspond to the different conditions of these two parts, in contrast to the unified character of Stockholm or Bredenberg. These languages included all the elements of the building: structure, windows, walls, and handrails. Each language posited a different relationship of structure to plan. Each posited and solved architectural problems in different, sometimes contradictory ways. One language, that of the interior, is an extension of the International Style and Constructivist themes of Bredenberg, but the second, that of the exterior, was a reinterpretation of the Classical language in modern materials.

The main facade is roughly a square grid with columns and beams of equal width. The grid is distorted to align with the old building so that base matches base, window matches window, cornice matches cornice. The column spacing is roughly equal to that of the old building, yet the grid remains completely abstract except for two modifications. The columns are slightly enlarged at the bottom to imply a Classical base and at the top are slightly reduced in width and then flared. This does not suggest a cornice so much as it recalls one of Asplund's favorite buildings, the temple of Neptune at Paestum. The Gothenburg facade is one of Asplund's more appealing compositions, hovering between abstraction and literalness.

Many of these modifications to the frame, although they are part of the structure, are at the expense of clarity of structural expression. The column base and capital serve no structural purpose. The column spacing is grossly inefficient. The system employed could easily have spanned twice the distance. Even the abstract grid is a distortion; columns and beams allowed to seek their optimum dimensions are seldom of equal width. In short, the ideas of light and material efficiency that were the guiding principles of Asplund's work in the early 1930s are of minimal importance here.

Of course none of the structure, even the concrete, is really visible, as the columns, beams, and brick infill are all covered with a thin layer of plaster. The whole facade is a highly layered construction, and Asplund uses this fact to advantage by insulating the steel frame. He is closer to contemporary practice than Le Corbusier in this regard, for if material efficiency was a primary concern of International Style Modernism, thermal efficiency was not. It is a rare Modernist building of the mid-1930s that was designed with any concern for heat loss. Most of those that were are for obvious reasons in Scandinavia. Thus Asplund's design is perhaps more a product of necessity and local convention than of architectural sensitivity.

3.15

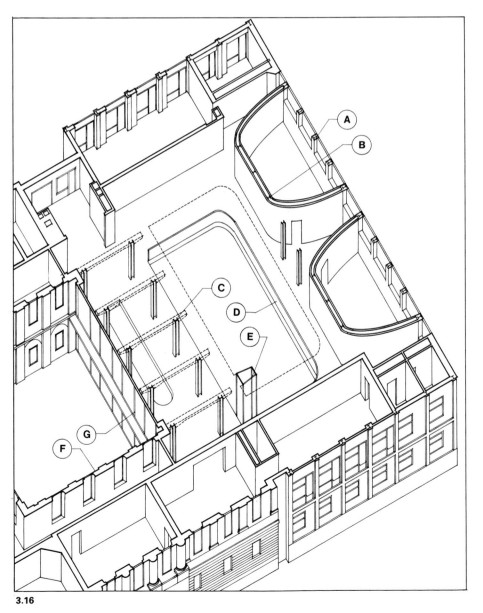

3.16

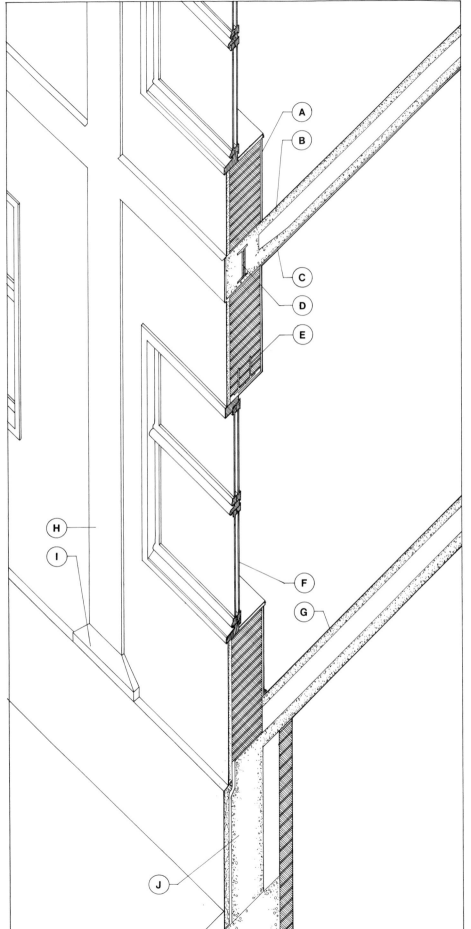

3.17

Gothenburg Law Courts Annex

Erik Gunnar Asplund

Gothenburg, Sweden, 1934–1937

3.15 View.

(Swedish Architecture Museum)

3.16 Framing.

A DIP 20 and DIP 22 steel columns. The structure of the U-shaped block is a composite steel and concrete replication of the Classical form of the older building, containing what are rather small spans.

B DIP 20 steel column hidden in courtroom wall.

C Steel beam encased in concrete supporting slab. The structure of the link uses freestanding columns, longer-span elements, and a minimum of material to minimize the mass of this part of the building.

D The railings are solid on the three sides facing the exterior and open toward the courtyard.

E Glass-enclosed elevator.

F Existing courthouse and courtyard.

G Courtyard curtain wall (see figure 3.20).

(SAM AM-88-02-2237, 2441, 2252)

3.17 Wall section.

A Brick masonry wall with stucco facing and copper flashing at base.

B Double composite steel and concrete floor with filling.

C Heating pipes in ceiling. These heat the entire surface of the ceiling, which then radiates the heat into the space.

D Dimmel 72 steel beam encased in concrete with cork insulation on inner face, framing into column.

E Steel T lintels to support masonry over opening.

F Oak window frame with teak sash. Double windows are used to minimize heat loss.

G Oak floor on concrete composite slab with filling.

H Steel column encased in concrete and faced with plaster. While not exposed, the structure is described by the stucco facing.

I Pedestal. This serves no functional purpose except to recall the pedestals of the older building.

J Granite base on concrete wall. This creates a base suggestive of but not identical to the base of the older building.

(SAM AM-88-02-2282)

The conservative nature of the facade is more than skin-deep. The tightly spaced columns create a small-scale cage that corresponds generally to the plan divisions of the building (each room has a column at its four corners). This was the precise opposite of the principles of Le Corbusier's free plan, where structural steel and concrete were used to establish the independence of structure and space. In the Corbusian system the plan was free to seek its own form with no limitation imposed by walls or beams. As Louis Kahn was to point out later, this was exactly the problem, that architecture and structure were no longer closely related, that Modern plans lacked the discipline imposed by structural limitations. Asplund, like other conservative architects of the 1930s, was attempting to relate more closely structural plan and spatial plan by means of the cage concept, in which each major room is defined by four columns.

None of this is true of the second of these languages, that of the glazed courtyard. This was a refined version of the ideas developed at Bredenberg: a minimal use of material, maximum transparency of the pieces, and the further development of the dematerialization of opaque planes through light. This is not done for the sake of adhering to Modernist dogma, but to conceptually link the new interior courtyard with the old exterior one by minimizing the mass of the link between the two.

The structural system is the same composite of steel and concrete used at Bredenberg, but with even more sculpting and carving to minimize the material. The structure is of the double cantilever type used by the German and Dutch Rationalists. It is an assembly that, at least in theory, uses the minimum amount of concrete since the loads on the cantilever offset the stresses created by loads between the columns. The columns are steel wrapped in concrete but the covering is much thinner than at Bredenberg. The beams have a similar treatment and are also carved out to show the location of the flanges and taper toward their cantilevered ends as the bending moment of the beam decreases.

The floor itself is also made of steel beams, here encased in a single slab at the second floor and a double at the third, a sandwich of two concrete slabs with a nonstructural lightweight filling in between. This was not an Asplund invention but a typical method for increasing the strength of a slab by increasing its depth while avoiding an increase in weight. As in any beam or slab it is typically the top and bottom that do most of the work, not the middle.

Despite the apparent directness of the structural expression of this frame, there is a difference between the structure one sees and the one that exists, albeit a logical one. No steel members are visible, only the concrete jackets, and of these only the column and major beams are shown, with the minor steel beams unexposed and unexpressed. Although this is not a true clad system in that the concrete is part of the structure, as in any analogous system the structure that is perceived is an abstraction of a more complex reality.

Between the exterior courtyard and the atrium is a wall almost entirely of glass. The logical window material to maximize transparency would have been steel because of its minimal frame size, and Asplund had used such a system, sheet-metal-clad iron bars, in the large windows of the Stockholm Public Library. But here he wished to use wood to match the other windows, and so compromised. Thus the window wall is actually a steel-reinforced wood system in which thin steel plates are clad in wood (figure 3.20). The resulting profile is larger than an all-steel section, smaller than an all-wood section, and vastly superior to the steel in term of maintenance. Asplund's intent was probably to unify the fenestration by matching these windows with the smaller wood windows of the exterior, which in turn were meant to match those of the old building. He may also have meant to create a kind of metaphorical trellis since he planted vines at the bottom of the window wall.

The interior of the atrium develops the theme of mass dematerialized by light. It is lit by a shed roof skylight, but the light enters the room through the filter of the open roof structure created by continuing the steel roof beams across the opening. The steel beams are as always encased in a thin layer of concrete slightly rounded

3.18

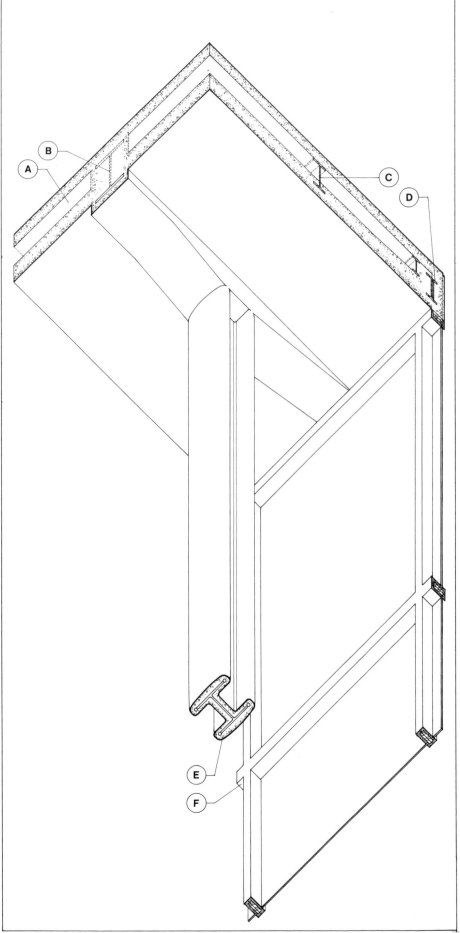

3.19

Gothenburg Law Courts Annex

Erik Gunnar Asplund

Gothenburg, Sweden, 1934–1937

3.18 **Wall facing courtyard**.

3.19 **Structure of link at upper floor.**

A   Double concrete slab with filling. Most of Asplund's slabs consist of two layers of concrete separated by a lighter filling. Since the top and bottom of the slab take most of the load, this creates a thicker slab while reducing its weight.

B   Steel beams encased in concrete, tapered toward the edge to coincide with bending moments.

C   Steel purlin framing into beam. While the major beams are exposed, the small ones are not.

D   Steel beam at edge with insulation on exterior face.

E   Steel column encased in concrete. As in the Bredenberg store, the concrete is carved away to reveal the steel profile, but here the concrete is much thinner.

F   Steel-reinforced teak curtain wall. See figure 3.20.
   (SAM AM-88-02-2450)

3.20 **Curtain wall details.**

A   6–8 mm plate glass.

B   Typical maple or oak mullion.

C   Steel reinforcement with 2 mm cork wrapping to allow a smaller profile of mullion and thus maintain transparency.

D   Exterior trim and glazing bead. Oak is not typically used on the exterior with a clear finish. This window has been rebuilt to accommodate double glazing.

E   Anchor to tie window mullion to concrete.

F   Masonry wall and plaster finish.

G   Oak sill sloped to drain water from condensation.

H   Oak floor on concrete slab with steel bulb T reinforcing.

I   Window flashing to drain water away from the horizontal joint at the base.

J   Waterproof membrane to intercept the water that penetrates the floor boards.

K   Wood slat floor at balcony. The open joints allow water to drain.
   (SAM AM-88-02-2364)

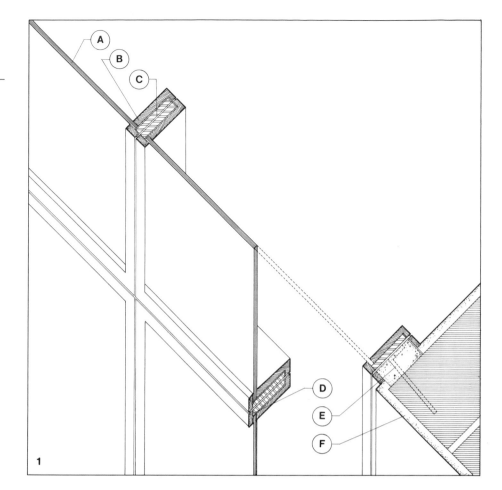

1

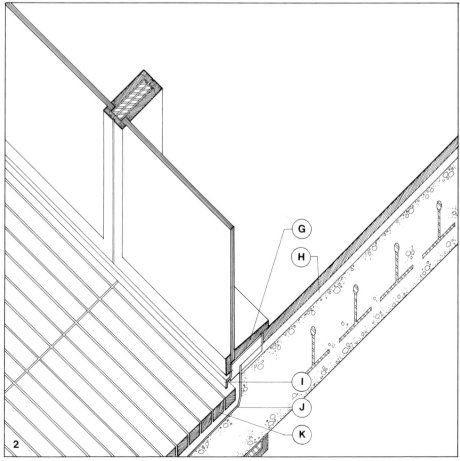

2

3.20

3.21

3.22

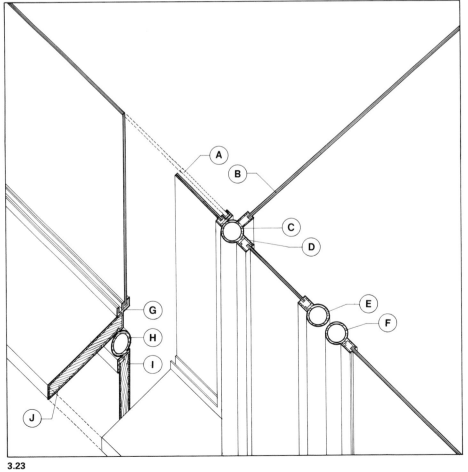

3.23

Gothenburg Law Courts Annex

Erik Gunnar Asplund

Gothenburg, Sweden, 1934–1937

3.21   **Drinking fountain with transparent bowl.**

3.22   **Interior showing elevator cage.**

3.23   **Section of elevator cage door at ground floor.**

A   Sliding glass window at porter's office.

B   6–8 mm plate glass.

C   5.5 cm galvanized steel tube painted white. All structural members of the cage are of the same cross section, regardless of the very different structural loads.

D   Nickel-plated glazing bead and frame.

E   Door jamb of 5.5 cm tube.

F   Elevator door frame of 5.5 cm tube.

G   Track for sliding window.

H   Horizontal 5.5 cm tube supporting counter.

I   Ash-veneered wood panel.

J   Wood counter with 8 mm nickel-clad support rods.

(SAM AM-88-02-2436)

at the corners. This assembly is one of a number of louvered screens, many perforated by light, that occur throughout the building. Another is the railing, but this particular design occurs only on one side of the atrium, that facing the courtyard. The remaining three railings facing the outside walls of the U-shaped extension are solid wood screens. Again Asplund radically changes detailing method to link the atrium and courtyard through transparency while connecting the two building masses with opacity. The railing is formed of tightly spaced 3.5-cm round steel tubes supporting an organically shaped Oregon pine rail. As at the Bredenberg railing, where the body touches the handrail it loses its mechanical form and takes on an organic one. Asplund rarely used the horizontal pipe rails favored by Le Corbusier that suggested nautical and industrial associations, preferring the vertical type that formally resembles his other louvered screens.

The wood railings of the three sides that correspond to the exterior walls adapt the system used in the marble walls at Bredenberg. Each ash-veneered panel is held between steel plates anchored to the edge of the slab. The width is constant but the depth tapers toward the top as the load decreases. A steel plate connects them at the top, but the surface the hand touches is again an organic-shape strip of Oregon pine. At several locations a table is hung from this rail by means of steel tubes.

The system of round steel tubes holding glass developed at Bredenberg is used here to the same purpose, giving transparency and lightness to a number of elements traditionally opaque and massive. The most spectacular is the trapezoidal, transparent elevator cage that is placed in the central space. The steel tubes are always the same diameter and shape—5 cm round—regardless of structural load, simplifying fabrication but denying it any structural expression. This tubular system might be called a furniture language, that is, a language in which articulation of the forces identified with building—bending, compression, gravity—is secondary to that of connection and standardization of sizes of structural members. Asplund uses this tubular system for a number of elements that may be seen as furniture or architecture or something in between, such as the telephone booths and the porter's lodge (figure 3.22).

The ash-plywood and steel handrails are one of several wood panel types used in the building. The three walls facing the atrium are made from ash panels 2.5 cm thick covered with a veneer of curly birch, the only solid pieces being at moldings between panels, door jambs, and other trim pieces. In places this wall becomes itself a balcony railing. Here the detail is similar to the steel and panel infill system described above, except that the panel covers the face of the steel piece.

The walls of the courtrooms themselves are curved in organic shapes. The paneling of these curved walls is not plywood veneer but solid tongue and groove ash planking run vertically. The reasons for this may have been either technical or aesthetic. The method of curving plywood was well developed by 1936, but it may not have been available to Asplund or may have been prohibitively expensive. The solid tongue and groove boards can be used in a faceted arrangement to approximate the curve, but it is possible that Asplund wanted to use solid rather than veneered wood here to indicate the programmatic importance of these rooms.

Late Modernism and contemporary architecture are both filled with attempts to reconcile the conflicting demands of Modern and traditional construction, to evolve a Modern language out of the Classical in a rational way, to build in a way sensitive to context without resorting to ersatz historicism. Most of these attempts are failures, some abysmally so, but Gothenburg succeeds better than most, struggling to reconcile opposites on every level. Strangely, it was a system Asplund rarely used again. The frame and infill system of the exterior occurs in only two other unbuilt projects. The minimalist structure of the interior is used somewhat less in subsequent work, but Asplund did continue to use multiple solutions to identical problems and to mix different languages of materials, not always with the same success.

3.24

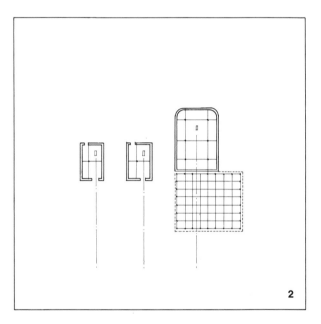

3

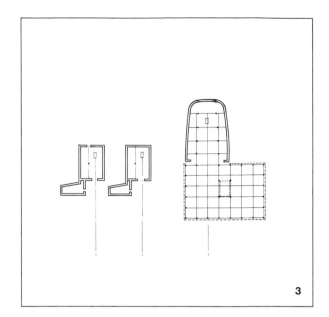

2

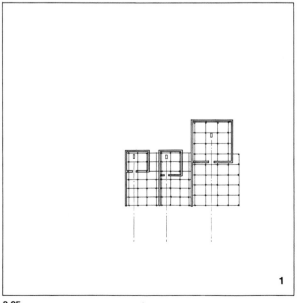

1

3.25

Woodland Crematorium

Erik Gunnar Asplund

Stockholm, 1935–1940

___

3.24 View.

3.25 Plan alternatives.

1 Early version showing uniform column grid. Note that while the bay sizes are the same, there is a different grid for each chapel.

2 Intermediate version, with a single center column for each small chapel.

3 Final version, with single column offset with catafalque on entry axis. Note omission of column at entry to large chapel.

(SAM AM-88-02-3610, 5135, 5708)

THE WOODLAND CREMATORIUM

Work on the Crematorium at Woodland began in earnest in 1935, twenty years after Asplund and Lewerentz had won the competition. The program called for one large chapel, two small ones, a connecting portico and vestibules, and the rather grim technical support facilities required for cremation. Although construction began less than two years later, the process of design and the number and complexity of solutions that were considered seem almost as great as at Gothenburg. The reasons for this are in this case and perhaps in all cases Asplund's working method of exploring a number of alternatives in detail and slowly reaching a personal sense of the best solution.

There are a number of Classical elements in these later alternatives and in the finished design. (There are a number of aggressively Modernist elements as well.) But the evidence suggests that Asplund was neither moving steadily toward Modernism nor returning to Classicism. Ironically, the main chapel developed from abstraction toward literal Classicism, while the Great Hall did the opposite, beginning as a Neoclassical portico and evolving toward the abstract minimal structure that was built.

The view that Asplund was uncertain as to the final forms for Woodland is supported by the mass of alternatives that were generated, some developed in great detail, many as interesting as the final result. But one must admit the possibility that Woodland today appears as Asplund wanted it to be, and that, by however convoluted a route, he arrived where he wanted to go: i.e., that he deliberately mixed literal Classical columns with abstract Classical columns with concrete-clad steel beams with stone-clad concrete; that, as at Gothenburg, he used the language of detail appropriate to the condition.

Old themes are also present: the universal but interrupted continuous column grid and the image of columns against a metaphorical sky. The basic layout is organized around a road, "the way of the cross," flanked by the crematorium, chapels, and porch on one side and the cross, the meditation grove, and a grid of trees on the other. It is clear from Asplund's drawings that he equated the grid of trees with the grid of columns and that he equated the roof of the main chapel with the vault of the sky, both representing types of sacred grove.

Asplund explored a number of placements of the chapels within the grid as well as displacements and distortions of the grid (figure 3.25). An early solution, similar to the final in spirit, made the main chapel into two rows of columns within walls, recalling the Greek temple plan, while placing a single column in the center of the two square smaller chapels. Although not used in the final design, the square chapel with one central column was used twenty-five years later by Lewerentz in the church at Klippan. Despite his uncertainty, Asplund was from the beginning intent on articulating the columns as independent elements.

The final arrangement has a single column and beam in each small chapel, a single column and beam in each small chapel vestibule, two rows in the main chapel, and two concentric rows forming the inside and outside edges of the portico or Monument Hall. The locations of most of the columns are in some way distorted from the basic grid. The small chapel columns are offset from the center a distance equal to the offset location of the entry. The rows of columns in the main chapel converge slightly toward the altar. The portico is missing one column at the entry of the main chapel, here on its central axis.

Each of the columns is of a different design. Some are representational, some are abstract, some are Classical in origin, some are the concrete-steel composite type used at Gothenburg, some are simple squares with chamfered corners. Each type was at some point considered for each position, but the final arrangement, although somewhat unresolved in its detail, forms a definite pattern, a conscious mixing of languages in which the most modern techniques and images are used on the exterior and the most traditional ones on the interior. It is as if the Gothenburg system had been turned inside out, but not without purpose. As one precedes from the exterior toward the sarcophagus and altar, the light becomes heavy, the minimal

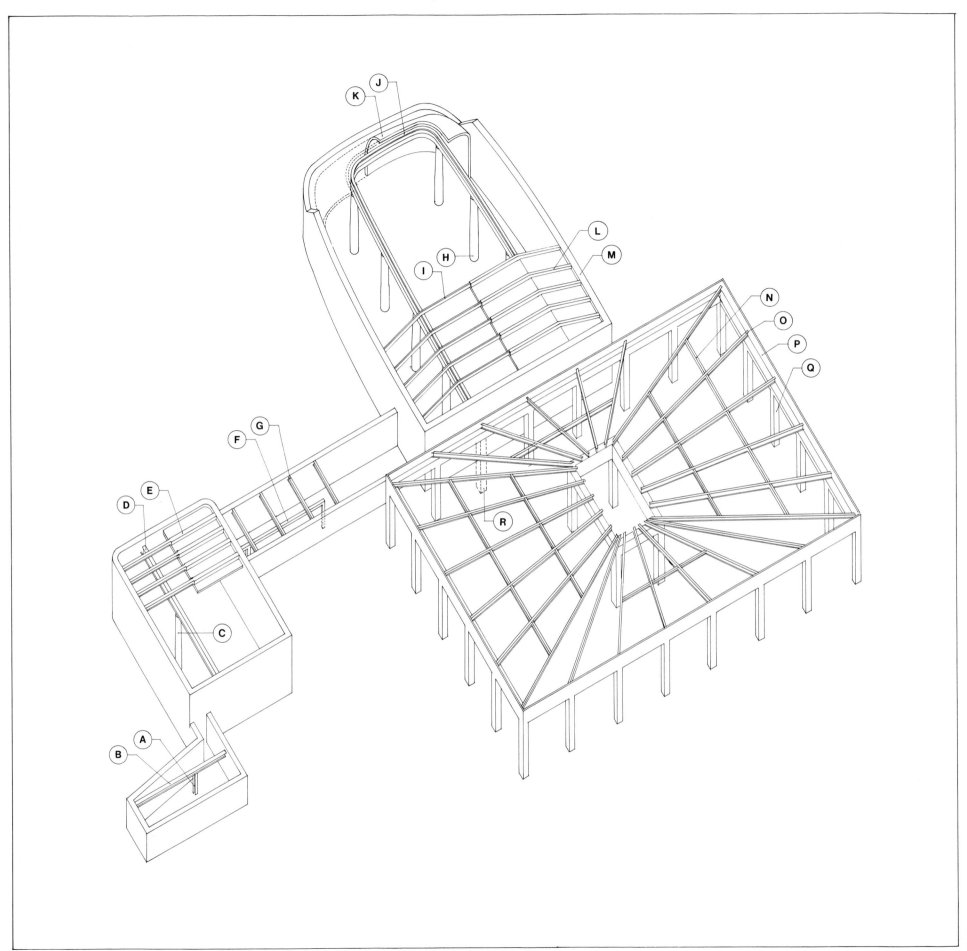

3.26

Woodland Crematorium

Erik Gunnar Asplund

Stockholm, 1935–1940

3.26   Framing.

A   Dimmel 22 steel column at vestibule encased in concrete. These are the only steel columns in the public spaces.

B   Dimmel 24 steel beam. The beams are progressively detached from the supporting columns as one moves toward the catafalque.

C   Hellikis limestone column from 4.5–6 cm disks at Chapel of Hope. The structure of the chapel resembles that of the vestibule structure but with a stone column.

D   22.5 cm deep steel beam bolted to stone column encased in concrete.

E   Steel beams encased in concrete. Wood-framed roof above not shown.

F   Beam at main chapel vestibule.

G   Steel beams encased in concrete at vestibule.

H   Solid marble column at main chapel.

I   INP 18 and Dimmel 25 steel beams.

J   INP 30 main steel girder encased in concrete with pedestals to support roof.

K   Concrete apse screen creating slot for air supply from basement. The air is returned at the floor through slots in the altar railing.

L   Concrete casing around steel beam. Wood roof framing not shown.

M   Masonry bearing walls. All spaces are framed with exterior bearing walls and interior columns.

N   Dimmel 14 steel bridging with wood ceiling below.

O   Portico steel beams, 312 Dimmel 42.5 largest and 50 INP 34 smallest.

P   Steel perimeter beam encased in concrete faced with marble.

Q   Concrete column with 3 cm marble facing.

R   Column omitted at entry.

(SAM AM-88-02-5945, 5966, 6818, 6817)

becomes the massive, the veneered becomes the solid, and, up to a point, the modern becomes the traditional.

The design of the portico perhaps generated the greatest number of alternatives, but generally followed a development from a literal Classicism to a light, abstracted one. Asplund's initial sketches explore the idea of stone columns supporting a wood trellis. Other designs were fairly traditional, including one with a gigantic if somewhat flat pediment. It is hard to believe this came after and not before Bredenberg. A more refined version used a simple arrangement of concrete columns and beams supporting a simple flat trellis floating above.

In the final design the columns are square with chamfered corners, considerably more minimal and abstract than the I sections of Bredenberg and Gothenburg, and considerably less descriptive of structural forces. There is no sense of the whittling away of material to minimize weight. They are built of marble veneer on composite concrete and steel construction; while there is considerable stone veneer at Woodland, this is the only veneered column. Those in the interior, the more sacred spaces, are of solid stone.

The "entablature" of the parapet is also considerably more abstract in its final form, but perhaps for pragmatic reasons. Several authors have pointed out that the visible wood roof of the portico is really a wood ceiling suspended from the true steel structure above, and that while the wood ceiling is an orthogonal grid, the actual steel structure is an irregular radial arrangement (figure 3.26). The wood ceiling, although framed with 5×6 teak beams, is incapable of spanning the large opening.

Asplund's assistant Lennart Bergvall recalled of this design: "Nobody could have been given a more Functionalist upbringing than we were. That meant, of course, that the form had to express the structure behind it. So it pained me, there being no connection between the two at the crematorium. I sketched a number of different alternatives which would have looked smart but still not belied the structure behind. But then Asplund said: 'You know, that business about the expression of the structure, you have to take it with a pinch of salt!'"[9]

The only modifications to the rectilinear form of the portico are the chamfered corners, but the reason for this is probably related to the stone joints. Since the stone is a 3-cm-thick veneer on a concrete column, a joint is required at each corner. If the shape were a simple rectangle with mitered corners, the corner and joint would coincide exactly. This is rarely a satisfactory detail, giving the form a soft look and making the stone look paper-thin. The chamfered corner disassociates corner from joint without making the column appear to be solid stone.

This was a common problem of the day: the detailing of stone columns in a way that would maintain their apparent solidity without concealing the fact that they were veneered. Eliel Saarinen in his Cranbrook portico avoided the problem altogether by using solid stone. Lewerentz, Asplund's one-time partner, faced a similar problem at his crematorium chapel at Malmö, which he solved by using different thicknesses of marble with staggered joints (figure 3.42). It was a clever solution, but one that, like his stone and concrete campanile at the same cemetery, suggests wood rather than masonry.

The portico is only one of several "orders" that Asplund used at Woodland. Each of the other major public spaces had its own order, a system of columns and beams, usually one of each. There is a clear hierarchy of these systems between Modern and traditional, between archaic and industrial. The most Modern version occurs in the two vestibules adjacent to the small chapels. It is the by now familiar composite order of steel and concrete developed for Bredenberg and Gothenburg, using the minimum quantity of material and, as a result, describing the structural forces at work. All of the other columns and beams are more traditional in form and material than those of the vestibule. Did Asplund use the Modern columns here because this was the most public space, its link with the outside world, or because it was the least important? In either case, he clearly felt that the more private,

3.27

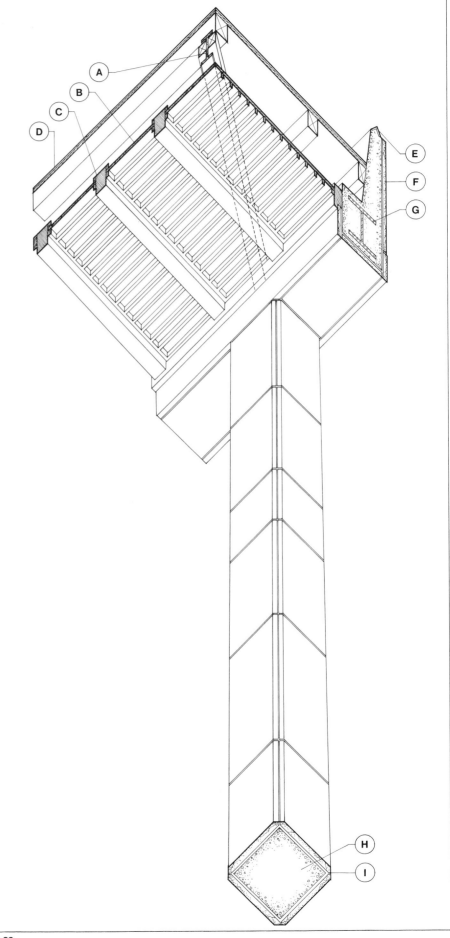

3.28

Woodland Crematorium

Erik Gunnar Asplund

Stockholm, 1935–1940

Portico

3.27 View.

(C. G. Rosenberg: Swedish Architecture Museum)

3.28 Section.

A Steel beams. These are oblique to the walls since they span from the interior columns to the perimeter beams. See figure 3.26.

B 1 × 4 wood boards and 1 × 1½" batten and trim.

C 5 × 6 redwood beam. The ceiling is not structural but supported by the steel beams above.

D Copper roofing on 25 mm boards resting on wood and steel beams.

E 6 × 40 mm steel angle set into notch in stone and bolted to steel insert in concrete to close joint at top of stone wall.

F 3 cm and 4 mm marble facing.

G Steel beam encased in concrete.

H Concrete column.

I 3 cm marble column facing. The chamfered corner avoids placing a joint at the corner of the two slabs of stone. All internal stone columns are solid.

(SAM AM-88-02-5790, 6921. 5942)

sacred spaces should have the more traditional columns. The small Chapels of Faith and Hope are identical save for one feature. Each has a single column; both columns are solid stone, and both are tapered in a conventionally Classical way (figure 3.36). Neither, however, has a base or capital but is topped with a steel plate to connect to the structure above. The only difference between the chapels is the size and type of stone used in the two columns. The Chapel of Faith uses large drums of marble. The Chapel of Hope uses thin disks of limestone. Both, however, are solid, without veneers or underlying steel structures.

The roof structure of the small chapels, however, like that of the vestibules, is a concealed steel composite system. Only one of the beams is exposed, or rather expressed, the long girder supported by the column; the numerous cross beams are hidden within the slab. There is a subtle but important difference with the vestibule, where only the bottom half of the beam projects. In the chapel the beam is almost detached from the slab above by a rectilinear extension, so that the slab appears to float rather than being engaged.

In his Italian trip in 1913, Asplund visited the Greek temple ruins at Agrigento and Paestum. Here he was transfixed by the image of the vault of the sky above the freestanding columns. The columns at Agrigento have no entablature. The interior of the temple of Neptune at Paestum consists of a small Doric order atop a larger one. Elias Cornell has shown the importance of this image in a quite literal way to Asplund's later work. The vault of the sky, usually represented by plaster, above columns without entablature or above a two-tiered colonnade is an element in a number of works from his Classical and Modern phases, from the Skandia Cinema to the Woodland Crematorium. At Woodland it became the basis of a series of details that elaborate on this theme. As one moves through the building, the vaults become progressively abstract and disassociated from the columns and entablature on which they rest, growing out of the beams in the vestibules while floating blithely above in the main chapel.

The most traditional columns were reserved for the main chapel, the Holy Cross Chapel, where they are solid stone and contain a surprising last-minute addition, column capitals and bases. The bases are small and easily overlooked, but they are unmistakably the Classical torus shape. There are only two explanations for this mixture of Modern and Classical: indecisiveness, or that Asplund wished to deliberately contrast the minimalist steel frame language of the vestibules with the massive masonry and somewhat traditional nature of the main chapel. This space also went through a large number of variations in design, many developed in great detail. Although Asplund explored such options as columns flaring out into a smooth flat vault, and vaults running perpendicular to the main axis, most of the others, like the final version, employ two trusses or beams running parallel to the main axis, supported by stone columns. In only a few of these designs is there an expression of the smaller beams running across the nave. If one equates the roof with the sky, which is hard not to do, the result is very close to the image of the Greek temple interior with the sky above.

The difficulty with this concept was how to connect the real and the symbolic, how to join the very literal structure of beam and column to the metaphorical vault above. All of the beams are the familiar composite steel and concrete sections. Obviously Asplund wanted the vault to float almost free of the girder below. In each space along the main circulation route the ceilings are progressively more detached from the structure. In the vestibule the ceiling is half-engaged. In the Chapels of Faith and Hope it is separated from the I-shaped beam by a rectilinear beam. In the Holy Cross Chapel vault and beam are separated by some type of pedestal. If one considers the vault as real concrete, not metaphorical sky, the vault and capital simply collide.

Other details of the complex follow similar hierarchies and employ similar mixtures of languages. This is particularly true of windows. There are at least five systems, two of steel, two of wood, and one a combination of the two. The places where each is used is in part determined by functional and in part by symbolic

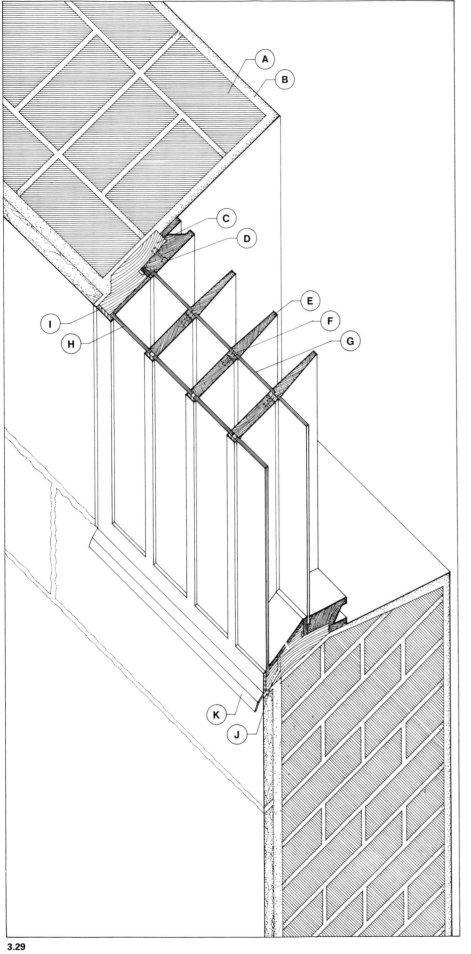

3.29

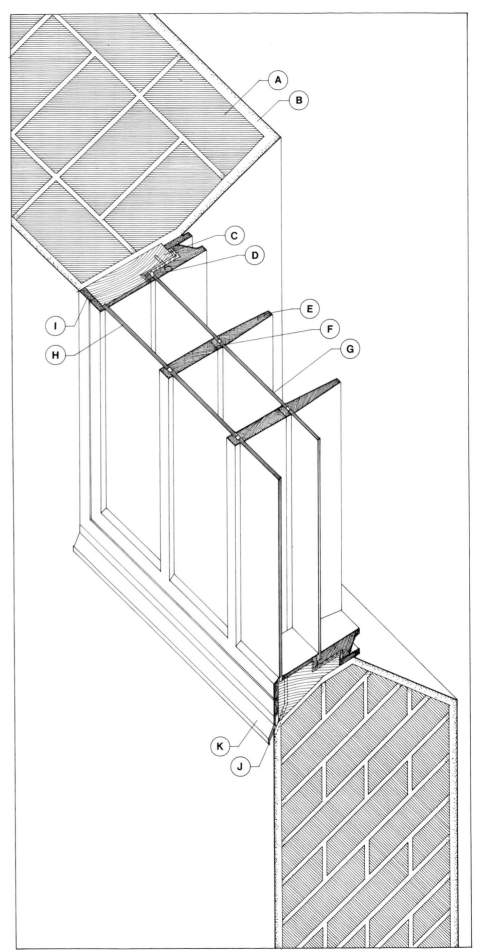

3.30

Woodland Crematorium

Erik Gunnar Asplund

Stockholm, 1935–1940

Chapel of Hope

3.29 **Detail of windows above entry.**

A Brick wall with 3 cm marble facing.

B Plaster interior finish.

C Pine jamb with oak facing anchored to brick wall. The less expensive pine is used for the bulk of the mullion, while the more richly grained and durable oak is used for the facing.

D Oak trim with anchor and screw. An oak plug covers the screw hole.

E Tapered oak mullion. Unlike the side window in figure 3.30, the fins are at 90° to the wall.

F Fasteners and oak glazing stops.

G 6 mm plate glass.

H 8 mm plate glass. The outer pane, which takes larger loads, is thicker.

I Bronze facing and glass stop. The bronze facing visually unites the window with the door below.

J Pine sill with oak facing and 6 mm air hole to ventilate the cavity and prevent trapped water vapor from condensing.

K Copper flashing to prevent water that accumulates at the bottom of the window from penetrating the joint between window and wall.
(SAM AM-88-02-6068)

3.30 **Detail of side window.**

A Brick wall.

B Plaster interior finish.

C Pine jamb with oak facing and anchor.

D Oak trim with 6 mm steel plate inserts.

E Angled oak mullion to direct light toward the catafalque and altar.

F Fasteners and oak glazing stop; since this is the side wall there is no bronze facing.

G 6 mm plate glass inner pane.

H 8 mm plate glass outer pane. The two layers of glass retard heat loss and condensation on the glass.

I Oak facing and stop. Unlike in the front window, the stop is oak.

J Oak-faced pine sill.

K Copper flashing to prevent water from accumulating at the bottom of the window and penetrating the joint between window and wall.
(SAM AM-88-02-5883)

3.31 **View.**

3.32 **Detail of window above entry.**

3.31

3.32

3.33

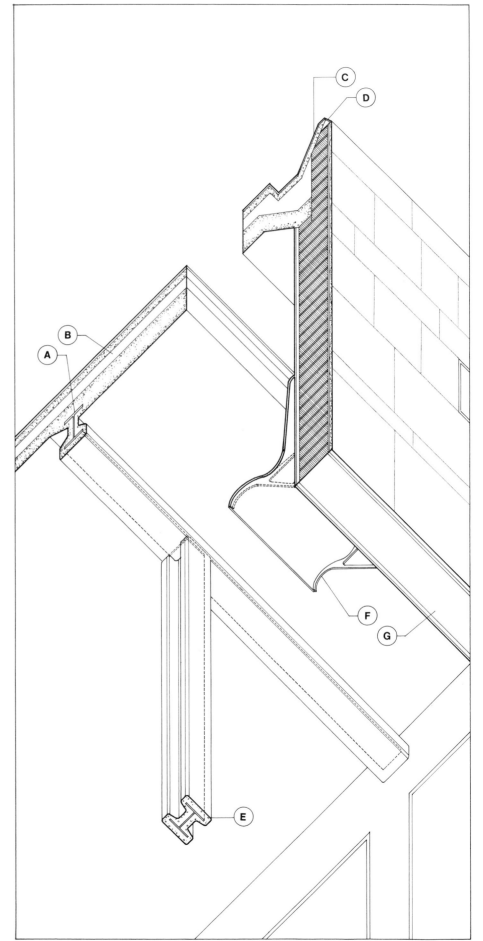

3.34

Woodland Crematorium

Erik Gunnar Asplund

Stockholm, 1935–1940

3.33 **Vestibule.**

(C. G. Rosenberg: Swedish Architecture Museum)

3.34 **Wall section at vestibule.**

A Dimmel 24 steel beam. The relationship of beam to slab varies from space to space. Here in the least "sacred" space the two are most closely engaged.

B Double concrete slab construction of protective concrete set on gas concrete with a membrane between.

C Gutter.

D Metal coping to cap stone and cover roof membrane edge.

E Dimmel 22 steel column. Only the vestibule columns are steel; the remainder of the spaces use solid or veneered stone.

F Plywood bench with metal support. The wood veneer of the wall panel continues down to form the surface of the bench.

G 3 cm marble on brick wall. See figure 3.38.

(SAM AM-88-02-6805, 5941, 5964, 6132, 6173)

reasons. As with the structural elements, the most abstract industrialized system is at the perimeter serving the most public areas. The most private and sacred spaces have the more traditional window systems.

The most industrial of the systems is that of pivoting double steel units similar to those used at Bredenberg. While extensive, they are used only for the service and secondary areas, most of which are on the back side of the complex. (Ironically and sadly, the units used were provided by Idesta, a company owned by Lewerentz.) A more complex mixture of windows occurs in the vestibules serving the three chapels. Here there are two systems, one wood, one metal. The metal windows face the exterior; the wood windows face the inner courtyard. The metal windows are fixed; the wood windows are operable.

All three chapels have large oak windows, again evoking the image of material dematerialized by light. The perforated louvered screens used at Bredenberg and Gothenburg are here greatly enlarged and made into fixed windows. The fins become mullions, thin but tightly spaced slabs of oak holding two sheets of glass. The outer layer of glass is flush with the wall. The inner layer is set so deep that it is barely visible. Although hardly traditional, they are certainly the least industrial of the window types and are used with the traditional columns of the chapels as the steel windows are used with the composite I sections. The window of the chapel front uses a bronze stop to match the door and outer vestibule windows below. The same window facing the courtyard has a wood stop to match the adjacent oak vestibule windows.

The deep fins allow light to enter but allow only for partial view, as in a traditional church. Asplund warps and distorts these louvered screens depending on their location. Those on the southwest side of the Faith and Hope chapels, facing the entry, are perpendicular to the wall. Those on the southeast are aligned east-west, at an angle to the wall, but allowing direct penetration of the morning sun. The opening in the main chapel is also skewed so that it is slanted to align with the sun's rays.

Perforated screens are used for many other details. Glass block and concrete partitions are used in the wreath room and as a roof around the parapet of the organ loft. The most spectacular screen is the gigantic door to the main chapel, which can be lowered into the floor to literally connect inside to outside, eliminating the whole east wall of the chapel and opening into the portico. Although it appears to be a metal grating, it is made of metal-clad wood window mullions; although a traditional gate by implication, it also is a screen perforated by light. The same type of detail is repeated at the doors between the vestibules and small chapels, where a wood screen is placed over the light in the door.

The same contrasts and transitions of styles and techniques—Modern to traditional, industrial to primitive, light to massive—can be seen more subtly in the stone details as well. The chapel columns are of monolithic stone. In contrast the forecourts are partially shaded by thin marble screens hung from steel brackets like awnings. The typical stone walls are somewhere in between. The stone is never more than 4 cm thick and mounted on brick or concrete with concealed clamps. But while the face of the stone has a smooth factory finish the joint edges are irregular, suggesting natural stone.

It is tempting to interpret Woodland as a kind of metaphor of the last ten years of Asplund's life, moving from Modern to Classical as he moved toward death, particularly since he died in the same year that the chapel was dedicated, but as with almost all generalizations about Asplund there are plenty of facts to contradict this. In these same years he was simultaneously pursuing designs devoid of Classical elements, mixing Modern and vernacular images and in some cases using vernacular elements only. The other buildings of his late career use more archaic and vernacular construction systems, although often in combination with concrete. They lack the Classical overtones, the symbolic references and the quotations of the earlier work. Asplund was not alone in this. His work of this period recalls the spirit and sometimes the forms of contemporary work of Le Corbusier

3.35

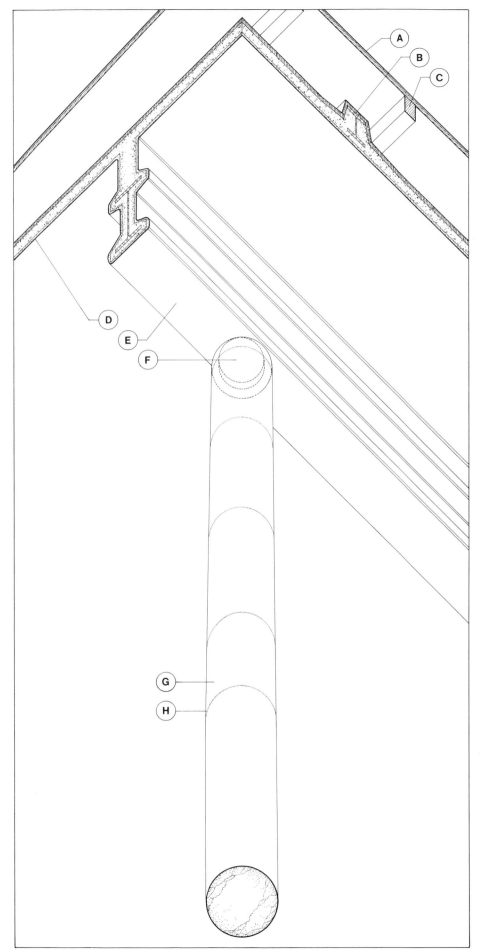

3.36

Woodland Crematorium

Erik Gunnar Asplund

Stockholm, 1935–1940

3.35 Chapel of Hope, interior.

(C. G. Rosenberg: Swedish Architecture Museum)

3.36 Chapel of Faith, column detail.

A Copper roof supported by wood boards.

B Steel beams encased in concrete. In all the main rooms, the major beam is exposed while the minor ones are concealed by the flat ceiling.

C 3 × 5" wood beams supported by wood posts. These rest on the concrete slab and are not structurally independent of the slab below.

D Concrete slab faced with plaster, with 5 cm insulation above.

E 22.5 cm deep steel beam encased in concrete. The roof slab is visually detached from the beam, unlike that of the vestibule.

F Two bolts to attach the steel beam to Ekberg marble cap of stone column.

G Ekberg marble column. Like a Classical column it is tapered from a point one third up its height to the top. The column at the Chapel of Hope is made of Hellikis limestone disks 4.5–6 cm thick.

H Joints are doubled in size at the edge.

(SAM AM-88-02-5838, 5848, 5945)

and Aalto, who were also exploring juxtapositions of vernacular and industrial methods.

If the early historians of Modernism admired Asplund, he also made them somewhat uncomfortable. His conversion to Modernism in the 1930 exhibition was too glib and facile, his subsequent Modernist work a bit too Classical, his previous Classical work not easily forgotten. Aalto's short Neoclassical phase can be written off or ignored, but Asplund's Classical period went on too long, and the work was perhaps too good. He was too hard to pin down. He would not stay put.

Asplund's career as a Modernist was thus a short one. It was only in the years 1930–1935 that he seemed anywhere near the mainstream of International Style Modernism, but it was a significant five years. The Bredenberg Store and the Gothenburg Law Courts have a stylistic similarity rare in Asplund's work. Between them they constitute a language of elements—composite frame, infill panels, projecting windows expressed but not exposed—that is perhaps one of the more successful, aesthetically if not technically, in Modernism. It was responsive to local conditions environmentally and economically. It avoided structural expression at the cost of impracticality, and the law courts and crematorium at least have stood up better over the years than many contemporary International Style buildings. And they were built. They stand in stark contrast to those of Le Corbusier, who proposed elaborate industrialized building systems while constructing houses in a technology often primitive at best. This makes it all the more curious that Asplund abandoned this style almost as soon as it was established. After 1936 he seemed to take a technical step backward, using materials and systems of a more traditional nature, though at the same time he moved forward in other areas, particularly the integration of mechanical services.

Asplund wanted the best of Classicism and the best of Modernism, and he succeeded far beyond what he had a right to expect. Like most of his Modernist contemporaries, he is criticized more for what he inspired than for what he himself did. Some, like Sverre Fehn, see him sending Scandinavian architecture off on a wrong course, obsessed with detail at the expense of substance. Asplund's eclectic approach to form and language has been used to justify many a Postmodern pastiche; his attempts to reconcile the constructional as well as the visual inconsistencies between the traditional and the modern have gone largely unnoticed.

Asplund was one of a significant minority of Modernists who sought to evolve a language of Modernism out of the language of Classicism, the Classical orders in particular, and whose work, unlike much of that of like-minded architects today, suggests that this reconciliation of opposites was possible. (He was perhaps unique in believing that this language could exist alongside that of an aggressively modern one that cut all ties with the past.) The argument that modern technology made Classicism impossible was never a very plausible one in any case. Whether or not this course was an appropriate one was not ultimately a technical question. To many Modernists it was not so much impossible as unnecessary, since the language evolving out of the design of industrial objects was too powerful to be ignored.

3.37

Woodland Crematorium

Erik Gunnar Asplund

Stockholm, 1935–1940

3.37 **Holy Cross Chapel.** Note the pedestals holding the slab above the beam.

(Studio Eisen: Swedish Architecture Museum)

3.38 **Stone details.**

A   6 mm Z hook to laterally brace the top of the stone panel.

B   3 cm marble. The stone is cut as thin as possible, as determined by the stresses created in transport and the thickness required for attachment.

C   2 cm mortar fill and joint. Although the marble panels are smooth on their faces, the edges are given irregular finish to give the joint a rustic appearance.

D   Brick or concrete wall.

E   13 mm bronze rod, two per panel, to transfer the weight of the stone back to the support wall. The bronze, unlike the steel used at Bredenberg, will not corrode.

(SAM AM-88-02-5942, 6882)

3.39 **Door of main chapel.**

A   Steel tube to house mechanism that allows the door to be recessed into floor.

B   Teak mullion with bronze cover and screws.

C   Steel plate reinforcement.

D   Bronze-covered teak double mullion.

E   6 mm plate glass.

F   8 mm plate glass.

G   Steel base rail and wood blocking to support the weight of the door with bronze cover.

(SAM AM-88-02-5855, 6919, 6120)

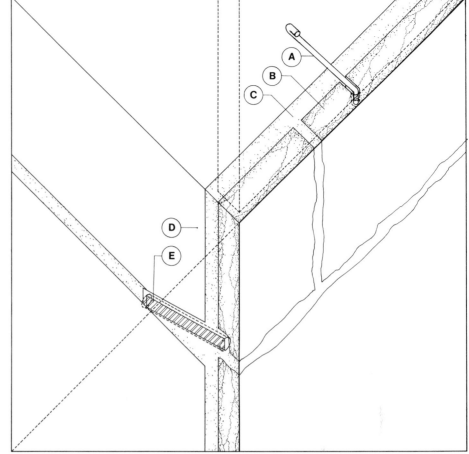

3.38

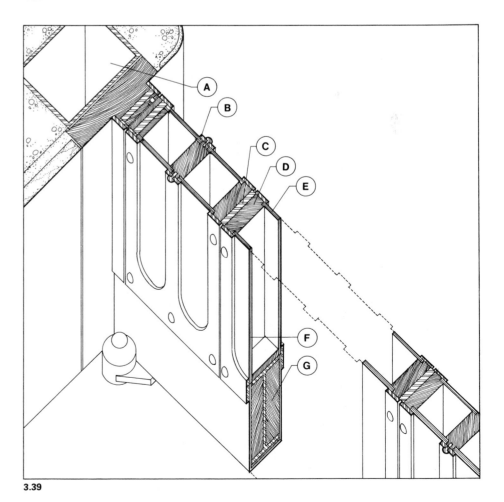

3.39

3.40

3.41

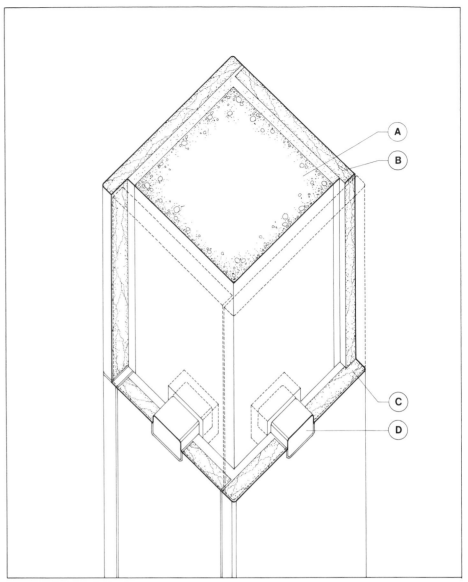

3.42

Chapel of St. Knut, Malmö Cemetery

Sigurd Lewerentz

Malmö, Sweden, 1943

3.40   **View.**

3.41   **Column.**

3.42   **Column detail.**

A   Concrete column.

B   3 cm stone. The thin and thick slabs
alternate sides at each horizontal
course to avoid continuous vertical
joints.

C   4 cm stone slab.

D   Stone plug.
(SAM MK 62)

4   Richard Neutra and the Architecture of Surface: 1933–1952

It is not far-fetched to think Neutra came to America because America was the home of Henry Ford. Ford was more amazing to Europeans than to us who saw in him our own likeness. In our minds, standardization of design and interchangeability of parts did not lead inevitably to a machine dominated civilization. Americans were already at home with machines and machines did not overly impress them. But Europeans were inclined to fear machines. Recently defeated and feeling the old order had let them down, they were looking for a new order. Machines, as a wave of the future, promised that new order. Europeans were prepared to worship the machine.

Harwell Hamilton Harris[1]

If Richard Neutra's architecture is an architecture of surfaces, it is an architecture of surfaces in the best sense of the word. To some the machine imagery of his work is literally only skin deep. But like Asplund's, Neutra's architecture was to a large degree determined by a unique vision of light and its influence on materials, and a preoccupation with surfaces was one of its results. It was a preoccupation Neutra shared with a number of his contemporaries, from László Moholy-Nagy to Asplund. Erich Mendelsohn and Rudolph Schindler, Neutra's one-time employer and partner respectively, had similar interests. Mendelsohn made frequent use of innovative lighting in his commercial buildings of the 1920s, and in 1927 Schindler designed a "Translucent" house for Aline Barnsdall. Nevertheless, in Neutra's case it reinforced a lifelong concern. He wrote in 1954:

My first impressions of architecture were largely gustatory. I licked the blotter-like wallpaper adjoining my bed pillow, and the polished brass hardware of my toy cupboard. It must have been then and there that I developed an unconscious preference for flawlessly smooth surfaces that would stand the tongue test, the most exacting of tactile investigations, and for less open-jointed, and also more resilient flooring. I recall, that scantily dressed or naked as I was, I became uneasily aware of the surface on which I sat and moved.[2]

Neutra's interest in surfaces, metallic, reflective surfaces especially, was not superficial. He was obsessed with light, but light in all its manifestations, in transparency and reflection, in the way light responded to materials and the way materials responded to light. It was an interest that went beyond the visible spectrum into radiation—radiant heating, radiant cooling, and insulation by means of radiant surfaces—and like Asplund's, his interest penetrated below the surface to hollow out and dematerialize the walls and roofs of his buildings.

Because his interest in new materials such as steel was so focused on surface qualities, it might be assumed that Neutra's interest in their structural and industrial properties was superficial, in comparison, say, to Le Corbusier's more rigid ideas of the standardization and industrialization that steel would produce; but Neutra saw himself as performing the same task, working toward a standardization of types like that achieved in the automobile industry. He wrote in 1935: "The well-integrated, standardized, pre-fabricated, assembled house is in conflict with mass

4.1

4.2

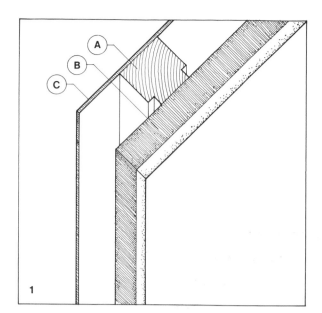

A
B
C

1

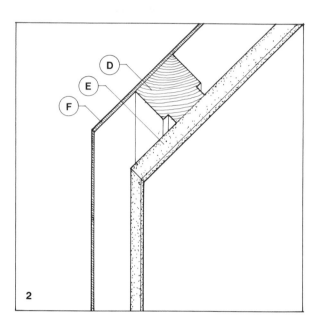

D
E
F

2

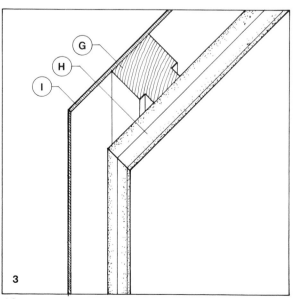

G
H
I

3

4.3

V.D.L. house

Richard Neutra

Silverlake, California, 1932–1933 (rebuilt 1966)

4.1 **View.**
(UCLA Special Collections, Dion Neutra, Architect)

4.2 **Stair detail of 1966 reconstruction.**
Note the treads hung with steel rods.

4.3 **Wall types.**
1 Type 1:
A 4 × 4 wood posts 3′ 3½″ oc. Unlike in the typical balloon frame, these posts are uninterrupted by openings, retaining their structural integrity.
B Lightweight pozzolan stucco exterior finish on 1″ steel netting set on Thermax insulation to retard heat loss faced with aluminum-foil-covered felt. The aluminum foil forms a vapor barrier to retard condensation on the interior cold surface of the exterior layer.
C Pressed panelboard interior finish.
2 Type 2:
D 4 × 4 wood posts 3′ 3½″ oc structural support.
E Cementlith exterior finish on asphalt on gypsum board with asphalt between.
F Pressed wood panelboard interior finish with aluminum-foil-covered felt vapor barrier on cavity face.
3 Type 3:
G 4 × 4 wood posts 3′ 3½″ oc.
H Cementlith stucco exterior finish on gypsum board with asphalt and aluminum-foil-covered felt vapor barrier facing cavity. The vapor barrier is placed on alternate sides of the cavity in types 1 and 2.
I Pressed wood panelboard interior finish.
(UCLA/DN 2-24-28)

---

prejudices, which have first to be dissolved. Obliging concessions to individualistic formal diversification threaten the manufacturer with economic failure. Model-consciousness would have to be created in consumers, as has been done in the automotive field. The hand-made house cannot be camouflaged, without losing prefabrication advantages."[3] This belief in standards is hard to reconcile with the absence of large-scale components or modules in Neutra's work, and if elements such as windows are all the same size on any given job, they are often not the same from one job to the next. Yet, in terms of materials and processes, Neutra's work is for more advanced industrially than that of many of his European Modernist contemporaries.

There is a Neutra system of standards and even types, but it is a different one from that of Le Corbusier or Gropius—one of small-scale grids based on tightly spaced columns with uniformly sized window units in between. The exact spacing varies with the structural material; there was one module for wood and two different modules for steel, based on the two types of steel structure used. The first of these systems was that developed for the Lovell house with steel H columns spaced at 5 feet 2 inches. The wood module was developed for his own house in 1932.

In 1930, following the completion of his house for Philip Lovell, Neutra took a world tour, in part to publicize the house's highly "industrialized" design. His stops included the Bauhaus, then under the directorship of Mies van der Rohe, where he taught for a month. While there he attended sessions of the preliminary course founded by Moholy-Nagy. Moholy-Nagy had departed by this time and the course was being taught by Josef Albers, but Albers's interest in light was no less intense than his predecessor's, and it is following this visit that Neutra's fascination with light comes to the forefront in his work.

Neutra's first major building following the tour was his own house in the Los Angeles subdivision of Silverlake. It was financed in part by C. H. van der Leeuw, owner of the van Nelle chocolate works in Holland, and Neutra, with his flair for self-promotion, convinced a number of material suppliers to donate material with the understanding that this would be widely published as the "V.D.L. (Van der Leeuw) Research House."

Despite the publicity the house received as being "revolutionary," and despite the fact that it incorporated a variety of new materials, the V.D.L. house is a variation on the standard American building type, the balloon frame, and its metallic finishes were only finishes. Neutra admitted this: "The basic structure of the house . . . was wood in a so-called *balloon frame,* which was to provide greater elasticity in case of earthquakes. 'Knock on wood'—earthquakes are never fully predictable, and I have since learned much more about lateral stresses. But thirty years of California shakes have not even cracked the cement plaster."[4]

The basis of the standard balloon frame is a cage of continuous studs and joists spaced at 16 inches on center, tied into a rigid box by means of sheathing and diagonal bracing let into the studs. Being essentially a load-bearing wall, it does not easily lend itself to the ribbon windows favored by Neutra and the International Style Modernists. Neutra's solution was to maintain the 16-inch joist spacing for the floor but to modify the wall by eliminating two of every three studs, creating a larger module of 3 feet 3½ inches, a little less than the standard 4 feet. Neutra compensated for the increased load on the remaining stud by increasing its section 4 × 4. The long slot in the wall created by this opening also reduces the lateral stability of the whole because it cuts through the sheathing, and this is accommodated by increasing the let-in bracing. Neutra liked to refer to this frame as a chassis, implicitly defending the fact that the frame is completely concealed in the finished building, as was the frame of an automobile. The walls are stuccoed on the exterior and plastered on the interior. The openings are filled with pairs of steel casements, let into the wood posts which are then covered with a curved wood strip. This assembly, along with the sill and the sheet metal fascia and gutter, is painted with an aluminum pigment, giving the house its reflective, mechanized appearance.

4.4

4.5

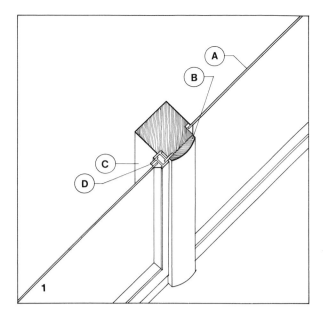

1

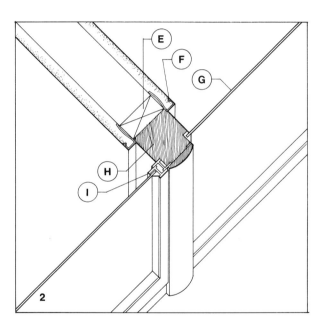

2

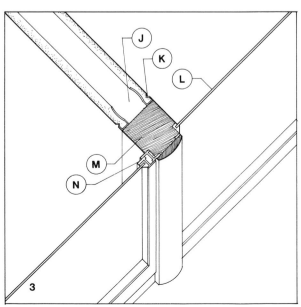

3

4.6

Strathmore Apartments

Richard Neutra

Los Angeles, 1937

4.4   **Window detail.**

4.5   **Window mullion.** This is detailed
       similarly to figure 4.6.1.

4.6   **Richard Neutra, column partition
       and window details.**
1   Miller house, Palm Springs, 1937:
A   Fixed glass.
B   Wood cover mold.
C   Typical milled wood posts 3′ 3½″
       oc. This is the typical window detail
       as used in the V.D.L. house system.
D   Outswinging steel casement
       window.
2   Kaufmann house:
E   2 × 4 wood stud interior partition.
F   Metal bullnose to end plaster. Here
       the plaster is outside the face of the
       post to create a layer between inte-
       rior and exterior.
G   Fixed glass.
H   Typical structural milled wood post
       and cover mold.
I   Operable steel casement window.
3   Moore house:
J   Wood stud and plaster wall.
K   Square metal plaster casing. This
       gives a hard end to the plaster and
       gives the plasterer a screed to work
       to. The plaster is flush with the
       post, unlike the detail in 2.
L   Fixed glass.
M   Typical 4 × 4 structural wood post.
N   Operable steel casement window
       and cover mold.
       *(B + W 12.54, UCLA/DN D-3-1o, DN 3-
       6789 BN 66)*

One of Neutra's American discoveries was aluminum paint, which he liberally applied to the finish wood and sheet metal parts of his wood frame buildings, creating the illusion that they were completely metal. His employee Harwell Hamilton Harris recalled: "'Mr. Neutra, what is the best material to build a steel house of?' was a question Ain and I were tempted to ask as we watched wood being finished with aluminum paint. Neutra excused such practice as 'educational'—getting people accustomed to the look of the future."[5] Harris's comment is perhaps not entirely fair, for this was perhaps less a desire to deceive than a desire to achieve reflectivity for its own sake. But if Neutra's interest extended below the surface it was also to a large degree focused on it.

There were technical innovations, or at least a variety of products, included in the V.D.L. house: resilient cork floors, pressed fiberboard, and a glass-aluminum sandwich panel. Neutra made much of the use of precast concrete beams in the house, but these are confined to the ground floors and basement. Many of the real technical innovations in the V.D.L. house were concealed. Neutra treated each wall of the house differently, partially as a response to microclimate, partially as an experiment. The wood "chassis" of 3⅝-inch posts was the same on all four sides. All the walls were insulated by facing the internal air cavity with foil. On the north side this was placed on the outside face; on the south side the foil was placed on the inside face of the cavity in one location, and in another location on the outside face but with the cavity filled with rockwool insulation (figure 4.3). A foil barrier facing the cavity from the outside will retard heat gain; placed on the inside facing the air space, it will retard heat loss. Presumably Neutra meant to measure the thermal efficiency of the building over time. Different types of stucco were tried in different locations as well.

Neutra's preoccupation with light, transparency, and reflections began to manifest itself in the details of the V.D.L. house. The most dramatic of these details is the strip of lighting added to the edge of the overhanging roof. It acts, at least in part, to reverse the normal condition where at night windows are transparent from the exterior and reflective on the interior by increasing the amount of light coming through the glass. At the same time, by increasing the exterior reflectivity he increased interior privacy. By increasing the interior transparency he maintained a connection to the exterior landscape in the evening. This detail also had the more subtle effect of describing the fascia as an external layer. It is similar to that used by Erich Mendelsohn in the Herpich & Sons Building in Berlin in 1924. Other details included collapsible transparent and reflective screens of glass and Bakelite. When Neutra rebuilt the house after a fire in 1963, he designed the roof to retain a shallow pool of rainwater. As the water evaporated it cooled the house but it also acted to turn the roof, visible from the interior, into a reflecting pool, supplementing the reflective qualities of the lake itself.

Although a modification of the balloon frame, the V.D.L. system was suggestive of two other precedents. It can be seen as the system of Neutra's Lovell house translated from steel to wood. At Lovell, Neutra used 4-inch steel H columns spaced at 5 feet, with the space between divided into three equal windows. The opaque walls were gunite (sprayed-on cement plaster), and it even has steel cover plates on the columns at the window strips corresponding to the curved wooden covers of the V.D.L. system. It can also be seen as a variation on the system developed by Frank Lloyd Wright, another former employer of Neutra's, for the Ready-cut Homes. This was a plan for mass-produced housing that Wright developed in 1915. It was a financial failure, but several examples were built in 1915–1916. It is possible that Neutra learned of it when he came to work for Wright in 1924.

Neutra was a believer in and practitioner of standardized detailing. He would accommodate most specific conditions by issuing 8½ × 11 standard sheets of details, such as the 4 × 4 post and window, which were the same for many buildings. The basic structure and wall system of 4 × 4 posts on a 3-foot-3½-inch module was used for numerous houses and apartments of the 1930s such as the Miller house and the Strathmore apartments, and the gutter detail occurs, with minor variations, in almost every Neutra building between the V.D.L. house and the Kaufmann house in 1946.

4.7

4.8

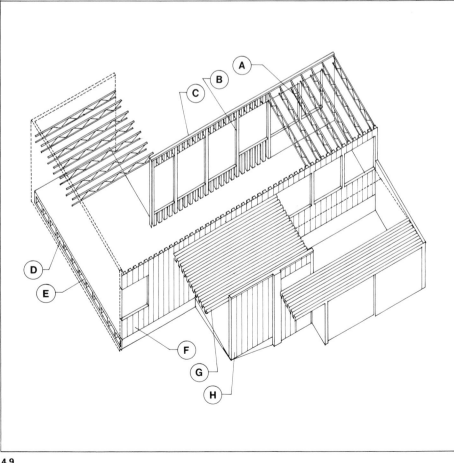

4.9

Beard house

Richard Neutra

Altadena, California, 1934–1935

4.7 View.
(UCLA Special Collections, Dion Neutra, Architect)

4.8 Construction photograph.
(UCLA Special Collections, Dion Neutra, Architect)

4.9 Framing.

A   2″ cement and metal roof deck on 9″ or 14″ trussed steel joists 24″ oc.

B   Column of single cellular steel section. Since there is no interior frame or columns, these members must extend up to support the roof.

C   Wall of Robertson cellular steel deck sections supporting joists, embedded in concrete footing with a ¾″ steel rod welded to the top for additional support.

D   2″ diatom cement floor slab on steel joists 2′ 6″ oc.

E   6″ cavity for circulation of warm air.

F   Air intake locations. The sun, by heating the walls and thus the air inside, was to set up a rising air current in the cavity drawing the heat out of the wall.

G   Robertson cellular deck sections. In order to demonstrate the capacities of the system, the smaller spans such as the porch and garage are made using the same sections as the wall.

H   Outer wall panels of flat steel sheets painted with three coats of aluminum paint.

(UCLA/DN 2-26-16, 17, 18)

THE BEARD HOUSE

It seems clear that Neutra was dissatisfied with the V.D.L. system, since it met so few of his criteria for an industrialized system of building, and it seems equally clear that he would have preferred a steel system. Since the Lovell house system was not repeated, despite its architectural success, we can assume excessive cost was the reason, and, although Neutra continued to use the V.D.L. house system, he also continued to look for a more "industrialized" alternative.

At some time in 1935 Neutra became familiar with a steel building system that Vincent Palmer, a Los Angeles architect and contractor, had designed and marketed the year before. The basis of Palmer's system was folded sheet metal decking. Structural steel is typically used either in rolled sections, the familiar I beam or wide flange, or in sheet metal bent into tubes, L's, or corrugated shapes. The latter system is weaker but uses less material, at least per unit. A typical steel frame building would use rolled sections for columns, girders, and beams, and sheet metal decking, usually covered with concrete, for the floors. Unlike the Lovell house wall, which used a frame of rolled steel sections, Palmer's wall had no frame per se, but used a type of metal decking, the Keystone, manufactured by the H. H. Robertson Company, to form what is essentially a load-bearing wall. Floors were a thin concrete deck on bar joists that were welded to the metal wall sections. Horizontal ¾-inch iron rods, welded to the decking, gave the wall lateral reinforcing.

Palmer's wall was plastered on the interior and given an exterior finish to suit the particular situation. Neutra chose to use a flat panel of the same copper bearing steel as the decking. These are in vertical strips, three cells wide, resulting in a vertically striped but highly polished exterior (figure 4.11). This also, however, received the by now familiar aluminum paint. The Palmer system gave Neutra a number of advantages. Unlike the Lovell system its steel was highly visible on the exterior, and although it was potentially weaker than the Lovell system, its capacities were more in scale with the comparatively minor structural problems presented by a house.

The first completed of Neutra's houses using the Palmer system was the Beard house in Altadena of 1934. The house is in two parts with two framing systems. The L-shaped house proper is framed with Palmer system walls and steel bar joist floors. The front porch and garage are also supported by the Palmer walls but their roof uses no joists, being made of the same metal decking as the walls. The second system, although simpler than the first, could only accommodate short spans.

Neutra wrote that the two systems were used for purposes of demonstration, and the whole house was meant to be a demonstration building. Nevertheless Neutra considered other systems during design development. One used the V.D.L. system of wood posts covered with plywood panels on the same 3-foot-3½-inch module, with metal battens covering the joints, a system he developed soon after in the GE Plywood house. He also asked the contractor for alternate bids omitting interior plastering, a decision that would have exposed the metal deck on the walls and ceiling of the interior. Fortunately perhaps, the plaster remained.

As in the V.D.L. system, the windows are pairs of rolled steel casements. The keystone metal section is covered with a flat plate on the outside and with a parabolic chrome sheet metal plate on the inside. The parabolic shape not only reduced the apparent size of the post but also recalled the shape of a metallic airplane wing, while the chrome surface continued Neutra's interest in reflections and light (figure 4.12).

For the smaller window openings he changed to a sliding metal window mounted on the exterior outside the plane of the wall. It is fabricated from sheet metal sections rather than the standard rolled section he used elsewhere. This produced some elegant details and some awkward ones. The elegant details occur at the sill, where the projecting plane gives the wall a kind of tautness similar to Walter Gropius's Bauhaus and Fagus buildings. The awkward detail occurs at the head, where the track and roller must be concealed and waterproofed. The deep projecting sheet metal hood does much to water down the crispness and slim elegance of the rest of the wall.

4.10

4.11

Beard house
Richard Neutra
Altadena, California, 1934–1935

4.10 **Interior.** Note the chromium-finished reflectors over the sheet metal columns. Neutra is at right. *(UCLA Special Collections, Dion Neutra, Architect)*

4.11 **Detail of cellular steel walls.**

4.12 **Window details.**
A Putty finish plaster on metal lath.
B Palmer cellular steel sections faced with flat plates and covered with three coats of sprayed aluminum.
C Parabolic reflector at jamb, soldered to cellular section.
D Rolling cadmium-plated sheet metal window with glass. These windows, being smaller and lighter than the doors, use sheet metal rather than rolled steel frames.
E 18 gauge galvanized iron stool.
F 1 × 1 × ⅛" angle to support sill.
(UCLA/DN 2-26-18)

4.13 **Rolling window details at coping.**
A Roof of 60 lb metallic cap sheet and 2 layers of 15 lb felt on 2" cement rock wool slab and 40 lb hyrib metal lath.
B Continuous ¾" iron rod welded to cellular section and angle to transfer loads from joist to wall.
C 20 gauge metal coping over 16 gauge compression channel welded to lintel top. The coping covers the edge of the felt. It is raised to prevent water from running over the edge onto the wall. The coping is filled with grout, except where open to ventilate the wall cavity.
D Steel joists 2' 0" oc.
E Putty-finish plaster ceiling on metal lath.
F Removable metal ceiling plate to provide access to the track and wheel of the window for adjustment.
G Steel track for sliding door with 18 gauge housing to protect the door track mechanism from water, removable for adjustment. Because of the weight of the doors they must be suspended from above rather than supported from below.
H Steel maple-lined trolley track with roller and hanger for steel-framed insect screen. This provides a slot for the wheel of the door hangers to run in.
I 16 gauge tension channel to support wall over window opening, covered with 18 gauge finish head jamb welded to lintel soffit below.
J Sliding steel door and glass.
K Fixed glass.
L Sliding insect screen.
(UCLA/DN 2-26-18)

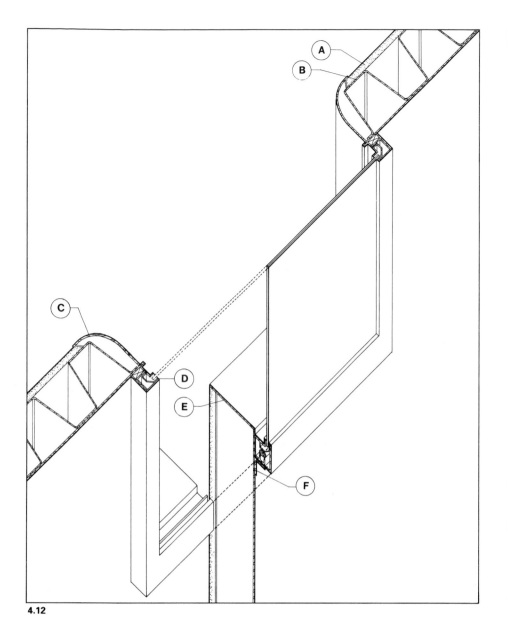

4.12

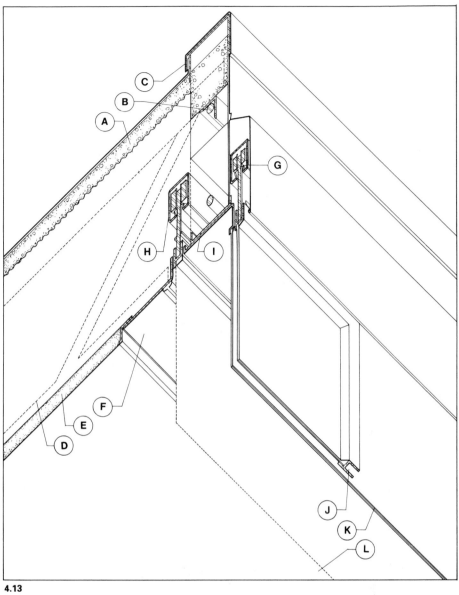

4.13

4.14

4.16

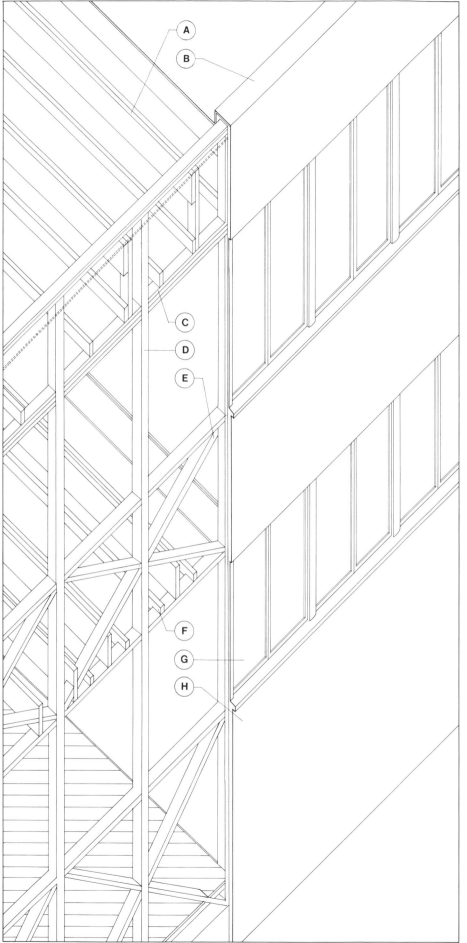

4.15

von Sternberg house

Richard Neutra

Los Angeles, 1935–1936

4.14 View.

(Julius Shulman)

4.15 Wall section of original design. The house was originally designed using a balloon frame system, similar to that of the V.D.L. house, but was built using the steel system in figure 4.17.

A   Roof construction. 2 × 8 or 2 × 10 rafters sloped to drain, with 2 × 3 cross bridging and 2 × 4 joists 16" oc below to support the ceiling. The bridging provides lateral bracing and ties the structure together. Neutra often used a separate system of rafters and joists.

B   Coping on 2 × 4 wood runner.

C   Three 2 × 4s at top of wall supporting joists.

D   4 × 4 posts 3' 3½" oc. These are the main vertical supports and run uninterrupted from foundation to roof.

E   2 × 4 diagonal bracing let in to posts to resist lateral loads.

F   2 × 12 floor joists and 2 × 8 ceiling joists 16 oc with ¾" finish floor on ¾" subfloor. The subfloor is structural and goes in first, tying the joists together. The finish floor goes in last.

G   Steel window with plate glass.

H   Wall construction. ⅞" lath and plaster exterior finish with insulated quilt between to retard heat loss. The interior finish is ½" plaster on 20 gauge galvanized iron netting.

(UCLA/DN f2-31a 3/15/38)

4.16 Ayn Rand, author of *The Fountainhead* and the third owner of the house, and Neutra in the courtyard in 1947. The steel cellular sections can be seen on the inside face of the wall.

(Julius Shulman)

Again Neutra uses many of the same details associated with light, reflection, and radiation—ponded water on the roof, the light strip at the edge of the fascia—but adds a dramatic new one, incorporating a radiant heating and cooling system in the hollows of the floors and walls. The ground floor is formed of two 2-inch concrete slabs with a 6-inch space between. The bottom slab rests on grade, the top slab on steel joists embedded in the slabs. Warm air is circulated in this void, radiating heat into the space above. This was similar to the system used by Frank Lloyd Wright at the Imperial Hotel in 1922, although in later work Wright favored liquid-borne rather than airborne systems. Both Wright and Neutra continued to be fascinated by radiant heating throughout their careers.

At certain points along the bottom of the metal walls Neutra left some of the cells of the metal deck open and, by means not clear, created openings at the top of the wall as well. As the air inside the cells of the deck was heated by solar radiation during the day, a convective current was set up, carrying away the heat. Neutra proclaimed: "The sun's rays themselves operate the cooling system,"[6] and rightly pointed out that this would have been impossible in a wood frame house, where "chimneys" in the exterior wall like those created by the cells would be potentially dangerous, since they would aid in the spread of fire. How well this cooling system worked is questionable; only about 10 percent of the wall cells are open at the bottom.

Neutra built only two other buildings using the Palmer system, only one of which was a house, but it proved to be one of his most memorable.

THE VON STERNBERG HOUSE

The 1971 demolition of Neutra's house for the film director Josef von Sternberg was particularly sad, in part because the house evoked so strongly Hollywood in the 1930s, but also because it was the largest and probably the finest of his all-steel houses. Its history, however, is a complicated one.

Despite its emphasis on lightness, transparency, and reflection, it is an intensely private and introverted space, reflecting, according to von Sternberg, his own desire for privacy and introspection, and was an intermediate stage in his eventual departure from Hollywood. There are few openings directly to the exterior that are not screened in some way by architectural or landscape features. The lower floor faces an enclosed terrazzo patio surrounded by a moat. The upper floors face outward either toward the distant landscape or toward the roof terrace, and the latter is made reflective by water. A desire for structural regularity played little if any role, and these spatial effects were not accomplished without major distortions to the structural system. The ground-floor opening to the patio required a wall three studs thick to span the opening, turning the wall above into a six-foot-deep truss.

The first design was not structured of steel but of wood. In the construction documents issued in March 1935 the major elements are shown as they were later built, except that the structure and details are the modified balloon frame system developed for the V.D.L. house. Although the wood version of the house proceeded as far as bid documents, it was not carried through, as it was during this period that Neutra became familiar with the Palmer system. Palmer was brought in to make a proposal for building the house of steel, producing a design for the von Sternberg house in shop drawing form, based on the wood and stucco drawings, that became the executed building. The building configuration remained remarkably similar to the wood design, the principal change being the dramatic difference in surface caused by the change from smooth stucco to the silver metal with its vertical lines.

The V.D.L. system and the Palmer system were in one important way remarkably similar: they were load-bearing wall systems. Although the Palmer system looked industrial and was industrial, it did not fit easily into the frame and skin preconception of International Style Modernism. Mies, Le Corbusier, and Gropius all predicated their architecture on the assumption that steel and concrete made the frame and curtain wall system inevitable. Developments such as the Palmer system confused the issue.

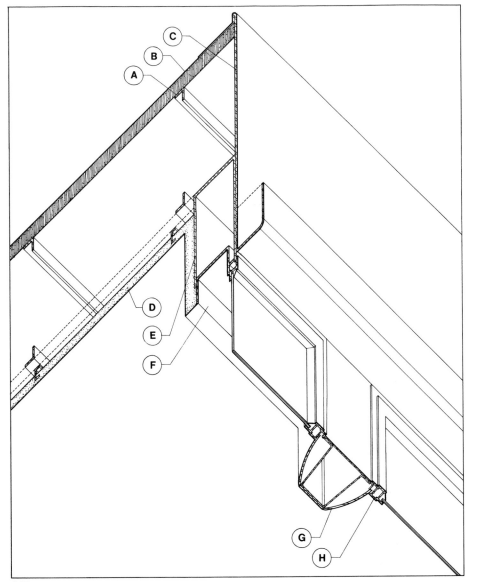

4.17

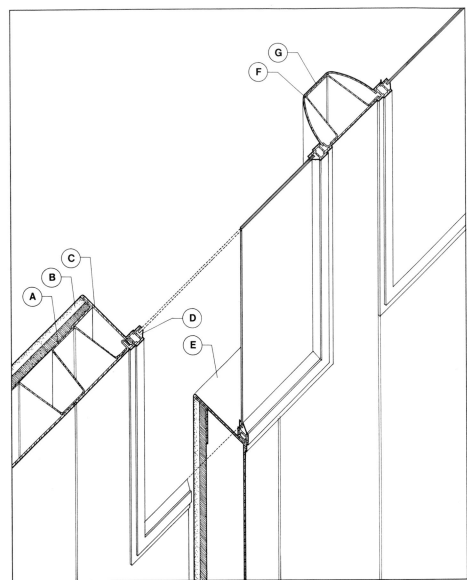

4.18

von Sternberg house

Richard Neutra

Los Angeles, 1935–1936

4.17   Palmer wall system coping.

A   Top chord of 10" joists from steel angles 18" oc.

B   Gravel on roofing on 1" Celotex insulation spanning between joists.

C   24 gauge galvanized iron apron and gutter welded to channel cap to terminate edge of roof membrane and prevent water from running over the roof and down the face of the wall.

D   ¾" plaster ceiling supported by ¾" channel furring strips attached to bottom of steel joists.

E   24 gauge sheet metal pocket for rolling copper screen.

F   10 gauge channel cap welded to window.

G   20 gauge sheet metal cover plate and FK section. The inner section supports the joists above, so that there are no steel columns. The cover provides a reflective, metallic finish.

H   Steel casement windows with plate glass. The inner L shape remains stationary while the outer one swings like a door.
(UCLA/DN 2-31a-143)

4.18   Palmer wall system window details.

A   Robertson cellular steel sections.

B   Plaster interior finish on ¾" Celotex.

C   20 gauge sheet metal jamb to close end of wall.

D   Operable outswinging steel casement window and glass.

E   20 gauge sheet metal stool.

F   Cellular steel section with 20 gauge sheet metal cover plate. These sections make up the structural support of the floors and roof. Some of them are extended through the window band to form a series of columns.

G   Parabolic chrome-plated steel cover.
(UCLA/DN 2-31a-143)

Another modification caused by the change to steel at the von Sternberg house was an increase in the module spacing. The strip windows Neutra favored were accomplished by extending one of the deck elements, or keystones, up through the window to the roof joists. This was not unlike the V.D.L. system, but these supports were more widely spaced at 6 feet instead of the 3 feet 3½ inches of the wood system.

Neutra used many of the V.D.L. details at von Sternberg, such as the strip light in the edge of the soffit, and added several more. In the interior he placed another light strip between the layers of a typical plaster partition, demonstrating the layered and hollow structural nature of the wall and implying that its hollows are filled with light (figure 4.20). The most dramatic reflective effects were in the bathroom, where the plumbing fixtures are monumentalized in a way that recalls the work of Neutra's friend Adolf Loos. Neutra added mirrors to the wall adjacent to the strip windows holding the fixtures (figure 4.19) so that both room and landscape are multiplied illusionistically in several directions.

While the multiple images and spatial ambiguities of the bathroom may seem the logical extension of Neutra's preoccupation with reflection and light, the idea may equally have come from the client, for mirrored images were no less important to von Sternberg than they were to Neutra. The former's biographer, Peter Baxter, notes that von Sternberg was fond of studying facial expressions in front of a mirror, and writes:

*The image of Sternberg scowling into a mirror accords exactly with scenes that were to turn up again and again in his films: Grand Duke Sergius Alexander catching in a mirror the reflection of his mistress, gun in hand, ready to assassinate him as an enemy of the people (*The Last Command*); Tom Brown realising, while trying on La Bessière's top hat in front of a mirror, that he is not the man to elope with Amy Jolly (*Morocco*); Raskolnikov before his looking-glass, flush with a publisher's advance, flinging a tie about his neck, a cigarette arrogantly clenched between his lips (*Crime and Punishment*). Whether it was the long heavy coat in which he took the leading role on his own set, the inscrutable expression, the arrogant, evasive remark, or the Belling portrait—half mask, half helmet—Sternberg confronted the world in the very act of disappearing behind an image of his own contrivance.*[7]

But if von Sternberg's house was a manifestation of his own artistic vision, it was not one in which he felt comfortable, and if it represented a new plateau in Neutra's career it represented something else to von Sternberg, one last, unsuccessful compromise between himself and Hollywood, from which he departed soon after its completion. He said of the house: "I sold the house and grounds for what the tennis court cost to build. Actually I was inclined to pay someone to take it off my hands." Von Sternberg's final comment on the house—"The house reflected me too much. Ideal environment and isolation were not for me"[8]—is perhaps deliberately ambiguous. Did he dislike its hermetic, monastic perfection or did it, quite literally, reflect him too much?

Neutra built one other building using the Palmer system, the California Military Academy of 1936, and most of his houses and apartment buildings of the 1930s are wood framed, built with modifications of the V.D.L. system. Perhaps this was in part an aesthetic choice, in that he preferred smooth stucco exterior walls, but there is little doubt that cost was a factor as well.

Like Schindler, Gropius, Wright, and the many others who sought to replace the standard American home building systems—the platform frame and balloon frame—with more industrialized systems of steel or concrete, Neutra not only found few converts but had great difficulty in using them in his own buildings. He continued to experiment but primarily with non-steel systems, and to the end of his life he continued to use concrete, large-scale wood framing, and other nonstandard systems in single-family houses. He rarely used steel framing in his subsequent houses, and when interest in steel framing was revived by Charles Eames, Pierre Koenig, Craig Ellwood, and others after 1945, Neutra was conspicuously

4.19

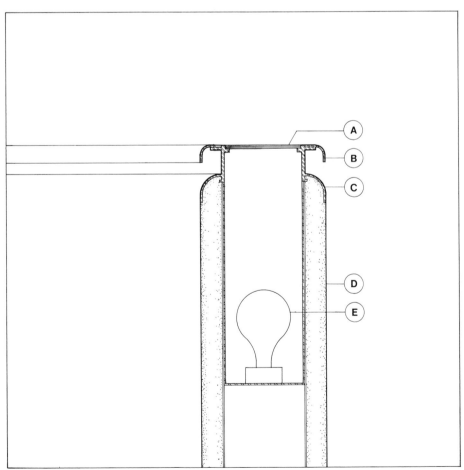

4.20

von Sternberg house

Richard Neutra

Los Angeles, 1935–1936

4.19 **Bathroom.** The mirror is juxtaposed
with a window of the same height
to create spatial ambiguities.
(UCLA Special Collections, Dion Neutra,
Architect)

4.20 **Light strip in plaster partition.**
A Lens to diffuse the light of the bulb
while reducing glare. This occurs
at the tops of the railing, like Asplund's bandstand detail in figure
3.7. It gives the impression that the
interior of the construction is filled
with light.
B Metal lens frame.
C Casing bead to provide a hard edge
to the plaster and a screed for the
plasterer to work against.
D Plaster on metal lath to hold the
first coat of plaster in place until it
dries.
E Incandescent light bulb.
(UCLA/DN BN 883 f.1)

absent. He did produce two other noteworthy systems before that time, however, the GE Plywood and the Diatom house projects.

The Diatom house was a series of projects based on concrete block using diatomaceous earth (a light fossil-bearing type) as aggregate, which produced a lightweight if somewhat soft concrete. Neutra became familiar with this system in the 1920s and produced a design for a prefabricated diatom house as early as 1923, but the most innovative of the series was the diatom dwelling published in 1934–1936.

The roofs and walls were sandwich panels of two diatom slabs with wood backing strips and insulation in between (figure 4.21). The most interesting part of the house was the steel skeleton, a series of cross-shaped masts in which a single column supported the beams via tension cables. Each column rested on a specially designed precast concrete footing. The masts were arranged in three parallel rows to provide flexibility in expansion.

Although the date of the design is uncertain, its debt to Fuller's 1927 Dymaxion house project seems clear. Neutra was an admirer of Fuller and had been one of the few customers for Fuller's Dymaxion prefabricated bathroom, using one in the Brown house in 1938. Although highly original and in some ways an architectural improvement on the Dymaxion house, whose internal spaces are rather awkward, the Diatom house seems out of character for Neutra. Although he had used tension cables in buildings like the Lovell house, the idea thus implied, an extreme allegiance to material efficiency, is not typical of him. His use of such elements as tension cables is usually confined to details, particularly stairs, rather than entire structures.

Neutra's work during and after the Second World War seems the antithesis of his work in the 1920s and 1930s. Brick and wood replace steel and stucco. The aluminum paint is gone. Tightly modular planning gives way to looser open arrangements, and there are few attempts at prefabrication. Like many of his contemporaries', his interest in industrialized systems waned as his interest in vernacular systems increased. Since the work of such well-known architects as Alvar Aalto and Le Corbusier had gone through similar transformations, the change in Neutra's architecture did not appear remarkable.

Yet Neutra may have been a more reluctant convert than his peers. In his first redwood house, the McIntosh house of 1939, Neutra asked for alternative bids on stucco finish, and the use of redwood siding was the preference of the client. The Nesbitt house (1942) uses walls of wood board and batten, but this was at least partly due to wartime limitations on the use of metals. Neutra never became the polemical spokesman for the new style that he was for the old, but his conversion was not temporary. When his colleagues in the Case Study House program of the 1950s were building steel houses and singing the praises of a prefabricated future, Neutra was not in the forefront. He wrote in *Arts and Architecture* in 1950: "A manufactured house must be sold to the customer as practically one indisputable whole—just like a car. To make prefabrication a true success a house must be produced in lots of about ten thousand each. . . . By reason of its tooling it cannot be small neighborhood business and survive."[9] Perhaps Neutra felt that having built several "prototypes" of mass production in the V.D.L., Beard, Plywood, and Diatom houses, he had no reason to do another steel house as a demonstration if it was never to be truly mass produced. He wrote in 1935: "We have faithfully endeavored to give many individual jobs entrusted to us a character which would easily lend itself to series production. . . . We have combed the housing field to demonstrate the advantages of typification, wherever least prejudice resists it. Standardization of the elementary school, of the drive-in retail market, of the highway auto court and restaurant, the vacation cabin, municipal beach resorts, gasoline stations, had been attempted."[10] But if Neutra seemed less engaged intellectually in his new "vernacular" style, he was engaged architecturally, and if this era produced some of his poorest larger buildings, it produced some of his finest smaller ones.

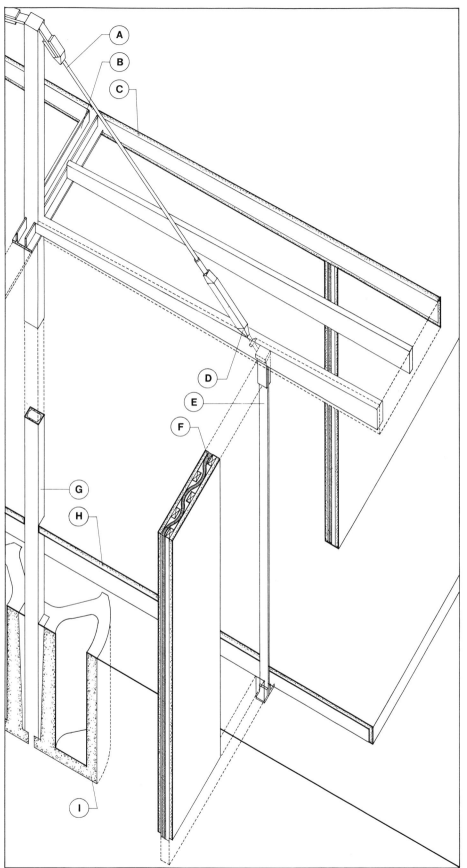

4.21

Diatom house (project)

Richard Neutra

1934–1942 version

4.21   Wall section.

A   Turnbuckle and supporting cables. The entire structure is suspended from the central columns to maximize the use of steel in tension.

B   Steel double T beam to support slab.

C   1½" diatom roof slab.

D   Cable adjustment.

E   Steel strap hanger to support floor beam below.

F   Sandwich wall panel of two 1¼" diatom slabs on wood strips with mineral wool insulation.

G   Supporting mast of two 5" steel channels.

H   Floor of 2" diatom floor slab on diatom joists.

I   Precast concrete footing.

(UCLA/DN 2-78-6, AMA 9.36)

THE KAUFMANN HOUSE

Neutra's golden opportunity came in 1946 with the commission for the Edgar Kaufmann house in Palm Springs. Kaufmann had a generous budget, a beautiful site, and a distinguished history as a client, having already built Fallingwater with Frank Lloyd Wright. The site, although spectacular, is more suburban and less exposed to the desert landscape than Neutra's drawings and Julius Shulman's photos imply. Neutra was no doubt thinking of Wright when he wrote emphatically that the Kaufmann house was not an organism: "There is no attempt made to make the building appear as though it has grown out of the sands or boulders, or the esthetically clean, heated pool as though it was a natural waterhole. It would be rather futile. Anybody who knows it all is not and cannot be."[11]

In the late 1930s architects such as Alvar Aalto and Le Corbusier had delighted in juxtaposing vernacular and industrial materials and techniques. Such surreal collages were foreign to the systematic Neutra, but the Kaufmann house is nevertheless filled with collisions of the high tech with handicraft, synthetic with natural materials, precise polished metal with rough stone and wood. This is one way to explain, or rather justify, the hybrid, ad hoc structural system of the Kaufmann house, a mixture of steel and wood framing. Most of the house is simple wood platform framing in which walls sometimes run past roofs and roofs sometimes overhang walls. The stone walls are a simple veneer applied to wood studs and sheathing. The steel occurs only in two locations, where special loading required its use. The first of these is the columns and beams of the "gloriette," a second-story porch whose primary purpose was to give vertical emphasis to a building in a city that permitted only one-story residences. The second is the steel supports for the sliding glass doors. Despite Neutra's attempts to distance himself from Kaufmann's previous architect, these doors give the house its most Wrightian qualities. The sliding doors comprise more than one quarter of the wall surface of the living room. When the doors are open, the living room, patio, and pool court are seamlessly connected, and the living room becomes an outdoor pavilion. Because of the weight of the doors and the fact that they must hang rather than rest on the ground, steel beams and columns are required. To preserve the openness of the corner, Neutra moved the column support off the corner and extended the beam outward so that the door slides out of rather than into the house, creating a kind of structural outrigger. This became another Neutra trademark and was used often in subsequent houses, with or without the sliding door.

The combination of steel and wood platform framing in the Kaufmann house is probably more a product of accommodation of practical requirements than a deliberate effort to juxtapose industrialized and vernacular systems. The platform frame, strategically reinforced with steel, was already a well-established building system when Wright used it in the Robie house in 1909. For Neutra, spatial organization and external material appearance took precedence over structural rigor and regularity. It should be noted that he was simultaneously designing the Tremaine house using a regularly spaced concrete frame, but with a less rich and complex floor plan.

Neutra explained the use of the hybrid system of the Kaufmann house as a response to climate:

For the space-forming bodies and enclosures, are used sandwiches of an exterior skin, fit to withstand or to react against the atmosphere; at the same time, a structural core is computed to resist the lateral stresses of earthquakes and storms, in spite of the fact that there must be great openings to enjoy intimacy with this strange landscape. Materials were used as present market conditions permitted; the low moisture content of the air leaves metals rather uncorroded, preserves timber. Glass remains unaffected but paint pigments fade out with speed and radiation softens and destroys asphaltic materials.[12]

The particular climate of the desert—intense radiation during the day, extensive heat loss through radiation at night—along with the aesthetic intensity of its sunrise and twilight dovetailed neatly with Neutra's interest in light, radiation, reflection, and transparency. He wrote in his description of the house: "Like the mirror surface of a pool, aluminum and plate glass will reflect the mood of the landscape

4.22

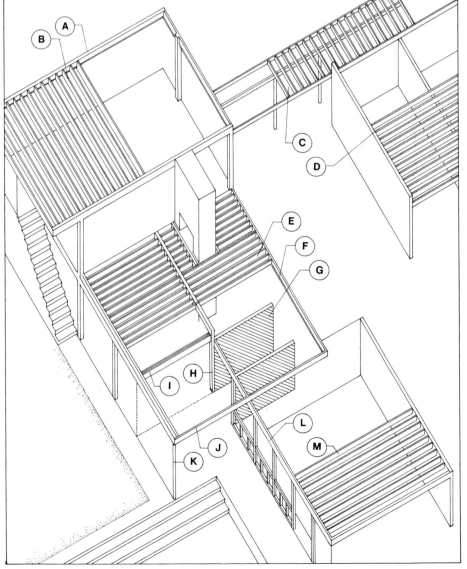

4.23

Kaufmann house

Richard Neutra

Palm Springs, California, 1946–1947

4.22 **View.**

(Julius Shulman)

4.23 **Partial framing at living room.**

A Steel framing for roof terrace and canopy of 8" and 12" steel channels, with columns from two 4 C 5.4 channels welded together.

B 2 × 10 wood roof joists at 16" oc with 2 × 6 ceiling joists 32" oc.

C Portico of 2 × 6 wood joists at 16" oc supported by 5 I 10 steel beam and 4" round steel pipe columns.

D Guest bedroom framing of 2 × 8s 16" oc supported by 2 × 4 wood stud bearing walls.

E Living room roof of 2 × 10 wood joists at 12" oc supported by steel beams.

F 10" steel channel supporting living room roof.

G 2 × 4 wood stud bearing wall with diagonal sheathing to provide lateral bracing.

H Steel tube column made from two 4" steel channels.

I Triple joist to support weight of sliding door below.

J 8" steel channels to support sliding door.

K 3" exposed pipe column.

L Wood frame bearing wall of 4 × 4 wood posts with let-in 1 × 4 bracing.

M Bedroom framing of 2 × 8 wood joists at 16" oc.

(UCLA/DN BN 66)

and the weather, the silver white moonlight, and the starry sky." As usual this concern extended to the building's construction: "Radiation from above was countered by radiation from below: The polished terrazzo floor inside and outside, around the pool, in patios, is made a radiant panel. . . . Aluminum heat mirrors were built into walls and roofs to protect the interior and aid other cooling devices. . . . Snow white crushed china and glittering mica glaze formed the exterior reflecting surface of these roofs and walls."[13]

Neutra conceived the Kaufmann house as Mies van der Rohe conceived the Barcelona Pavilion, as a composition of independent planes of contrasting materials. Each plane of Mies's pavilion responded to light in a different way—clear glass, tinted glass, obscure glass, reflective water, polished stone. Neutra took a similar palette of materials a step further. Each plane interacts with light and heat. The gravel roof reflects it. The glass allows it to penetrate; the water does both. The planes of the floor and roof radiate heat through coils, and heat penetrates or is reflected by the opaque walls themselves through adjustable louvers or aluminum accordion insulation.

Like Wright before him, Neutra shifted from a system of radiant floor heating through circulated air to one that worked through circulating water in pipes. The system at the Kaufmann house is considerably more complicated than that used by Wright in the Usonian houses of the 1930s, involving coils in the floor for both heating and cooling and heating coils in the plaster ceiling. The slab with the coils extends outside of the house to the pool at the corner with the sliding glass door, thus thermally as well as architecturally connecting interior and exterior. Although a potentially inappropriate system in the desert, since it is slow to respond to rapid changes in temperature, it seems to have worked to everyone's satisfaction after some initial difficulties.

The reason for Neutra's fondness for aluminum accordion insulation is obvious given his interest in light, heat, and radiation, and the fact that it presented the opportunity to tie the means of insulation to the rest of the house conceptually. Although popular for a time in the 1950s, accordion insulation never replaced the more standard mineral and glass wool types (which the contractor of the Kaufmann house repeatedly asked to use instead). The accordion type works on the same principle as the wood types, using a combination of foil to reflect heat and retard its loss through radiation and trapped pockets of air to retard convection and conduction of heat. Accordion insulation differs from wool in being made only of foil and having much larger air pockets, giving it a more mechanistic image, which is of course not visible in the finished house.

Opinions as to whether the second Kaufmann house was at all comparable to the first (Fallingwater) have varied over the years with changes of taste and the opinion of individual critics, but the house is certainly emblematic of an attitude toward technology and its relationship to nature. This was best expressed and best criticized by a writer with a somewhat different view of the Southwest, Wallace Stegner. He wrote of the house and its architect:

He had built of cinderblock, in the form of Bauhaus cubes, the only right angles in that desert. He had painted them a dazzling white. Instead of softening lines between building and site, he had accentuated them, surrounding his sugary cubes with acres of lawn and a tropical oasis of oleanders, hibiscus, and palms— not the native Washingtonia *palms either, which are a little scraggly, but sugar and royal palms, with a classier, more Santa Barbara look. Water for this estancia, enough water to have sustained a whole tribe of desert Indians, he had brought by private pipeline from the mountains literally miles away.*

The patio around the pool—who would live in the desert without a pool!—would have fried the feet of swimmers three hundred days out of the year, and so he had designed canopies that could be extended and retracted by push button, and under the patio's concrete he had laid pipes through which cool water circulated by day. By night, after the desert chill came on, the circulating water was heated. He had created an artificial climate, inside and out.

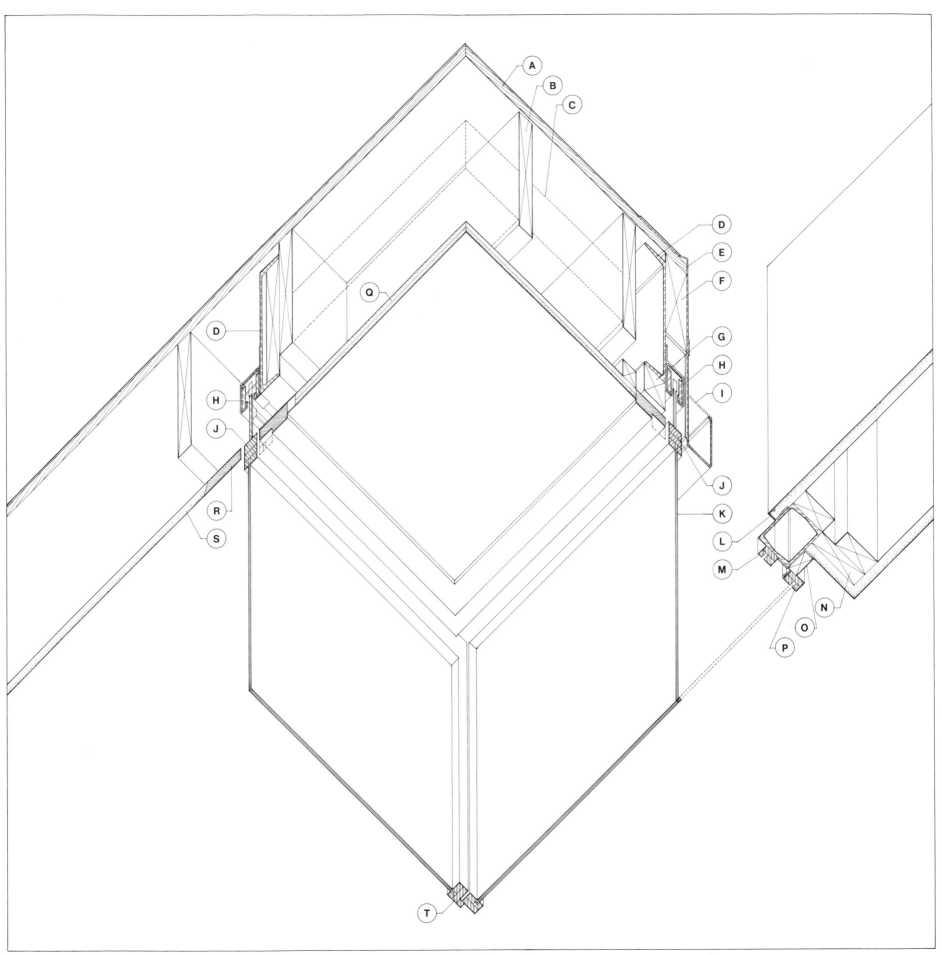

4.24

Kaufmann house

Richard Neutra

Palm Springs, California, 1946–1947

4.24 **Sliding glass door details at intersecting corner.**

A Roofing on wood deck set on wood wedges to achieve slope.

B 2 × 10 wood joists.

C 4″ mineral wool insulation to retard heat loss through the roof.

D 10″ channel lintel. This takes the weight of the door back to the column or wall.

E Galvanized iron fascia and gravel guard to protect and cover end of roofing membrane and fascia. The slope of the roof and the quantity and location of gutters were insufficient, and the house leaked badly after its completion.

F Wood beam to frame out fascia.

G Wood blocking to support wood trim below.

H Steel track and hanger for wheels of sliding window.

I Gutter with extension to interlock with gravel guard. This detail and many others in the house are identical to those used in Neutra's industrial houses.

J Sliding glass door.

K Glass.

L Plaster and casing bead interior finish attached to side of 3½ × 4″ steel tube column from two channels.

M Steel frame from two ½ × 1½″ bars with ⅜ × ⅜″ and ⅜ × ¾″ glass stops with fixed glass.

N Plaster on wood studs.

O Wood blocking and flashing.

P Sliding glass door jamb with weather strip.

Q Plaster ceiling with gypsum lath.

R Wood trim to provide hard edge to plaster at opening.

S Exterior plaster soffit.

T Meeting rail of sliding doors with weather strip to provide air seal. When both doors are retracted, the corner is open to the exterior.
(UCLA/DN BN 66)

4.25 **Night view.**
(Julius Shulman)

4.25

4.26

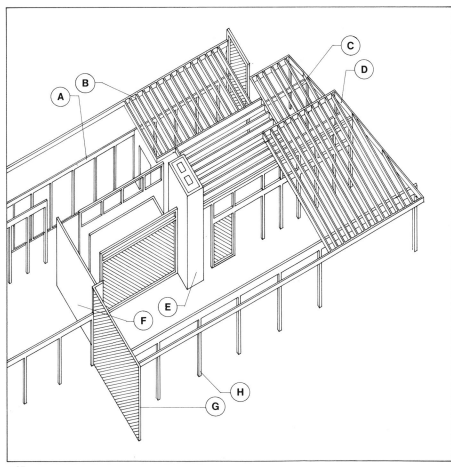

4.27

Moore house

Richard Neutra

Ojai, California, 1952

4.26 **View.**

(Julius Shulman)

4.27 **Partial framing at living room.**

A Typical frame wall of 4 × 6 wood beams supported by 4 × 4 posts 4′ 0″ oc.

B Low roof of 2 × 6s at 16″ oc and 2 × 8s at 16″ oc.

C 4 × 8 wood beams exposed at the screen porch.

D Upper roof of 4 × 6 wood beams and 4 × 12 typical laminated beam supporting 2 × 10 Douglas fir joists with 2 × 3 bridging.

E Fireplace.

F 2 × 4 stud bearing wall.

G 2 × 4 studs 16″ oc with 1 × 6 let-in bracing to resist lateral loads.

H 4 × 4 redwood posts 8′ 0″ oc supporting 4 × 16 laminated wood lintel. The post spacing is increased to provide greater transparency toward the garden.

(UCLA/DN 2-336-28, 2-336-24, DN 3)

Studying that luxurious, ingenious, beautiful, sterile incongruity, I told its creator, sincerely, that I thought he could build a comfortable house in hell. That pleased him; he thought so too. What I didn't tell him, what he would not have understood, was that we thought his desert house immoral. It exceeded limits, it offended our sense not of the possible but of the desirable. . . . That desert house seemed to me, and still seems to me, a paradigm—hardly a paradigm, more a caricature—of what we have been doing to the West in my lifetime. Instead of adapting, as we began to do, we have tried to make the country and climate over to fit our existing habits and desires. Instead of listening to the silence, we have shouted into the void.[14]

THE MOORE HOUSE

The rigorous application of the concept of light, heat, and reflection that characterized the Kaufmann house is missing from the James Moore house of five years later. Neutra seems to have lost interest in industrialization in his late work. Though his later career saw a general decline in his work, the Moore house is one of his finest houses; but it is clearly the product of a more hermetic aesthetic.

As in the Kaufmann house, the plan is a pinwheel, but here an elongated one, and again it seems directed toward gaining transparency at the external corners of the major spaces, the living room and the bedroom. Although formally similar to the Kaufmann house corners, those of the Moore house are technically dissimilar. The walls are not sliding doors but fixed glass. The structural outrigger is also used here, but it serves no functional purpose, as the window does not slide out from the house, and it represents only a symbolic extension into the landscape. Also missing from the Moore house are the stark juxtapositions of industrial and vernacular materials. The structure is entirely of wood, although of two types: standard platform framing for roofs and walls and larger-scale post and beam members for the window wall, including the outriggers. The steel window–wood column detail (figure 4.6) is familiar from Neutra's earlier work, the aesthetic difference being a matter of paint and wood species. Little of this structure is exposed. The platform framing is completely concealed. The post and beam members of Douglas fir are for the most part wrapped in redwood to match the siding and soffit boards.

Although Neutra's interest in light, transparency, and reflection here is largely confined to the aesthetic realm, it met with spectacular success. The mitered glass corner of the living room reflected in the pool is certainly one of the finer moments in his architecture. The design of the pool itself, which acts as a retention pond for the irrigation system, is curious in light of his comments on the Kaufmann house pool. There he ridiculed the idea of giving a manmade pool a naturalistic appearance, but this is exactly what he did at the Moore house. It is placed in an unnatural location, half cut into the hill, half on a berm of fill, and, although paved in concrete, it is edged with rocks and given an irregular shape. Neutra's declining interest in industrialization and its products and his increasing acceptance of purely symbolic details are seen in his comments on the pool: "Water that mirrors space is one of the earliest experiences. Is it utilitarian or beautiful to have a reflecting pool? Is it comfort to have water evaporate and cool the air in an arid climate or is it all just a cheap way of storage and irrigation? Is perhaps the so called 'practical' approach a hangover of nineteenth century materialism which makes it necessary to rationalize every design in something primarily useful?"[15]

It is curious how many standard Neutra details appear here, but deprived of function, or at least watered down. The soffit edge light detail of the V.D.L. house, for example, is replicated here, but the light is eliminated in favor of an empty slot (figure 4.28). While it asserts more elegantly the layered forms of the composition, its only functional purpose is as a sunscreen, which could easily have been solid. Some flashes of the old Neutra remain: the implied hollowness of the walls, for example. Compare the Kaufmann house column-partition detail with the same detail in the Moore house. At Kaufmann the plaster is flush, creating a uniform plane. At Moore the plaster projects beyond the post, implying that the hidden wood structure of the wall is emerging (figure 4.6).

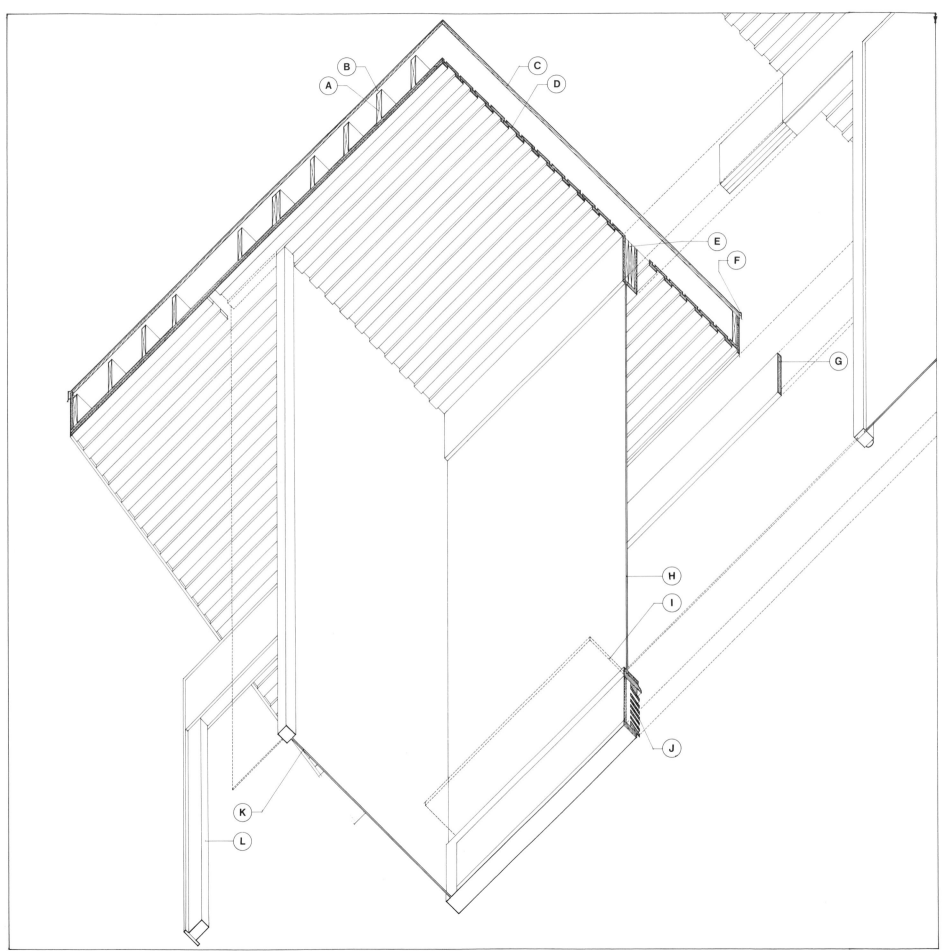

Moore house

Richard Neutra

Ojai, California, 1952

4.28 Section at corner of window of living room.

A 2 × 10 Douglas fir joists. Since these are concealed they are fir rather than redwood.

B Wood deck lifted on wedges to achieve a slope for drainage.

C Gravel on four layers of 15 lb roofing felt mopped with hot asphalt for waterproofing.

D Ceiling of 1 × 6 redwood strips 7″ oc nailed to 1 × 6 redwood board above. Staggering the board eliminates the need for tongue and groove joints.

E 4 × 16 laminated lintel from 2 × 16s.

F Galvanized iron gravel guard and ¾″ redwood fascia.

G 2 × 10 redwood outrigger.

H Frameless ¼″ plate glass set into column and ceiling.

I Operable ventilation panel and seat.

J ¼″ × 4″ redwood louvers. Since the glass is frameless and fixed, ventilation must be provided elsewhere.

K Glass set in groove of wood ceiling beyond.

L 4 × 4 solid redwood post to provide structural support for the beam. It is extended to visually engage the landscape beyond. The exterior exposed wood is made of redwood, which has a better appearance and a natural resistance to decay.
   (UCLA/DN BN 84 D-13-1, D-13-9, D-3-43)

4.29 Corner window of living room.

(Julius Shulman)

4.29

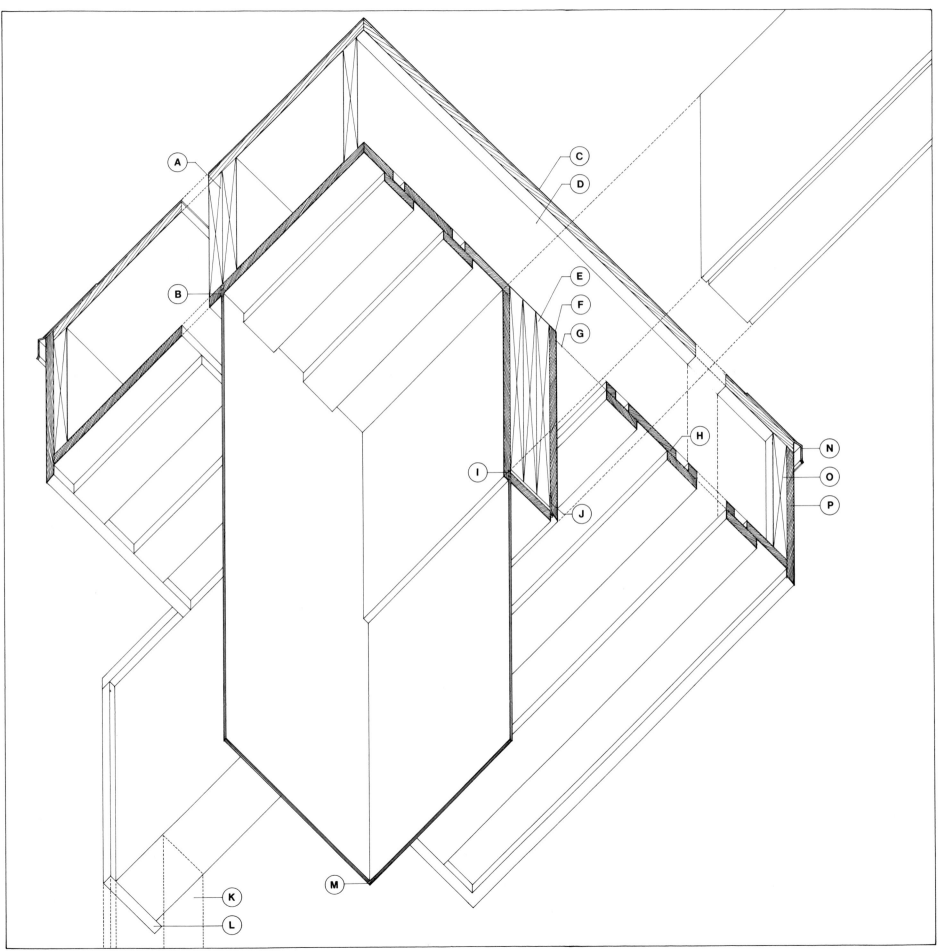

Moore house

Richard Neutra

Ojai, California, 1952

4.30   **Details of corner window.**

A   Douglas fir joists.

B   ¼" plate glass.

C   Pea gravel on four layers of 15 lb roofing felt mopped with hot asphalt. This provides the waterproof surface to the roof. The asphalt both seals the joints in the felt and binds it to the roof deck.

D   4" mineral wool batt insulation (not shown).

E   4 × 16 laminated girder from 2 × 16s to support joists. The column is exposed, the girder is clad, and the joists are concealed.

F   ¾" redwood casing. This could have been a solid redwood beam but it is more economical to case a less expensive wood in redwood.

G   Screen vent to circulate air in roof cavity to prevent condensation.

H   Ceiling of staggered 1 × 6 redwood strips at 7" oc.

I   The glass is set without a frame so that it disappears into the beam.

J   Flashing to prevent water from traveling along the soffit of the beam.

K   4 × 4 solid redwood post to provide structural support for the beam. Unlike in the Kaufmann house, where the extended beam supports the sliding door, this column had no functional reason to extend beyond the structure.

L   ¾" redwood finish head.

M   Mitered glass corner. Eliminating the frame increases the sense of transparency.

N   Galvanized iron gravel guard to prevent water from penetrating under the roofing or running over the edge.

O   Douglas fir joist to support fascia.

P   ¾" finish wood fascia.

(UCLA/DN BN 84 D-13-1, D-13-9, D-3-43)

Although Neutra did not pursue the heavy timber frame with the same ideological passion as he did the industrial V.D.L. and Palmer house systems, it was used in many of his finest houses. These houses inspired many similar houses in California but their closest relatives were in Scandinavia, where Jørn Utzon, Arne Jacobsen, and others were building houses quite similar in construction and spatial character, although their debt to Neutra is less than the mutual debt of all of them to Mies van der Rohe.

One of the better-known examples is not a house but a museum. Jørgen Bo and Vilhelm Wohlert were asked in 1958 to design the Louisiana Museum in Humlebæk, Denmark, as an extension to an existing estate and house. They created a series of pavilions composed of walls, roof slabs, and heavy timber columns and beams, arranged in an elemental fashion similar to the Moore and other houses. This kept the museum dispersed and small-scale while allowing the pavilions to respond to specific landscape situations.

The refinements of the type are in the details, particularly those of the roof. The structural system consists of bearing walls supporting glued and laminated beams which in turn support pine joists. The main beams are exposed while the joists are concealed beneath a tongue and groove wood ceiling. The beams sit atop a masonry wall and the space between is glazed without frames. The beam ends, where water is most damaging to the wood, are covered with gold leaf. In an equally elegant detail, the two ends of the wood fascia covering the joists are joined with a dovetail rather than a standard miter.

It is odd that this kind of special attention and high craftsmanship is so rare in Modernism. There are few details in Neutra's work anything like it. Perhaps this is because it required a very frank recognition of the very different levels of craft that go into building. The other wood connections at the Louisiana Museum are not made with dovetails but butted and nailed or bolted, and the level of craft below the surface is far below what we see on the outside, all, needless to say, containing no gold leaf. But strangely, the concept that building requires widely varying levels of craft, and that these variations could be exploited, has rarely found acceptance.

Neutra's Moore house, along with other of his houses of the 1950s—the Tremaine house, the Perkins house, and the Singleton house—suggest a different Neutra than do the Lovell, Beard, and von Sternberg houses. Although the former are among his finest works, he seemed reluctant to discuss their finest qualities, their transparency, their interior-exterior relationships, their use of natural materials, and when he did so he often used scientific reasoning. Much of his later writing is focused on biology and perception and attempts to give a scientific justification for what seem to be purely aesthetic impulses.

The Moore, Tremaine, and Perkins houses also suggest a different Neutra than do the Los Angeles Hall of Records or the graduate dorms at the University of Pennsylvania, two dismal Neutra buildings of the 1960s. Like Marcel Breuer and many early Modernists, Neutra saw his reputation suffer a decline in the 1960s, and in his case, as in Breuer's, the decline was perhaps deserved. Both suffered a strange paralysis in the large commissions that came with the financial success of their later years. Even Neutra's admirers, such as Thomas Hines, speak of the "general sense of fatigue that characterized Neutra's later larger buildings" and describe some as "bland and lifeless."[16]

Neutra's reputation declined in part for the same reason that the reputation of his long-neglected former partner Rudolph Schindler ascended. The industrial polemics and manifestos of the 1930s, Neutra's finest period, rang hollow in the last third of the twentieth century. The odd juxtapositions of Schindler's work, of precision and rudeness, of industry and craft, seemed a more appropriate response to the ambiguous relationship of American society to industrialization.

4.31

4.32

Louisiana Museum

Jørgen Bo and Vilhelm Wohlert

Humlebæk, Denmark, 1958

4.31 **View**.

4.32 **Corner**. Note the dovetailed corner
and the metal cover (originally gold
leaf) on the beam end.

4.33 **Wall section**.

A High roof construction. Four-ply
built-up roof on 5 × 5 pine joists at
2' 7" oc with ventilation holes to
allow air circulation to prevent condensation. Ceiling is of tongue and
groove Colombian pine boarding,
with 8 cm insulation.

B ¾" insulating glass with built-up
teak mullion with ¾" pine glazing
bead at head and pine sill with teak
glazing bead. The top mullion is
eliminated to make the ceiling appear continuous between interior
and exterior. Teak is naturally resistant to decay.

C 6 × 12 laminated pine beam. It is
difficult to obtain quality timbers of
this size, and glued-together sections are often stronger in any case.

D The low roof is identical to the high
roof except that joists are 2 × 5 and
the roof is raised on wedges to
achieve a slope for drainage.

E 6 × 12 laminated wood beam supporting low roof joists, with pipe
columns to support high roof. Gold
leaf on lead is applied at the beam
end, where the end grain of the
wood being more absorbent is
more susceptible to rot.

F The head and jamb are frameless
so that the glass disappears.

G 1 × 11 teak fascia dovetailed at corner. The dovetail holds the corners
together as the two long pieces of
wood expand and contract.

H Copper flashing. The flashing is terminated in a groove at the back of
the board rather than bringing it up
over the top.

I 36 cm brick wall.

J 2 cm brick tiles and 6 cm grout, 10
cm clinker concrete, and 20 cm
gravel.

(Arkitectur *10.58*)

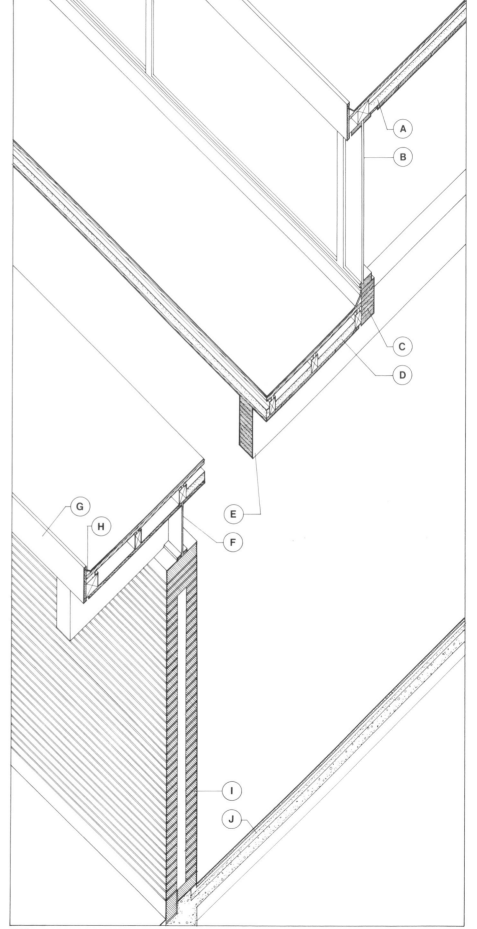

4.33

5   Alvar Aalto and Marcel Breuer: Light, Industrialization, and the Vernacular, 1928–1963

But cloud in stead, and ever-during dark

Surrounds me, from the cheerful waies of men

Cut off, and for the Book of knowledg fair

Presented with a Universal blanc

Of Natures works to mee expung'd and ras'd,

And wisdom at one entrance quite shut out.

So much the rather thou Celestial light

Shine inward, and the mind through all her powers

Irradiate, there plant eyes, all mist from thence

Purge and disperse, that I may see and tell

Of things invisible to mortal sight.

John Milton, *Paradise Lost*

Alvar Aalto made his first airplane flight in 1920. Like his contemporary Le Corbusier, he liked to draw while flying, but his sketches were usually more impressionistic than formal. In February of 1947, on a flight from Finland to the U.S. over Newfoundland, he made a sketch of the northern lights through the propeller of the plane in a letter to his wife.

Aalto's drawing tells us more about Aalto than it does about the plane. He is less concerned with the construction of the plane than with the image of light coming through the filter of the propeller. He is less concerned with the form of the airplane than with the form the rotating propeller implies. Aalto loved flying more than he loved airplanes, and he loved machines not for their own sake but for what they made visible. As it was to his contemporaries Asplund and Neutra, light was to Aalto more than illumination. It could destroy forms or create them, and could at times be inseparable from the objects it defined. Aalto's drawing is certainly an image that Moholy-Nagy would have enjoyed. The propeller's disklike form is defined only by motion modifying light, in Moholy-Nagy's terms a "virtual" form.

Moholy-Nagy and Aalto might seem an odd pair, one a major proselytizer of the machine age, the other to become its severe critic. Yet they were friends and shared not only ideas but stylistic affinities. Although Moholy was neither the only nor perhaps the primary source of the idea, the dominant characteristic of Aalto's architecture through its many manifestations is literal transparency, and a physics of light that paralleled closely Moholy-Nagy's own.

In the late 1920s and early 1930s Aalto experimented with and quickly abandoned most of the elements of the International Style Modernist vision—standardization, geometric forms, mechanistic finishes, and the doctrine of material efficiency

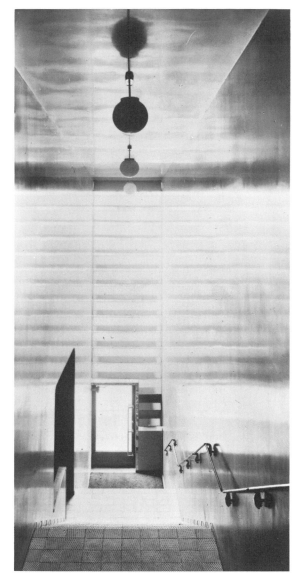

5.1

5.2

through minimal forms in steel or concrete. The images of light, of mass dematerialized, of material interchangeable with energy and its attendant forms—the louvered wall and the perforated screen—were to remain key devices of Aalto's architecture, leading ultimately to a spatial conception similar to Moholy-Nagy's, of space bounded not by mass or surface but by layers of perforated or transparent screens, mediating between exterior and interior.

If these elements are not readily perceptible in Aalto's work, it is because they are executed in the medium of venacular and natural materials. Of all the Modernists, Aalto is seen as the hero of regionalist architecture, responding to climate, site, and above all material, and gaining insight into the proper relationship between these through the study of vernacular forms, which had, in the view of many, already solved the problem. While this image of Aalto is not inaccurate, it is important to realize that to him the industrial, the natural, and the vernacular were not mutually exclusive languages. At the level of detail Aalto was the great humanizer, the enemy of rigid and arbitrary standards, responding with sensitivity to the most minute of functional concerns, softening the harshness of industrialization. Yet despite his frequent criticism of industrialization and its effects, he adhered to a system that could be equally rigid, a concept of industrialization that paralleled both the natural world and vernacular building.

Aalto's interest in vernacular and natural forms as sources of architectural inspiration undoubtedly owed much to the National Romantic style popular in Finland in the early 1900s, but when Aalto completed his education National Romanticism was passé, and he set off for Sweden, determined to work for Asplund. Though he was unsuccessful in this, his early work is in the mainstream of Nordic Classicism and has many of its faults. Aalto's Seinäjoki Defense Corps building (figure 3.2) is faced with Corinthian wooden pilasters with no entablature and no structural function or meaning. They are merely ornaments on a load-bearing wood wall. His church in Muurame has false plaster vaults hung from wood trusses and is redeemed only by the exposure of the bottom chords of the trusses, which penetrate the vault and are thus visible.

There were architects of the 1920s, notably Auguste Perret, who sought to reconcile the Classical language with the demands of rational building, but Aalto was not one of them. As in Asplund's work, the naive use of Classical elements included a structural naiveté, and although Aalto was to acquire the language of Modernism, his aquisition of Modernist structural principles was far more tenuous.

AALTO AND THE INTERNATIONAL STYLE

Aalto's 1928 Turun Sanomat newspaper building is perhaps his purest International Style work, containing all the style's familiar elements—ribbon windows, white stucco walls, freestanding columns—and equally familiar International Style strategies—standardization and the free plan. Aalto's interest in International Style architecture brought with it an interest in International Style materials, and while his early buildings emphasize wood structure, wood windows, and wood siding, Aalto turns here to concrete structure, steel windows, masonry, and stucco walls. The building also contains some concessions to Finnish tradition (the wall vents) and to Finnish climate, as the spandrels are insulated, unlike many typical International Style walls, which were commonly masonry plastered on both sides and nothing else.

The building's standardization existed mostly in Aalto's mind. Many of the detail drawings—lights, windows, and other repetitive elements—are labeled as standard and numbered. Aalto gave many of his details this designation in the late 1920s, implying that, at the very least, they would be reused form job to job, but he did not let this prevent him from designing a particular detail to suit a particular condition, and his library of standards grew rapidly. These details show the key elements of Aalto's response to industrialization, a standardization so varied and small-scale as to be capable of responding to the most minute concern, and the use of those small-scale elements to achieve a tight fit between form and a particular function.

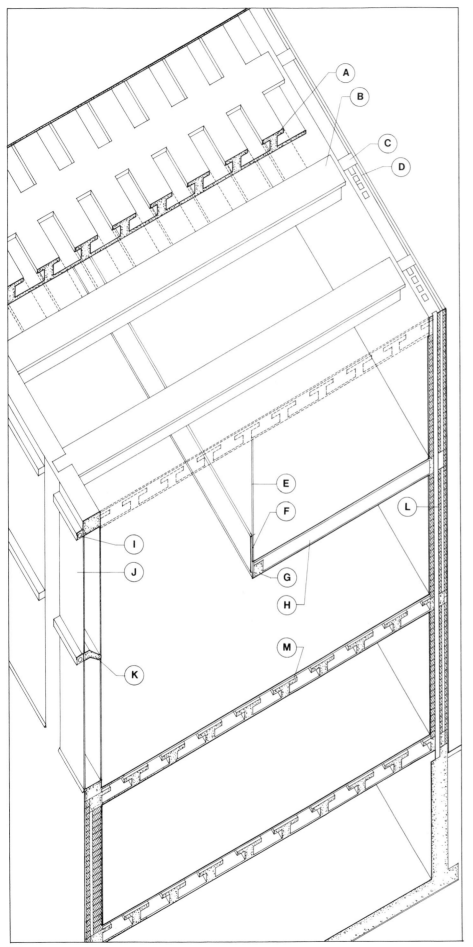

5.3

5.4

Paimio Sanitorium

Alvar Aalto

Paimio, FInland, 1929–1932

5.3   Cafeteria framing.

A   Concrete slab and inverted T beams with coke slag fill and concrete topping. This creates a flat ceiling while preserving the efficiency of a ribbed slab.

B   Concrete T girder with slab above.

C   Concrete column.

D   Brick wall with voids for services.

E   Steel hanger. This eliminates the need for columns below and uses the material, steel, in a more "economical" way.

F   Radiant heating panels in spandrel.

G   Concrete beam supported by hanger.

H   Radiant heating panels in ceiling.

I   Retractable awning in metal housing.

J   Double window. The two layers of glass both reduce heat loss and add a second layer between interior and exterior.

K   Concrete fin to support window and awning.

L   Voids in masonry wall for services. Aalto called this the negative skeleton of the building.

M   Floor construction identical to A above.

(AAA 50/303, 311)

5.4   Cafeteria.

(Finnish Architecture Museum)

Another Aalto trademark, the use of light to both dematerialize and define form, is present in the main window and entry of the Turun Sanomat building, a construction possibly inspired by Moholy-Nagy, Russian Constructivism, or both. The large window was for the projection of the front page of the newspaper. The slot next to it is the main entry leading to a stair. The tall transom is filled with louvered glass sheets on which are printed the names of the tenants.

The walls of the narrow interior stair hall were covered with highly reflective paint and lit in a way that makes the space appear to expand horizontally (figure 5.2). All of these elements approach the Moholy-Nagy and Malevich ideas of virtual form, forms defined by light, a minimum of transparent material, and spaces that exist only in perception. Unfortunately the entry was only partially executed and subsequently altered. Aalto only rarely used so literal a virtual form in his later work, and he quickly abandoned reflective surfaces, light sculputre, and transparent graphics, but the principles remained intact and were in fact expanded, particularly in his next work, the Paimio Tuberculosis Sanitorium.

The concern with light at Paimio is more than aesthetic; it is the functional rationale of the building. Tuberculosis in the early twentieth century was closely associated with dense urban areas and the absence of sunlight and fresh air, and before the development of drugs in the 1940s sunlight and fresh air were the only treatment.

For many architects of the 1920s light was the great purifier and cleanser. No quantity of light was excessive, and the ability of light to reach the most remote part of any room often took precedence over visual or acoustic privacy. The concepts of minimal material and maximum transparency, and the architectural devices with which they are associated such louvers and perforated screens, were thus given an additional functional rationale. On a small scale this produced some of Modernism's finest buildings, Pierre Chareau's Maison de Verre, Johannes Duiker's Open Air School, and Mart Stam's van Nelle Factory. On a larger scale it produced some of Modernism's most disturbing visions, such as the mass housing schemes of Walter Gropius and Ludwig Hilberseimer, with their seemingly endless rows of identical parallel apartment blocks. In any case, when Aalto entered the Paimio competition in 1929 the typical Modernist program for a sanitorium was well defined.

Many historians have pointed out the influence of Johannes Duiker's Zonnestraal (Ray of Light) Sanitorium on Aalto's Paimio Sanitorium. To Duiker in particular, abundance of sunlight and fresh air were key factors of the new architecture. But despite the similarities of functional approach and formal vocabulary, there are critical differences between the buildings in the relation of structure to program and in the relationship of structure to finish materials and form.

Duiker's structural layout is determined not by interior functional requirements but by the desire to use a minimum quantity and volume of concrete. The columns are pulled inward to reduce the bending moments at midspan. The beams are tapered as their stress decreases. The internal plan is accommodated to the skeleton. The structure is in fact the architecture and there is no ambiguity as to what is structure and what is not. Other than glass and the stucco facing on the concrete, Duiker's sanitorium has few nonstructural materials; most of the opaque sections are concrete. That this resulted in an enormous quantity of glass and sunlight is not seen as a problem but a virtue. While Aalto's building is concerned with material economy and light, its idea of what constitutes economy is far more complex than Duiker's, and Aalto does not shy away from distorting the structure to accommodate light. By contrast the structural frame of Aalto's building is hidden and at best implied.

While there is much regularity at Paimio, there is little structural standardization, at least in the sense that a building by Le Corbusier is standardized. The main building has four wings, each of which has a different bay spacing and structural system. There are regular bays within each wing, but they are largely determined by the programmatic requirements of the rooms, and each wing of the building is given a slightly different orientation, presumably determined by the requirements of sunlight and ventilation.

5.5

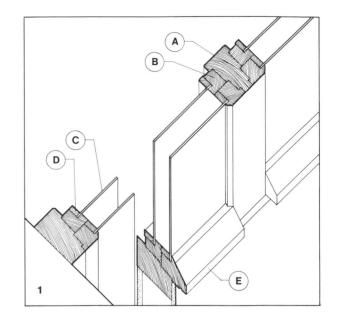

1

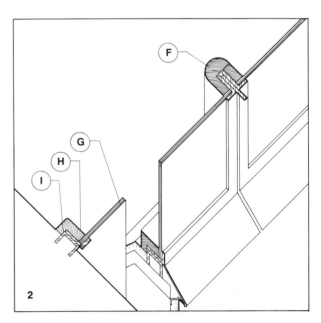

2

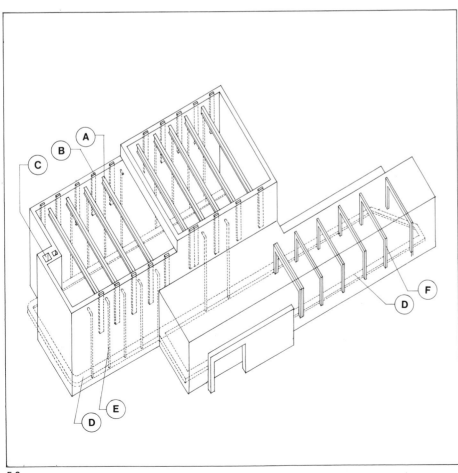

5.6

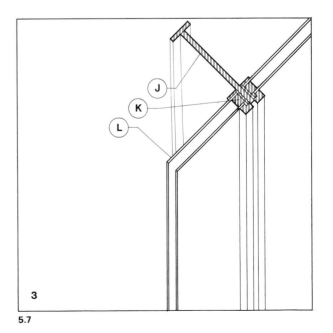

3

5.7

Viipuri Library

Alvar Aalto

Vyborg, Russia, 1927–1935

5.5 View.
(G. Welin: Finnish Architecture Museum)

5.6 Framing and mechanical systems.
A Reading room wing with steel beams supported by 2′ 6″ masonry bearing wall with concrete slab above and radiant heated ceiling below.
B Exhaust air ducts.
C Fresh air intake.
D Main air supply duct.
E Fresh air supply ducts. The air supply and returns are contained within the hollows of the bearing walls.
F Composite steel frame and concrete column. The lecture room/office portion of the building is a frame rather than a wall structure. The upper portion is apparently concrete.
(NA, AAA 43/115, 147, 151)

5.7 Window details.
1 Standard window used for smaller openings:
A Wood intermediate fixed mullion.
B Operable wood window sections. The double window and double layer of glass reduces heat loss in cold weather.
C Glass.
D Wood glass stops to allow reglazing.
E Sill. The bottom surface slopes and projects to shed water away from the joint and off the horizontal surface.
2 Lecture room window (see figure 5.10):
F Intermediate mullion of steel with teak cladding on interior.
G 8 mm plate glass. This larger window is single-glazed.
H Teak stop to retard condensation by insulating the cold interior surface of the steel section.
I Steel window frame.
3 Curtain wall at main lobby:
J The flat part of the mullion is in the shape of a catenary tapering toward its ends as the load decreases.
K Glass stops.
L Glass.
(AAA 43/201, 43/211)

The structure is seldom exposed, being enclosed in a series of complex layers of finish materials, and when it is exposed it is often done in a deceptive way. The floor slabs, for example, are not flat as they appear, but inverted ribbed slabs. The spatial module determines the bay size, not structural efficiency, and in fact the structure is distorted to accommodate the program. For example, in the patients' wing the edge of each slab is turned up at the exterior, allowing for a higher window and thus deeper penetration of light into the room. Equally meticulous thought was given to lighting and the effect of surfaces on light in both the visible and nonvisible spectrum. Radiant heating panels are located above the patients' beds and various parts of the walls are painted to reflect the light in various ways.

The cafeteria wing shows similar concerns applied in a slightly different manner (figure 5.3). The principal structure is also an inverted slab, although the bay spacing is different to accommodate the different program requirements of the cafeteria (longer spans). Aalto employs a minimalist solution in the mezzanine, hanging it from the beams above and eliminating the columns below. He would occasionally make use of such "engineered" devices, but he never sought or achieved the structural rigor of a Duiker or even the structural standardization of a Le Corbusier. The effect of the hung balcony is one Moholy-Nagy would have approved of, since, combined with the widely spaced double glazing of the facade, the mezzanine is separated from the interior by three transparent layers, and in Aalto's subsequent work it was light and not structure that was to dominate.

Aalto won the competition for the Viipuri Library in 1927, but the building was not finished until 1935. As at Paimio, the program, and with it the structure, are split into parts. The main reading room and children's library are housed in a block of load-bearing masonry supporting a composite roof of steel beams and concrete, while the lecture room and offices are housed in a concrete-framed block. The reading room is the most massive of the enclosures, with 2-foot-6-inch-thick masonry bearing walls and a 5-foot-deep roof structure. Aalto was repeatedly to use the combination of load-bearing and frame block, and, more than Paimio, Viipuri is the beginning of Aalto's own brand of Modernism.

There is little exposed structure in the building, and although the differences between the two blocks are only subtly perceptible, they are clearly deliberate. Structural expression is secondary to the delamination, perforation, and dematerialization of the wall surfaces, especially by means of light.

Both structures are heavily eroded, by light in the roofs and by air in the walls. There is little indication of this in the ceiling, which is flat plaster, but structure and ceiling are perforated by a grid of truncated cones that admit reflected light into the interior (figure 5.12). Aalto thought of this as "a series of suns," but they bear a strong resemblance to the perforated screens of Moholy-Nagy's work. Nor is the function of the slab as a modulator of light limited to the visible spectrum, for it also contains one of the building's major heating systems, a radiant one consisting of a circuit of pipes embedded in plaster through which is circulated heated water, heating the slab and thus radiating heat to the space below. The analogy of the suns is thus extended into the mechanical system.

If the roof is dematerialized by the light, the wall is eroded by air. The thick masonry walls contain numerous shafts for air distribution and return. Air is drawn in from the roof via a chimney, conditioned in the basement, and distributed to the reading room through small ducts in the walls, located so as to fall in the centers of the piers below (figure 5.6). Exhaust ducts are located between the supply ducts, and discharge at the roof. The use of wall cavities as vents is common in Finnish construction, but Aalto uses them as a means of hollowing out the mass of the wall in a systematic way. Although there are numerous windows in the children's library below the main reading room, there are none in the main reading room above.

The lecture room/office wing, although it appears similar to the reading room from the exterior, is apparently framed in an entirely different way, with steel wide-flange columns supporting a ribbed concrete slab. These columns are visible only

5.8

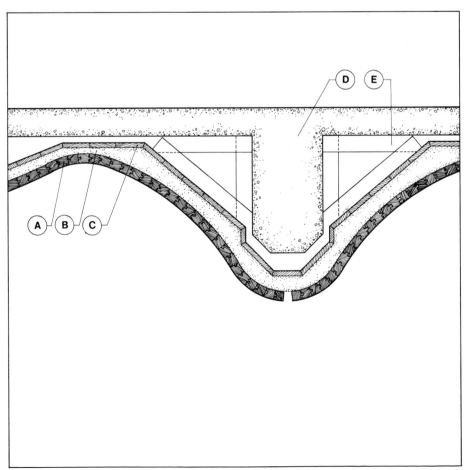

5.9

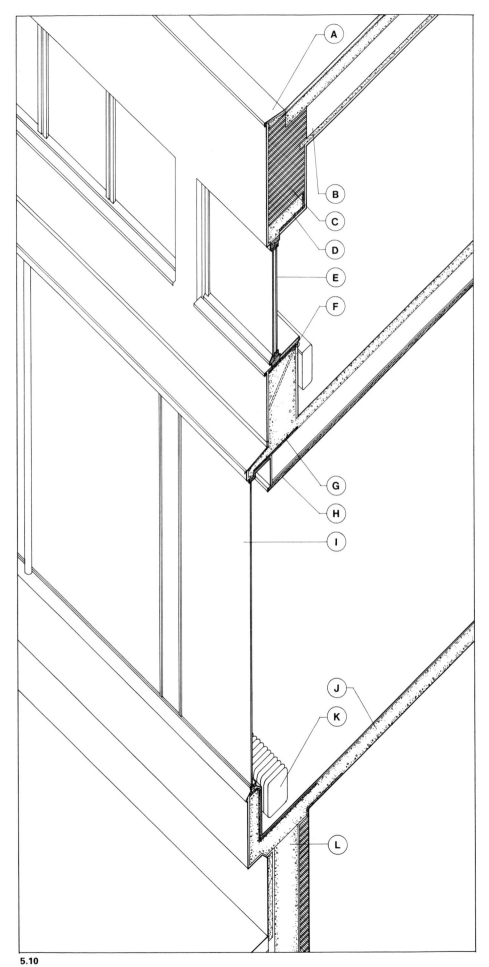

5.10

Viipuri Library

Alvar Aalto

Vyborg, Russia, 1927–1935

5.8   **Lecture room.**

(Finnish Architecture Museum)

5.9   **Lecture room ceiling.**

A   Red pine tongue and groove boards. The undulations are to reflect sound to the audience from the speaker.

B   Slag wool insulation.

C   Wood board to receive insulation.

D   Concrete beam and slab. The pattern of the undulations roughly follows that of the concrete beams above, which are concealed by the ceiling.

E   Wood framing to support wood ceiling and connect it to the concrete structure above.

(NA, AAA 43/312)

5.10   **Wall section.**

A   Copper coping on steel clip. This covers the edge of the built-up roof and protects the plaster-wall joint from penetration by water. The wood blocking acts as a nailer for the copper and built-up roof. The roof is a bituminous membrane covered with a protective concrete layer.

B   Double concrete slab with filling. The double slab achieves the strength of a deeper slab with less weight.

C   Brick wall with plaster interior finish and stucco exterior.

D   Reinforced concrete lintel. This supports the masonry over the window opening.

E   Double wood window. See figure 5.7.

F   Concrete sill with fresh air vent.

G   Concrete slab with cork insulation at edge to retard heat loss.

H   Undulating ceiling of red pine boards. See figure 5.9.

I   Steel and glass curtain wall with wood glazing stops and copper flashing. See figure 5.7. The larger window is single-glazed, with a metal frame because of its greater size and hence greater load.

J   Linoleum floor on concrete floor slab.

K   Radiator to create a rising current of warm air on the glass to retard heat loss and condensation.

L   Concrete wall with granite facing. The stucco is a poor finish at grade, where it is subject to additional wear and water penetration.

(NA, AAA 43/148)

in one location, the exterior wall of the lecture room, which projects beyond the plane of the solid wall to allow the steel columns to become freestanding. The contrast of load-bearing wall block with frame block is actually still more complicated, as the latter is actually a hybrid with bearing walls on the second floor.

The concrete beams of the floor structure above the lecture room are not visible, being hidden by an undulating wood ceiling. Aalto's explanation of this ceiling as an acoustical reflector, which was given so much credence by early Modernist historians, is dubious. In any case a concern with acoustics would hardly have led to the design of an auditorium 3½ times as long as it is wide.

There are three fenestration systems at Viipuri, determined not so much by the needs of the spaces that they serve as the size of window that the spaces require (figure 5.7). The smaller openings are inswinging double wood windows. The large two-story glazed area at the entry lobby is framed with rolled bronze sections, fabricated in sections very similar to steel. Aalto's curtain wall makes use of the resemblance of the bronze sections to industrial steel sash to create an International Style curtain wall.

Steel sash was industrial both in its method of production and in one of its typical applications, the factory, but also fit precisely the laws of economy of material as exemplified by the airplane and the bridge, having the smallest profile of any available window, barely one quarter that of wood sash. Like the bridge and plane, it could seem to dematerialize. Aalto carries this a step further by tapering the mullions in accordance with their stress, further minimizing their size and weight. The tall vertical mullions are in the form of a very flat catenary deepest at the center where maximum bending and deflection occurs, smallest at the ends.

The third fenestration system, that of the long lecture room window, is a hybrid of steel and wood. The steel profile was the typical Modernist solution to the larger window because of its lightness and association with factories and industrialization. It was not entirely appropriate to Scandinavia because steel is a better conductor of heat than wood and thus a poorer insulator; and since the steel windows are single-glazed, the assembly is subject to greater heat loss and condensation.

Aalto ameliorates if not eliminates this problem by using internal teak glazing beads so that no metal is exposed on the interior, and by lining the edges of the projecting bay with cork. The teak, besides being a better insulator, is less cold to the touch, a criterion that was always important to Aalto. As in the stair handrail (figure 5.11), Aalto adopts almost a different language when the building is touched. This window projects forward of the wall to stand free of the columns, creating a shallow glazed bay on the exterior, and is only a section of a general layering of the facade perpendicular to the axis of entry.

In 1929 Aalto constructed a series of "laboratory experiments in wood," which, according to his biographer Göran Schildt, were inspired by Moholy-Nagy's and Josef Alber's explorations of materials at the Bauhaus. Aalto's experiments utilized the same processes of shaping and forming as his furniture—laminating wood strips and rods, slicing an end piece and laminating the resulting strips into curves (figure 5.17)—but served no functional purpose, and throughout the 1930s he continued an exploration into the nature of material, to discover those natural characteristics that revealed the key to form. Yet while pursuing this abstract exploration without reference to precedent, he began or perhaps continued another, a study of vernacular form as the key to the nature of material, most specifically the architecture of the Finnish province of Karelia.

In a 1941 essay on Karelian architecture, Aalto explained in part his change of focus from an abstract treatment of material qualities to material qualities as they are manifested in vernacular traditions:

It is forest architecture pure and simple, with wood dominating almost one hundred per cent both as a building material and in jointing . . . generally left naked, without the effect of immateriality given by coloring. A tumbledown Karelian village is externally somehow related to Greek ruins, where the unity of material

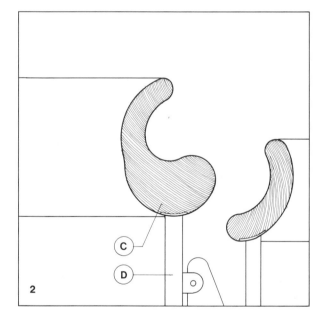

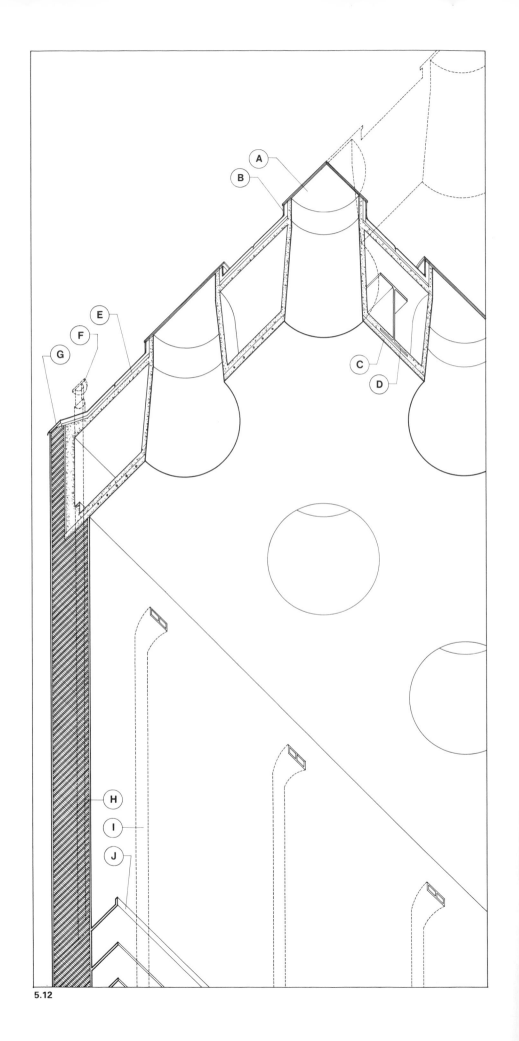

5.11

5.12

5.11 Alvar Aalto handrails.

1   Paimio Sanitorium stair railing. In his "industrial" phase Aalto used simple geometric shapes.

A   Wooden railing. Although it is painted to appear metallic, only the external railings are metal.

B   2 cm round nickel-plated steel support.

2   Viipuri Library. Here Aalto has changed to a shape that is both organic and wooden.

C   Beech handrail.

D   Pipe support.

3   Säynätsalo Town Hall:

E   Wood handrail.

F   Steel angle and square vertical support.

(AAA 33/297, 50/242, 43/235)

Viipuri Library
Alvar Aalto
Vyborg, Russia, 1927–1935

5.12   Interior wall section at reading room.

A   Skylight lens of 16 mm roughcast glass on 5 mm glass. Since a broken skylight is potentially more dangerous than a broken window, provision is made to prevent broken glass shards from falling into the space below.

B   Copper flashing with concrete slab and cone below. The cone ensures that only reflected and not direct sunlight will reach the interior.

C   Plaster ceiling with radiant heating pipes.

D   Steel beams. Despite the structural importance of these elements, they have no expression, direct or indirect.

E   4 cm concrete paving slabs on waterproofing and 1″ softboard insulation. The entire roof was to be accessible, but the insulation over time proved to be of insufficient strength to support the pavers.

F   Exhaust air vent.

G   Copper coping.

H   Load-bearing brick wall.

I   Air supply duct and diffuser. The air is directed across the heated ceiling before dropping to the space below.

J   Bookcases.

(NA, Alvar Aalto Foundation Restoration Report)

is also a salient feature, though in them wood is replaced by marble up to the entablature. In a way the Karelian house is a building which begins with a single small cell or dispersed, embryonic shacks—shelters for people and animals—and grows, figuratively speaking, year by year.[1]

Aalto saw perhaps too glibly in these buildings all his formal and ideological interests: respect for material, biological organization based on cellular growth, and the picturesque qualities of Classical ruins.

Vernacular wood forms appear more and more in Aalto's work in the 1930s: pitched, irregular roofs, wood siding, and sometimes even log cabin construction similar to that of Karelia. He saw these as being in the nature of the material, based not on abstract form derived from structural qualities but on vernacular form based on constructional tradition.

THE PARIS PAVILION AND THE VILLA MAIREA

Aalto's interest in vernacular forms and construction was not unique in the late 1930s. Le Corbusier, Walter Gropius, Marcel Breuer, even Mies van der Rohe held similar attitudes, but they typically used vernacular forms in combination with, rather than opposition to, International Style forms. Likewise Aalto's interest in vernacular forms did not decrease his interest in volumes dematerialized by light, and if the laminated wood curves of the mid-1930s are seen less and less frequently in subsequent work, the perforated and louvered wood screens are seen more and more. Perhaps becuase this methodology required the juxtaposition of opposites seemingly incapable of reconciliation, the irrational combination of radically different techniques, and the simultaneous consideration of multiple variables, it was one at which Aalto excelled.

The buildings of this period are rich in juxtapositions: the international and the regional, the industrial and the hand-crafted, the archaic and the modern, frame with wall, wood with white brick. The possible reasons for these characteristics— the general decline of faith in industrialization, the emergence of nationalism and regionalism, the impact of Surrealism, or in Sigfried Giedion's terms, the "irrational" element—were rarely addressed by Aalto in writing or lectures. He saw himself as simply humanizing the impact of industrialization on modern life.

In his pavilion for the 1937 Paris Exposition, Aalto began to systematically explore the effects of light on surfaces not explicitly transparent. While his interest in light continued to increase, his interest in structural expression, or at least accurate structural expression, continued to decline, and his mechanisms for articulating the effects of light, while remaining formally similar to those he had previously used, were not executed in the machine finish elements of Moholy-Nagy but in vernacular and organic components used in similar configurations.

The Paris building combined what appears to be a wall building with frame buildings. The main pavilion was composed of one large windowless block with skylights surrounded by the frame buildings, a series of one-story pavilions and open walkways. In reality the structure of both parts is a hybrid of wood and steel. In the wall building it is completely concealed; in the frame building it is only partially exposed. At this point in his career Aalto had come to the conclusion that, however important the frame was to the realization of Modern architecture, the expression of that frame was of secondary importance. In an essay from 1938, one year after the pavilion was completed, he wrote:

In primitive times the supporting skeleton was almost the only problem, and it was also the basic element of architecture. . . .

Today, on the other hand, the basic element of architecture at that time—the skeleton—is, for example, reduced to a light metal grid, and the production of this grid is only a small part of the whole building process. It may well be that a metal construction of this kind is, in its character, similar to the tent construction of primitive times; yet it differs from this in one important way: The skeleton of a modern building is often in its volume, but above all in its importance, certainly a smaller part of the whole building than formerly.[2]

5.13

 5.14

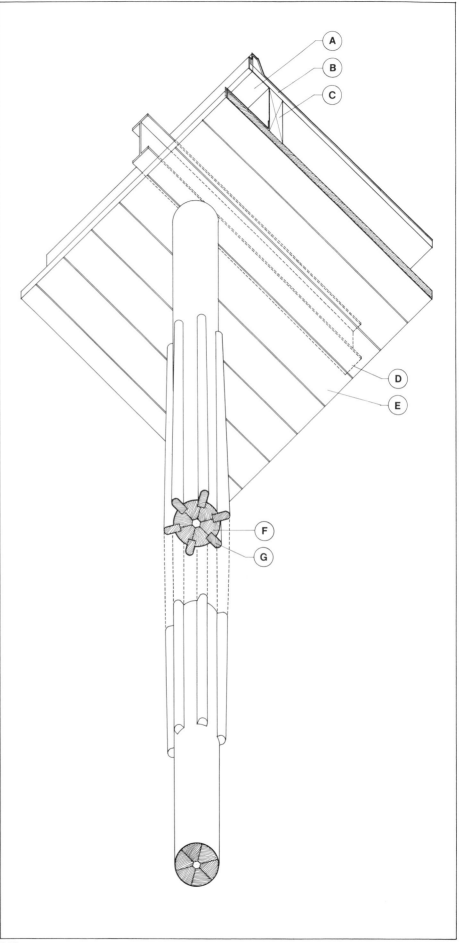

5.15

Finnish Pavilion for 1937 World Exposition

Alvar Aalto

Paris, 1936–1937

5.13 View.

(A. Heinonen: Finnish Architecture Museum)

5.14 Portico.

(A. Heinonen: Finnish Architecture Museum)

5.15 Column detail at portico.

A   Sheet metal coping and flashing to protect the structure from water penetration and the top of the projecting soffit from standing water.

B   Roof deck of 3 × 12 cm boards.

C   S 22 wood beams.

D   J 18 steel beam. This projects through the wood fascia to show that the underlying structure is steel. The remainder of the extensive steel framing is concealed.

E   Soffit of 3 × 15 cm wood boards. As he was to do in many buildings, Aalto exposed the columns while hiding the beams.

F   Wood column from wedged shaped fir segments. These taper toward the ends as the loads decrease. The diagonal cross bracing of the structure makes the pinned connection possible at the base.

G   Ash reinforcing fins.

(AAA 68/181, 68/211)

This is one of the more unique aspects of Aalto's Modernism, the only occasional exposure of the structural frame and the only occasional expression of the structural qualities of materials.

If the frame is subdued it is to allow the effects of light to emerge, and if the means and materials of the execution of this idea are vernacular and organic, the forms and themes are born out of Moholy-Nagy's objects of industrialization. The only real source of natural light in the main block is the grid of cylindrical skylights creating a perforated screen like that of the *Light-Space Modualtor.* The opaque walls could have thus only metaphorical transparency, achieved in part by applied photomontages, but more effectively by modulating the surface to diffuse the light while dematerializing the mass.

Here Aalto adapted a common vernacular device, board and batten siding, but by deepening, adding to, and modeling the profile, he heightened the shadows cast by the battens. The curved fins in figure 5.16 have no technical function, as the siding, even without the secondary batten, is watertight. Stripped of the two battens, the wall is similar to that of the Villa Aalto (figure 5.16). The only purpose of the batten was thus to make what was an opaque wall appear as a semitransparent screen. Aalto also proposed a deeper batten of a more organic shape that would have cast an even deeper shadow, but this was not realized.

In the surrounding pavilions and arcades the theme of light is subdued and the theme of structure more apparent, but, as in many Aalto structures, the apparent complexity is different from its real complexity, which is largely concealed. Also as with many Aalto structures, the column is expressed to the point of overarticulation, while the structure of the roof is largely suppressed.

There are three types of columns used, one natural, one venacular, and one industrial. The natural columns are birch tree trunks brought from Finland. The vernacular columns are clusters of poles lashed together. Most critics assume that these are inspired by Karelian construction, but they also resemble the tied stone columns of northern Italian Gothic and the iron-bound double columns occasionally used by Saarinen, Gesellius, and Lindgren. The industrial columns, although built up of wood segments, appear to be inspired by airplane struts, with fins tapering toward their pinned ends (an arrangement that works only if diagonal bracing is used). Like airplane struts they use the minimum material, and unlike traditional architectural columns they are the same upside down.

The structure of the roof is, at least in appearance, much simpler than that of the columns. The actual structure is a deck of wood boards supported by steel I sections or round or rectilinear wood sections. All are concealed from below by a flat wood ceiling, creating a typically Modernist free-plan space, but are allowed to project on the ends. The I sections or pairs of round beans projecting through the fascia thus imply, if not exactly reveal, the real structure. Both upper and lower wood decks also project (figure 5.15) so that we perceive the roof in its reality, not a monolithic slab, but a frame wrapped in a series of layers.

The Paris pavilion was in many ways the beginning of Aalto's mature style. The themes of dematerialization of mass through light, articulation of the building envelope as a series of layers, and the combination of organic, industrial, and vernacular forms, along with the devices for accomplishing these themes—the louvered and perforated screens and the doubled bound and tapered columns—all were to continue in his subsequent work.

In the Villa Mairea these themes achieved perhaps their most systematic expression. The major spaces of the villa are articulated not as traditional masses, not as International Style volumes but as spaces loosely defined by layers of porous and transparent screens in both floors and walls. The screens never seem to join, particularly at corners; many of them are mobile and most are transparent or perforated literally or symbolically, by light, by heat, or by air. The configuration of these screens is sometimes the perforated grid of circles or more often the louvered

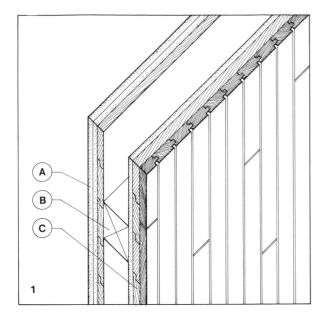

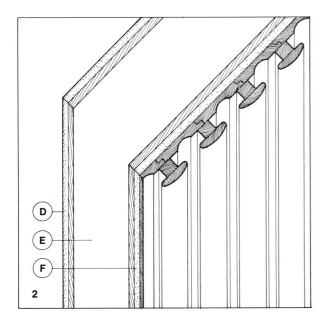

5.17

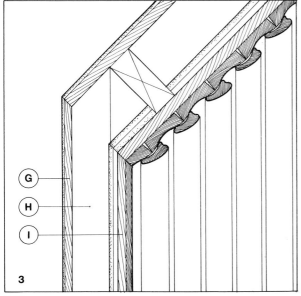

5.16

5.16 Alvar Aalto, siding types.

1 Villa Aalto. Here Aalto uses standard tongue and groove siding with a small space between, a type he was rarely to use again.

A Interior facing of two layers of ½″ insulation board on ¾″ horizontal wood sheathing.

B 3 × 3 wood girts at 50 cm oc.

C Outer facing of 1 × 2 red pine tongue and groove boards on ⅞″ shiplap horizontal sheathing and ½″ insulation board.

2 Paris Pavilion:

D Inner layer of 18 mm sheathing and 13 mm insulation board.

E Wood framing.

F ¾ × 5″ shiplap siding with battens on 1 × 1 blocking, and 13 mm insulation board, 18 mm board behind. The batten and blocking are unnecessary to waterproof the wall. Battens are applied to the wall to cast shadows and create the illusion of a perforated screen.

3 Villa Mairea, siding at studio. Although Aalto experimented with deeper profiles (figure 5.19), he finally settled on a shallow organic profile.

G Inner layer of ¼″ asbestos board on sheathing.

H 2 × 5 wood stud framing with 1″ insulation between. The studio wall, unlike the remainder of the building, uses wood framing.

I 1″ tongue and groove sheathing at 45° and 1 × 4″ red pine vertical boards with curved red pine battens cut from one 2½ × 3.
(AAA 60/220, 222, 84/582)

5.17 Alvar Aalto, Paimio chair (variation), 1932.

screen of Moholy-Nagy, but the components are usually nonmetallic, composed either of industrial forms translated into wood, vernacular wood forms, or organic ones.

The structure is a load-bearing masonry box (the kitchen/service wing) combined with a concrete and steel composite frame (the living room/study wing). The bar between, the entry/dining area, is a hybrid of concrete and masonry. The structural expression of these systems is hardly pure. The wall system invades the frame block to displace columns; the frame system invades the load-bearing block to create openings. The frame is constantly being distorted, eroded, or otherwise changed to accommodate some programmatic or spatial need, as in the dining room, where the beam is dropped to create a stepped terrace above, or in the studio, where it breaks out of its rectangular grid to create an organic shape, or in the living room, where hollow load-bearing walls that distribute air displace columns. Surrounding the house are other pavilions, each with a unique structure: the concrete and wood trellis that extends the dining area, the primitive log and lashed-pole frame of the sauna, and the entry canopy, actually a steel frame entirely wrapped and concealed by rectangular milled sections, organic milled sections, and sections of saplings.

There is a structural expression in the building, particularly the living room, but it is a structure in which much is concealed, particularly by the ceiling, and in which what is revealed, particularly by the columns, is far more complex than structural logic would dictate. The room is roughly a grid of nine squares with sixteen supports (figure 5.21). Four of the columns are replaced by walls containing ductwork. In general there are single columns on the perimeter and double columns in the interior. This has a certain logic, as the interior column supports twice the floor area, but given the large size of the columns, 16 cm in diameter, and the small size of the floor area, 25 square meters per column, this seems hardly necessary. In the study the double column is replaced by a single larger concrete column, again perhaps logical given the tighter spatial arrangement of the smaller room. There is no apparent logic, however, to the one cluster of three columns at the edge (except that one of them extends upward and is exposed on the second-floor balcony). Other differences also appear to be alterations for the sake of nonstandardization. Some columns are wrapped with caning, some clad with beech strips, some are left alone, but few are treated in the same manner.

The first-floor structure is a simple one-way ribbed slab whose ribs are often not as wide as the double columns that support them. The roof structure is a doubled ribbed slab with filling. Neither is visible. The roof, being double, appears flat; the first-floor slab is covered entirely by a wood slat ceiling. This was by now the typical Aalto method of structural expression. The layers of screens that make up the walls and roof for the most part conceal the structure except for the columns, which are given elaborate treatment and are in effect visually isolated by the suppression of the remainder of the structure under a flat ceiling. The ceiling is hardly a deception; it is obviously nonstructural, is revealed at its edge, stops short of the wall, and is permeated by air if not by light, since it is by means of a grid of ¼-inch holes drilled in the grooves of the wood that air is supplied to the space.

The villa was Aalto's first air-conditioned house, and its method of distribution and integration is sometimes systematic, as in the living room, and sometimes ad hoc, squeezed into voids created by closets or with ducts simply allowed to run along the ceiling. In the living room the architecture, by contrast, is altered considerably to accommodate the services. The walls adjacent to the fireplace and study are hollowed out to accommodate risers and returns to the central plant in the basement. Some of these supply air to the ceiling plenum, where it is diffused into the room through the small holes in the wood ceiling. Others simply end in diffusers on the wall. These are covered with wood-louvered screens or by vertical boards with slots between. This was a happy marriage between Aalto's conception of the floors and walls as a series of layered porous screens and the need to accommodate a large number of diffusers and return air grilles.

5.18

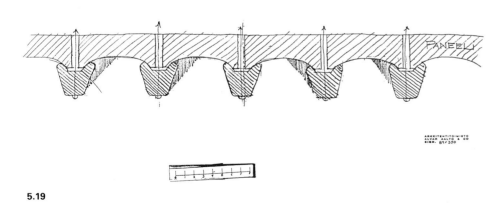

5.19

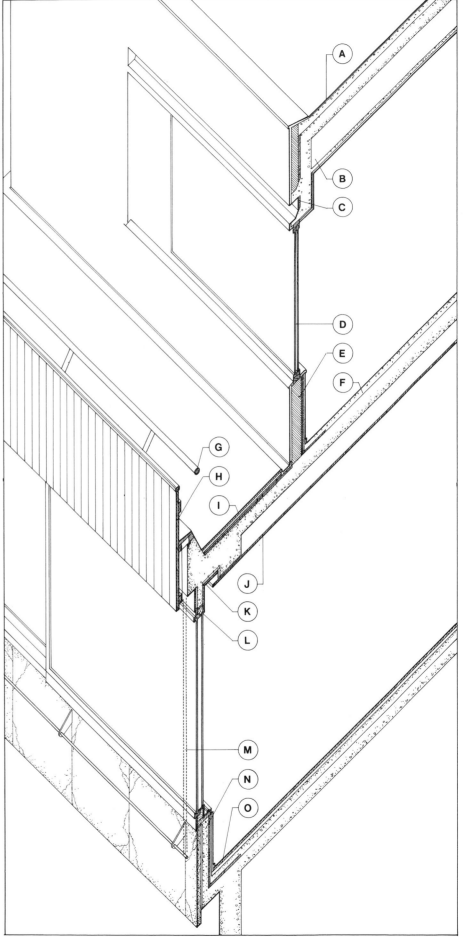

5.20

Villa Mairea

Alvar Aalto

Noormarkku, Finland, 1938–1939

5.18 **View.**
(Finnish Architecture Museum)

5.19 **Siding experiments.**
(Alvar Aalto Archive)

5.20 **Wall section at living room.**
A Roofing and copper flashing.
B Double concrete slab with protective concrete covering.
C Pocket for blind.
D Teak window.
E Typical wall construction of stucco on masonry with 4 cm cork insulation.
F Concrete floor slab.
G 7 cm teak handrail on 5 cm steel tube.
H 2.5 cm teak boards.
I Balcony slab with 15 × 15 cm tile on grout and bitumen waterproofing, with expanded cork insulation between grout and slab. The bitumen intercepts any water that penetrates the tiles. Since the room below is interior and the balcony exterior, it must be insulated.
J Wood ceiling.
K Blind pocket. This also makes the ceiling appear as an independent plane.
L Teak window.
M Blinds with hold-down.
N 5.5 cm granite on 10 cm concrete wall with 4 cm cork insulation and plaster interior finish.
O Wood flooring on concrete slab with basement below.
(AAA 84/461, 610, 914)

The walls of the load-bearing service wing are for the most part stucco-covered solid masonry with punched openings. The living room by contrast seems devoid of opaque or smooth surfaces. The studio/living room wall in particular seems made entirely of louvered screens—the real louvers of the trellis, the horizontal exterior wood blinds, and the vertical boards of the studio railing which have a small gap between each to emphasize each member. Even the horizontal siding sometimes has long grooves cut between boards to allow for ventilation. There is a stone base to the wall, but it is also a hanging plane with exposed edges. In fact the edges of all the planes of different materials are extended and exposed so that each seems an independent floating layer, each modulating the light in a different way.

The studio received the most elaborate treatment, being the room in which light is the most critical. The illumination is provided by a large skylight and window facing the courtyard, but Aalto wished here to articulate the other walls as undulating and porous screens of thin verticals, a concept considerably at odds with the constructional reality (25-cm-thick walls and a 55-cm-deep ribbed concrete slab). His solution was to warp walls and roof and extend the wall facing to form a paper-thin parapet, then to apply to the vertical surfaces the type of deep profiled siding he had used at Paris. Aalto sketched out the projection of the shadows on various profiles (figure 5.19) before finally arriving at one of a shallow organic shape.

The window details are no less complex. At this point in his development Aalto's details had lost most of their International Style and industrial imagery and are far more reconciled to local building tradition (although teak is hardly a Finnish vernacular material). Aalto considered some aircraft-like punched I sections for mullions at the projecting bays. The final solution is, in appearance, all doubled wood windows of the typical Scandinavian type.

The most interesting of these are the projecting bays of the bedrooms and the large windows of the living area. The bays have considerable steel to support the projection, but this, like most of the structure, is concealed and unarticulated, leaving only the effect of weightlessness. The various glazed and louvered panels that make up the living room walls are all to some degree adjustable to allow changing nuances of light, but also to alter interior-exterior relationships. The southeast wall has two oversize sliding windows and a louvered wood ventilator, the southwest wall has exterior blinds and interior sliding screens, the winter garden has large swinging doors, and at the northwest wall facing the courtyard, one half of the entire wall—windows, doors, and wood siding—can be slid into the double wall of the winter garden to connect living room and courtyard. The character of the room is more Japanese than industrial or Finnish.

The most elaborate mechanism for modulating light and space is the stair, a kind of static version of Moholy-Nagy's *Light-Space Modulator* with louvered screens at the bottom and a grid of perforated circles at the top. Although the final version of the stair is wood, it began as a series of vertical steel cables from which the treads were hung (fig 5.29). The movement in this case is supplied not by a mechanism but by the diagonally moving observer, who simultaneously views both garden and living room through passing bars of the trellis.

The principal virtues of the villa—its contrasts and juxtapositions of seemingly contradictory levels of craft, finish, and precision, and the inclusion of elements that are simultaneously organic, industrial, and vernacular—are qualities Aalto seldom achieved or even attempted to achieve in subsequent work. While the themes of light and dematerialization were to continue, the industrial references of the triad continued to decline, while the vernacular and organic references rose to dominance.

THE MASONRY BUILDINGS OF THE 1940s AND 1950s

In 1945 Aalto visited the office of Saarinen, Swanson, and Saarinen near Detroit. There Eero Saarinen made him an offer; Aalto could have one-half the commissions in the office if he would be willing to move to the United States. This was only one of many offers made to Aalto to lure him to America, especially after the

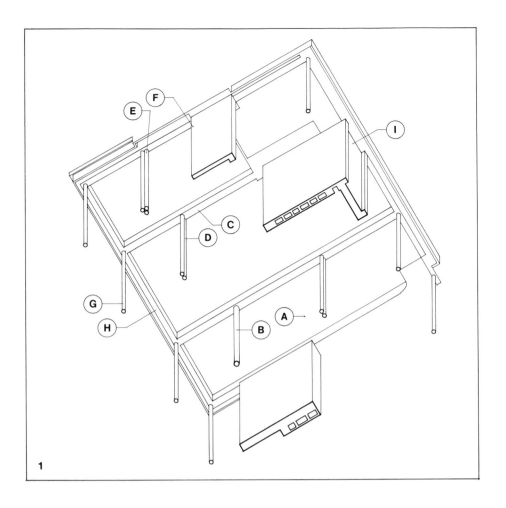

1

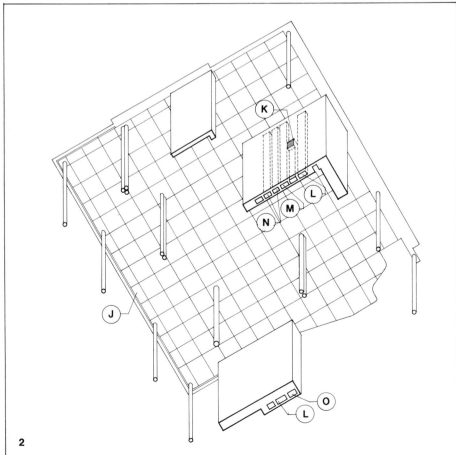

2

Villa Mairea

Alvar Aalto

Noormarkku, Finland, 1938–1939

5.21 **Framing and ceilings.**

1 Structure:

A 16 cm concrete slab.

B Concrete column in library.

C 30 × 45 cm concrete beam.

D Two 15 cm steel columns with concrete fill and 6 mm asbestos cover. See figure 5.23.

E Three 13.5 cm steel columns with 6 mm asbestos coating. See figure 5.25.

F Concrete bearing walls.

G One 15 cm steel column with concrete fill and 6 mm asbestos cover at perimeter.

H Perimeter concrete beam.

I Fireplace.

2 Finishes and ventilation:

J Ceiling of 10 × 30 mm red pine tongue and groove boards in 1 m square panels. This exposes all the columns while concealing all the beams.

K Air supply shaft and wall diffuser to porch.

L Air supply shaft to wall diffuser in living room.

M Air supply shaft to plenum above living room ceiling. The air is distributed to the space through holes in the ceiling.

N Air supply and return shafts to studio above.

O Air return shaft from living room.

(AAA 84/435, 467, 507, 508, 510, 541)

5.22 **Living room.**

(Havas: Finnish Architecture Museum)

5.22

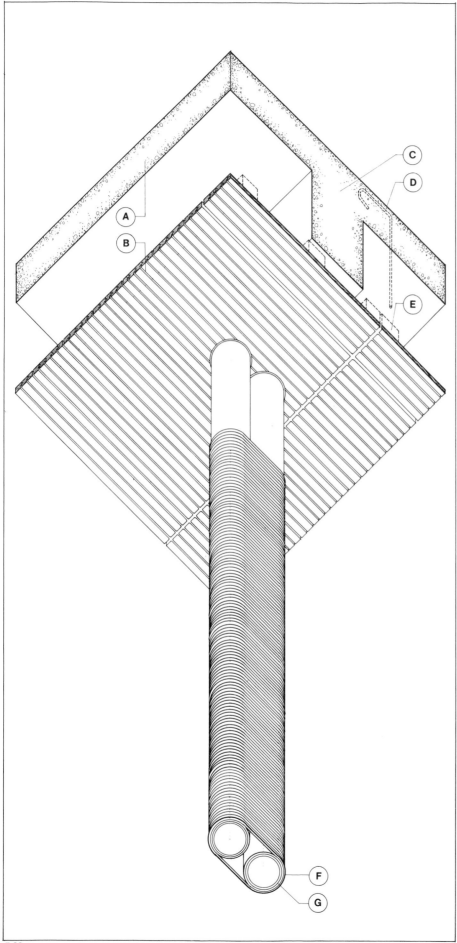

5.23

5.24

Villa Mairea

Alvar Aalto

Noormarkku, Finland, 1938–1939

5.23 Double column at living room.
- A Concrete slab.
- B Red pine ceiling with ¼" holes for air distribution, shop-fabricated in square panels.
- C Concrete beam. The beam is hidden by the wood ceiling.
- D ⅜" threaded rod cast in slab to support ceiling.
- E Wood blocking to support ceiling panels.
- F Wood wrappings.
- G 15 cm steel column with concrete fill and 6 mm asbestos cover.
  (AAA 84/541, 800)

5.24 Double column at living room.

Second World War, all of which he declined. How American architecture might have been different had Aalto taken Saarinen's job is impossible to say, but the anecdote tells us something about Aalto. Eliel Saarinen is perhaps more strongly identified with Nordic Regionalism and Finnish Nationalism, but it was he who emigrated, not Aalto.

Although Aalto's relationship to National Romanticism was always equivocal, he and the elder Saarinen became good friends. Like many architects of the 1930s Aalto's outlook was that of a regionalist, while his personal development was dependent on international influences, both ancient and modern. But his role as the leading "regionalist" and "organic" architect (along with Frank Lloyd Wright) was particularly important after 1945.

The Baker House dormitory at MIT is the first in a series of Aalto buildings that are primarily, if not entirely, exposed brick: The Finnish Pensions Institute, the Säynätsalo Town Hall, and the Otaniemi Institute of Technology. All are institutional buildings with complex programs, all use concrete frames and mix in other materials—marble, granite, copper, and wood—in various ways. While unquestionably Modern, they stand in stark opposition to the pure white abstract volumes of Aalto's International Style buildings of the 1920s. While all of these buildings have certain similarities in their treatment of brick, each has its own particular language, particulary in the way in which the detailing describes, or sometimes fails to describe, the structure below by means of the brick cladding.

Although a highly original work, Säynätsalo had two important precedents, as Malcolm Quantrill has pointed out, Ragnar Östberg's Stockholm City Hall and Willem Dudok's Hilversum Town Hall. The three buildings are formally similar—all have brick, all have courtyards, all have asymmetrically placed towers—but they have radically different attitudes toward the use of brick.

Östberg's city hall, which Aalto visited as it was nearing completion in 1920, is a load-bearing-wall building and wastes no time in making this fact plain. The openings, narrow in the extreme, are arched, linteled, or corbeled in every case. Despite its open arcade at the base, it is a monument to massiveness in contrast to Hilversum and Säynätsalo. What probably interested Aalto was not the walls but the roofs. Most are spanned with steel or wood trusses, all of which are concealed, with one exception: the exposed wood trusses of the council chamber, which is in fact identical to the structural conception of Säynätsalo.

Dudok's building, in contrast to Östberg's, is concrete-framed, and although it contains a number of large openings, there are no exposed lintels or arches, and the frame is nowhere to be seen on the exterior. Dudok's comments on this issue could have been made by Aalto: "Why only visible construction should be considered as honest work has never become clear to me. It is neither necessary nor important that construction should always be visible; such is not even the case in nature. . . . I also, naturally, think it important to build so that full justice is done to the character of the material used and to the method of construction, even if the material like the skeleton is hidden from view."[3]

Aalto's similar nonstructural attitude toward the material is evident in the openings of the brick walls at Säynätsalo, which are made entirely with concealed lintels. To earlier traditionalists and to later Modernists such as Louis Kahn, concealed lintels were taboo, since they concealed the structural support and implied that the brick had structural properties that it does not possess. This detail is typical of the general lack of structural expression in Aalto's work of the period, although his treatment of brick was to undergo subtle transformations.

Säynätsalo is famous for the wood trusses, or rather non-trusses, of the council chamber, but, except for the attic framing, they are the only independent wood structure in the building, the remainder being concrete. The wood trusses are only one of three structural types in the building. Aalto again combined frame and wall bulidings, using the frame to open the building where desired. The council chamber uses load-bearing brick walls with wood trusses; the library structure is of U-shaped

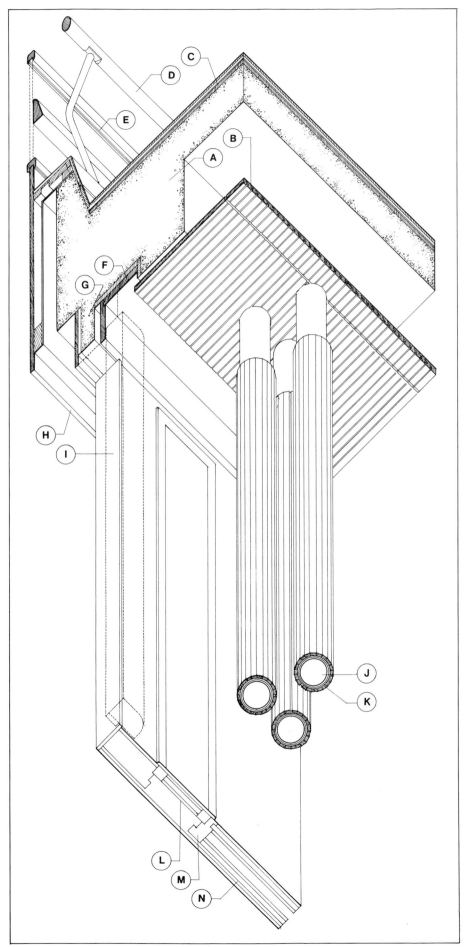

5.26

Villa Mairea

Alvar Aalto

Noormarkku, Finland, 1938–1939

5.25 **Triple column at living room.**
- A Concrete beam.
- B 1 × 3 cm red pine tongue and groove board ceiling.
- C Tile on grout and bitumen waterproofing, with expanded cork insulation between grout and slab.
- D 7 cm round teak handrail.
- E 2 cm teak parapet. At this location there is an opening in the solid parapet with steel C supports attached to parapet.
- F Recess for curtain.
- G Wood-faced concrete fin to receive mullion.
- H Wood facing of railing.
- I Sliding window at living room (not shown).
- J 13.5 cm steel column with concrete fill and 6 mm asbestos facing.
- K 1.5 × 2.5 cm red beech slats connected with wire and joined with a brass square.
- L Operable ventilation panel.
- M Teak frame for operable panel.
- N Typical wall of two layers of insulation board with ¾″ teak facing.
  (AAA 84/541, 610, 800)

5.26 **Triple column at living room.**

concrete frames; the office portions are load-bearing brick supporting concrete flat plates, except for the corridor around the courtyard which is framed with columns. The most public spaces—library and corridor—are given concrete columns. The most ceremonial space is given a traditional structure of wood and brick.

Aalto explained the complex trusses of the council chamber as a response to two contradictory requirements, the need to triangulate the structure and the need to have a double-layered and vented roof as is typical of Scandinavian construction. The truss does both these things, but Aalto had never found it necessary to design this type of truss before, nor did he after. A great part of its effectiveness is that the top chords of the trusses are hidden by the double roof, although they are articulated by wood strips. The concrete beams of the library are clearly related to raising the roof and tilting it toward the southern light, as well as making it possible to glaze most of the south wall. This is only one of three structural elements—council chamber trusses, library beams, and columns facing the courtyard—that are exposed in the building.

There is certainly little expression of the structural forces at work in the brick walls, whether through arches, lintels, or exposed slab edges. The larger openings, such as those into the council chamber, are supported by concrete beams concealed within the monolithic walls. The cantilevered brick masses and the typical window openings are supported by internal concrete beams, and the bottoms covered with a thin soffit of copper and wood. The brick masses explain the presence of the concrete frame by their disposition, not by exposing the frame or by explaining its specific location. A few other features of the walls are treated structurally. There is a granite base to the brick walls, tile at the base of the curtain wall, and those portions of the wall that correspond to the attic created by the sloped wood roof are given special grooves, in part to visually lighten the top of the wall and to mark the location of the attic, but also to bring the louvered screen motif into the wall design.

The trellis/perforated screen motif continues to grow in prominence at Säynätsalo, and finds some new applications. As he had gone often before, Aalto contrasts a horizontal trellis, that at the building entry, with vertical ones. In this case the screens are not placed in front of the windows but become the windows themselves, particularly in the major public spaces. There are four window types at Säynätsalo (figure 5.42). All are of a double wood type used by Aalto in the 1930s. Those in the simple rectilinear openings for the offices are straightforward, and there is a storefront system serving the shops on the ground floor with large glazed openings. The two major systems, those used in the major public spaces, the library and the corridor, are adaptations of the trellis motif into a curtain wall.

The library is glazed completely on its south side from top of book cases to roof. The horizontal sash is a standard profile, but the verticals are tapered and extended beyond the face of the horizontal. It could be argued that these distortions are structural, since the vertical mullion must span the opening and take the wind load on the glass, but the need for additional depth is certainly exaggerated. The curtain wall that surrounds the courtyard also has projecting mullions, but they are square in section, more regularly spaced, and darker in color. Their height is the same as those of the library and they are only slightly more widely spaced; thus their load is about the same. These mullions, however, are shallower than those of the library wihle being twice as wide, being made in two segments. Nevertheless, like those of the library, these verticals extend both beyond the wall face and past the edge of the opening to create a series of independent vertical elements.

Although the council chamber is by use the most public space, it is in an architectural sense the most private, being lit only by one small window and a larger one admitting light but without view. The small window is blocked by the fins of a tightly spaced louver. Its blades are directed toward the adjacent wall where a painting commissioned from Fernand Léger, but never purchased, was intended to hang.

The perforated louvered screen is used in a number of other locations, often for the same purposes, to imply or create transparency between interior and exterior or to

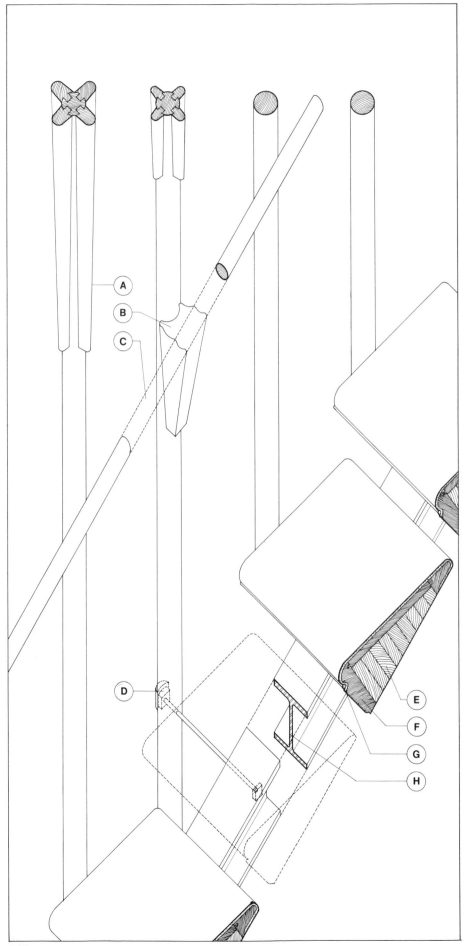

A

B

C

D

E

F

G

H

5.27

5.28

Villa Mairea

Alvar Aalto

Noormarkku, Finland, 1938–1939

5.27 Stair details.

A 65 mm red pine poles. These serve only to support the rails, although they are attached to the treads.

B Red pine bracket to support handrail.

C 35 mm red pine handrail. An organic shape was considered.

D ⅜" bolts with red pine plugs to tie poles back to steel beam.

E Laminated pine core boards. A softer, less expensive wood is used for the internal frame.

F 25 mm beech facing on tread.

G Carpet held in place with 12 mm brass rod.

H 10 × 10 cm steel I section supports. These elements, rather than the wood poles, support the treads. *(AAA 84/566, 568, 832, 835)*

5.28 Stair.
(Havas: Finnish Architecture Museum)

5.29 Preliminary stair design. Note the cable-suspended treads.
(Alvar Aalto Archive)

5.30 Stair columns and handrail.

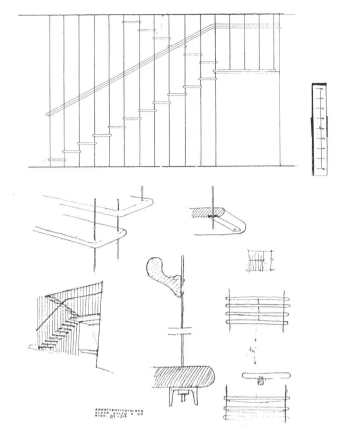

5.29

5.30

5.31

5.32

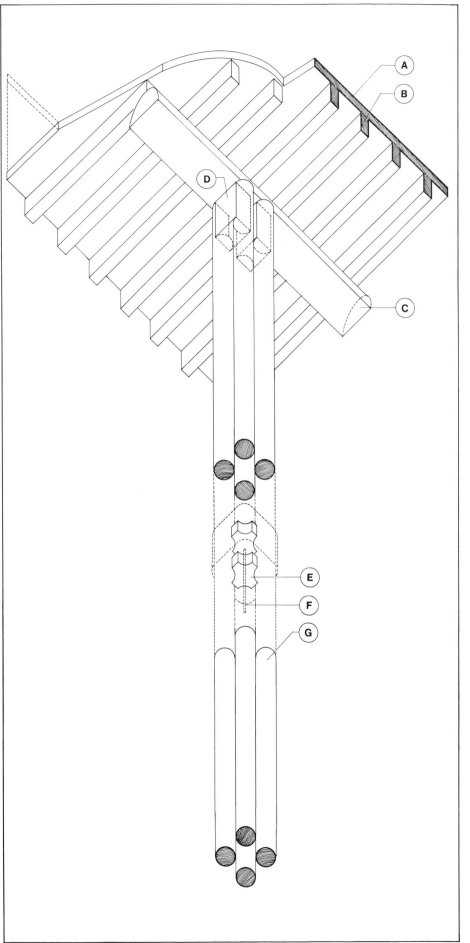

5.33

Villa Mairea

Alvar Aalto

Noormarkku, Flnalnd, 1938–1939

5.31 **Sauna column.** Note that there is no cross beam to connect the semicircular beams to the column, implying that the column is nonstructural.

5.32 **Sauna column detail.**

5.33 **Sauna column.**

- A Sod roof (not shown).
- B 2 cm wood planks on 4.5 × 7 cm purlins.
- C 10 cm semicircular beam. Some of the beams have column supports while others of equal or longer span do not.
- D Blocking to connect column and beam, attached with ¼″ bolts.
- E 4.5 cm wood diaphragm to separate columns.
- F ¼″ bolt. These bolts, and not the wrapping, are the actual connectors for the columns. The wrapping serves no functional purpose.
- G Column from four 3½″ round poles.

(AAA 84/591)

connect semipublic and public spaces, or to filter and diffuse light. The light from the clerestory serving the stair to the council chamber is filtered through a short wood screen (figure 5.40). Almost all of the doors are made to resemble the screen, but since the openings in the slats must be closed this is done by making the slats in two pieces to hold a thin sheet of glass and by placing the horizontal rails on the inside where they cannot be seen. Like many of Aalto's elements it implies both a rough vernacular wood gate and at the same time one of Moholy-Nagy's louvered screens. In the courtyard corridor these screens are extended to form the adjacent walls, again connecting the interior rooms with the courtyard without fully glazing them.

Much of the appeal of Aalto's postwar buildings is the subtle combination of red brick and copper. The latter is used somewhat sparingly at Säynätsalo, probably because of cost. Only the corridor roof is copper, the others being covered with galvanized iron. The necessary separation between iron and copper to prevent galvanic action is made a virtue, corridor and rooms being visually separated on the exterior by placing the joint at their juncture. Like many Finnish roofs it is divided into two layers to avoid a large temperature drop across a single material, with an inner layer of concrete and an outer layer of copper supported by wood. Aalto clearly preferred the knife edge roof detail to the more technically responsible gutter. The gutters are left entirely off of small roofs, while larger roofs have only minimal gutters, and in many locations, such as the library roof, water is channeled toward a single point to avoid complicated roof edge details.

The largest building of Aalto's brick and copper phase, the Finnish Technical Institute at Otaniemi, has a more complex program than its predecessors, and it was a complexity he was quick to exploit in his use of structure and materials and his treatment of light. The basic vocabulary is a concrete frame with upturned spandrels clad with brick and copper. The structural grid has some regularity but is distorted and varied to accommodate differing program requirements. The copper is again used to call out some but not all of the structural features—exterior columns, for example, but not beams. The concrete ledges supporting brick are clad and thus expressed, but Aalto stops these at certain locations so that the floors are not continually expressed on the exterior.

There is considerable stone used at Otaniemi, mostly a dark gray granite forming the building base, but surprisingly one of the courtyards, that facing the architectural school wing, is clad in marble. The courtyard was intended to house marble classical fragments, and the marble facing to link them visually with the building. In addition to being a reminder that Aalto was as much influenced by northern Italy as he was by Scandinavia, the marble is a harbinger of Aalto's future work, as his last buildings are dominated not by brick and copper but marble.

The theme of the building mass dematerialized by light had been somewhat subdued on the exterior of Aalto's postwar work, despite the use of innumerable louvered screens. At Otaniemi he perforated the brick wall in a number of locations, typically at junctions between building masses, through screens that seem to be dematerialized brick walls. These are constructed of round hollow tile, the same color as the brick, filled with grout and steel reinforcing and used to cover the numerous air intake and exhaust louvers. The screens serve no functional purpose, but visually unify the wall and hide the standard but obtrusive metal louvers typically used for these openings.

In the interior, by contrast, louvered and perforated screens abound. In the main lobby below the auditorium there are few surfaces or objects not activated by these elements. The stair treads and railings are supported by a screen of regularly spaced struts, each a sandwich of metal and two layers of wood, that modulate the vision of a person moving up or down the stair in a manner similar to the stair at the Villa Mairea. The walls are covered with two kinds of tiles, a flat one and a projecting oval white tile that is applied to the columns and pier ends.

The two auditoriums served by these lobbies are among Aalto's finest spaces. Here the structure, hidden or of secondary importance in the other parts of the building,

5.35

5.36

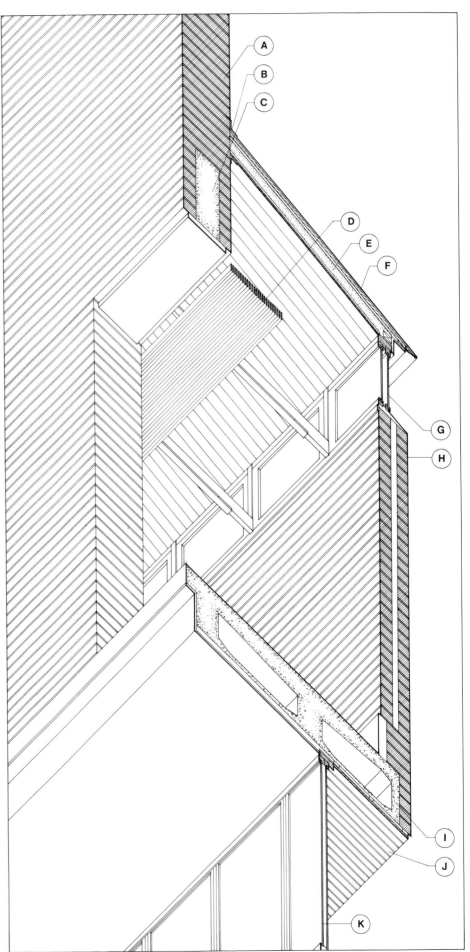

5.37

Säynätsalo Town Hall

Alvar Aalto

Säynätsalo, Finland, 1949–1952

5.35   **View.**

(Moser: Finnish Architecture Museum)

5.36   **Council chamber.**

5.37   **Wall section at council chamber.**

A   Solid brick wall of 26.5 × 7 × 13 cm bricks.

B   Flashing to prevent water running down the face of the wall from penetrating the roof.

C   Concrete beam inside brick wall to support masonry over opening. Aalto felt no need to express the structural forces in the lintel.

D   12 mm wood trellis supported by 1½ × 4″ wood beams. This is another of the numerous wood screens used to filter light into the building.

E   Roof construction of 2 × 4 joists with 3″ cork insulation and ¾″ board on blocking with wood deck below.

F   Copper roofing.

G   Window.

H   Brick cavity wall of two 13 cm brick wythes with 7 cm insulation and cavity. This is the only cavity wall in the building, probably to decrease its weight since it is suspended.

I   Double concrete slab.

J   Wood soffit of shiplap boards ⅞ × 1½″ on blocking with copper edge.

K   Double wood window.

(AAA 33/247, 220, 221, 243)

but rather a very diversified standardization. In architecture, the purpose is not to aim at identical types, rather to aim at change and creative richness which in the ideal situation is to be compared with the inexhaustible gift for nuances posed by nature.

What methods are needed to bring this about?

The most striking of all standardization committees is nature herself. Nowhere else is there so complete a standardization system. Let us take for example a plant or a tree. We can see from a fruit tree flowering in spring that each large flower in it is different. Upon closer examination, we find that this variety is in no way arbitrary. The blooms face in different directions, are in the shadow of different branches, leaves and neighboring blooms. . . . All this inexhaustible richness of function and form, this uninterrupted change, is achieved through a most exact "standardization system." Every flower is constructed of a million apparently monotonous cells, except that within them lies a property that permits an extraordinary variety of alternatives in the combining of these cells. In the end product we have a richness of form that is inexhaustible and moreover in accordance with a given system.[6]

The element Aalto specifically designed to demonstrate this type of standardization was a stair tread, almost identical to that used at Villa Mairea, which could be adjusted to different floor heights, but the cellular idea gave new impetus to the by now familiar tiles, screens, and other repetitive linear elements of his work.

THE WHITE BUILDINGS OF THE 1950s and 1960s

Despite the success of Säynätsalo, the Pensions building, and Otaniemi, Aalto seemed dissatisfied with his brick and copper buildings, and in the late 1950s and early 1960s he was continually experimenting with other finish materials. The reasons for this are not clear. On the one hand there is a tendency toward greater monumentality and the use of marble. At the same time he continued the theme of dematerialization and a layering of the wall and the use of the screen motif, which would seem to defy construction in a material so massive and brittle.

Aalto experimented with all copper-facades and with facades of specially made brick, but after the marble courtyard of the architectural school at Otaniemi he became progressively more interested in white, especially marble, buildings. One of the best of these, technically and aesthetically, is the Wolfsburg Cultural Center. The Italianate historical references of the Otaniemi courtyard are even more explicit here in the alternating horizontal layers of dark and light marble. But again Aalto delaminates and dematerializes the massive wall implied by this model, denying it its traditional structural role and appearance.

The structure of Wolfsburg is concrete, and the base material of the wall is concrete or concrete masonry; the stone is only a thin veneer. Aalto goes to great lengths to make the nonstructural nature of the stone explicit. In addition to lifting the wall off the ground, he transforms it into louvered screens at some locations. The stone pattern is literally turned sideways so that not only the stripes but the grain of the stone is at 90 degrees to its orientation in its natural bed. Interestingly enough Aalto's conception of stone as a material is not radically different from his conception of wood. He wrote in 1969: "Stone is also a natural product, only much older still than the trees growing around us. But one cannot work on these ancient materials without a feeling for the material. The different kinds of porosity require different architectural as well as different sculptural shapes. The 'biological phenomenon' in stone is perhaps not as apparent to us as that in wood, but it exists."[7]

Aalto built a number of marble buildings and experimented with a number of treatments of the veneer. In the Enso-Gutzeit building the slabs slide past each other at the corners almost like shingles. At Finlandia Hall the entire building becomes a louvered screen. Few critics consider these buildings the equals of their brick predecessors, and a number of the Finnish marble buildings have had technical problems, particularly Finlandia Hall. Here, through a number of factors including a low-grade marble, inappropriate attachment, and sheets too thin for their large

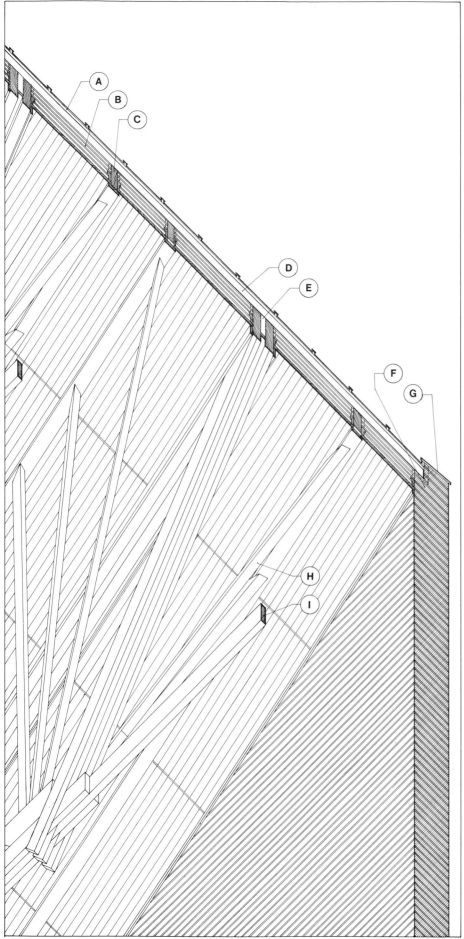

5.38

5.39

Säynätsalo Town Hall
Alvar Aalto
Säynätsalo, Finland, 1949–1952

5.38 Interior wall section at council chamber roof.

A Standing seam galvanized metal roof supported by wood decking.

B Four layers of insulation board with ceiling of 1.8 cm wood boards below.

C 10 × 14.5 cm wood beam with 2 cm thick beam cover. While the bottom members of the truss are exposed, some of the top chords are covered with trim to match the ceiling.

D Vent space. An opening just below the coping allows air to penetrate this cavity.

E Two 12.5 × 22 cm wood beams. Unlike the small beams, these are exposed.

F Monolithic brick wall.

G Copper coping. The edges of the roof, which are visible, are copper, while most of the roof is the less expensive galvanized steel.

H Radiating intermediate truss members. Aalto explained the complex design as the result of differential thermal movements between the interior and exterior of the roof.

I Bottom chord of truss.
(AAA 33/289, 290, 353, 264, 265)

5.39 Trusses in council chamber.
(Ingervo: Finnish Architecture Museum)

surface area, the slabs have warped like so much plywood, giving a sad confirmation of Aalto's analysis of the "biological" nature of stone. More successful were the white tile buildings, and Aalto did product at least one white masterpiece (albeit a stucco one), the church at Vouksenniska.

Ironically one of Aalto's most industrialized buildings was completed after his death, a church in Riola, Italy. It was for him a new structural type, a series of concrete frames supporting a series of asymmetrical vaults that become progressively larger toward the top. The building has a highly irregular geometry, and Aalto intended it to be cast-in-place concrete, but when finally built in the late 1970s it was a condition of the donor, the owner of a concrete precasting plant, that it be built of that material. So it was that two years after his death Aalto realized simultaneously one of his most industrialized and least standardized buildings. The precast system uses far more off-site labor than any comparable Aalto building, yet due to the geometry of the original plan there are probably no two identical precast pieces in the building. A series of adjustable steel forms were built to form the vaults so that, posthumously and perhaps unintentionally, Aalto realized his dream of elastic standardization.

MARCEL BREUER

Aalto was only one of many architects of the 1930s who explored the juxtaposition of vernacular and industrial elements. Although the vernacular began to dominate the industrial in Aalto's postwar work, this was not true of some of his contemporaries. In America Marcel Breuer's postwar houses continued to pursue these seemingly contradictory themes that he had begun in his work with Walter Gropius in the late 1930s, and the controversy that surrounded some of his later, larger buildings should not detract from the achievement of his domestic work, particularly that of 1945–1955.

In 1941, following a faculty meeting at the Graduate School of Design at Harvard, Marcel Breuer wrote to Walter Gropius requesting that their architectural partnership be immediately terminated. The letters between the two do not indicate the cause, except that Breuer was offended by some action of Gropius. Yet if their partnership ended for academic reasons, it could just as easily have ended for architectural reasons, for they were to pursue different, even opposite constructional directions in their postwar work. Gropius returned to his preoccupation of the 1920s, mass-produced factory houses; Breuer continued the effort begun in the Gropius and Breuer houses of 1938 to 1942, the design of Modern housing using vernacular American construction techniques.[8]

The relationship between Aalto and Breuer was not close and may have been a bit hostile, but there was certainly a relationship. Aalto's early wood furniture is clearly based on transformations of Breuer's tubular steel designs into laminated wood, while Breuer's laminated wood furniture of the late 1930s certainly draws on Aalto's techniques. (When Breuer designed a similar chair of wood in the 1930s, P. Morton Shand, the English representative of Aalto's furniture company, accused him of patent infringement.)[9]

As in Aalto's work, there is little direct formal connection between Breuer's furniture and his buildings, but they have close conceptual ties. Both utilize similar structural principles, such as the cantilever; both combine industrial and vernacular elements, and the industrial objects drawn on for inspiration, such as the bicycle frame that inspired the metal tubular furniture, are in a way vernacular. Of Breuer's mature furniture, the Cesca chair is one of the more structurally determined pieces, using the tensile strength of steel tubing to achieve a cantilevered seat. The seat itself is vernacular, of traditional wood and caning. Breuer's Wassily chair uses the same steel tubing, but not in a particularly structural way. It seems in some ways to deny its structural character, in the twists and turns taken by the tubing and in the way that the tubes are joined (seeming at times not to be joined at all). The Wassily chair is rather an exercise in elementalism, the use of intersecting yet independent planes. These two types, the structural tour de force and the elemental composition, occur in all of Breuer's houses, particularly in the work of the late 1940s.

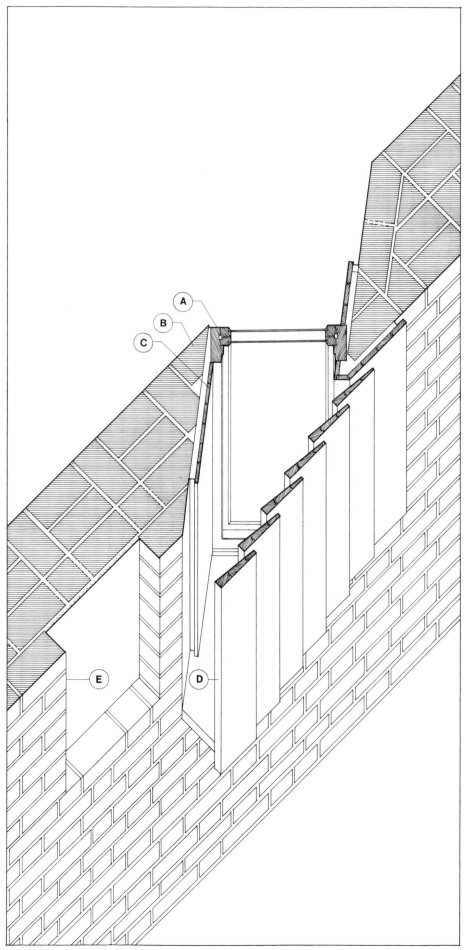

5.40

5.41

Säynätsalo Town Hall

Alvar Aalto

Säynätsalo, Finland, 1949–1952

5.40 **Council chamber window.**

A Double wood window.

B Brick wall.

C Tongue and groove pine paneling.

D Pine fins from tongue and groove boards.

E Niche. This was to hold a painting by Fernand Léger, and the finned screen was a method of providing indirect natural light.

(AAA 84/313)

5.41 **Council chamber interior showing window.**

(Eino Mäkinen: Finnish Architecture Museum)

Breuer's early furniture was in the vernacular wood craft tradition. He said of his first, somewhat crude chair that it was an attempt to see "how far can you go in the romantic, handicraft tradition."[10] Breuer's contact with Bauhaus ideas was far more direct than Aalto's, the former being one of its best-known students, and he shared with Moholy-Nagy a fascination with light and virtual volumes. Some of Breuer's early work, such as the screen he exhibited at the 1930 Deutsche Werkbund exhibition incorporating a grid of circular lenses, could as easily have been designed by Moholy-Nagy. In his later work, like Aalto, he adapted the same elements of Moholy-Nagy's floating louvers and perforated screens to vernacular rather than industrial forms.

Breuer's two basic house types, the structural box and the elemental volume, have no better illustration than two of his first postwar commissions: his own house in New Canaan, Connecticut, the structural box par excellence, and the Robinson house in Williamstown, Massachusetts, which rambles along the ground, opening out to the landscape in contrast to the compact elevated box of the New Canaan house.[11]

Breuer's own house adapted the American platform frame, a system that was industrial and vernacular at the same time, and pushed it to its structural limits, forming the walls as trusses and cantilevering all four faces of the wood box from the foundation below. No steel is used for these cantilevers, but marine steel cable and hardware is used to support the balcony. (Whether using vernacular or industrial components, Breuer preferred the off-the-shelf type, whether it was marine hardware or a 2×4.) In fact he took the platform frame beyond its limits, as the balcony and both ends of the cantilever began to sag almost immediately after completion; as the house appears today, several strategically placed stone walls support these elements.

In 1951 Breuer sold the cantilevered house and built another for himself only a short distance away in New Canaan. The second Breuer house is clearly of the elemental variety, using extensive planar fieldstone walls. It is as welded to the earth as the earlier house was liberated from it. Given the problems of the first house and Breuer's short stay there, one might assume that he had abandoned the structural type, but he returned to it almost immediately in other houses, usually of smaller size and simpler program.

Following his discharge from the army Sidney Wolfson bought an Airstream style trailer and placed it in a lot in rural New York. In 1949 he commissioned a house on the lot, but on the condition that Breuer incorporate the trailer into the new design. The trailer was given a wood trellis and fieldstone foundation; the house proper is a cantilevered wood rectangle above a fieldstone and concrete masonry subfloor. The plan is a simple box and may account for the choice of the structural over the elemental type, as almost all houses of the former type are planned around single living spaces.

Probably because of his bad experience in the first New Canaan house, Breuer supported the cantilevers with a steel and wood frame rather than using the diaphragm action of the cantilevered walls. The frame consists of a pair of wood beam supporting the roof and a pair of steel beams supporting the floor. These in turn are supported by three double wood columns each, an arrangement that places a column exactly in the center of the long facade. The wood beams are exposed on the interior as are the columns, but the steel floor beams are clad in cypress boarding. The choice of steel was probably due to the greater loads imposed on the floor and/or the cost of the large wood timbers, and the choice to clad the steel was undoubtedly in order to minimize maintenance, but the result might be seen by some as a deception. While the beam is clearly visible, particularly in the way the bottom edge of the box is cut out to show the beam profile, one might assume the beam to be wood. Despite Breuer's use of structure as a primary determinant of form in many of his buildings, he was not adverse to cladding the structure, particularly the wood frame. The majority of the structural elements in the majority of his houses are hidden; usually only major structural members are exposed, if any are exposed at all.

5.46

5.47

Otaniemi Institute of Technology, main building

Alvar Aalto

Helsinki, Finland, 1953–1966

5.46 **View.**

5.47 **View.**

5.48 **Section at auditorium.**
- A Hollow concrete beam.
- B Double concrete beam with air supply duct and diffuser between.
- C Vertical leg of concrete frame.
- D Wood screen for acoustic absorption to prevent sound from reflecting to the audience or back to the speaker in ways that would blur speech. See figure 5.49.
- E Projection booth.
- F Solid wood screen on lower portion of wall.
- G Exterior masonry curtain wall with insulation behind.
- H Concrete structure.
- I Coping.
- J Copper roof with openings for mechanical system.
- K Wood clerestory windows.
- L Copper roofing on wood boards with air space and insulation. The concrete structure is not exposed on the exterior.
- M Stone on concrete steps.
- N Acoustic screen to reflect sound to the audience.
- O Retractable projection screen.

  (AAA DN 339, 442)

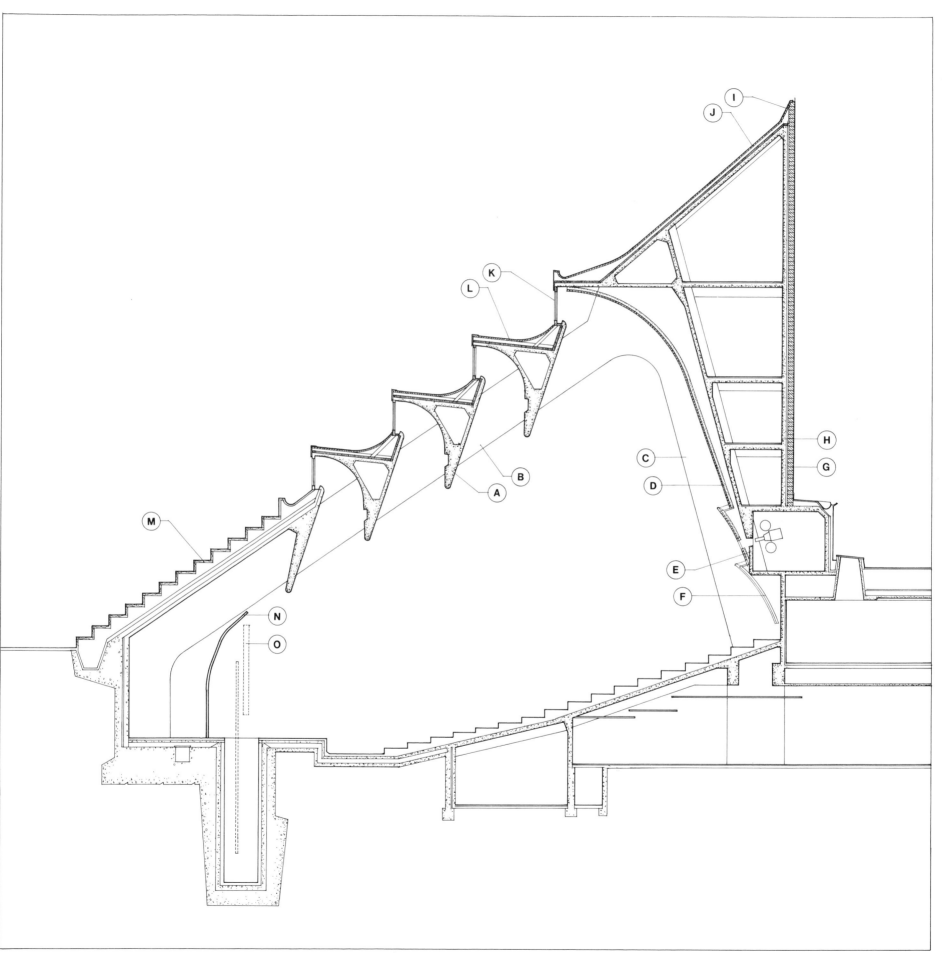

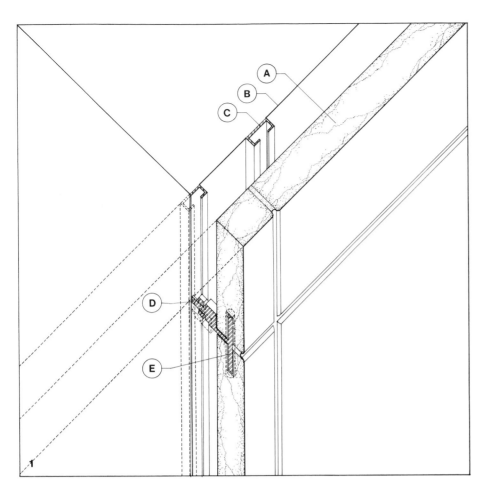

5.51

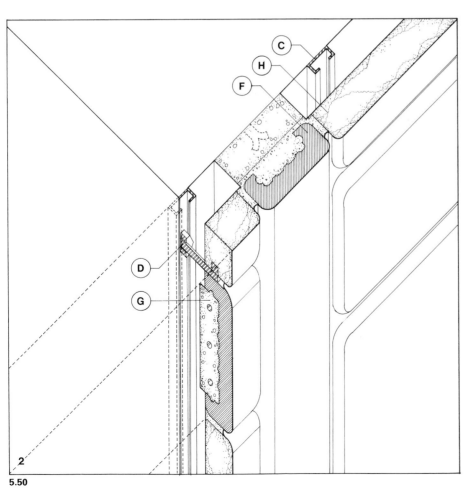

5.50

Wolfsburg Cultural Center
Alvar Aalto
Wolfsburg, Germany, 1958–1962

5.50 **Stone details.**
1 Typical stone detail:
A 4 cm white travertine stone panel. Although Aalto experienced many problems with his stone buildings, the details are not generally different from those of most modern stone veneers. See figure 10.17.
B Backup masonry or concrete with parging. As in most modern stone buildings, a minimum thickness of marble is used with a less expensive masonry or concrete support.
C Metal channel to receive bolts for anchor.
D Bolt to secure stone to support wall.
E Dowel attached to clip set into drilled edge of stone panel.
2 Stone detail with tile. (This was a detail that was evidently not implemented.)
F Ceramic tile.
G Grout and reinforcing to bind the tile to the back up wall.
H 4 cm polished marble.
(AAA DN 175, DN 179)

5.51 **View.**
(Finnish Architecture Museum)

5.52 **Tile screen at telephone booth.**
A Tile. The C shape helps key the grout into the tile.
B Grout to secure the tile to the masonry wall.
C Oak window and oak trim.
D Glass.
E Oak slat screen with brass rod frame to hold the slats together. This is one of many louvered screens in Aalto's late work.
F Desk on plaster and masonry wall.
(AAA DN 289)

5.53 **Finnish Pensions Institute**
Alvar Aalto
Helsinki, Finland, 1952–1956
Tile screen

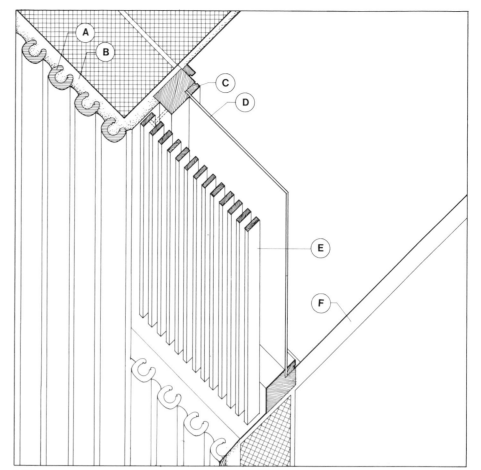

5.52

5.53

5.54

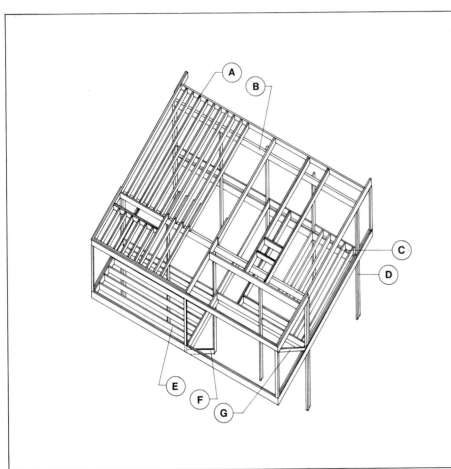

5.55

Caesar cottage
Marcel Breuer
Lakeville, Connecticut, 1951–1952

5.54 **Interior.**
(Archives of American Art/Ben Schnall)

5.55 **Framing.** (The house has been greatly enlarged over the years.)
A   Roof construction. ⅝″ plywood on 2 × 10 joists 16″ oc.
B   Roof girder of two 1 × 12s supporting roof joists and supported by 4 × 8 wood columns.
C   Floor construction of ⅝″ plywood on 2 × 12 joists 16″ oc.
D   Column and floor girder.
E   2 × 12s 16″ oc.
F   Diagonal brace to carry point load to column.
G   Lattice truss and diagonal brace below with 3 × 5½ corner post. The lattice is nonstructural, although the entire wall acts as a diaphragm to support floor and roof.
(ARL/SU DN 3)

5.56 **View of rear balcony.**
(Archives of American Art/Ben Schnall)

5.57 **Wall section.**
A   Composition roofing.
B   ⅝″ plywood roof sheathing.
C   2 × 10 roof joists 16″ oc.
D   Roof girder of two 1 × 12s supporting roof joists.
E   Edge of openings in roof deck.
F   Fixed wood frame with frameless sliding glass pane.
G   Wall construction of 1 × 4 tongue and groove siding and building paper on ⅝″ plywood sheathing on wood studs, insulated with reflective foil and interior finish of ¼″ birch plywood.
H   Floor of 25/32″ walnut on ⅝″ plywood sheathing and 2 × 12 wood joists.
I   Fascia and gravel stop.
J   Lattice truss siding.
K   Floor girder supporting joists covered with 1 × 4 cypress siding.
L   2 × 12 joists supporting 2 × 4 planed duckboards.
M   4 × 8 columns supporting girder.
N   Steel cable railing.
O   Wood railing.
(ARL/SU DN 3)

5.56

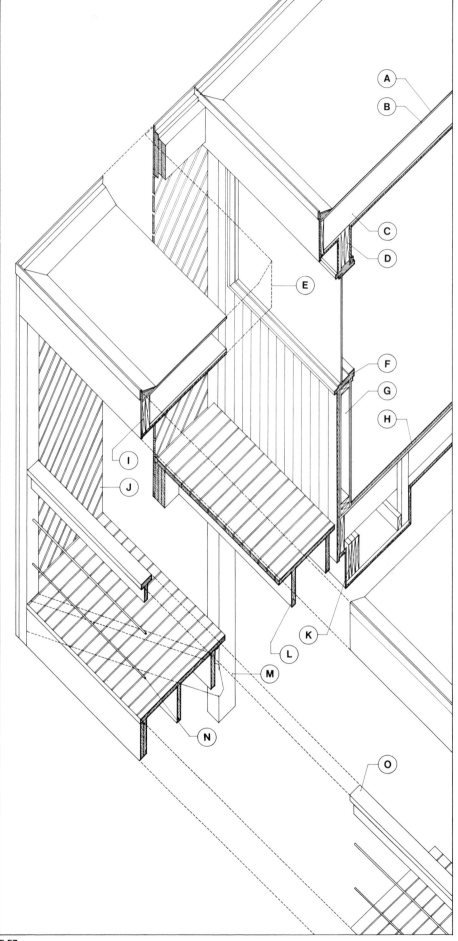

5.57

5.58

5.59

Wolfson house

Marcel Breuer

Pleasant Valley, New York, 1949–1950

5.58   **View.**

(Archives of American Art/Ben Schnall)

5.59   **View.**

(Archives of American Art/Ben Schnall)

5.60   **Framing.**

A   Roof construction of insulation board and plywood on 2 × 12 wood joists at 16″ oc.

B   Existing trailer.

C   Beam supporting trellis of slanted 2 × 8 boards 10″ oc.

D   Trellis from 2 × 8s and 2 × 4s at 16″ oc to connect trailer and house.

E   4 × 12 wood beam and column from two 3 × 8s. Splitting the column facilitates connection to the beam.

F   Steel tie rod to transfer load from the floor beam to the roof beam.

G   Floor joists, 2 × 12s at 16″ oc. 1 × 3 bridging braces the bottom of the joists to resist buckling and ties the ends together.

H   12 W 22 steel beam supporting floor joists.

(ARL/SU DN 3)

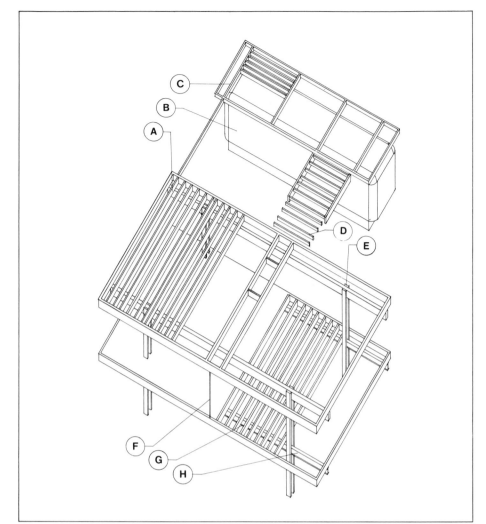

5.60

6   Le Corbusier after 1928: 1928–1965

I will always remember that one year, showing at the Salon d'Automne, I had the advantage of being next to the Aviation Show,

which was about to open. Through the partition, I listened to the hammers and mechanics' songs. I jumped over the barrier, and never,

in spite of my familiarity with these spectacles, had I been so impressed. Never had such a stark contrast assailed my eyes. I left vast

surfaces, dismal and gray, pretentious in their frames, for beautiful, metallic objects, hard, permanent, and useful, in pure local colors;

infinite varieties of steel surfaces at play next to vermilions and blues. The power of geometric forms dominated it all.

Fernand Léger, *The Machine Aesthetic*

Henri Farman was one of the pioneers of French aviation, and like many of them he was simultaneously entrepreneur, designer, and pilot, and was perhaps less of an inventor than he was a sportsman. His first aircraft design, a modified Voisin biplane resembling a box kite (figure 1.10), was more of an aesthetic than an aerodynamic success. Although quickly superseded by other designs, it gained immortality through the attention that painters gave to it, particularly Robert Delaunay in his *Équipe de Cardiff* (figure 1.11).

Farman's greatest aeronautical success, however, was the F-60 Goliath (figure 1.5). Developed as a bomber late in the First World War, it had as large a capacity in size and weight as any plane of its day, and became one of the first passenger aircraft. Not surprisingly it was one of the stars of the 1921 Salon L'Aéronautique exhibition in Paris.

From 1909 to the 1920s the Salon L'Aéronautique was held at the Grand Palais, simultaneously with the Salon d'Automne exhibition of art. Not a few visitors who came to see one visited the other, including Fernand Léger and Marcel Duchamp who, upon seeing a wooden propeller, proclaimed the death of art given its inability to compete with such beauty. Two others equally depressed by the comparison were the editors of the newly founded review *L'Esprit Nouveau*, Le Corbusier and Paul Dermée. Le Corbusier, writing in *L'Esprit Nouveau* in 1925, tells the story of two friends and their reaction to the two exhibitions:

He, the companion, had nothing to say against Paul's enthusiasms; he shared them himself. But he was too much of an artist not to have searched long for an explanation of the emotion that he had also felt and not, in particular, to have long since sought to triumph over the profound demoralization that overcame him when, for example, in 1921, he went directly from the Salon d'Automne *to the* Salon de L'Aéronautique—*both in the Grand Palais: he had felt crushed by the splendor of the machine and had returned to his studio filled with feelings of doubt and negation. He had fought against this by his realization of the fruitful relationship that could unite the work of art, which was his goal, with the machine, which was the object of his admiration.*[1]

However depressing they may have found their visit, there is no doubt that the exhibition at the Salon L'Aéronautique was important to *L'Esprit Nouveau*, for its short catalogue was to provide eight illustrations for future articles, most of which appeared again later in *Vers une architecture.* It provided some ideas as well.

The 1921 show does explain in part the collection of aircraft images that appear in Le Corbusier's books of the 1920s. *Vers une architecture* contains eighteen photographs of airplanes: three of a Caproni triple hydroplane; one each of a Caproni triplane, a Farman Mosquito, a Farman F-44, a Caudron GIII, a Handley Page 0/400, a Spad XIII and a Spad 33; and eight, nearly half the total, of a Farman Goliath.

Le Corbusier's fondness for the Goliath is easy to understand. Even for a plane of the 1920s it has remarkably little streamlining, and most of its modeling is in single curves. Its wings, rather than being rounded and tapered at their ends, maintain a uniform profile as if they had been extruded. It was said of Farman that his wings were "built by the mile and cut off by the yard."[2] While this design was aerodynamically inferior, it was obviously more standardized and easier to build. Likewise the fuselage had only a mild taper at its rear and a single curvature at the nose. These simple curves brought the Goliath far closer to the geometric solids—cones, cylinders, and cubes—that Le Corbusier thought the basis of ideal form.

It is generally felt that Le Corbusier's interest in objects such as the Goliath was literally superficial, i.e., confined to the surface, and did not include any structural analysis. Reyner Banham, Martin Pawley, and others have pointed out the disparity between the light, taut engineered structures of the aircraft that Le Corbusier admired and the heavy, wet masonry, concrete, and stucco of his houses of the 1920s, and there has been a general assumption that the influence of objects such as the Goliath on Le Corbusier's architecture is limited to geometric similarity and a few direct quotes, such as the porter's lodge of the Villa Cook, which resembles the Goliath's nose. Yet Le Corbusier was aware of and not infrequently commented upon the construction of planes such as the Goliath, and he did undertake a kind of structural analysis, albeit a shallow one.

Le Corbusier's *L'Art décoratif d'aujourd'hui* featured a Goliath fuselage with one side stripped away to show its construction and interior, and a set of wings without their canvas covering, so there is no doubt that Le Corbusier understood the basic construction. The uniformly sectioned wings are built with a series of trussed ribs supported by wooden spars leading back to the fuselage (figure 1.7). The top and bottom spars are connected by tension wires and aerodynamically shaped wood struts, which are the only structural parts visible from the exterior. The fuselage is of the truss type almost universal at the time. In the early models the Goliath's sides were faced with canvas while the top and nose were plywood. In later versions, particularly those used for passengers, the cabin was faced entirely with plywood, while the tail and wings remained canvas.[3]

The constructional virtues of the Goliath are obvious. They are the same as those of the cathedral and the suspension bridge: economy of material and minimum weight through the configuration of those materials into forms appropriate to their nature. More ticklish is the subject of structural exposure. Less than half the structure is visible, although much can be inferred because of the canvas facing and the fuselage structure is visible on the interior of the cabin. This lack of literal structural expression did not trouble Le Corbusier. He wrote in *Vers une architecture:*

One commonplace among architects (the younger ones): the construction must be shown . . .

But . . . To show the construction is all very well for an Arts and Crafts student who is anxious to prove his ability. The Almighty has clearly shown our wrist and our ankles, but there remains all the rest! . . .

Architecture has another meaning and other ends to pursue than showing construction and responding to needs (and by "needs" I mean utility, comfort, and practical arrangement).[4]

Le Corbusier here uses an old argument for the concealment of structure, that the human body does the same. The anthropomorphic argument was more than an expedient; it confirmed a Corbusian preconception as to the nature of modern building, that it consisted of skin and bones. Le Corbusier had determined through his analysis of concrete construction that modern buildings must be constructed of frames and curtain walls of thin or transparent materials. Certain aspects of the Goliath, the canvas and wood frame portions, confirmed this analysis.

The Goliath had a constructional similarity to another Corbusian paradigm, the primitive tent (or temple) that Le Corbusier had sketched in 1911 and illustrated in *Vers une architecture*. The juxtaposition of the vernacular tent with the high-tech airplane might seem an odd one, but the image of plane and tent are to a large degree one image. The planes illustrated in *Vers une architecture*, with their canvas, wood, and wire construction, use the same materials in the same way as the ship and the primitive tent, substituting wire for rope, and in the same way: the canvas as a suspended membrane, the wood as compressive struts, and the wire cables in tension, conforming to a concept of materials adhered to not only by Gothic rationalists such as Viollet-le-Duc but by Russian Constructivists.

Metal aircraft construction, while featured at the 1921 exhibition, was not prominent, mainly because the French lagged behind the Germans in this field. Le Corbusier was not unaware of German developments, as he had cut out and saved an article on metallic construction in Germany in the early 1920s. An important concept in this field was the Junkers J series wings, consisting of a series of steel pipe trusses wrapped in corrugated metal (figure 6.17). It was to provide an inspiration to Le Corbusier for a number of future constructions at both the large and small scales.

As a model of mass production, the airplane was a dubious example. In the 1920s it was not often that enough planes of any given type were being built to speak of mass production. Only 60 Farman Goliaths were built during its long life, and many of these varied in detail. Le Corbusier may have been unaware of this, and the airplane factory remained to him a model to emulate. He wrote in the second issue of *L'Esprit Nouveau:* "Made with machine tools in factories, assembled as Ford assembles on the assembly line the parts of automobiles. Aviation, during this time, realizes the wonders of mass production, an airplane is a small house that flies and resists tempests."[5]

There would seem to be little constructional kinship between the canvas and wood Goliath and the sheet-metal-covered steel chassis of the Model T, but to Le Corbusier the automobile also seemed to confirm the idea that geometric simplicity and shapes of a single curvature equaled rational construction. In this he may have been unduly influenced by an article by Gordon Crosby, who wrote in *The Autocar* in 1921: "for as a general rule it may be taken that where curved surfaces are necessary in design, they should be used with the utmost simplicity; and that Restraint should be the keynote."[6]

Crosby presented a diagram of the development of the automobile body that showed it evolving toward geometrically simple forms, a diagram Le Corbusier published in *L'Esprit Nouveau*. But the automobile confirmed another preconception as well; it consisted of chassis and body, a structural frame concealed beneath a skin, a skin that was not necessarily designed to express the structure of what it concealed. If the role of structural expression in airplane design was not clear in 1921, it was well codified in automobile design, in that it hardly existed at all.

Of course the construction of those buildings executed by Le Corbusier prior to 1930 had little resemblance to the construction of any type of airplane or automobile, making no use of metal or canvas and little of wood. These buildings were for the most part concrete frames with masonry infill covered with stucco, a solution that was hardly economical and was industrial only in the most superficial way. It was also a "wet," high-tolerance system with intensive on-site labor. If it was Modern, it was Modern in its structure rather than its means of production.

Many of Le Corbusier's post-1930 buildings make even less use of industrialized processes. Industrial objects and geometric simplicity had lost much of their appeal to artists by 1930, and many artists and architects had abandoned the highly pol-

6.1

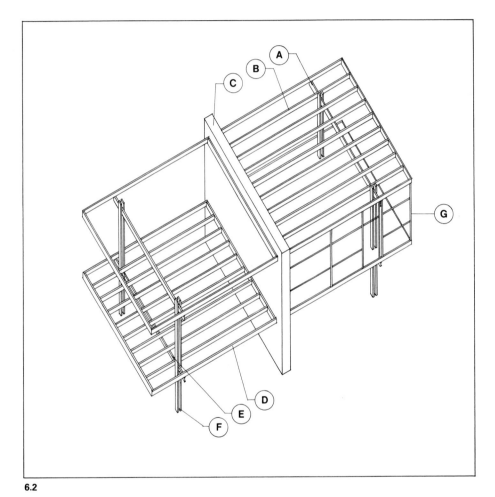

6.2

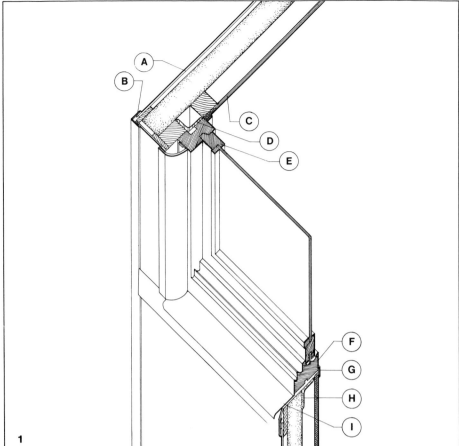

1

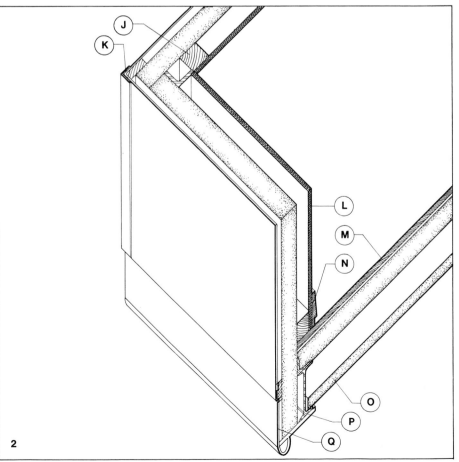

2

6.3

Maisons Loucheur (project)
Le Corbusier
1928

6.1 View.
(Fondation Le Corbusier)

6.2 Framing.
A Roof beam supporting purlin.
B Steel beam purlins with Solomite (wood fiberboard) deck.
C Load-bearing masonry wall to be built by local workmen. The rest of the structure was to be factory-produced.
D Floor construction of Solomite on steel purlins.
E Steel floor beam.
F Columns from two steel channels. This is the only exposed structure.
G Horizontal girts to support wall panels, partially shown.
(LAV 0.29)

6.3 Wall details.
1 Detail at corner:
A Zinc or iron sheet metal facing and wood blocking set on Solomite to provide both insulation and a structural backing for the thin sheet metal.
B Corner batten to close sheet metal joint.
C Plywood interior finish.
D Steel angle girt connecting wall panels to structure above and below.
E Sliding wood window, a patented Corbusian invention similar to that used at the Villa Savoye.
F Fixed sill of sliding window.
G Molding to cover joint between plywood and window.
H Horizontal steel angles supporting window and Solomite.
I Sheet metal sill to shed water and close joint.
2 Detail at base:
J Wood furring.
K Corner batten to close sheet metal joint.
L Typical wall of zinc panels on Solomite with plywood interior finish.
M Floor of tile or wood on sand and cement supported by Solomite plank.
N Wood base.
O Soffit.
P Steel I section supporting girts and frame.
Q Drip molding to throw water off the face of the wall.
(LAV 0.29, AR 8.30)

ished geometric shapes of the machine art of the 1920s for the rough organic shapes of Surrealism, an aesthetic that was more likely to celebrate the vernacular than the industrial. Le Corbusier was with them, at least in part, but he did not see the industrial and vernacular as incompatible. In 1935 he wrote in *Aircraft* of his flight over Algeria:

With my friend Durafour, I left Algiers one sun-drenched afternoon in winter and we flew above the Atlas toward the towns of the M'Zab in the third desert to the south. . . .

Durafour, steering his little plane, pointed out two specs on the horizon, "There are the cities! You will see!" Then, like a falcon, he stooped several times upon one of the towns, coming round in a spiral, dived, just clearing the roofs, and went off in a spiral in the other direction; then, high in the air, he started farther off. Thus I was able to discover the principle of the towns of the M'Zab. The airplane has revealed everything to us, and what it had revealed provided a great lesson. . . .

The lesson is this: every house in the M'Zab, yes, every house without exception, is a place of happiness, of joy, of a serene existence regulated like an inescapable truth, in the service of man and for each. Up in the air this can be clearly seen. The many arcades of the town open out on as many gardens. In the M'Zab it is not admitted that any family should be without arcade and garden.

Such is the gulf which separates the natural creations of the desert people from the cruel and inhuman creation of white civilization.[7]

However important the form of the airplane, its construction, design, manufacture, and performance are less important to Le Corbusier than what it enables him to see, the superiority of primitive vernacular architecture over Modern academic architecture. But to Le Corbusier this was neither paradoxical nor contradictory, for the virtues of the plane and the virtues of the primitive dwelling, particularly the tent, were one. He wrote in 1953: "So is the nomad's tent and the aeroplane, flying over the desert, can claim kinship with it. It will find different styles of tent in different regions, each adapted to the conditions of its environment (to the winds, for instance). Like the aeroplane the native's hut and the nomad's tent are not arbitrary in form. They are the dwellings of men bowing to a rule of law."[8]

These two images, the airplane and the primitive building, particularly the tent, were the constructional models, in theory at least, of much of Le Corbusier's work after 1928. One might be ascendant while the other was in decline, but neither was ever completely absent. Nor was the nature of these two models fixed; that is, the perceived construction of airplanes and the type of vernacular dwellings being emulated were to change considerably over the years.

Yet however great Le Corbusier's interest in vernacular low-tech buildings, he never lost his faith in the model of the airplane and the airplane factory as the course that architectural construction should follow. This accounts in part for another radical change of the early 1930s, his switch from concrete to steel as the preferred construction system for mass-produced housing. He wrote in *L'Architecture Vivante* in 1930:

In 1926 Auguste Perret speaking of reinforced concrete in a series of lectures at the Bourse du Travail at Paris affirmed: "It is mad to dream to use reinforced concrete in the construction of small houses. Only large constructions can be economically built in reinforced concrete." This assertion of an illustrious builder shows that opinions can differ profoundly.

We proceed from another point of view, not the present state, but that of the future. Having demonstrated that the ideal solution requires framework and therefore free plans and facades. We say that steel and reinforced concrete lend themselves to these necessities. Concrete for large works, and steel for standardized houses of dry construction.[9]

Although the architectural results of this conclusion were not immediate, it does explain the rather unsystematic exploration of the series of houses Le Corbusier

6.4

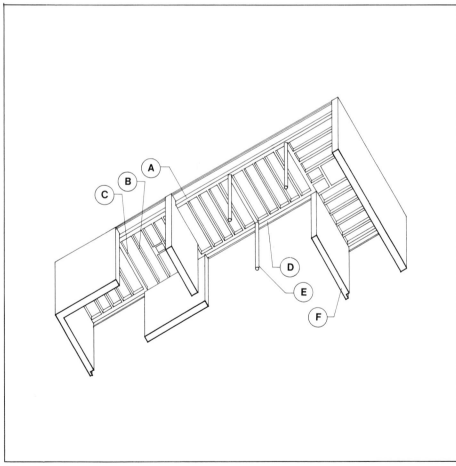

6.5

Villa de Mandrot

Le Corbusier

Le Pradet, France, 1929–1931

6.4   **View.**

(Fondation Le Corbusier)

6.5   **Framing.**

A   22 × 34 cm concrete beam at
     perimeter.

B   11 × 28 cm concrete ribs 80 cm oc.
     These are covered by plywood in
     the finished building. The structural
     system of the houses of the 1920s
     was the lost tile system. The sys-
     tem used here is a ribbed slab in
     which the forms are removed so
     that the underside is ribbed.

C   22 × 28 cm concrete girder connect-
     ing columns or bearing wall.

D   6 cm concrete slab cantilevered at
     edge. The beam is pulled to the inte-
     rior so that only a thin portion of
     the slab is exposed and the walls ex-
     tend to the parapet.

E   Round concrete column. Although
     the column grid is regular, the col-
     umns are sometimes replaced by
     load-bearing walls.

F   Load-bearing masonry walls 45 cm
     thick, using native stone. The build-
     ing has suffered from considerable
     condensation and leakage in the
     walls.

(FLC 22172, 22176)

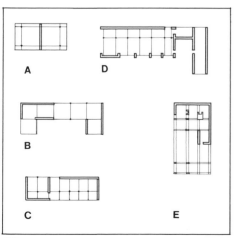

6.6   **Le Corbusier, framing plans of villas
       of the 1930s.**

A   Maisons Loucheur.

B   Villa de Mandrot.

C   Maison aux Mathes.

D   Errazuris house.

E   Weekend house at La Celle-St.-
     Cloud.

6.6

designed in the 1930s. Gone is the desire to achieve a universal system of building, as described in *Une maison—un palais* in 1928, in which the same materials and the same components would be applied to the most diverse building problems, from a small house to a large institution. Instead there is a mix of highly industrialized unexecuted projects, highly vernacular executed buildings, and several that combined the two. Having built a number of prototypes for mass production, he perhaps felt no need to do more and, in single-family houses at least, felt free to respond to individual technological needs. At the same time there is, at least on paper, a desire to produce a building system that would be truly industrial in its materials and components and that would be truly mass-produced.

In 1928 Le Corbusier and his partner Pierre Jeanneret had neither the technical knowledge nor the resources to implement a large- or even small-scale system of steel industrialized buildings, but were soon provided with both in the form of a client, the Swiss industrialist Edmond Wanner. Wanner commissioned several buildings from Le Corbusier and served as engineer and fabricator on one that was executed, the Immeuble Clarté in Geneva, as well as providing steel components for several Le Corbusier's other buildings. He was deeply committed to industrialized building in steel, and his influence on Le Corbusier accounts for the radical departure from previous work of Le Corbusier's next attempt at mass-produced housing, the Maisons Loucheur.

In 1928 the French government passed the Loi Loucheur, a financial assistance program for housing that was also meant to stimulate the steel industry. In response Le Corbusier produced the design for the Maisons Loucheur. He had previously designed systems for mass-produced housing, all unimplemented, and he was to produce many more after, also unimplemented, but none of them was as evocative as the Maisons Loucheur, none was as enduring a concept in Le Corbusier's own work, and none was so perplexing as to what was his intention. Tim Benton and other historians have long noted the importance of this work, particularly in its mixture of radically different styles and crafts of building. Each unit is two houses framed in steel. Separating the units and acting as the central structural support is a masonry wall to be built by local craftsmen of fieldstone, brick, or other material appropriate to local conditions. There is no question that the inclusion of this wall, at least initially, was a political and not an aesthetic act. Fearing that local workers would protest the extent of off-site labor, the law encouraged the inclusion of at least some local labor.

The remainder of the structure would have been Le Corbusier's most technologically sophisticated construction to date, and would have done what he claimed to be doing all along, build houses in the manner of airplanes or automobiles. The structure was to be steel wide flanges for the floor and roof, and paired channels for the columns (figure 6.2). Only the latter would have been exposed, as only the vertical struts of the Goliath were exposed. The basic wall, floor, and roof material was Solomite, a processed wood product. The walls were given a cladding of zinc, and this, combined with the steel horizontal girts that support it, gives the wall construction a strong resemblance to the sidewalls and nose of the Goliath.

The wall system of the Loucheur houses, despite its conceptual resemblance to the Goliath and other planes, is ultimately less an incorporation of aircraft technology than a modification of architectural construction. It is essentially a modified version of a German metal building system, that of the Wöhler Brothers, which had been published in *L'Architecture Vivante*.[10]

The double steel channel column was a favorite device of Wanner. Like many of his contemporaries and followers, Le Corbusier was rarely able to adapt actual aircraft construction techniques but was forced instead to adapt standard building techniques to aircraft-like arrangements.

Despite the odd combination of circumstances that produced them, the Maisons Loucheur were a harbinger of Le Corbusier's subsequent work of the 1930s. The new elements that characterize the work done after 1930—the mixture of load-bearing and frame structures, the juxtaposition of handicraft and high-tech con-

6.7

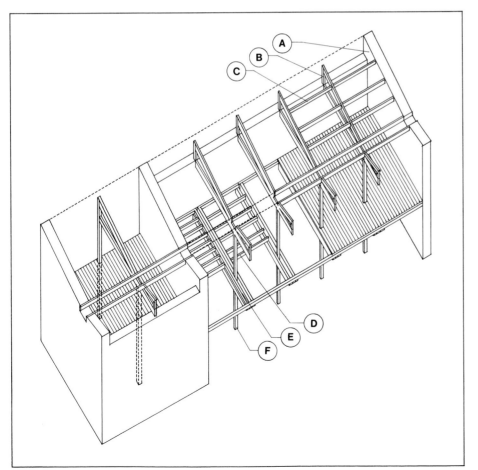

6.8

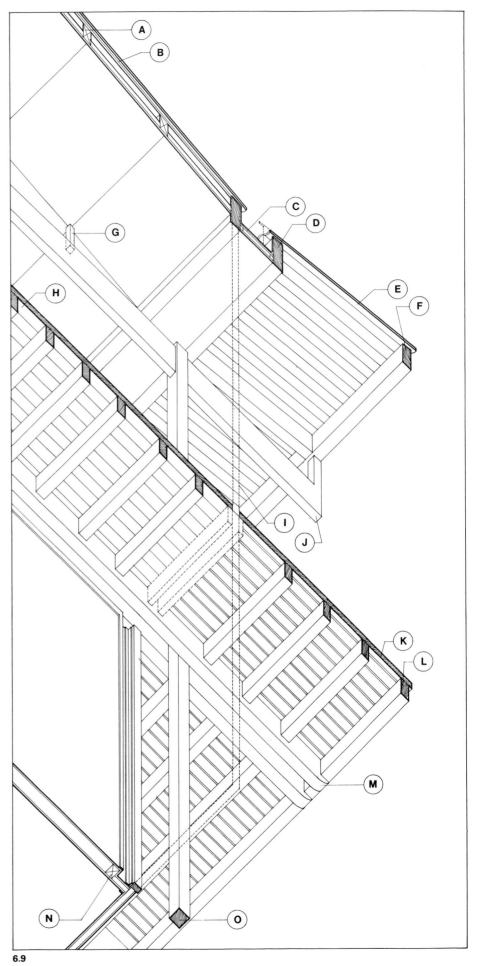

6.9

Maison aux Mathes

Le Corbusier

Les Mathes, France, 1935

6.7 View.

(Fondation Le Corbusier)

6.8 Framing.

A 1′ 6″ thick load-bearing masonry wall of local stone. The masonry, carpentry, and millwork (composed of windows, panels, and doors) remain independent to allow separate erection.

B Wood truss with 8 × 22 cm and 8 × 16 cm chords.

C 8 × 11 cm or 8 × 15 cm purlins.

D 8 × 11 cm floor purlins.

E Two 8 × 16 cm floor girders.

F 14 × 14 cm wood columns. The columns are evenly spaced although sometimes replaced by bearing walls.

(NA, FLC 8401, 8447, 8412)

6.9 Wall section.

A 8 × 11 cm purlin. Unlike the typical American platform frame, Le Corbusier used a system of larger, more widely spaced components that maintain their visual and structural identity.

B Corrugated asbestos 1.8 cm thick on two layers of plywood, with granulated cork roof insulation and interior finish.

C Zinc-lined wood gutter.

D 8 × 22 cm wood girders supporting plywood.

E Exposed corrugated asbestos (Everite) 1.8 cm thick on 8 × 11 cm purlins.

F Edge beam.

G Post connecting purlin to beam below.

H 36 mm pine parquet flooring.

I Sandwich panel of two layers of plywood and one layer of asbestos sheeting.

J 8 × 22 cm chord of wood truss.

K 36 mm pine deck with open joints to drain water.

L Edge purlin (railing not shown).

M Two 8 × 16 cm wood beams.

N Natural finish plywood internal partitions.

O 14 × 14 cm wood column.

(NA, FLC 8401, 8447, 8412)

struction techniques, the interest in vernacular forms, and the attempt to borrow construction techniques directly from airplane and automobile manufacturing—are all present here.

The failure to realize the Maisons Loucheur was not the end of the idea, for Le Corbusier repeatedly attempted to resurrect the scheme in the 1930s and even the 1950s, but these and other efforts to use a truly industrialized steel system were confined to large-scale projects. His single-family house designs were simultaneously moving in the opposite direction, for if the former saw the ascendancy of the industrial metaphor, the later saw the ascendancy of the vernacular.

In 1928 Le Corbusier published *Une maison—un palais,* which, although an apology for the Villa Stein and the League of Nations project, contained considerable references to vernacular buildings. Like his analysis of airplanes, his analysis of vernacular buildings was not a structural analysis but a formal analysis with structural implications. None of the vernacular buildings are seen as incompatible with a production system like that of automobiles or airplanes, but in fact as confirming the structural and formal lessons of industrial objects.

Structurally the vernacular examples in *Une maison—un palais* may be divided into three groups: tent buildings (the primitive temple mentioned above); masonry-walled buildings with timber roofs and sometimes partially framed with timber columns, such as the Breton farm house; and third, the most common, load-bearing masonry buildings with timber roofs. The most important of these for Le Corbusier's future work were a farm near Calvaire de Tregastel, a heavy timber frame with a sod roof, and log frame structures such as the primitive lake dwellings. This was a selective group, confirming or at least suggesting structural types that Le Corbusier had already selected. The tent was equated with the airplane, and the timber-framed structures, particularly those of the fishing village, suggested concrete framing with pilotis. Le Corbusier rarely imitates these vernacular buildings in a formal way, but they appear as structural systems in his buildings of the 1930s. What was to be the most important of these systems, the vault, had yet to be developed in its vernacular form.

HOUSES OF THE EARLY 1930s

The completion of the Villa Savoye in 1930 clearly marked the end of a series, and although Le Corbusier was to continue his pursuit of high-tech ideals, particularly in the curtain walls of his larger buildings, his houses eliminated all but a few references to industrialization and standardization in favor of either rustic materials such as fieldstone, or industrial materials such as concrete used in a "rustic" way. The first of this series of houses was the unexecuted design for the Errazuris house in Chile in 1930, but ironically the first house to be built in the new style was for Hélène de Mandrot, the benefactor of the progressive International Congress of Modern Architecture (CIAM).

Elements from Le Corbusier's Purist works of the 1920s are present in the Villa de Mandrot, but in modified form. The structure is hybrid, juxtaposing a traditional structural material, rubble masonry, with a modern one, concrete. The structural bays are equal squares as in the houses of the 1920s, but the bays are supported sometimes by columns and sometimes by walls. Unlike in the earlier houses, the window modules neither fit within nor coincide with the lines of the structural bay. The surreal juxtaposition of plaster and stone on the exterior is the result of the literal expression of the structural system. The bearing walls are stone; the nonbearing walls are two layers of concrete masonry, plastered inside and out.

Of the primitive houses of the 1930s none was more primitive than the villa at Mathes, so much as that Le Corbusier felt obliged to explain the circumstances: that the site was distant from Paris, that the budget did not allow for architect's site visits, and that he was forced to use a local contractor. All of this is undoubtedly true, although site supervision was never Le Corbusier's strong point, even with the most generous of budgets. In the Villa at Carthage (1928–1931), certainly a remote site, he was willing to build in the abstract Purist style. It is hard not to believe that other factors not wholly pragmatic were at work, and that Le Corbusier

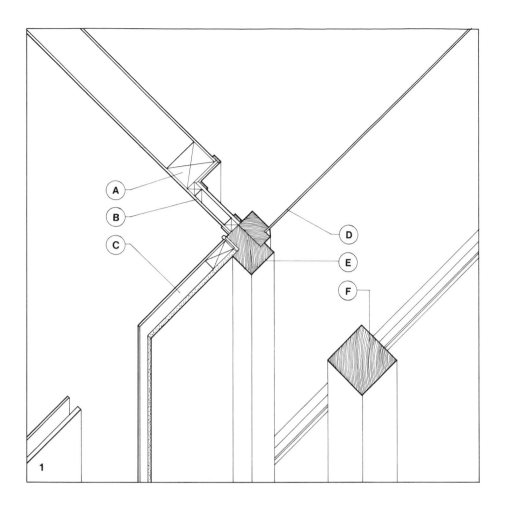

1

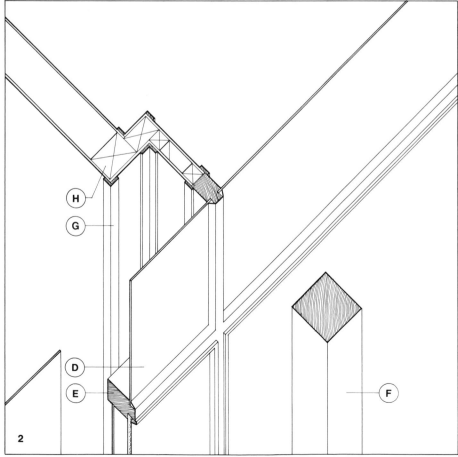

2

Maison aux Mathes

Le Corbusier

Les Mathes, France, 1935

6.10   Wood curtain wall.

1   Detail at partition between bathroom and daughter's bedroom at upper floor:

A   Internal partitions of natural finish plywood on wood framing.

B   Since the mullion spacing is slightly different from the partition layout, the transition pieces are necessary.

C   Sandwich panel of two layers of plywood and one layer of asbestos sheeting.

D   Glass.

E   Wood door and window frame.

F   14 cm square wood column.

2   Detail of partition between bathroom and servant's bedroom at ground floor:

G   Corner batten to cover plywood joint.

H   This wall is off center to align with the double beam above.

(NA, FLC 8420, 32095)

wished to build a completely vernacular building. He wrote in his description of the house: "The history of architecture (the past with us, or sometimes even the present in other climates) shows us that there exist or have existed methods of building infinitely more flexible, more profoundly and richly architectural than those imposed on us by present practice (the lake dwelling, the Gothic wood house, the Swiss blockhouse, the Russian isba, the Indochinese straw hut, the Japanese tea pavilion)."[11] It was this desire to emulate the quality of vernacular building that led Le Corbusier, perhaps unwisely, to a rather simplistic structural concept of solid masonry walls without cavities or interior and exterior finish. He assured the contractors of the villas at St.-Cloud and Mathes that a solid stone wall with no covering on either side could be built without condensation or leaks, but the Villa de Mandrot has experienced severe problems with both over the years.[12]

Despite its vernacular imagery, Mathes is more industrialized than it might at first appear. On the one hand it uses few modern materials. The structure is timber and stone, the nonbearing walls glass and wood. There is no concrete or steel. Yet these traditional materials are used in standard, even industrialized ways. Like his houses of the 1920s, this one uses a uniform structural bay, although the supports are sometimes stone walls and sometimes timber posts. The wood curtain wall is perhaps the most interesting aspect of Mathes. It is geometrically determined but in a highly complex way, and it appears both related and unrelated to the column spacing. Despite its materials it certainly could not be called a vernacular element and is in fact no less a factory-made component than the wood windows of the villas of the twenties or the steel windows at de Mandrot.

The best of this series of prewar vernacular houses is the last one built, the weekend villa at La Celle-St.-Cloud (1935). Located in suburban Paris, there could be no circumstantial justifications for its primitive construction techniques. Although it contains the same juxtapositions of frame and wall, machine-made and handcrafted, rusticity and precision, its principal virtue is in the use of a structural system that could be vernacular, industrial, or both simultaneously. This was the result of Le Corbusier's discovery of another vernacular element, the vault.

Many have traced the development of Le Corbusier's vaulted house projects, from their origin in Auguste Perret's Casablanca warehouses of 1914–1916 to the Maisons Jaoul of 1951. The Casablanca warehouses were built of masonry bearing walls and concrete roofs. Le Corbusier's proposed Monol Houses of 1919, inspired by Casablanca, were to be built of curved sections of corrugated asbestos sheets covered with a layer of concrete (figure 6.11), neither a true masonry nor a concrete vault. Le Corbusier, however, was soon presented with several more dramatic examples of the latter.

Although these projects inspired the exterior form of St.-Cloud, its technical origins lay elsewhere in a far more sophisticated system, the recently developed technology of thin-shelled concrete vaults. It had always been recognized that thin layers of concrete configured in curved shapes could span great distances, but the 1920s brought rapid technical advances in the use of such systems. The French pioneer of this system, Eugène Freyssinet, was well known to Le Corbusier, and the former's hangars at Orly were illustrated in *Vers une architecture*. The origin of the St.-Cloud design is another Freyssinet building, the conical (half of a truncated cone) vaults of his National Radiator Factory in Dammarie-les-Lys. This inspired Le Corbusier's project of 1929, Ma Maison, which used a single conical vault. This in turn became the first design for St.-Cloud, also a single conical vault, and the final design was the adaptation of this technology to the forms of the Monol houses, a series of parallel shallow cylindrical vaults.

The structurally ambiguous system of hybrid wall and frame support that began at de Mandrot reached its apogee here. Only the freestanding vault of the garden is supported by four simple concrete columns; the others are supported partly by columns and partly by masonry bearing walls. The lack of structural clarity is only complicated by the interior finishes. The vault interiors are covered in plywood, as

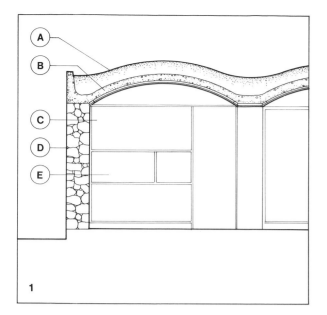

1

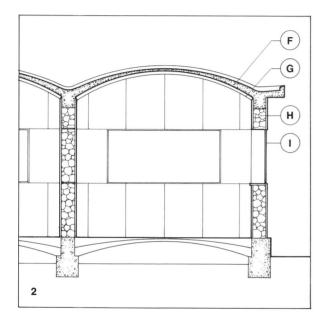

2

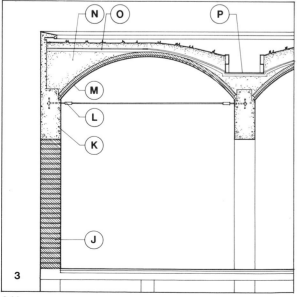

3

6.11

6.12

6.11 Le Corbusier, vault types.

1 Weekend house at La Celle-St.-Cloud:

A Earth on waterproofing.

B Concrete vault. Most of Le Corbusier's subsequent vaults were masonry rather than concrete.

C .34 cm fir plywood attached to concrete with wood blocking.

D Stone bearing wall.

E Plywood interior paneling and casework.

2 Maisons Monol:

F Concrete.

G Corrugated asbestos sheeting. This serves as a formwork for the concrete and remains in place.

H Rubble between asbestos sheets.

I Window.

3 Villa Sarabhai:

J Brick wall.

K Concrete beam.

L Steel tie and anchor.

M 5 cm layer of structural bricks and 2 cm layer of finish tiles.

N Crushed rubble fill.

O Earth on screeds and waterproofing.

P Gutter.

(FLC 6842, 9247, Patent drawing No. 496,013)

6.12 Weekend house at La Celle-St.-Cloud

Le Corbusier
Paris, 1934–1935
Interior
(Fondation Le Corbusier)

are many of the walls, and the concrete columns are sometimes faced with plywood to match the adjacent flush cabinets, with the column articulated only by a single joint.

These vaults had vernacular as well as industrial precedents, in what Le Corbusier was to call Catalan vaults. On a lecture trip to Barcelona in 1928, he came into contact with the work, including the vaults, of Antoni Gaudí. Memories differ as to his reaction. According to Salvador Dalí, Le Corbusier called Gaudí "the manifest disgrace of the city of Barcelona"; but Le Corbusier wrote in 1957: "What I had seen in Barcelona was the work of a man of extraordinary force, faith and technical capacity, manifested throughout his life in the quarry."[13] In any case he sketched two vaulted buildings, the first Gaudí's school of the Sagrada Familia, the second a vernacular warehouse, and noted that both were constructed without the use of centering (temporary timber formwork spanning the width of the vault).

Catalan vaulting, which is the origin of the Guastavino tile method used by McKim, Mead & White and many others, uses thin successive layers of tile in lieu of heavier masonry blocks. Le Corbusier's understanding of the process was somewhat imperfect, as subsequent work was to show, and he did not make immediate extensive use of the system, but Catalan vaults were to become a Corbusian trademark of the 1950s.

Between the completion of St.-Cloud in 1935 and the end of the Second World War, Le Corbusier built few buildings and almost no single-family houses, which accounts in part for what seems another reverse of direction. The influence of the airplane, seemingly dormant, returned to the ascendant, displacing vernacular building. But the aircraft in question had by now undergone their own transformation. In 1935 Le Corbusier wrote *Aircraft* at the request of the English magazine *The Studio*. It contains none of the planes illustrated in *Vers une architecture*, and those it does contain are of a different type altogether. There is an Henri Farman design, the 221, but this is structurally a completely different plane from the Goliath. There is no exposed structure, no canvas skin to hint at the structure behind, and there is no suggestion of skin and bones. There is not, from the outside, any indication of what the plane structurally is or is not. Most of the planes illustrated in *Aircraft*, like the Farman 221, are metal skins on metal frames. There are some hybrid designs—the tensile cables and the compression struts on the Curtiss A-12—but this type exhibits a more integrated structural behavior, in which the skin and frame, being the same material, act together structurally. It was a type, of course, not so clearly analogous with the tent, but like the tent it is a structural membrane in implied and sometimes real tension.

Aircraft design had evolved rapidly during the 1920s and 1930s; biplanes became monoplanes, exterior struts began to disappear, and canvas skins were replaced by wood or metal, and in many cases these materials took on a structural role. Le Corbusier had seen the beginnings of this technology at the 1921 air show, where the fuselage of a Nieuport-Deluge was displayed. Rather than a canvas-covered truss, it was a plywood shell without a frame. He wrote: "[Here is the] fabrication of a monocoque fuselage. And calculation and economy are accused of leading to meanness! In fact, here is a new craft for which we are unprepared, unequipped."[14] A monocoque or single shell fuselage is one in which strength is derived from the external skin rather than interior bracing. First developed in 1911 by the British designer Handley Page, its best known example was the de Havilland Mosquito of the late 1930s (see figure 7.23). Monocoque construction was not structurally appropriate to wing design, but here another related development, the stressed skin, brought other major changes. The stressed skin has a long history dating from the metal wing designs of the German engineer Adolph Rohrbach. In a stressed skin design the metal skin and the enclosed beams are codependent, so that one cannot conceive of a structural frame and nonstructural skin.

Both developments led to a type of plane whose structural expression was far more subdued than the traditional type, if it had any structural expression at all, since the actual frame was partially or totally concealed by the streamlined metallic skin. A building constructed in this way could hardly be structurally descriptive in

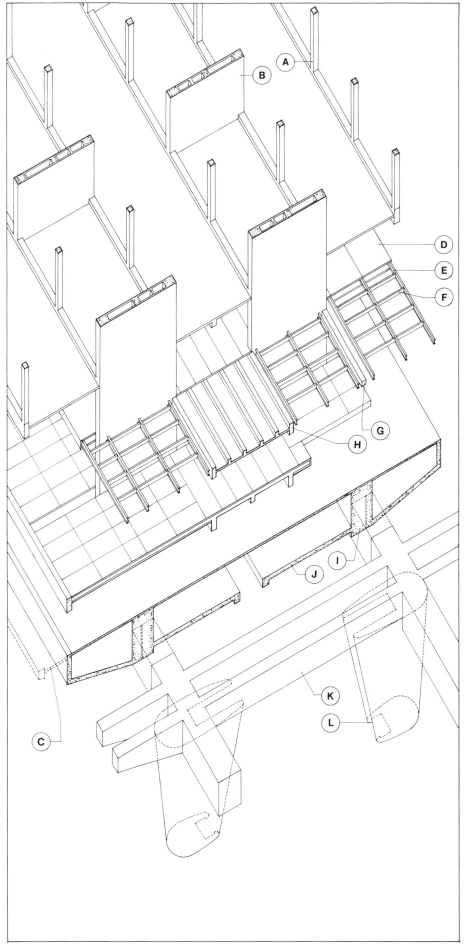

6.21

6.20

Unité d'Habitation

Le Corbusier

Marseilles, 1945–1952

6.20 Framing.

A Concrete column.

B Concrete utility core with voids for services.

C Precast and cast-in-place concrete balcony (not shown).

D Prefabricated wood panels, typically 90.6 × 203.8 cm. These constitute the "bottle" of the "bottle and rack."

E Rolled steel beam.

F 30 × 80 cm braked sheet metal steel beams.

G Concrete beam.

H Inverted ribbed concrete slab at corridor.

I Main concrete girder.

J Hollow concrete slab for transfer of structure and utilities.

K Double concrete beam to allow penetration of services from utility core.

L Pilotis hollowed out to contain services. These and the base are the most visible cast-in-place portions of the structure.

(LHA 11.14.47)

6.21 View.

(Fondation Le Corbusier)

6.22 Wall section at balcony.

A Cast-in-place concrete sunshade.

B Precast facing slab.

C Concrete shelf with tiled surface.

D Precast pierced balcony front. The perforation increases the cross ventilation somewhat but mostly serves to decrease the mass of the wall.

E Tiled flooring and asphalt on precast floor plank. The floor may be cast in place.

F Intermediate concrete beams.

G Folding wood doors.

H Floor construction (see figure 6.23).

I Rolled steel floor beam supporting wood floor plank.

J Concrete beam.

K Concrete platform at last floor.

(LHA 11.14.47)

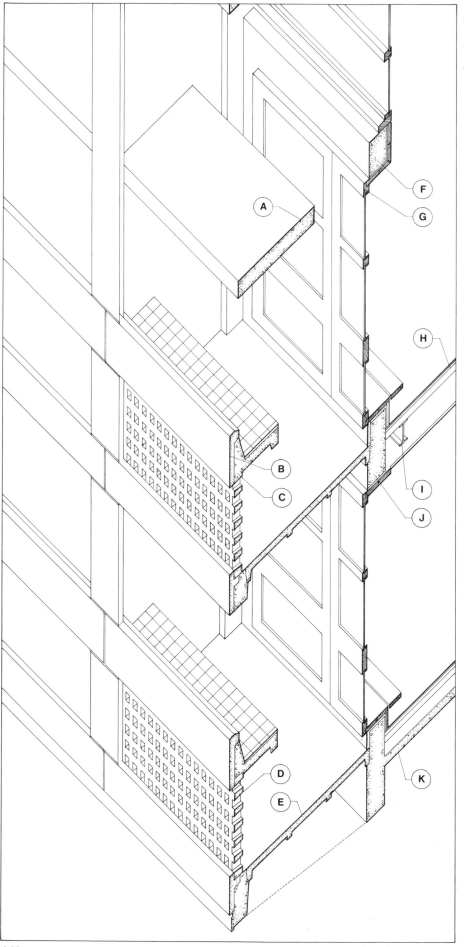

6.22

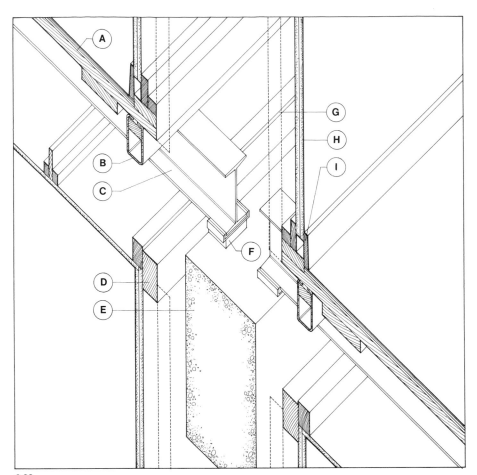

6.23

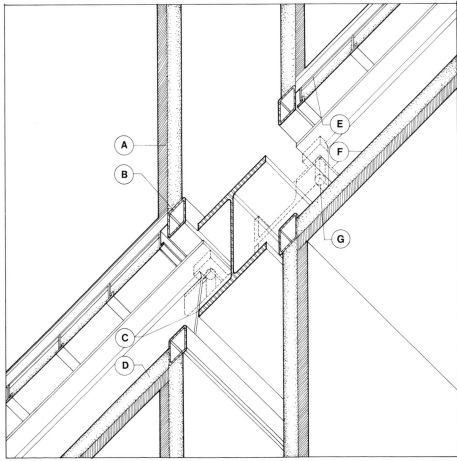

6.24

Unité d'Habitation

Le Corbusier

Marseilles, 1945–1952

6.23 **Typical beam and panel intersection.**

A 3 mm linoleum finish floor with 6 mm and 12 mm Isorel underlayment on 5 mm plywood and 2.8 cm pine subfloor. The wood panels form the "bottle" to fit in the concrete and steel "rack" and are prefabricated.

B 30 × 80 cm braked sheet metal beams.

C Rolled steel beam supporting sheet metal beams.

D Rough pine wall framing. Modern American building codes would probably not allow this construction because of the fire hazard created by the tall, wood-lined cavities.

E Concrete beam.

F Lead acoustic isolating pad 10 cm thick.

G Glass wool insulation for sound isolation.

H Wall construction: two layers of gypsum wall panel.

I Wood base with passage for electrical conduit behind.

(LHA 11.14.47)

Unité d'Habitation, steel system (project)

Le Corbusier

1959

6.24 **Typical beam and panel intersection.** This was a prototype developed in conjunction with Renault that was never realized.

A 2.5 cm interior finish on 5 cm insulation.

B Steel tube set with adjustable bolts on lead pad to prevent the transfer of sound. This is the intersection of the bottle and rack.

C 150 cm steel beam. This replaces the concrete used at Marseilles.

D Ceiling construction of 2.5 cm interior finish on 5 cm insulation.

E Floor construction of 4 mm and 14 mm plastic flooring on metal deck, filled with felt insulation. Rather than the small panels used at Marseilles, this system used one large prefabricated steel unit for the bottle.

F Silicone protection on inside of insulation.

G Adjustable mount to connect apartment unit to steel beam.

(Zodiac 7.60)

never fulfilled."[18] Although Prouvé was to fabricate some of the steel components of the Unité, his ultimate contribution to the design was minimal.

The Second World War had ended Le Corbusier's partnership with Pierre Jeanneret, who had handled most of the technical aspects of the practice, but, as was often the case in his career, Le Corbusier was soon presented with an expert who seemed to be ideal in possessing the necessary experience. This was Vladimir Bodiansky, who had actually worked for Renault and the aircraft manufacturer Caudron and had also worked with Jean Prouvé, who was then doing in reality what Le Corbusier was doing in theory, building houses like airplanes. What was ultimately to be more important to the Unité, Bodiansky had worked with the Mopin system of precast concrete construction.

According to A. E. J. Morris, Le Corbusier, through Bodiansky, was investigating a system designed by Eugène Mopin, a proprietary system that utilized precast concrete elements as forms for a composite system of cast-in-place concrete and steel.[19] This system was far closer to the final constructional system than Prouvé's, although there are few rolled steel sections in the finished building. According to Le Corbusier they had little choice, as steel was unavailable in 1945.

The Marseilles Unité as it was eventually constructed contains every common structural material—cast-in-place concrete, precast concrete, steel, and wood—in a variety of forms (figure 6.20). The platform and pilotis on which the structure rests are cast-in-place concrete. The main block is divided into three-story-high units by a series of cast-in-place concrete slabs. The two floor structures in between have concrete beams and columns but no floors except for the corridor at the center. This forms the "rack" to receive the "bottle" of the housing units. These "bottles" are not installed as single units but fabricated from a number of steel and wood pieces. The major floor structure is of rolled and braked sheet steel beams (these were the elements produced by Prouvé) and the remainder of the walls, floors, and ceilings are panels made from wood fiberboard or fibercement.

Although subdividing the "bottle" unit into so many diverse elements detracted from the concept of large-scale prefabrication, Le Corbusier went to great lengths to preserve the independence of the units, particularly their acoustical independence. The steel beams are set on lead pads to discourage vibration, and the cavities between wall panels are filled with glass wool acoustic insulation (figure 6.23).

The result is, at least in the units, a completely clad structure in which little or no concrete, cast in place or otherwise, is visible from the interior. There is in fact no structural expression of any kind inside the units. There is considerable concrete visible on the exterior, but little is truly structural and most of it, except for the base, is precast. The solid walls are concrete block spanning between concrete beams faced with ribbed precast panels hung from the floors or from precast brackets set into the block (figure 6.25). That these panels are often mistaken for cast-in-place concrete is understandable given the poor quality of their finish.

The balcony unit also uses precast concrete extensively, but in a more complex configuration. The column covers, beam covers, and railing facings are precast. They are not hung from the structure but installed prior to pouring to act as the formwork for the cast-in-place concrete, thus in theory saving the cost of formwork and bonding the precast concrete directly to the structure. The floors and ceilings themselves are concrete, although the walls between units are concrete block. The balcony railings are made from a fine-grained precast lattice grid.

This was not the first and certainly not the last of many large-scale prefabricated-component concepts of building, and like all of them it faced the same problems—transport and lack of programmatic flexibility—but the fundamental difficulty with the bottle and rack system is structural redundancy. The rack must be large enough to support itself without the unit; the unit must be strong enough to support itself without the rack and to withstand transport. The result is often a structure that, when completed, is literally twice the necessary size, hardly an efficient building system.

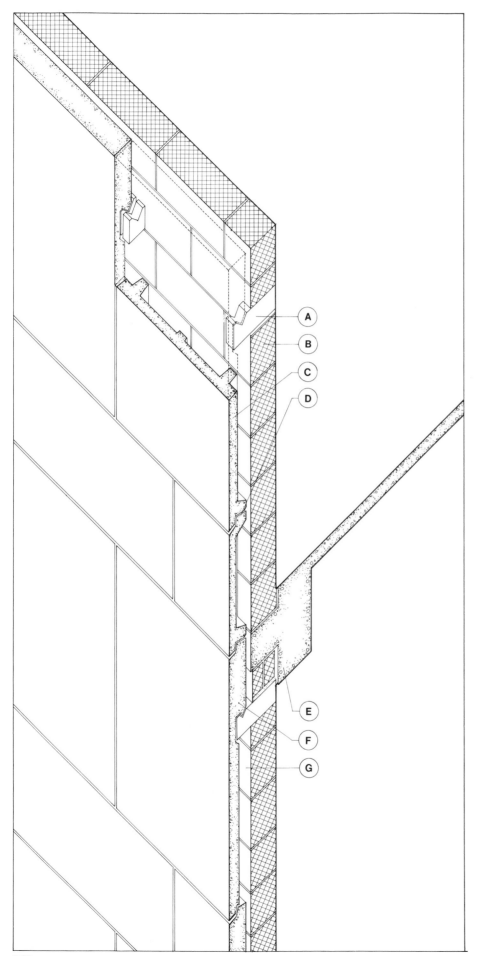

6.25

6.26

Unité d'Habitation

Le Corbusier

Marseilles, 1945–1952

6.25 **Wall section at precast panels.**

A Precast concrete fixing nibs to support the face panel.

B 18 cm concrete unit masonry to transfer the load of the panels to the floor structure.

C 4 cm "vibrated" precast panel faced with gravel with 9 cm rib. This is a variation of the Mopin system. The wall is not monolithic but functions much like a brick cavity wall.

D 1 cm cavity sloped for drainage and filled with mastic and then cement.

E Concrete beam and slab.

F 9.5 cm haunch on panel. This panel is thicker above the nib to strengthen its resistance to shear.

G Cavity to drain condensation and water that penetrates the joints.
(LHA 11.14.47)

6.26 **Under construction.** Note the rolled and braked steel beams framing into the concrete.
(Fondation Le Corbusier)

Le Corbusier built five more Unités, each less interesting than the last. Each new scheme ironed out and simplified the problems of Marseilles, but as the rough edges disappeared, so did the vitality. Le Corbusier had less control of some of these buildings than he had at Marseilles, and was perhaps not allowed the same latitude with building codes and regulations, and this may account in part for the odd deterioration of the concept.

The most interesting of the subsequent Unités was never built. In a 1959 project Le Corbusier attempted to recover the concepts lost in the original Unité—steel framing, the bottle and rack concept, and true mass production of the housing units. Although the project was designed in consultation with Renault engineers, it bears only a conceptual resemblance to an automobile chassis and steel cover (figure 6.24). The structure is entirely steel, with a series of V-shaped pilotis that recall the similar nineteenth-century work of Viollet-le-Duc and Hector Guimard. The concrete beams of Marseilles are replaced by steel wide flanges, and the bottle units are framed with smaller wide flanges and tubes. The floors are steel metal deck, covered with panels and layers of insulation. This Unité, like many others, went unbuilt, and the last realized Unité (Firminy in 1967) was concrete like all its predecessors.

One suspects that Le Corbusier felt as frustrated in his built housing schemes of the 1950s as he had been with his unbuilt housing schemes of the 1920s and 1930s, but in any case, good or bad, industrialized or not, they were eclipsed by the large-scale institutional buildings that came in the 1950s, particularly the chapel at Ronchamp and the capital at Chandigarh.

RONCHAMP

Like Marseilles, Ronchamp appears to be one of Le Corbusier's more low-tech buildings, massive, hand-crafted, even crude, and in a form that seems the antithesis of industrialization. But also like Marseilles, its technical development underwent a significant transformation, and the metaphors of tent and airplane play a surprisingly important role in its origins.

Figure 6.27 shows one of the first models of Ronchamp, built of wire and paper. The resemblance here to a wood and canvas airplane is remarkable but could be written off as an accident of model making techniques, except that the drawings of the same date show a similar conception. The design has at least part of its origins in industrial objects. It has four parts: the convex roof, the towers, the curving but uniformly thick walls of the north, east, and west sides, and the triangular (in section) south wall (figure 6.28). The south wall is the same shape as its final profile but appears to be a trussed pylon. The roof is also shown as a metal truss. Other early sketches show these trusses parallel to the main axis, although each is different in shape. It is a construction identical in concept and approximately in form to an airplane wing. Maxwell Fry visited the office at this time and wrote that Le Corbusier wanted to build the entire structure of gunite on expanded metal lath, thus giving the whole form a thin hard shell.[20]

In addition to the airplane wing, there were other analogies that played a role in determining the final form of the roof, which was not gunite but a thin concrete shell. Le Corbusier wrote: "The shell of a crab picked up on Long Island near New York in 1946 is lying on my drawing board. It will become the roof of the chapel: two membranes of concrete six centimeters thick and 2m. 26 cm. apart. The shell will lie on walls made of the salvaged stones."[21] There is of course an important structural difference between the canvas airplane and the crab shell. The crab shell is much closer to the stressed skin concept of aircraft design, in which skin and ribs act together as a structural unit.

Though the wire model is lighter and tauter than the concrete and stucco of the finished building, the spirit of both tent and plane is still present in the finished structure. (Originally there was even to have been a light metal framework attached to the building forming a campanile and containing a rotating sunshade.) The final form of the roof, for example, follows closely the scheme shown in figure 6.28 except that the parallel supports are concrete girders, not steel joists. These are

6.27

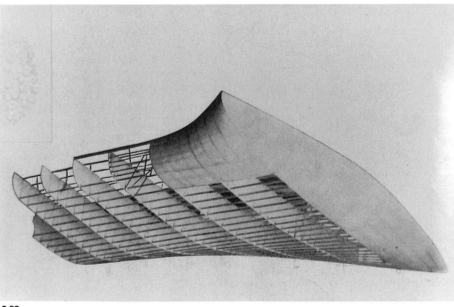

6.29

Notre-Dame-du-Haut

Le Corbusier

Ronchamp, France, 1950–1955

6.27 **Wire and paper model.**
(Lucien Hervé)

6.28 **Original construction scheme.**
A Aluminum roof covering.
B 4–5 cm cement gunite covering.
C Metal framework of parallel trusses resembling an airplane wing, covered with 5 mm of cement. This was changed to concrete in the final design.
D Rotating joint.
E Trussed pylon.
(FLC 7510)

6.29 **Wire and paper roof model.**
(Œuvre Notre-Dame-du-Haut)

6.30 **View.**

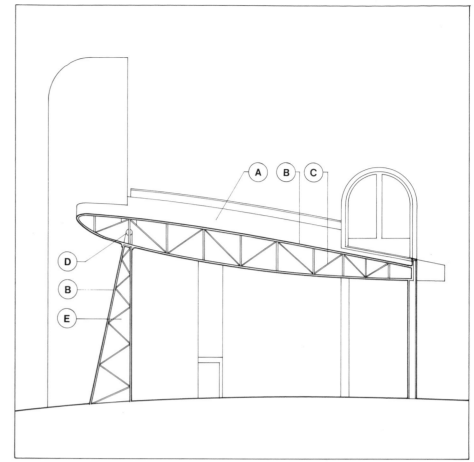

6.28

6.30

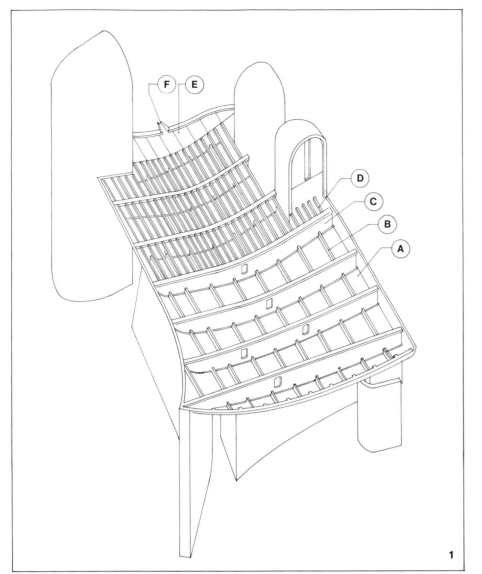

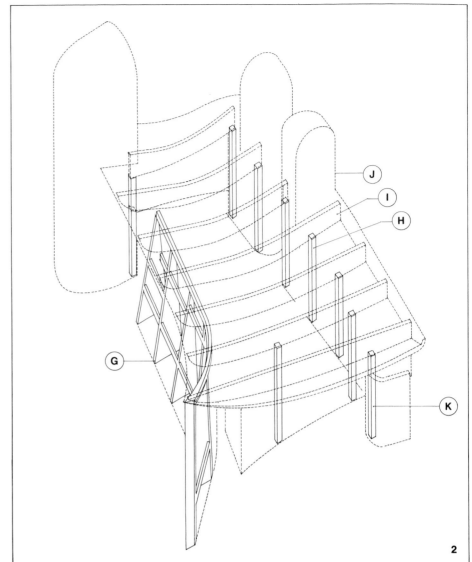

6.31

Notre-Dame-du-Haut

Le Corbusier

Ronchamp, France, 1950–1955

6.31 Framing.

1 Roof framing. Although the steel frame airplane wing–like concept was abandoned, the finished structure is in the same spirit.

A 6 cm concrete shell. This is the only visible part of the concrete structure.

B 10 × 30 cm cast-in-place lower beams.

C 17 cm thick girders with thickened top and bottom flanges bearing on columns and south wall. The profile varies.

D 5 × 27 cm precast upper roof beams. Precasting eliminates the need for formwork, which is difficult to build in this location.

E Roof deck 4 cm thick.

F Scupper for rainwater.

2 Roof supports:

G 15 cm concrete pylons and 40 × 15 cm beams with pinned connection to the main beams at the south wall.

H Reinforced concrete columns inside wall.

I Girder (shown dotted) bearing on columns and north wall, with a rigid connection at north wall.

J Masonry walls.

K This is the only exposed column.
(FLC 7569, 7574, 7591, 7592)

6.32 View.

6.33 Window detail.

A Precast concrete window frame. The precast elements are set in the rough rubble wall to provide a uniform opening and groove size in which to set the glass.

B Lead glazing compound.

C Glass.

D Plaster on wire mesh covering precast concrete and stone.

E Rubble wall.
(FLC 7155, 7564)

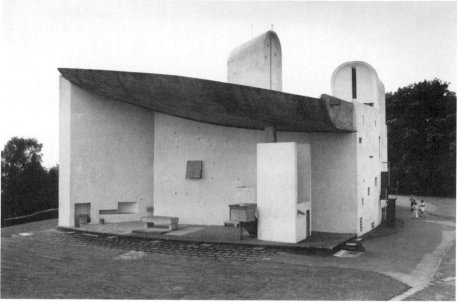

6.32

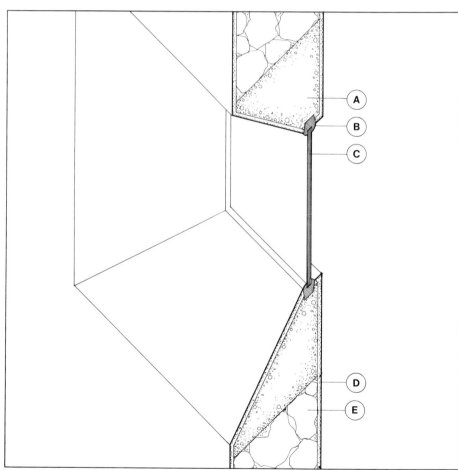

6.33

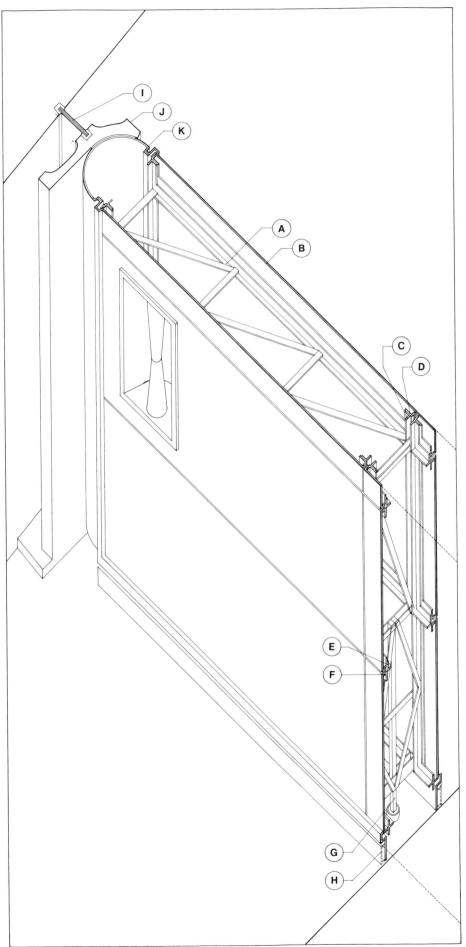

6.34

6.35

Notre-Dame-du-Haut

Le Corbusier

Ronchamp, France, 1950–1955

6.34 **Section at main door.**

A Truss section. The construction is based on the principle of the Junkers airplane wing.

B 15/10 mm or 18/10 mm enameled sheet metal panels.

C Typical truss chord of two 30 × 30 × 4 mm angles.

D Two 30 × 20 × 4 mm face angles.

E Horizontal truss member from 30 × 30 × 4 mm steel or bronze angles.

F Typical joints between panels with mastic and fasteners with lead washers.

G Pivot.

H Base trim panel.

I Frameless glass.

J Concrete frame. This may have been changed to another material.

K Metal end panel and trim.
   (FLC 7225, 7552)

6.35 **Main door.**

invisible from the church below, where one sees only the curve of the roof. It recalls not only an airplane wing but a specific tent, the Pavillon des Temps Nouveaux of 1937, and in fact it is easy to misread the structure as a cable-suspended roof, similar to Eero Saarinen's Dulles Airport. The spirit of airplane technology is present in the wall construction as well, but in more subtle ways. As in the first design, there are two wall types. The first, comprising the north, east, and west walls, is of uniform thickness although curving and of irregular height. The south wall also curves in but is much thicker and tapers toward the top. This difference is obviously due to solar orientation, as the south wall has numerous pyramidal openings for stained glass. The north, east, and west walls, made from the stone rubble of the old church, are solid. Despite its apparent mass, the south wall is hollow, an internal concrete frame covered with a thin membrane of gunite.

The door and window systems at Ronchamp make use of concrete, wood, and steel in no less than five different systems employing radically different materials and levels of craft. In their juxtaposition of industrial and vernacular techniques, they recall Le Corbusier's work of the 1930s. The most airplane-like of the systems is literally an airplane wing except in function. The large opening that separates the south wall from the west is filled with a metal-sheathed airfoil that pivots to form the main door. Its frame is a series of horizontal and vertical trusses, forming something like a space frame, which is sheathed in steel panels with enameled finish. Although it is not a stressed skin, it duplicates the construction of the Junkers metal airplane wing that Le Corbusier studied in the 1920s. The pivoting airplane wing door was to become a feature of most subsequent Le Corbusier buildings. Other door and window frames are far less technologically sophisticated. Some are built from frames of tapered wood mullions. The clerestories of the towers are steel. Most of the windows have no frames at all. The colored windows of the tapering south wall and the fixed glass of the other walls are set directly into notches in precast blocks set into the masonry and covered with plaster. Like all the other elements at Ronchamp, the fenestration systems have their own internal logic, but it is a different logic for each system.

This logic and the building as a whole went unappreciated by many of Le Corbusier's contemporaries and by younger Modernists, who saw Ronchamp as arbitrary and a betrayal of Modernist principles. James Stirling wrote: "There is little to appeal to the intellect, and nothing to analyse or stimulate curiosity. . . . The initial structural idea of outlining the form by a tubular metal frame wrapped over with wire-meshing on to which concrete was to be sprayed for some reason was not carried out. With no change in the conception, this outline was filled in with masonry, rendered over and whitewashed to the appearance of the initial ideal." And Craig Ellwood: "The chapel at Ronchamp is a profound statement of rebellion against machine building. . . . But can we, with our machine economy, truly justify a crafted architecture? I think not."[22]

Le Corbusier did not abandon his pursuit of the more literal aircraft technology in his subsequent work. But although this was the most productive period of his life in terms of executed commissions, the majority were in India where little of this technology, and certainly less of the more sophisticated European building technology, would be at his disposal. Nevertheless the structure of airplane, particularly that of the stressed skin, was to continue to play an inspirational role.

CHANDIGARH

Le Corbusier began work on the Chandigarh buildings in 1950, the same year he began Ronchamp, and work on the architectural design of the main buildings (High Court, Secretariat, and Assembly) started in earnest in 1951. Like the Marseilles block, the buildings at Chandigarh are commonly thought of as examples of the *béton brut* style—great, massive, yet simple structures of solid reinforced concrete—but, as at Marseilles, this is a gross misreading of both the intention and the reality. Some of the buildings are solid concrete; many are not. Much of the structure is exposed; much of it is concealed. There is a desire to use concrete as a kind of modern stone, solid and massive, but, as at Ronchamp, there is also a desire to inform concrete with the qualities of canvas and metal, the tent and the airplane.

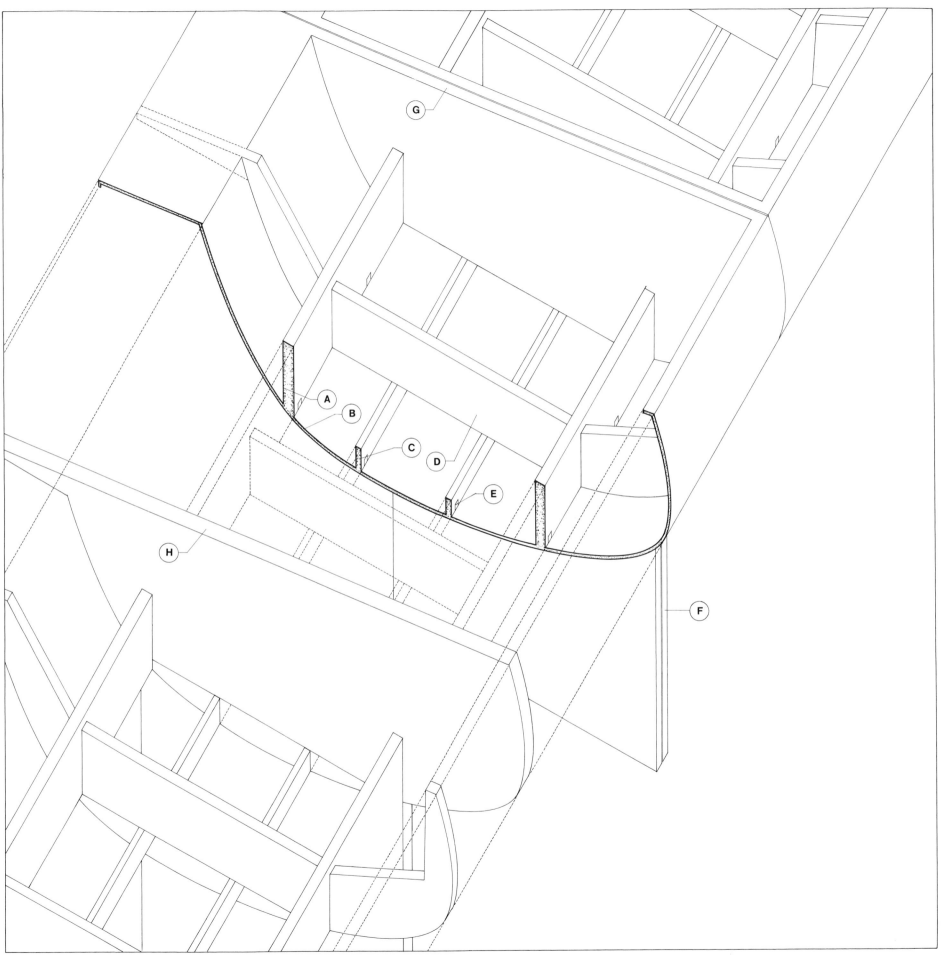

Assembly Building

Le Corbusier

Chandigarh, India, 1951–1962

6.36 Portico framing.

A 30 × 170 cm longitudinal beams spanning between concrete piers below.

B Concrete shell 8 cm thick.

C 16 × 64 cm small longitudinal beams.

D 20 × 140 cm transverse beam. This and the diaphragm do not extend to the concrete shell to allow the water to run to the ends for drainage. These beams can only be seen at the portico ends.

E Drainage holes for rainwater.

F 50 cm concrete pylon at expansion joint.

G Double diaphragm. The great length of the portico makes an expansion joint necessary.

H 43 cm concrete diaphragm with concrete pier below. There is a diaphragm at each pier for lateral bracing.

(FLC 3242, 3245, 3258)

6.37 View.

(Fondation Le Corbusier)

6.37

The first of the main buildings, the High Court, utilized both of these; a concrete substructure is covered by a larger umbrella. The parasol concept had definite advantages in the climate of India, since it shaded the building proper. The concrete structure is visible primarily in the *brise-soleil* and the ramp; the structure of the umbrella and the subbuilding, although concrete, are for the most part concealed under various types of cement plaster. The actual concrete is on top, while the vaults, as Le Corbusier called them, are really suspended ceilings of cement plaster. By nineteenth-century rationalist standards this is a sham, a false vault, but if one recalls the points Le Corbusier made in *Vers une architecture* regarding the lack of structural expression in airplane design, the thinking becomes clearer.

The Assembly building, finished in 1962, is much closer to our expectations of a Corbusian concrete building. There is a great deal more exposed concrete structure than in the High Court and a great deal less Gunite and cement plaster, yet there is still a great deal of concealed and even deceptive structure, and although the thin membranes of Gunite are missing, the spirit of canvas and metal is infused into the concrete.

Le Corbusier began with the umbrella concept used in the other Chandigarh buildings. In an early scheme the entire roof is a thin double vault with porches at either end supported by Y-shaped frames and propped against the main building. This idea proved unwieldy and Le Corbusier opted for a single square grid with attachments. The umbrella became a portico, extending the length of the building along the southeast side. The assembly hall itself became a large hyperbolic paraboloid shell set within the square grid. Although the structure of the square grid was always envisioned as concrete, the structure of the porch and main assembly chamber began with entirely different images, again mimicking much lighter steel and skin structures of planes or tents, which could be seen as a type of stressed skin.

The hyperbolic shape of the assembly room was inspired by cooling towers that Le Corbusier had seen at Ahmedabad. Although he had used both concrete frames and concrete vaults in previous buildings, this was the first of many juxtapositions of the two. His intention was also that the flat roof of the hall itself be mobile, sliding back one day a year to open the chamber to the sky and allow the sun to enter. This proved impractical, but the vestige of the idea inspired bridge truss and other objects that adorn the top of the assembly chamber.

The porch followed a far more complex course of development. Like the other parasols it was seen as a collector of water, and William Curtis has pointed out the similarity of the final form of the portico to the horns of a bull as drawn in Le Corbusier's sketchbook. Given his method of drawing formal inspiration directly from the shape of stones, shells, and other organic objects, this is more than plausible, but it is clear that Le Corbusier thought of it as an airplane wing as well. In an early sketch he drew it as a literal airfoil shape, acting to direct air into the block of the building. Le Corbusier explored a wide variety of aircraft-like solutions to the portico—a metal truss cantilevered from a tapering pylon covered in Gunite, contrasting pyramids similar to those used later at the Centre Le Corbusier in Zurich, V-shaped supports and airfoil-like pylons—before arriving at the final solution, simple flat slabs of concrete with irregularly spaced openings supporting a single-curvature airfoil shape.

Again the building refers to aircraft construction not in the literal use of materials and systems but in the adaptation of aircraft structural principles to concrete. The canopy as built is structured as a kind of inverted ribbed slab, with a smooth curved surface on the underside and a complex assembly of beams and ribs on top (figure 6.36). Two deep beams run the length of the canopy, a diaphragm is located above each pier, and two additional transverse ribs are added at each bay. To those schooled in Gothic rationalism this is an unacceptable deception (the structural skeleton is concealed and presented as something else). To the designer of aircraft this is a logical stressed skin design. The only literal application of aircraft technology, as was to become typical of late buildings by Le Corbusier, was at the small scale, in this case in the ventilating panels. There are no operable windows per se

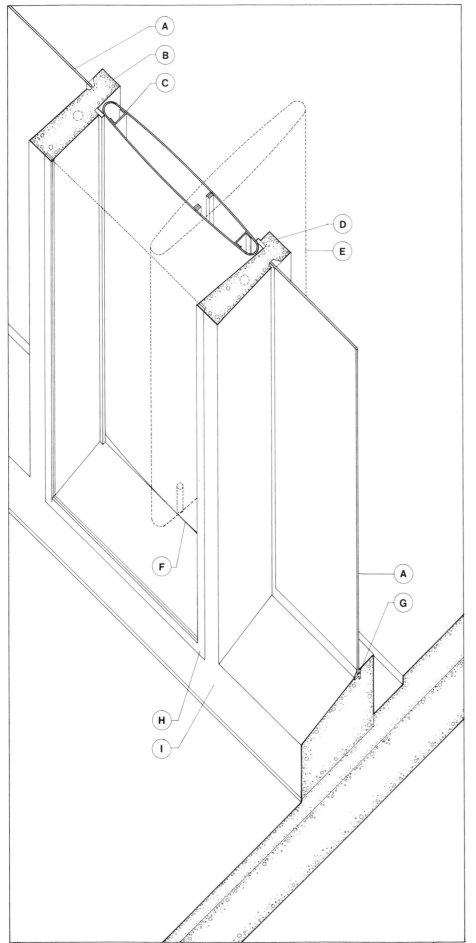

6.38

6.39

Assembly Building
Le Corbusier
Chandigarh, India, 1951–1962

6.38 **Window details.**

A Fixed glass set without frame in an oversized opening to allow replacement of the glass.

B Precast concrete mullion. It is easier to cast these horizontally and then install them than to cast them in place. By use of fixed glass and opaque operable panels, the need for window frames is almost eliminated.

C Aluminum *aérateur* shutter.

D Rubber weather strip.

E *Aérateur* in open position.

F ½″ diameter pivot with ¾″ diameter steel pin fastened to cast-in-place slab with wood wedges.

G Steel T to receive fixed glass. This is the only frame.

H Two ¾ × ⅛″ steel plates to hold screen.

I Precast concrete sill on topping with ½″ diameter weep hole. Both are sloped to drain water.
    (FLC 3570)

6.39 **Carpenter Center for the Visual Arts**
Le Corbusier
Cambridge, Massachusetts,
1961–1964
Precast window mullions

but fixed areas of glass and operable opaque panels for ventilation called *aérateurs*. This was an idea that dated back to the "Roq" and "Rob" housing project of 1949, where he had proposed a horizontally pivoting aircraft-shaped panel similar in design and construction to the Junkers wing he had studied in the 1920s (figure 6.17). The *aérateur* of the Assembly has a smooth skin with no internal frame but preserves the airfoil shape. It was set between the precast concrete mullions holding fixed glass, thus eliminating metal frames altogether. This was to become a standard system in most of his subsequent buildings.

The structure of the unbuilt Governor's Palace was to be a grid of 10-meter squares with cruciform columns. The floors are of different and irregular shapes, creating a number of cantilevered balconies and canopies. Here Le Corbusier executed a clever if somewhat deceptive inversion. The typical floor consists of beams connecting the columns, infilled with a plaster ceiling. When this extends beyond the building envelope it is turned upside down, giving the impression from the exterior that it is a flat concrete slab. The appearance of the wall is equally deceptive. The cast-in-place concrete exterior, often assumed to have been monolithic and exposed, is actually the thin outer layer of a far more complex arrangement, faced on the interior with an air space, aluminum foil vapor barrier, glass wool insulation, and wood finish. Even in the context of India Le Corbusier could not escape the tendency of modern construction toward layered and specialized components, and its resistance to the use of monolithic concrete walls that cost and weighed so much and did so little technically.

As at Marseilles, the actual construction systems used at Chandigarh were widely misunderstood, and as at Marseilles the image was far more influential than the reality. This was unfortunate, as the layered and stressed skin aspects of the real construction would have proved a far more appropriate model for future construction than the monolithic exposed concrete structure that it was assumed to represent. For several generations of architects, Chandigarh demonstrated the principles of "good" architectural construction: that walls should be monolithic, that structure should be exposed, that cladding was bad, that buildings should rely on natural ventilation, that buildings could not and should not have waterproofing or insulation, interior finish, or any other of the modern layered elements and specialized components that respond to a variety of engineering problems and an increased use of environmental conditioning. This influence is particularly evident in the work Le Corbusier inspired in Japan, which in some ways improved the Chandigarh model and in some ways imitated its shortcomings.

An improvement, at least technically, is the work of Kunio Maekawa, who worked for Le Corbusier in the 1930s before returning to Japan, where he became one of Japan's pioneer Modernists. In the late 1950s they collaborated on the National Museum of Western Art in Tokyo, formally one of Le Corbusier's weakest buildings but one that resolved a number of technical issues that Le Corbusier, working alone, was apt to ignore. The walls are not solid cast-in-place concrete but concrete faced with precast panels. This design provides a waterproofing cavity, air space, insulation, and an exterior finish easier to achieve. Maekawa's 1979 addition to the museum, although it appears to match the older wall from a distance, takes the concept considerably further in technical performance. The joints between panels are left open, and an air cavity is created behind the panels with insulation on its inner face. This is a rain screen design, in which a layer of air is captured inside the wall to reduce sharp drops in pressure across openings between inside and outside, and the resulting construction is far less likely to leak. While allowing for the fact that the building was completed fourteen years after Le Corbusier's death, it is far more technically sophisticated in design and certainly far better in technical performance than any building designed by Le Corbusier, and represents a far more responsive model for imitation than the other Corbusian legacy in Japan, the monolithic, cast-in-place, uninsulated, and unwaterproofed wall.

Kenzo Tange, in contrast to Maekawa, began by building in reality what was only implied at Chandigarh. The roof of his Totsuka Golf Club follows closely the form of the Chandigarh portico, but with a real thin-shell vault; unlike many buildings

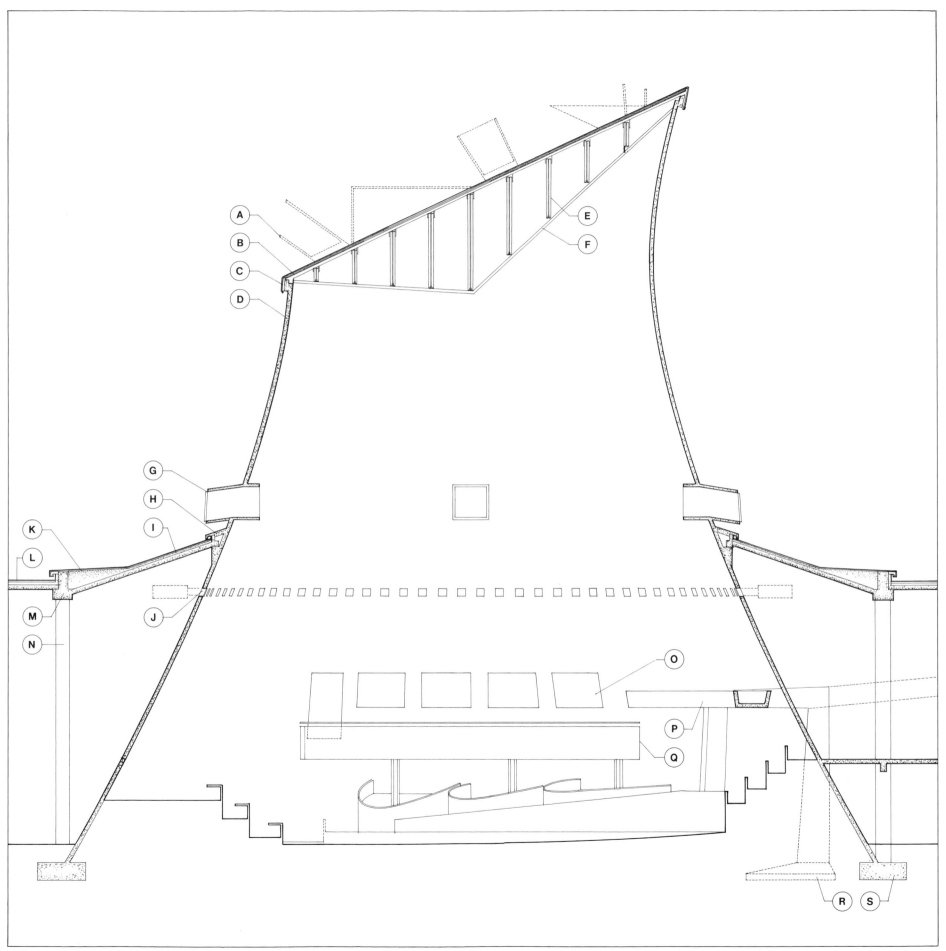

Assembly Building

Le Corbusier

Chandigarh, India, 1951–1962

6.40 **Section at main assembly chamber,** taken on north-south axis at an angle to column grid.

A Roof ornaments (not shown).

B Roof construction of aluminum sheet on a sandwich panel of two thicknesses of 5 cm wood planks with glass wool insulation between.

C Concrete edge beam with pockets to receive steel trusses.

D Hyperbolic concrete shell of 20 cm uniform thickness. The curvature makes possible a long span with a thin shell.

E Steel trusses supporting roof from two $10 \times 10 \times 1.2$ cm angles at top and two $9 \times 9 \times .9$ cm angles at bottom, with double channel and angle diagonals.

F Steel angle bridging.

G Windows facing cardinal directions. The assembly chamber is oriented north-south but the building is not.

H 20 cm concrete cap and concrete edge beam to cover joint between vault and frame, while allowing the shell and the sloped roof to move independently.

I Sloped concrete slab 25 cm thick covered with 10 cm pozzolan concrete, with 3 cm cement and aluminum roof.

J Openings provided for mechanical system that was never installed.

K Pozzolan concrete fill and roofing.

L Typical roof construction, 25 cm concrete slab and beams covered with gravel, asphalt, and 10 cm insulation.

M Circular T beam to support slab around opening between sloped and flat roofs.

N 70 cm round concrete columns supporting circular beams.

O Openings in shell for ladies' gallery.

P Press gallery.

Q Ladies' gallery.

R Press gallery footing.

S Shell footing.

(FLC 3067, 3069, 3270, 3076, 3077)

by Le Corbusier, Tange's Kagawa Prefecture Building is built of monolithic exposed concrete walls, frames, and floors with little or no plaster, Gunite, or precast components. Tange's most controversial work began when he combined the raw concrete language of Chandigarh with forms derived from Japan's traditional architecture. His Kurashiki City Hall is a kind of log cabin of precast components sandwiched between poured-in-place frames (figure 6.46). To his admirers Tange clearly explored the similarities of precast concrete and wood construction. Precast concrete, unlike cast-in-place, must be made up of discrete parts and joined in the field either with welded steel plates or by pockets of grout around interlocking reinforcing members, and has a certain resemblance to a heavy timber frame. Tange's solution has some odd details, particularly the corners where the alternating precast logs hide the true column; to his detractors this is its shortcoming, a glib visual connection of two different materials.

Much of Le Corbusier's subsequent work led toward the monolithic Chandigarh Assembly Building and away from the airplane wing systems of the High Court and Ronchamp, and he built buildings of the former type in a variety of climates from Cambridge to Firminy, but in the most innovative work of his late years he returned to older themes, particularly the vault and the parasol pavilion.

LA TOURETTE

The Corbusian building that perhaps comes closest to the *béton brut* ideal is the monastery of La Tourette, begun in 1953. It has none of the vaulted membranes of Chandigarh or Ronchamp in concrete or in plaster. Nevertheless, the building is far more complex structurally than it first appears. Much of the structure is not cast-in-place concrete. The balconies of the monastic cells use a precast system similar to that at Marseilles, and most of the walls are masonry covered with gunite. The floors are of the lost tile system Le Corbusier used in the 1920s, which achieved the appearance of a flat slab while retaining the structural advantages of a ribbed one (figure 6.48). The airplane construction method is not totally absent, however, particularly in the fenestration.

The glazing system continues the typical method of Le Corbusier's later buildings. One might say that his intention was to eliminate fenestration altogether. His previous concrete buildings had relied on heavy wood window frames, as did the High Court. At La Tourette he used a variation of the system used at the Assembly building at Chandigarh, where fixed glazing is set directly into irregularly spaced precast ribs with opaque ventilation panels (*aérateurs*) occasionally taking their place. In many buildings Le Corbusier made the *aérateurs* rectilinear in section; here he gave them a shape that is both organic and airfoil-like. Setting the glass directly in the concrete has a number of technical difficulties—tolerance, reglazing, expansion and contraction of the glass—but has two advantages. Conceptually it separates the functions of the window, light and ventilation, into two different mechanisms. Visually it dispenses (almost) with the need for window frames. For the most part La Tourette and the later buildings at Chandigarh either have no glass or have the glass and frame placed well within the building envelope, giving the whole the quality of a windowless ruin. Eliminating the frame was another way of minimizing the visual impact of the environmental envelope.

Having demonstrated, not without some difficulties, the possibilities of cast-in-place concrete, including the vault, at Chandigarh and La Tourette, it might be expected that Le Corbusier would do likewise in his domestic work. Interestingly enough, although he returned to the residential-scale vault, he did so not in concrete but in masonry.

THE MAISONS JAOUL AND OTHER LATE BUILDINGS

Simultaneously with the development of the Chandigarh plan and buildings, Le Corbusier returned to a theme of the 1930s, the shallow masonry barrel vault. He had made numerous attempts to use the form after 1945, but none were realized until the Jaoul houses of 1951.

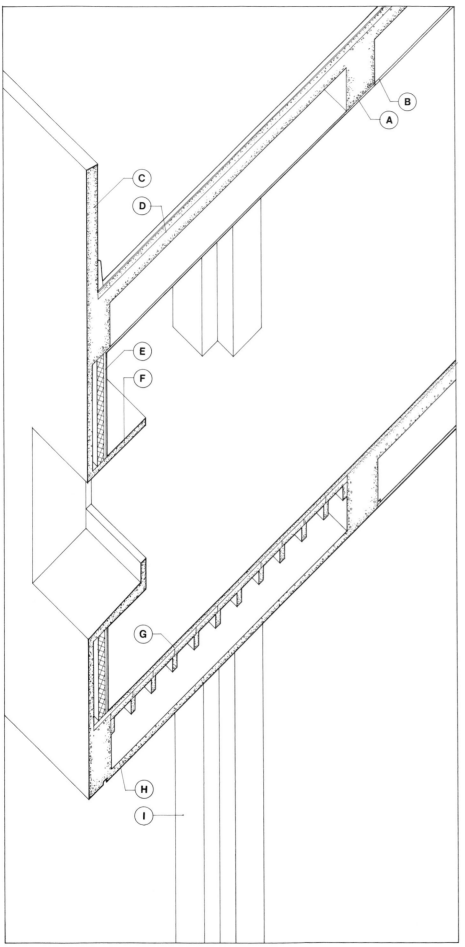

Governor's Palace (project)

Le Corbusier

Chandigarh, India, 1951–1954

6.41   Wall section.

A   Concrete beam.

B   Lime plaster suspended ceiling.

C   Concrete parapet.

D   Roof fill.

E   Wall of 7 cm concrete with air space, aluminum foil vapor barrier, and glass wool insulation to retard heat gain and loss.

F   Cast-in-place concrete window surround.

G   Terrazzo finish flooring.

H   The concrete structure at the exterior balcony is inverted, with the slab at the bottom, creating the appearance of a monolithic slab at the exterior. Bricks spanning between precast concrete beams form the top slab.

I   Cruciform concrete column.

(FLC 3782)

These vaults were not concrete, as in the villa at St.-Cloud, but masonry composed of two layers, a top structural layer of 5.5-cm structural tile and a bottom facing layer of 2-cm tile. Le Corbusier referred to these as Catalan vaults, like those he had seen in Barcelona in 1928, which required no centering and produced considerably less lateral thrust than conventional masonry.

Le Corbusier's understanding of this system was evidently imperfect, as he had hoped it would not require tie rods. A circular vault resolves its load into two vectors, one vertical and one horizontal, the latter resulting in lateral thrust which must be counteracted with buttresses, walls, or tie rods. Le Corbusier had hoped that end beams would take up the thrust, but such was not the case; after consultation with an expert in Catalan vaults, steel tie rods were added.[23]

Although there are a substantial number of end beams at Jaoul to absorb the vaults' thrust and the pull of the tie rods, there are no concrete columns, and the building is composed entirely of bearing walls. In the process of pouring there was considerable leakage, resulting in concrete pouring down the face of the brick. This contributed even more to the rustic quality of the building, which has none of the industrial elements found at St.-Cloud.

The increased rusticity of this building, located only a short distance from Le Corbusier's International Style Villa Cook, seemed to many, as did Ronchamp, a betrayal of principles. James Stirling wrote in the *Architectural Review*:

There is no reference to any aspect of the machine at Jaoul either in construction or aesthetic. These houses, total cost £30,000, are being built by Algerian laborers equipped with ladders, hammers and nails, and with the exception of glass no synthetic materials are used; technologically, they make no advance on medieval building. . . . It is disturbing to find little reference to the rational principles which are the basis of the modern movement, and it is difficult to avoid assessing these buildings except in terms of "art for art's sake." [24]

Stirling neglected to mention one industrial element that was present at Jaoul, the steel tie rods, and for whatever reason Le Corbusier's next vaulted house, the Villa Sarabhai, eliminated them, at least in part. The scheme is similar in concept to Jaoul, with vaults spanning between parallel bearing walls. The vaults are also the Catalan type, composed of a bottom layer of 2-cm tiles topped with a layer of 5-cm tiles. Several aspects of the design ameliorate the need for steel ties. The parallel vaults are aligned so that their lateral thrusts in many cases push against each other, canceling themselves out, except of course at the ends. The end beams are not curved to follow the vault but are rectilinear, in theory acting to tie the ends together. Nevertheless steel ties were required in certain locations, particularly the second floor.

The rustic quality of these houses, along with the apparently low-tech quality of Chandigarh, seemed to indicate to many, as it did to Ellwood and Stirling, that Le Corbusier had abandoned industrialization and its products as a source of inspiration. In print Le Corbusier continued to praise simultaneously the industrial and the vernacular, and if he felt any paradox he kept it to himself. Nor do his buildings give a clue to his true beliefs, for, just as he seemed to have abandoned industrial imagery altogether, he revived it with a vengeance: first in a project for a high-tech addition to the Maisons Jaoul that, according to John Winter, would have placed a steel and glass enclosure above the existing building; second in one of his last buildings, completed after his death, the pavilion of the Centre Le Corbusier in Zurich.[25]

Given that the precision of detail in the pavilion is lacking in most other Corbusian buildings, it is tempting to attribute it to the fact that the details were developed after his death. Such may be the case, but the building was a culmination of several of his ideas, notably the parasol exhibition type that had begun with the airplane wing at Liège in 1938. This had been refined in subsequent unexecuted projects, evolving into a pair of shallow opposing pyramids, but in Zurich the structure finally achieved the reality of the stressed skin prototype. Like all of his parasol buildings, it had two separate components. The umbrella is something like a steel

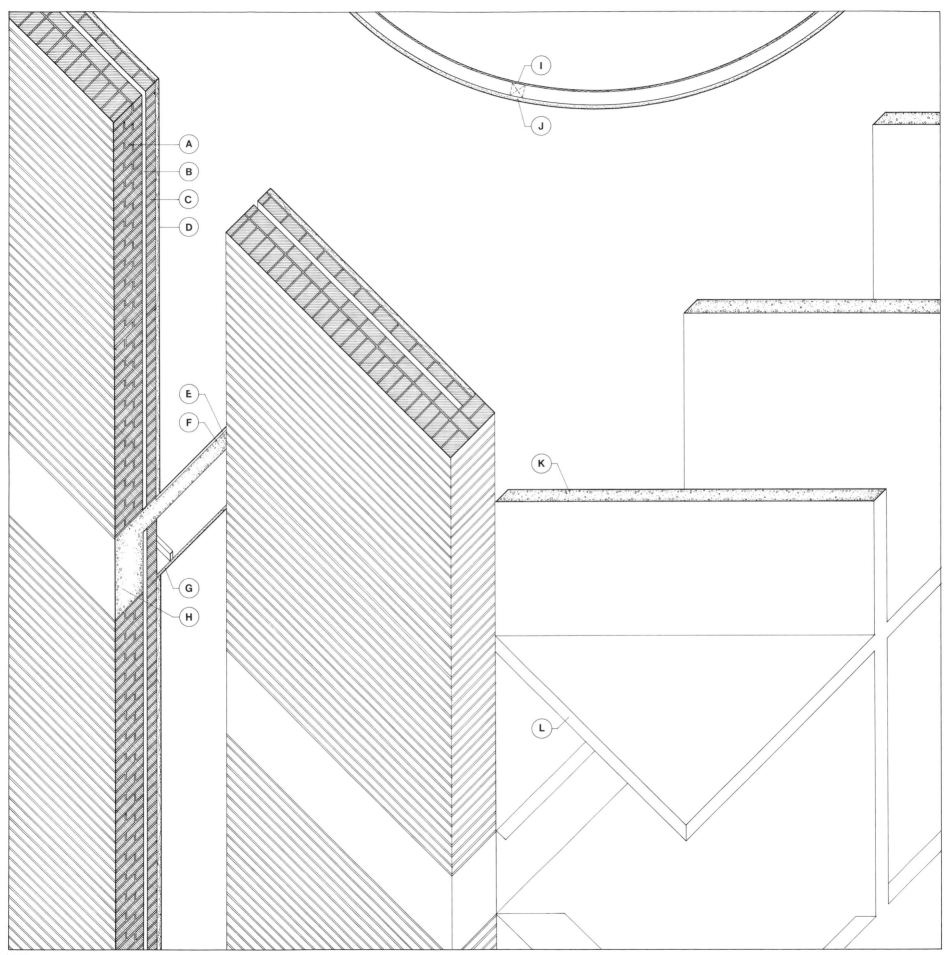

6.42

Millowners' Building

Le Corbusier

Ahmedabad, India, 1951–1954

6.42 Wall section.

A 33 cm brick.

B 4 cm cavity.

C 10 cm brick.

D 5 cm Morak stone lining.

E Finish floor.

F 70 cm deep concrete beams and 15 cm concrete slab.

G Plaster of Paris or plasterboard suspended ceiling.

H 70 cm edge beam.

I 7 cm Burma teak plywood on 2.7 cm blocking to form inner wall of curved meeting room.

J Gunite on metal lath on 10 × 10 cm wood framing.

K Vertical blade of cast-in-place concrete sunscreen. The screen is separated from the wall to allow air to circulate between the two.

L Horizontal blade of concrete sunscreen.

(FLC 6782, 6807, 6825, 6839, 6840, 6827)

6.43 View.

(Fiske Kimball Fine Arts Library)

6.43

6.44

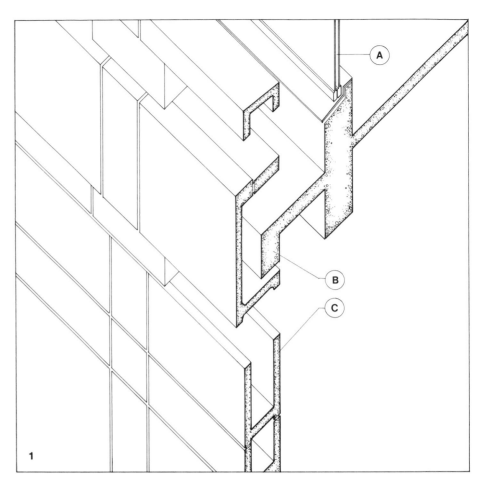

1

6.45

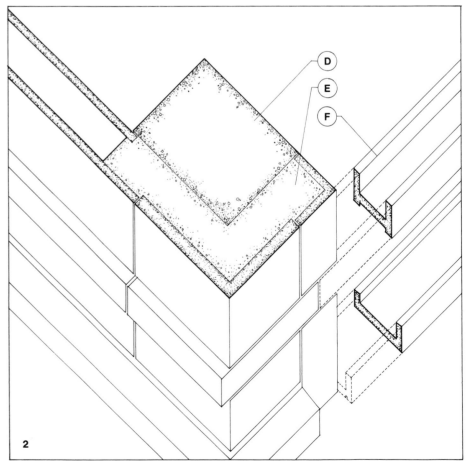

2

6.46

Kurashiki City Hall

Kenzo Tange

Kurashiki, Japan, 1958–1960

6.44 **View.**

(Fiske Kimball Fine Arts Library)

6.45 **Corner.**

(Fiske Kimball Fine Arts Library)

6.46 **Wall section and corner plan.**

A Window and glazing.

B Cast-in-place concrete beam and slab.

C Hollow precast concrete facing panels.

D 86 × 112.5 cm cast-in-place concrete column.

E Concrete fill.

F Precast concrete facing panels with 20 mm joints. These are open above and below; from the outside they appear identical to the thinner panels covering the corner. Note that the column is hidden by the loglike precast facing.

(JA)

folded plate, the descendent of the Liège parasol. The understructure is the realization of another old idea, the 223-cm cube first proposed for the "Roq" and "Rob" project of 1949. All major beams and columns are of a uniform cruciform cross section, made of four steel angles with spacers. This of course is a decidedly antistructural expression as it denies completely the different forces acting on beam and column. This is not a technical problem, given the small span, less than nine feet, and acts to minimize the secondary structure and allow the umbrella to dominate. The cruciform frames are infilled with a variety of components: porcelain enamel steel panels with an inner layer of plywood; braked sheet metal windows sometimes infilled with an operable sash. Both glass and metal are detailed so as to make their outside faces align with the outside of the column, giving the lower volume a precise articulation while maintaining the perception of a crisp volume.

The conspicuous success of Le Corbusier's individual buildings has obscured the conspicuous failure of his attempts to realize industrialized building and the relatively small number of buildings that drew in a literal way on the actual construction of airplanes or automobiles. Le Corbusier's later executed buildings are seen as a kind of self-criticism of his earlier mechanistic work. Yet the facts do not entirely support this view. Neither his polemical writings, which remain steadfast in their hopes for the industrialized future, nor the history of the individual buildings, many of which began as thin, lithe mechanisms, even if they reached realization as massive concrete structures, are consistent with this analysis. Recent scholarship has implied that Le Corbusier's advocacy of modern technology was merely an expedient, that he had no real interest in it and was merely enlisting a useful argument in support of a cause whose intentions were largely formal. This is hard to believe given his lifelong advocacy of industrialization, which although sometimes wavering was never abandoned.

There is, however, a troubling pattern in Le Corbusier's work. A number of individuals who were prepared to assist him in realizing his stated goals of mass production and metal construction emerged from their collaboration feeling that he had abandoned this intention for no strong reason. A number of buildings, particularly the Marseilles Unité and Ronchamp, began with systems that adapted the industrialized techniques of automobile and aircraft production and ended as massive, rustic, low-tolerance, wet-constructed buildings with extensive on-site labor. The obvious conclusion is that he either felt no obligation put into practice his utopian programs or could not reconcile his aesthetic feelings with his theoretical positions. If he felt that economy of material and precision construction would lead to "style," it was perhaps not the style that he desired; perhaps intuitively he preferred the quality of mass, apparent stability, and craft construction that site-cast concrete achieved or suggested.

Le Corbusier's writings also leave little doubt as to who he feels is to blame for this failure: shortsighted bureaucrats, greedy, narrow-minded industrialists, a misguided public; those with "eyes that do not see." Clearly he was given few opportunities to implement his industrial ideas, but he may bear some responsibility for his own failure. The evidence for this is not so much that of his own career but the success of the careers of others, particularly that of his sometime collaborator Jean Prouvé.

Prouvé's later career may be seen as a kind of realization of the Corbusian dream, for in many instances he was able to bring to realization, albeit in modified form, ideas that for Le Corbusier remained on paper. The two collaborated several times starting in the late 1930s, most notably on the Écoles Volante (a project for prefabricated schools), a housing project at Lagny (1956) based on the Maisons Loucheur, and the Marseilles Unité d'Habitation itself. None came to fruition, but all were the basis for future, and often realized, work by Prouvé.

The Écoles Volante project seems to be the product of a true collaboration, as it more closely resembles Prouvé's other work than Le Corbusier's. There is a single row of A-shaped columns supporting a ridge beam; the aircraft-like side walls appear to be load-bearing as there are no columns there. This is a structure more

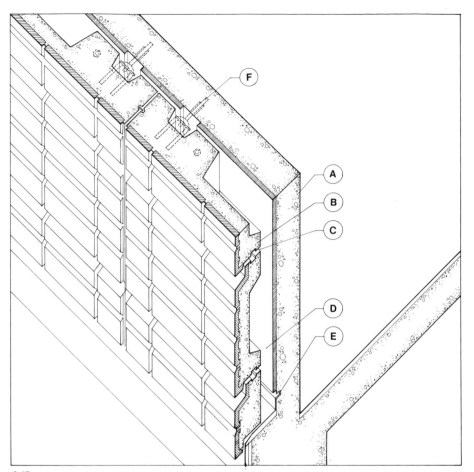

6.47

National Museum of Western Art addition

Kunio Maekawa

Tokyo, 1979

6.47 Wall section.

A Cast-in-place concrete wall.

B 15 cm thick (with ribs) precast concrete panel faced with tile. Unlike in the original building, which had closed joints and insulation on the warm side, this wall does the opposite, creating a "rain screen" to eliminate large drops in air pressure across joints.

C 2 cm open horizontal joint to allow air penetration.

D Cavity for drainage with 35 mm insulation on cold side.

E Metal flashing to lead water out of cavity.

F Anchor to fix panel to wall.

(Process *43.84*)

characteristic of Prouvé than of Le Corbusier, who generally used complete frames in his more high-tech buildings. While this joint project went unbuilt, it became the basis for a series of executed designs by Prouvé. His temporary school buildings at Villejuif utilized a similar structural concept, with a series of pinned tapering steel frames supporting a plywood sandwich panel roof, the beams of which were supported by the window mullions. These mullions were perforated V sections with vents to permit ventilation and to eliminate the need for operable windows (see figure 11.6). The sandwich panel and the perforated mullion are direct adaptations of aircraft technology.

The design is remarkable for its lack of clarity as defined by International Style Modernists such as Mies or the young Le Corbusier, in which each functional role must be accomplished by a single element. The schools seem designed to confound these expectations, as there is little consistency of this type and each element is assigned as many roles as possible. Thus the window mullions are also columns and ventilators, the building is part frame and part wall, and there is no clear articulation of skin and bones or frame and wall. This was Prouvé's principal achievement: not just that he successfully incorporated techniques from other industries into architecture, but that he felt little obligation to make them conform to existing architectural languages of structure and envelope.

While Le Corbusier's projects for small-scale metal houses remained on paper, Prouvé built several, most notably the houses at Meudon in 1949–1953. These bear a resemblance to the Maisons Loucheur in size and material, particularly in that they use both metal and fieldstone. This was a condition forced on Prouvé, as it was on Le Corbusier, but unlike Le Corbusier Prouvé was unhappy with the requirement. The first house type built at Meudon, in its ideal form, used sheet metal construction and was designed around the principle of a frame that could be erected without the use of a crane. This was accomplished by the use of a central portal frame that was erected first, to which were attached a series of sheet metal box beams. Interior and exterior partitions were given a slightly bowed shape to prevent oil canning without the use of thicker sheet metal (see figure 11.3). In the houses executed at Meudon a number of these features were replaced with more conventional methods; the floors for example were concrete rather than the sheet metal of the prototype, and the lower portal frames are replaced by fieldstone walls. The change to concrete floors may have been economic or aesthetic. Most laymen and not a few architects prefer the tactile solidity of a concrete floor to the bouncy resilience of a steel deck. Although the latter is perfectly safe, it is not reassuring. This is no small point, as it is at the heart of Prouvé's aesthetic of the minimal use of material, which produces work that while functional and sound does not express itself as solid and stable.

A later series of houses, dubbed the *coque* or shell type, were a direct application of the stressed skin approach to building and have no frames at all, using long, thin hollow structural shells sitting on load-bearing fieldstone walls. This design is also remarkable for its nonarchitectural character. Le Corbusier's Loucheur wall, although complex, remains a relatively flat plane forming a uniform volume. Prouvé's wall is more configured and more complexly profiled to respond to needs of strength or fabrication.

The Meudon houses were not a financial success. Prouvé ended up giving parts of them to his employees as compensation, but they were built, and several years later a similar project was planned for Lagny, this time in collaboration with Le Corbusier. (Prouvé almost always collaborated with other architects.) The point of departure was, not surprisingly, the Maison Loucheur design. This version was given more styling than the earlier design, using windows with round corners, sloping roofs, and preformed sheet metal gutters, yet it is a far more flat volume than earlier work by Prouvé.

The highly configured, nongeometric curtain walls typical of Prouvé's work and its nonstructural character demonstrate his tendency to allow the conditions of the problem to determine the result. For example, one of the chief problems of sheet

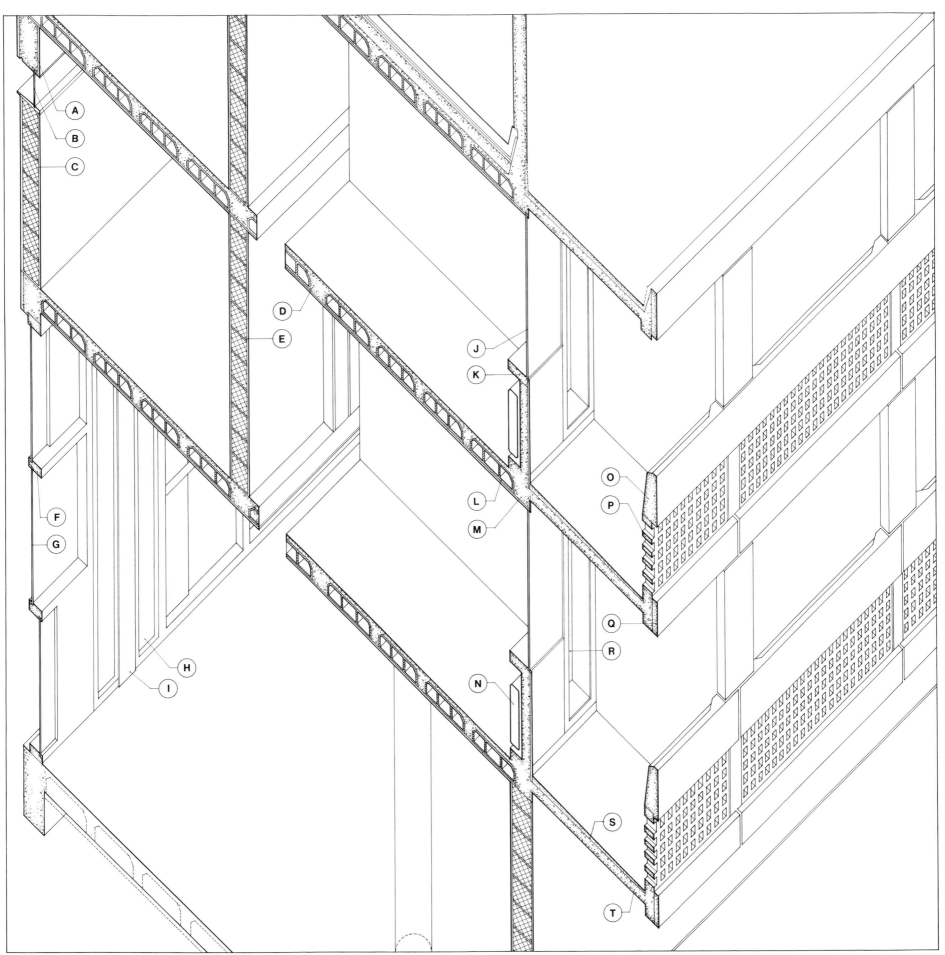

6.48

Monastery of La Tourette

Le Corbusier

Éveux-sur-l'Arbresle, France, 1953–1959

6.48 **Wall section at typical cell and corridor.**

A Concrete beam covered with gunite on exterior.

B Fixed glazing or operable steel window. See figure 6.52.

C Gunite on concrete masonry exterior wall. Although commonly thought of as cast-in-place concrete, the building uses a great deal of concrete masonry and precast concrete.

D Internal concrete beam flush with slab so that it remains hidden.

E Internal partition, plaster on concrete masonry.

F Precast concrete window frame bolted in place.

G Fixed glass set in precast frame. The glass is sometimes at the front and sometimes at the rear of the mullions.

H *Aérateur.* See figure 6.53.

I Cast-in-place concrete column.

J Fixed glass at cell window.

K Concrete sill.

L Lost tile concrete slab. This creates the appearance of a flat slab, with the efficiency of a ribbed one.

M Cast-in-place concrete beam.

N Radiator.

O Precast concrete rail with exposed aggregate finish.

P Precast screen.

Q Precast spandrel facing panel.

R Wood *aérateur* ventilation panel.

S Balcony slab topping, sloped to drain.

T Concrete structural slab.
   (FLC 1099, 1092, 1095)

6.49 **View.**

6.49

metal curtain walls is oil canning—the tendency of flat metal surfaces to bow out and warp with changes in temperature. A typical Modernist would try to eliminate this action and maintain a flat wall. Prouvé's response in his best-known curtain wall design, that of the market at Clichy, was to curve the panel outward and place springs behind it. This controlled the bending action and brought it into the design, though admittedly at the expense of the formal definition of the building; and what is a virtue at the small scale may become a shortcoming when multiplied innumerable times.

The production of large-scale standardized components proved the most elusive of Le Corbusier's ideas for industrialized construction. Prouvé began where Le Corbusier had left off at Marseilles and continued to develop the bottle and rack conception as a metallic language. His entry in a 1952 competition for housing at the University of Nancy is not radically different from his concept sketches of Marseilles, but neither this nor any other variations were built, at least by Prouvé. There have been isolated examples by others. Moshe Safdie's 1967 Habitat in Montreal was to be a much more articulated concrete version of the bottle and rack, and Kisho Kurokawa's Nagakin capsule tower built in Tokyo in 1971 achieved the idea through the use of cargo container technology. Despite the difficulties in achieving construction using large-scale standardized and mass-produced components, its power and appeal kept it alive and it became a tenet of the High Tech architects of the 1980s.

If Prouvé succeeded where Le Corbusier failed, however, it is only from a certain viewpoint. Both having reached the limits of the minimal use of material, Prouvé took a step forward while Le Corbusier took a step, perhaps more than one, back. Many find Prouvé's work too minimal, too flimsy, not to mention too repetitive, and the lack of a reference to conventional architectural languages is after all not always an asset. Even Reyner Banham, who in the 1960s was the chief critical advocate of the rigorous application of vehicular technology to architecture, took Prouvé to task for both these shortcomings, finding that some of his details had the "thin and flimsy air of bent metal section" and noting that "the basic difficulty raised by Prouvé is that his thin, bent details so often usurp functions previously performed by traditional usages."[26]

If one believes that Prouvé exceeded the desirable limits of minimalism, it is easier to sympathize with Le Corbusier's ultimate conservatism. While utilizing in a largely poetic way the concept of the frame and skin, the monocoque fuselage and the stressed skin, Le Corbusier still sought a solidity, permanence, and regularity that far exceeded the merely functional. While he adopted the principle of minimal material, it is rather an attitude that informs details of a more substantial character, and while he may have indulged in the ambiguities of architectural language that vehicular structures suggested, he never abandoned architectural language altogether. Ultimately his work was informed, but not controlled, by the objects he chose to emulate.

6.50

6.51

Monastery of La Tourette

Le Corbusier

Éveux-sur-l'Arbresle, France, 1953–1959

6.50 **Elevation at courtyard.**

6.51 **Windows at cell corridors.**

6.52 **Window at cell corridor.**
- A Concrete beam over window, This is not only a lintel but supports the floor above.
- B Fixed section of steel window. The distance from window to column is shortened for clarity.
- C Operable steel window and glass.
- D Typical wall construction of gunite and plaster on masonry.
- E Sheet metal sill. This was not an original detail but probably added during construction.
- F Concrete column hidden in wall.
- G Concrete extension to column. Since the column interrupts the continuous slot of the window, the beam is given an ornamental projection.
  (FLC 1012)

6.53 **Window at main spaces and corridors.**
- A 50/10 sheet aluminum *aérateur*.
- B Wood handle above. When closed, the *aérateur* is held in place with dead bolt (not shown).
- C Rubber strip to seal opening between aluminum and concrete.
- D Precast concrete fin to support fixed glass.
- E Glass set without frame.
- F Sill.
- G 20 cm pivot in bronze socket.
- H Grout pedestal. This was a construction addition, probably related to placing the pivot.
  (FLC 1011)

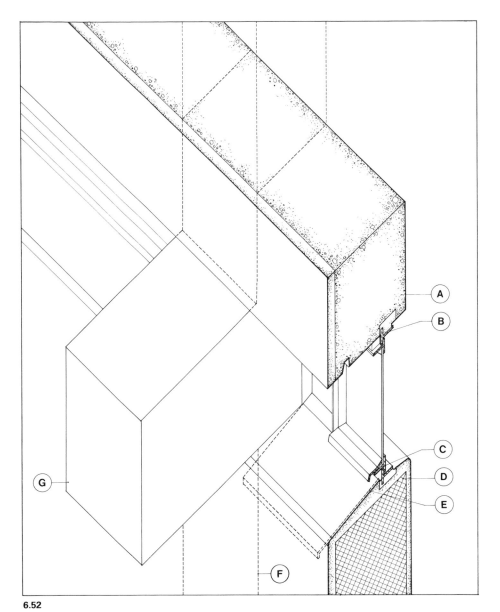

6.52

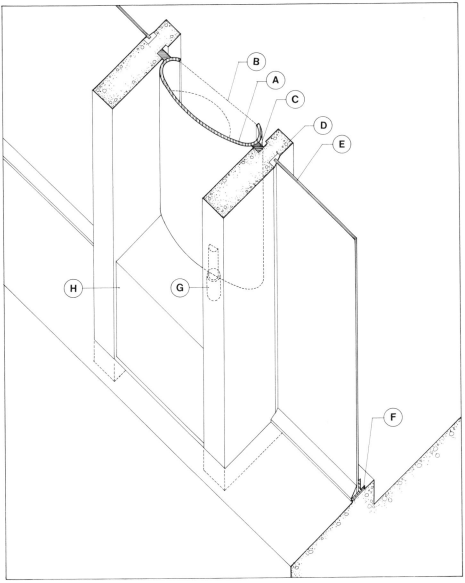

6.53

7.1

7.2

Willow Run Bomber Plant

Albert Kahn

Ypsilanti, Michigan, 1941–1943

(Henry Ford Museum & Greenfield Village)

7.1 **B-24s on the final assembly line in March 1943.**
(Henry Ford Museum & Greenfield Village, P.883-77581)

7.2 **Assembly line.** Aft fuselage sections in foreground moving from left to right in assembly line, with nose sections being assembled in rear, on September 11, 1944.
(Henry Ford Museum & Greenfield Village, P.80710-14)

need for housing for displaced workers. Given that the government was financing and building large numbers of low-cost units, industrialized building seemed an obvious answer. The first priority of American industry and government, however, was to build war material and equipment, not housing, and even when housing was built, metal was an unlikely choice of material, since most metals, particularly structural steel, were reserved for war use.

This paradox is apparent in the difference between the conceptual projects and realized buildings of 1940–1945. The numerous proposals for factory-made housing show an obsession with adapting the new materials—steel, plywood, aluminum—and the new processes of industry, particularly the aircraft industry—the stressed skin, tension cables, etc.—to problems of building construction. Yet while this type of industrialization of the building industry was never close to realization, numerous large-scale modular housing projects were executed. Although a number of new materials were used, particularly processed wood products, and although some of the projects used new techniques, such as plywood sheathing incorporated into stressed skin panels, they are for the most part slimmed-down prefabricated platform frame modules, built at low cost, and if they used new materials they did so in conventional ways. Most are of minimal aesthetic interest.

The need for massive quantities of housing has no better illustration than the Willow Run plant itself. It was to be located in what was then the small town of Ypsilanti, which lacked even adequate water supply for the influx of workers. Ford had probably chosen Willow Run for political reasons. As the site was outside the city of Detroit, the company hoped to minimize conflicts with the United Auto Workers, conflicts that had been frequent and violent in the late 1930s. While many had assumed that the workers would simply commute from Detroit, the UAW decided to bring the city, government and all, to the factory, and proposed to build a town of 6,000 housing units adjacent to the plant. In 1941 they hired Saarinen, Swanson, and Saarinen to develop a master plan.

If the Willow Run factory was one of the great successes of American industry, the city of Willow Run was one of the great failures of American architecture and urban planning. The town proposal collapsed due to a complex set of political and economic concerns. Most buildings never got beyond the planning stage, only small fragments were built, and if the pressure of time and economy brought out the best in American industry, it cannot be said that it did the same in the architects. It was not for want of talent. At the very least Willow Run was a dress rehearsal for postwar American architecture. Eliel and Eero Saarinen, along with Ralph Rapson, worked on the town center and master plan. Neighborhoods were given to various other firms, among them Skidmore, Owings and Merrill and Oscar Stonorov and Louis Kahn. Yet if one examines the sketchy plans and drawings made, it seems that not much was lost of lasting value. Strangely, there is little in them to suggest the interest in industrialization and its products that many of these architects shared at the time.

One might think from this that the interest of these architects in the architectural implications of the industrialization that Willow Run symbolized were minimal, were it not for the unexecuted projects of the same years, particularly those of Eero Saarinen.

EERO SAARINEN

Saarinen had spent a short but important time in the office of Norman Bel Geddes in the 1930s. While Geddes's interest in industrial objects now appears superficial, Saarinen saw these objects as the source of functionalism, which he defined as "the doctrine of making the physical requirements of architecture establish the form, of making everything—as in a clipper ship or an airplane—as convenient and economic as possible and letting these conditions determine form."[2] It might seem odd, given his interest in a highly assertive machine age style, that he would return to the Arts and Crafts community of Cranbrook in the late 1930s, but if Eero's interest in machine imagery was not shared by his father, it was by his other colleagues there: Charles and Ray Eames and Ralph Rapson.

7.3

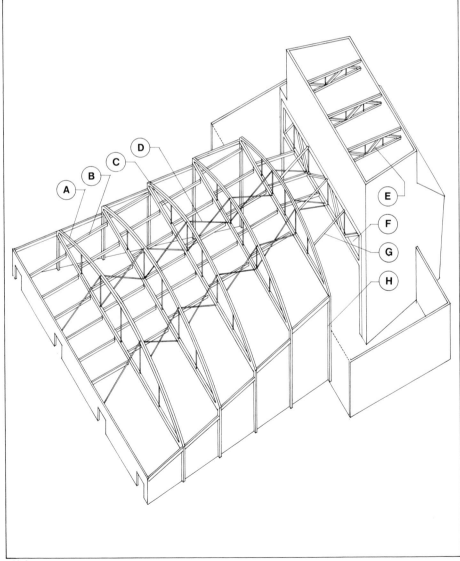

7.4

Opera House, Berkshire Music Center, Tanglewood

Saarinen and Saarinen

Lenox, Massachusetts, 1940–1941

7.3 View.
(Prints and Photographs Division, Library of Congress/Gottscho-Schleisner)

7.4 Framing.

A 8 × 16 (8 × 22 at longer spans) laminated wood arches made from 2" yellow pine boards, joined at the center, with 8 × 8" laminated wood chord below hung from steel rod.

B 4 × 12 purlins attached to chord with joist hangers and hung from the adjacent chord. The structure collapsed under a heavy snow load in 1958, and rotting of the wood in the beams around the suspension cables was a factor.

C ⅞" steel rod. The smaller cables here eliminate the need for a second beam.

D ⅞" steel rods to diagonally brace the structure against lateral loads.

E Truss at fly loft.

F Special truss to form proscenium.

G 3" steel pipe to brace the shed against the fly loft.

H 8 × 10 or 8 × 12 wood columns.
(KRJD&A, A-4, 7)

The first prominent manifestation of Saarinen's and Eames's interest in industrial objects was their winning entry in the Museum of Modern Art's Furniture Competition of 1940, which employed plywood curved in two directions. Two of the jurors, Alvar Aalto and Marcel Breuer, had pioneered in the design of furniture using single-curvature plywood. Eames and Saarinen, however, were drawing directly from industrial sources. Double-curved plywood had been frequently used in aircraft manufacture. In the late 1930s the de Havilland Company had produced some spectacular plywood designs, particularly the Mosquito, a plane completely of wood utilizing a sandwich panel skin of two layers of three-ply birch with a core of balsa (figure 7.25). In the early 1940s Eames and Saarinen had contacted the Packard Company to explore a process they were developing called "cycle welding," a method of laminating plywood to metal, rubber, and glass. Packard's primary interest was the manufacture of automobile seats, and the adaptation to furniture seemed obvious.

About the time that Sorensen and Kahn were planning Willow Run, Eero Saarinen was producing one of the more industrially inspired designs of the war years to be built, albeit in wood, the Tanglewood Opera House. In 1938 the firm of Saarinen and Saarinen had built a large shed for Serge Koussevitzky and the Boston Symphony Orchestra in their summer home near Lenox, Massachusetts. In 1941 a much smaller building, largely the work of Eero, was added for opera. Although enclosed on all sides with windowless partitions, the building had numerous openings for natural ventilation. The two side walls taper toward the stage, while the roof steps up to provide slots for ventilation. The spans required are considerable, 80 feet at the longest point, and Saarinen, perhaps restrained by limitations on the use of steel, chose instead a structure primarily of wood; but it was a structure in the spirit and forms of steel.

Each section of the roof is hung by steel cables from a laminated wood arch, which in turn is supported by laminated wood columns. It is obviously inspired by Le Corbusier's Palace of the Soviets competition entry, while the technology is that of the suspension bridge and primitive aircraft, a technology that was well established in 1941. These precedents, however, were not commonly associated with wood framing. The wood framing of Tanglewood was not solid but laminated, with larger timbers produced by gluing smaller strips of wood together. Laminating did not originate in aircraft design but had contributed to aircraft design, and the technology was similar to that used by Eames and Saarinen for their 1940 chair designs. The shed was certainly a thorough exploitation of the material. The 80-foot span would have been impossible for a single piece of timber, and Saarinen's laminated piece had to be made in two pieces so that it could be transported to the site.

Saarinen and Eames parted company in 1941. Charles and Ray Eames moved to California, where they manufactured plywood splints and aircraft parts for the armed forces. (Although all of their work after 1940 is in some way collaborative, Charles was trained as an architect and Ray as a painter, and the former is generally credited with their architectural work.) Eero Saarinen spent 1942–1945 in the OSS (despite the fact that his native Finland was an ally of Germany), but he continued his architectural practice, sometimes alone and sometimes with his father Eliel and brother-in-law Robert Swanson.

In 1942 the U.S. Gypsum company sponsored a series of designs by Eero Saarinen and a number of other architects "to show how research has developed new materials and construction methods." Saarinen's contribution was a prototypical community center, and although it appeared only in an advertisement, it is developed in fairly elaborate detail. The building's steel structure employs a roof suspended by cables from a central mast containing utilities. The exterior wall is made of 4-foot-by-6-foot sandwich panels of two layers of plywood separated by a core of Weatherwood, with an exterior finish of canvas glued to the plywood. The building was clearly designed around basic industrial principles—minimum weight, minimum material, maximum exploitation of structural properties such as tension, and components precisely made and joined—but it also makes reference, deliberately or not, to a number of precedents, including the suspension bridge and early aircraft

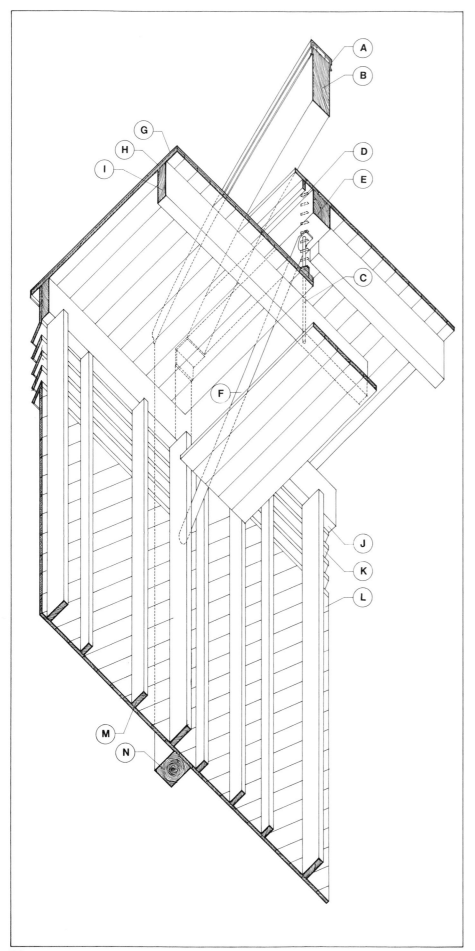

7.6

Opera House, Berkshire Music Center, Tanglewood

Saarinen and Saarinen

Lenox, Massachusetts, 1940–1941

7.5   Interior wall section.

A   Metal flashing to protect top of truss from rainwater and rot.

B   8 × 16 southern yellow pine laminated wood arch.

C   ⅞″ steel rod to connect the truss and beam.

D   Wood louvers to vent the unairconditioned space.

E   8 × 8 laminated wood bottom chord.

F   3″ steel brace to laterally brace and triangulate the structure.

G   Composition roofing.

H   2 × 6 tongue and groove yellow pine roof deck.

I   4 × 12 purlin.

J   4 × 12 edge beam.

K   Wood louvers.

L   2 × 6 diagonal yellow pine siding.

M   2 × 4, 6, or 8 long leaf yellow pine wood studs. Both the size and the spacing of the studs are varied for visual rather than structural reasons, perhaps to suggest musical rhythms.

N   8 × 10 wood column. The columns increase in size as their height or unbraced length increases.
(KRJD&A, A-7)

7.6   Interior.
(Prints and Photographs Division, Library of Congress/Gottscho-Schleisner)

in the cables, and the aircraft sandwich panel in the walls. Its debt to Fuller's 1927 Dymaxion house (figure 7.44) is a bit too strong. Closer to home it recalls the cable-supported tent that Charles Kettering, General Motors's chief engineer, designed for traveling exhibitions in 1941.

Saarinen and Eames each participated in a number of competitions and proposals during the war in which the technology of industrial objects, particularly airplanes, played an important if not dominant part. *Architectural Forum*'s September 1942 issue featured "Houses for 194X," the proposals for which included Neutra's Diatom house, with its mast-and-cable-suspended roof. The most evocative and most technologically adventurous entry, by David Runnels and Ralph Rapson, a former Cranbrook student (figure 7.9), recalled Le Corbusier in its fusion of the tent and airplane analogies. The walls and roof were sandwich panels of two layers of canvas with a core of insulation, supported by 1-inch round pipes. The major beams were stamped metal girders tapered and with round openings in imitation of aircraft structure. The columns were double-tapered wood struts.

This was followed the next year by the "Buildings for 194X" issue, featuring buildings by Eames, Mies, and Stonorov and Kahn, but these three were less literally inspired by industrial objects than was Pietro Belluschi's proposal for an office building, which featured a series of aluminum sandwich panels riveted together. The honeycomb sandwich panel had been developed by the aircraft industry as a means of dissipating heat; the fate of Belluschi's design illustrates the difficulties of adapting the techniques of aircraft manufacture to building construction. The design was eventually built in 1948 as Belluschi's Equitable Building in Portland, Oregon. Although the curtain wall is aluminum, the honeycomb panel is replaced by thick aluminum plate (figure 7.11) and most of the rivets are replaced by concealed clips; the design thus lost in translation most of those elements that specifically linked it to aircraft.

California Arts and Architecture magazine's 1943 competition, "Houses for Postwar Living," was incestuous from the start. Eames was on the jury (as was Neutra) and Eero Saarinen was the winner. It is telling that all the premiated and exhibited entries make some reference to industrialization and aircraft. Saarinen's entry, done with Oliver Lundquist, involved a series of PACs (pre-assembled components), 3-by-9-meter boxes to be mass-produced in factories and towed to the site. Saarinen wrote that "the economic and social demands for post-war housing must be met by extensive utilization of assembly line potential." The units were to be built of stressed skin plywood with an integral radiant heating system. Saarinen continued to develop this project during the war, which grew into the "unfolding house," a design similar to the PAC but with a metallic skin.

Saarinen's design was inspired in part by the TVA house, a prefab wooden system that was produced by the government on a modest scale in the late 1930s, essentially of the type that we would call a modular house or trailer. Saarinen explained his design in a letter to Buckminster Fuller in 1945:

It is a 8′ wide trailer package which unfolds to 3 or 4 times its original size. This, of course, is an advantage over the TVA house where you have to ship too much air to ever make it economical. . . . The system fits well a long term development where at first a more conventional looking house with immediate consumer acceptance value is manufactured with a smaller investment in presses, etc. Later, as a logical development, a skin stressed curved surface takes the place of clumsier flat wall and roof panels.[3]

The PAC design, in both its wood and metal manifestations, almost unconsciously called into question one of the basic tenets of International Style Modernism—the idea of modern buildings as frame and skin assemblies—but it followed instead the aircraft fashion of the day, the stressed skin, in which frame and skin merged into one.

The second prize entry by I. M. Pei and E. H. Duhart was designed around the General Panel system developed by Walter Gropius and Konrad Wachsmann. This involved prefabricated 3-foot-4-inch-wide wood panels clipped together on site. Un-

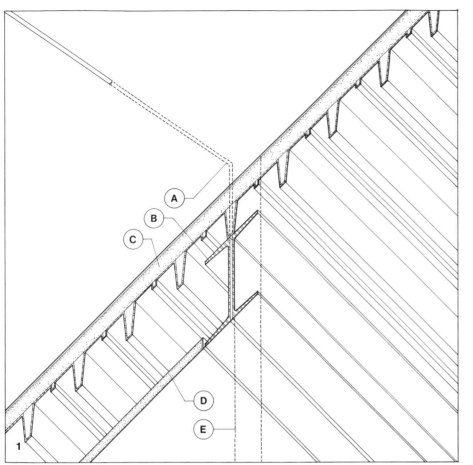

1

7.7

7.8

2

7.9

The drawings on these pages show details of the proposed pipe and fabric construction, and a suggested plan which reflects in an interesting manner the flexibility of shape permitted by the system. The scheme adopted for the packaged mechanical unit leaves little choice in the location of the bathroom, but it may be assumed that for larger houses separate bath units could be provided without difficulty. As developed on the facing page, the mechanical core is extremely compact, measuring about 5' x 14'. The basic plan, more conventional in its outlines than the scheme directly above, is shown at the bottom of the opposite page.

1" INSULATION
1" DIA. POST. light metal tube
1¼" FABRIC WALL
exterior fabric water repellent
interior any fabric.
THIS SURFACE ALUMINUM PAINT
POST SPREAD

WATER REPELLENT FABRIC
ROOF
INSULATION
1" PIPE TILE BETWEEN POSTS
STAMPED LIGHT METAL
ROOF GIRDER
POST and GIRDER CONNECTOR
ROOF LAP and WIPED WITH WATERPROOF MASTIC

ROLL-FAB WALL
INSULATION
CLIP FABRIC LAYERS HERE
LINO FLOOR COVERING and COVE
CHEMICALLY TREATED TAMPED EARTH
1" METAL POST TUBE
SAND or CRUSHED ROCK BED FOR HEATING COILS
POST SPREAD
TARVIA SHOULDER

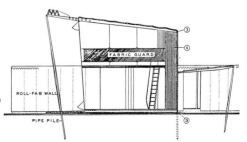

Community Center (project)

Eero Saarinen

1942

7.7 Wall section. Due to the hypothetical nature of the design, many of the details are uncertain or unresolved.

1 Detail at roof beam:

A Ring bolt and spun steel tension cables attached to center mast.

B Two 7 C 9.7 steel channels.

C 12' × 12' roof panel with two-ply 15 lb asphalt-saturated felt roofing on 1" weatherboard insulation and steel roof deck.

D Ceiling. Exposing the steel deck was optional.

E Interior wall (not shown).

2 Detail at junction of floor and wall:

F 4' × 6' and 2' 6" wall sandwich panels of 1½" weatherwood with plywood on both sides and glued canvas exterior finish.

G Radiant floor heating coil.

H Floor of pressed steel panels 5" deep with ½" weatherboard insulation (location uncertain) and covering of battleship linoleum on saturated felt and ½" underlayment.

(AF 1942)

7.8 Model. Some units of Saarinen's PAC industrialized housing system are visible in the foreground.

(Courtesy of Cranbrook Archives)

7.9 A Fabric House (project), Houses for 194X Competition, Ralph Rapson and David Runnels, 1942.

(AF 9.42)

7.10 Competition entry (project), Houses for Post War Living Competition, Raphael Soriano, 1943.

(AF 9.43)

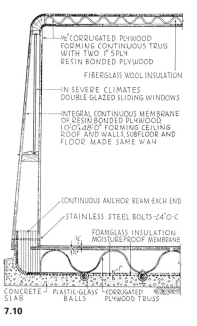

7.10

like Saarinen's single-unit standard type, Pei's uses small-scale wood elements, infinitely more flexible but lacking the qualities of Saarinen's design that evoke the Model T and the B-24. The most literal of the aircraft designs is Raphael Soriano's series of prefabricated U-shaped boxes (figure 7.10), formally suggestive of an airplane with its tapering form and rounded corners, and aircraft-like in structure as well. The U shape had no frame per se but, like monocoque plane construction, used structural membranes made from two sheets of 1-inch plywood encasing a sheet of corrugated half-inch plywood. The technique of bonding a corrugated sheet to a flat sheet (the corrugated center sandwich panel) is another assembly developed in the 1930s. Sadly, few of these ideas found their way into real buildings during or even after the war. Saarinen's PAC proposal stands in sharp contrast to his Centerline Housing Project (done with his father), finished in 1941, which is of conventional wood construction.

But Eero Saarinen's future was not in housing or wood buildings, whether in the form of Centerline or of Tanglewood. His first postwar project, the General Motors Technical Center, was a design that symbolically, technically, and economically demanded steel, and housing of any kind is rare in his subsequent work. Charles Eames's exploration of house construction, on the other hand, was just beginning.

CHARLES EAMES AND THE CASE STUDY HOUSES

Charles and Ray Eames arrived in Los Angeles in July 1941, four months before Pearl Harbor, where Charles went to work as an architect for MGM. Working in the bedroom of their home in Neutra's Strathmore Apartments, he continued his experiments with double-curved plywood for chairs on a homemade device, the Kazam machine, that employed plaster casts, a bicycle pump, and an automobile battery.

After the beginning of the war Eames designed a molded plywood split system for the military and in 1942 established the Plyformed Wood Company to manufacture the splints and other plywood products. In an interesting reversal of the flow of technological information, they were soon making parts for plywood aircraft. In 1943 they produced vertical and horizontal stabilizers for the Vultee BT-15 trainer. Designs for plywood pilot seats and gas tanks were made but not mass-produced. The largest component was the blisters for the nose and other round end pieces of the CG-16 experimental glider, which was also never put into production.

John Entenza, owner of *Arts and Architecture* magazine, had been a supporter of and collaborator with the Eameses, and they in turn became involved in the editing and design of the magazine. In 1944 an entire issue was devoted to industrialized housing, to which the Eameses, Eero Saarinen, and Buckminster Fuller all contributed. Eames and Entenza wrote: "Because of the enormous acceleration of world industry for military purposes we now know that insofar as the design, engineering, and production of the house on an industrialized basis is concerned that reality only awaits the desire." And Buckminster Fuller: "The beauty of scientific dwelling machines is as certain as the beauty of an airplane, a square-rigged vessel; this aesthetic point needs no consideration provided best science and technology are employed."[4]

Entenza was not content merely to write about housing and in January 1945, six months before the end of the war, announced the Case Study House program for the support of the design and construction of innovative housing, to be financed by product manufacturers and from the sale of the houses themselves. Although the original eight architects selected included Eames, Neutra, Rapson, and Eero Saarinen, the program's primary concern was not the industrialization of building. Few of the houses were industrialized in any meaningful way, and most were not steel-structured. But if the program was perceived to be both of these, it was in large part due to the Eames house.

The focal point of the first series of Case Study Houses was to be numbers 8 and 9, designed by Eames and Eero Saarinen in collaboration and to be occupied by Eames and Entenza respectively. Although Saarinen's involvement diminished as

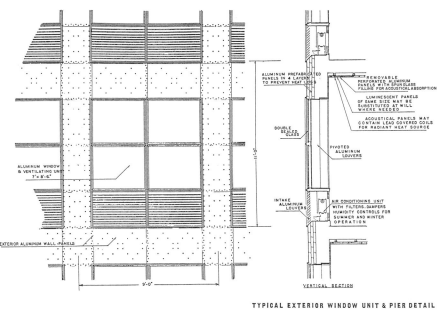

ALUMINUM PREFABRICATED
PANELS IN 4 LAYERS
TO PREVENT HEAT LOSS

REMOVABLE
PERFORATED ALUMINUM
PANELS WITH SPUN GLASS
FILLING FOR ACOUSTICAL ABSORPTION

LUMINESCENT PANELS
OF SAME SIZE MAY BE
SUBSTITUTED AT WILL
WHERE NEEDED

ACOUSTICAL PANELS MAY
CONTAIN LEAD COVERED COILS
FOR RADIANT HEAT SOURCE

DOUBLE
SEALED
GLASS

PIVOTED
ALUMINUM
LOUVERS

ALUMINUM WINDOW
& VENTILATING UNIT
7'x 8'-6"

INTAKE
ALUMINUM
LOUVERS

AIR CONDITIONING UNIT
WITH FILTERS, DAMPERS
HUMIDITY CONTROLS FOR
SUMMER AND WINTER
OPERATION

EXTERIOR ALUMINUM WALL PANELS

VERTICAL SECTION

TYPICAL EXTERIOR WINDOW UNIT & PIER DETAIL

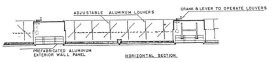

ADJUSTABLE ALUMINUM LOUVERS

CRANK & LEVER TO OPERATE LOUVERS

PREFABRICATED ALUMINUM
EXTERIOR WALL PANEL

HORIZONTAL SECTION

7.11

7.12

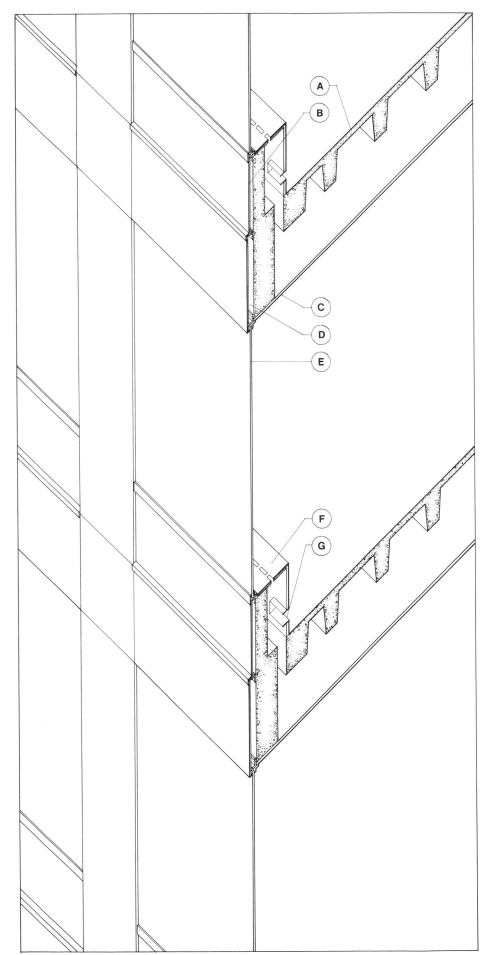

7.13

7.11 Office Building for 194X project,
Pietro Belluschi, 1943. The opaque
portions were to be built of riveted
aluminum sandwich panels.
(AF 5.43)

Equitable Building

Pietro Belluschi

Portland, Oregon, 1948

7.12 View.
(Ezra Stoller ©Esto)

7.13 Wall section.
A   Ribbed concrete slab.
B   ³⁄₁₆″ cast aluminum spandrel.
C   Suspended ceiling of metal lath and
plaster on furring channels.
D   Sheet aluminum beam cover.
Rather than being exposed, the concrete frame is clad and expressed,
an arrangement that is superior in
terms of tolerance, infiltration, and
heat loss.
E   ³⁄₄″ green-tinted insulating glass in
aluminum frame.
F   Aluminum sill with openings for air
conditioning exhaust.
G   Three 4 × 16″ openings for mechanical system in metal lath and plaster
wall.
(AF 9.48)

7.14 Curtain wall.
1   Mullion and window sill detail:
A   ³⁄₄″ insulating glass inside-glazed in
aluminum frame with green-tinted,
heat-absorbing outer layer. The use
of insulating glass was not standard
at this date.
B   Extruded aluminum T mullion.
C   Extruded aluminum glazing stop
screwed to mullion.
D   Internal partition.
E   ¹⁄₈″ sheet aluminum sill.
F   Opening for air distribution.
G   Angle supporting typical T mullion.
H   Concrete spandrel.
I   ³⁄₁₆″ cast aluminum spandrel. The
sandwich panel of the 1942 design
was replaced by a single thicker
sheet.
2   Detail at spandrel and column
cover:
J   ¹⁄₈″ sheet aluminum covering con-
crete beams and columns.
K   Aluminum extrusion.
L   ³⁄₁₆″ cast aluminum panel.
M   Aluminum sill extrusion.
N   2½ × 2½ × ¼″ clip angle allowing
adjustment of the panel to accom-
modate inaccuracies in the concrete
frame.
O   Concrete wall.
(AF 9.48)

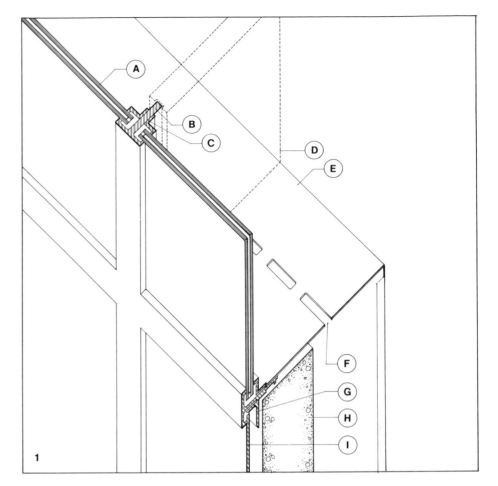

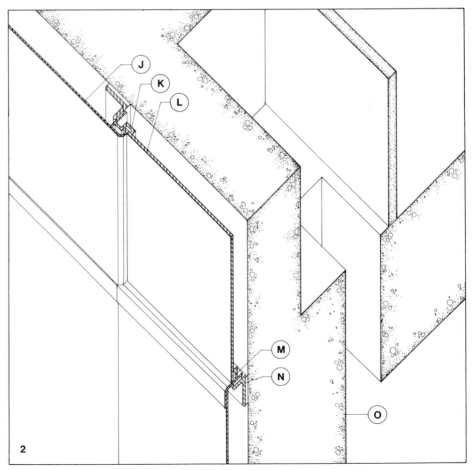

7.14

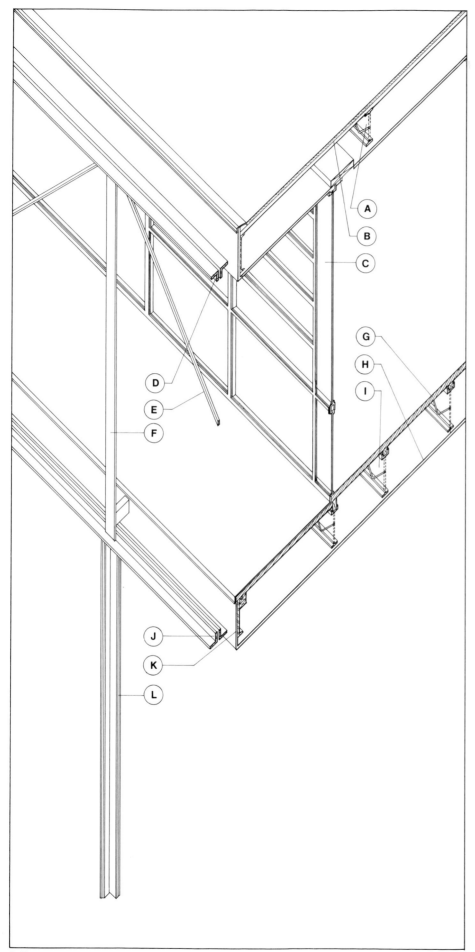

A

B

C

G

H

I

D

E

F

J

K

L

7.15

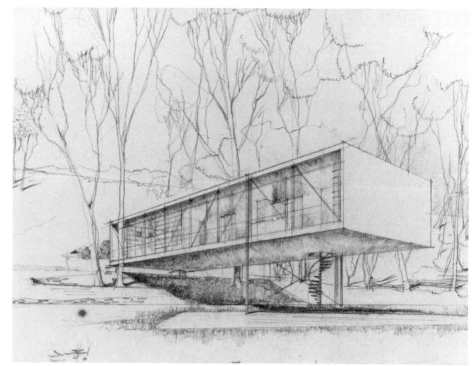

7.16

Case Study House No. 8 (Eames House), initial design

Charles Eames and Eero Saarinen

Pacific Palisades, California, 1945–1947

7.15 Wall section.

A Roof structure of 1¼″ metal deck on Trusscon OT 125 steel joists with 12 C 10.6 edge channel supported by truss and steel beam beyond.

B Built-up roof and insulation on 1¼″ metal deck.

C Trusscon intermediate steel windows.

D Two 3½ × 3 × ½″ steel angles forming top chord of steel truss.

E 1 × 1″ square steel bar truss member.

F ST 4 I 94 steel T intermediate truss member. The two pairs of angles are tied together with triangulating supports so that the entire assembly acts as a single unit.

G 2 × 6 wood tongue and groove flooring.

H Cement plaster soffit concealing joists.

I Trusscon OT 141W floor joist and 12 C 10.6 edge channel.

J Two 3½ × 3¼″ steel angles forming bottom chord of truss.

K 12 C 10.6 edge channel.

L Steel column.

(LOC DN 4)

7.16 Perspective.

(Lucia Eames Demetrios dba Eames Office © 1989)

his postwar practice grew, his initial involvement was significant, and he was listed as codesigner of both houses in the original contract drawings. The two houses were conceived from the outset as contrasting applications of industrialized, steel construction. The Eames house was a cantilevered trussed bridge while the Entenza house was a square pavilion on grade. The frame of the Eames house was to be exposed; that of the Entenza house was to be concealed. The Eames house was to be glazed and outward-looking; the Entenza house with its walls of solid brick was to be introverted. The Eames house was to float above the ground; the Entenza house sat firmly upon it. Edgardo Contini, the engineer for the first design, explained the difference: "In the cantilever bridge house the emphasis was on structure, and it was designed for the structure to be exposed; the intention of the Entenza house is to eliminate structure—to be anti-structural, to be as anonymous as possible. In the Entenza house no beams are expressed, no columns visible."[5]

The initial design of the Eames house was a quite literal application of what architects perceived as the principles of engineering rationalism: the minimum of material to achieve the maximum span. It configured the material to exploit its primary structural virtue. It derives its form not from the program nor from the site but from its own structural order.

Contini however, somewhat overstates the differences. While almost all the Entenza house structure was to be concealed, not all of the Eames house structure was to be exposed. The house was to be supported by two floor-deep trusses set outside the envelope of the house, between which spanned bar joists to form the floor and ceiling. While the two trusses were exposed, the floor and ceiling joists were concealed by plaster ceilings and soffits. This was done, no doubt, to facilitate the placement of interior partitions, as a ceiling of exposed bar joists cannot easily be joined to the tops of the partitions in a way that permits acoustic privacy. The side walls were layered bands of horizontal steel windows.

There were numerous delays in getting under way and in the interim a number of changes. Saarinen dropped out, a different engineer was brought in, but principally Eames rethought the entire conception of the house, particularly the ideal of material efficiency. Esther McCoy describes what happened next:

A last minute change was made in the Eames house after the steel had been delivered to the site. Eames was disturbed by the fact that he was employing the largest amount of steel to enclose the smallest amount of space. His wish to lift the house above the ground to capture the full sea view became of less importance than enclosing more space. While the steel waited in the yard, Eames began working on a new design. The problem was to make the stock pile serve the revised plan. After a new scheme was developed and McIntosh and McIntosh, structural engineers, were consulted, every piece of steel had found its way into the new design; only one additional beam was required.[6]

This oft-repeated story does not seem wholly plausible. It is difficult to visualize how these two designs could be built using identical parts and only those parts. A comparison of the working drawings of both houses reveals that the reuse of components was probably considerably exaggerated. There are clear correspondences between many of the old and new components—the bar joists of the roof and floor are the same, although turned 90 degrees; the steel angles of the top and bottom chords of the bridge truss became the edge of the new roof and floor—but many new components were required, notably 38 4-inch H columns and base plates. Likewise many sections in the old design, particularly the rolled sections, were not reused. The 12-inch-deep edge channels at the floor, although of the same cross section as used in the first design, are of different lengths and punched or drilled with different openings. If they were salvaged from the original design, they must have required considerable modification.[7]

The image of a warehouse full of building components that can be ordered from a catalog, as one might buy something from Sears, is hardly an accurate one in the case of the Eames house or of any other steel building. Some components are available in certain predetermined standard sizes—steel windows and bar joists, for

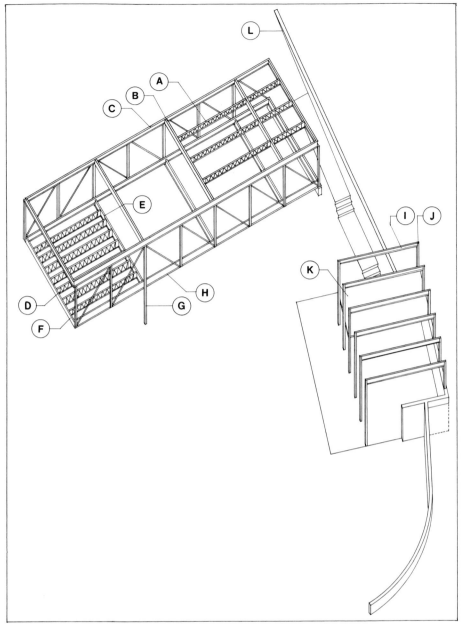

7.17

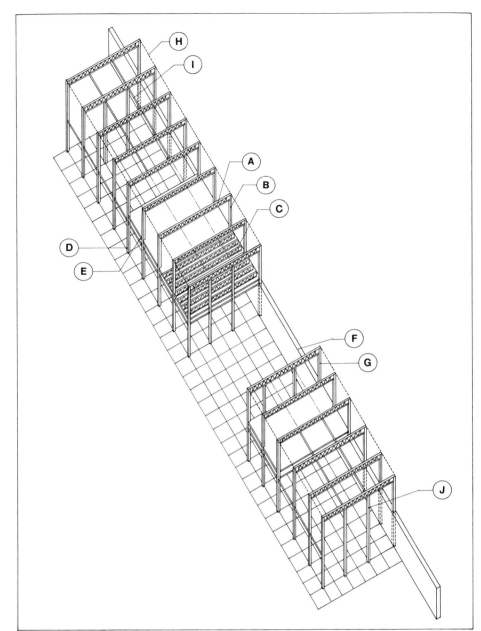

7.18

Case Study House No. 8 (Eames House), initial design

Charles Eames and Eero Saarinen

Pacific Palisades, California, 1945–1947

7.17 Framing.

A Trusscon OT 125 steel bar joist (RJ-1) supporting roof with metal deck above.

B 12 WF 27 steel beam (RB-1) and 12 I 16.5 steel beam (RB-2) at edge supporting joists.

C 12 C 10.6 edge channel (RJ-2).

D Trusscon OT 141W steel bar joist (FJ-1). The joists span the long dimension of the box so that they can be lowered where the deck occurs. See figure 7.15. The floor joists are more closely spaced than the roof joists because of their greater load.

E 14 WF 43 steel beam (FB-1).

F 12 C 10.6 edge channel (FB-2).

G Steel column.

H Story-high truss from steel angles.

I 8 × 4" I section at studio. Although the framing of the studio is similar in the final design, it is much lighter.

J Steel column at studio.

K Studio floor framing of 6 × 4" I section with Ferroboard metal deck.

L Retaining wall.

(LOC DN 1–3)

Eames House, second design

Charles Eames

Pacific Palisades, California, 1948–1949

7.18 Framing.

A OT 125 roof joists 7' 4" oc (RJ-1). Numbers in parentheses refer to elements from the initial design in figure 7.17.

B 4 × 4" × 10 lb. column partially embedded in concrete wall.

C OT 141 floor joists 1' 10" oc (FJ-1).

D Two-story 4 × 4" × 10 lb. column. Although columns occur in the first design, there are only two, whereas the second uses 18.

E 12 C 10.2 channel at second floor to support floor joists. Although a similar member is used in the first design, it was of a different length with different connections.

F Concrete retaining wall.

G Studio framing similar to house.

H 3 × 3 × ¼" continuous steel angle at top. This was a truss part in the initial design.

I Bridging partially shown.

J Nonstructural 4 × 4" columns at ends. These do no support beams or joists, only windows.

(LOC DN 4)

example (although they are often made only on demand)—and the number of sizes available is considerable. This is not true of the rolled steel sections, i.e., wide flanges, channels, etc. The cross-sectional shapes themselves are standard because of the rolling process. The lengths are not rigidly standardized, nor are the means of connection, which must be custom-made for each individual condition.

The windows and joists were the only two "standard" components that could be used without some modification to meet specific requirements. The truss was to be custom-made, and the columns, wide-flange beams, and other steel components, although standard rolled cross sections, had to be cut to specific lengths, punched with holes, and fitted with clips to make connections; although these components appear similar, two are rarely alike. The image of the house as somehow a giant erector set that could be disassembled and rebuilt in a different configuration gave rise to many of the misconceptions about the house, particularly in what happened in the redesign.

But if Eames exaggerated the "kit of interchangeable parts" aspect of the design, his perception regarding efficiency was true. The concept of minimal material as exemplified by the bridge design was not yielding truly efficient results. Although the second design does not contain all that much additional space (3,000 square feet versus 2,500 square feet in the original, an increase of 20 percent), it does use considerably less steel. The house lost much of its industrial styling in the process, but it was replaced with a more subtle and certainly more pragmatic view of steel construction. Like many of his predecessors, Eames began with a conception of steel construction drawn from outside of architecture, in this case from the bridge. In the end he adapted what was really the steel system used in small commercial buildings to residential design.

Yet the house was not devoid of references to aircraft technology. The parallel construction of closely spaced bar joists is not unlike that of some airplane wings of the period. Eames himself stated that the cross bracing was aircraft-inspired and produced the same result, minimal material. The *Architectural Forum* correspondent wrote in 1950:

One of Eames' many surprise discoveries as the house went up was that light steel is a distinct material, very different from its familiar, heavy parent. A delicate tracery of thin rods 12 in. deep can span more than 20 ft.; a cleverly bent sheet can bridge more than 7 ft. and still carry the usual roof loads; a 4 in. column can rise 17 ft. without wavering; a few crossed wires and turnbuckles can pull together an entire bolted frame. This, he decided, is a material inspired by the daring of aviation engineers, rather than the more timid techniques of traditional building.[8]

The steel structure of the first design was entirely concealed on the interior; in the new design it is largely exposed, primarily because there are fewer ceilings. But if Eames went to great lengths to expose more of the structure, he felt no obligation to clarify the structural expression, and strangely enough that of the second design is in some respects less clear than that of the first. While all of the H columns, cross bracings, and angles are visible, Eames goes to great lengths to disguise the largest structural members, the 12-inch channels that support the floor joists. Where there are walls above the channel, the finish is extended to the bottom of the floor structure to cover the channel. Where the walls above are glazed, a typical window frame is set into the space inside the channel. An opaque panel is set into the frame so that insofar as possible, it is identical to the window above (figure 7.22).

The reasons for this rather strange detail are not entirely clear. The channel supporting the second floor is discontinuous, and Eames may have wished to regularize the facade by making the one-story walls identical to the two-story walls. More importantly, this detail makes the apparent beam depth almost equal to the column, which makes the black lines of the facade of equal width and thus reinforces the sense of a black grid of rectangles with various types of infill. (If the first design was the bridge design, the second might be dubbed the Mondrian.) While this is undoubtedly one of the house's more appealing qualities, it is also achieved at the

7.19

7.20

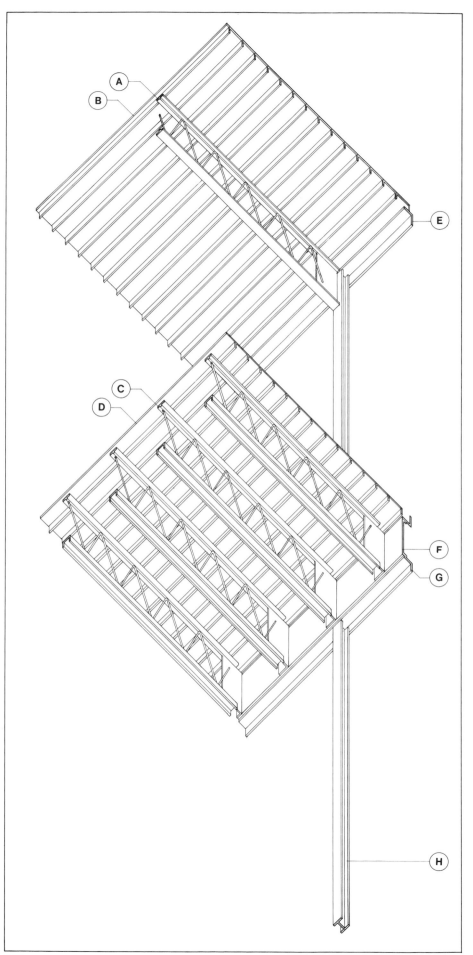

7.21

Eames House, second design

Charles Eames

Pacific Palisades, California, 1948–1949

7.19 **View.**

7.20 **Interior.**
(Julius Shulman)

7.21 **Interior wall section with structure only.**
A OT 125 roof joists 7′ 4″ oc. Since there is one joist per column, no edge beam is required.
B Steel roof deck.
C OT 141 floor joists 1′ 10″ oc. There are more joists at the floor than the roof because of their greater loads.
D Steel floor deck.
E $3 \times 3 \times \frac{1}{4}''$ edge angle for attachment of windows.
F 12 C 10.2 channel transferring floor joist load to column.
G Steel angles at floor to facilitate attachment of windows.
H $4 \times 4'' \times 10$ lb. column.
(LOC DN 4, 5)

7.22 **Interior wall section with finishes.**
A Built-up roof on $1\frac{1}{2}''$ insulation.
B Metal gravel stop.
C Steel window with double-strength glass and opaque panels.
D 2×6 tongue and groove wood floor on metal deck.
E Gypsum wallboard ceiling covering floor joists.
F Steel window frame and opaque panel covering web of edge channel. This effectively hides the largest structural member on the exterior.
G Plaster interior finish and ferroboard metal deck wall. This was changed to or covered with gypsum board or plaster in the finished building.
H Steel window with obscure glass.
(LOC DN B, C, E; UND 3.14.45)

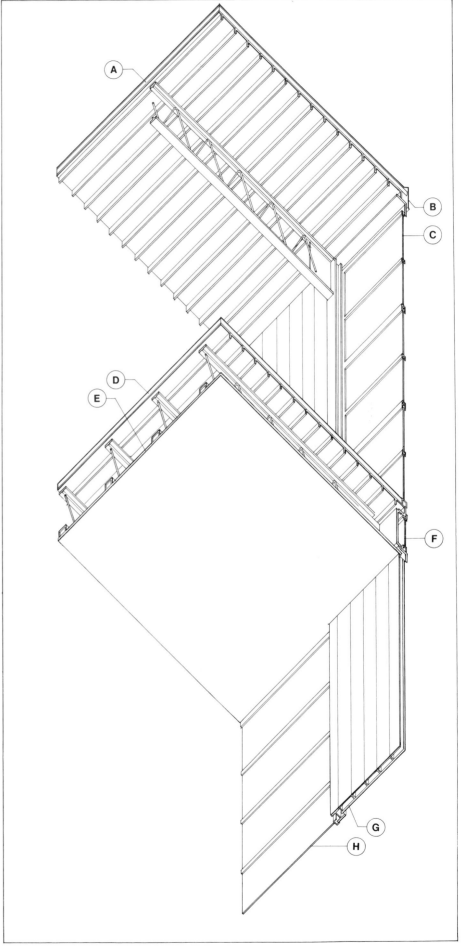

7.22

7.23

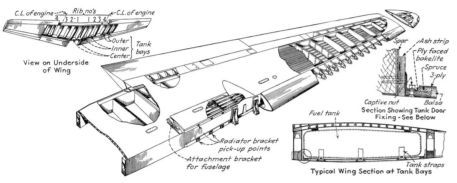

C.L. of engine → ← C.L. of engine
Rib no's
4 3 2 1 1 2 3 4

Outer
Inner
Center

Tank
bays

View on Underside
of Wing

Spar — Ash strip
— Ply faced
bakelite
— Spruce
3-ply

Captive nut — Balsa
Section Showing Tank Door
Fixing - See Below

Radiator bracket
pick-up points

Attachment bracket
for fuselage

Fuel tank

Tank straps

Typical Wing Section at Tank Bays

7.24

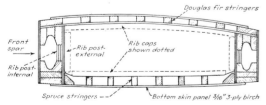

Spruce
edge boom

Top inner skin
¼" 3-ply birch

Top outer skin
¼" 3-ply birch

Continuous stringers
Douglas fir

Spruce
edge boom

Front
spar

Dural connection angles
woodscrewed to spar

Balsa core

3-ply birch skins

Rear
spar

Ash tension
member

Longitudinal
ash tension member

Bottom removable
panel

Section Through Spar Box Near Wing Root

Douglas fir stringers

Front
spar

Rib post-
external

Rib caps
shown dotted

Rib post-
internal

Spruce stringers

Bottom skin panel 3/16" 3-ply birch

Section Through Spar Box Outboard of Removable Panels

Spruce stringers

Front
spar

Spruce stringers

Section Through Spar Box Near Tip

7.25

7.26

7.27

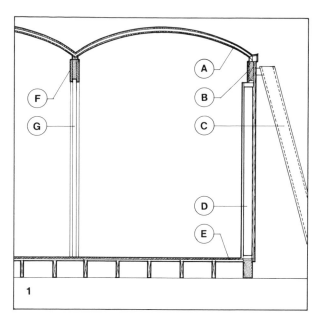

1

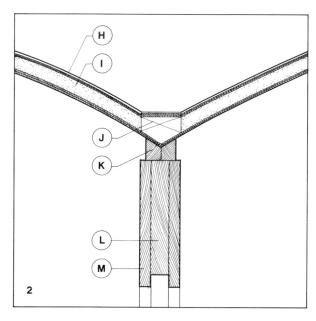

2

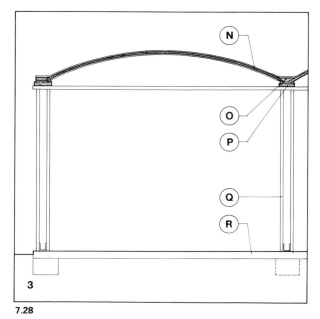

3

7.28

Mosquito

Geoffrey de Havilland

1938–1940

7.23 **View.**

(National Air and Space Museum, Smithsonian Institution, SI Neg. No. 94–8823)

7.24 **Structure.**

(Neville, Aircraft Designer's Data Book*)*

7.25 **Detail.** The typical skin is a sandwich panel of two layers of birch plywood with Douglas fir stringers between.

(Neville, Aircraft Designer's Data Book*)*

7.26 **Hook house,**

Paul Rudolph, Siesta Key, Florida, 1953.

(Paul Rudolph/Ezra Stoller)

7.27 **Sanderling Beach Club,**

Paul Rudolph, Sarasota, Florida, 1952.

(Paul Rudolph/Ezra Stoller)

7.28 **Paul Rudolph, vault sections.**

1 Hook house:

A Plywood vault. Curving the plywood gives it greater strength.

B Edge beam.

C Strut to counteract the lateral thrust of the vault.

D Wall construction.

E Wood floor deck and joists with edge beam.

F Beam.

G Column.

2 Detail:

H ¼" plywood at top and bottom.

I Insulation.

J Blocking.

K Blocking.

L 2 × 10 wood beam.

M Two ¾ × 10½" wood boards.

3 Sanderling Beach Club:

N Built-up roof on two layers of ⅜" plywood glued together, with galvanized iron gravel stop at ridge.

O Wood blocking bolted to plate below.

P 2 × 8 wood plate.

Q Column from two 2 × 4s with steel U support at base.

R 3" concrete slab with 12 × 12" footings.

(PR DN 4)

7.29

7.30

7.31

Case Study House No. 16

Craig Ellwood

Los Angeles, 1952–1953

7.29 View.
(Marvin Rand)

7.30 Under construction.
(Julius Shulman)

7.31 Framing.

A 6 I 12.5 steel beam 8' oc and 2½" square steel column site-welded to beam.

B 2 × 8 wood joists 24" oc. These are concealed in the finished construction.

C Screen from 2½" square steel tubes. The same section is used for the screen as for the columns.

D Steel trellis from 2½" steel tubes.

E Perimeter heating duct below.

F Forced air heating unit.

G Carport.

(CSH, AAR 6.53)

expense of expression of the structure and expression of the internal spatial arrangement. Like many examples of "honest" building, the Eames house goes to considerable effort to hide certain aspects of its construction in order to glorify others.

Pat Kirkham has suggested that as Saarinen's role in the project diminished, Ray Eames's increased, and that as the importance of structural expression receded, the importance of the more painterly aesthetic advanced; but he also suggests that the interest of Ray, the painter, in Mondrian was no less than that of Charles, the architect.[9]

In retrospect, history seems to have assigned to Eames the role of an apostle of prefabrication, a role that he did not reject but did not particularly relish. His primary interest was not in the industrialization of building but the determination of an abstract idea of "good" building under a given set of circumstances. It can be said of the Eames house that it required less than a standard amount of on-site labor. (It cannot be said of Mies van der Rohe's Farnsworth house, which could hardly have required more.) This was at the expense, of course, of considerably more shop labor. Eames claimed that the entire time required for the erection of the frame was 16 hours with a five-man crew and crane. This characteristic, speed of erection, was the argument consistently used by many architects of the day to justify the additional cost of planning, engineering, preparation of shop drawings, and off-site fabrication that steel houses required.

Ironically, the industrialized aspects of the house seemed of little interest to Eames. In fact he thought this attitude something of a mistake. The *Architectural Forum* reported: "An avid reader of catalogues on marine and aviation equipment, he is now sorry he stuck so close to the building industry, neglected several offerings from outside quarters. If he could do it all over again, he might treat this house more as a job of 'product-design,' less of architecture in the traditional sense."[10]

There are other buildings by the Eameses, but they are as obscure and unknown as the Eames house is famous, and in some respects strangely lacking in those qualities that made the house so unique. Their project for a prefabricated house for the Kwikset company (1951) is notable for being their only building that attempts to use the technology of the Eames plywood chairs to architecture. The roof is a vault of single-curved plywood panels supported by glued and laminated beams. They did build a wood house in 1954 for Max De Pree, but it is a heavy-handed reinterpretation of the Eames house in timber.

The Eameses devoted most of their subsequent careers to films and exhibitions, and the closest thing to a replication of the Eames house in their later work is the short segment of film Charles made as the second unit director of Billy Wilder's *The Spirit of St. Louis,* which depicts the building of the plane with shots of bar joist ribs, wood gusset plates, and metal cowlings being installed on the plane. It fell to others to translate the technology of the Eames chairs and the wood technology that grew out of the de Havilland Mosquito into building, notably Paul Rudolph, who had already made far more profitable use of plywood vault technology in several buildings in Florida (figure 7.26). There was one Case Study house to utilize plywood vault technology, Case Study House No. 20, built in 1958 by Buff, Straub, and Hensman.

Although the Eames house is the best known of the Case Study houses, and although Raphael Soriano deserves credit for being one of the first to use steel, it is the houses of Craig Ellwood and Pierre Koenig that, for many, define the movement. Ellwood's life story might have been written by Vasari. In 1947 he was working as a cost estimator for the contractor building the Eames house, and his experiences with Eames underscore his work. Although he had no formal training as an architect, within a year he opened his own firm. In his first Case Study House, No. 16, finished in 1953, Ellwood continued the structural cage and infill system used in other Case Study houses. Although he began the design using steel H sections, he later switched to 2½-inch square steel tubes spaced at 8 feet supporting 6-inch-deep I sections. Only the bottom section of the beams is exposed, the rest of the

7.32

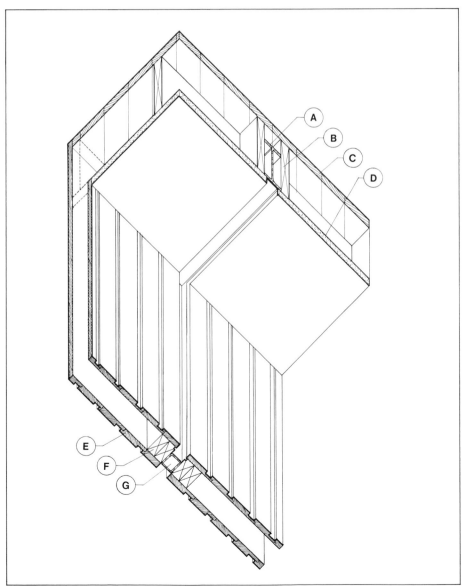

7.33

Case Study House No. 16

Craig Ellwood

Los Angeles, 1952–1953

7.32 Interior.

(Marvin Rand)

7.33 Wall section.

A 6 | 12.5 steel beam punched to receive bolts. Only the bottom flange is visible, which is equal in width to the column.

B 2 × 8 wood joists 24″ oc and 2 × 8 wood blocking bolted to steel beam. The blocking acts as nailers for the wood joists.

C Roofing on 1 × 6 diagonal wood sheathing.

D Plaster ceiling with casing bead.

E 1″ select fir siding with 15 lb. felt on inside of exterior face. Typical practice is to place wood sheathing behind the exterior siding.

F 2 × 4 wood studs attached to bolts welded to steel tube.

G 2½″ square steel tube column covered with 26 gauge flashing on exterior to seal joints.

(CSH, AAR 6.53)

---

roof structure being covered by plaster (figure 7.32). Since the widths of beam and column are the same and since the length of the bays varies from 12 to 24 feet, the effect is a space that appears to be divided by 2½-inch-wide black lines, a spatial or perhaps a graphic arrangement similar to that used by Eames.

The house is industrial primarily in its imagery. It is doubtful that there was less on-site labor than in conventional construction (there was perhaps more), and although the major structural members are steel, there is an almost equal amount of wood framing. The joists spanning across the 8-foot bays are wood 2 × 6s 16 inches apart, completely concealed by the ceiling. Although unquestionably elegant, the visible structure is highly misleading in relation to the real one. In a case of circular logic, Ellwood argued that the use of steel reduced the cost of the house by reducing the size of wood joists required. All structural welding of columns, beams, etc., was done on the site. While there was certainly much preplanning required, there was little prefabrication.

Ellwood did not use the frame to create a true free plan, but filled in between the tubes with panels so that few columns are free standing. In fact he used a large number of additional tubes to support the freestanding partitions, particularly those of glass (figure 7.31). He argued that the tubes were superior to H sections in this regard, that a simple steel plate could attach glass, plywood, etc. Although Ellwood is often associated with Mies, nothing could be less Miesian than this detail. From the Miesian point of view, as the ceiling detail is misleading as to the structure of the house, so is this detail misleading as to what is structure and what is not. There is no clear distinction between the tubes that support the roof and those that support the glass screens, nor is there a distinction between the tube and the stop that holds the glass. Mies went to great lengths to distinguish all these elements—column, beam, window, and glass—as semi-independent elements. Ellwood's system has its own logic, and his intention was not so much ambiguity as simple economy. "Standardization" required all tubes to be the same size, regardless of function. It is more "economical" to make a column function as a window frame as well. It is in fact this ambiguous quality of Ellwood's early work, its messy vitality, that gives it a quality lacking in Mies's Farnsworth house, which although undoubtedly clear contains little mystery.

Ellwood's subsequent Case Study houses clarify some of these issues. Number 17 switched to H sections and achieved a Miesian clarity. Number 18 eliminated on-site welding and returned to square tubes used ambiguously as bracket, buttress, and column, but to Ellwood the loss of clarity is offset by the increase in economy through standardization. He wrote: "With this system, detailing has been minimized. . . . One connection method applies to all in-line exterior wall conditions: panels, glass, sash and sliding door units all attach to structural tubes in the same manner." Ellwood showed an unbounded optimism for the future of industrialized building: "More and more the increasing cost of labor is forcing construction into the factory. Eventually the balloon frame will tend to disappear, and within possibly 10 or 15 years houses will be built from pre-cut and prefabricated components manufactured for fast assembly. Catalogs will offer a choice of metal, wood or plastic structural frames which will be easily and quickly bolted together."[11]

Ellwood's statement seems a bit naive forty years later. Wood framing still makes up 94 percent of the single-family house construction in the United States; most of the remainder is built of concrete masonry with wood joists. The steel house type that has emerged is based almost entirely on sheet metal studs and joists which are essentially wood substitutes having few of the characteristics of Ellwood's large-scale frame and infill system, and in which no more factory labor is used than in a balloon or platform-frame house, which in fact they closely resemble.[12]

Unlike Ellwood, Pierre Koenig trained as an architect, but through his work in Soriano's office and by his own efforts he came into contact with the small-scale steel building industry early on. Like Eames and Ellwood his approach was to apply the techniques of that industry to the single-family house, not to introduce radically different techniques inspired by the aircraft or automobile industries.

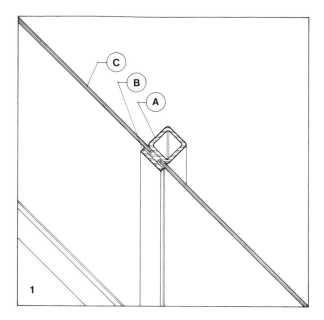

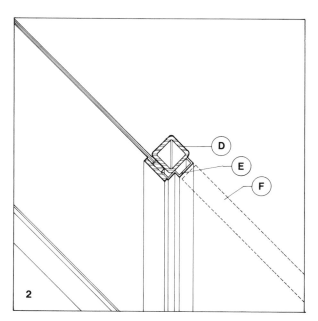

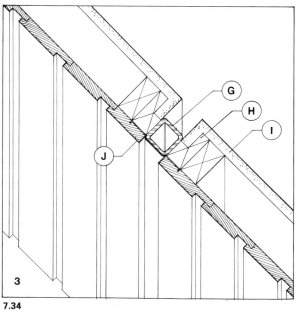

7.34

7.35

Case Study House No. 16

Craig Ellwood

Los Angeles, 1952–1953

7.34 Column details.

1 Glass screen:

A 2½″ square steel tube column.

B 2½″ cover plate.

C Glass.

2 Door jamb:

D 2½″ square steel tube column.

E Sheet metal door frame.

F Door.

3 Exterior wall:

G 2½″ square steel tube column faced
with metal flashing on exterior.

H Wood stud.

I Plaster.

J 1″ vertical shiplap fir siding.
(CSH, AAR 6.53)

7.35 Glass screen.

His first Case Study house, Number 21, is one of the purest in terms of the ideas of the day as to what constituted industrialization. Structural sizes and spans were not only standardized but used the elements to their maximum spans. It minimized, if it did not eliminate, on-site welding. The main structure is a series of steel U shapes 9 feet by 22 or 44 feet, consisting of two or three 4-inch H columns and 8-inch-deep beams spaced 10 feet apart. The U's were shop-welded, and the elements connecting them, channels at the floor and roof, were welded at the site. It is also one of the purest Case Study houses in structural expression. The span between the frames is accomplished by steel deck. There are no wood joists, no ceiling, and the entire steel structure is exposed. The only structural elements not visible are the studs supporting the exterior wall, which are not structural in the conventional sense of the term. Koenig's column is an H rather than a tube and at 4 inches is twice the size of Ellwood's. It interfaces with the infill components in different ways as well. The exterior wall is made of the same steel deck as is the roof and is set into the flanges of the H column (figure 7.39). The interior plaster finish is stopped at the column edge as in Ellwood's detail, so that the column is visible from the interior and exterior.

If Koenig's Case Study House No. 22 is perhaps not so pure in its geometry, it did provide the movement with its most memorable images, Julius Shulman's night views showing glass box and pool suspended above the lights of a distant city. Like Ellwood, Koenig used the recently introduced long-span steel deck to eliminate purlins or joists—a 5-inch-deep deck that would span 20 feet, then as now approaching the maximum span for this type of construction. Although it lacks the formal regularity of its predecessor, the steel frame of Number 22 is likewise completely exposed.

John Entenza sold *Arts and Architecture* in 1962, although the Case Study House program continued until 1966. Craig Ellwood's house commissions grew into a practice that included a number of larger commercial and institutional buildings, but they have little of the spirit and spatial and material richness of his houses. Finally in the 1980s he gave up architecture for painting and moved to Italy, where he died in 1992. Koenig has continued to build steel houses, expanding the themes of his earlier work. The fate of the Case Study legacy is sadly illustrated by the fate of Ellwood's Case Study House No. 17, which was redecorated with Classical elements in 1962. Charles and Ray Eames went on to international success as filmmakers and designers of furniture and exhibitions, but it was a practice that included few buildings. The Eames house stands, like Chareau's Maison de Verre and Rietveld's Schröder-Schräder house, as one of the unique and puzzling masterpieces of Modern architecture.

The Case Study architects were not alone in their desire to revive the dream of mass-produced housing, or at least a housing that exploited the new technologies of aircraft and automobiles. Almost simultaneously with the beginnings of the Case Study House program, a similar effort was under way in an unlikely location, Wichita, Kansas, where Buckminster Fuller was developing the prototype for the Dymaxion house, a concept that had already gone through several metamorphoses over two decades.

BUCKMINSTER FULLER

Like Henri Farman, Starling Burgess was a pioneer aviator and aircraft manufacturer. Unlike Farman he was well established in another profession before he began his career in aviation. The son of one of the premier racing yacht designers of the nineteenth century, he was well on his way to becoming the same for the twentieth century when he began designing and manufacturing airplanes in 1909. His most successful design was a modified version of the Dunne Flying Wing, but after a career of mixed success in designing planes for the Gordon Bennett Races, he returned to yacht design. His designs included three America's Cup defenders, beginning with *Enterprise* in 1930.

In 1932, not long after his success with *Enterprise*, Burgess attended an exhibition of Buckminster Fuller's first (1927) Dymaxion house in New York, where he met

7.40

7.40 **Case Study House No. 22,**
Pierre Koenig, Los Angeles, 1959–
1960. Number 22 uses a deeper
metal deck than No. 21 to achieve a
longer span.
(Julius Shulman)

the designer. Although Burgess was 17 years older than Fuller, their backgrounds were remarkably similar. Both had attended Milton Academy, both had dropped out of Harvard, both had served in the Navy, and both had a lifelong interest in the design of boats and planes. It was an opportune meeting. A short time later the owner of the Bath Ironworks, a major shipyard, offered Fuller the use of his shop and equipment to build the Dymaxion house, provided Fuller could obtain financing. To Fuller, who did not always follow through in the development of his ideas, Burgess would be the ideal collaborator.[13]

That Fuller, Burgess, and the shipyard were interested in one another is not surprising, for what Fuller was attempting to do with the first Dymaxion house was to apply the principles of vehicular design and construction to buildings. He wrote in his autobiography: "What hit me very hard was that the building world was thousands of years behind the art of designing ships of the sea and air. On land, for instance, the thicker and heavier walls were constructed, the more secure people felt—exactly the opposite of doing more with less. At sea and in the sky you had to do it more with less."[14]

The Dymaxion house in its 1927 version (figure 7.44) was intended to correct these defects, to achieve minimal material and minimum weight through the use of the appropriate structural system. He wrote of its variation, the 4D tower: "Conventional buildings, constructed stone on stone, are almost completely compression structures and weigh as much as when they built the pyramids. The 4D Tower House was stressed like airplanes, with compression and tension parts separated out-again, of continuous tension and discontinuous compression, with compression islands floating in a tension web."[15] The house is based on two simple structural principles. The first was the resolution of structural loads into tension and compression rather than bending (the action in a typical beam). While there is no evidence that Fuller ever read Viollet-le-Duc, it is not surprising that he arrived at the same conclusion as the followers of the French historian, given the examples of the suspension bridge and the early airplane as models of the compression-tension form of structure. The second principle was the triangulation of the structural frame, triangles being inherently more stable than rectangles.

The design of the house, however, was far closer to the airplanes of the 1920s than to those of 1930. Its tension cables were exposed; its exterior sheet metal skin followed the triangular pattern of its structure. In 1945 Fuller explained many of the house's characteristics in terms of the limited technology of the time—that stainless steel and aluminum were not available, that the cost of curving sheet metal was prohibitive, and that the low tensile strength of the steel used necessitated that the tension members be kept toward the vertical, which placed them outside the building envelope. Nevertheless the results in terms of structural expression are in principle, if not in form, what an architect trained in Gothic Revival principles might expect. The structure is exposed and the exterior envelope conforms to the frame in shape.

Unfortunately, the financing for the 1927 house never materialized and Burgess never worked on the design. Nevertheless Fuller and Burgess formed a partnership and did secure financing for another Fuller project, the Dymaxion car. They obtained a small factory in Bridgeport, where the car was designed and several prototypes built simultaneously with a Burgess yacht design.

Fuller's initial design for the car adhered to certain basic principles. The outside was aerodynamically shaped for minimum drag, and the structure was to obtain maximum strength with minimum material, however complex the result. These were the basic criteria of aircraft and ship design and, to Fuller, of any design. A third principle, stability through triangulation, was less rigidly adhered to as Burgess began to develop the design.

Fuller's conceptual sketch had called for a triangular wheel base and a triangular, apparently tubular frame. As Burgess developed the idea the frame became far more complex and empirical in design. The internal frame of chrome-molybdenum aircraft steel is angled, curved, and tapered to meet individual conditions, mostly to

7.41

7.42

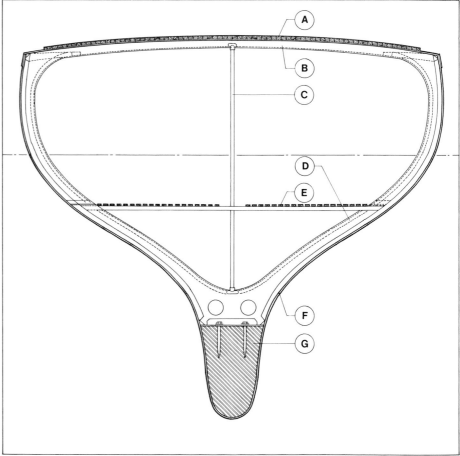

7.43

Enterprise

W. Starling Burgess

1930

7.41 **View.**

(© Rosenfeld Collection, Mystic Seaport Museum, Inc.)

7.42 **Interior.**

(© Rosenfeld Collection, Mystic Seaport Museum, Inc.)

7.43 **Section.**

A 2½″ white pine deck planking.

B Deck beams amidships from pairs of 3″ × 1¾″ × 6.7 lb angles and plates 24″ oc forming the main ribs of the hull structure.

C 2¼″ hollow tube .275″ thick.

D Frames with 9½″ × .22″ webs with flanges from two angles, 24″ oc.

E ⅞″ white pine slats to form cabin floor.

F Strakes .23–.25″ thick riveted to beams to form hull.

G Cast lead keel attached with bronze keel bolts.

(MIT Museum, Hart Nautical Collection, Herreshoff/Paine Collection)

7.44 **4D Dymaxion house (project),**
R. Buckminster Fuller, 1927.
(© 1994 Allegra Fuller Snyder, courtesy Buckminster Fuller Institute, Santa Barbara)

7.45 **Dymaxion car frame,**
R. Buckminster Fuller and W. Starling Burgess, 1933–1934. Note the wood framing of the body and the tapered steel beam with punched-out webs connecting the wheels and engine, the radiator of which is visible.
(© 1960 Allegra Fuller Snyder, courtesy Buckminster Fuller Institute, Santa Barbara)

7.44

7.45

7.46

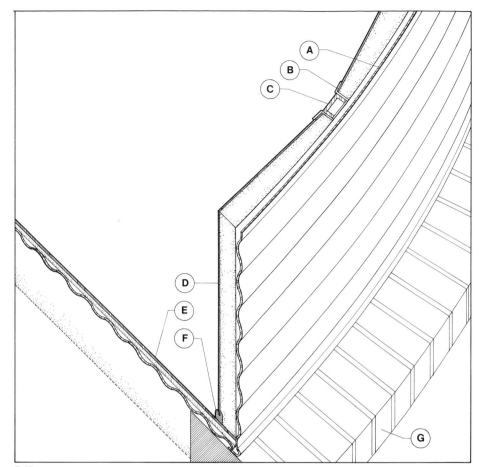

7.47

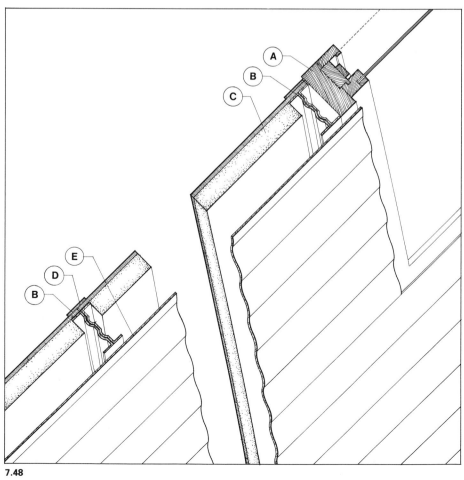

7.48

Dymaxion Deployment Unit

R. Buckminster Fuller

1940–1941

7.46   View.

(© 1960 Allegra Fuller Snyder, courtesy Buckminster Fuller Institute, Santa Barbara)

7.47   Wall detail.

A   20 gauge corrugated metal siding. Corrugating the metal makes a thinner sheet stronger.

B   Wall channel trim strip.

C   Channel with keyholes to receive shelving units holding Masonite in place with ¼ × ½" stove bolts, waterproofed with asphaltic emulsion.

D   ³⁄₁₆" or ⅛" Masonite or presswood panels with 2" Celotex insulation glued to back.

E   Floor of 20 gauge corrugated metal with ⅛" Masonite and ½" insulation board.

F   Rubber molding.

G   Sand and brick foundation below. This is a foundation system that is both heavy and "wet," which Fuller avoided in other designs.

(BFI DN 7, 1-127)

Quonset hut

U.S. Navy

1941

7.48   Wall detail. There were several versions of the Quonset hut of varying diameter. This is the 1944 version manufactured by the Stran Steel Division of the Great Lakes Corporation.

A   Wood window frame with plastic glazing and insect screen.

B   Nailable double steel arch rib. Width varies to span 20'. Unlike the Dymaxion Deployment Unit, the Quonset hut had a frame and non-bearing skin.

C   Insulation held in place with wood blocking.

D   Masonite interior finish with 2" Masonite batten nailed with 6d nails 8" oc.

E   Corrugated galvanized iron siding with corrugated asphalt filler strip to close ends of corrugation.

(AF 2.44)

carry the weight of the engine and driver to the three wheels. The webs of its I-shaped members are hollowed out, giving it a close resemblance to an aircraft frame, but the shell of the car was another matter. Built of plywood sheets reinforced with wood ribs, it had little formal similarity to the steel frame that it covered, while it did have a close resemblance to the hull of the cruising racing sloop Burgess was constructing in the same space. Each of these complex elements had a single purpose, maximum strength with minimum weight and material.

If the rigid adherence to principles of aircraft and ship design is a notable quality of the car, another is equally notable: its deviation from the principles of architectural design. The frame is not expressed, and the outside shell of the car is completely unrelated to the frame that supports it. In his short description of the car, Burgess's concern is solely with its aerodynamics:

First of all the Dymaxion is supremely different from any vehicle of the land that has ever gone before. It is more of a change from the automobile as we know it than was ever taken from ship to ship in the whole science of naval architecture.

So complete is the Dymaxion's streamlining that literally nothing protrudes from the surface other than the segments of her three wheels, her cooling scoops, and her periscope. Her form is cleaner than the best of submarines; compared with which the ordinary automobile is to the resistant air as a dragging fish net is to the sea.[16]

This concern with the shell and indifference to expression of external structure is not surprising coming from the designer of the *Enterprise*. While the aluminum mast superstructure of the *Enterprise* represents the exposed structure par excellence, the steel frame and sheet hull demonstrates the principle of independence of internal structure and external shape.

The Dymaxion car never saw mass production and the Fuller-Burgess partnership ended unhappily. Burgess went on to design the greatest of his J-boat series, *Ranger.* Fuller returned to the problem of mass-produced housing, but took with him a different attitude toward the relationship of structure and form after his experience with Burgess. The idea of mass production suggested the analogy of the car, but this, like everything else, was to Fuller a question of weight, for whom the key to industrialization was not just standardization but minimum weight as well: "I could already see then that if everyone was to get high quality shelter, houses must be mass-produced industrially, in large quantities, like automobiles. At the time it cost little more per pound than a Ford did, or a Chevrolet—installed for living—through the use of mass-production techniques. And I could see that we might really be able to do more with less."[17]

In 1940 Fuller introduced his first and only housing scheme actually to be mass-produced. The Butler Company was a manufacturer of prefabricated agricultural buildings, in particular of a circular galvanized steel grain bin with a conical roof that varied in diameter from 10 feet to 20 feet. Fuller convinced Butler to investigate the conversion of these units to emergency housing, and thus the Dymaxion Deployment Unit (DDU) was born. Historians have stressed the similarity between the DDU and the Dymaxion house: its circular form, its metal skin, its central opening for ventilation, and its method of erection by means of a central mast. Equally important are the differences between the two. The DDU had no frame, and the curved steel panels are the actual structure, unlike either of the Dymaxion houses, which use structural frames with curtain wall skins. Fuller's modifications to the Butler unit included a roof of segmented panels to simplify erection and lining the inside of the corrugated steel with insulation-backed Masonite panels held in place by shelving brackets. The floor was of similar construction: Masonite panels on insulation board and metal deck.

Fuller said of the DDU what many Modern architects were saying about their structures, that they achieved economy of material by exploiting the primary structural characteristics of the material: "The solution consists of employment of light sheet steel in its most efficient design form, i.e. curved;—involves only conversion of

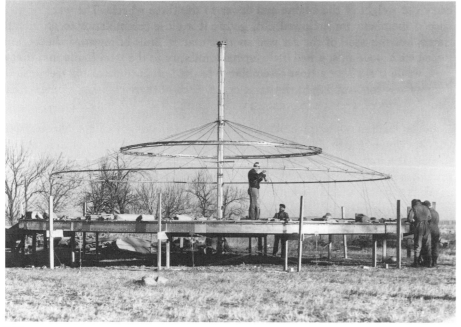

7.49

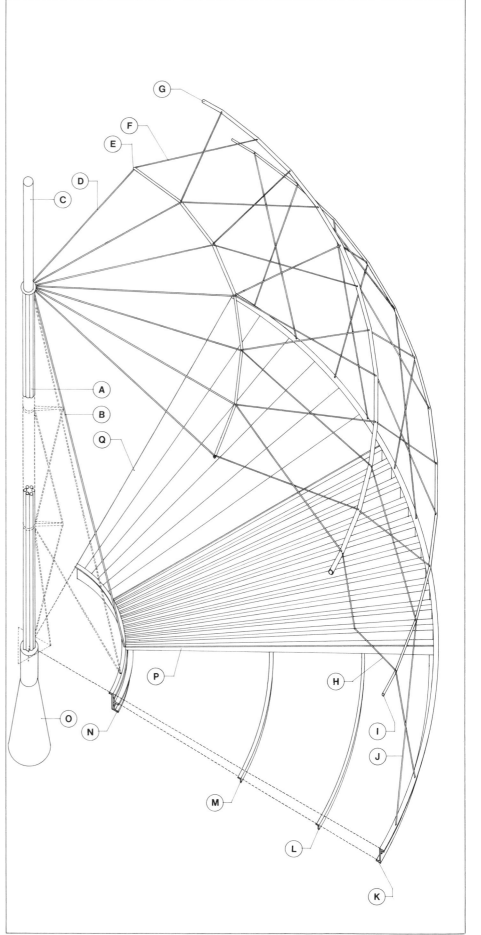

7.50

Dymaxion house

R. Buckminster Fuller

Wichita, Kansas, 1944–1946

(Currently being reconstructed in the
Henry Ford Museum & Greenfield
Village)

7.49   Under construction.

(© 1960 Allegra Fuller Snyder, courtesy
Buckminster Fuller Institute, Santa
Barbara)

7.50   Wall section showing frame only.
There were five different prototype
houses, with variations on some of
the assemblies shown here.

A   Mast of six 2⅛″ tubes bound in a
cluster.

B   Inner cable mast bracing.

C   Mast extension.

D   ⁵⁄₁₆″ chrome moly steel rod cables.

E   A ring 1″ corrosion-resistant steel
tube with .035″ wall spliced with ¾″
tubes.

F   ¼″ chrome moly steel rod cables.

G   B ring 1½″ corrosion-resistant steel
tube with .058″ wall spliced with
1⅜″ tubes.

H   ³⁄₁₆″ chrome moly steel rod cable.

I   C ring 1″ corrosion-resistant steel
tube with .035″ wall spliced with ¾″
tubes.

J   ³⁄₁₆″ chrome moly steel rod cable.
The rods decrease in diameter as
the load decreases.

K   Outer deck ring of two 2½ × 2 ×
¼″ aluminum angles and .064 ×
7¾″ aluminum plate. There were
two versions of this component,
one using rolled sections and one
using braked sheet metal.

L   2 × 2 × ¼″ aluminum angle floor
beam support.

M   2 × 2 × ¼″ aluminum angle floor
beam support.

N   Inner deck ring of three 2½ × 2 ×
¼″ aluminum angles and ¼ × 7½″
aluminum plate with ¼″ splice
plates.

O   Concrete foundation.

P   R-301-T aluminum floor sections.

Q   Five-ply fir plywood.

(BFI/AF UND Artifacts of R. Buckminster
Fuller, *p. 127, Henry Ford Museum &*
Greenfield Village)

galvanized (or painted) steel grain bins, which encompass not only ample volume of space for ready adaptation to dwelling units—but also the maximum cubage mathematically possible of enclosure for dwelling purposes with the least possible material."[18]

All of the DDUs produced were sold to the Army, which used them for temporary housing for aircraft mechanics in Alaska and the Persian Gulf. Then, according to Fuller, production was stopped, due to the fact that the steel required was reserved for more strategic uses. Given wartime conditions this seems credible, but the fact remains that the humble Quonset hut, manufactured of the same corrugated steel, was produced on a much larger scale during and after the war. One might ask whether, given the Army's criteria or even Fuller's, the Quonset hut was not a better solution. The Butler units did not exceed 20 feet in diameter, presumably because this was the upper limit of self-supporting curved steel panels. If more floor area was needed, and it often was since a 20-foot circle contains only 314 square feet, two or more units had to be combined. The Quonset hut panels were not self-supporting, but used curved ribs made from back-to-back sheet metal C channels, giving it a structural if not necessarily an economic advantage and enabling it to span from 28 up to 40 feet.[19] The Quonset hut with its single curvature and rectilinear plan could provide the same space as two DDUs with less material, and allow for more flexible room arrangements as well. The military in fact was dissatisfied with the curved cross section of the Quonset Hut, and Butler, without Fuller, produced a rectangular model of similar dimensions.

Fuller's next steps were predictable: first to develop a frame for the DDU to make possible a larger unit, and then, if steel was not available, to do what the aircraft industry was doing, build in plywood. Neither the framed nor the plywood DDU was ever produced, but the approach of the end of the war brought Fuller a far more promising endeavor. In 1944 he was given the gift, or perhaps the curse, offered to few visionaries, the opportunity to implement his ideas. He was asked by the International Association of Machinists to produce a design for an industrialized house to be manufactured by the Beech Aircraft Company of Wichita, Kansas, to go into production at the end of the war.

The euphoria for industrialized building of 1942 had given way to something else by 1944, at least in the aircraft industry: the fear that the end of the war would bring factory closings and unemployment. The proposal for the Beech factory was not an exercise in public relations but a genuine desire on the part of labor and management to survive by conversion to mass production housing. The result was an updated version of the Dymaxion house, sometimes called the Wichita house. Conceptually it follows the first Dymaxion house of 1927, employing a central mast for structure and the use of steel both in tension and in triangular configurations, but its form, particularly its external form, was modified heavily, in part to conform to the techniques of aircraft production, but also to conform to the principles of aircraft design.

By this point Fuller was articulating what has become a central philosophy of High Tech Modernism: the linkage of minimal material and minimum weight to maximum industrial efficiency. He wrote in 1946: "So you will find that throughout the whole world of industry the basic economic or accounting unit, or constant, is the pound."[20] Perhaps because of the cost of transport, perhaps because strength per unit was so crucial in airplane and automobile design, Fuller became convinced that minimal weight was the key to the economics of mass production, regardless of the cost of the material or the complexity of the design.

Thus the form of the Wichita house adhered rigidly to certain criteria: (1) the achievement of minimum weight through minimum use of material; (2) the minimization of air resistance on the exterior both by means of its shape and by the nature of the connections (e.g., the cables are concealed within the construction and the panels fastened with flush rivets); (3) enclosure of maximum volume with minimum surface; (4) the use of tolerances far less than those usually found in building construction. Other conventional industrial criteria were applied as well:

7.51

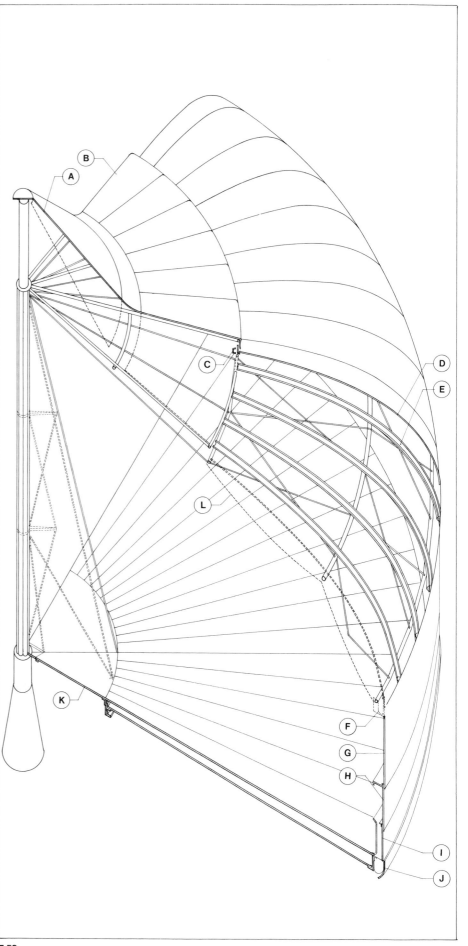

7.52

Dymaxion house

R. Buckminster Fuller

Wichita, Kansas, 1944–1946

7.51 **View.**

(© 1994 Allegra Fuller Snyder, courtesy Buckminster Fuller Institute, Santa Barbara)

7.52 **Wall section with finish panels.**

A Ventilation cowling supported by ¾″ ring tube of 24 ST aluminum. There were two versions of this, one of trapezoidal sections, the other formed from a single sheet cut in a spiral. All aluminum sheet is 24 ST.

B Lower cowling skin.

C Gasket to seal cowling.

D Gore cowlings of .020″ aluminum alloy R-301-T at same spacing as ring segments.

E C-shaped rib supporting gore. This intercepts any water that penetrates the joint and carries it to the gutter.

F Gutter, window head, and trim. The construction at this point is uncertain.

G ¹⁄₁₆″ Plexiglas.

H Sliding .025″ sidewall skin for ventilation.

I .025″ sidewall skin.

J Gutter attached to outer deck ring.

K Floor of five-ply fir plywood.

L Inner skin of neoprene-backed glass cloth.

(BFI/AF ID-1 2.27.46, UND Artifacts of R. Buckminster Fuller, p. 127, Henry Ford Museum & Greenfield Village)

minimization of on-site labor and elimination of "craft" (that is, less accurate) trades such as masonry, carpentry, etc. Also as in aircraft design, the accommodation of other, more standard architectural criteria—efficiency of internal arrangement, adaptation to site through manipulation of form or fenestration, even internal privacy—are all secondary to these goals.

The house consists of a steel frame enclosed by an outer aluminum shell and an inner shell of lightweight nonmetallic elements with a layer of insulating foil between. The frame is suspended from a central mast of stainless steel tubes and consists of compression rings of round tubes or channels hung by triangulated tension cables (figure 7.50). Like Fuller's previous structures, it attempts to reduce structural forces to tension and compression while minimizing bending stresses. A primary concern was not only the use of tension, but, insofar as possible, the minimizing of foundations. Conventional foundations would have required, as in the DDU, either masonry, a craft system, or concrete, a wet one. Both for Fuller were taboo.

The inner and outer shells are nonbearing, and are designed in different configurations according to their span and location. The exterior envelope design is based on the principle of keeping the surface absolutely smooth, and thus the outer panels above the level of the windows are smooth aluminum trapezoidal segments (gores) reinforced at their joints with aluminum sheets bent into semicircular shapes (carlings). The inner shell was originally to be supported by W-shaped ribs. In the patent drawings these were to be sheets of plastic or plywood. In the mock-up the inner carlings were eliminated and a tent of fibrous neoprene made up the inner ceiling. The lower exterior wall panels are simply curved aluminum sheets .025 inch thick fastened to the supporting rings and to Z-shaped rings that make up the window sill. Some of these could slide horizontally to allow for ventilation in conjunction with a rotating roof ventilator. Since the triangulated support cables must pass through these supports at various angles, the wall takes on a rather complex configuration. The floor is made in analogous fashion. The bottom layer is assembled of pie-shaped aluminum sheets in W-like corrugations onto which plywood sheets are laid, held down by metal battens. The continuous strip window is Plexiglas, riveted together at its vertical joints. Plexiglas is lighter, more flexible, and less easily broken than glass and was the principal material in aircraft glazing at the time. It has the distinct disadvantages of flammability and short life.

Like most prefabricators and aircraft designers, Fuller wanted a dry construction, and the joints, insofar as possible, are all made without caulking, many with gaskets or clips. Isolators, "dielectric gaskets," were used to prevent contact between the steel and aluminum, which in the presence of water and acid rain are subject to deterioration through electrolytic action. Rather than attempting perfect watertightness, the grooves in the outer carlings were put to use as gutters for any water that leaked through the joints (figure 7.52), and the outer wall has circular U-shaped internal gutters at the top and bottom to collect water off the wall surface and whatever leaks through the joints. The water was to be drawn off and drained to a cistern for reuse.

Extensive wind tunnel tests were made on the model, in part to test the extensive provisions for natural ventilation and in part to locate any pockets of air pressure that would be generated by high winds. Fuller stated correctly that the main cause of leaks in buildings is differential air pressure between interior and exterior, and that by eliminating these one could eliminate leaks. In this he anticipated the rain screen principle of design frequently utilized today. In fact every detail seems to have the goal of creating the aerodynamically perfect shell. Hence the concealed gutters, the flush rivets, and the total concealment of the cable structure by the aluminum shell. But the overriding reason for this obsession with aerodynamics seems to be that it is a primary concern in aircraft design.

With his flair for the dramatic, Fuller brought Marian Anderson to Wichita to "test the acoustics" of the house. What precisely was being tested is not recorded—that one of the most powerful contraltos in America could be heard 40 feet away? That

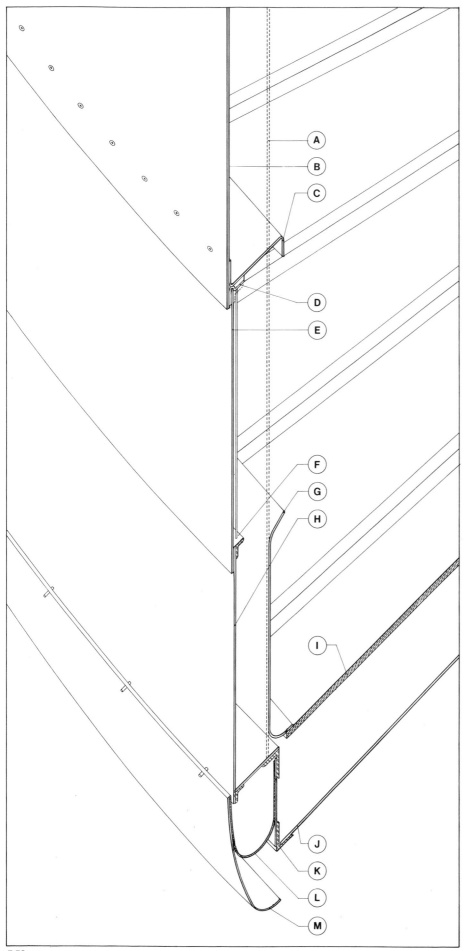

Dymaxion house

R. Buckminster Fuller

Wichita, Kansas, 1944–1946

7.53 **Wall section at base.**

A Cable (at angle).

B ¹⁄₁₆″ Plexiglas window.

C Window sill.

D Clip for sliding skin.

E Sliding sidewall skin. All aluminum sheet is .025″ 24 ST. This, along with the rotating cowling at the top, provides for ventilation.

F Cable and clip for sliding skin.

G Inner aluminum wall.

H Sidewall skin.

I Five-ply fir plywood sound one side.

J R-301-T aluminum floor support.

K Outer deck ring of two rolled or bent angles and plate.

L Gutter.

M Aluminum gutter cowling.
  (BFI/AFI CDS-2 8.8.45, Henry Ford Museum & Greenfield Village)

the interior, with its ceiling and walls of light fabric, was totally lacking in acoustic privacy? The only benefit would seem to be to demonstrate the absence of focusing echoes that a dome would inevitably produce.

Fuller explained the transformation of the house from its 1927 prototype in pragmatic terms. Stainless steel made it possible for the tension members to be more horizontal, bringing them inside the building envelope. Aircraft tools made possible the double curvature of the aluminum sheet exterior, greatly strengthening the sheet in the process as well as minimizing its weight. Yet Fuller had clearly abandoned the more conventional architectural qualities of the 1927 house—exposed structure and the coincidence of exterior envelope and frame—in favor of the vehicular principles used in the Dymaxion car—concealed frame with frame and skin formally independent of each other, each seeking its own shape according to its specific function.

It is difficult, although by no means impossible, to fault the internal logic of the Wichita house. It does enclose the maximum space with the minimum envelope, being roughly a half sphere. It does achieve a maximum structure with a minimum weight of material through steel tension cables and curved and braked aluminum sheets. It does minimize the quantity of on-site labor. One might well ask whether, industrialization or no industrialization, these are the criteria of rational building. Is it logical to sacrifice convenience of room arrangement in favor of minimal aerodynamic resistance? Is it logical to achieve minimum weight at the expense of acoustic privacy? (Fuller's argument, of course, would be that we accept all these things when we travel in a Pullman car, so why not in a house?) And then, does minimum weight really equal minimum expense? In the building industry as it presently exists, the actual cost of material in place may or may not be directly related to weight. Structural steel is often purchased by the ton, concrete by the cubic yard. At the same time while an aluminum curtain wall may be as little as one-thirtieth the weight of a masonry wall, its cost may be less than, equal to, or, if it is a sophisticated design, ten times as much as the masonry wall. Weight and structural strength per unit weight are only two of a number of factors, not necessarily the primary ones, in determining cost.

This is not a logic Fuller would have accepted. The conventional values of building were to him a reflection of the misplaced values of society. He was no more a pragmatist than John Ruskin or William Morris. In addition to all the other things these men were, they were critics not just of architecture, of construction, of style, but of the societies in which they lived. Fuller quoted Theodore Larsen in *Arts and Architecture:* "The proper activity of the architect-engineer is purposeful. It is not to devise a better society so as to arrive at finer architecture; it is to provide a better architecture in order to arrive at a more desirable society."[21]

In the *Grunch of Giants,* Fuller wrote that the Wichita house failed because of external resistance: the refusal of banks to finance the houses, the unwillingness of lenders to provide the tooling-up costs. But Fuller had 37,000 advance orders, the Army had already purchased the first two prototypes, and the Beech company was anxious to proceed. Martin Pawley in his biography of Fuller argued the contrary, that Fuller contributed to the demise of the project by delaying the start of production.

Whatever the reasons, the effort would probably eventually have failed in any case in the long term, for it was only the most interesting of many such projects of the time. The Consolidated Vultee Aircraft Corporation undertook a similar proposal, the Vultee house, designed by Edward Barnes and Henry Dreyfuss, which made extensive use of sandwich panels. Lockheed investigated its own housing proposal. In 1944 Kaiser Aluminum proposed the manufacture of a component system of 50 types of aluminum panels for prefab houses. In Britain the Aircraft Industries Research Organization for Housing produced the AIROH house, fabricated from aluminum components by aircraft manufacturers. The most conspicuous of these projects and the most successful was the all-steel Lustron house, of which 2,500 were manufactured before that company's demise. These efforts had few significant

7.54

7.55

R-100 Airship

Barnes Wallis

1930

7.54 **Interior.**
(National Air and Space Museum, Smithsonian Institution, SI Neg. No. 94-7907)

7.55 **Lounge.** The novelist Nevil Shute, who was Wallis's chief assistant, is standing on the landing.
(National Air and Space Museum, Smithsonian Institution, SI Neg. No. 94-7911)

short-term and no long-term results. Neither Kaiser, Lockheed, Consolidated Vultee, nor AIROH ever produced metal houses in quantity, and all soon abandoned these efforts for other endeavors. The Lustron Company eventually ceased production in 1950. The cause was not so much a failure of the factory house as it was the success of other enterprises: most of these manufacturers found other more accessible markets for their services after the war, in larger-scale building components or the manufacture of cars or planes.

While Saarinen, Eames, Rapson, and Soriano all abandoned the airplane as a literal construction model in favor of Miesian clarity, commercial steel building techniques, or minimal abstraction, Fuller persisted, and aircraft technology continued to inform his work. After the collapse of the Dymaxion house project he joined Black Mountain College, where he began to develop the construction with which he is most identified, the geodesic dome. Despite Fuller's lengthy analysis of the idea of the geodesic dome, it may have a far more direct source of formal inspiration in aircraft design, specifically "geodetic" aircraft design.

Geodetic construction had been a well-established practice in aircraft design for some time, although it was certainly not common. It originated in the design of airships, specifically the first of the Schütte-Lanz ships of the early 1900s, but its best-known applications were those of Barnes Wallis, one of the chief designers of the British aircraft manufacturer Vickers. In the late 1920s Wallis had applied similar principles to the design of the airship R-100. (If minimum weight is a primary feature of aircraft design, it is the central criterion in airship design.) In order to hold the gas bags in place, Wallis designed a series of crisscrossing cables laid out on the principle of the geodetic, the shortest distance between two points on a curved surface. In the 1930s he applied the idea to aircraft frames, first in the Wellesley, and later, most prominently, in the Wellington bomber (figure 7.57). This was made of a lattice of braked C sections. As explained in the *Encyclopedia of Aviation:*

A geodetic, (strictly, a "geodesic") is the shortest line that can be drawn between two points on a curved surface. Wallis saw that an aeroplane can be made with fairly regular surface curvature all over, and he developed a metal basketwork in which the entire airframe is assembled from quite small geodetic members pinned together at the joints (structurally called nodes, because the loads are applied only at the nodes). Each member experiences pure tension, as a tie, or pure compression, as a strut, with no bending load at all. All of the flight loads could be carried wholly within this basketwork lying in the surface (thus forming a kind of monocoque), though spars and longerons were added to take the bending loads, because the unsupported basketwork could be bent an unacceptable amount.[22]

The similarity of the first geodesic dome to the construction of the Wellington goes well beyond the basic structural principle of pure tension and pure compression to the methods of joinery and fabrication, which are similar and in some cases identical. The early domes Fuller built in North Carolina were small makeshift assemblies, using materials such as venetian blind slats. His first commission for a large-scale dome called for more sophisticated techniques, and the formal similarities would indicate that these may have come from Wallis's work.

The object of this commission, the Ford Rotunda, has a curious history. In 1933 Henry Ford asked Albert Kahn to design an exhibition pavilion for Ford cars at the Century of Progress Exhibition in Chicago. The building, meant to suggest the form of a gear wheel, was a series of concentric cylinders with serrated walls, supported by a light steel frame. Although the building was probably meant to be temporary since it is open at the top and the steel is unprotected, Ford decided to reconstruct it, and after the exhibition it was moved to Dearborn (outside the Rouge Plant) and reassembled. Twenty years later Henry Ford II decided to cover it over, but this presented considerable problems, as the structure, underdesigned to begin with, was incapable of supporting the weight of a steel roof. Since this was a problem that called for minimal material and minimum weight, Fuller, his theories, and his methods seemed an ideal answer.

7.56

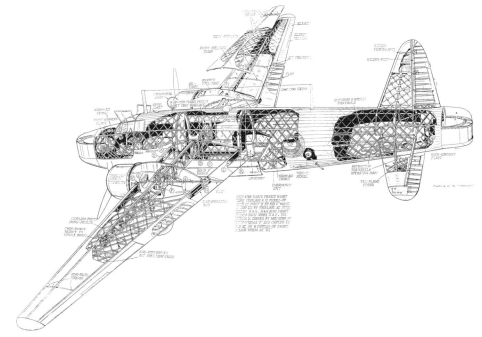

7.57

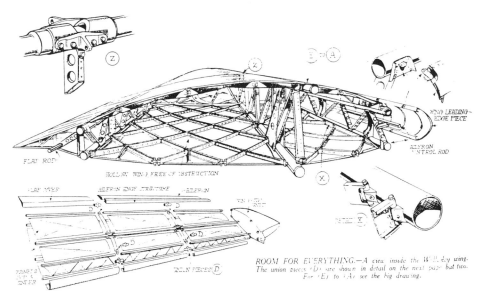

ROOM FOR EVERYTHING.—A view inside the W.B. dry wing.
The union pieces 'D' are shown in detail on the next page but two.
For 'E' to 'A' see the big drawing.

7.58

Wellington bomber

Barnes Wallis

1937

7.56 **View.**
(National Air and Space Museum, Smithsonian Institution, SI Neg. No. 94-7908)

7.57 **Structure.**
(Aeroplane 7.5.39)

7.58 **Barnes Wallis,** Wellesley bomber, 1937, wing structure.
(Aeroplane 12.7.38)

7.59 **Rouge Ford Plant,**
Albert Kahn, Dearborn, Michigan, 1917–1938. Albert Kahn's Rotunda, which was covered with Buckminster Fuller's first large-scale geodesic dome in 1953, is visible in the foreground.
(Henry Ford Museum & Greenfield Village, P.99210-90)

7.59

For his first large-scale geodesic dome Fuller utilized both the experiences of Black Mountain College and the methods of aircraft manufacture. The dome is not a pure sphere but is composed of triangular segments, each of which in turn is composed of another Fuller invention, the octet truss. Construction began with a series of braked aluminum sections riveted together to form equilateral triangles. Three of these triangles along with additional struts are joined to form an octahedron (figure 7.63). The octahedrons, when combined, form a series of tetrahedrons in the spaces between; thus the "octet." Ten octahedrons are joined with various connectors to form the triangular truss segment. The actual dimensioning of the construction is far more complex; since the segments must taper to form the segments of the sphere, the octahedron dimensions must vary slightly, requiring a variety of different lengths of elements. The shape of the individual members that make up the triangles is similar to those used by Wallis, but also to the type of duralumin girders used in American airship design.

The method of construction is not that of buildings but of airplanes and follows the same principle of minimal weight. The structure was not steel but aluminum, the glazing material was plastic, not glass, and the assembly was riveted, not bolted or welded. The design of the individual members was similar to established aircraft techniques, particularly those used by Wallis. Of course both dome and truss have numerous other inspirations. The truss is similar to the diagram of a U-235 atom that Fuller had cut out and saved, while the dome resembles certain biological forms such as radiolaria.

The Ford dome had a short but spectacular life. It attracted a great deal of attention but burned in 1960. Precisely those qualities that minimized its weight—the use of thin members of plastic and aluminum, its lack of mass—made it more susceptible to fire.

Fuller built many other domes using a variety of methods and materials, and this interest, along with many others, displaced his concern with the mass-produced single-family house. The dome in fact became to Fuller an acceptable form for city or house, and for almost any other building problem in between. His popularity with the public has always been greater than his influence with the architectural profession, yet he helped popularize the use of both tension cables and tetrahedrons, and the work of Neutra, of Saarinen, and of Kahn all shows, at certain periods, a considerable Fuller influence. As late as the 1970s he was collaborating with Norman Foster. Perhaps ultimately more important was his codification of the principles of aircraft and automobile design—minimum weight, minimum material, exploitation of material qualities, and energy conservation—as the qualities of rational building.

CONCLUSION

All modern movements in architecture fail in some way; no failure is more disappointing than that of the Case Study Houses. They seemed to offer a genuine American version of modern life that still seems ripe with unexplored possibilities. Perhaps this failure was inevitable. The movement rarely recognized its purely aesthetic characteristics, and certainly overstated its technological ones. There is a popular notion that the steel frame house died out due to stylistic unpopularity. This was certainly a factor; magazines of the day are filled with advertisements for companies such as Bethlehem Steel aimed at overcoming an ill-defined prejudice toward steel as a domestic building material. But the failure of the Lustron house indicates otherwise.

The fate of the Ford dome and the similar fate of Fuller's dome in Montreal suggest to some that he may have crossed the line between the minimal and the inadequate, although many Fuller domes have survived and functioned adequately with no problems. The line between the two is a subjective one in any case. A case in point is Fuller's Dymaxion bathroom, a stamped metal tub and shower of which only a handful were produced. It is nevertheless the ancestor of numerous sheet metal and fiberglass units today. Although they are functionally the equivalent of the traditional porcelain units, they are unacceptable to many because of the perceptible deflection of their surfaces.

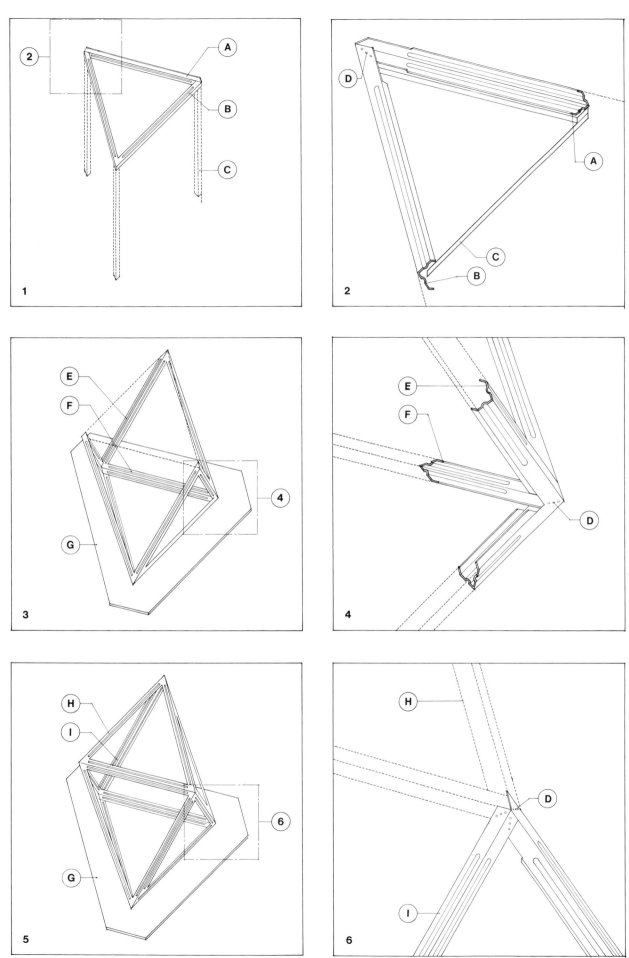

1

2

3

4

5

6

7.63

Ford Rotunda

Rotunda by Albert Kahn, 1933

Dome by R. Buckminster Fuller, 1953

Dearborn, Michigan

7.63   Truss assembly.

Steps

1–2   Three aluminum sections are riveted together to form an equilateral triangle.

A   70° aluminum strut facing up.

B   120° aluminum strut facing down.

C   Jig table. The parts were assembled to a tolerance of .055".

D   Rivets.

Steps

3–4   Three triangles are joined to begin the octahedron.

E   120° internal aluminum strut legs of triangle projecting upward.

F   70° aluminum struts flat on jig table.

G   Jig table (typical).

Steps

5–6   Three additional 70° aluminum struts are riveted in place to complete the octet.

H   Additional 70° aluminum struts to form top of octet.

I   120° internal aluminum strut leg of triangle.

Steps

7–8   Octahedrons are joined with aluminum angle connectors.

J   120° strut at edge of octahedron. The 70° struts are all at the top and bottom, while the 120° struts are all internal.

K   Aluminum angle connector to hold octets together.

L   Large jig table to form truss.

Steps

9–10   10 octahedrons are joined to form a triangular octet truss section. The voids between the octahedrons are tetrahedrons, hence the name octet.

M   Triangular gusset plate.

N   70° aluminum strut top of octet.

Steps

11–12   The truss section is connected to the channel frame.

O   70° aluminum strut at edge of triangular truss.

P   Aluminum channel.

Q   Cast aluminum hub.
Additional struts are added when in place to complete the triangular section.

(BFI UCM)

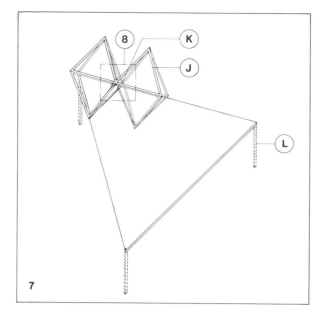

7

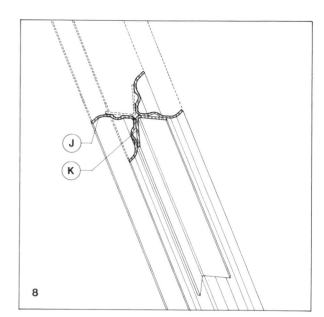

8

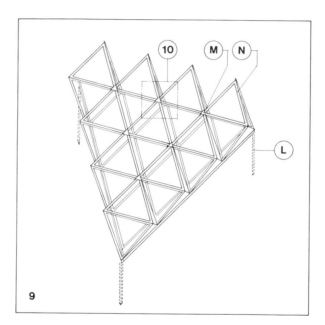

9

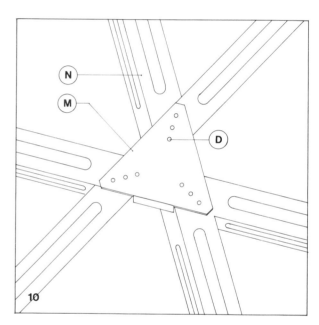

10

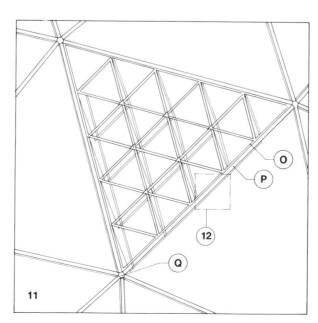

11

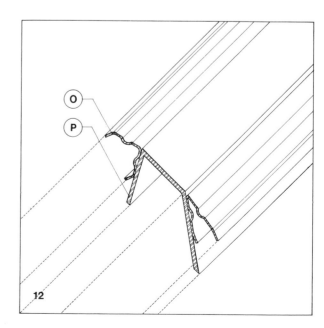

12

8.3

8.4

General Motors Technical Center, second design

Eero Saarinen

Warren, Michigan, 1947–1956

8.3 **Aerial view.**

(Balthazar Korab)

8.4 **Cars outside the styling auditorium.**

(General Motors Corporation)

buildings at IIT, it is high in maintenance and low in thermal performance, since the steel is uninsulated and unprotected from corrosion. This was, however, a fairly standard construction system of the time, particularly for shop and factory buildings. The most evocative feature of the building is the exterior chimneys. Engine testing produces large quantities of carbon monoxide, which is exhausted through slots into the floor to the basement, pulled to the exterior by fans, and exhausted above the building by means of a series of tubular chimneys a short distance to the side. Although faced with metal, they are in fact built of fire brick. An extensive but largely hidden mechanical system provided fresh air through the ceiling. The requirements of the Dynamometer Building are fairly unique, and the exhaust stacks were not duplicated elsewhere, nor did Saarinen seem to feel that what he had done was significant; the building is largely hidden from the central area of the complex. Nevertheless it is one of the most memorable of any at the Tech Center and was to have an important influence on Louis Kahn.

The second part of the Engineering Complex, the drafting and administration wing, despite its Miesian inspiration significantly departs from his work structurally. The standard buildings at Mies's IIT campus use 24-foot column bays and planning modules of 4, 6, or 12 feet. In the Engineering Building there is only one module, since every column is a mullion and every mullion a column (figure 8.7): the structural module and the planning module are one. It is a system that has little in common with the work of Le Corbusier or Mies, but it is one Saarinen was to pursue throughout his career. Understandably this system of tightly spaced columns is rarely used, since a system of columns on 5-foot centers, as opposed to one on 30-foot centers, requires five times as many column footings and connections. Perhaps for this reason, Saarinen increased the column spacing in subsequent buildings at GM. Although the system of tightly spaced structural columns was less economical than the Miesian system in the quantity of material and number of connections required, it had important beneficial effects in the design of the floor-ceiling sandwich, particularly in allowing for a tight integration of mechanical systems and structure.

The need to integrate mechanical ductwork into a structure and ceiling assembly was still a relatively new one in 1950, although the standard system for doing so was well established. A ceiling containing lights was hung from the structure and the ductwork placed between the two. The system had the advantage of allowing the different components to remain independent of each other. It had the disadvantage of requiring the most vertical depth and thus space, and often increased the height and the cost of the building. Saarinen's space frame structure is deeper than the conventional wide flange and bar joist arrangement, but its voids are sufficiently large to allow ductwork (at least some ductwork) to be placed inside the space frame (figure 9.6.3).

The curtain wall produced by these tightly spaced columns is unique as well. Although the structure is steel, the curtain wall itself is aluminum. The column, a steel tube, is wrapped on the exterior by an aluminum plate extrusion. A sheet of double glazing is held in place by aluminum extrusions on the interior and the space between column and extrusion is packed with insulation. Unlike Mies van der Rohe's buildings at IIT (and the all-steel curtain wall of the Dynamometer Building), this curtain wall has both double glazing and thermal breaks (the insulation) and, since it had no exposed steel, low maintenance. Although commonplace today, these features were rare in 1950.

Like Mies, Saarinen desired to express the structure, preferably by exposing it, but his fundamental concepts of detailing are different, favoring the multifunctional and perhaps ambiguous element rather than the functionally specific but perhaps redundant elements favored by Mies. Miesian buildings all distinguish clearly between structure and curtain wall—between skin and bones. Sometimes this separate articulation of elements is carried even further, distinguishing between the structure that supports the glass and the structure that supports the floor. The GM Technical Center is much more integrated: what appear to be the major window mullions are indeed the window mullions, but are also the structural steel columns of the building.

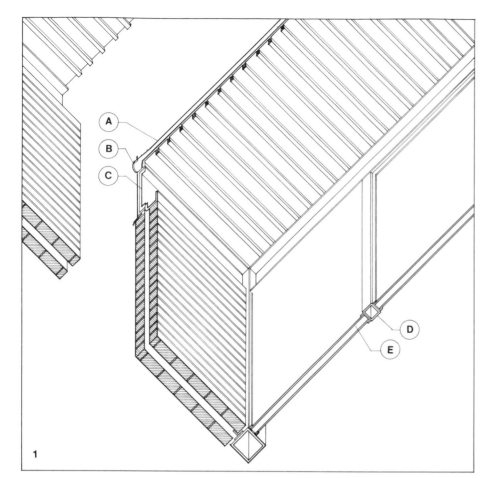

1

8.6

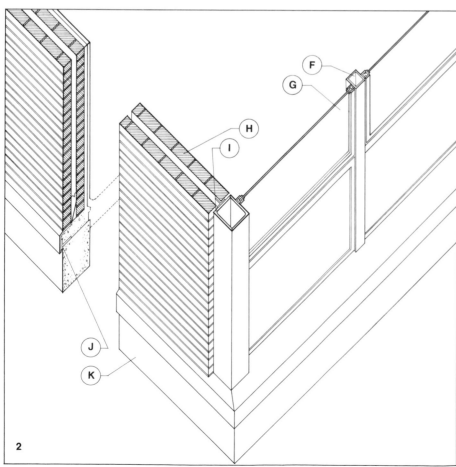

2

8.5

General Motors Technical Center, Dynamometer Building

Eero Saarinen

Warren, Michigan, 1949–1951

8.5 Wall section.

1 Section of coping at corner from interior:

A Composition roofing and 1½" rigid insulation on 1½" metal deck.

B Extruded aluminum coping.

C 14" steel channel with 1" sprayed-on insulation.

D 4 × 4" steel tube column.

E 2¾" porcelain enamel sandwich panel.

2 Section at base of corner from exterior:

F 4 × 4" steel tube column.

G Out-swinging steel windows with ⅛" polished, heat-absorbing glass.

H Masonry wall of 4" glazed brick, with cavity to intercept water that penetrates the wall and wall ties to structurally connect the two wall layers.

I Steel tube column from two 8 × 8½" steel angles welded at corners.

J Flashing and ¼" weep holes 4' 0" oc. Water that collects in the cavity drains to the outside through the weep holes. Sill from ¼" bent steel plate below.

K Concrete foundation.

(SHG A-5, A-8)

8.6 View. The vertical cylinders are exhaust stacks for the engines being tested.

(Ezra Stoller © Esto)

Besides a wider column spacing, the Styling Building of 1952 had another important change. The early curtain walls at GM relied heavily on caulking to achieve watertightness, and often failed. There was particularly a problem in bonding the caulking to the porcelain panels. At this point, at the instigation of the architect or client or both, they began to investigate the possibility of a dry or gasketed system, gaskets being the primary method of glazing in automobiles. This was not a new idea; the dream of a completely dry system of building assembly had been in the air as long as architects had been admiring cars and planes, and Walter Gropius and Le Corbusier repeatedly proclaimed the virtues of dry construction. The Tech Center was one of the first real applications of this idea to architectural glazing, a traditionally wet system. GM's bus division used its extrusion machinery to produce H-shaped rubber gaskets. These worked by means of a zipper that forces the legs of the H to press against the glass and a metal flange attached to the window frame (figure 8.10). The first mock-up ended with rubber strips on the floor of the shop, as the expansion and contraction of the sharp-edged sheets of glass sheared the assembly apart. The gaskets were changed to neoprene (stronger than rubber), the glass edges were softened, and the first assembly was installed in the Styling Building. This is the origin of the structural glazing gasket in architecture and one of the many innovations the Saarinen office developed or popularized.

Although various types of gasketed systems are in common use today, wet systems are still common as well, with a number of improvements having been made in wet glazing compounds. At the same time, gaskets have experienced certain difficulties such as installation in cold weather and the problem of joining and sealing corners, and while gaskets have become extremely popular in factory-glazed windows, their use in field-glazed windows is still less common than wet glazing.

The opaque portions of the curtain wall were drawn not from automobiles but from aircraft. The honeycomb sandwich panel, in which two sheets of metal are separated by a honeycomb-patterned core, had been developed as a cladding system that would allow for the rapid dissipation of the heat that builds up at high air speeds. The sandwich configuration gives great strength with little weight, placing maximum material at the faces where the stress occurs. It was adapted in the Styling Building with porcelain enamel on steel face panels. The honeycomb core provides insulation as well.

Another of the Center's technical innovations, the glazed brick end walls, also drew on automobile technology, as a spark plug manufacturer provided the glazing compound. They required several attempts to achieve success. Bricks and mortar are both to some degree porous and allow water to move in and out. If a brick wall is sealed, it runs the danger of trapping any water that does penetrate the wall, where it can freeze and pop off the sealed outer layer. Glazing the bricks had the effect of sealing the surface. The mortar, however, remained porous, and water quickly penetrated to the interior and froze; as a result, the glazed surface soon delaminated from the brick. The problem was solved by applying a sealer to the mortar after the wall was laid up.

The primary role of the different-colored brick walls, in addition to giving a De Stijl-like flavor to the complex, was to give identity to the individual buildings and divisions. The curtain wall, despite its subtle modifications, obviously failed to do this, which is perhaps why Saarinen placed so much emphasis on giving individual identity to the interiors as well. He wrote: "Each of the staff organizations prides itself on its own individuality and its range of activities. Each wanted its own 'personality.' We tried to answer this desire architecturally in the main lobby of each of the five groups. In four of these, the visual climax to the lobby is the main staircase. These staircases are deliberately made into ornamental elements, like large-scale technological sculptures."[3] While these stairs also probably failed in their stated purpose—the different divisions and their individual buildings are identifiable only to the initiated—the stairs are the most interesting architectural pieces in the complex. Many make use of steel cables in tension, and the ideas of the 1942 Community Center begin to reassert themselves.

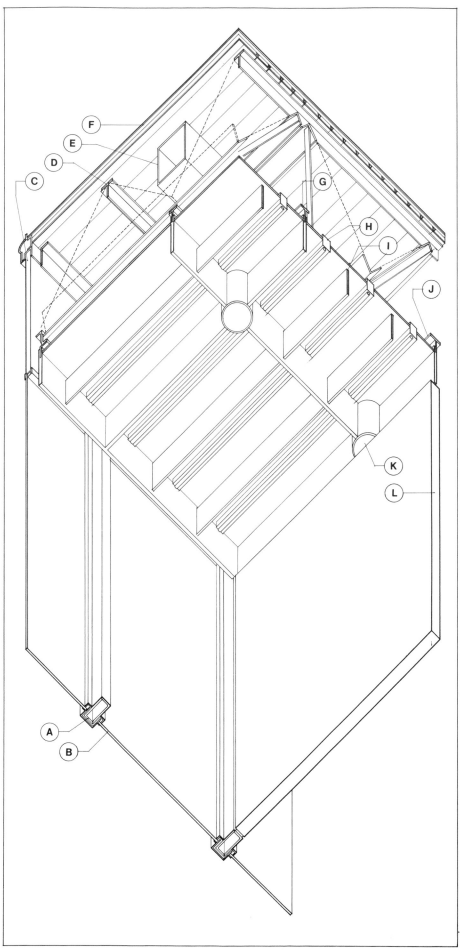

8.7

General Motors Technical Center, Engineering Complex

Eero Saarinen

Warren, Michigan, 1949–1951

8.7   Interior wall section.

A   4 × 8½″ steel tube column with aluminum cover and insulation. Unlike in most glass curtain wall buildings, the columns and mullions are the same structural element.

B   Curtain wall with 1″ insulating glass.

C   Porcelain enamel panel.

D   Top chord of steel-angle space frame.

E   High-speed supply duct in trusswork.

F   Composition roofing, 1½″ insulation, and 1½″ metal deck.

G   Steel T and sheet aluminum baffle with suspended metal acoustic panel.

H   Fluorescent lighting tubes. There are four types of ceiling in addition to that shown here. The drafting room type has exposed lamps; the other three have Plexiglas lenses.

I   Minor aluminum baffle.

J   T supporting major baffle at partition.

K   Diffuser in aluminum cylinder.

L   Partition.

(SHG A-18, 19, 20)

The most spectacular is the spiral stair in the Research Laboratory. Independent granite slabs are suspended by stainless steel rods from the roof and floors, the structural principle being to use the steel in its most efficient form, that of pure tension. The outer edge of each tread is suspended from the handrail around the openings, but the cable then continues to the floor, turning the handrail bracket into a compression strut. Each cable engages the leading edge of one tread and the rear edge of the next to reduce the number of cables, a detail conceptually similar to the double-functioning cable-suspended roof at Tanglewood. The treads themselves were originally designed in reinforced terrazzo, but at the last minute tests were made on Norwegian granite that showed it capable of withstanding the bending stresses, and the treads as built are solid stone. The inner edges of the tread are hung from a round plate in the ceiling plane. The specific references to automobile construction in the stair (such as to wire wheels) are less important than the more general ones. The stair uses the same principle as Fuller's Dymaxion house and Neutra's Diatom house, but it is also the direct descendant of the tension cable and compression mast language of the suspension bridge and the clipper ship.

In the executed complex, only two fragments remain of the airplane wing technology of the early schemes, the water tower and the Styling Auditorium, the latter built in 1954. In aircraft terminology, Saarinen referred to the auditorium as a blister. Taking the form of a dome, the building raises the question of the appropriate method of construction of a modern dome in relation to the traditional construction of masonry domes, and to an extent the principle of rational building as determined from aircraft construction came into conflict here with the principle of rational construction as derived from masonry construction.

The purpose of the Auditorium was to unveil each year the new-model cars. Conventional lighting gave odd reflections and shadows on the highly reflective cars, and the dome is designed to give uniform illumination from all sides, functioning as a giant reflector for the auditorium below. There are actually two shells of different radii, architecturally necessary to create the circular lobby, which had its own parabolic light reflector (figure 8.18). The double shell concept is close to that of Norman Bel Geddes's Little Theater in the Round, which also uses a metallic double shell.

Saarinen also referred to the Auditorium as a thermos, i.e., two thin shells inside each other. The outer shell is itself a double shell: an inner structural steel shell clad with insulation and a second shell of aluminum plates. Of these, the structural shell is of ⅜-inch-thick steel plate reinforced with steel angle stiffeners. The considerable lateral thrust developed by this steel dome is taken up by a tension ring, a ⅜-inch steel plate box beam. The structure is very much like a traditional masonry structural dome translated into steel. The steel shell is of course hidden by the inner shell and the outer layer of aluminum plates. These are .081-inch-thick plates supported by aluminum clips, which overlap almost like shingles.

The inner shell of 12 and 14 gauge perforated sheet metal is suspended from the structural steel shell above and is thus nonstructural. The sheets are not bent into pans, as is usually the case in this type of ceiling, but left flat and, like the exterior, overlapped like shingles. Focusing echoes are a potential problem in a space of this shape, and the acoustic absorption of the dome is increased by setting the actual acoustic insulation in perpendicular rings behind the perforated metal, creating a void to further absorb the sound.

The technical source of many of these details was pressure vessel technology, and several pressure vessel manufacturers were consulted to study techniques. The contractor for the auditorium was a major manufacturer of pressure vessels, refinery tanks, etc., and had used this type of technology in the construction of its own headquarters in Chicago in 1942, but its appeal to Saarinen was undoubtedly that it suggests in image and construction automobiles and aircraft. (It is, among other things, another example of stressed skin structural design.) Judged by the Gothic Revival or early Modernist principle that structural expression and structural honesty are paramount, it is a kind of sham. A masonry form, the dome, is executed in steel and aluminum. Logically the steel ought to be allowed to seek its own

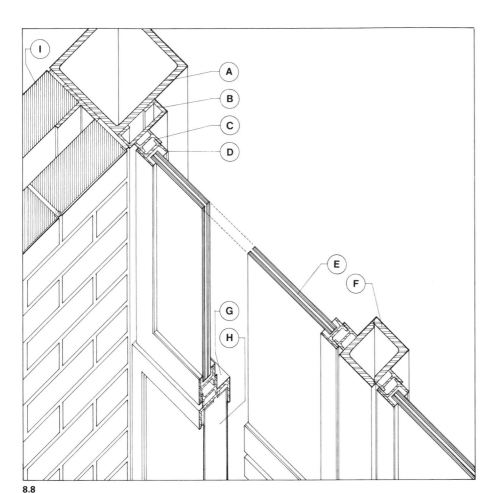

8.8

General Motors Technical Center, Dynamometer Building

Eero Saarinen

Warren, Michigan, 1949–1951

8.8　**Curtain wall details.**
A　Steel tube column from two 8 × 8½″ steel angles welded at corners.
B　Steel closure. The shop areas of the complex use steel curtain walls while the remainder use aluminum.
C　Fixed steel sash.
D　Out-swinging steel sash.
E　Insulating glass.
F　4 × 4″ steel tube column.
G　Trim.
H　2¾″ porcelain enamel sandwich panel.
I　Masonry wall: two layers of 4″ glazed brick with cavity.
(SHG A-5, A-8)

8.9

General Motors Technical Center, Styling Studios and Shops

Eero Saarinen

Warren, Michigan, 1952

8.9   Curtain wall.

8.10   Curtain wall details.

A   5¾ × 12″ steel tube column from two channels. The large tube supports the beams of the floor above.

B   ⅛″ extruded aluminum cover with black porcelain enamel finish attached with hanger clip. This protects the steel from rust while providing space for insulation, although only some of the buildings at GM insulated the columns.

C   Extruded aluminum mullion.

D   Extruded rubber gasket. This was later changed to neoprene for additional strength.

E   1″ insulating glass.

F   ⅛″ aluminum cover.

G   3¼ × 6″ steel tube. This tube is nonstructural and serves only to support the curtain wall.

H   Aluminum closure fastened with stainless steel oval-headed screws 24″ oc.

I   Insulated porcelain-faced sandwich panel attached to aluminum mullion with gaskets.

(SHG A-11)

8.11   Curtain wall at brick end wall.

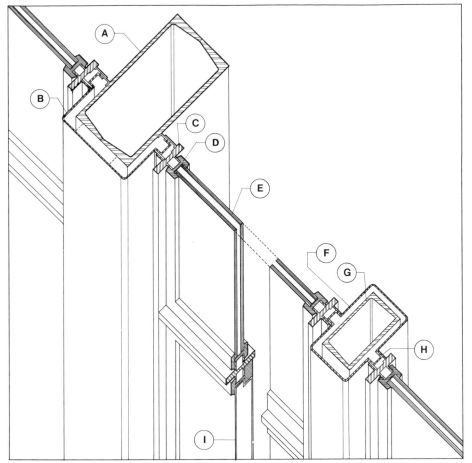

8.10

8.11

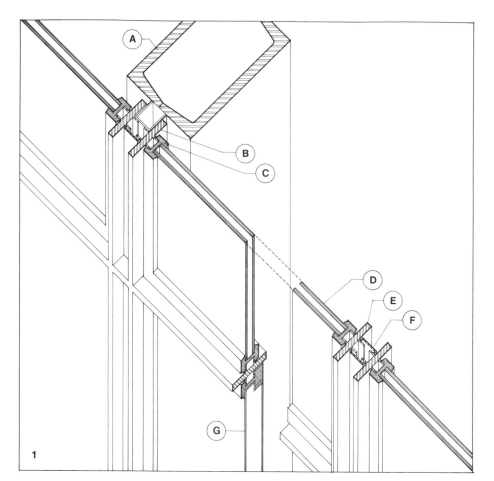

8.13

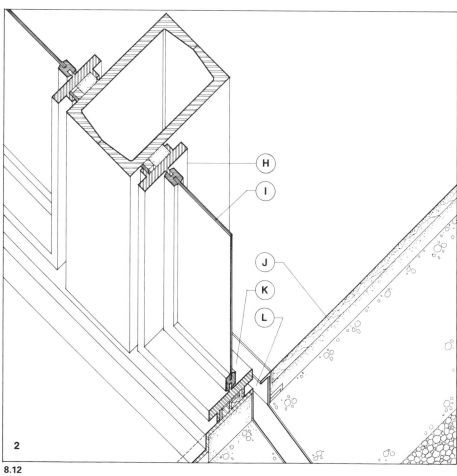

8.12

General Motors Technical Center, Styling Administration Building

Eero Saarinen

Warren, Michigan, 1955

8.12 **Curtain wall details.**

1 Typical office wall at upper story:

A 8 × 12″ steel column from two channels. Unlike in the earlier GM buildings, the curtain wall here is semi-
independent of the structural
column.

B 5″ extruded aluminum mullion.

C Extruded rubber or neoprene
gasket.

D 1″ polished plate glass double
glazing.

E Intermediate mullions 5′ 0″ oc.
These are identical to the mullion at
the column.

F Extruded aluminum strip with slot-
ted screw hole for vertical
expansion.

G Porcelain enamel-faced spandrel
sandwich panel.

2 Sill at ground-floor lobby:

H 5″ extruded aluminum mullion, here
placed outside of the 8 × 12″ steel
column, with ⅝ × ¾″ steel bar
welded to column to receive aluminum mullion.

I ¼″ polished plate glass with extruded rubber gasket. The lobby is
single-glazed, unlike the office wall
shown above.

J Finish floor on grout on concrete
slab.

K Typical aluminum mullion on ⅛″
bent sill plate separated from steel
with nonmetallic shims.

L 16 gauge metal duct with 1 × ⅛″
aluminum edge angle.

(SHG A-7)

8.13 **View with Styling Auditorium in
background.**

(Balthazar Korab)

8.14 **Office of Harley Earl.**

1 Corner of Styling Building:

A Curtain wall (see Figure 8.12).

2 Detail:

B Extruded aluminum bars.

C Cherry wood slats.

D ½″ plywood.

E Sheet cork.

F 2″ plaster.

G 2 × 4 wood studs.

H Door.

(SHG A-64)

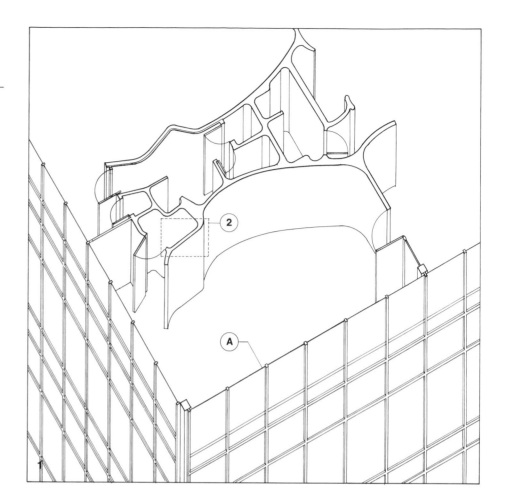

1

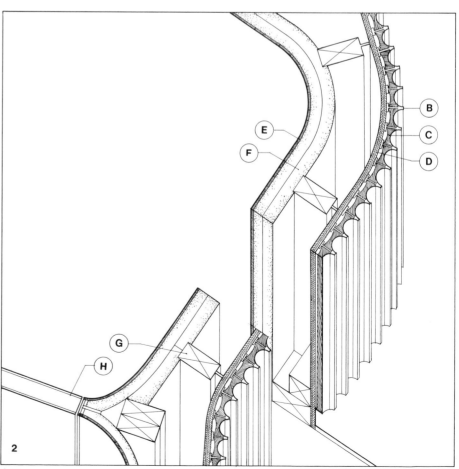

2

8.14

8.15

8.16

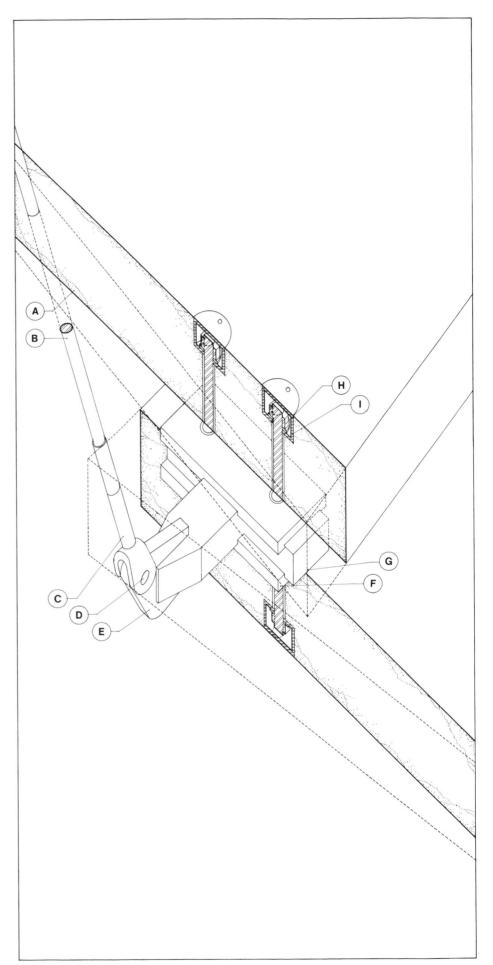

8.17

General Motors Technical Center, Research Laboratory

Eero Saarinen

Warren, Michigan, 1952–1954

8.15 **Stair.**

(Balthazar Korab)

8.16 **Detail at inner edge of stair tread.**

8.17 **Detail at outer edge of stair tread.**
- A Stone tread (shown cut away).
- B ⅜" stainless steel rod supporting stone tread. These were heated and tightened during assembly.
- C Stainless steel jaw terminal with threaded end attached to rod.
- D ½" bolts.
- E Stainless steel billet attached to jaw.
- F ½" stainless steel plate welded to billet, drilled to receive ½" bolts.
- G Billet.
- H ½" bolts in 9/16" hole drilled in granite.
- I 20 gauge stainless steel sleeve with 1/16" lead washers and stainless steel cover.

(SHG A-57, 58, 59)

appropriate form and then to express it. Judged as an application of aircraft technology to building, however, the dome makes perfect sense. The thin exterior and interior skins are supported by an internal concealed skin and framework of struts. Structural expression is not a criterion in aircraft design. In the modern aircraft, exterior and interior pressures shape the outside and inside, and the framework is adapted to accept these conditions. Of Saarinen's many attempts to reconcile modern technology, drawn from airplanes and automobiles, with the language and systems of traditional building, this is undoubtedly one of the more successful. Its lack of recognition over the years is perhaps due to the secrecy that surrounds its function as the place of unveiling of the new GM designs.

There is one other fragment remaining from the 1945 design, and in a location that is not surprising, the office of Harley Earl. Trapped within the Miesian grid of the Styling Administration Building, its undulating wood and plaster curves seem to contain on a small scale all those that were taken out of the building (figure 8.14). By the time construction of the auditorium was under way, Saarinen had moved on to a number of other commissions that often utilized these structural forms: tension cables, thin structural shells, and structural grids, sometimes in steel and sometimes in other materials.

THE VAULT AND CABLE BUILDINGS OF THE 1950S

If the streamlined metallic forms of the early GM scheme were largely missing from the final, they were to return in a more important context. In a 1948 competition in which the entrants included, among others, his father Eliel and Louis Kahn, Eero won the commission for the Jefferson National Expansion Memorial, or as it has come to be called, because of his solution, the St. Louis Arch. Since its development runs the length of Saarinen's career (it was finished in 1965) and since its technical history alone could fill a single book, it is not easily summarized, but essentially it was a simple form, constructionally logical, simply detailed, but extremely difficult to execute due to sheer size: a catenary arch 630 feet wide and 630 feet high. Unlike a semicircular arch, a catenary has no lateral thrust. The structural concept is equally simple, a sandwich panel of two stressed skin steel sheets with a concrete infill. The cross section is an inwardly turned triangle, tapering toward the top. As was to become typical of his later work, Saarinen was not content with the form of the pure catenary and slightly altered its shape for purely sculptural reasons.

The realities of construction and execution were considerably more complicated but follow the same principles. The typical arch wall is ¼-inch stainless steel on the outside, ⅜-inch carbon steel on the inside, the space between concrete. Steel tension bolts tie the two outer skins together and force the bond between concrete and steel. Both steel layers have additional stiffeners and the concrete is prestressed. The wall panels were prefabricated in segments and welded together on site. At a point on the arch 300 feet above the ground, where lateral loads decrease and dead weight is more critical as the arch becomes more horizontal, the concrete is eliminated and steel diaphragms connect the inner and outer steel layers.

The numerous problems of assembly—how to make and transport the segments, how to support the legs when the arch was incomplete—are best summarized by a single example, the insertion of the keystone. The last segment was 8½ feet wide (and weighed 80 tons), but the gap separating the two legs was only 2 feet, since they naturally leaned toward each other in their incomplete state. Nor was the gap always 2 feet, as the thermal expansion and contraction of the more than 400-foot-long segments was considerable. A special horizontal jack was used to pry the legs apart (figure 8.21) while fire hoses poured water onto their stainless steel covering to minimize thermal expansion, and finally, after several lawsuits, a wildcat labor strike caused by fear of collapse, a civil rights protest that attempted, unsuccessfully, to climb the arch, and as workmen raced against time as the legs began to expand in the afternoon sun, the last segment was set in place on October 20, 1965, with 10,000 people, including Saarinen's widow, looking on.

Despite the problems, the arch in its form and construction comes the closest of any of Saarinen's buildings to realizing the idea of applying stressed skin airplane

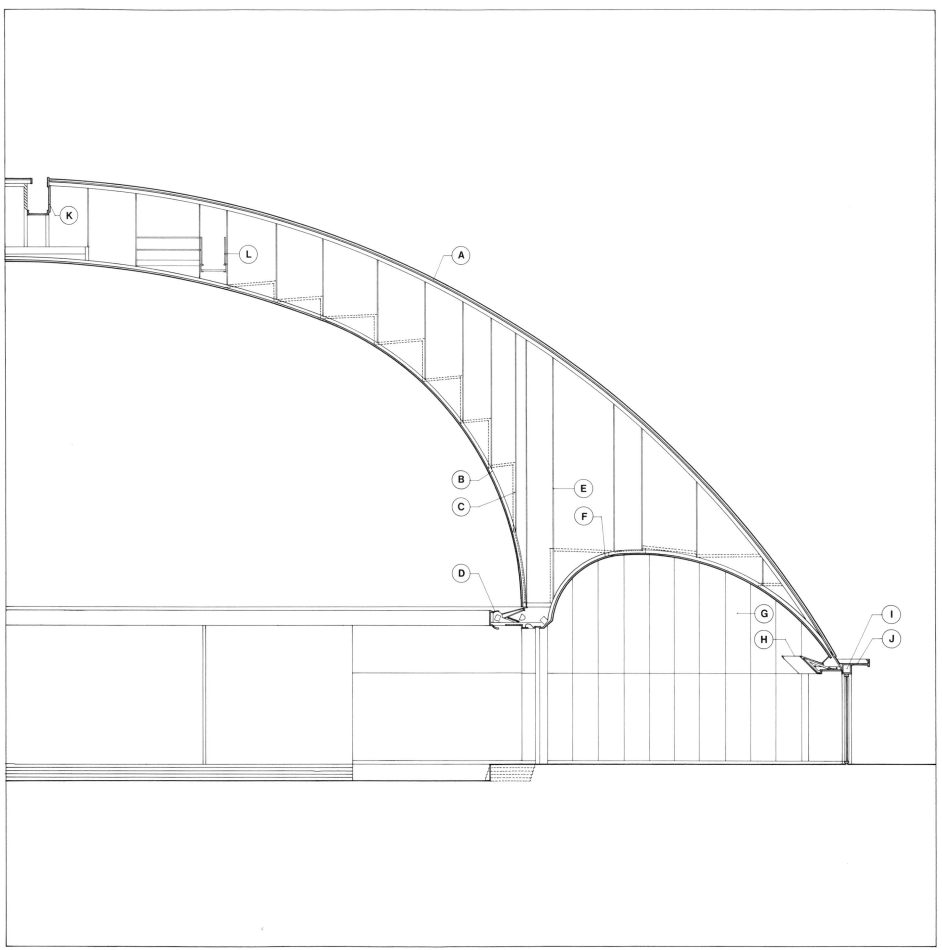

General Motors Technical Center, Styling Auditorium

Eero Saarinen

Warren, Michigan, 1954–1955

8.18 Section.

A Outer shell of aluminum shingles on ⅜" steel plate structural shell, with steel angle stiffeners and 1" rigid insulation between.

B ⅛" aluminum sheet inner shell with 15% perforations. This shell is non-structural and is suspended from the steel shell above.

C Concentric rings of insulation to absorb sound.

D 12" steel channel to support inner shell with 14 gauge cover to form shield for floodlights and spotlights.

E Inner shell hangers.

F Parabolic 16 gauge metal ceiling with 2½ × 2½" radial stiffeners. The parabolic shape will diffuse the light, unlike a circular shape which will focus it.

G Wood veneer on ¾" plywood paneling.

H 14 gauge metal shield for floodlights.

I Steel tube tension ring with columns beyond to take the lateral thrust of the dome as well as transfer its weight to the columns.

J Gutter 8" steel channel with membrane flashing.

K Recess for exhaust fan. This hides the fan from view from the ground.

L Catwalk.

(SHG A-7, GM Journal 5.56)

8.19 View.

(Balthazar Korab)

8.20 Outer shell.

A ⅜" structural steel plate shell.

B Stiffening angle beyond.

C 1" rigid insulation.

D Stainless steel stud welded to steel plate.

E Aluminum washer, neoprene washer, and stainless steel washer. The neoprene prevents electrolytic action between aluminum and steel, and the assembly is designed so that the two metals never touch each other.

F Waterproof membrane to intercept any water that penetrates the roof.

G Aluminum shingle stamped from .081" thick aluminum. Rather than butting the edges together, the outer window panels are overlapped to prevent water penetration.

(SHG A-5)

8.19

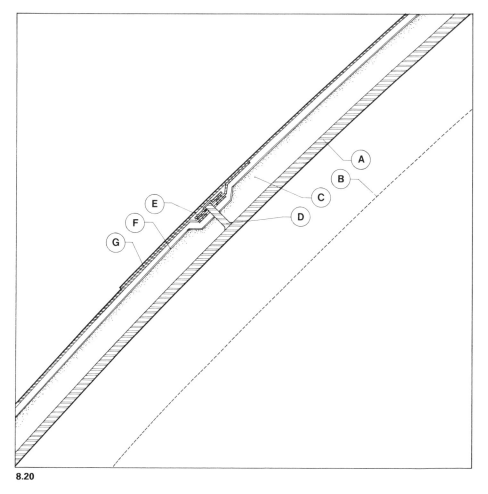

8.20

8.21

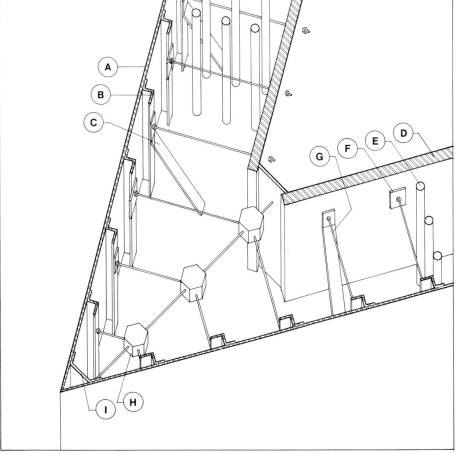

8.22

Jefferson National Expansion Memorial

Eero Saarinen

St. Louis, 1948, 1958–65

8.21 Under construction.
(Robert Vickery)

8.22 Typical arch wall at lower section.
A ¼" stainless steel facing.
B 2½ × 2½ × ⅛" steel Z stiffeners fastened to steel facing with ³⁄₁₆" steel studs and bolts.
C 2" strap at mild steel bolt, connected to bolt on opposite side below.
D 12' × 54' section (concrete fill not shown). The arch is constructed of triangular prefabricated elements 12' high. Like the GM dome, it has no frame in the lower portion and acts as a load-bearing structural shell.
E 1¼" round prestressing rods.
F ⅜" mild steel stud bolt. The two bolt types alternate.
G Tensioning bolts to compress skin and concrete to create composite action.
H Octagonal fastener to receive bolts at corner.
I ¼" perforated corner stiffener plate.
(KRJD&A S 107B, S 112)

technology to building. Like Le Corbusier before him, in his later buildings Saarinen began to apply the sensibility of metal airplane design to other more purely architectural materials, specifically concrete in the form of the thin-shelled vault. The reasons for the popularity of concrete shells in the 1950s have as much to do with style as technique. To some, shell technology was not a welcome development. Vaults are totally absent from the work of Mies van der Rohe, who maintained to the end a post and lintel, skin and bones attitude toward modern construction. To many others, Saarinen in particular, the structural shell offered endless possibilities within the bounds of rationalism. It could be used to build the modern equivalent of the Gothic or Roman vault, as Perret had done; it could be used to recall vernacular vaulted buildings, as Le Corbusier had done; or it could be used to build a concrete equivalent of the stressed skin airplane wing, as Le Corbusier and Saarinen were to do.

The first of Saarinen's shell experiments was a modest one, the Irwin Union Bank and Trust building in Columbus, Indiana, finished in 1955, but his next shell was far more challenging, the Kresge Auditorium at MIT, built, along with the MIT chapel, adjacent to Aalto's Baker House dormitory between 1953 and 1955. Although to the contemporary eye they are oblivious to their surroundings, Saarinen considered the two buildings to be contextually responsive:

We felt that a box-like structure in these surroundings, differing from the adjacent dormitories and apartment buildings only by the absence of windows, would be an undistinguished anticlimax. We believed that what was required was a contrasting silhouette, a form which started from the ground and went up, carrying the eye around its sweeping shape. Thus, a domed structure seemed right. There were other reasons, too, that influenced us toward a dome. There was the large dome of Welles Bosworth's central building at M.I.T. . . .

It seemed right to use a traditional material, such as brick, for the chapel—for brick would be a contrast to the auditorium and yet the same material as the surrounding dormitories.[4]

The MIT dome was actually conceived before the Styling Auditorium at GM, and the two form an interesting contrast, since they represent the same structural principle in concrete and steel respectively.

But the structural shell in concrete or steel raised another difficult question, particularly in this case. The shell was a form determined by structure rather than internal use. A dome is often a poor shape for an auditorium, since it tends to create focusing echoes. The conventional wisdom held that the proper auditorium was fan-shaped, as Saarinen himself had used in previous projects. Saarinen's approach was to configure the outside on the basis of structural demands and build an inner nonbearing shell tailored to acoustic demands. His desire was not functional (i.e., programmatic) expression, but structural expression by using the minimum of material. He said of the MIT auditorium that it was his most Miesian building, since it was "doing the most work with the least concrete."[5]

Saarinen was not content to use a simple dome, but insisted on modifications. The dome is one-eighth of a sphere, but it is also triangular in plan, so that it rests on three points. In a pure shell structure, there would be no ribs or beams. At MIT the shell proper is sometimes as thin as 3½ inches, despite its 160-foot span. Largely for acoustic reasons, the shell was doubled (to prevent sound from the exterior from reaching the interior). The 3½-inch concrete shell is covered with 2 inches of glass fiberboard and a second nonstructural layer of lightweight concrete 2 inches thick. Additions had to be made to this structure, since Saarinen's sculptural cutting of the shell created edge disturbances that had to be counteracted by an edge beam. There were also large stresses created at the three points of support. These were reinforced with tapered H-shaped steel ribs, which in turn were connected to a steel hinge allowing for movement. In the end Saarinen's modifications proved excessive, and after the formwork was removed it was discovered that the edges were deflecting an unacceptable amount. Additional supports were added in the form of 4-by-9-inch steel tubes spaced at 11 feet. As these are also used to support the window wall, they are, while noticeable, not prominent in the interior.

8.23

8.24

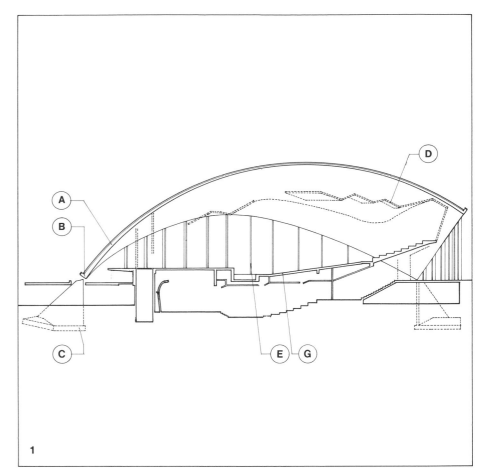

1

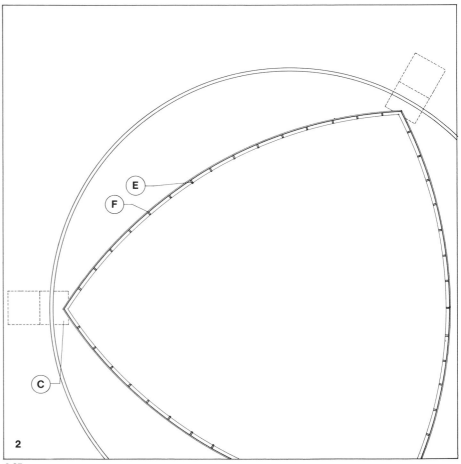

2

8.25

Kresge Auditorium, MIT

Eero Saarinen

Cambridge, Massachusetts, 1953–1957

8.23 **View.**

8.24 **Interior.**

8.25 **Section and plan.**

1 Section at center.

2 Plan.

A Structural shell with an average thickness of 4.8″, 3.5″ at edges. It is given a 2″ nonbearing concrete covering for acoustic isolation, then 2″ fiberglass insulation and neoprene roofing. This was later replaced with lead-coated copper roofing and then copper roofing.

B Edge beams.

C Footing. The entire load of the shell comes down to three points.

D Acoustic "clouds." The fact that the hemisphere is a poor acoustic shape and the acoustic need for an auditorium of a certain volume dictate that the inside surfaces be configured very differently than the outside.

E 3 × 12″ steel tubes. These were added later to support the edge beams after excessive deflection of the shell following removal of the forms. They are only slightly larger than the tubes originally included to support the curtain wall.

F Steel tubes of various sizes. The size of the tubes decreases as their height decreases with the curve of the shell.

G Concrete floor of auditorium.
(KRJD&A A-8, A-9)

Kresge Auditorium was a building in which everything seemed to go wrong, and the roof was no exception. Drainage was a particular problem. The roof shape and the edge beams naturally brought all the rainwater down to three support points. An elegant lead-coated copper gutter pours it into a less elegant grating-covered drain in the pavement. Due to an improper substitution of concrete topping mix, the original roof covering of acrylic plastic began to leak not long after the building's completion. This was replaced with a copper roof in 1954, but this only lasted until 1961, when it was replaced with lead-coated copper. The continued water penetration over the years created yet another problem, as the steel reinforcing in the shell began to corrode, and in 1979 a major structural renovation was required.

Critical response to the Kresge Auditorium was not good. Bruno Zevi, J. M. Richards, and Pierluigi Nervi variously attacked its failure to respond to context, its structural shortcomings, or the inappropriateness of the form to the function. The noted theater designer George Izenour wrote: "an architectural *tour de force* on the outside is a theatrical and acoustical *tour de farce* on the inside, proving only that an eighth of a sphere is far from being an ideal shape into which can be shoehorned a room intended for either speech or music."[6] Leo Beranek, the acoustical consultant, assembled a number of favorable opinions as to the auditorium's acoustics, but few wished to come to its architectural defense.

Like the auditorium, the chapel has met with much criticism. Louis Kahn said that it has all the paraphernalia of a chapel—altar, stained glass, etc.—without having any of the essential qualities of one. Constructionally, it expresses a great deal of structure and material in the wall but none of either in the steel roof with its plaster ceiling. (In this respect, although far more abstract, the building is very much in the spirit of the buildings at Cranbrook.) The walls are solid brick without waterproofing cavities or insulation, but they are layered in other ways. The outermost layer is a cylinder of 8-inch solid brick. The second layer is an undulating wall that intersects with the outer shell. Brick-sized openings in this inner wall, in combination with the acoustic insulation in the voids between the inner and outer layers, act to create sound-absorbing chambers, lowering the reverberation time and softening the space acoustically so that speech can be heard. Both walls are supported on brick arches of varying size which rest on granite posts in a pool of water. The innermost layer is an undulating concrete upstand, set 8 inches away from the inner brick wall, leaving an 8-inch horizontal window allowing light reflected from the pool to enter the chapel from below.

Saarinen's conception of material expression was to articulate the material's structural limitations. The structure and materials of the wall are precisely explained; all openings have arches, no lintels are concealed, or so it appears. There is considerable concealed reinforcing within the wall in the form of a concrete bond beam and concrete diaphragms stabilizing the 30-foot-tall brick walls. The roof structure, although requiring a 60-foot span at its longest point, is simply structured, with parallel wide flange steel beams of varying depths spanning the cylinder. There is no hint of this on the interior, with its suspended plaster ceiling and circular skylight.

The image of the cable-suspended tent, which Saarinen had first elaborated in his 1942 Community Center, also recurs in a series of later works. In 1949 he designed a literal tent to serve as a concert hall for the Goethe Bicentennial Music Festival in Aspen. There are many types of tents, but Saarinen made a particular point of contrasting masts in compression with steel in tension. His fondness for the luminous ceiling was also manifest; the lights are located above the canvas so that it would glow uniformly. The ideas of the Community Center resurfaced dramatically in the Ingalls Hockey Rink at Yale, begun in 1956. One reason for this was the general popularity of cable-suspended structures at the time, particularly Matthew Nowicki's Livestock Pavilion at Raleigh, North Carolina, in 1953. This was a pure structural form based on a hyperbolic paraboloid, which has the quality of being generated out of straight lines, a useful characteristic in buildings built of sections of steel, wood, etc.

8.26

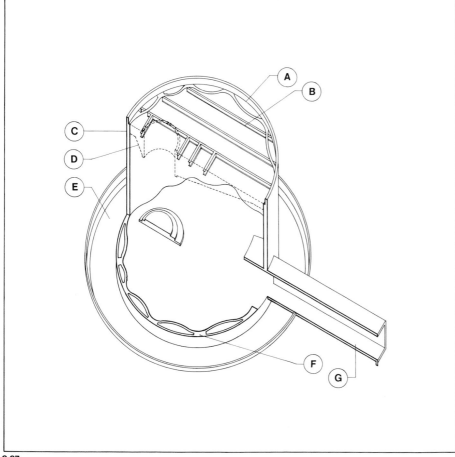

8.27

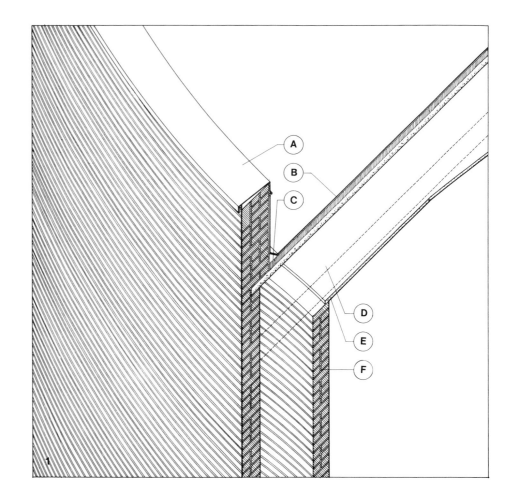

1

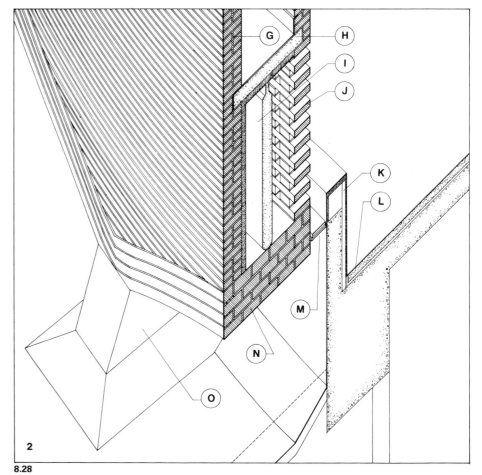

2

8.28

Chapel, MIT

Eero Saarinen

Cambridge, Massachusetts, 1953–1957

8.26 **View.**

8.27 **Framing.**

A 2″ precast concrete slab roof deck (not shown).

B Steel beams. The smallest is a 12 WF 76; the largest a 16 WF 50. All structural steel is concealed by the plaster ceiling.

C Load-bearing masonry wall of two layers of 8″ brick. The inner layer undulates. The outside layer is re-inforced with two ¼″ pencil rods every sixth course and a continuous reinforced concrete bond beam.

D Plaster ceiling.

E Pool to reflect light through openings.

F Granite piers supporting arches.

G Concrete slab at entry supported by steel tube column.
(KRJD&A A-6)

8.28 **Wall section.**

1 Section at parapet:

A Parapet and coping.

B Roofing and insulation on 2″ pre-cast concrete planks.

C Cant strip on through wall mem-brane with flashing to intercept water.

D Steel beams.

E Suspended plaster ceiling.

F Undulating 8″ inner wythe rein-forced with concrete bond beam.

2 Section at base:

G 8″ outer brick wythe reinforced with two ¼″ pencil rods every sixth course.

H Concrete slab on Transite formwork reinforced with four no. 9 bars at edge and no. 4 bars at 12″ radial.

I 4″ sound insulation wrapped in loose-woven fabric.

J Perforated brick wall to absorb sound.

K Wood panel on concrete wall.

L Travertine flooring on concrete slab.

M Window (see figure 8.29).

N Brick arch reinforced with nine no. 4 reinforcing bars. Because of the height of the thin wall, additional horizontal bracing is necessary, which is not visible from interior or exterior.

O Granite pier in asphalt-paved pool.
(KRJD&A A-6)

8.29 **Window detail.**

A Brick with openings for sound absorption.

B 1½″ laminated oak strips.

C Concrete wall.

D ²⁵⁄₃₂″ thick × 2¼″ vertical tongue and groove oak boards.

E 1″ insulating glass and $3 \times 3 \times \frac{3}{16}$″ eggcrate louvers of 16 gauge sheet metal to allow light reflected from pool to reach inner surface of walls.

F Sheet metal welded glass frame of $\frac{5}{8} \times \frac{17}{8} \times \frac{1}{8}$″ bent plate on $\frac{3}{4} \times 1\frac{1}{2} \times \frac{1}{8}$″ continuous bent plate support, lag-bolted to brick wall.

G Brick wall and arch reinforced with nine no. 4 bars.
(KRJD&A A-13)

8.30 **Base of wall.**

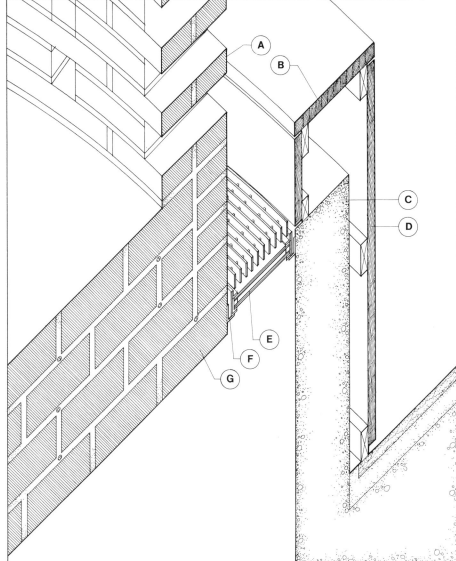

8.29

8.30

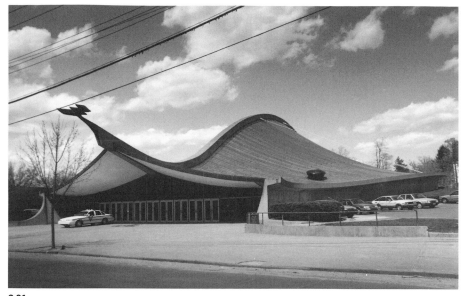

8.31

8.32

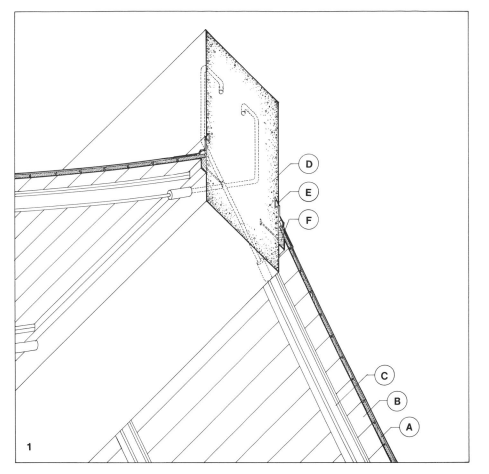

1

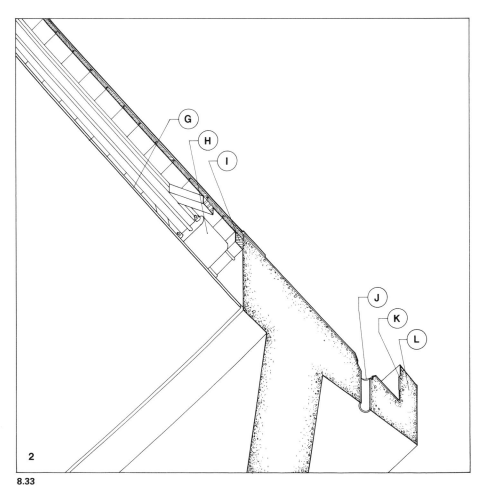

2

8.33

David S. Ingalls Hockey Rink, Yale University

Eero Saarinen

New Haven, Connecticut, 1956–1959

8.31 **View.**

8.32 **Interior.**

(Ezra Stoller © Esto)

8.33 **Roof details.**

1 Detail at concrete arch:

A ¹⁄₁₆″ sheet neoprene roofing.

B 2 × 8 wood decking on 2 × 6 nailers clipped to cables.

C ¹⁵⁄₁₆″ steel bridge strand cables 6′ 0″ oc spanning from concrete wall supporting roof.

D Reinforced concrete arch.

E Reglet and caulking sealing joint between roof and arch.

F 4 × 6 nailer bolted to arch.

2 Detail at wall:

G Suspended metal lath and plaster ceiling for fireproofing.

H ¹⁵⁄₁₆″ bridge strand socket tied to beam with four no. 8 reinforcing bars to transfer load of cables to wall.

I 4 × 6 wood nailer.

J Roof drain.

K Reglet and sheet neoprene flashing with liquid neoprene over concrete to terminate roof membrane.

L Reinforced concrete fascia beam.

(KRJD&A A-7, A-11, S-13)

While adapting the structural principle, Saarinen insisted on major sculptural modifications to the basic structural form. The main roof support of Ingalls is a low, parabolic concrete arch with cantilevered ends spanning the long axis of the rink. Cables are strung from the central arch to the concrete side walls, with a roof of tongue and groove wood boards. Both concrete walls and roof beam are sculpted, sometimes for structural purposes and sometimes not. The exterior walls slope outward, helping to counter the pull of the cables. The main beam is extended over the main entry for purely aesthetic reasons. The references to bridge technology are not metaphorical; the cables used are bridge cables. Saarinen declared: "We were able to achieve this structure, based on tension rather than compression, which is unique to twentieth-century technology. We hope that architectural character, growing out of its structure, will be both expressive and appropriate to our time."[7]

While conceptually impressive, the building is marred by problems not sufficiently thought out in the conceptual phase and resolved later by ad hoc solutions. Nowicki's slanted arches required no additional bracing because of their angle and location. Saarinen's upright arch had no such advantage, and additional cables were placed on the exterior above the roof to stabilize the arch along the short axis of the rink. The exposed steel and wood roof structure is a potential fire hazard, but the code will allow it in this situation if the roof is a sufficient distance above the seats. At its low end Saarinen's roof is not, and a plaster ceiling was added extending to a point where the roof was sufficiently high above the rink.

Most critics of the day saw the Ingalls Rink as a tour de force marred by sloppy execution, the arch bracing and fireproofing details, and an apparent whimsy in Saarinen's manipulation of form independent of any structural logic; this attitude was symptomatic of what was to put an end to rationalism, in this form at least, for the time being. To some, the building was so obsessed with its own form and structure as to be oblivious to its surroundings. Vincent Scully, a Yale faculty member, wrote: "It embodied a good deal that was wrong with American architecture in the mid-1950's: exhibitionism, structural pretension, self-defeating urbanistic arrogance. It should in all these ways be contrasted with Kenzo Tange's otherwise rather similar Olympic stadium in Japan, where the conception was developed three-dimensionally, with integral structure, and with an understanding of the larger urbanistic responsibilities involved."[8]

Yet if Tange's Gymnasium and Pool for the 1964 Olympics in Tokyo is superior to Ingalls, the latter was its inspiration. The Olympic complex is actually two buildings, a large-span arena and a smaller one for swimming pools. The span of the large auditorium was much greater than Ingalls, and Tange indulges in his own sculptural modifications to the form. The principal difference is that while Saarinen's central element was a concrete arch, Tange's is a series of cables, making the resemblance to a suspension bridge all the stronger. The two main supports, cables woven from small ones in the manner of a bridge and containing as many as 127 elements, are suspended from two concrete masts. (They run parallel from the mast, then separate to form a skylight.) Spanning from the main cables to the perimeter wall, a series of hanging steel girders spaced at about 4 m are the roof proper. Little of this structure is visible from the floor below. The main cables are wrapped in concrete, then clad in aluminum jackets. The bottom of the hanging girders seems to support the ceiling so that only the bottom flange is visible. Yet it is a remarkably clear structure for one in which the literal elements are hidden, and the finish elements do a great deal to simplify what is a structure of extreme complexity. Tange was no more content to leave the pure engineered form unaltered than was Saarinen. The two halves of the arena are not symmetrical but form a pair of interlocking ear shapes, and the main cables follow slightly curved paths; but Tange's manipulations, unlike Saarinen's, do not add anything structurally unnecessary and make no distortions counter to basic structural behavior.

Saarinen was to return to cable-suspended structures in what many consider his finest building, the terminal for Dulles Airport, but his first attempt at an airport building utilized another by now familiar system, thin-shelled concrete vaults. In

8.34

8.36

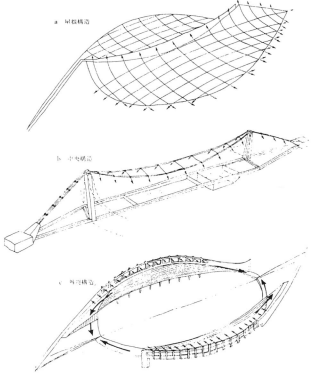

a 屋根構造

b 中央構造

c 外周構造

图-1 主体育館構造系

8.35

8.37

National Olympic Gymnasium

Kenzo Tange

Tokyo, 1961–1964

8.34 **View.**
(Kirk Martini)

8.35 **Framing diagram.**
(Kenchiku Bunka 65)

8.36 **View.**
(Kirk Martini)

8.37 **View.**
(Kirk Martini)

8.38 **Roof detail.**

A Main roof plate 4.5 mm thick with corrosion-resistant coating and 20 mm spray-applied mineral wool.

B Steel beam suspended between central cables and concrete beam at edge.

C Roof plate splice cover.

D Restraint cables. Wind and pressure may cause the roof to uplift and its loading to shift in the opposite direction to the norm. These act to hold it down.

E 200 × 75 × 20 mm steel C purlin.

F Aluminum ceiling section: expanded aluminum sheet with glass wool acoustic insulation above.

(Kenchiku Bunka 65)

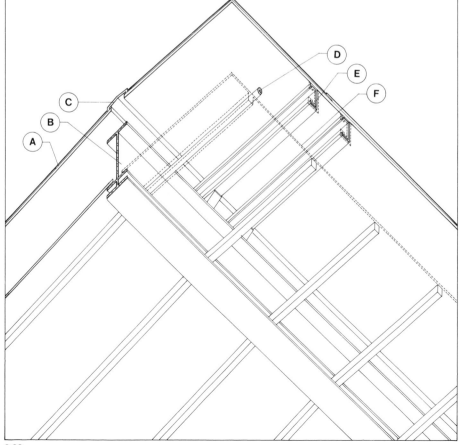

8.38

the TWA Terminal at Kennedy (then Idlewild) Airport, as at the Kresge Auditorium, he insisted on considerable modifications to this structural form. According to legend, the form of the vault was not arrived at by structural analysis, nor by imitating the form of a bird, but was discovered one morning at breakfast when Saarinen turned his grapefruit upside down and pressed in the center. His first design had been a spherical shell supported on four points, not unlike Kresge, but he wanted something more open-ended, and structural determinism was quickly left behind in favor of sculptural exploration.

The building consists of four separate but structurally dependent vaults, separated by skylights but connected by a center plate for structural bracing. Each shell is a quadrilateral with two opposite corners resting on Y-shaped supports, one corner held by the center plate, and one corner cantilevered (figure 8.41). The vaults are all generated from sections of circles and in some ways are not unlike barrel vaults. The shell is not so thin here as at Kresge, never less than 7-inches (at the tip of the front shell) and more typically 11 inches (the tip of the side shell). Again extensive edge beams were required because of the shell's not entirely structurally logical shape. Originally Saarinen wished to bush-hammer the supports and edge beams, leaving the shell smooth. In the end the concrete was uniformly finished and sealed.

The method of constructing the formwork, although laborious, was quite simple, a grid of adjustable U shapes, supported atop scaffolding adjustable to the desired height. Wood timbers set in the U's and covered with plywood make up the formwork itself. Upon removal of the forms the maximum deflection was 1½ inches and three months later was only 2 inches, which was within acceptable limits. Thus, unlike at Kresge, the curtain wall was not burdened with the problem of incorporating structural supports. Nevertheless, it did present considerable problems.

The glazing had to both slope outward and curve, and spans of typical mullions ranged from 4 feet up to 22 feet. Had typical tube mullions been used, they would have approached and perhaps exceeded the size of small steel columns. Saarinen's solution was a series of trusses, resembling bar joists, which, although deeper than tubes, give a more transparent appearance due to their open webs. The bar joists taper at both ends as their maximum bending is at the center. This tapering also makes it clear that the trusses are not supporting the shell, and facilitates the connection at the end points, which must be flexible. There are 38 types of truss mullion, none of which are at 90 degrees to the shell, the glass, or the ground, and the angle of any of these relationships is seldom the same.

Despite the complexity of the curtain wall, it contains the most intriguing set of details at TWA, in part because they are so unlike the rest of the building. Of the latter Saarinen wrote: "Having determined the basic form of the building, our next challenge was to carry the same integral character throughout the entire building so that all of the curvatures, all of the spaces, and all of the elements would have one consistent character. As the passenger walked through the sequence of the building, we wanted him to be in a total environment where each part was the consequence of another and all belonged to the same form-world."[9] Unfortunately, he succeeded only too well, and with dubious means. Even if one accepts the desirability of streamlining everything in sight, benches, counters, clocks, and stairs, and to a degree that Harley Earl might have found excessive, it cannot be called good detailing to fabricate these shapes out of so many different materials and imply that they are the same. Take for example the two canopies that extend along the entry drive. Although they are sculpted to resemble the concrete shell, only the top half is concrete; the vault below is suspended cement plaster, and the actual structure of the building behind is a one-way ribbed slab on columns. One may condemn Saarinen outright for this, but one should recall that similar details are used at the Guggenheim Museum and at Chandigarh. The question, as Ruskin pointed out long ago, is whether honesty is the absence of deception.

At the time Saarinen was seen as not following the internal logic of the shell structure. Many preferred the work of engineers such as Pierluigi Nervi or Felix Candela,

8.39

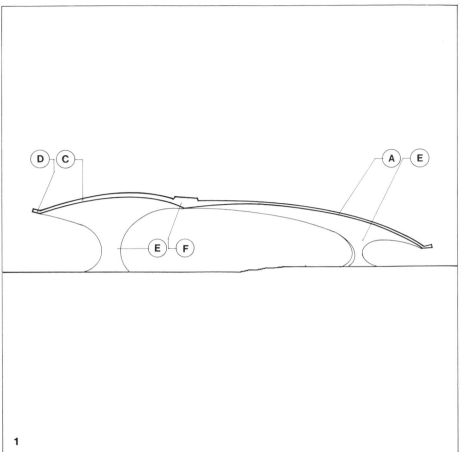

1

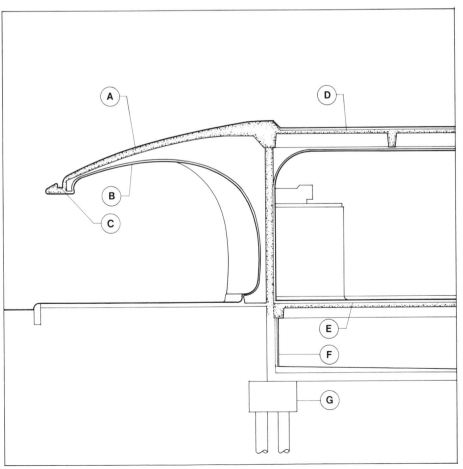

8.40

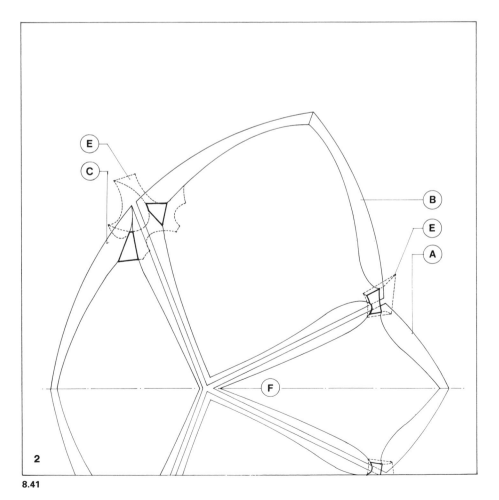

2

8.41

TWA Terminal

Eero Saarinen

New York, 1956–1962

8.39 **View.**

8.40 **Canopy section at entry.**
- A Concrete shell.
- B Ceiling of ¾" cement plaster on metal lath, suspended by ¾" furring channels and 1½" carrying channels at 4' 0" oc. Although it appears to be structural concrete like the outer shell, it is actually a plaster imitation.
- C Flashing and gutter.
- D Marble chips and built-up roof with rigid insulation on one-way concrete slab. The ribs are concealed behind a flat plaster ceiling.
- E Terrazzo on concrete floor slab.
- F Tunnel plenum wall with metallic waterproofing and ⅜" cement plaster cover.
- G Concrete foundation and pilings.
  (KRJD&A)

8.41 **Shell section and plan.**
- A Front shell, 7" thick at crown. All shells are covered with silicone sealer on lightweight aggregate concrete.
- B Side shell, 11" thick at crown.
- C Field shell.
- D Exterior edge beam.
- E Y buttresses of stone aggregate concrete.
- F Center plate holding the shells together, which lean away from each other.
  (Design and Construction of Shell Roofs, KRJD&A A-15, 17, 18, 22)

as it lacked the aesthetic meddling with structural form so common to Saarinen. There was in 1950, and is perhaps today, a widespread belief that if one simply uses architectural forms in a straightforward and logical way, using engineering techniques as the determining factor, beauty will follow. It was a belief Saarinen did not share:

The principle of structure has moved in a curious way over this century from being "structural honesty" to "expression of structure" and finally to "structural expressionism." In my opinion, it is a potent and lasting principle and I would never want to get very far away from it. Here, just as in the principle of function, the degree to which structure becomes expressive depends to a large extent on the problem. To express structure is not an end in itself, it is only when structure can contribute to the total and to the other principles that it becomes important. The Yale Hockey Rink and the TWA terminal are examples of this.[10]

Dulles Airport, completed after Saarinen's death, brings together ideas from older projects—material efficiency, the exploitation of structural forms—while at the same time allowing for sculptural modification to the structure. Although they are concealed, the essential elements of the buildings are the cables of the roof. Saarinen referred to the structure as a hammock. The roof is supported by 16 pairs of cast-in-place columns supporting two horizontal concrete slabs that act as edge beams. Strung between the edge beams on 10-foot centers are pairs of steel cables, five in each bay. The cables are encased in poured-in-place concrete for protection and stability and to facilitate connection with the roof itself, which is made of precast concrete planks that span the 10 feet between cables. The entire roof structure is concealed by a nonstructural plaster ceiling, hung immediately below the bottom of the T's.

For the most part these elements take their logical structural forms, but Saarinen modifies parts of the structure as well as concealing a great deal of it. Some modifications are functional, some are visual. The leaning outward of the columns helps them to resist the pull of the loaded cables, but the enlargement of the columns at the base is purely sculptural. The simplicity of the roof form masks the true complexity of its construction. Not only does the ceiling hide cables, concrete, and ribs, but it erases the difference between the edge beam and the roof proper. The connection of column to edge beam, however elegant, is grossly deceptive, making the edge beam appear to be part of the suspended roof.

Dulles perhaps suggests that the sculptural manipulation of structural forms will not invariably lead to problems, that if done well it might produce more than acceptable results. But Saarinen was able to demonstrate in another posthumously completed building that this level of formal quality could be accomplished in a much more structural way.

THE JOHN DEERE HEADQUARTERS

Many have remarked on the Japanese quality of the John Deere Headquarters, but its immediate inspiration is perhaps not traditional Japanese architecture. Saarinen was a friend of Kenzo Tange, and there is little doubt that the structural inspiration of Tange's Olympic Halls of 1964 is the concrete arch and cable structure of the Ingalls Rink. Saarinen visited Tange in Japan just before he began the Deere Company. One can see the porches and screens of Deere as a translation of Tange's concrete balconies, at the Kagawa Prefecture offices and elsewhere, into steel.

The use of steel was a response to the specific nature of the client. Saarinen wrote:

Deere & Co. is a secure, well-established, successful farm machinery company, proud of its Midwestern farm-belt location. Farm machinery is not slick, shiny metal but forged iron and steel in big, forceful, functional shapes. The proper character for its headquarters' architecture should likewise not be a slick, precise, glittering glass and spindly metal building but a building which is bold and direct, using metal in a strong, basic way.

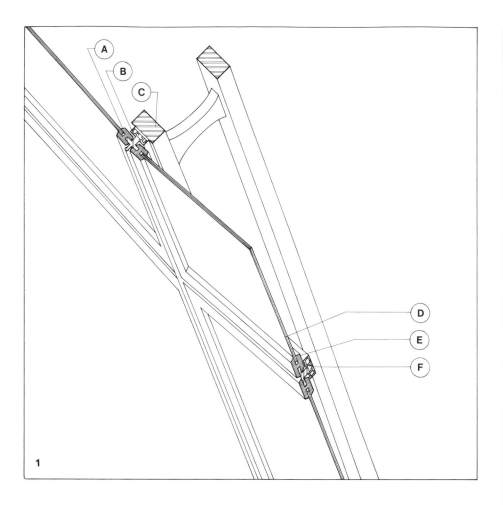

1

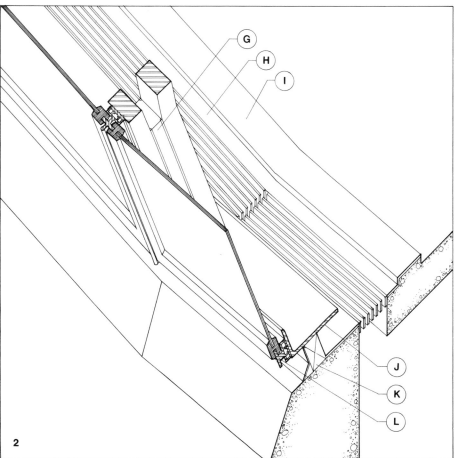

2

8.43

8.42

TWA Terminal

Eero Saarinen

New York, 1956–1962

8.42 Curtain wall details.

1 Section at typical vertical mullion:

A Neoprene gasket sealing joint and attaching glass to mullion.

B Aluminum extrusion bolted to steel truss to receive gaskets.

C Inner chord of mullion truss of 1½ × 2½″ steel bar. Outer chord of truss also 1½ × 2½″ steel. The large height of the glass opening and the angle require a large structural support. The truss is field-assembled.

D ¼″ glass; angle to the mullion varies.

E Longitudinal asymmetrical gasket.

F Horizontal aluminum extrusion. Unlike the vertical mullion, this is not visible on exterior.

2 Section at sill:

G 1½ × 2½″ steel truss connector. The truss depth decreases away from the center as its load decreases.

H Plenum and diffuser grating. This sets up a current of warm air rising above the inner face of the glass to prevent condensation and heat loss.

I Ceramic tile curb or carpet.

J Sill cut from 6 × 2½ × ¼″ steel angle.

K Wood filler and roof flashing.

L Aluminum extrusion with weep holes.

(KRJD&A DN 45A)

8.43 Interior.

(Balthazar Korab)

8.44 Curtain wall.

8.44

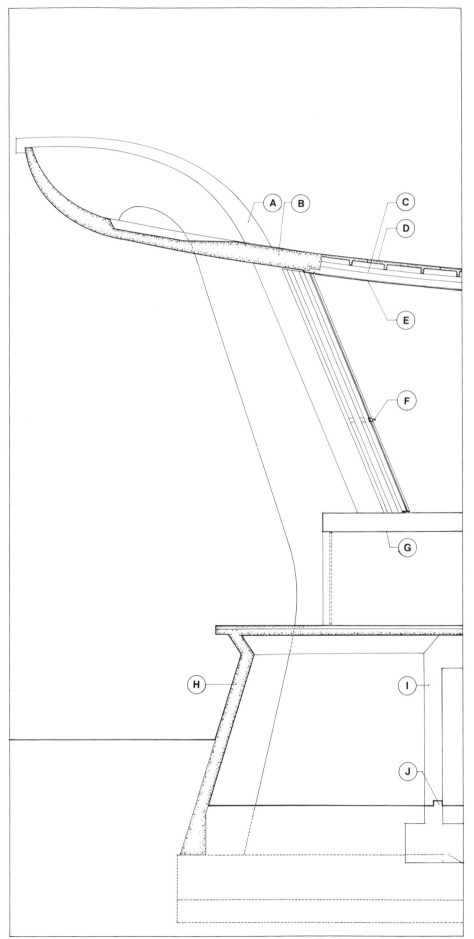

A
B
C
D
E

F

G

H
I

J

8.45

8.46

Dulles Airport

Eero Saarinen

Chantilly, Virginia, 1958–1962

8.45 Section at field side.

A Cast-in-place concrete column, sloped outward to counteract pull of cables. The flair at the base serves no structural purpose.

B Cast-in-place concrete edge beam to transfer the load of several cables to the column.

C Two 1″ steel cables with cast-in-place concrete casing to minimize flutter.

D Lightweight precast concrete units fixed to cable beams. Panels are precast to minimize formwork, lightweight to minimize dead load.

E Plaster ceiling. This hides the complexity of the structure above.

F Aluminum-clad steel curtain wall.

G Vestibule connecting to mobile lounges.

H Cast-in-place concrete wall.

I Concrete structure of ground floor.

J Foundations and floor slab.
(KRJD&A A-16, A-19, S-16)

8.46 View.

(Balthazar Korab)

Having decided to use steel, we wanted to make a steel building that was really a steel building (most so-called steel buildings seem to me to be more glass buildings than steel buildings, really not one thing or the other). We sought for an appropriate material—economical, maintenance free, bold in character, dark in color.[11]

The architect wishing to build a seven-story office building with an exposed steel frame faces all the same problems as an architect wishing to build an exposed steel frame house, and many more: (1) the deterioration of the steel through corrosion, (2) the loss of heat through thermal bridges created by the exposed steel, (3) the need to fireproof the steel, (4) the need for higher levels of craft and joinery to keep out water and present an aesthetically acceptable appearance, however crude this acceptable level might be.

Had Saarinen been required to thoroughly resolve all four of these problems he probably would not have succeeded. To prevent corrosion he used a type of steel, now commonly called Cor-ten, that develops a protective coating of rust. It had been developed for rails, and Saarinen adapted it to buildings. Under the terms of today's BOCA code an unfireproofed frame would not be allowed in a building of this area, height, and use in any location without a variance. The inside face of the spandrels and concealed floor beams are sprayed with fireproofing insulation where it would not show, since it is hidden by the ceiling, and presumably it was agreed that the outside steel was safe from fire. But what gives Deere its unique character comes from Saarinen's solution to the last problem, the way that the steel is joined, or rather the way that it is not joined.[12]

Conventionally, steel wide flanges are connected web to web and flange to flange, so that the center line of the column is the center line of the beam and the top of the beam is the top of the purlin. These are joined either by clip angles bolted to the webs or by welding. This minimizes the structural depth and width and assures that load will not be eccentrically transferred. At Deere, by contrast, nothing seems to be quite connected to anything else. The purlins sit atop the beams, the beams slide by the columns. The ends of all the sections are visible. Every member seems independent of every other, without connection or support. The individual structural members maintain their own visual identity. It is a detail that manages to be Classical, Constructivist, and Japanese all at once.

The use of this type of detail was no doubt in part to simplify connections. All the steel connections at Deere are welded, or more accurately bolted and then welded. Field welding requires that the members be held in place until the weld is complete. Placing the purlins atop the beams and sitting the beams on a box protruding from the column simplifies the need for temporary support. Both connections were made by bolting the members together, welding the connection, and then burning off the bolt. The problem of eccentric loading created by attaching the beam to the side of the column is solved by doubling the beam and placing one on either side. The primary reason that the configuration is not commonly used is that it greatly increases the depth of the structure, since none of the beams are in the same horizontal layer. Many other structural members are doubled as well, but largely for the purpose of closing the envelope. The typical spandrel beam is too deep in the envelope to close the building, so another projecting one is added (figure 8.51). The problem of waterproofing considerably aggravated the welding problem, as seen in the detail of the closure plate where a single ¼-inch plate of steel is welded to one W 29, two W 6s, one W 21, and two more ¼-inch plates (figure 8.51).

But as in a steel house, the fundamental problems of craft and tolerance—the skill and accuracy of the welding and the dimensional accuracy of the steel members—remain. Elements such as exposed exterior columns could be no more than ⅜ inch out of position in their height, while window mullions, where accuracy is the most crucial since they must interface with the glass, were accurate to within ⅛ inch in every dimension. The tolerance problem at Deere is well illustrated by the window mullion, a simple W 6 section with glazing gaskets fastened to its flanges. It is a simple and direct detail, provided the member is placed in precisely the right location to create precisely the correct opening. Mies's similar detail in the Toronto

8.47

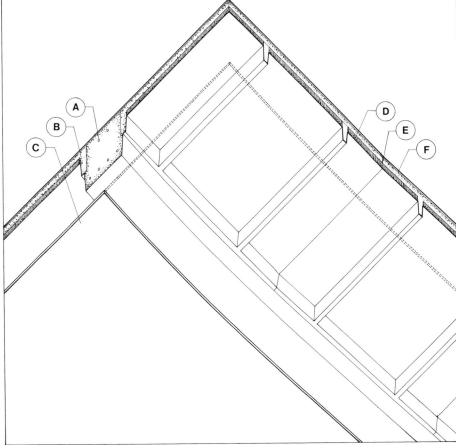

8.48

Dulles Airport

Eero Saarinen

Chantilly, Virginia, 1958–1962

8.47 Roof detail.

8.48 Roof section.

A Two 1″ steel cables encased in concrete 10′ 0″ oc with additional conventional reinforcing.

B Precast lightweight concrete double Ts with bridging, 5′ 11″ wide × 7½″ deep.

C Plaster ceiling.

D 1½″ rigid insulation fixed to underside of precast slab.

E Joint of double T.

F Neoprene roofing.

(KRJD&A A-16, A-19, S-16)

Dominion Center is far more forgiving in this regard in allowing for field adjustment to accommodate dimensional error.

The only piece of awkwardness in this superbly worked out building is the ceiling plenum. Saarinen used an egg crate ceiling with lights and reflectors above. The egg crate extends to the exterior to form part of the sunshade, creating an interior-exterior continuity. The result is an 18-inch band on the outside between bottom of steel and top of ceiling behind which is only the unoccupied space of the plenum. Covering this band with steel would have made the structure appear much heavier, so it is glazed in the same way as a window, but then blanked out with a metal panel behind.

Dulles and Deere are certainly the finest of the many Saarinen buildings finished after his death, and if Dulles was the fulfillment of the many cable and shell projects of the 1950s, Deere promised something else. There is little in any of his many previous office projects that connects them with the details of the Deere Headquarters, which suggests a world of unexplored possibilities. Saarinen died in 1961 at the age of 51. He never saw his best buildings in complete form. Although a large number of Saarinen employees went on to become major practitioners of the 1970s and 1980s, and while they remained dedicated to his memory, his reputation suffered a marked decline in these years.

Saarinen received a number of commissions for academic, institutional, and office buildings following the GM Technical Center. In most cases they seem to be a retreat from the high-tech promise of GM. Although almost always technically innovative in some way, their imagery, particularly the exteriors, seems often to be an unhappy compromise between their surroundings and the possibilities of modern construction. This was perhaps not a real change from Saarinen's earlier work at all. His use of airplane and automobile imagery at GM was perhaps because he thought it appropriate to the client rather than because he saw it as the universal direction for Modern architecture. Depending upon one's evaluation of these buildings, one can say that Saarinen was one of the first architects to try to make Modernism contextually responsive, or with Vincent Scully, that Saarinen's attitude toward building was a kind of packaging design, making superficial responses to context while failing to find any universal links between the buildings themselves.

His least successful buildings were often his most ambitious, those that used traditional materials—granite aggregate at the Oslo embassy, Portland stone facing at the London one—while articulating the mass-produced repetitive nature of the facade elements. His attempts to employ modern materials toward traditional ends often pleased neither Modernists nor traditionalists, and to some degree combined the worst qualities of both. Vincent Scully lambasted the Ingalls Rink for its self-referential insensitivity to its urban context, while ten blocks away at Stiles and Morse colleges Reyner Banham mocked Saarinen's attempts to reconcile concrete and stone with the traditional architecture of Yale. To make a building respond to its historical context, demonstrate the methodology of its production, and reflect the nature of its client may be a goal that cannot be consistently met by the best of architects.

Saarinen's contribution to architectural construction was a redefinition and to an extent a refutation of some principles of 1920s Modernism. After experimenting with standardization of large-scale components in the Unfolding house and of small-scale components in the GM Tech Center, he abandoned both in favor of a custom-engineered response to each problem, however idiosyncratic the result. Certain ideas remained: the ideal of material minimalism and efficiency. Some preconceptions remained unchallenged: the expression of the opaque structure and the suppression of the transparent. Most significantly he challenged and to a degree displaced the traditional skin and bones structural concepts of Mies and Le Corbusier, and in so doing challenged the idea of the open plan. But if this desire to reconcile structure and space in a way that would make them interdependent produced some of his weakest buildings, they perhaps inspired the efforts of a friend who was to excel at this endeavor, Louis Kahn.

8.49

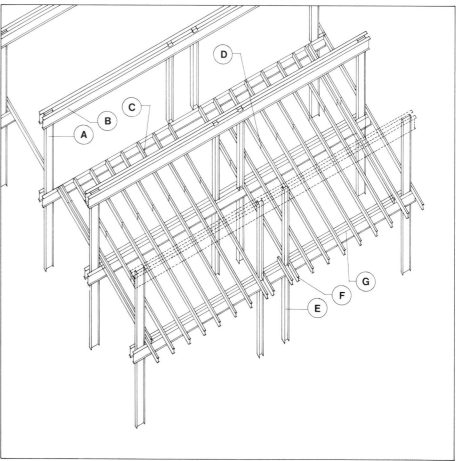

8.50

John Deere Headquarters

Eero Saarinen

Moline, Illinois, 1957–1964

8.49 View.

(Julius Shulman)

8.50 Framing.

A 30 WF 108 steel column. Beams and columns are joined at their sides rather than at web and flange. See figure 8.54.

B Two 21 WF 82 main girders. All exposed steel is Cor-ten.

C 10 WF 29 purlins 6' 0" oc. The purlins sit on top of rather than flush with the girders as in conventional construction; they are spaced according to the structural span of the steel deck they support.

D Beam splice.

E 10 WF 39 column at center.

F Double 10 WF 29 at corridor.

G Two 21 WF 82 floor beams.

(KRJD&A S-106)

8.51 Wall section.

A 10 WF 29 steel beam.

B Two 21 WF 82 main girders. Doubling the beams serves to maintain a symmetrical structure while allowing the connections on the beam and column sides rather than ends.

C 6 JR 4.4 beam holding sunscreen.

D 3 × 3 × 3" metal eggcrate sunscreen.

E Sunshade of 1/8" steel blades with 1/4 × 5 1/4" hanger.

F 10 WF 29 purlin.

G 30 WF 108 column.

H 1/4 × 11" steel plate for coping.

I Built-up roof and insulation on 1 1/2" metal deck.

J 10 WF 29 purlin with fireproofing.

K Glass.

L Eggcrate ceiling.

M Neoprene gaskets holding 1/4" laminated glass attached to 6 B 12 steel mullions behind. See figure 8.55.

N Continuous grille for air supply.

O 2 1/2" concrete topping on 2" cellular deck.

P Two 10 WF 29 steel beams. The outer beam is fireproofed on its inside face. All concealed steel receives fireproofing.

Q Metal acoustic panel.

(KRJD&A 109, 111, 113)

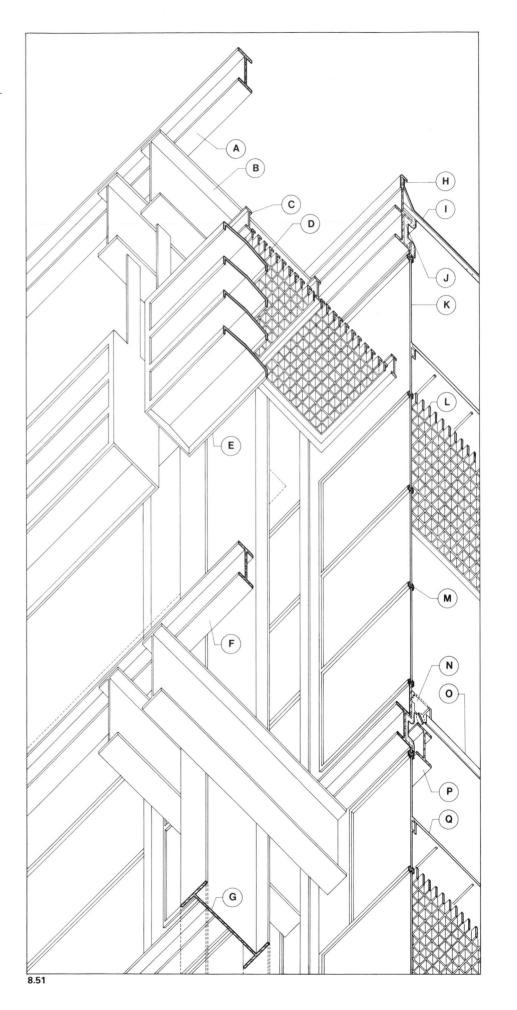

8.51

8.52

8.53

John Deere Headquarters

Eero Saarinen

Moline, Illinois, 1957–1964

8.52   **Detail.**

8.53   **Detail.**

8.54   **Steel connections at column.**
  A   30 WF 108 Cor-ten steel column.
  B   Two 21 WF 82 steel main girders,
      one shop-welded to column, the
      other field-welded.
  C   10 WF 29 typical purlin.
  D   Two 10 WF 29 purlins weather-
      welded to WF 21. The outer purlin
      forms the base of the curtain wall.
  E   ⅞″ erection bolts to hold beam in
      place temporarily. They are re-
      moved after completion of welding.
  F   ⅜″ thick steel box to support girder
      in place during welding.
      (KRJD&A S-106)

8.55   **Curtain wall detail.**
  A   6 B 12 steel mullion. Unlike in simi-
      lar Mies van der Rohe details, there
      is no frame between mullion and
      glass.
  B   Neoprene gasket. After GM, Saari-
      nen rarely used any method other
      than gaskets for fixing the glass.
  C   ¼″ laminated glass.
  D   Continuous air grille. This provides
      a warm current of air rising on the
      face of the glass to prevent conden-
      sation and minimize heat loss
      through the glass.
  E   2½″ concrete topping on 2″ cellular
      deck.
  F   Damper to regulate air flow.
  G   Steel beam.
  H   ¼ × 11″ steel plate with 1
      ½ × 1½ × ⅛″ steel angle.
      (KRJD&A A-109)

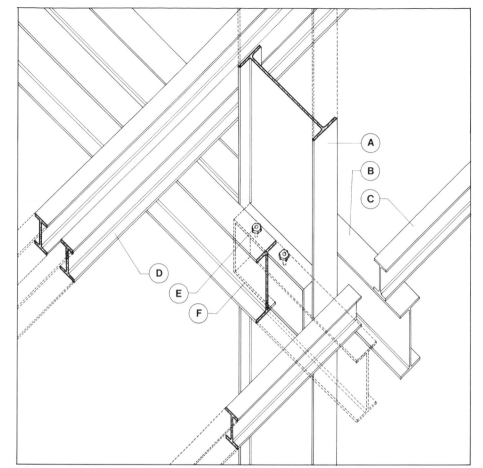

8.54

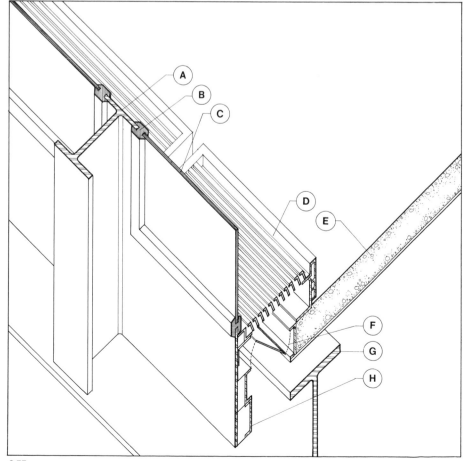

8.55

9 Louis Kahn, Sigurd Lewerentz, and the New Brutalism: 1954–1974

"Lou, do you consider this building an architectural or a structural success?"

Eero Saarinen to Louis Kahn, on seeing the Richards Building

If the work of Eero Saarinen illustrated for Vincent Scully the shortcomings of American architecture in the 1960s, then the work of Louis Kahn illustrated its virtues. Scully wrote in *American Architecture and Urbanism* of Kahn's dormitories at Bryn Mawr: "The whole is limpid with the sweetness of its program, and it flows with the land, beautifully sited there. . . . One should contrast, in terms of the institution, Saarinen's packaging conception for a girl's dormitory for the University of Pennsylvania: Château d'If outside, Blanche DuBois within."[1]

In 1969, when this was written, it seemed obvious that Kahn was everything that Saarinen was not. Saarinen's architecture was slick, smooth, seamless, skin-deep, arrogant, and insensitive. Saarinen was the architect of General Motors and IBM, a packager for corporate America. Kahn seemed the opposite. His buildings were crude, direct, timelessly archaic, and solid. They hid nothing (or it appeared so); they showed all that Saarinen's packages concealed. Kahn was the architect of institutions, the man who asked questions of them; what were they really? Yet if one were to assume from this view (at most a partial truth, perhaps underestimating Saarinen's abilities and overestimating Kahn's) that Kahn and Saarinen were antagonists, one would be wrong.

The Saarinen-Kahn friendship went back as far as the Willow Run town plan and continued until Saarinen's death. One of Kahn's most important commissions was obtained in part through Saarinen's efforts, and, unlikely as it appears, there was a close architectural relationship between the two. In retrospect those aspects of Modernism that Saarinen's work implicitly criticized—the disassociation of spatial organization from structure caused by the free plan, the disassociation of facade from scale caused by the free facade, the disassociation of buildings from context caused by structural determinism—can be seen as the same aspects of Modernism that Kahn's work sought, and to a degree succeeded, in correcting.

Despite the differences in surface appearance, the mutual influence between their work carries into the realm of form as well. The concepts of structure, space, and services are often the same in the work of both architects, and in many cases Saarinen's buildings provided the conceptual point of departure for those of Kahn.

9.1

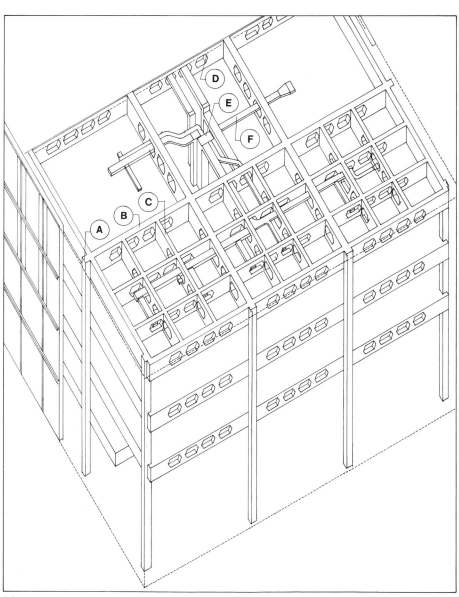

9.2

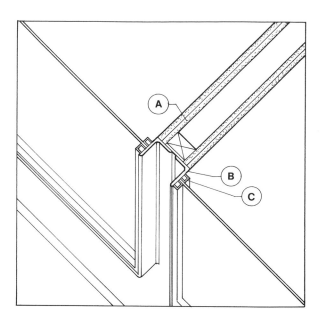

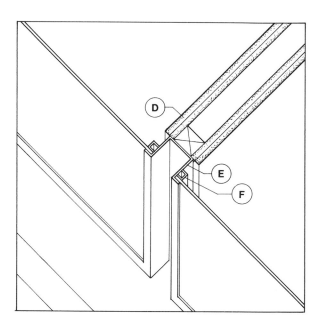

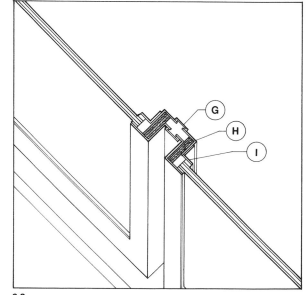

9.3

AF of L Medical Services Building

Louis Kahn

Philadelphia, 1954–1957

(demolished)

9.1   View.

(Robert Dripps)

9.2   Framing and mechanical systems.

A   Offset concrete column. Note the varying relationship of column to edge beam.

B   Major concrete Vierendeel truss, 22″ wide × 3′ 9½″ deep. The slab forms the top chord of the truss.

C   Secondary concrete Vierendeel truss, 8″ wide × 3′ 9½″ deep (partially shown).

D   6″ and 8″ concrete slab tapering to 4″.

E   Main supply duct risers.

F   Supply air ducts set in openings in truss.

(LK/UP A-2, 3, 4, 9, 12, M-7, S-8)

9.3   Louis Kahn, curtain wall development.

1   First AF of L design:

A   4½″ metal stud and gypsum board partition.

B   Two 2 × 2½″ steel angles. The first design used rolled steel sections.

C   ⅝″ square steel glazing stops.

2   Second AF of L design:

D   4½″ partition.

E   Stainless steel braked metal frame. The second design reduced the quantity of steel by using sheet metal, while the stainless steel reduced the maintenance problem. This system made possible a "taut" wall as the braked stainless steel mullion can be glazed from the inside, placing the exterior face of the glass closer to the outside face of the wall.

F   Stainless steel glazing bead.

3   Kimbell Art Museum:

G   Splice cover plate.

H   12 gauge stainless steel and plywood mullion.

I   12 gauge stainless steel glazing stop.

(LK/UP A-14, 14B)

Kahn's advocacy of the archaic, or perhaps his anti-Modernism, was more apparent at the perceptual level than at its ideological core. While his work appears to replace the light, precise, metallic, sometimes eggshell-thin forms of Modernism with the heavy, thick, sometimes crude, sometimes natural, usually rough forms of traditional construction, Kahn did not question many of the basic tenets of Modernist rationalism. For Kahn as for his precursors the key to style was economy of material, however complex the resulting form. He wrote in 1944:

The combination of safety factors . . . and standardization narrowed the practice of engineering to the se[le]ction of members from handbooks recommending sections much heavier than calculations would require and further limited the field of engineering expression stifling the creation of the more graceful forms which the stress diagrams indicated. For example, the common practice of using an I-beam as a cantilever has no relation to the stress diagram which shows that required depth of material from the supporting end outward may decrease appreciably.[2]

A beam designed to reflect its stress diagram is one that uses the minimum quantity of material, and in 1944 Kahn was interested in minimum weight as well. Minimum weight was a concern he was quick to abandon, but he retained the principle of economy to which it was attached. It had been the contention of John Ruskin and others that modern materials could never provide a suitable architecture for want of mass. Kahn seemed determined to prove them wrong. Many of his buildings have a strangely contradictory nature in that they seek to use minimum amounts of massive materials such as brick and concrete. His early structures, and many of his late ones, are transpositions of Modernist steel forms, particularly those used by Saarinen, into heavier materials.

One of the first of these forms, mentioned in the same 1944 essay, is based on hollow metal structures:

To attain greater strength with economy, a finer expression in the structural solution of the principle of concentrating the area of cross section away from the center of gravity is the tubular form since the greater the moment of inertia the greater the strength.

A bar of a certain area of cross section rolled into a tube of the same cross section (consequently of a larger diameter) would possess a strength enormously greater than the bar.

The tubular member is not new, but its wide use had been retarded by technological limitations in the construction of joints.[3]

In 1948 Eero Saarinen won the competition for the Jefferson National Expansion Memorial in St. Louis with a proposal for a 630-foot arch. Kahn's entry also contains arches of a sort, although considerably smaller, that have a structural relation to Saarinen's, as both employ the concept of the hollow structural tube. Saarinen's steel and concrete sandwich panel was an indirect expression of his interest in stressed skin airplanes, automobiles, and pressure vessels, while Kahn's smaller arches and thin-shelled round tubes in irregular forms seem more organic in inspiration. Although he was rarely to use steel again, Kahn's fascination with hollow structures continued into his later work, expanding first to house utilities and then into occupiable space.

Another steel idea from this period was the hollow steel umbrella that Kahn used in his Parasol House project. Sponsored by the Knoll Furniture Company, it was to be built by an aircraft manufacturer. The house was a series of square canopies each cantilevered from a single column, while the roof itself was a sort of eggcrate sandwich panel with open webs. The parasol concept was one of several Kahn ideas that began as steel structures but were later transferred into concrete, and the deep, hollow floor was to be the point of departure for some of his major buildings.

THE EARLY WORK

Kahn's first major executed commission, the new art gallery at Yale (obtained through Saarinen), was the first of these steel-to-concrete transformations, as the

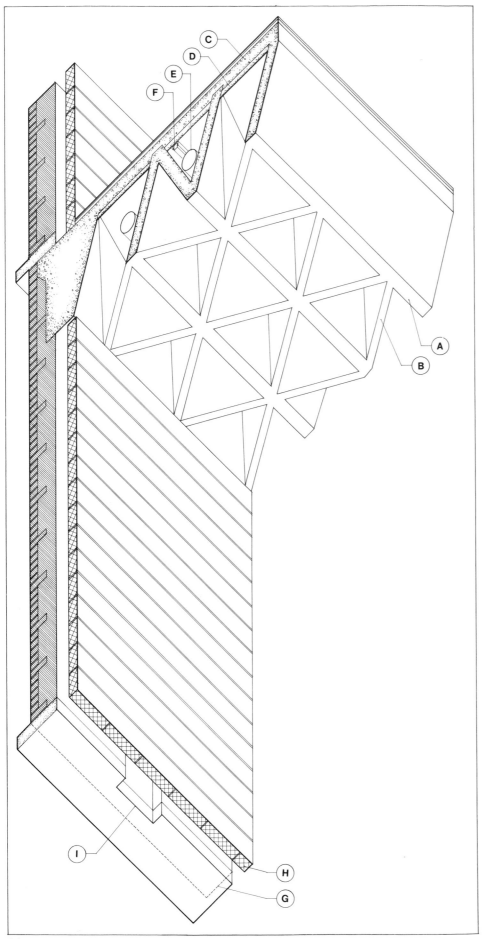

9.4

9.5

Yale University Art Gallery

Louis Kahn

New Haven, Connecticut, 1951–1953

9.4   Wall section.

A   Main beam of tetrahedral concrete structure. Although it appears to be a space frame, the pattern of reinforcing assures that it acts as a series of beams.

B   Minor beam.

C   4" concrete slab with 1¼" finish wood floor.

D   2" acoustic panel serving as formwork for the concrete slab.

E   Heating and air conditioning duct; diameter varies. A number of smaller ducts are used in lieu of fewer, larger ones to make it possible for them to be contained in the concrete structure.

F   Electrical duct.

G   Face brick and cement brick.

H   Concrete masonry wall.

I   Space for horizontal heating pipes.
    (YU A-11, 55, D-4)

9.5   Interior.

building's principal feature, its tetrahedral floor structure, was essentially a form associated with steel—the space frame—executed in concrete.

Kahn was at this time working almost entirely in triangular structures. His Philadelphia City Hall project of 1952–1957, for example, contains no right angles (figure 9.6). He had been heavily influenced by the ideas of Buckminster Fuller and Robert Le Ricolais, who both were working with triangular rather than quadrilateral structures. Fuller in particular felt that triangles were inherently stable under loads from any direction while rectangles were not. Kahn argued that the triangular structure gave equal expression to lateral loads, and was fond of taking Mies van der Rohe to task for going to such lengths to express vertical loads while going to equally great lengths to hide lateral bracing.

While the triangular structure of the Yale Art Gallery is a product of this thinking, it is, on a less philosophical level, a translation of the space frame of Saarinen's Engineering Building for GM into concrete. Both structures use the deep triangular voids created by the space frame to house round ductwork so that the structure and services are unified into a single volume in which both are visible. Kahn was simply changing Saarinen's thin steel pipes into massive concrete tetrahedrons.

This gives the building its greatest appeal but also creates something of a problem; it is ultimately a rather absurd structure. It is the purpose of the space frame to use minimum material to obtain maximum spans, sacrificing simplicity in the process. Kahn's structure uses a massive quantity of concrete in a complex arrangement to achieve what is ultimately not a particularly impressive span (the bays are 20 by 40 feet). This component of the building, at least, had the kind of mass that many found lacking in Modernism. Nevertheless, as a manifestation as a space frame it has something of a Dadaist appeal.

Kahn did not use this type of structure again, probably because of the neutral character of the spaces it produced. The building is one of the more elegant expressions of the free plan, in which space was to be independent of structure and thus liberated. Kahn immediately began to move away from this idea, and his future development is a progression toward tighter and tighter relationships of all the components of buildings.

His 1954 AF of L Medical Services Building in Philadelphia pleased no one, then or now, and when it was demolished in the 1970s Kahn said, "I'm glad it's torn down."[4] Strangely enough this building, so unlike his mature work, was a moment of crystallization for many of his ideas about detailing and the integration of structure and services. The structure of the building is another translation of a steel form into concrete: in this case the interlocking Vierendeel trusses of Kahn's Parasol House became a two-way hollow concrete truss. The web openings are hexagonal, recalling the geometry of the Yale building, but also resemble a castellated steel beam. The purpose of this carving out is not purely economy but again the integration of mechanical services. The ductwork runs through the beam openings, allowing both structure and mechanical systems to be exposed while also giving a flat ceiling grid that allows the space to be subdivided, albeit with little acoustic privacy.

Although the slick, thin wall of the exterior seems out of character for Kahn, it is ironically the origin of one of his most commonly used details. The solution here reappears in only slightly altered form in almost all of his subsequent work. Kahn's first design for the curtain wall was Miesian in inspiration, and resembled the windows made from rolled steel sections used at IIT. Why he abandoned this system is not known, but it can require a great deal of maintenance and an excessive quantity of steel. The most economical use of steel is in bent sheets, which enables a smaller amount of material to be configured in a larger, deeper, and hence stronger section. This system is in common use for interior door frames where maintenance is not a problem. The problem of exterior use can be solved easily but not economically by the use of stainless steel. A typical solution is Gordon Bunshaft's Lever House mullion, in which two standard steel channels are wrapped in stainless

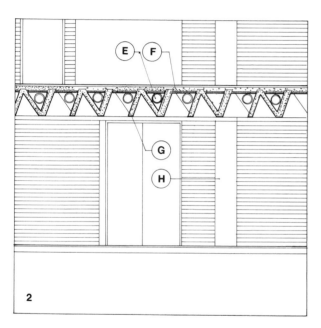

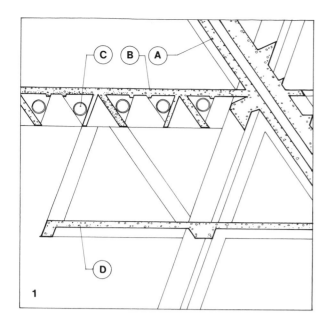

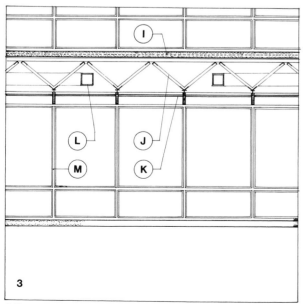

9.6 **Louis Kahn and Eero Saarinen, comparative sections.**

1   Louis Kahn, Philadelphia City Hall tower (project):

A   Concrete column with voids. The triangular section is more expressive of the lateral loads, which are the major structural concern in a tower.

B   Concrete tetrahedral floor structure.

C   Ductwork for heating and ventilation.

D   Intermediate concrete floor slab.

2   Louis Kahn, Yale University Art Gallery:

E   Ductwork.

F   Concrete floor slab.

G   Tetrahedral concrete floor structure. See figure 9.4

H   Concrete column. Although these are vertical, Kahn later said that he wished they had been tetrahedral as well.

3   Eero Saarinen, GM Engineering Building:

I   Concrete slab on metal deck.

J   Steel angle space frame made from V-shaped shop-fabricated joists, shown here in section, welded together at site.

K   Acoustic baffles and lights.

L   Caldwell high-velocity heating and air conditioning duct. The high-speed system requires a duct of smaller cross section. Its drawbacks are noise and air turbulence.

M   Column at curtain wall mullion. See figure 8.7.

(Perspecta 4, YU DN 11, SHG DN A-5, 20)

steel, thus minimizing the quantity of stainless used. However, Kahn was in this instance uncomfortable with the system of hollow tubes:

I was looking for an answer to the window, which, when made of stock members, did not please me. I also thought it was technologically false because you were trying to make it look like a familiar molding which would be applied more to wood than it would be to metal. Wood is complete, it's full. If you make a hollow column in metal, it must be a container. It's completed and it's right. But when you're dealing with nothing on the inside, you're suspicious of the metal that's helping it on the interior which you don't want to show, or it is a limitation of another material.[5]

Kahn was not abandoning the idea of hollow structure, simply indicating that the window mullions were not structure. In the conventional Modernist wisdom, beams, columns, and slabs were structure, window supports were not, and he was following the typical Modernist practice of articulating the primary structure while suppressing the secondary ones.

Thus his second curtain wall design uses bent sections of stainless steel sheets, but in the form of exposed L's and U's rather than as wrappers for steel tubes (figure 9.3). Although Neutra and several others had used similar systems in the 1930s, the inspiration was probably Eero Saarinen, who used a similar system at the MIT chapel (figure 8.29). Since this required the metal to be self-supporting, it also required the use of thicker sheets of stainless steel than those used in the Lever House type of mullion. Although the building was built using this second system, it was accomplished only with considerable difficulty. The additional thickness of the sheet metal made the braking, or bending, of the metal much more difficult, and the subcontractor who made the sections swore he would never attempt to fabricate this type of mullion again. Despite its difficulties, Kahn was fascinated with this system and used it on many other buildings, including his next where it played a critical role.

THE RICHARDS BUILDING

The commission for the Richards Medical Building at the University of Pennsylvania almost went to Saarinen but was ultimately given to Kahn and was to become the commission that made him famous. Despite its importance to Kahn's career, it is atypical of his mature work. It is ironic in any case that Kahn came to prominence by designing two research laboratories, the Richards Building and the Salk Institute, a type not easily adapted to his architectural principles.

Except for the service towers Richards has no load-bearing walls. It does contain the typical Kahn materials—brick, precast and prestressed concrete, and stainless steel windows—but they are not used in the configurations typical of his later work. Each tower of the Richards complex consists of a series of square, concrete-framed floors. At the center of each side of the square is a masonry tower, sometimes containing exhaust ducts and sometimes containing fire stairs. These towers were another transformed Saarinen element, being inspired by the exhaust towers of Saarinen's Dynamometer Building at GM, but again transformed into more massive elements.

Each floor is composed of three largely independent squares arranged around a service core. Each of the squares is divided into nine smaller squares by cross beams, and each of the nine is subdivided into four smaller squares by minor beams. Like Wright, Kahn preferred to support the beam by placing the columns at its third points rather than at the ends, thus opening up the corners while equalizing, at least in theory, the bending moments in the beams. The concrete beams are exposed on the exterior, where they support cavity walls of brick and concrete masonry.

The structure of nine squares is not determined by any particular programmatic aspect of the building, but is the result of Kahn's desire to find the most "efficient" way to use concrete. Like the Modernist architect's before him, and like the High Tech architects' that came after him, his overriding principle was minimal material through appropriate form. The strategy adopted to accomplish this in the Richards

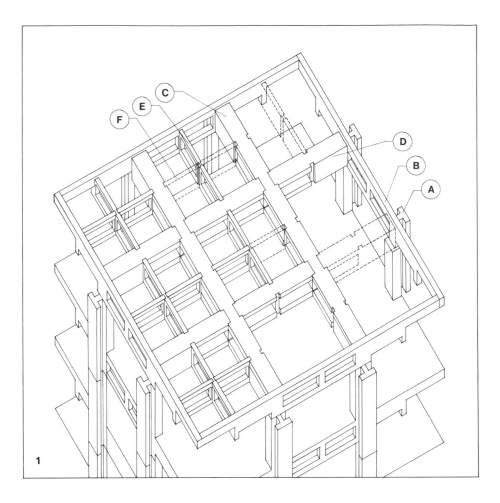

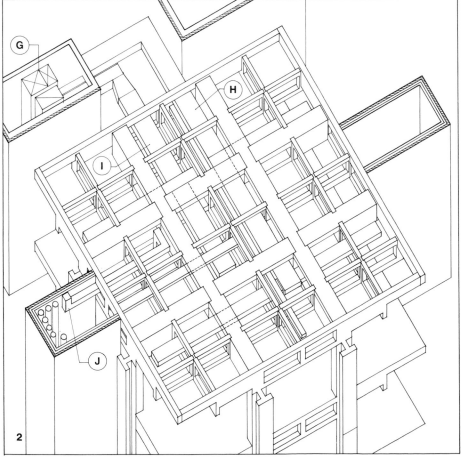

9.7

9.8

A. N. Richards Medical Research Building

Louis Kahn

Philadelphia, 1957–1965

9.7   Framing and mechanical systems.

1   Structure:

A   Precast concrete column.

B   Precast prestressed edge truss.

C   One-piece main truss with twelve ⅜″ prestressing strands in the top flange and twenty-eight ⅜″ pre-stressing strands in the bottom. These receive a slightly greater pretensioning stress to carry the three-part trusses until they are post-tensioned.

D   Three-part post-tensioned truss with three 1¼″ post-tensioning rods. Despite the symmetrical struc-tural arrangement of the system and the fact that in the finished structure the main trusses appear identical, the method of construc-tion is entirely different.

E   Secondary trusses 13′ 4″ long. The secondary trusses serve no struc-tural purpose other than to support the pipes and ducts.

F   Secondary trusses 6′ 0″ long.

2   Complete structure with mechanical systems:

G   Main supply and return ducts.

H   Air supply duct.

I   Air return duct.

J   Exhaust air duct. Only a small por-tion of the ductwork is located in the towers.
    (LK/UP S-4A, 7A)

9.8   View.

9.9   Louis Kahn, comparative sections.

1   Parasol House:

A   Two-way eggcrate steel roof with hollow web and steel top plate.

B   Steel pipe column. Each steel para-sol was cantilvered from a single column.

C   Field splice of square parasol roof sections.

D   Voids in steel web.

2   AF of L Building:

E   6″ concrete slab thickened to 8″ at columns.

F   22 × 44″ concrete beam.

G   10 × 44″ concrete beam with voids.

H   10 × 4″ concrete beam in section.

I   Supply duct and air diffuser.

J   Offset concrete column.

3   Richards Medical Research Building:

K   4″ cast-in-place slab.

L   Precast beam.

M   Small nonstructural beams to hold ductwork.

N   Beam in elevation.

O   Precast post-tensioned columns.

P   Supply air duct.
    (LK/UP M-7, S-8, A-22)

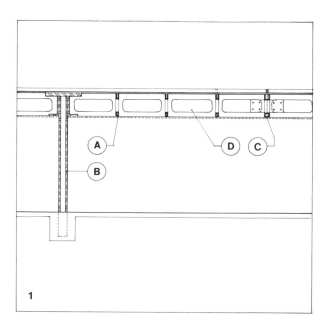

1

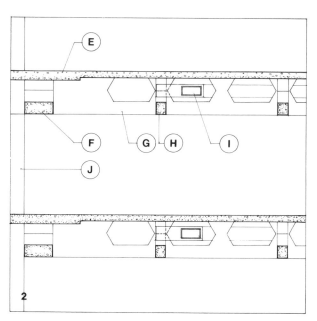

2

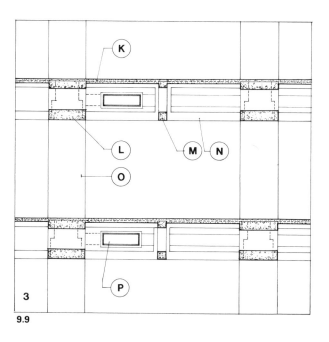

3

9.9

9.16

9.17

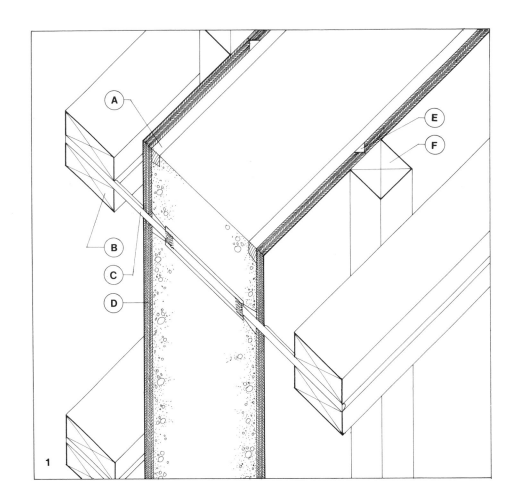

1

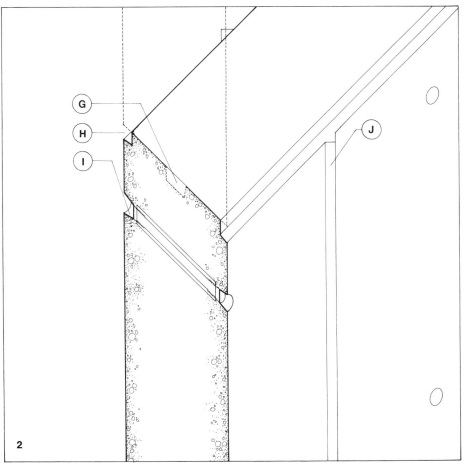

2

9.18

Salk Institute for Biological Studies
Louis Kahn
La Jolla, California, 1959–1965

9.16   **Courtyard.**

9.17   **Study.**

9.18   **Formwork of typical concrete wall.**
   1   Section of typical wall with forms in
        place:
   A   ¾ × ¾″ tapered wood rustication
        strip inserted at joint between
        pours. It is tapered to facilitate re-
        moval and to create a slope to drain
        out water. The shadow thus created
        hides the color differences that may
        occur because the two tiers of con-
        crete are poured at different times.
   B   Two 2 × 6 beams to counteract the
        outward pressure of the wet
        concrete.
   C   Screw-type form ties. The ties also
        hold the two plywood panels to-
        gether, resisting the outward pres-
        sure of the wet concrete.
        (Reinforcing bars not shown.)
   D   ¾″ plywood formwork.
   E   Joint between two plywood panels.
        The edges are beveled ⅝″.
   F   4 × 4 structural wood support.
   2   Section after removal of forms:
   G   Key to tie the two levels of wall
        together.
   H   Notch created by rustication strip.
   I   Conical shaped opening left by
        form ties. The tie remains embed-
        ded in the wall. Its ends are covered
        with lead or other material to pre-
        vent rust.
   J   Ridge created by beveled plywood
        panel. Since this will show up as a
        joint in any case, Kahn elects to ac-
        centuate it rather than attempting
        to hide it.
        (LK/UP DN 303)

tory. The studies by contrast use wood windows, many of which are operable. One of the more elegant details is the way in which the wood panels meet and do not meet the concrete walls and floors. At the head they are butted, at the base is a drip cap, at either side are frameless windows. The reveal was a detail Kahn used sparingly, wisely, and often intuitively. He might let two dissimilar materials collide or he might separate them with a reveal, and he felt no need to be consistent in his use of this element.

Kahn is often associated with monolithic concrete and masonry walls, and is thought of as one who resisted the layered development of modern construction. He certainly liked solid walls, he certainly disliked veneers, and many of his walls are monolithic, although not nearly so many as it appears. (Many are actually cavity walls.) But Kahn was not so simple-minded as to ignore the reality of layered construction, and he struggled with the problem of how to build layered walls without sacrificing literal structural expression by means of exposed construction. In the conference center and in the original lab design he developed a detail of stone walls with concrete backup; rather than trying to turn the stone veneer around the corner to hide the backup, he brings the concrete around the corner to expose it.

In the end the conference center was not built and construction on the lab proceeded with exposed concrete finishes. For these walls Kahn in part copied and in part developed what has become a standard system of exposed concrete finish. Popular concrete finish systems at the time included sandblasting, bush hammering, and other techniques to even out the irregularities in finish inevitable in cast-in-place concrete. Kahn, however, wanted "the marks of the tool" left on the wall. The basic system involved nonabsorbent plywood sheets beveled at the edges, notched with rustication strips between forms and with plugged form-tie holes (figure 9.18). Because this deprived the contractor of any means of correcting defects and errors (patching was not allowed), his job became all the more difficult. This apparently did not bother Kahn, nor did the fact that the system could hardly have been less industrialized, requiring a quantity of skilled on-site labor that William Morris might have found excessive. The contractor throughout the course of the design development argued that a steel system ought to be used rather than the one employed.

In the end the cost of the finished building was comparable to that of other labs built with clad steel frames, but this did not make exposed concrete a popular substitute for clad steel. By this point American medium- and large-scale construction was moving relentlessly toward clad, layered, independent, and specialized systems of building, and was not about to be convinced that the system used at Salk, which had none of these qualities, was an acceptable substitute, even at the same price. It presented too many opportunities for mistakes that could not be corrected, placed too much pressure on a single building component to perform too many tasks, allowed little margin for error, and caused too many headaches.

But Kahn was committed at this point to pursue his own and not society's idea of "order." He had said as early as 1954:

We should try more to devise structures which can harbor the mechanical needs of rooms and spaces and require no covering. Ceilings with the structure furred in tend to erase the scale. The feeling that our present-day architecture needs embellishment stems in part from our tendency to fair joints out of existence—in other words, to conceal how parts are put together. If we were to train ourselves to draw as we build, from the bottom up, stopping our pencils at the points of pouring or erecting, ornament would evolve out of our love of the perfection of construction and we would develop new methods of construction. It would follow that the pasting on of lighting and acoustical material, the burying of tortured unwanted ducts, conduits, and pipelines would become intolerable.[7]

Although Kahn used exterior exposed concrete infrequently in subsequent buildings, he built more and more in ways that were implicitly critical of typical American construction techniques.

9.19

9.20

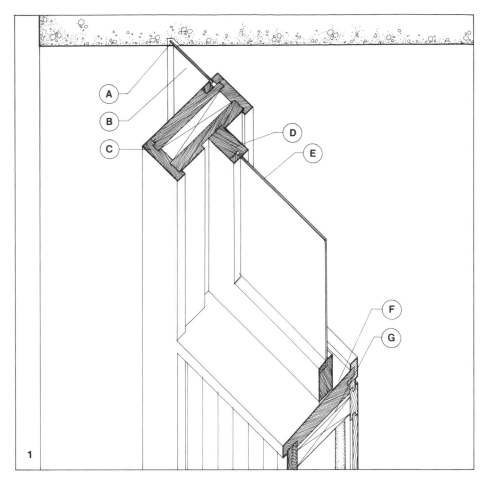

1

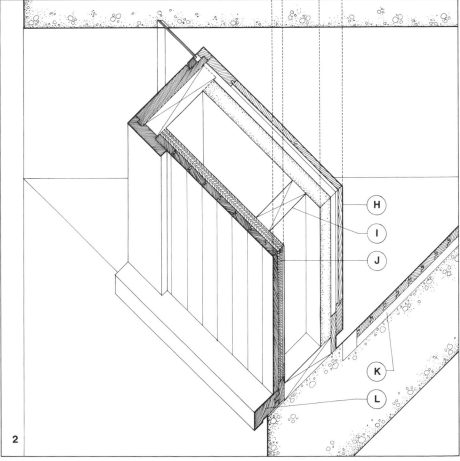

2

9.21

Salk Institute for Biological Studies

Louis Kahn

La Jolla, California, 1959–1965

9.19 Wood panel at study.

9.20 Window detail.

9.21 Window details.

1   Jamb detail:

A   ¾ × ¾" slot in concrete formed from Plexiglas insert.

B   Glass set in slot.

C   Teak exterior frame. Teak will retain its natural finish and does not receive paint.

D   Teak window.

E   Glass.

F   Teak sill sloped to drain, with track for sliding shutter.

G   Rough wood framing.

2   Sill detail:

H   ¾" oak inner wall panel on 1¼" cement asbestos board. Oak is a more beautifully grained wood but less suitable for exterior use than teak. These panels could have been concrete, but the wood indicates that they are nonstructural.

I   Wood studs 12" oc to support panels.

J   Outer wall panels of ¾" teak tongue and groove boards. Teak may be exposed on the exterior without paint or varnish.

K   Oak flooring on concrete slab.

L   Teak sill and copper flashing on ⅛" waterproof setting bed.

(LK/UP LA 56)

Between the completion of the first phase of the Richards Building and his death Kahn completed thirteen major buildings, seven of which have brick or unit masonry exterior walls (six of the seven are bearing walls) and one of which, a concert barge, is steel. He seemed unable to deal with steel and even had difficulty accepting what he called the "generosity" of concrete. He came to dislike the concept of frame and curtain wall entirely, and in his subsequent buildings progressively tried to eliminate it.

THE MASONRY BUILDINGS AND THE EXETER LIBRARY

After the Richards laboratory Kahn executed a number of brick buildings, beginning with the Unitarian Church at Rochester. This was in part inspired by Saarinen's chapel at MIT, although Kahn's response to the chapel was largely negative. Saarinen's chapel used load-bearing brick masonry and brick arches at a time when both were taboo in the Modern movement, providing a precedent for what Kahn was to do next, not just the revival of archaic masonry techniques but a rethinking of the relationship between structure and space in Modernism.

This relationship in typical postwar American buildings was a highly bastardized version of Le Corbusier's free plan. While the steel and concrete frame had made possible the independence of structure and plan, the major aesthetic consequence of this—the ability of spaces to interconnect and interlock, to "flow" together— was rarely used for obvious functional reasons. The net result was not "a new world of space," but simply that structural and spatial divisions of the building became independent. Spatial layouts, while retaining traditional cellular character, lost the order imposed by load-bearing structure, while the structure itself was likely to go completely unnoticed. Kahn was not alone in finding this unacceptable, but he went further than others in insisting that the structural divisions of a building and its spatial divisions must coincide, however small those divisions might be. A person standing in a space must perceive the structure of that space.

Coupled with Kahn's revival of interest in traditional spatial and structural systems was an increased use of traditional masonry assemblies. To him there were definite rules about the way brick could be used. Steel lintels or other types of concealed reinforcement were rarely acceptable, and in his later work openings were invariably made with arches, usually segmented. In some early masonry experiments, such as the Tribune Review Building in 1958, he differentiated between bearing and nonbearing walls by the use of different types of concrete block, but after 1965 masonry is seldom used as a curtain wall. The basic structures used at the Rochester church—modern, open, concrete-framed space on the interior and traditional, cellular, masonry space on the exterior—provided the best of both worlds and were to form the basis for numerous subsequent Kahn works.

Kahn said of his library for Phillips Exeter Academy: "I felt that a reading room would be a place where a person is alone near a window . . . a kind of discovered place in the folds of construction."[8] The order of space at Exeter, as at Rochester, is concentric rings of different structures of different materials—in Kahn's terms, doughnuts. The innermost has no assigned use: a concrete cube with a large circular opening on each side is supported by four concrete piers at 45 degrees to the primary grid. An X brace of one-story-deep concrete beams spans the top and supports the skylight above (figure 9.28). In theory this structure is a folded plate acting to laterally brace the entire building. At a glance it seems somewhat structurally excessive for an eight-story building, and perhaps owes more to a desire for structural expression than to structural necessity. The second doughnut holds the books. Concrete flat plates are supported by concrete columns in square bays on the four sides. On the ground floor this area is used for the circulation desk, card catalogue, and a grand stair, and the three square bays of each side are merged into one by means of eliminating the two center rows of columns. This requires a transfer structure at the second floor to pick up the load of the lost columns. Here the concept of one structure for one space is carried to extreme if not excessive limits. Is a 40-foot free-span space really necessary for a space housing a card catalogue? The outer layer is composed of brick bearing walls supporting a flat-plate concrete

9.22

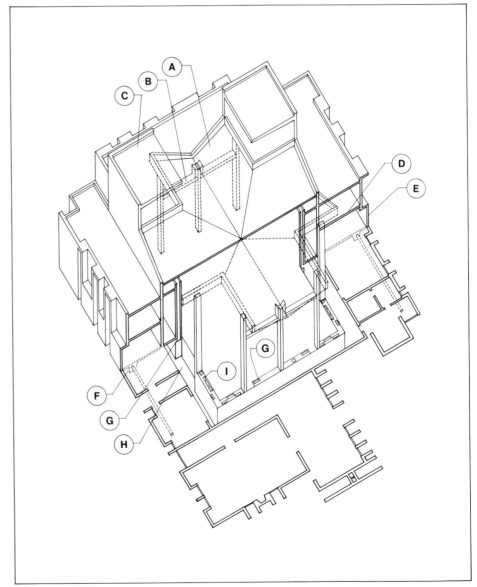

9.23

First Unitarian Church, Rochester

Louis Kahn

Rochester, New York, 1959–1969

9.22 View.

9.23 Framing.

A Thin-shell concrete post-tensioned folded plate, 9″ thick at bottom, 6″ thick at top with edge beam.

B Concrete column and beam plate support. These are largely hidden by the masonry walls.

C Concrete slab at light monitor, tapering from 10″ at wall to 4″ at edge.

D 6⅝″ concrete flat-plate slab with 12 × 22″ beams at brick piers.

E Load-bearing masonry walls.

F Perimeter air supply duct.

G Air supply shafts to sanctuary. Air travels up these shafts from the utility corridor to a diffuser at the top of the wall.

H Utility corridor to provide space for ductwork.

I Air return shafts. Air is returned from the corridor and sanctuary through continuous slots in the masonry wall and returned to the utility corridor through shafts in the wall. The doors to the classrooms have special frames that allow the return air to pass into the corridor. (LK/UP A-3, S-5, 6)

slab. Lateral bracing is provided by brick crosswalls dividing the doughnut into a series of rooms, each containing two windows and four built-in carrels.

Like Frank Lloyd Wright, Kahn desired monolithic exterior walls, unfinished so that the interior and exterior surfaces were the same, but like Wright he faced the difficulty of the layered nature of the modern wall. Although solid brick walls are often used in contemporary construction, the typical contemporary masonry wall contains within its thickness a cavity for waterproofing, insulation to retard the flow of heat, a vapor barrier to prevent condensation, and metal reinforcing to tie the whole thing back together again. In addition to hindering Kahn's simple desire for monolithic building, this complicated assembly did not fit easily into his philosophy. A wall was not to him a machine. Each material and component—brick, concrete, ductwork—had its own "order." An assembly of specialized components, such as the modern brick wall, was not easily reconciled with this way of thinking.

When conditions permitted, Kahn built monolithic walls, such as in India and Pakistan, where construction and standards of building performance were less specialized. The Indian Institute of Management has monolithic brick walls 8 to 24 inches thick laid in bonded patterns. (Interestingly enough, the Millowner's building built by Le Corbusier in the same city ten years earlier had used a cavity wall.) Almost all Kahn's American buildings use cavities and rigid insulation. He rarely used the same solution to his problem more than once, and the development of these walls (figure 9.26) shows an ongoing effort to reconcile his philosophy of construction with the realities of contemporary American practice.

Before Exeter Kahn had used two types of brick exterior wall. The first, used in India and Pakistan, was a true monolithic wall, and had the richness of detail and bonding patterns of traditional brick walls. The walls of Richards and Rochester were modern, specialized, and sophisticated, but lacked the visual qualities of the first wall type, particularly the absence of bonding patterns. At Exeter Kahn sought to combine the two.

The Exeter wall has two layers, an outer layer of 12-inch-thick brick and block which is a bearing wall and an inner layer of 4-inch-thick brick which is a curtain wall. The cavity between holds insulation, vapor barrier, and waterproofing as in a traditional cavity wall. The outer wall is bonded in a pattern resembling common bond, while the inner, being only one brick thick, is in simple running bond. This is an inversion of the wall type used at Rochester, or for that matter the typical masonry cavity wall, where the thinner layer is placed on the outside. The advantage of the Exeter wall is purely visual, since it exposes the bonded structural portion of the wall to the exterior. This may seem to many a result so subtle as to be hardly worth the effort, but to Kahn's eye the Exeter wall was everything that the Rochester wall was not.

Exeter is the purest of Kahn's brick structures. Rarely is brick used here as a curtain wall material. At least conceptually, every brick contributes to the structural support of the building. There are no steel or other concealed lintels. Each opening in the bearing wall is a frame with a flat arch (an arch with a very shallow curve). In traditional masonry structures a wall often becomes thicker toward the base as the load increases. The Exeter wall is of constant thickness, but each pier is one brick wider in its face dimension than that of the floor above. As a result there is a noticeable taper to these piers that makes them appear something like Egyptian pylons. There are many places where the openings between piers are opaque, but here the voids are filled with wood paneling, not brick, to indicate that they are nonstructural. According to Jay Wickersham the entire exterior wall is nonbearing since the pattern of reinforcing in the slab carries the load to the cross walls between cubicles. Like all structural rationalists, however, Kahn expresses some things while concealing others. The floor slab, for example, meets the wall in a fairly complex way. At the piers it turns down several feet for additional support; at the arches between these piers it is held back so that the slab does not bear on the arch. No hint of this complicated assembly appears on the facade.[9]

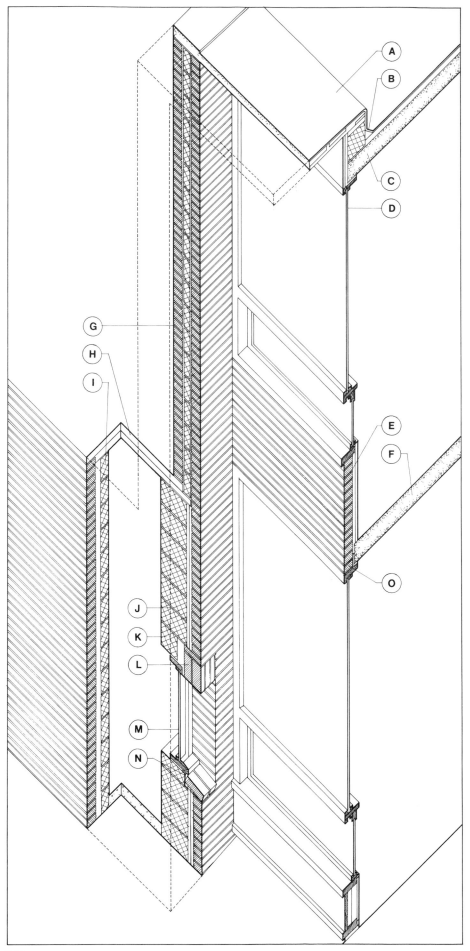

9.24

9.25

First Unitarian Church, Rochester

Louis Kahn

Rochester, New York, 1959–1969

9.24 Wall section.

A Terra-cotta and prefabricated concrete cap with terra-cotta coping.

B Roof flashing, built-up roof, and waterproof membrane on 2″ rigid insulation.

C Concrete roof slab.

D Wood windows and glass.

E 4″ brick wall with wood panel interior facing.

F 6⅝″ concrete floor slab bearing on interior concrete masonry walls.

G Two layers of 4″ brick and 4″ concrete masonry with no cavity, since both sides are exterior and separated from the wall below with flashing.

H Concrete slab and terra-cotta coping.

I 4″ brick and 4″ concrete masonry with 1″ insulation and air space to intercept water that penetrates the wall.

J 4″ brick and 12″ concrete masonry with 1″ insulation and air space.

K Concrete masonry lintel to support masonry over opening.

L Reinforced brick lintel with reinforcing bars in brick joints. In subsequent projects, including the addition to this church, Kahn used jack arches.

M Wood window.

N Sill flashing to prevent water that penetrates the sill from entering the cavity.

O Steel lintel to support masonry above with spandrel flashing.
(LK/UP A-11)

9.25 Wall detail.

9.26 Louis Kahn, development of wall types.

1 Indian Institute of Management, Ahmedabad:

A Solid brick wall.

2 First Unitarian Church:

B 4″ brick.

C 1″ insulation and cavity.

D 8″ concrete masonry. The two masonry layers are connected with metal ties so that they act as a structural unit.

E Wood window frame.

3 Exeter Library:

F 12″ CMU (concrete masonry) and 4″ brick exterior bearing wall.

G Insulation and cavity.

H 4″ inner face brick. This wall is nonstructural and serves only to create the cavity.

I Teak and oak window with flashing below.
(LK/UP A-7, A-19)

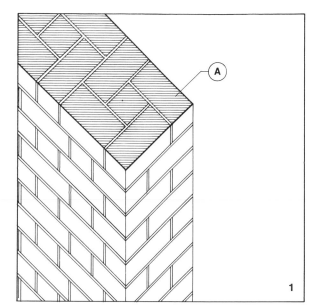

1

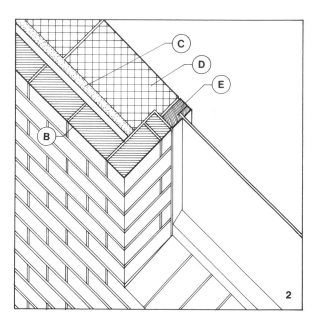

2

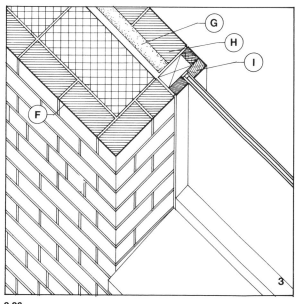

3

9.26

9.27

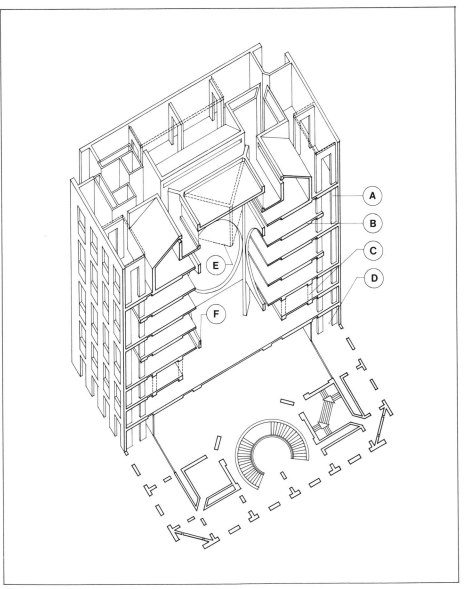

9.28

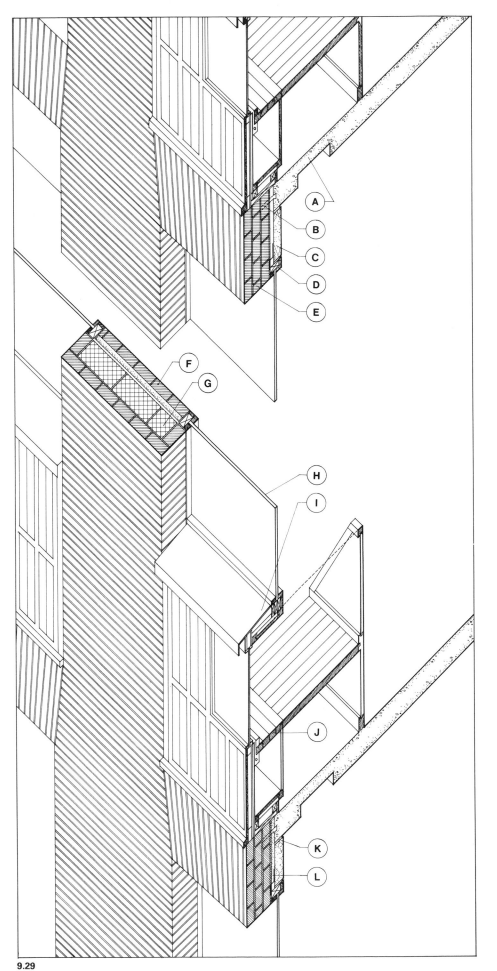

9.29

Library, Phillips Exeter Academy

Louis Kahn

Exeter, New Hampshire, 1965–1972

9.27 View.

9.28 Framing.

A Exterior masonry wall and cross walls supporting 8¾" flat-plate concrete slab on brick and concrete masonry bearing walls. The library has suffered from leaks for many years since its completion, especially at the roof terrace, as well as from uneven settlement of the foundation, and portions of the wall have been rebuilt since the building's completion.

B 3½" concrete slab with 11½ × 30" beams and 18 × 18" concrete columns in stack area.

C Transfer structure to allow desk and catalogue area to be free of columns.

D Open air gallery at ground floor. The structure is also open to the weather at the top.

E Diagonal bracing at top of central space.

F Concrete pier and diaphragm wall with circular opening.
(LK/UP AC-3, S-4, 8)

9.29 Wall section.

A Concrete slab with slot for light fixture.

B Anchors 12" oc to tie arch back to continuous dovetail anchor slot in concrete slab.

C Sandstone lintel.

D Teak and oak window frame with flashing to divert water out of cavity.

E Brick arch.

F Inner wall of 4" brick with cavity filled with 1½" rigid insulation fastened to ¾" galvanized furring channels.

G Brick-faced concrete masonry with headers every fifth course.

H 1" insulating glass.

I Stainless steel sill on wood frame to drain water off horizontal surface.

J Carrel of 1" teak boards, 1" rigid insulation, ¾" oak plywood, and ½" insulating glass.

K Compressible filler to ensure that the slab does not bear on lintel.

L Flashing to drain water from cavity to exterior.
(LK/UP A-20, 36)

The details that show Kahn at his best are those that describe what the building is not. Due to the need for lateral bracing one would expect this building to have heavy solid corners. It does not; the corner is broken open to show the edges of each wall, thus demonstrating that there is an internal concrete frame bracing the building and making the solid corner unnecessary. A similar condition occurs at the inner wythe of the exterior wall. This layer of the wall is nonbearing—in fact it is separated from the wall by a compressible filler to ensure that the concrete slab does not bear on the wall—and it is in this wall that the only lintels in the building, the red sandstone ones over each opening, occur. This opening could have been spanned with an arch as is the outer layer, and perhaps it would have looked better if it had been, but Kahn does not want to mislead us as to the nature and function of this wall, i.e., he does not want the arch to appear to support the slab. The wall could have been made to appear to be monolithic, and most observers probably assume that it is, but Kahn refuses to deliberately deceive us.

The system of exposed and integrated utilities used at the Richards Building and Rochester was not abandoned but heavily modified, primarily because Exeter is an eight-story building. Like other buildings of comparable size, it has two mechanical systems, one for the perimeter and one for the interior spaces, due to the differing conditions of their heating and cooling loads. The perimeter system, rather than air, uses water, which requires only small pipes for distribution and thus does not pose the same problems of spatial accommodation as an air system with ductwork.

Each corner of the building contains a core for fire stairs, toilet rooms, etc., that also contains vertical shafts to distribute air to each floor. The air is distributed on each level by two round horizontal ducts running above the corridor that separates the book areas and the reading areas. The diffusers that distribute the air are for the most part located in the ducts themselves, but occasionally a duct will turn, penetrate the wall, and reemerge as a linear diffuser. These diffusers, unlike the simple slots used at Rochester, can be modified to control the flow of air. It should be noted that, appearances to the contrary, the ductwork is rarely exposed.

The fenestration system at Exeter is a variation of that developed for Salk, although the method of forming structural openings is in some ways the opposite. The typical opening in the exterior wall is two stories high, with a carrel at its base containing a small view window and a large single light above to light the reading room interior. The glass of the larger high window is set as deep into the wall as possible, and the wood frame is recessed into the brickwork. Kahn sought to make the glass almost invisible, to achieve the quality of a ruin. By contrast the lower window is placed flush with the face of the exterior wall, and the small view window is set only as deep as the glazing detail requires. This window is not operable but an interior wood panel may be slid across the opening, omitting the view but preserving the light above. As at Salk, all exterior wood is teak; all interior wood is clear-finished white oak.

If Exeter was the typical Kahn building, the Kimbell Museum was to be the opposite, violating most of the rules he had set out to this point but losing nothing in quality in its deviance from his own standards.

THE KIMBELL MUSEUM

The Kimbell Museum is one of Kahn's finest buildings, in spite or perhaps because of the fact that it breaks so many of his own rules. There are none of the tightly defined structural elements that Kahn defined as "rooms," there is no direct correlation between the structural order and the spatial order, and there are no intermediate spaces between interior and exterior. The walls are not monolithic and do not appear to be monolithic.

The two-story building is set on a hill so that it is one story tall at the rear, which faces a park. The roof structure of the upper floor is composed of concrete vaults, relatively narrow in their short dimension but spanning over 100 feet in their long dimension. There are two interior courts which interrupt the vaults, a slit in the top of each vault to allow light into the interior, and windows facing the park.

9.30

9.31

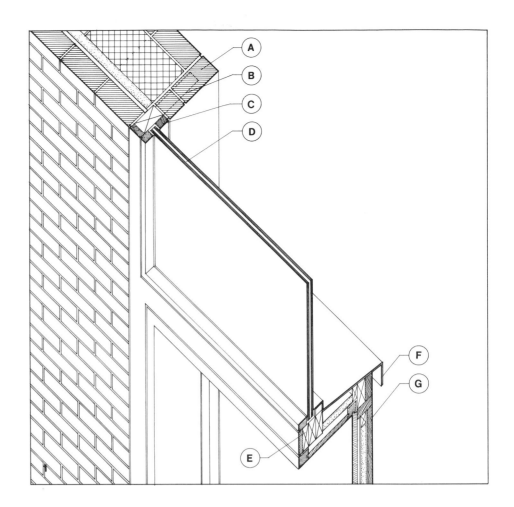

9.32

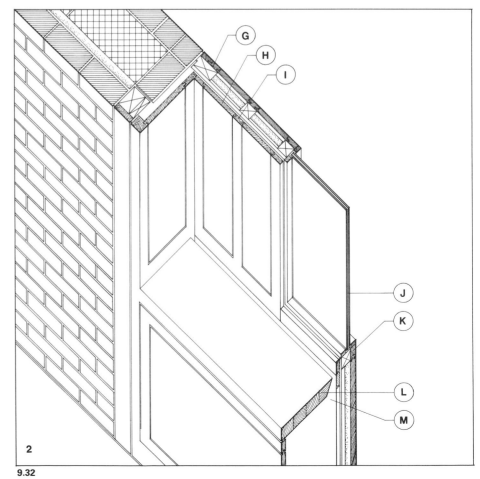

Library, Phillips Exeter Academy

Louis Kahn

Exeter, New Hampshire, 1965–1972

9.30　**Window at study.**

9.31　**Interior.**

9.32　**Window details.**

1　Window jamb at clerestory:

A　Brick and concrete masonry.

B　Strap anchors 16″ oc to tie window to masonry.

C　Teak glazing bead.

D　1″ insulating glass.

E　Wood framing to support glass with oak finish trim.

F　Projecting stainless steel sill above each carrel. If this horizontal surface were made of wood, even if sloped, rot would be inevitable, so stainless steel is substituted.

G　Carrel of 1″ teak boards on exterior, with ¾″ solid oak on interior and insulation between.

2　Window jamb at carrel:

H　Interior and exterior oak panels with solid oak infill panels. Teak is not as fine or as prominently grained as oak, and due to its softness does not have as crisp an edge. Exterior panels are thinner, and are randomly matched according to grain.

I　Solid oak rail.

J　½″ insulating glass.

K　Teak rail to cover ends of tongue and groove teak boards.

L　Solid oak desk.

M　Slot for circulation of heated air.

(LK/UP A-20, 36)

The concrete vaults are cycloids in section, the shape generated by a point on a rolling circle. This shape was an aesthetic choice rather than a structural one, and the shape has few precedents in architectural history, although Edwin Lutyens used it in rather flattened form in his arched bridges, such as the one at Hampton Court. The vaults achieve their long spans by means of post-tensioning rods that run in long sweeping curves along their lengths. Kahn responded to Komendant's first drawing of the design by saying, as most architects would, that the edge beams seemed too small to carry the vault over such a long span. Komendant's response was that Kahn's perception was correct; it is the vaults that carry the beams, not the beams that carry the vaults.

The floor below, although flat, is also post-tensioned despite the smaller bay size. Here Kahn used something similar to a waffle slab, but with flat slabs of concrete at both top and bottom. The formwork of the coffers could thus not be removed and was made from foam blocks that remained within the structure.

At Rochester, Exeter, and Salk, the structural order is tightly matched to the program of rooms. Thus the card catalogue at Exeter has its own particular structure and its own particular space. At the Kimbell the structure is dominant; rooms that have little or nothing in common with exhibition spaces are placed within a structural system designed for that purpose. The library and auditorium are shoehorned into the long narrow spaces created by the cycloid vaults. The results are not unpleasant, but are arguably inappropriate, particularly in the auditorium where the concave vaults focus rather than diffuse the sound as is desirable.

While Kahn was fond of the old adage "the joint is the beginning of ornament," he made less use of it at the Kimbell than elsewhere. A number of joints are concealed, some in rather elusive ways, whether through economic necessity or a general sense of restraint. He chose a flat-seam lead roof rather than the standing-seam copper popular at the time. A more curious detail occurs at the caps at the end of the prestressing rods. In their raw form these ends are unsightly, and in any case need to be covered to prevent rust. A typical solution to this problem was to place a chrome cap over the rod ends "ornamenting" the joint, a common detail in buildings of the 1960s. The condition of rod ends occurs frequently at the Kimbell, notably at the tops of columns and at the ends of the vault. Kahn had wanted to cover these with marble plates, but the budget, which was by no means generous, would not allow this, and the end strands were set in pockets later filled with concrete (figure 9.38). Viewed from close up the detail appears somewhat crude.

The Kimbell, like most museums, has a large number of occupants and a large quantity of incandescent lighting and thus requires frequent air changes and hence a large quantity of ductwork. The public parts of the Kimbell are essentially a one-story building and the air could conceivably have been distributed through the floor slab as it was at the Rochester church, but Kahn chose a more tightly integrated system, placing the ducts within the structure of the gallery. There is no exposed ductwork as there is at Richards and there are no ducts encased in concrete as at Salk. Between each vault at the Kimbell are shallow U-shaped concrete channels from which are suspended a series of linear metal pans. The space created holds two supply air ducts, one for the gallery on each side of the channel. The central mechanical room is on the floor below, and the ducts reach the roof structure through the small bays between the long spans. A linear diffuser between the concrete U and metal pans distributes the air, as well as serving as a bracket to brace the tops of partitions. Return air is accomplished by slots at the bottom of some interior partitions which lead to shafts in the basement. This system appears simple when seen from the gallery space, but requires considerable modifications to the concrete structure in order to support the wall above the slot.

This is one of the happier solutions to Kahn's desire to integrate the utilities while exposing the structure. The ductwork, being concealed, requires no special craftsmanship. The utility space is easily accessible through the metal ceiling, and allows for later adjustments and modifications to the system. The supply diffuser and return air grilles, being unobtrusive, do not visually compete with the art for

9.33

9.34

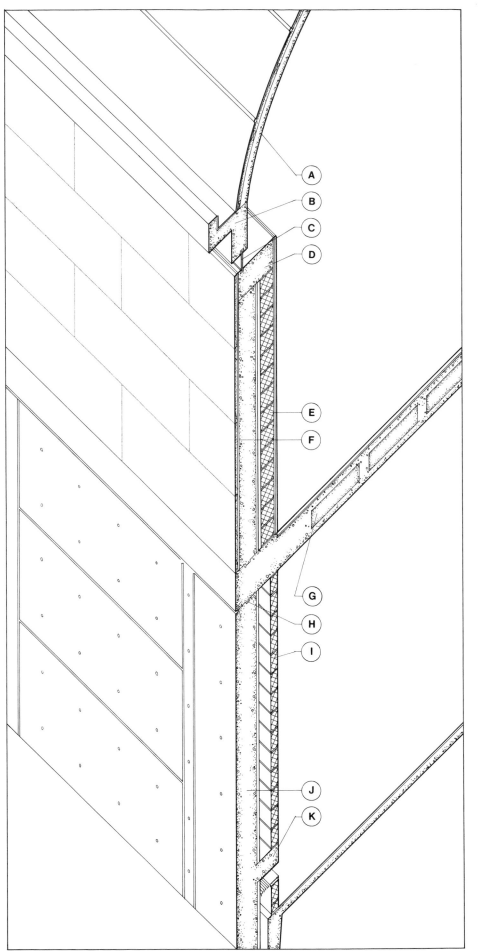

A
B
C
D
E
F
G
H
I
J
K

9.35

Kimbell Art Museum

Louis Kahn

Fort Worth, Texas, 1966–1972

9.33 **View.**

9.34 **Vault at portico.**

9.35 **Wall section.**

A   Roof construction of lead sheet and two layers of ⅜″ plywood on 2 × 4 wood nailers 24″ oc with 2″ rigid insulation between, on 4″ concrete shell. The two layers make the curve possible.

B   Concrete support with three-ply elastometric roofing in gutter.

C   ⁹∕₁₆″ glass, with 2½″ cement wash with wire fabric reinforcing on wall below to create sill.

D   Concrete beam.

E   8″ block interior wall with 2″ rigid insulation behind.

F   Outer wall of ⅞″ travertine on concrete. The backup wall is concrete rather than masonry in order to form a beam over the entry beyond.

G   Concrete slab with foam block inserts finished with ¾″ wood parquet floor on ¾″ board underlayment.

H   Concrete key and rustication strip, similar to figure 9.18.

I   4″ concrete masonry with air space and insulation beyond.

J   Cast-in-place concrete wall with form tie holes and panel joints.

K   Concrete support to create slot for air return.

(LK/UP A-12)

attention. But again this solution was somewhat unique to the problem at hand, and Kahn did not use it again.

Although the structure is atypical of Kahn's work, the relationship of structural to nonstructural elements is not. Throughout the building the infill elements are held back from the vault and columns with reveals and windows. The reveals serve a functional purpose where precision finish materials must join with relatively crude concrete, but they and the windows serve chiefly to clarify what is supporting the vault and what is not. Thus at the short end of the building, where the travertine and concrete block curtain wall meets the concrete vault, a tiny tapered slot separates the two. The opening is filled with frameless Plexiglas. Kahn wrote: "Travertine and concrete belong beautifully together because concrete must be taken for whatever irregularities or accidents in the pouring reveal themselves. Travertine is very much like concrete—its character is such that they look like the same material. That makes the whole building again monolithic and doesn't separate things."[10]

The nonbearing walls on the main floor are travertine on the exterior and sometimes on the interior as well. In fact they are concrete block walls faced with 1-inch travertine. There is nothing inelegant about the way in which they are detailed, but they presented Kahn with a problem with which he was uncomfortable, that of veneering. He went to great extremes to avoid the use of veneers whether in brick, wood, or stone. His insistence on solid oak panels in the carrels at Exeter is only the most extreme example. Kahn's problem at the Kimbell was that, given the technology of modern stone construction, some type of veneering was almost inevitable. Monolithic stone walls in travertine were simply out of the question. Of course he had faced this problem before, particularly at the AF of L Building, the Bryn Mawr dormitory, and the early studies for the Salk Institute. At the Kimbell he developed a solution that was somewhat atypical of his mature style. The concrete is exposed on the face of the wall at the edge and at floor levels, attempting to make it clear that the stone is only a facing. This could be an awkward detail, since it requires the joining of a precision material, stone, with a crude and sometimes inaccurate one, concrete, but this type of juxtaposition is common in Kahn's work as a whole.

The Kimbell is filled with many other materials that are veneered, but all are detailed in a way to show that they are veneers. The interior freestanding partitions are clad in wood and fabric but have metal ends to show the thinness of the surface. The travertine walls are more ambiguous. The ends are not exposed or even revealed, and the joint pattern resembles that of a traditional stone wall. It could be argued that this is not dissimilar to the Salk-type detail, but it cannot be argued that the Kimbell detail is consistent with Kahn's other work.

Like the nonbearing partitions, the windows are clearly separated from the structure that contains them. A deep reveal sets off the window from the surrounding concrete so that the windows seem to float in the openings, and once again the reveal is used to join a smooth precision material with a crude and rough one, concrete, while preserving the geometric purity of the volume. Once again Kahn uses an inside-glazed stainless steel system (here reinforced with plywood) to achieve a taut precise membrane whose tension is broken only by the pattern of reveals at the mullions. Once again the windows are shop-fabricated in frames and field-joined at the reveal with a splice instead of the more common stick system. It is surprising to note how rarely a steel frame joins with a travertine wall. All of the large windows are in structural openings in the concrete; the stone walls are never punched or penetrated by openings. The only junctions of glass and stone occur at the small reveals at the tops of walls, where no frames are used.

The most remarkable aspect of the Kimbell, however, is not the windows but the skylights. They are much less extensive in area than the windows, a narrow strip at the top of each vault, but they are much more dramatic in effect, particularly on partly cloudy days when shadows travel across the floor of the museum. Kahn had hoped to use this slot to light the paintings, but this proved impossible, and the

9.36

9.38

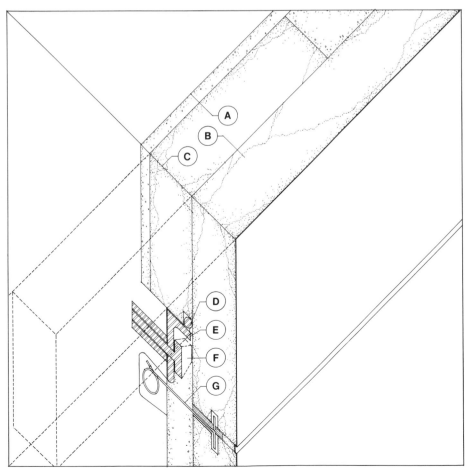

9.37

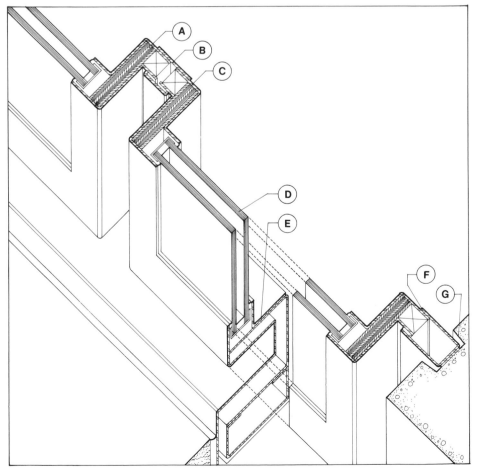

9.39

Kimbell Art Museum

Louis Kahn

Fort Worth, Texas, 1966–1972

9.36 **Window between columns at vault ends.**

9.37 **Stone details.**
A   Blocked-out area of concrete wall to receive anchor.
B   1¼″ travertine panel.
C   4 × 8 × 1¼″ support panel epoxied to rear of travertine to transfer the weight of the panel to the steel clip.
D   Bead welded to angle to prevent lateral movement of the stone.
E   Support cut from 2 × 1¼ × 10″ long steel angle to take the weight of the stone panel to the concrete wall.
F   Expansion bolt anchoring clip to concrete wall.
G   Wire anchor to laterally support the top of the stone panel below.
    (LK/UP A-26)

9.38 **Column and vault end.** The rectangles of concrete of different color cover the pockets that house the ends of the post-tensioning strands.

9.39 **Window details.**
A   Frame from braked stainless steel sheet.
B   Stainless steel splice plate and bolts. The frames are shop-fabricated in panels requiring field splicing.
C   12 gauge mill finish (104) stainless steel inner frame epoxied to ½″ plywood with glazing bead. The wall's taut appearance is a result of inside glazing.
D   1″ insulating glass with stainless steel glazing bead.
E   Stainless steel sill.
F   Stainless steel sleeve to allow inaccuracies between wall and frame to be taken up.
G   Notch in concrete column to receive sleeve.
    (LK/UP A-10)

irony is that this light never reaches the paintings, being deflected by a perforated metal diffuser and thrown onto the vault to avoid damage to the paintings that uncontrolled sunlight could cause.[11]

Patricia Loud has pointed out that while response to the Kimbell was and remains enthusiastic, several critics have questioned the structural appropriateness of the vaults. Kahn, interestingly enough, was criticized for the same reasons as Eliel Saarinen had been sixty years earlier, that he had taken a form inherent to masonry, the vault, and executed it in concrete, and while the result was not inappropriate, neither was it expressive of the material or the process. The great success of the building was in its introduction of natural light, however compromised in the finished building, and it was a concern that was to dominate his next, and last, building.

YALE CENTER FOR BRITISH ART

Unlike the typical Kahn building, the Center for British Art is composed in a subtractive rather than an additive way. Although it contains a variety of types of space, they have little effect on the building's structure. The primary structure is a cage of structural bays of uniform size. If a space larger than one cell is needed, as at an auditorium, it is carved out by the removal of columns or beams. It is a system that has little in common with the free plan or with Kahn's previous work. (Kahn died when the Yale Center was beginning construction, but the building was finished by Anthony Pellecchia and Marshall Meyers, who had detailed many of Kahn's other buildings.)

As always Kahn faced the dual problems of exposing the structure and integrating the utilities, and here he came closest to achieving his idea of "hollow stones." Much of the ductwork is completely encased by the concrete structure. In fact the vertical risers for the ducts make the only modifications to the structural grid. At two locations on the column grid one column is split into four columns to create an opening approximately the shape of a rotated square. The main supply (and return) ducts are in this space and the horizontal ducts branch out from them. On the first and second floors this is accomplished by pairs of ducts in round stainless steel casings, as at Exeter. On the third and top gallery floors the ducts are housed in V-shaped, hollow concrete beams. Return and minor supply ducts are housed in the double-slab airfloor system. As at Exeter and the Kimbell the diffusers and grilles are elegant but almost invisible.

The edges of the columns and slab are exposed on the exterior, and the voids between filled with matte finish stainless steel panels or glass. From a distance it is a system that seems totally foreign to Kahn's thought and work; closer up, familiar details begin to appear: braked stainless steel mullions, inside glazing, shop-made frames joined with reveals, and projecting metal sills. Atypical of Kahn are the thinness of the wall, the absence of transitional spaces, and the relatively small windows in the panels themselves.

After the mixed success of his experience with natural lighting at the Kimbell, Kahn wisely decided to consult with the lighting designer Richard Kelly at a much earlier stage in the design process. The result is a system for the top-floor galleries that truly lights the paintings, not just the building. It is a system simple in conception but rather complex in execution. An acrylic skylight of four square domes covers each opening between concrete beams. On top of the domes, outside the building, is a series of aluminum louvers looking something like a venetian blind to block the most damaging direct sunlight into the galleries. From the complexity and awkward appearance of this system one can assume that it owes more to Kelly than to Kahn, but one cannot argue with the results on the interior, which seems flooded with sunlight.

At the time of Kahn's death in 1974 he enjoyed an immense popularity, and a number of his buildings, such as the Kimbell Museum and the Salk Institute, proved in the final analysis to be comparable in cost per square foot to buildings of similar program built by more conventional techniques; but it was also clear that he was

9.40

9.41

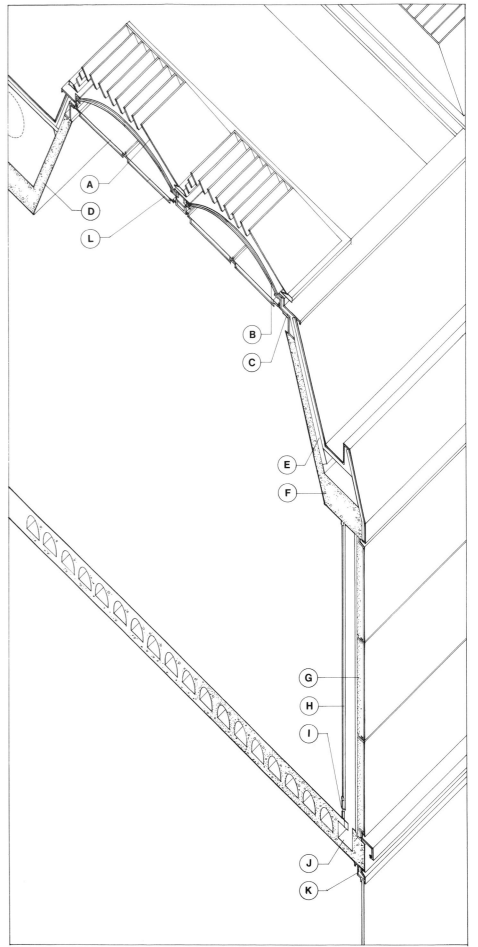

9.42

British Art Center, Yale University

Louis Kahn

New Haven, Connecticut, 1969–1974

9.40   **View.**

9.41   **Wall detail.**

9.42   **Wall section.**

A   Aluminum louver. This is asymmetrical because of solar orientation.

B   Acrylic dome skylight with double lens. The inner layer of the dome has an ultraviolet light filter.

C   Aluminum skylight frame, slot for air return, and steel bracket.

D   Concrete V beam. The voids house air supply ducts.

E   Terne-coated stainless steel roofing on 1½″ rigid insulation and ¾″ plywood on concrete wall.

F   Concrete edge beam.

G   12 gauge matte finish stainless steel panel filled with urethane insulation and .040″ galvanized steel backing.

H   Interior finish of oak or fabric-covered panel on ⅝″ gypsum board and 2½″ metal studs.

I   Oak base with slot for return air.

J   Void for air return in airfloor slab.

K   12 gauge stainless steel window frame.

L   Holophane pyramidal diffuser with sand-blasted acrylic cover.

(LK/UP A-14, 15, 15a)

becoming increasingly alienated from the mainstream of American construction. His office left over $500,000 in debts, and it had only survived as long as it had through the personal financial sacrifices of many of his employees. Kahn's attitude was one of gentle but firm defiance, and was ultimately utopian: architecture could not wait for a better world to come, one must build correctly now.

It was clear by the early 1970s that what Kahn considered to be a good building and what the American building industry considered to be good building were diametrically opposed. It wished to separate utilities; Kahn wished to integrate them. It wanted independent building components; Kahn wanted them interdependent. It wished to conceal structure and services; Kahn wanted to expose them. It sought maximum flexibility; Kahn sought a tight fit of form and activity. These philosophical differences led to conflicts at a smaller scale. The building industry wanted veneers; Kahn wanted bearing walls. It wanted steel; Kahn wanted concrete. Kahn wanted all to be monolithic; it wanted it layered. Thus the paradox of Kahn's influence. He inspired countless formal imitations of his work in the 1970s but few of these had any constructional similarity to his own work, and all too often the massive brick walls, arches, and lintels surrounded steel frames and acoustic tile ceilings.

On the positive side it can be said that Kahn succeeded where Saarinen so conspicuously failed. Those buildings in which Saarinen tried to use the processes of industrialized building—standardization and material economy—to achieve the character of traditional architecture were among his weakest. This was by contrast Kahn's greatest success; if he eschewed standardization, he adhered to principles of material economy, however massive the result, however archaic the means, and in the end perhaps disproved Ruskin, who thought that the want of mass in modern materials would bring architecture to an end. But Kahn was not alone in his intransigence; others were attempting to reverse the trends of modern construction using methodologies, and sometimes forms, similar to his.

SIGURD LEWERENTZ

Lewerentz's career was in many ways similar to Kahn's, beginning in Classicism, going through International Style Modernism, and ending in the New Brutalism. Unlike Kahn, Lewerentz excelled at all three. His Resurrection Chapel at the Woodland Crematorium, designed when he was 37, would be sufficient to establish his historical importance. But not even the vicissitudes of history can explain the difference between this church and his last, the church at Klippan which differs from it so fundamentally in every way.

If Lewerentz's life was similar to Kahn's, it differed greatly from that of his one-time partner, Erik Gunnar Asplund. Asplund's career was short and successful, Lewerentz's was long and erratic. For much of its middle part Lewerentz supported himself through his ownership of the Idesta window company, which supplied the steel windows for Asplund's Bredenberg store and Woodland Crematorium. He executed a variety of buildings in these years, notably the cemetery and crematorium at Malmö.

Lewerentz's reputation today rests largely on his first building, the Resurrection Chapel at the Woodland Cemetery, and his last two, the churches of St. Mark in Björkhagen, near Stockholm (1956), and St. Peter in Klippan, near Copenhagen (1963). The last two, while not unnoticed at the time of their construction, have recently achieved a cult status following their rediscovery by Colin St. John Wilson and others.

It is entirely possible that Lewerentz was unaware of Kahn's work, and the similarities in style are perhaps the inevitable result of similarities of intention. Both wished to discover and to evoke the qualities of archaic masonry construction while scrupulously avoiding any overt historical references. Both came ultimately to have a spiritual reverence for the nature of the material they were working with, attributing to masonry an inner life of its own. Neither was content to use brick alone, for both structural and perhaps financial reasons. Kahn's answer was to structurally combine brick with concrete, Lewerentz's to do the same with steel.

9.43

9.44

St. Mark's

Sigurd Lewerentz

Björkhagen, Sweden, 1956–1960

9.43 View.
(Per Bonde/Swedish Museum of Architecture)

9.44 Interior.
(Tomas Mjöberg/Swedish Museum of Architecture)

The floors and roofs of St. Mark's are supported entirely by brick bearing walls. Most of the former are precast planks, while the main sanctuary has brick vaults, but vaults that are traditional neither in form nor construction. The vault form is composed of long, thin conical sections tapering in alternate directions, giving the structurally necessary curved form and also giving a slope to the valley between the segments for drainage. The interlocking segments rest on a series of Cor-ten steel wide flanges that carry the loads back to the bearing walls, similar to the ribs in a Gothic cathedral. The vault, while not necessarily an economic form in cost or weight, is a form "in the nature of brick," utilizing brick's inability to take tension stresses to structural advantage.

Like Kahn, Lewerentz set down a rigid set of rules for the use of bricks. They could not be cut, they could not be used as veneer. The accommodation of this first rule is made possible through the use of extremely wide mortar joints, 1 inch or larger in many locations. Unlike Kahn, Lewerentz felt no obligation to articulate the forces acting around windows or other openings; where Kahn would inevitably use an arch, Lewerentz made frequent use of concealed concrete lintels and beams. The larger opening that separates the chapel from the chancel is framed with what appears as a brick beam, a sight that would pain a number of rationalists, from Viollet-le-Duc to Kahn himself.

The oversized, handmade brick and wide mortar joints contribute greatly to the building's archaic appearance, but the windows presented a problem. Wishing the quality of a ruin, Lewerentz no doubt would have preferred to dispense with glass altogether. His solution was the same as Kahn's, to pull the glass as deep into the thick masonry wall as possible. Lewerentz went a step further, for the glass is not in the opening at all but mounted to the inside face of the wall and framed only on its sides so that the top and bottom edge of the glass are exposed. The head and jambs of the brick opening remain untouched, although a thin copper sill is necessary at its base to shed water.

St. Peter's in Klippan, although similar to St. Mark's in program and construction, differs in form, using a square sanctuary surrounded by an L-shaped school and office wing. In this it is remarkably like a fragment of Kahn's Rochester church. In addition to their mutual obsession with the nature of brick, St. Peter's gives us Lewerentz's version of Kahn's "hollow stones" concept.

The structures in both wings of the building are refined from those of St. Mark's. Bearing walls are used again; the secondary buildings are roofed with laminated timber beams and wood decking. The sanctuary uses the conical segmented brick vaults, but given its large square shape, 20 by 20 meters, additional support was necessary, and Lewerentz took the structurally logical but functionally questionable step of placing a column in the center of the space. Column is a poor word for this complex component, a T shape of welded I sections. That it succeeds as both a symbol (the cross) and support (it must pick up the two I sections supporting the vault ribs) is perhaps due to the complex and indirect methods of support. None of the main structural members are directly connected to each other, but are either supported by small pedestals of cruciform steel sections or rest on top of each other rather than being welded or bolted in the same plane.

This theme of discontinuity of elements, which remain visually separate while being physically connected, was applied to a number of other details. Lewerentz wished to dissociate the glass from the wall to give the building an archaic character. Rather than placing it inside the wall, as he had done at St. Mark's, he does the opposite, placing an unframed piece of glass outside the wall. The tinted glass is held in place by four small clips and seems to deny the transparency of the glass altogether. From the inside the effect is the opposite, as the building appears to have no glass at all, only openings in the masonry. A similar detail is used in some of the doors, where the wood door frame, instead of being set inside the masonry opening, is mounted on the surface of the brick wall so that the opening remains just that, while the door takes on a certain visual independence. At the main sanctuary door the same door is set flush with the brick wall (figure 9.56).

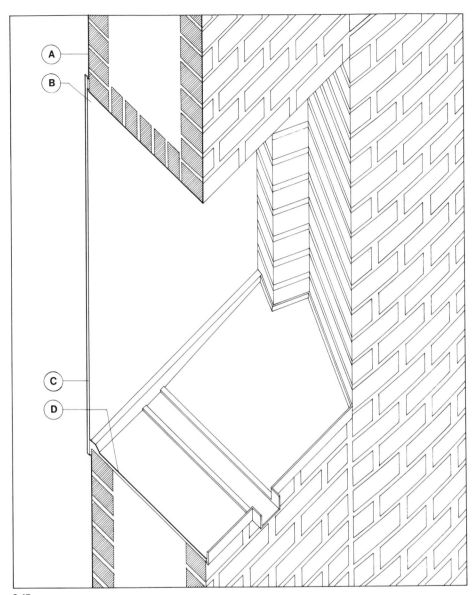

9.45

9.46

St. Mark's

Sigurd Lewerentz

Björkhagen, Sweden, 1956–1960

9.45 Window details.

A   Brick wall with internal concrete lintel. Despite his reverence for brick, Lewerentz is willing to use concealed lintels.

B   2 mm hard copper glazing stop beyond the glass. It is set inside the building rather than in the masonry opening. See figure 9.47.

C   1 cm glass.

D   Copper sheet sill.
    (SAM DN 194)

9.46 Window.

9.47 Window attachment.

A   Masonry wall.

B   1 cm glass.

C   5 mm glazing support at base.

D   2 mm hard copper glazing stop.
    (SAM DN 194)

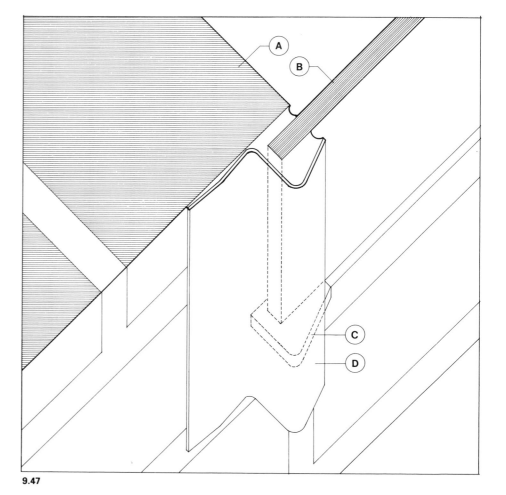

9.47

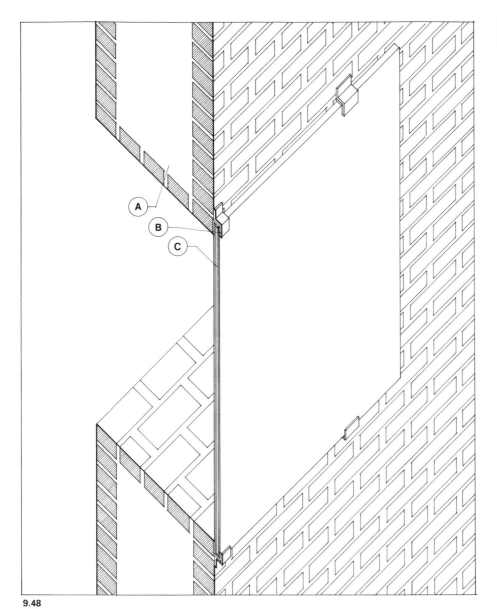

9.48

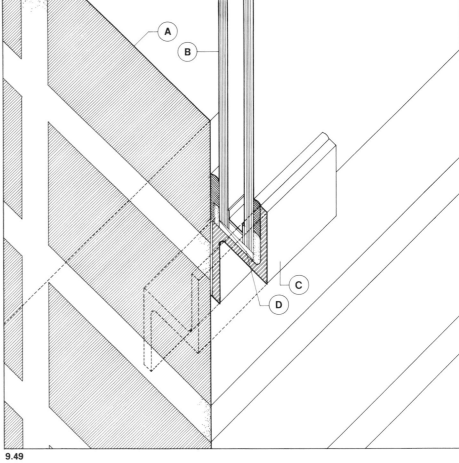

9.49

9.50

St. Peter's

Sigurd Lewerentz

Klippan, Sweden, 1963–1966

9.48   Window details.
- A   Brick wall with internal concrete lintel.
- B   4 × 4 × .5 cm steel angle 10 cm long holding glass in place. Setting the glass outside the wall eliminates the sill in figure 9.45.
- C   2.5 cm thermopane glass of two sheets of 66–67 mm glass with metal spacer.
    (SAM DN 49)

9.49   Window attachment.
- A   Masonry wall.
- B   2.5 cm thermopane glass of two sheets of 66–67 mm glass with metal spacer. The edge of the glass is not typically designed to be exposed to the weather.
- C   No. 4 steel angle 10 cm long, 4 × 4 × .5 cm, attached with ½ × 2″ screw, hot-dip-galvanized and painted with two coats roofing paint.
- D   40 mm neoprene setting block. There is considerably more caulking in the existing building than that shown on the drawing.
    (SAM DN 49)

9.50   Window.

Another reason for reversing the position of the glass from that of the earlier church is that at Klippan Lewerentz was using the window sills for air supply. In this Klippan has another remarkable similarity to Kahn's Rochester church, as all air supply to the sanctuary is through the hollows of the massive brick walls. Lewerentz used this detail throughout the building, so that one sometimes has the impression that a layer of air surrounds the building in the wall cavity. Most of the ducts are located in a utility trench under the building from which they rise to voids in the walls. This detail, along with the undulating floor which breaks open to form the baptismal font, gives less the impression of a monolithic wall than of a liquid sculptural mass barely contained by a thin coating of brick.

Lewerentz died in 1975, and St. Peter's was his last work. In retrospect his work was not so much ignored at the time as it was misinterpreted, for both he and Kahn were seen not just as reversing the trends of Modernism but as part of a much larger movement, the New Brutalism, which, if not anti-Modern, was certainly critical of the International Style. Perhaps Kahn's and Lewerentz's aims and those of the New Brutalists were not so similar, but the confusion is understandable given that their tools were often the same.

STIRLING AND GOWAN

Kindred spirits, if not direct influences, can be found in European work of the period. Stirling and Gowan's Engineering Laboratory at the University of Leicester has a curious conceptual, if not formal, affinity with Kahn's work. Each programmatic element of the building has its own volume, its own structure, its own window system, and its own materials. The administration tower has a flat-plate concrete slab and wall of patent glazing and tile. The laboratory tower has a two-way ribbed concrete floor, brick cavity walls, and specially projecting jalousie windows for ventilation. The workshop has a steel truss and skylight roof with translucent glass and a brick base, and the lecture theaters are concrete boxes faced with tile. These elements are assembled in a way that is both picturesque and Constructivist, and many of the details, such as the pipe rails, recall nautical and industrial images, which are totally absent from Kahn's work. On the other hand most of the structures are exposed concrete and many of the utilities are exposed as well.

Stirling's History Faculty building at Cambridge (designed with Michael Wilford and without Gowan) shows a similar division of and articulation of programmatic elements but a greater dependency of these parts when reassembled. The triangular trusses of the reading room lean against the L-shaped office wing, so that while in sharp contrast in form and material, the reading room is structurally dependent on the brick, tile, and concrete tower.

Stirling's attitude toward structure, space, and services was similar to Kahn's; it was their attitude toward material, particularly exterior materials, that was different. Brick and tile in Stirling's work have no mass, no weight; they may be carried by lintels or veneered onto other structures and sit atop glass walls. Glass is not a material that fills voids but a taut membrane that in the Modernist tradition sits in front of and not behind the wall.

Unfortunately the two materials that gave these buildings their taut, industrial quality, the tile-covered walls and patent glazing, have both proved problematic over time. A number of tile-clad concrete buildings have suffered problems of delamination. Many of the older patent glazing systems are well below standard American systems in structural performance. A contemporary American curtain wall of this type would require double glazing and a deeper and wider mullion.

The specific problem with the New Brutalism was its dependence on the building program as a determinant not only of form but of structure and detail. These architects sought a tight fit between structural space and institutional use. Similarly details were altered or completely changed to suit different parts of the building. This often proved more inflexible than accommodating, but in any case there were an increasing number of buildings being built without specific programs, if they

9.51

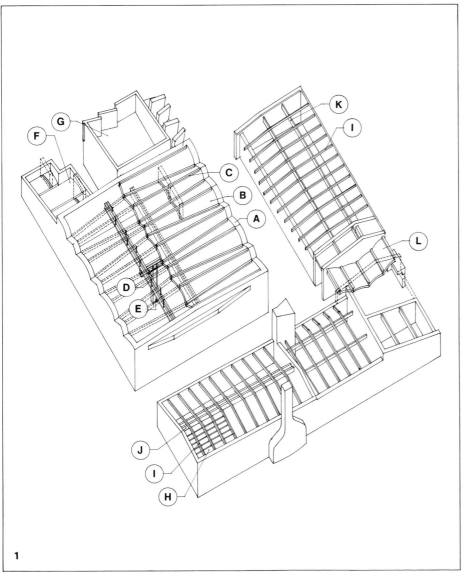

1

9.52

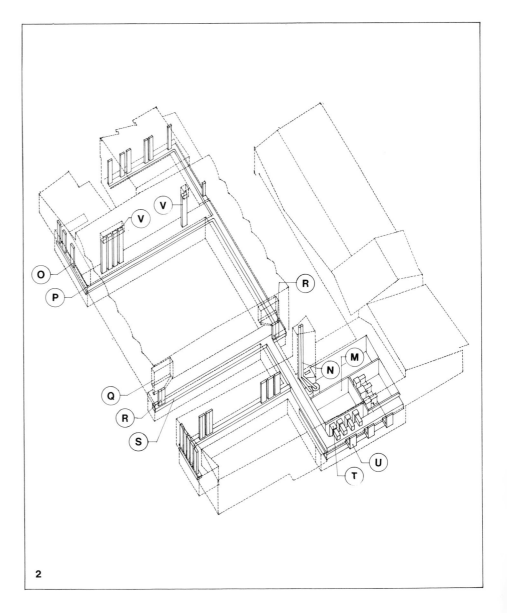

2

St. Peter's

Sigurd Lewerentz

Klippan, Sweden, 1963–1966

9.51 **View.**

9.52 **Framing and mechanical ventilation.**

1   Framing:

A   70 cm brick bearing wall.

B   12 cm thick brick vault.

C   INP 34 steel beam vault ribs.

D   Two pairs of INP 50 steel beams forming main girders bearing on wall and column, with pedestals to support ribs from two ST 120 × 60 × 10 mm steel Ts.

E   Two steel sections forming column. See figure 9.55.

F   Brick-vaulted narthex with light monitor above.

G   Bell room.

H   Typical roof deck of 1 × 4 wood planking on 2 × 4 wood purlins.

I   116 × 224 mm or 90 × 224 mm laminated wood beams 160 cm oc.

J   Double concrete support beam.

K   90 × 364 mm wood beam.

L   Brick vault at parish council room.

2   Partial layout of heating and ventilating ductwork. Many more ducts were shown on the original drawings than appear to be included in the executed design.

M   Fan room.

N   Chimney from boilers in basement.

O   Air supply to narthex in brick wall.

P   Perimeter supply duct in utility corridor below.

Q   Recess in masonry wall for air supply.

R   Two 20 × 40 cm supply ducts.

S   40 × 50 cm main supply duct at perimeter below-grade utility corridor.

T   Fan or air-handling unit.

U   Two ducts supplying air to window sill. See figure 9.56.

V   Series of 20 × 40 cm nonducted return air slots in wall to utility trench below.

(SAM DN 64–617/1–4, 41–46)

had any programs at all, while the abandonment of standard details led to greater expense and returned little in the way of real benefits to the users. This is not to say that these buildings were functionally inadequate; most of them were not, but few were used in the specific way that the architects anticipated.

It is no accident that the movements that followed the New Brutalism attempted to dispense with two of its basic tenets altogether. Where the New Brutalism sought a tight fit between program and construction, High Tech sought the opposite, an almost unlimited flexibility, and if the New Brutalism sought the expression of construction through purely literal means, Postmodernism sought the opposite, an architecture whose structural expression was entirely symbolic.

9.53

9.54

St. Peter's

Sigurd Lewerentz

Klippan, Sweden, 1963–1966

9.53 **Interior showing central column.**
(Swedish Museum of Architecture)

9.54 **Beam and column detail.** Note the doubling of all the structural members.

9.55 **Beam and column details.**
A   Metal roof.
B   Brick vault.
C   INP 34 steel beam vault ribs.
D   Pedestals to support ribs from two ST 120 × 60 × 10 mm steel Ts.
E   Two pairs of INP 50 steel beams forming main girders bearing on wall and column.
F   Cross bar from two INP 50 steel beams.
G   Column from two steel sections.
H   Steel plates to tie column sections together.
    (SAM DN 64–617/1–4, 41–46)

9.56 **Door and window details.**
1   Window at offices:
A   Double glazing set outside of wall. See figure 9.48.
B   Opening for air distribution.
C   Cavity in wall for air supply.

2   Door at sanctuary:
D   Wood door with jamb on surface of wall.
E   Solid wood door with spline.
F   Screw and wood plug.

3   Door at offices:
G   Wood jamb flush with wall.
H   Solid wood door.
I   Screw and plug.
    (SAM UND)

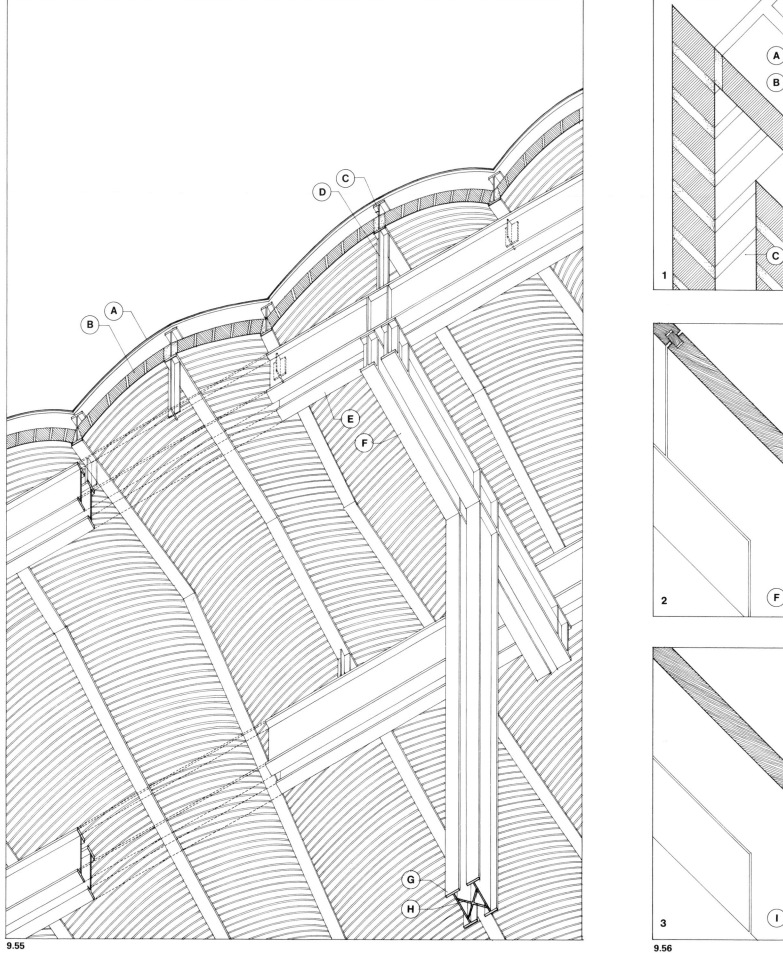

9.55

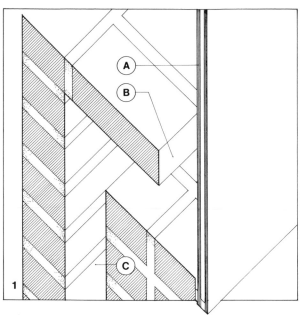

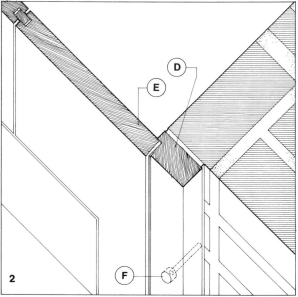

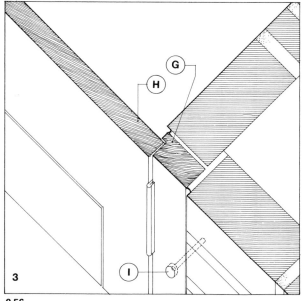

9.56

9.57

9.58

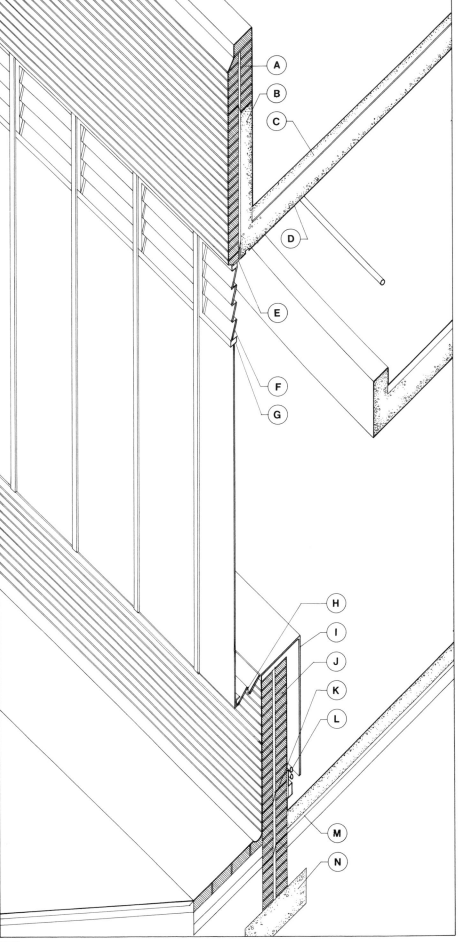

9.59

Cambridge University History Faculty Building

James Stirling with Michael Wilford

Cambridge, England, 1964–1967

9.57 **View.**

(William Wischmeyer)

9.58 **Curtain wall.**

(William Wischmeyer)

9.59 **Wall section.**

A 11″ brick parapet wall facing.

B Concrete upstand. The face of concrete behind the brickwork is painted with two coats of waterproofing.

C Asphalt on insulating screed, sloped to drain. The asphalt is carried over upstand beam.

D Insulation board ceiling finish.

E Steel angle supporting brick facing.

F Ventilation louvers.

G Aluminum patent glazing.

H Aluminum panel and aluminum louvers and sill.

I Metal heater with ½″ wood base.

J 11″ brick cavity wall.

K Damp-proof courses.

L Heating pipes.

M 6″ waterproof concrete slab with 2″ blinding and 4″ hardcore.

N Concrete footing.

(AD 10.68, SW)

10 The Venturis, Graves, Scarpa, and the Layers of History: 1963–1984

I did not say that [history] was bunk. I said . . . I did not need it very bad.

Henry Ford

What is an arch? Is it a tool? Is it a symbol? Is it a method for spanning an opening or is it a sign for a door? Can it be both? If it is a symbol, what difference does it make?

This is in essence the question of Postmodernism, at least as far as the issue of construction is concerned. Can a language of architecture exist independently of the technology that produces it? If a set of elements that originates in the characteristics of one type of building system and materials is executed in another, are the ability of these elements to communicate meanings enhanced or denied?

The question is not merely a stylistic one, that is, whether traditional architecture is superior to Modern architecture, since these same questions had been asked within the Modern movement itself. By 1970 many historians, notably Reyner Banham, had pointed out the inconsistencies between Modernist dogmas of building and realities. The forms of International Style Modernism came to be seen not as the inevitable result of technological development but as simply another set of aesthetic signs, like Classicism or any other style, that existed independently of the technology that inspired it, if it had been technologically inspired at all.

Those who provided something in the way of an answer to this question, Colin Rowe, Robert Venturi, and Denise Scott Brown, probably had no intention of doing so. Their primary concern was with how architecture communicates, regardless of how it is technically accomplished. But none of them was indifferent to constructional concerns, and their theories on the subject, whatever their intentions, were to define attitudes toward building for many in the 1970s and 1980s. Rowe's influence came from a series of essays of the late 1950s and 1960s, notably "Transparency: Literal and Phenomenal" (written with Robert Slutzky) and "The Mathematics of the Ideal Villa." Venturi's book *Complexity and Contradiction in Architecture* was published in 1966 with considerably more fanfare and controversy. Although the subject matter of the two authors is generally different—Rowe focuses on Le Corbusier, Venturi on "Mannerist" architects such as Nicholas Hawksmoor and Edwin Lutyens—the impact of these essays was felt in much the same way in the early 1970s, and understandably so, since they share a common concern: the idea of layered space and layered buildings in architecture.

10.1

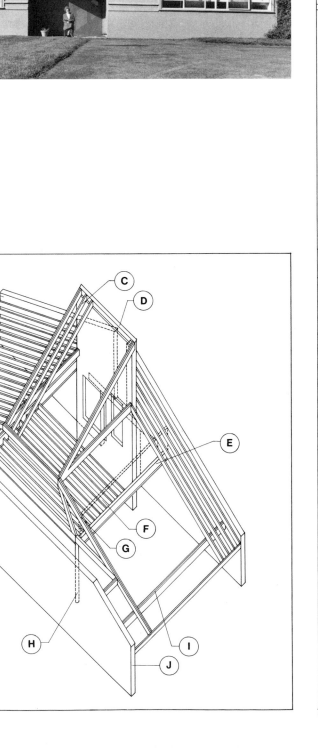

10.2

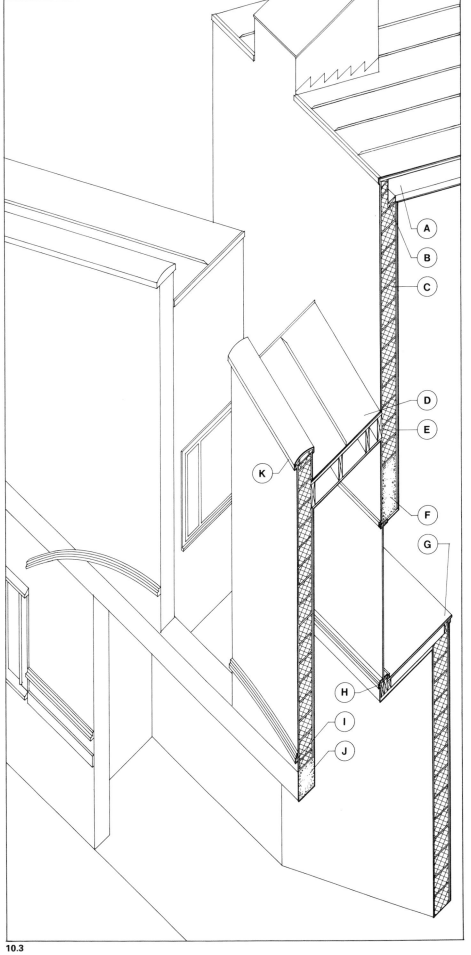

10.3

Vanna Venturi House

Venturi and Short

Chestnut Hill, Pennsylvania, 1962–1963

10.1 View.

(VSBA/Rollin R. La France)

10.2 Framing.

A   8″ concrete masonry walls reinforced with 16″ concrete bond beams and 9 × 12″ concrete lintels over doors.

B   Roof framing of 2 × 10s at 20″ oc.

C   High roof framing 2 × 12 rafters 16″ oc bearing on wall and truss.

D   Concrete masonry bearing wall.

E   14 WF 30 steel beam, supporting 2 × 4 wood stud bearing wall.

F   Floor framing of 2 × 12s at 16″ oc supported by steel beams.

G   Wood truss with 18 WF 50 steel beam below. This takes the load of the high roof down to the two steel columns while making possible the large segmented window at the rear of the house.

H   6″ steel column. This is the only exposed steel and the only freestanding column.

I   Two 2 × 12s to support rafters.

J   8″ concrete masonry bearing wall.

(VSBA DN 8)

10.3 Wall section.

A   2 × 10 wood rafters at 16″ oc supporting high roof.

B   2 × 4 wood plate to receive rafters.

C   8″ concrete masonry wall with ¾″ exterior stucco and interior finish of ⅜″ plaster on ⅜″ lath, with reflective insulation in cavity.

D   Metal roof on ⅝″ plywood sheathing with metal flashing to close the joint between roof and concrete masonry.

E   2 × 12s at 16″ oc.

F   Cast-in-place concrete lintel to support masonry over opening.

G   2 × 3 wood joist soffit framing with insulation in voids.

H   Wood frame with fixed glazing.

I   Wood trim. This serves no functional purpose, and was controversial at the time.

J   9 × 12″ exposed cast-in-place concrete lintel over door.

K   Terra-cotta coping and grout to protect the wall from water penetration. Walls parallel to the layers receive parapets. Those perpendicular have metal copings.

(VSBA DN 8)

Although his work is often described as the antithesis of Kahn and Saarinen, Venturi was the employee and to an extent the protégé of both. He was able to join Saarinen's office through Kahn's influence where he worked on the project with which one would assume he had the least affinity, the General Motors Technical Center, and later he both worked and taught with Kahn in Philadelphia.

Complexity and Contradiction in Architecture is neither devoid of interest in construction nor necessarily incompatible with much of Kahn or Saarinen's work. In the early small projects of his own that Venturi describes at the end of the book, there is a desire to apply the same principles of ambiguity and multiple readings to structural problems as are applied to formal problems in the first part, and one of his primary formal concerns, the idea of layered space, is to an extent inspired by both his mentors. In the chapter "The Inside and the Outside" he takes as his starting point an idea of Eliel Saarinen: "Eliel Saarinen said that just as a building is the 'organization of space in space. So is the community. So is to the city.' I think this series could start with the idea of a room as a space in space. And I should like to apply Saarinen's definition of relationships not only to the spatial relationships of building and site, but to those of interior spaces within interior spaces."[1] The idea of layered space was also in part inspired by Kahn's technique of building ruins around buildings to create layers of concentric space:

Redundant enclosure, like crowded intricacies, is rare in our architecture. With some significant exceptions in the work of Le Corbusier and Kahn, Modern architecture has tended to ignore such complex spatial ideas. . . . Contradictory interior space does not admit Modern architecture's requirement of a unity and continuity of all spaces. Nor do layers in depth, especially with contrapuntal juxtapositions, satisfy its requirements of economic and unequivocal relationships of forms and materials. And crowded intricacy within a rigid boundary (which is not a transparent framework) contradicts the modern tenet which says that a building grows from the inside out.[2]

THE VENTURI HOUSE

One of the earliest and perhaps the best example of Venturi's layered space, illustrated in *Complexity and Contradiction*, was his 1962 house for his mother in Chestnut Hill, Pennsylvania. The Vanna Venturi house is a rectilinear prism with its gable on the long side forming the front and rear facades. The volume of the house is then eroded and articulated so as to emphasize the two large planes perpendicular to the axis of movement. Venturi wrote:

The protrusions above and beyond the rigid outside walls also reflect the complexity inside. The walls in front and back are parapeted to emphasize their role as screens behind which these inner intricacies can protrude. Indentations of the windows and porch on the sides at all but one of the corners, increase the screen-like quality of the front and back walls in the same way that the parapets do their tops. . . .

This method of walls—layered for enclosure, yet punctured for openness—occurs vividly at the front center, where the outside wall is superimposed upon the two other walls housing the stair. Each of these three layers juxtaposes openings of differing size and position. Here is layered space rather than interpenetrated space.[3]

The structure of the house, although seldom exposed, reinforces this spatial organization. The two long front and rear walls are load-bearing concrete masonry. Spanning between these are steel beams and wood joists supporting the floors and roofs (figure 10.2). Because the back wall is considerably eroded to form a balcony, there is a secondary system of steel columns and beams forming a second line of structural support at the inside face of the balcony, including a steel pipe column, the single piece of exposed structure. This column, along with the corresponding pillar of the bookcase, forms a third plane between the two long walls. Thus the concept of the house as a series of parallel planes perpendicular to the axis of movement is reinforced by a structure of two parallel walls and a frame perpendicular to that axis. At the same time, it is hardly a rigidly ordered system.

10.4

10.5

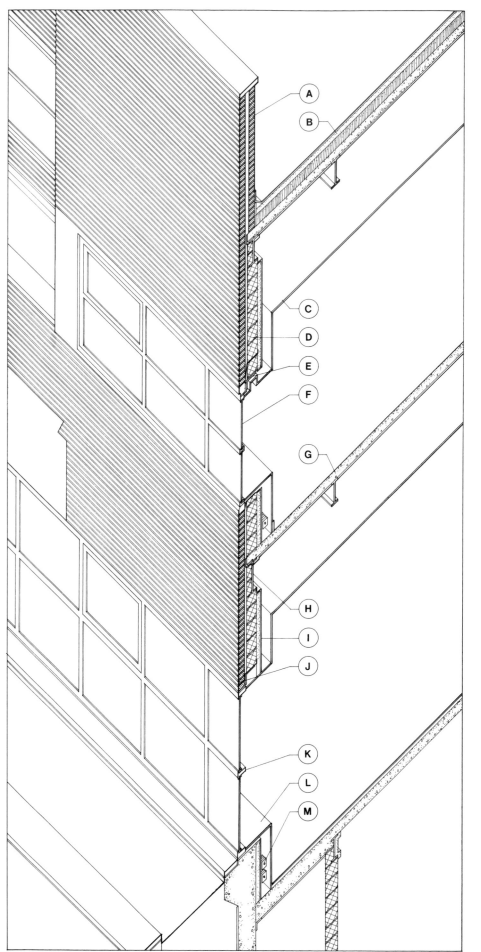

10.6

Gordon Wu Hall, Princeton University

Venturi, Rauch and Scott Brown

Princeton, New Jersey, 1980–1983

10.4 View.
(VSBA/Tom Bernard)

10.5 Under construction.

10.6 Wall section.

A Parapet of two wythes of 4″ face brick with marble coping.

B Built-up roof on 2½″ concrete topping slab sloped to drain, with 4½″ insulation on 5″ structural concrete slab.

C Gypsum wallboard ceiling and interior finish. This is pulled back into the building to make the wall appear thicker.

D Typical wall construction of 4″ face brick, air space, and ¾″ parge on 8″ concrete masonry.

E Steel angles with brace supporting brick. Because of the long strip window below, the brick must be hung from the beams above.

F ½″ insulating glass in aluminum window frame.

G 3″ concrete slab and metal deck on steel beam.

H Steel beam. This is the major structural member carrying all the brick between the two horizontal windows.

I 2½″ rigid insulation with, ⅝″ gypsum board facing to prevent a fire in the cavity from reaching the insulation.

J Flashing and weep holes 24″ oc to drain water from the cavity.

K Aluminum curtain wall.

L ¾″ veneer plywood sill and ¾″ wood wainscot on ⅝″ plywood on 1⅝″ metal studs.

M Fin tube radiation to create a warm current of air traveling up the inside face of the glass.
(VSBA DN A-7, 9)

The distinction between the front and back of the house and the sides, and the subsequent layering, are reinforced by differences in detailing. Three of the four corners are cut away to transform the front and back walls into planes. (Since the corners of load-bearing buildings are structurally its most important parts, this is not necessarily advantageous.) The roof at the front and a portion of the back ends with a parapet and terra-cotta cap so that the planar quality of these walls is further emphasized. At the two sides the wall is suppressed and the metal roof projects to form eaves. The gutter at the sides is recessed and concealed, unlike the typical projecting gutter that is used on the rear wall. In his description of the building Venturi points out his frank acceptance of the gutter and downspout as saying "life is like this" but does not mention the length to which he goes to hide the gutters on the sides.

It was intended that the architectural elements of the front and rear planes—windows, trim, etc.—distort the perceived scale of the building. Thus there are two different fenestration systems, one for the front and rear "billboard" facades and another for the walls that are perpendicular to them. The front facade is composed of a row of square steel hopper windows held in wood frames with trim. The clerestory and the other windows that connect the billboard back to the house are fixed glass in concealed wood frames so that they act, at least conceptually, to set off the front and back planes. In theory these distort the scale of the house, but the square steel windows have no scale and the doors are approximately 3 feet by 6 feet 10 inches, a fairly standard size. It is in the trim that most of the "distortions" occur.

Venturi was instrumental in reviving trim as an architectural tool, but the trim design in this house, at least in profile, is unlike anything that might be found in traditional architectural work. The reasons for its simplicity are not solely economic, as the design as well as the placement of the trim act to distort the scale. The trim design reinforces the front/side distinction, as the exterior stringcourse occurs only on the front and back, not on the sides, and the trim ends abruptly at the corner rather than turning the corner. All of these details strengthen the reading of the front and back walls as billboardlike planes in which the signs of architecture are displayed. The stringcourse is set higher than normal (3 feet 6 inches) to make the house appear smaller than it is, while the window sill in fact remains at standard height.

The interior trim is finer and scaled down from that of the exterior. The interior window jamb uses a three-quarter diameter round wood section, the exterior a larger one-half round section. Despite their historic references, they are decidedly un-Classical. They are complete geometric curves, "spent" as Lutyens would say. Their convex shapes do not contrast with convex curves, only notches. The shapes are not multiplied but occur singularly. They seem to deny two of the most important roles of trim—to affirm scale and to create a play of light and shade—but this is precisely what Venturi wished to do, to confuse, or at least make ambiguous, the scale of the building. Perhaps he did not want the viewer to appreciate the sensuous qualities of trim, only to see it as sign. By depriving it of its purely aesthetic qualities he enhances its symbolic qualities.

While the concept of layered space occurs in many subsequent Venturi buildings, it is by no means a mandatory feature, and other architects were to make far more extensive use of the concept. Venturi's interest in the shallow detail was to lead ultimately to an interest in the two-dimensional detail. It was for him a small step from Lutyens's flattened-out shaftless capitals to capitals that were only flat silhouettes.

Venturi has had several partners who were important to his work, most notably Denise Scott Brown who shared equal responsibility on his subsequent work. She was also coauthor, with Venturi and Steven Izenour, of a second important book, *Learning from Las Vegas*. Like *Complexity and Contradiction, Learning from Las Vegas* is more about structure than one might suppose, but it is not about the literal reality of structure but rather what might be called the symbolic language of structure. The decoration of the Renaissance palazzo is an example:

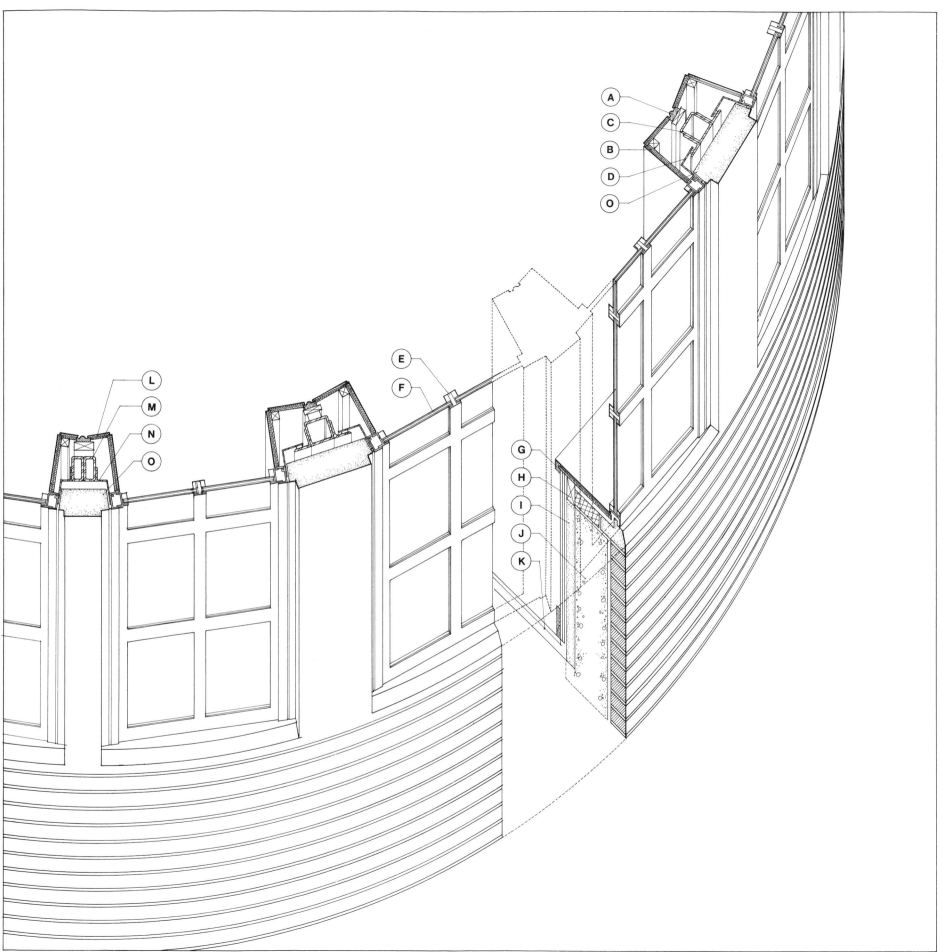

10.7

Gordon Wu Hall, Princeton University

Venturi, Rauch and Scott Brown

Princeton, New Jersey, 1980–1983

10.7 Window details at north bay.

- A Solid oak trim.
- B ¾" oak veneer plywood.
- C 4 × 4 × ¼" steel tube and 3 × 3 × ¼" continuous steel angle.
- D Continuous ⅛" steel plate to directly attach the window to the frame rather than the limestone.
- E Inside-glazed aluminum frame.
- F ½" insulating glass.
- G ¾" veneer plywood sill.
- H Wood blocking.
- I 2½" rigid insulation with ⅝" gypsum board interior finish.
- J 4" face brick, air space, ¾" parging on 8" concrete and concrete masonry wall with flashing and weep holes 24" oc.
- K Floor slab and finish floor.
- L Oak-veneered plywood. Note unequal trim and mullion widths.
- M Two 2 × 4 × ⁵⁄₁₆" steel tubes with continuous ⅛" steel plate attached to frame and tube.
- N ⅛" steel plate anchors to connect stone to steel tubes.
- O Limestone facing.
  (*VSBA DN A-10*)

10.8 Bay window.

10.8

Its ornament, literally based on the Roman, Classical vocabulary, was to be an instrument for the rebirth of classical civilization. However, since most of this ornament depicts structure—it is ornament symbolic of structure—it is less independent of the shed it is attached to than ornament on medieval and Strip architecture. The image of the structure and space reinforces rather than contradicts the substance of the structure and space. Pilasters represent modular sinews on the surface of the wall; quoins represent reinforcement at the ends of the wall; vertical moldings, protection at the edges of the wall; rustication, support at the bottom of the wall; drip cornices, protection from rain on the wall; horizontal moldings, the progressive stages in the depth of wall; and a combination of many of these ornaments at the edge of a door symbolizes the importance of the door in the face of the wall. Although some of these elements are functional as well— for instance, the drips are, but the pilasters are not—all are explicitly symbolic, associating the glories of Rome with the refinements of building.[4]

Although the structural expression of Venturi, Scott Brown and Associates' (VSBA) subsequent work was to be largely symbolic, and although exposed structure was to become a rarity in their work, they were not content to leave the structure alone, as evidenced by their academic buildings.

WU HALL

The program and budget of Wu Hall offered VSBA opportunities to which they had not often had access, but a number of problems as well. The building forms the nucleus of a residential college, containing a dining hall, small library, and offices; its budget was generous enough to allow oak windows and limestone trim. There was a clear context in the late Gothic Revival and Tudor style of the Princeton campus and a clear prototype in the older dining halls of Ralph Adams Cram and Day and Klauder. But the site itself was in a crowded section of the newer, less stylistically unified portion of the campus, and the building is pressed up against a variety of nondescript Modern buildings. There is no axial approach to the building, but its ends acts as visual punctuation points for two major paths of movement through the campus.

As in much of VSBA's work, the solution is sometimes determined by external and sometimes by internal conditions. The plan is an elongated lozenge with a large bay window at each end. The lozenge is inflected and sometimes stepped back to respond to the immediate context, and the bay windows, besides recalling similar windows in older Princeton dining halls, act to terminate visually the approaches to the building. The bay windows are clearly a response to external conditions: one contains a stair; the other is split in half to serve an office and library. The windows on the long side are located more in accordance with interior function.

The principal difficulty with the design is the complexity of steel framing required to accomplish the inflected and eroded envelope. Figure 10.5 shows the frame of Wu Hall during construction. The steel is nowhere directly exposed in the finished building, but there are a number of freestanding columns clad with reinforced gypsum covers so that there is almost a free plan arrangement in some of these areas. The economic difficulty of this approach is the increased quantity of steel required by the distortions of the envelope. Setting back the library wall required an additional row of columns less than 5 feet away from the perimeter columns. There are several other conditions where jogs or cuts required duplication of structure. This is not to say that VSBA were wrong in their approach. Wu Hall is a superior building to its neighbors, which have no such structural distortions, but it does show that it is more "duck" (to use VSBA's terms) than "decorated shed," and that despite the architects' acceptance of the realities of concealed structure, layered construction, and independent systems, a large number of deviations from the norm were necessary to satisfy its complex architectural demands.

The exterior wall uses two subtly different architectural languages. The first, that of the bay window, uses brick, limestone mullions, and deep-set windows and is generally in the vocabulary of traditional load-bearing construction. The shadows on the glass produce the massive, material-conscious quality of pre–steel frame buildings, with details that recall not only the nearby work of Ralph Adams Cram

10.9

10.10

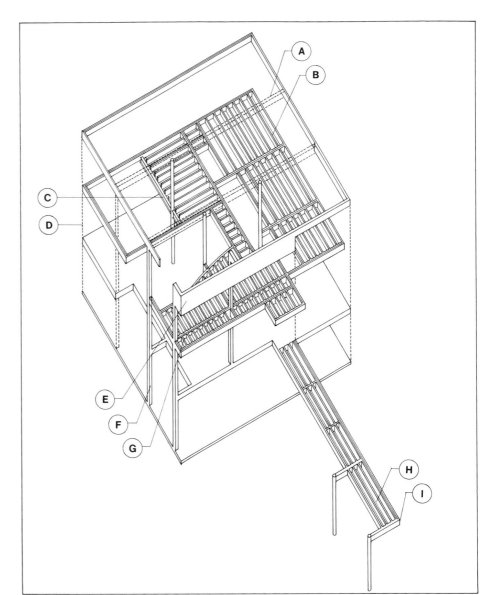

10.11

Hanselmann House

Michael Graves

Fort Wayne, Indiana, 1967

10.9 View.
(Michael Graves)

10.10 Side view.
(Michael Graves)

10.11 Framing.
A Roof construction of 2 × 12 wood joists supported by girders from two 2 × 12s.
B Floor construction: girders from two 3 × 12s and two 2 × 12s with 2 × 12 joists 16" oc and ⅝" plywood sheathing.
C Girder from two 7" C 9.8 steel channels and steel pipe column.
D Bearing wall of 2 × 4 wood studs.
E Plywood box beam.
F Typical 4 × 4 wood column.
G 2 × 6s.
H Walkway framing of 2 × 10s.
I 4 × 12 beam and column.
(MG DN SM)

but also Edwin Lutyens. The other language is that of the side walls. Here brick and glass are flush, and the wall brick is used with the membranelike quality that we associate with Modernism.

The differences between VSBA's bay window and a traditional bay window are a result both of changes in the technology of stone and glazing and of their desire to flatten out traditional detail in order to enhance its symbolic qualities. The traditional stone mullions of the older academic buildings that were the model for VSBA's mullion approximated the profile of a medieval window by placing a steel sash in a stone mullion. The Wu Hall windows were subject to technical constraints that its predecessors were not. The stone was veneered, not solid, and required steel supports. Insulating glass was required to reduce heat loss, which can require a larger mullion profile, and, perhaps for economic reasons or perhaps to unify the building's fenestration, aluminum was used instead of steel. The net result is a profile that is thicker and heavier than the traditional models nearby.

The details of the long, flush west wall that connects the two bays recompose the same elements of brick, stone, glass, and aluminum frame in a different configuration, stressing the weightless, membranelike quality of the wall. There are contextual and historical references (the flat marble keystones and the entry mural), but they are purely two-dimensional and have little relationship to the fenestration, which, unlike the bay window, is largely determined by internal requirements. In the bays the mullions are set deep in the stone. In the west wall they are flush with the face of the wall, putting glass and brick in almost the same plane and giving the wall the taut quality desired. The disposition of the brick control joints reinforces this reading, cutting through keystones and revealing the thinness of the wall at the corner. There are no lintels or stringcourses; nothing visibly supports the brick above the long dining room window, unlike at the bay windows, where a limestone lintel appears to support the brick. In fact both walls are supported by concealed steel lintels.

Despite the similarity of certain of their ideas, Colin Rowe was initially perceived and to a degree is still perceived as the Venturis' antagonist; but they are separated more by subject matter than ideology. Rowe's focus, in the 1950s at least, was Le Corbusier, but it was a different Le Corbusier than that studied by Sigfried Giedion and Reyner Banham. Rowe was indifferent to or even dismissive of both the social and technological aspects of Le Corbusier's work, focusing rather on its connections to both Classicism and Cubist painting. Rowe's version of "layered space" (as described in "Transparency: Literal and Phenomenal") occurs in both Cubism and Le Corbusier. He wrote of the Villa at Garches:

Thus, throughout the house, there is that contradiction of spatial dimensions which [Gyorgy] Kepes recognizes as characteristic of transparency. There is a continuous dialectic between fact and implication. The reality of deep space is constantly opposed to the inference of shallow; and, by means of the resultant tension, reading after reading is enforced. The five layers of space which, vertically, divide the building's volume and the four layers which cut it horizontally will all, from time to time, claim attention; and this gridding of space will then result in continuous fluctuations of interpretation.[5]

Rowe sees this same layered space, with the same virtues, in some of Le Corbusier's larger buildings, particularly the project for the League of Nations: "These stratifications, devices by means of which space becomes constructed, substantial, and articulate, are the essence of that phenomenal transparency which has been noticed as characteristic of the central post-Cubist tradition."[6]

Although Rowe's essay was no manifesto, either in style or content, it helped inspire, along with others of his essays, something of a Corbusian revival. One result was the 1972 publication of *Five Architects* containing a number of small buildings by Richard Meier, Peter Eisenman, John Hejduk, Charles Gwathmey, and Michael Graves, all of which drew heavily on the formal vocabulary of Le Corbusier.

But it was the formal vocabulary alone that was used, certainly not the technical. If the buildings showed geometric organization, they deliberately avoided the

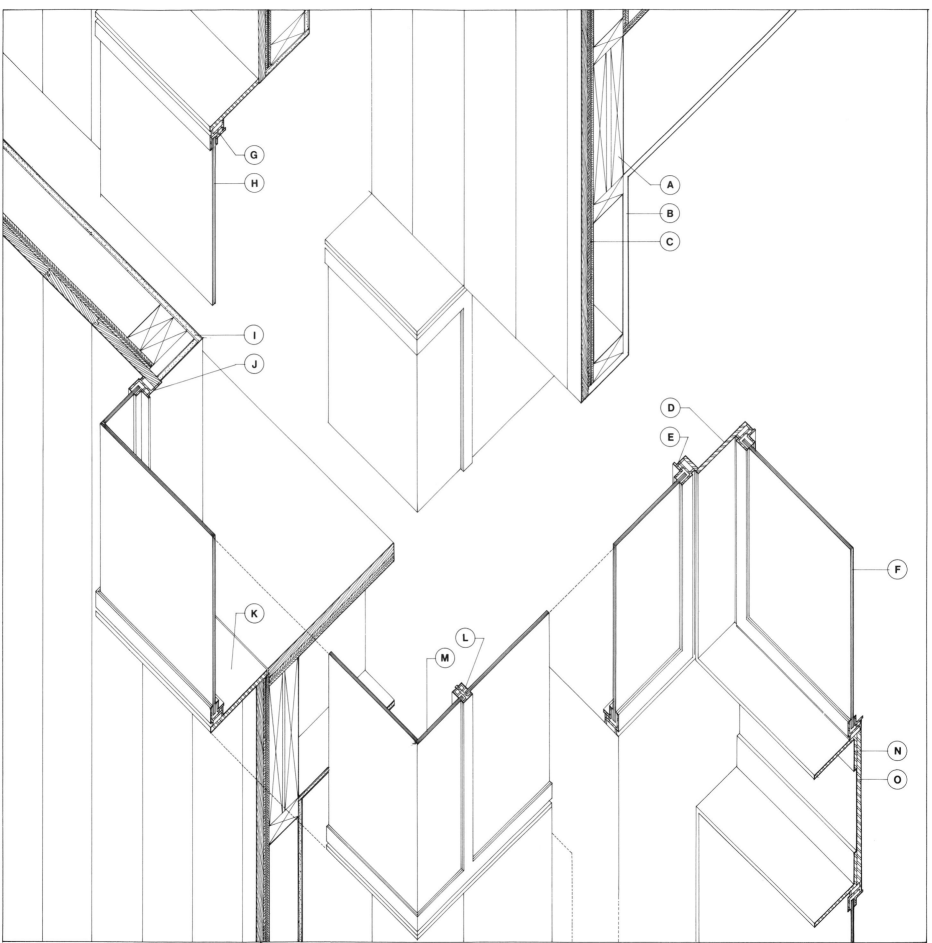

Hanselmann House

Michael Graves

Fort Wayne, Indiana, 1967

10.12 Window details.

A Wood framing.

B Typical wall construction of 2 × 4 studs and exterior finish.

C ⅝" plywood sheathing and ¾" vertical wood siding.

D ¼ × 5½" steel plate.

E Fixed steel vertical window section.

F The glass here is not only recessed behind the plane of the wall but disassociated from this plane by allowing it to extend beyond the opening into a pocket.

G Removable glazing bead.

H ¼" polished plate glass.

I Typical exterior wall: ¾" vertical wood siding on 2 × 4s at 16" oc and ⅝" plywood sheathing, with ½" drywall interior finish.

J Note that this part of the glass projects beyond the face of the wood wall.

K Steel plate sill.

L Small steel mullion at point where glass aligns with wall face.

M Butted glass corner.

N Two 3 × 5 × ½" steel angles.

O 13⅜ × ½" steel plate.

(MG D2, 4)

"standardization" of the villas of the 1920s, and if they employed the free plan, the free facade, and pilotis, these were accomplished without the Corbusian material vocabulary of concrete and masonry. Most were in fact simple platform frame buildings with the odd steel wide flange or pipe column for the long span or glazed facade. There was no attempt to hide this, nor any apparent embarrassment on the part of the architects in their use of traditional systems. The fact was commented upon by Kenneth Frampton in his introductory essay: "In all these projects, except Hejduk's there is an allusion to concrete forms and to so called 'post-Corbusian' space; that is, there are certain syntactical references to Le Corbusier and hence direct allusions to building in concrete. Yet, most of these structures are, of course, projected to be built in wood."[7]

There was little or no interest in implementing any of the building systems of Le Corbusier, which would have been foolish in any case, and there was no attempt to justify formal ideas on the basis of industrialization, machine age imagery, or even structural rationalism. Having thus admitted by fact or omission that International Style Modernism had no constructional superiority to other styles, and that its virtue lay in its use as an aesthetic language, it was only a short step to the exploration of other aesthetic languages, richer in historical associations but often more difficult to reconcile with late twentieth-century technology.

MICHAEL GRAVES

To return to the question that began this chapter, what is an arch? Is it a tool? Is it a symbol? Is it a method for spanning an opening in masonry or is it a door? Can it be both? If it is a tool to use with masonry, can it be used with wood? If it is only a symbol what difference does it make? Graves's answer was given in an interview, referring to the giant keystones of his Fargo-Morehead Cultural Center project: "The keystone was my attempt to use an architectural element that is in the public domain. The window and the door are similar elements. Of course, the architect used the keystone as symbol. The keystone is not necessary to the actual construction of that building. If you eliminate the pragmatic value in any form, you tend to heighten its symbolic value."[8] For Graves the answer is clear. In architecture (as opposed to building), an arch is a sign. The Venturis might say it can be either or both, or perhaps all three in one building, but for many there are moral imperatives involved. Wagner might use an arch as a symbol, but if it were nonstructural, he would detail it accordingly. The Venturis and Graves feel no such moral imperatives. The Venturis might enjoy the Wagner detail, but out of a love of ambiguity, not a sense of ideological obligation.

The Hanselmann house, which was thought at the time of *Five Architects* to be a rather literal formal translation of Le Corbusier's buildings of the 1920s, seems in retrospect to be far less so. Certainly not technically—it uses wood joist framing for the most part—nor in its basic formal arrangements—the column spacing and fenestration arrangements are unlike anything in Le Corbusier's work of the Purist period.

Structurally the building is rather accepting of standard American house-building technology, using steel tube columns, wood joist floors, and wood siding. A square plan subdivided into nine smaller squares by columns is extruded into a cube. Although it appears a pure frame and skin structure at first glance, it is in reality a steel-reinforced platform frame, and while there are freestanding columns to create a free plan, there are an almost equal number of load-bearing walls, and the resulting order is more geometric than structural (figure 10.11). While the real structure beneath the ceilings and walls is a complex hybrid, the revealed structure is only slightly less ambiguous. For example, at the column and wall detail at the perimeter, instead of placing a round column behind the wall membrane, as Le Corbusier would have done, Graves makes the column square and flush with the wall itself. The walls and floors are eroded considerably to manipulate the ambiguous reading of layers and along the main axis of circulation, assisted by a second negative cube defined by a freestanding wall in front.

10.13

10.14

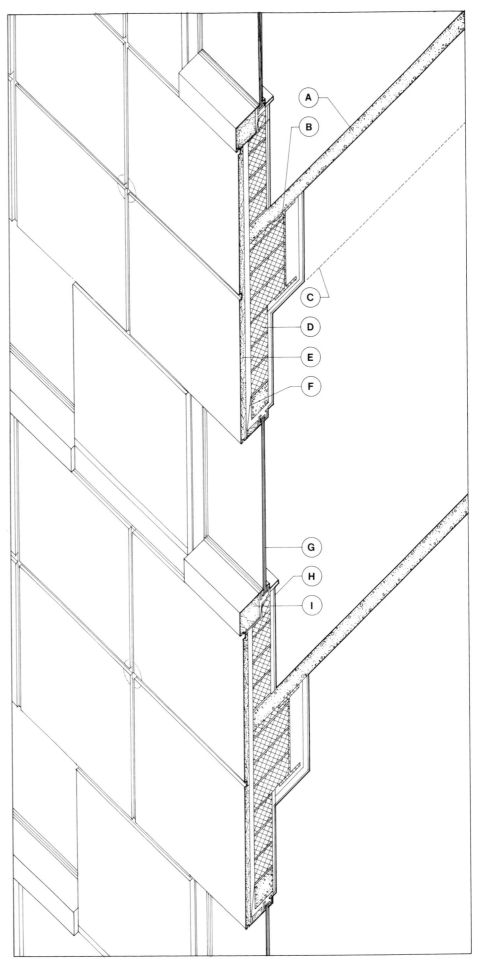

10.15

Humana Building

Michael Graves

Louisville, Kentucky, 1982

10.13 View.

(Paschall/Taylor)

10.14 Rear view.

(Paschall/Taylor)

10.15 Wall section.

A Concrete slab on metal deck.

B Steel beam. Size varies.

C Suspended ceiling. Location varies.

D 8" masonry wall to support the stone and transfer wind loads back to the slab and structural frame.

E 2" granite panel anchored to masonry wall with false joint. The false joint divides the large panel into sizes associated with traditional masonry. The real joints when caulked would almost disappear, so they are cosmetically enlarged as well.

F Concrete lintel with flashing to intercept any water that penetrates the wall and lead it back to the outside.

G Aluminum window with 1" insulation glass and thermal break recessed to hide frame.

H Interior finish on 2½" metal studs with 2½" insulation between.

I Solid granite sill with flashing below.

(MG A140)

The fenestration uses none of the repetitive modular components that were the key to Le Corbusier's work of the 1920s. Rather a steel and glass curtain wall fabricated out of standard steel sections and flat steel plates is used to create an independent membrane, usually recessed behind the outer surface of the building envelope, as in the front, but sometimes projecting forward, as at the side, emphasizing the outer wood wall as an independent layer and then projecting to become a layer itself.

Graves's Plocek house illustrates the disassociation of the architectural element from its structural origins even at the most conceptual level. In order to enhance its symbolic qualities the famous "missing keystone" is relocated to the garden, where it terminates the sequence of movement through the house. (The keystone was in fact never built.) Thus both keystone and lintel have no structural purpose. Even the entry is deprived of its function, since the real entry is on the side. But this hardly matters. The keystone is an element of masonry construction and the Plocek house for the most part is stucco on wood frame, although the base is stucco on concrete masonry.

Graves's early work achieved much of its evocative power through the painterly nature of its language. The use of stucco and painted wood gives these houses an abstract, ideal nature that heightens our sense of their constituent elements as symbols. Thus while the rusticated base of the Plocek house suggests stone, we do not think for a minute that it is stone. In his larger buildings, given the opportunity, even the necessity, of using more durable materials than stucco, this distinction between materiality and symbol is blurred, and when the material in question is stone, the answer is far less clear.

THE HUMANA BUILDING

Graves won the commission for the Humana Building in a limited competition, and it is telling perhaps that his entry, however radical its forms, generally accepted the conventional technology of the American office building, unlike the High Tech entries of his fellow competitors Norman Foster and Helmut Jahn. Stripped of its projections and stone cladding, Graves's building would reveal a skeleton not all that different from Lever House or the Seagram Building. Its structural frame, its core layout, its elevators and mechanical systems all conform to what was by then an established type. Nor is this surprising. The acceptance of such types, and the acceptance that an architectural language could exist independently of them, was a de facto tenet of Postmodernism, as was its corollary, that an attempt to radically alter these types might do more harm than good. Thus while there are a number of structurally suggestive elements, they are largely symbolic; the steel frame is covered beneath a stone cladding, and where it appears to be exposed it is simply a metal cladding instead. The great exception to this is the large exposed steel bracket that appears to support the 24th-floor terrace, meant in part to recall the bridges on the nearby Ohio River.

The design of the stone wall, however, raises the most questions, since the technical considerations at Humana, or in any other steel-framed building faced with stone, would lead to a solution that was the reverse of expectations raised by tradition. In traditional buildings where stone was used as a bearing wall, structural stability was dependent on mass and thickness; the heavier and thicker the wall, the stronger it would be. Openings in such walls were, out of necessity, narrow and deep, revealing the thickness of the wall. When stone was used as a curtain wall, all of these characteristics are reversed. Since the wall is borne by the structure, the stone should be as light and as thin as possible. The minimum quantity of stone is used, usually a 2–3-inch veneer on a less expensive masonry backup. Openings are correspondingly thin and easiest to build if the window is flush with the wall plane, to avoid exposing the edge of the veneer.

Thus, while stone might be used for its traditional associations, it could be used to create a traditional appearance only with difficulty. Like many stone-clad buildings of the period, Humana is a building in which the reality of the material and our expectations of that material are at odds. The architects had two choices: to use

10.16

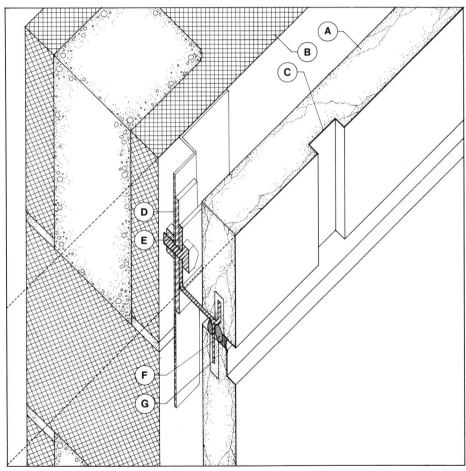

10.17

Humana Building

Michael Graves

Louisville, Kentucky, 1982

10.16 Wall detail.

(Michael Graves/Terry Smith)

10.17 Stone detail.

A 2" granite panel.

B Concrete masonry with voids filled with concrete at anchors.

C Notch in granite to create false joint.

D Adjustable anchor support.

E Stainless steel support angle and galvanized shim with plastic separator.

F Seal and bond breaker. Note that the joint is artificially enlarged.

G Anchor.

(MG A140)

the stone in what appears to be a traditional way by a series of clever deceptions, or to try to revise the traditional elements in a way that reveals the nature of the modern stone and as a result transform the old language into a new one. Most architects, Graves included, would probably argue that they are doing the latter, but Humana seems to take both approaches, sometimes recreating the appearance of traditional stone construction and sometimes revealing the nature of the modern.

The primary problem areas were the corners, edges, and sizes of the panels. Modern stone panels are much larger in area and thinner in depth than traditional stone. The typical panel at Humana is 2 inches deep and 80 square feet in surface area. The illusion of a traditional wall is created by using a number of false joints so that the stone appears to be about four feet square. This is a detail that will work only with a stone of homogeneous texture and color, as veins or different shades will easily show the false and real joints.

But the greatest problem is at corners and edges of windows and other openings, where the thinness of the stone is visible and must be dealt with technically and visually. The window detail presented several alternatives. Setting the frame flush with the wall surface would hide the veneered edge but eliminates any shadows, depriving the building of the massiveness associated with stone. Recessing the window would expose the block backup and thus require the stone to be butted or mitered in order to turn the corner. The miter joint seems the obvious solution but in reality is often the least satisfying, as the joint between the two panels, which is caulked, appears "soft" and again deprives the building of its massive character. At Humana there are butt joints at the head and jambs so that the joint is on the inside surface, and a massive 8-by-8-inch solid granite piece used at the sill, eliminating the joint at the horizontal surface where it is most vulnerable to leakage. At the corners of the piers at the base a different option is used, probably because these joints are more easily seen by the passerby. Here another solid piece, this time set at 45 degrees, is used to move the soft caulk joint away from the corner.

Despite elements such as the false joints, there is at Humana a desire to accommodate the realities of the material; but there is also clearly a demand that this accommodation not compromise the symbolic function of the element that the materials compose. The success or failure of Humana in reconciling its imagery with the means of its realization is more fairly judged by comparison to some of its contemporaries, as many architects were struggling with this same problem, given the popularity of stone as a finishing material and the requirement that it be veneered onto a steel frame. In Johnson and Burgee's AT&T Building, in a detail that caused much derision at the time, the upper corners of the building are made from L-shaped pieces of stone to give the appearance of a massive corner block. Graves's wall, by contrast, is a model of honesty.

Other architects, notably James Stirling and J. P. Kleihues, while making use of traditional imagery go much farther in adapting and exploiting modern stone technology. Both make use of a development of the 1960s known as the rain screen principle, a method developed to minimize leakage in buildings by eliminating the extreme drops of air pressure between the exterior and interior of buildings. The method requires that an air cavity be created in the wall that is vented to the exterior and insulated on its interior face, creating an air pocket of intermediate pressure between inside and outside.

Stirling and Wilford's Staatsgalerie in Stuttgart is a bearing-wall building, although not a stone one; the walls are concrete and the roof is steel, and the stone of the wall is only a thin veneer. From a distance this might be deceptive, as the wall is composed of alternating colors of stone laid in a bond pattern that recalls northern Italian traditions of building. On closer approach the stones appear to be floating in front of the structural wall. This is not an aesthetic conceit, but the rain screen principle in application (figure 10.21). The concrete wall is faced with insulation and an air barrier. The stone is then mounted just in front of the insulation with clips that allow the joints to remain open, creating the air cavity and rain screen.

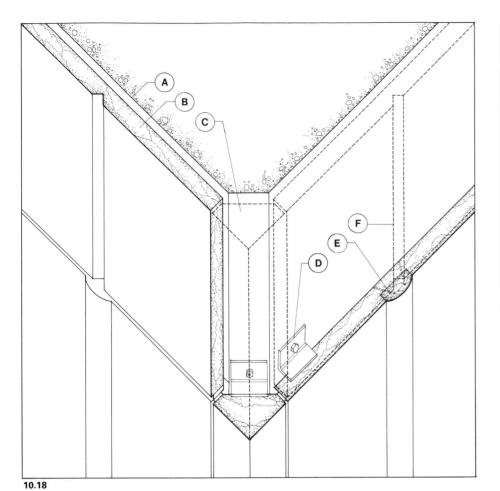

10.18

10.19

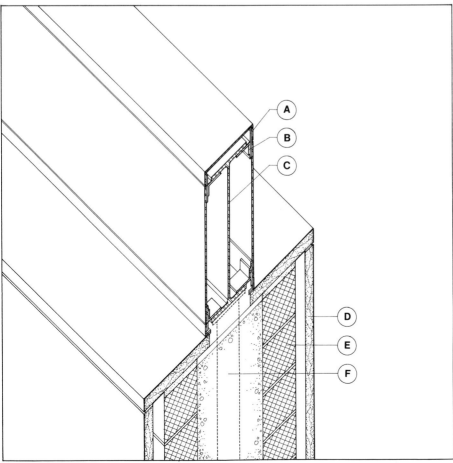

10.20

Humana Building

Michael Graves

Louisville, Kentucky, 1982

10.18 Stone detail at corner.
- A Steel column encased in concrete.
- B Granite facing.
- C Solid corner piece to move the soft joint away from the corner, to give a greater impression of solidity.
- D Clips to support stone panel.
- E Black granite rib attached to granite with stainless steel dowels.
- F Groove lined with shop-applied gold leaf.
  (MG A141)

10.19 Stone-faced concrete columns at base.
(Michael Graves/Terry Smith)

10.20 Detail at beam cover.
- A Steel box beam.
- B Clip angle.
- C Steel wide flange beam with fireproofing.
- D Granite panel.
- E Concrete masonry and solid cement fill.
- F Steel pipe column below.
  (MG 141)

Kleihues uses the same technique in a series of German museums (figure 10.22). To Stirling's detail used at Stuttgart Kleihues adds the use of exposed fasteners, drawn from early Modernism and recalling the work of Otto Wagner. It should be noted that only half the fasteners are shown (the lower clips that do most of the work are concealed), and the part that is visible is actually a cover on the fastener.

Kleihues's solution would seem to offer the best possible alternative to the problem of the contradiction of aesthetic expectations and technical realities. It certainly comes the closest to reconciling Modernist ideas of good building with contextural requirements and technical needs, but it is not necessarily the best technical solution, and it is certainly not the most economic. Exposed fasteners are generally more expensive than concealed ones, requiring a higher level of craftsmanship, and are more exposed to water than concealed ones (admittedly less of a problem in a rain screen wall). Graves's solution, however mute or potentially deceptive it might be in terms of technical expression, is sometimes the only choice that contemporary architects have.

Nor can one say that any of these buildings are really "honest" in conventional terms. They sometimes tell the truth and they sometimes lie, and sometimes say nothing at all about their construction. They all describe to some degree the nature of their materials and its fabrication, whether by accident or design. None of them describe completely, either literally or symbolically, all that is happening constructionally, nor would this be possible. Any language, by definition, cannot utter all facts simultaneously; any building by its nature must show some things while concealing others. The best we can say is that Kleihues's detail is a more accurate description of the forces at work than Johnson's.

It is an unalterable fact that much of modern construction is layered, not monolithic, and that it often can be structurally expressive only in symbolic ways. Nonetheless the orgy of symbolic excess ignoring constructional realities that is often blamed on Postmodernism was perhaps not inevitable. It is a virtue of the Venturis' thought in particular that they recognized not only the layered nature of modern building but the fact that architects cannot control and reinvent every constructional aspect of their work. But what might have been a more constructionally correct Postmodernism, one in which the design of layered space developed into an expression of layered construction, was suggested elsewhere, notably in the work of Carlo Scarpa.

CARLO SCARPA

One could hardly write about detailing without writing about Scarpa, who in recent years has joined Mies van der Rohe and the Greene brothers as the quintessential modern detailers in the conventional wisdom. But in many ways neither he nor his work fits easily into this role. Commentary on his work has centered on its details in part because the totality of much of his building is so elusive. In some cases they seem to be assemblages of brilliant fragments lacking an organizing idea, and what the elements do have in common is often equally disturbing, the use of motifs. Certain Scarpa details, seen in isolation, seem virtuoso responses to technical requirements. Yet, on viewing the whole, one often finds the same formal configurations used at vastly different scales, rendered in different materials, and serving totally different constructional tasks. The result is to raise doubts as to whether either detail is a response to conditions and problems or simply the repetitive use of styling motifs.

Both perceptions are to a degree true. Scarpa's work often lacks formal cohesiveness; it is sometimes weakened by the overuse of motifs. But in his best work, it is these motifs that provide unity, not solely in the service of clever joinery but to create an architecture that can accommodate history without aping it. Scarpa succeeded in many ways that his Postmodern colleagues failed. He was able to treat the elements of Modernism as a language without depriving them of their constructional identities; he was able to adapt the concept of layered space and the reality of layered construction without the loss of three-dimensional character.

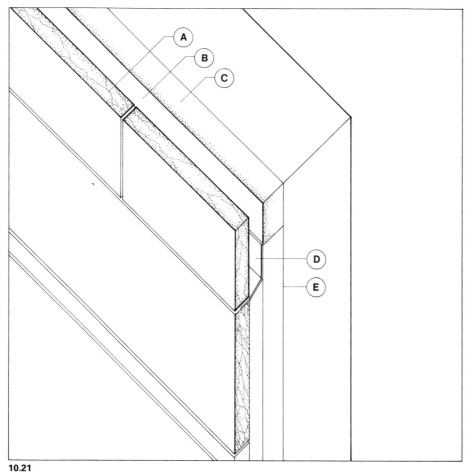

10.21

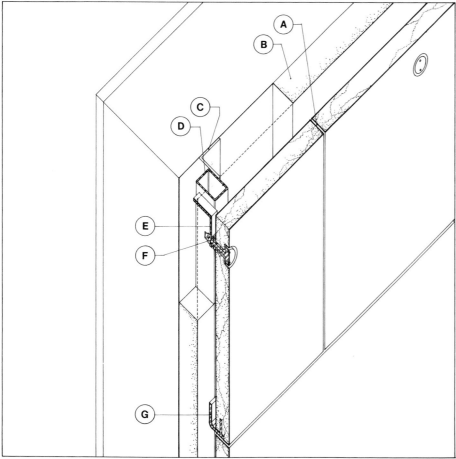

10.22

Staatsgalerie

James Stirling and Michael Wilford

Stuttgart, Germany, 1977–1983

10.21 Stone detail.

A Alternating bands of 4 cm travertine and 4 cm sandstone with 10 mm open joint and stainless steel T bar fixing brackets.

B 4 cm air space to create rain screen.

C 6 cm insulation.

D Flashing.

E Concrete wall.

(SW DN 5.41.103, AJ 5.13.87)

Sindelfingen Civic Gallery

J. P. Kleihues

Sindelfingen, Germany, 1986–1989

10.22 Stone detail.

A 4 cm stone with open joints and 5 cm air space behind designed on the rain screen principle. This allows the air to circulate to the cavity behind the stone, creating a pocket of air at an intermediate air pressure between exterior and interior and eliminating sharp pressure drops across openings and consequent leaks.

B 6 cm insulation.

C Clip angle to attach tube to structural wall while allowing for adjustment.

D Steel tube to support the stone panel.

E Adjustable clip to receive bolt. The arrangement of three clips and tube allows adjustment of the face of the stone in three dimensions.

F Exposed bolt to laterally brace the panel.

G Concealed base clip to support the weight of the stone panel.

(Detail 5.90)

Layered construction is the first and most important characteristic of Scarpa's work. Its near-universal expression and application in his work is not the result of an analysis of the contemporary constructional conditions, but of tradition. Scarpa was a Venetian, and Venetian construction had been layered since its inception. The reasons for this are in part functional and in part traditional themselves. The poor foundation conditions in Venice dictate the use of piles and thin masonry walls covered with stucco and, in more important buildings, thin layers of stone, but the use of mosaics and veneered marbles was also a Byzantine tradition that found its way to Venice. This is what Ruskin refers to as the "encrusted" style of building, which he found superior to the monolithic building traditions of the Italian mainland. But it was not always so popular. The Venetian Renaissance architects Sansovino and Palladio abandoned it in favor of solid Roman techniques, and many nineteenth-century thinkers, such as G. E. Street, thought it invited "falsehoods."

Scarpa's wholesale adaptation of the technique was only partially due to local inspiration. He felt an equally strong debt to the layered building tradition of Vienna, which at the turn of the century had made extensive use of veneered construction that was structurally descriptive solely through analogous means. He said in a lecture in Vienna:

The geography of my academic background inclined me naturally while being at school to feel closer to the modern trends from Vienna. . . . Josef Hoffmann had a great sense or feeling for decoration which students were also trained at the academies of Fine Arts (one has to recall, as Ruskin said, that art is decoration). This fact includes a very basic orientation for us both: I am a Byzantine at heart, and in Hoffmann you'll find something of an oriental too.[9]

It is a rare Scarpa work that is not layered and delaminated, with its edges cut back and exposed, in which no single layer seems to quite join with another. The technique is so pervasive that it is applied to materials that are in reality monolithic, concrete and solid stone (as in the walls of the Brion Chapel or Bank of Verona), revealing that although he accommodates the layered nature of modern construction, the two are not in Scarpa's mind inextricably joined.

Several other motifs—two intersecting circles, structural systems split in half and rejoined, and indirect structural support—occur in some form and at some scale in almost every Scarpa building. This type of detailing with motifs, although it also has Venetian origins, was probably inspired by Frank Lloyd Wright, as were some of the motifs themselves, particularly the two intersecting circles, which also pervade the Guggenheim Museum at every scale and at every level.

An early and revealing use of this double circle motif is the window at the Gavina Showroom in Bologna (1961). One of the main windows is a large single circle, the other a double intersecting circle. The glass has only a partial frame, being held against a gasket by an exterior clip that also takes the form of two circles (figure 10.27). From the exterior the circles appear to be bolts or disks, but the attachment is actually an F-shaped clip grasping the glass, and the circular shapes are irrelevant to its function; it would in fact probably have been easier to make as a rectilinear shape. Viewed in isolation and on the surface, the double circle fastener appears a simple revelation of the technology of making at work. Viewed in depth and in relation to the numerous other double circles, which appear as solid or void, in wood, metal, or concrete, it appears a superficially applied ornament.

Scarpa's 1954 Venezuelan Pavilion for the Venice Biennale is an example of the second of these motifs, structural doubling, used in the same perplexing way, sometimes to elegantly reveal and explain the nature of construction, sometimes superficially applied to nonfunctional devices. The actual structure of the building, although complex in places, is largely concealed and consists of three different systems. The main exhibit rooms themselves are two simple concrete cubical blocks, separated by a steel and wood walkway that connects to an open room for drawing exhibition covered with a hollow double concrete slab. The two main exhibit rooms are bearing-wall buildings; the drawing room and walkway are sup-

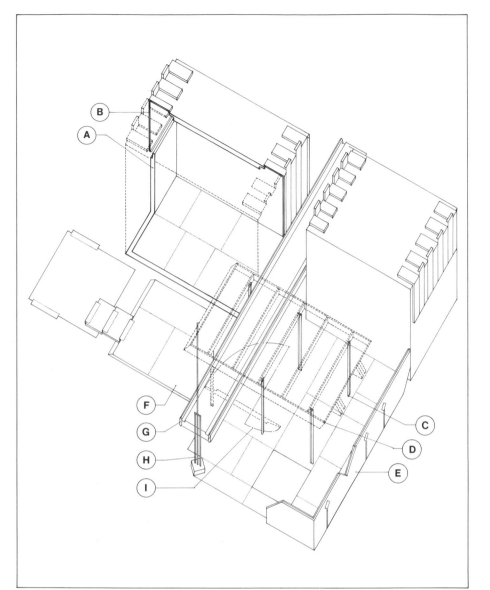

10.23

10.24

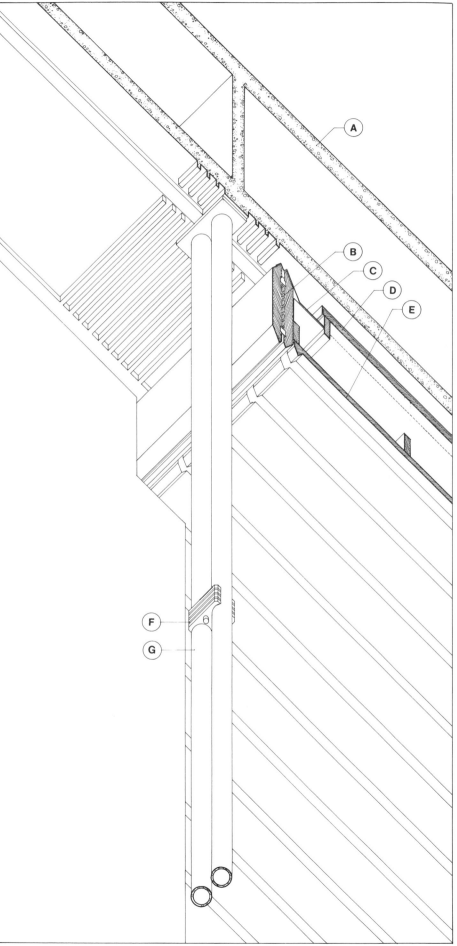

10.25

Venezuelan Pavilion for the Biennale

Carlo Scarpa

Venice, Italy, 1954–1956

10.23 Framing.

A Concrete bearing wall and slab.

B *Cristallo* glass with Vincenza stone panels between. The window turns over the parapet to become a skylight.

C Two steel tube columns with brass and iron connectors.

D Hollow concrete slab with gutters (shown dotted).

E Concrete garden wall adjacent to lagoon.

F Entry court.

G Wood-framed canopy.

H Flagpole supporting end of canopy.

I Rotating panels allow the room for drawings to be opened to the garden. Steel structure with burnt and brushed wood slats outside and white panels on interior.

(Casabella *212.58*)

10.24 Column detail.

10.25 Column detail at entry.

A Hollow concrete slab roof.

B Flitch beam from two *legno duro* boards with 8 × 200 mm steel plate between.

C ⁸⁄₁₀ mm lead sheet gutter and roofing.

D ⁸⁄₁₀ mm lead sheet roofing on wood boards.

E Wood soffit of oak or pitch pine.

F Brass and steel collar.

G Steel tube columns.

Casabella *212.58*)

ported by a grid of six pairs of pipe columns. These columns, along with the beams of the walkway, are the only readily visible parts of the structure, and both are doubled, or rather split and rejoined. The columns are steel tubes connected by brackets of alternating layers of steel and bronze (figure 10.25). There are potential advantages to splitting the column in that it facilitates connection to the beam, but Scarpa denies it this utility by alternately turning the pairs of columns at right angles to each other. Nevertheless, this is typical of Scarpa at his best. Although the detail is fairly abstract, it is highly evocative, both historically and symbolically. Is it a quotation of Aalto's paired columns at the Villa Mairea? Is it a modern reinterpretation of the knotted stone columns of Italian Gothic rendered in steel? Is it meant, like the double circle motif, to represent some kind of union or division and reunion, or did Scarpa simply want to make the column appear thinner and smaller by splitting it in half?

The walkway beams are also split and rejoined, as each is composed of a sandwich of two timbers with a steel plate between. This is a flitch beam in American terminology, a common builder's device for increasing the strength of a beam without increasing its depth. Scarpa's use of the device here could be technical, in that additional strength was required, or symbolic, in that it constitutes another division and rejoining of the structural elements. The chamfering of the beam corners is another Wright-inspired motif, and occurs throughout the pavilion at different scales and in different materials. This is the type of Scarpa detail that the structural purist finds so disconcerting, in which he seems blatantly to deny the qualities of materials by applying the same complex forms to them all.

The elements of layered construction, double structure, and intersecting circles appear in abundance in what is perhaps his most conspicuous work, the Olivetti Showroom on the Piazza San Marco. The basic solution was to strip the interior space down and rebuild the floor above, leaving only a few internal piers, and then hang a balcony from the floor above. All of the new finishes are of course new layers and are expressed as such. Few surfaces appear actually to touch each other at the corners, so that plaster never touches floor, terrazzo never touches wall; the stair and pool hang weightlessly. The whole sense of layering and delaminating is so pervasive that the whole seems in danger of coming apart. The cladding here is of course a historical comment; it literally separates new from old, making manifest the layers of history that make up this site.

Scarpa clad the remaining masonry piers with new stone. His solution to the problem of veneering and cladding, particularly at the corners, is enlightening in comparison with the solutions of Graves and Johnson to the same problem. Scarpa's corner joint is simply butted, so that the thickness (or rather the thinness) of the stone is always revealed. Although the face of the stone is always smooth, the edge is given a rusticated treatment to highlight the difference. Lest any doubt remain, holes are provided for access to the fasteners beyond. The stone slabs are arranged in a pinwheel, but the direction of the pinwheel is reversed at each horizontal joint so that there are no continuous vertical joints. This joint and the veneered quality of the stone are emphasized by a brass strip between the two.

The other structural elements, being new, are split in half and rejoined with another motif, the paired circles. The new floor is a concrete and steel composite of which Scarpa was fond. The steel projecting below the concrete is split, creating a notch to receive the balcony hanger. The hanger itself is also split and rejoined at the head, base, and railing by pairs of thin brass disks—double circles, but this time separated. The variety of ways in which these motifs are used is somewhat restrained in Olivetti, lending more technical credibility to these details, but the old Scarpa is still there. The exterior windows, for example, are simply the space defined by two intersecting circles.

Scarpa did not substantially add to this vocabulary after Olivetti, but the nature of his new commissions put the vocabulary to a more substantial use as a means of historical restoration. Strangely, his freestanding houses in rural sites where he

10.29

10.30

10.29 Wall of *androne*.

10.30 Travertine door.

method. The door in Christian iconography represents not only death but triumph over death through the resurrection. (John 10:9: "I am the door; by me if any man enter in he shall be saved.") In traditional Venetian art this has taken many forms— Sansovino's resurrection door panel in San Marco for example, but most commonly in the funerary monuments of the large Venetian churches, in which death is presented sometimes as a curtain or veil but most often as a triumphal arch merging classical and Christian iconography. Scarpa makes extensive use of the door as symbol, but without any of the traditional Venetian images.

If one travels through the cemetery beginning at the chapel entry, the path taken by the mourners as opposed to visitors, one traverses a series of doors and thresholds that lead from chapel to sarcophagus to meditation island at the end, crossing a number of bridges en route. The doors are of different materials, have different functions, and have different modes of operation, but follow a progression from heavy and dark to weightless and light.

The first of these, the door that penetrates the concrete wall that surrounds the private cemetery, is itself concrete rimmed with steel, but on steel wheels and rails so that it slides into a slot in the wall. It is the heaviest of the doors, the most opaque, and when closed is almost indistinguishable from the surrounding walls. The door to the chapel itself is ebony with white infill and is perhaps the midpoint. It has two L-shaped leaves and functions with offset pivots so that when open it does not appear all that different from when closed. It is set within the serrated edges created by Scarpa's 5.5-centimeter module applied to all the wall edges in the chapel which gives them a layered appearance at odds with their monolithic character. 5.5 centimeters is perhaps the smallest module one could use that would be of any consequence. Like Asplund and Aalto, Scarpa favored a standardization at the smallest scale possible.

There are a number of other windows and doors in the chapel. Behind the altar a low set of doors allows a view of the pool, but little else. In the side walls are a series of small brass-framed casement windows glazed with sheets of alabaster cut thin enough to be translucent. This is another Italian tradition. The windows of Orvieto cathedral, for example, have fixed sheets of alabaster. This series culminates in the door that permits access to the meditation island. This door, being glass, is the most transparent. Its mode of operation is by a series of cables and counterweights that submerge or raise the door into or out of the water below.

If Scarpa was not quite the quintessential detailer, he was the quintessential preservationist detailer. There were flaws in his approach: his restoration was confined to a narrow time period and systematically eliminated any nineteenth-century elements in any building he restored. In his favor is his unsurpassed devotion to the language of Modernism as a means of communication even in the most sensitive of historical contexts.

There is a widespread assumption that with the revival of interest in a nonhistoricist architecture, there would be a revival of interest in the principles of construction in architectural design. This assumes of course that the entire subject had been neglected during the Postmodernism of the 1980s. It is more accurate perhaps to say that Postmodern architects are not so much disinterested in construction as that construction had become for them primarily a set of symbols, in which a traditional structural element such as the keystone, having lost its structural function, either has become a false appliqué that outwardly conceals this change (Johnson) or is adapted to express its new function, or rather nonfunction, by being reduced to a two-dimensional cartoon of itself (Venturi) or by displacement or even downright removal (Graves). Changes in taste and aesthetics are not totally to blame for this phenomenon, for in many of the commissions of the 1970s and 1980s architects were reduced to supplying thin veneers for speculative, nonprogrammed buildings, over the contents of which they had little control. The decorated shed was very much the order of the day, and the popular finish materials of the era, quartzputz, thin stone veneers, tile, etc., were far too easily adapted to accommodate this practice.

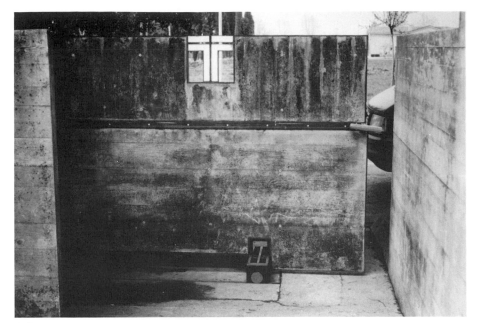

10.31

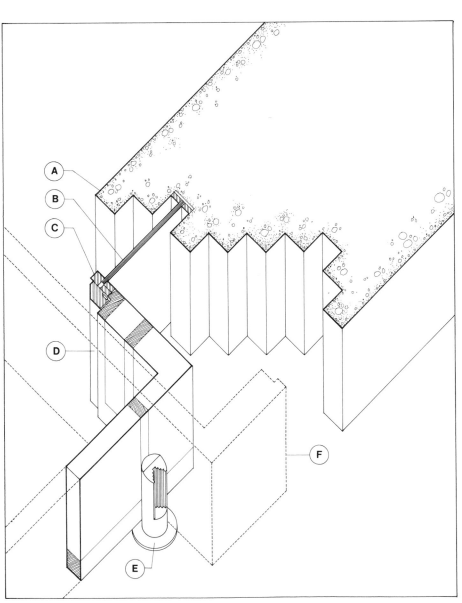

10.32

10.33

10.34

Brion Cemetery

Carlo Scarpa

San Vito di Altivole, Italy, 1970–1975

10.31 Concrete gate.
(Mitch Glass)

10.32 Detail of door to cypress grove at base.
A Concrete wall with steps on 5.5 cm module.
B Glass.
C Metal window frame.
D Infill panel door with ebony trim.
E Brass pivot hinge with echelon design that recalls the pattern of the concrete wall.
F When open, the door return is flush with wall (shown dotted).
(The Other City, 520, 525)

10.33 Door of chapel to cypress grove.

10.34 Chapel window.

There has been a strong reaction against this trend in recent years among architects, although it continues unabated in speculative work. Although there is a general agreement in the conventional architectural establishment that the Modern world requires a Modern architecture, in which historical models and associations are avoided if not eliminated, it is not because the technology of the Modern world directly requires it. The old Modernists argued that new material and industrialization required this change—Otto Wagner wrote that "it may therefore be deduced with certainty that new constructions must likewise yield new forms"—but Postmodernism proved that the imagery derived from fifteenth-century building methods could be hung all too easily on the framework of twentieth-century construction, albeit not always in a convincing way.

Initial criticism of Postmodernism in the late 1970s often referred to its "unbuildable" quality, a charge quickly refuted by a number of executed projects. Those who argued against the Postmodernism at the end of the 1980s had perhaps learned a lesson from their predecessors; while their objections were technologically based, they argued not that history and modern technology were irreconcilable with one another but that their relationship was irrelevant. For them it was the perception of the world that this technology had created, not merely its means of realization, that was irreconcilable with the languages of traditional architecture. The High Tech and Deconstructivist architects that came after perhaps felt, as did Henry Ford, that history was something they did not need.

10.35

10.36

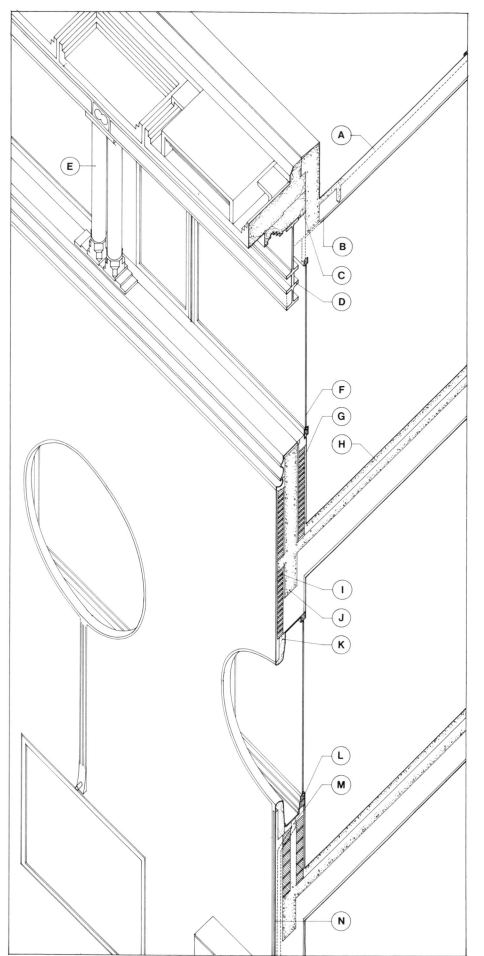

10.37

Banca Popolare di Verona

Carlo Scarpa and A. Rudi

Verona, Italy, 1973–1980

10.35 **View.**

10.36 **Double column.**

10.37 **Wall section.**
- A Concrete slab.
- B Plaster ceiling.
- C Stone cornice on 5.5 cm module.
- D Steel beams supporting cornice. The lower I section is filled in with ceramic tile to hide a fabrication error.
- E Double steel column. There are two pairs of these for every concrete column behind.
- F Wood and metal window and roll-down shutter.
- G Interior wall of plaster on masonry.
- H Concrete floor slab.
- I Stucco on masonry exterior wall.
- J Concrete frame and spandrel beam. The actual structural frame is nowhere exposed or expressed on the exterior.
- K Stone trim around window. The shape is actually two half circles with a small straight piece between.
- L Wood window.
- M Internal drainpipe to scupper below, marked with stone on surface of the wall. Rainwater drains behind rather than running off the sill.
- N Stucco finish.

  (A+U 2.82)

11 High Tech, Deconstruction, and the Present Day: 1972–1988

You believe in a crystal edifice, eternal and imperishable, an edifice at which one can never stealthily stick out his tongue or make a fist, even in one's pocket. As for me, I am perhaps afraid of this edifice just because it is crystal and forever imperishable, and because it will be impossible even stealthily to stick out one's tongue at it.

You see, if there should be a chicken coop instead of your palace, and it begins to rain, I may crawl into this chicken coop to avoid getting wet; yet I will not imagine that this chicken coop is a palace out of gratitude, because it gave me shelter from the rain. You are laughing, you even say that in such a case a chicken coup and a mansion are the same. Surely—I answer you—if the sole purpose of living is to keep from getting wet.

Feodor Dostoyevsky, *Notes from Underground*

In one sense the English High Tech movement can be said to have begun with the end of a partnership, the breakup of the firm of Team 4 in 1967, which included Norman Foster and Richard Rogers. The work of Team 4 had been largely concrete and concrete masonry single-family houses, and the difficulty in constructing these buildings is reflected in the tenets of Rogers's manifesto of 1969, which contains in its prescriptions some familiar phrases: "Constructed of the minimum number of prefabricated standard components," "Have joints of a yes-no variety," and "Use maximum spans with minimum internal structure to eliminate internal obstructions."[1]

Here in a capsule are all the lessons that Modernism learned from industrial objects: mass-produced standard parts (automobiles), maximum spans with minimal material (the airplane and the bridge), and minimum on-site labor using "dry" techniques.

After leaving Team 4, Rogers began a partnership with Renzo Piano, and in 1971 they won the competition for the Place Beaubourg, later renamed the Pompidou Center. (Not surprisingly Jean Prouvé, the "father" of French High Tech, was the chairman of the jury.) All of the maxims of Rogers's manifesto are applied in the Pompidou Center, and it became the work that brought the High Tech movement to prominence.

The design achieves flexibility of internal planning and mechanical systems by a combination of long-span trusses and a plan that locates all of the services outside the structural envelope. While the trusses achieve the requisite long span with minimum means and standardized, factory-assembled components, their great size, 3 meters by 45 meters, and the remoteness of the factory made their delivery to the site a political and social event. There are overt references to industrial objects as well—cable-suspended passageways, hollowed-out beams resembling aircraft girders, and a highly articulated curtain wall that seems to consist of moving parts—all used with a devotion to structural expression through exposure, an idea more closely related to the Gothic Revival than to aircraft design. Among the results are a number of clever but also misleading details. The columns, although exposed, are hollow cast-steel tubes filled with water for fireproofing, while the truss members are wrapped with mineral wool or ceramic fiber fireproofing. Only the round tension members and wide flange section are exposed steel.

11.1

11.2

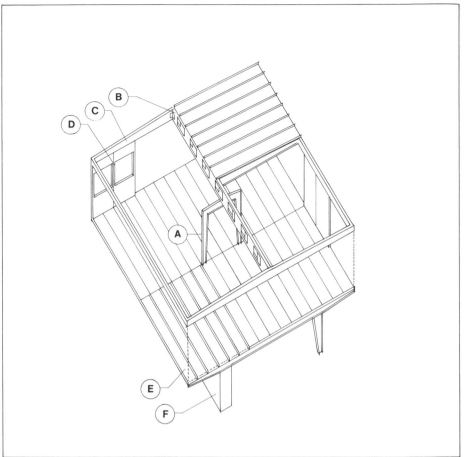

11.3

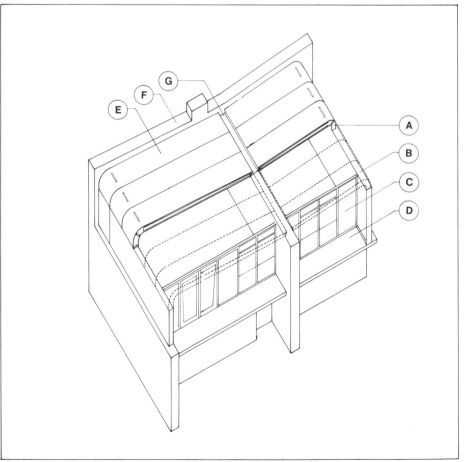

11.4

Housing at Meudon

Jean Prouvé with Andre Sivé and Henri Prouvé

Meudon, France, 1949–1953

11.1 **View of Type 1.** The executed houses, although similar in concept, were enlarged while eliminating many of the essential features.

11.2 **View.**

11.3 **Framing, first house type.**
- A Central steel frame, erected first. The assembly is designed of small lightweight components so that no crane is required.
- B Braked metal beam and metal roofing, erected second.
- C Edge beam, erected third.
- D Metal wall panels, see figure 11.6.
- E Metal floor decking. This was changed to concrete when the houses were erected at Meudon.
- F Masonry wall.
   (B + W 6.54)

11.4 **Framing, Type 2 (coque),** Jean Prouvé and Henri Prouvé, 1951.
- A *Coque* shell with Isorel ceiling filled with aluminum foil insulation. The roof has no frame per se but forms the metal skin into a structural shell.
- B 40 cm masonry walls covered with stucco.
- C Sheet steel wall (see figure 11.6).
- D Concrete balcony slab.
- E Sheet aluminum roofing.
- F Fieldstone walls.
- G Sheet aluminum gutter with sheet steel support.
   (B + W 6.54)

Although there had been many previous High Tech buildings, they possessed few of the Pompidou Center's customized elements. Its style is rooted in a number of Modernist precedents (the imagery of the Archigram group, the industrial nostalgia of the New Brutalism, the work and writings of Buckminster Fuller), but for the most part these roots were ideological rather than formal, as its forms were drawn not from Corbusian or Fulleresque interpretations of industrial objects but from the objects themselves.

It may be that the highly evocative forms of High Tech will be the beginning of a new architectural language, but there seems little doubt that ideologically it represents an end and not a beginning, that it is the culmination of the old Modernism, not the birth of a new one. For its contradictions are the contradictions of the old Modernism, and if the High Tech architects of the 1970s produced a multitude of new forms, they did so by reasserting the somewhat uncomfortable fusion of principles inspired by industrial products with the principles of nineteenth-century Gothic rationalism. For the dogmas of Gothic rationalism—the equation of architecture with structure, the equation of material efficiency with rationalism, the assertion of primary structures and the suppression of secondary ones—and the dogmas of industrialization—the minimal weight of aircraft design, the mass-produced, large-scale components of automobile manufacture, and the tension cables of bridge design—were not so coincident in 1970 as they were in 1920.

Following the completion of the Pompidou Center and the end of his partnership with Piano, Rogers built several smaller buildings in conditions that allowed more possibilities for literal structural expression. His PA Technology (PAT) Center near Princeton is as literal a translation of the suspension bridge into building as one could wish. If it minimizes the use of material with its steel cables in tension, it cannot be said to have minimized on-site labor. The large A frames, although repetitive, were too large to be fabricated and transported from elsewhere.

The frames are combinations of rigid and pinned joints, beautifully articulated but requiring a great deal of skilled labor on site. The rigid portions of the frames were each welded on site and then tilted to an upright position, the pinned connections made, and the suspension cables added. The cross beams were then bolted on by means of clip angles. In an ideal condition, all structural welding would have been done at the shop, where controlled conditions, ease of supervision, and organization of tasks usually produce superior work. However, since the PAT Center frames were too large to be easily transported, only the connecting plates were welded in the shop, and beams and columns were welded in the field to form the basic frames. Field welding of major structural joints is often avoided, precisely for the reason that made it so difficult here: over 40 percent of the welded joints were rejected for structural reasons after their first inspection.[2]

Another conspicuous problem caused by the exposed steel frame was that of tolerance. In the American construction industry it is accepted that dimensional perfection is impossible, and that there are varying degrees of acceptable inaccuracy or "tolerance" which are determined by the nature of the materials employed. Peter Rice, the engineer for the project, commented in another context:

One of the fundamental problems of any specification of tolerances is that, although intended as a definition of a reasonable upper limit by designers, it is interpreted as a license by the builders. . . . If you design with the upper limit as a norm you cumulate this and end up with a visually unacceptable system of details. . . . In the US the typical construction systems set out to resolve tolerance problems by providing a zone for adjustability between the cladding and the frame. In the UK and in high-tech the relationship tends to be more explicit, more visual . . . we have tried to identify a hierarchy of fits to be achieved and designed accordingly assuming a reasonable average and leaving room to resolve any extreme conditions which may arise when two separate elements meet each other.[3]

The construction of this frame is an excellent example of what Norman Foster referred to as the large amount of handicraft that goes into a High Tech building. But if the PAT Center did not deal with these issues entirely successfully, its difficulties paled in comparison to those of Rogers's next large work, the Lloyd's Building.

11.5

11.5 Housing at Meudon,
Jean Prouvé with Andre Sivé and
Henri Prouvé, Meudon, France
1949–1953, detail.

11.6 Jean Prouvé, curtain walls.
1 CIMT curtain wall:
A Inner sliding window section.
B Extruded aluminum track.
C Extruded aluminum mullion. This
carries the wind load to the floors
above and below. The projection
gives it additional depth and
stiffness.
D Extruded aluminum cover plate
attached with screws with nylon
washers, only partially a thermal
break.
E Outer sliding window section.

2 Meudon:
F Varnished aluminum sheet on inte-
rior and exterior faces.
G Plastic strip wrapped with edge of
aluminum sheet.
H Joint batten.
I Glass wool insulation between two
layers of corrugated aluminum.
J Plywood interior partition.

3 Villejuif prefabricated school sys-
tem, M. Novarina, architect:
K Aluminum mullion which also acts
as a structural brace for the roof.
L Openings for ventilation.
M Extruded aluminum ventilating
doors with plastic weather strip.
N Aluminum extrusion.
(Das Neue Blech, Domus, ADA)

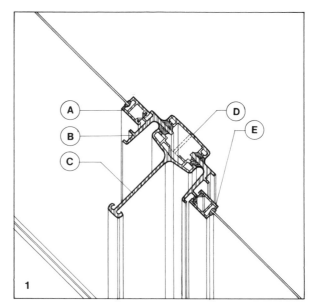

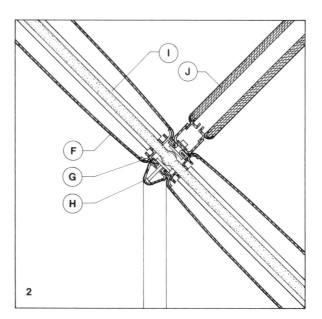

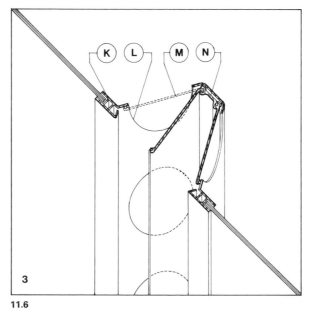

11.6

11.7

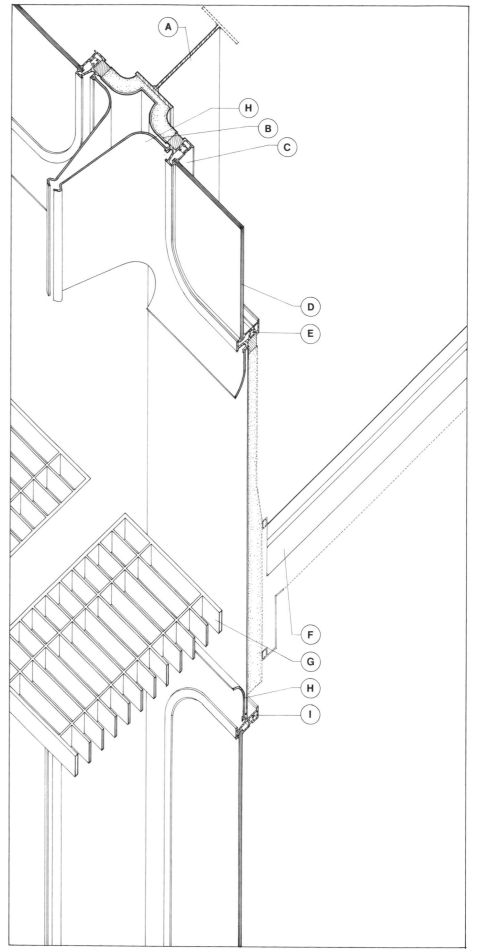

11.8

UNESCO Building V

Bernard Zephrus and Jean Prouvé

Paris, 1968–1969

11.7 **Curtain wall.**

11.8 **Curtain wall details.**
- A Steel support.
- B Insulation and anodized aluminum sheet.
- C Extruded aluminum window frame.
- D 15 mm clear glass with neoprene joint.
- E Nylon thermal break.
- F Floor structure.
- G Sunshade grating.
- H Sheet metal mullion. Rather than applying an extruded mullion, the metal sheet is bent outward to give the panel greater depth and stiffness.
- I The corner is curved rather than mitered so that the gasket may be continuous.

(Domus *6.89*)

THE LLOYD'S BUILDING

The commission for the Lloyd's Building, while prestigious, was also highly problematic, given Rogers's intentions. As a multistory urban office building, with no special code allowances as had been given at Pompidou, its frame had to be fireproofed, and here the combination of Gothic revival and industrial principles reached an impasse. The frame could be steel, light, and minimal, but not exposed. If exposed it must be concrete, which, however minimal the design, would be a heavy, site-intensive, and thoroughly "wet" system. After some attempts at a compromise steel frame, Rogers went with a mixture of precast and cast-in-place concrete. The constructional systems are ones that Kahn might have used, but the style of execution, in appearance if not in reality, was High Tech. Ironically, this was achieved by the use of highly skilled and not entirely repetitive on-site labor. Fireproofing the structure alone did not completely solve the problem of how to expose the structure, since, had the floor-ceiling assembly been built in the conventional way, it would still have been covered up.

In conventional American office buildings the space between the ceiling and the floor above is divided into a system of horizontal layers, each of which is assigned to a major component or trade, the uppermost for structure, the lower layers for ductwork, lighting, then ceiling (figure 11.13). In many contemporary office buildings, an additional layer is added: the computer floor on pedestals. Each layer is designed by a separate discipline—structural, mechanical, and electrical engineers, and architect—who may work independently of each other provided they do not violate the zones assigned to the others. Likewise the four separate subcontractors executing this work may operate independently of each other, which is extremely beneficial in terms of their schedules. Economically and functionally this system works well. It requires minimum coordination and thus less time for architect, engineer, contractor, and workman. For the client it provides reasonable flexibility, since changes in one system are less likely to effect the other three. Its drawback, of course, is that it is almost devoid of any possibility for structural expression (at least through literal means), and much of the drabness and lack of hierarchy in modern interiors is a result of the mindless application of this system with its uniform ceiling height and unchanging ceiling grid.

Rogers's solution was to invert this system, putting the structure on the bottom and the ductwork in a computer or access floor above (figure 11.13). In so doing he eliminated most of the system's independence. Lights and ducts occur in the structural zone, but, of course, independent system design is not an overriding criterion in aircraft or automobile design.

The building does have some highly industrialized components, despite the use of so much site-cast concrete. Some parts maximized off-site assembly, particularly the bathroom units, which were "mass-produced" stainless steel capsules plugged into the structure. This caused other problems, which are revealing of the differences between building construction and industrial fabrication. The factory-made building components were divided according to the parts of the building itself—bathrooms, mechanical units, stairs, etc., were supplied by different manufacturers. This seems logical but often is not. A standard American building specification would subdivide the building by materials—steel, concrete, ornamental metal, etc.—each of which might occur in any or all of the building's larger parts. There are, for example, four types of metal panel on the exterior at Lloyd's, three of which are stainless steel—those covering the bathrooms, the stairs, and ductwork—all of which are supplied by a different subcontractor and none of which match. An industrial designer might not consider this a problem at all, but an architect less so.

The curtain wall design is an expression of some very traditional Modernist ideals: that structure and nonstructure should be clearly separated and articulated, and that the optimum structure uses the minimum amount of material (thus the large quantity of glass to set off the concrete structure, and the exposure and expression of each layer of the floor system on the exterior). In the curtain wall itself there is a clear separation between the I-shaped aluminum mullions and the smaller beads holding the glass, a detail obviously Miesian in its origins. Rogers punches out

11.9

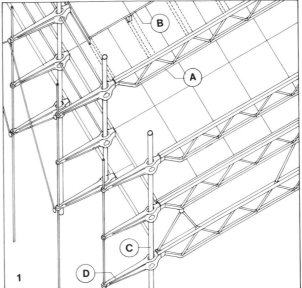

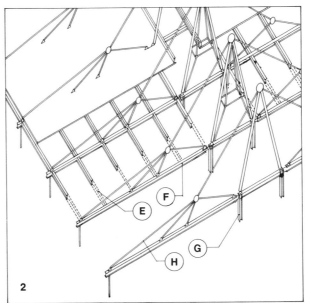

1

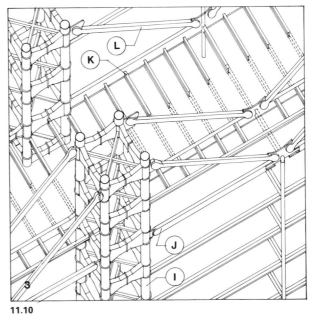

2

3

11.10

11.9 Pompidou Center,
Renzo Piano and Richard Rogers,
Paris, 1971–1977, view.

11.10 Comparative framing.
1 Piano and Rogers, Pompidou
Center:
A 3 × 45 m trusses with hollow tube
top and bottom chords and solid
round webs covered with
fireproofing.
B Concrete slab floor unit supported
by WF section.
C 850 mm hollow cast steel tube filled
with water for fireproofing.
D Cast gerbette to support escalator
and services.
2 Richard Rogers, PA Technology
Center:
E Wide flange supporting roof.
F Frame from wide flanges and tubes.
G Steel WF column. See figure 11.12.
H Tension support points, eliminating
the need for internal columns in the
main office area.
3 Norman Foster, Hong Kong and
Shanghai Bank:
I Mast. The loads travel up the cable
to the truss and then down the
mast to grade.
J Truss with hangers at ends and mid-
span to support floor beams below.
K Typical beams.
L Truss hanger.
(AJ 9.84, RR)

sections of the mullion web to reduce weight in imitation of aircraft design, a gesture that is aesthetically rich but not necessarily economically advantageous.

In subsequent office buildings Rogers has used steel framing, exposed where possible, but clad in aluminum where not, regaining some of the high-tech imagery of the Pompidou Center in the process but losing, in the eyes of traditional Modernists, some constructive validity. But Rogers has simply recognized a characteristic of modern building construction (and one might add, of aircraft and automobile construction as well), that layered construction with the primary structural frame concealed is inevitable in the tall steel building. It is a type of construction that Norman Foster, Rogers's one-time partner, had begun to experiment with somewhat earlier.

Foster has made no secret of his interest in the principles and the forms of aircraft design, nor does he deny that their appeal is aesthetic as well as intellectual. He said in 1983: "If you look at a racing sailplane in glass- or carbon-fiber, you'll see what I mean. They are unbelievable. Beautiful. That's why I took to gliding in the first place; the actual tactile quality of the machine, even if it never flew, frozen in space."[4] Foster's concern with flexibility, another canon of High Tech, is also traced to his study of aircraft:

The question of true flexibility is a search to define the long-life and short-life components of a building; this has many parallels in aviation. The Jet Ranger helicopter, for example, was introduced in 1965 and although the technology of many of the individual parts, such as the engine and electronics, has changed quite dramatically, it is still being made. Even though its appearance seems to indicate that of a fixed object, it is actually responsive to a process of continuous change.[5]

But if the principles of vehicular design—minimum material, factory labor—and its associated techniques—steel tension cables, large prefabricated components, and long spans—are ubiquitous features of any mature Foster design, there is a great deal of nineteenth-century theory present as well: the ideal of exposed construction, the equation of the building with the structural frame, and the use of large expanses of glass to set off the structure and exoskeletal frames to enhance structural expression.

Like Rogers, Foster found this philosophy easiest to apply in smaller buildings, such as his Renault warehouse in Swindon, where the one-story building allowed for an elaborate and exposed steel frame. Most of the conventions of Modernism drawn from aviation and engineering are here. The roof is cable-suspended; the webs of beams and mullions are hollowed out like so many aircraft ribs. Beams are tapered and otherwise formed to express the forces at work, using the minimum quantity of material in the process, however complex the resulting form. This economy of form and material did not readily translate into financial economy. The mullions and beams, for example, would have cost less with solid webs. Nevertheless the building's style is attributable to the rigorous application of aircraft principles to a building. The application of these principles at a larger scale was to prove more difficult.

THE HONG KONG AND SHANGHAI BANK

It was assumed from the beginning that the construction of the Hong Kong and Shanghai Bank would be different. Foster's office did extensive research and development on ideas for components that could easily have been supplied by readily available standard products, but, like Neutra, Fuller, and many others, Foster was frustrated by the low tolerance, heavy weight, and hand-crafted nature of the standards of the building industry. Attempts were made to import materials and techniques from aircraft and industrial fields, attempts that were, at least in a literal sense, unsuccessful. Stephanie Williams notes, for example, that during development Foster's office wished to adapt the technology of honeycomb sandwich panels, lifted from the aircraft industry, for the floor construction, and visited the Concorde engineering office at Bristol to research the possibility.[6] In the end the research provided more inspiration than useful information, and the floor is concrete and steel deck, probably due to the need for fire and acoustic insulation.

11.11

11.12

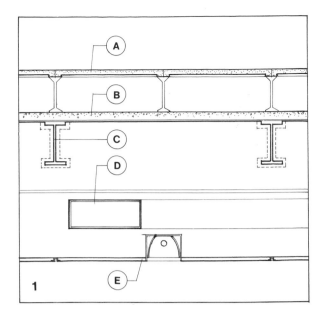

1

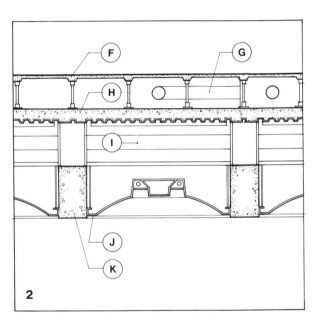

2

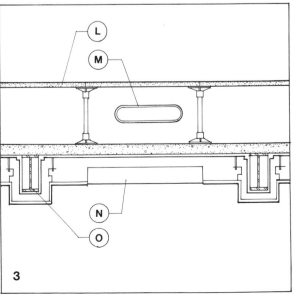

3

11.13

PA Technology Center

Richard Rogers

Hightstown, New Jersey, 1984–1986

11.11 View. The steel frame did not require fireproofing and could thus be exposed, as are the ductwork and rooftop mechanical units. There is little that is layered, covered, or concealed.

11.12 Steel connections. There are two basic joint types: rigid, which will transfer bending moments, and pinned, which connects beam and column with a single bolt so that when the beam deflects its end simply rotates and no twisting force is transferred to the column. The connections are field-welded.

11.13 Comparative floor depths.

1 Typical American office building:

A Access floor (partial or optional).

B Concrete on metal deck.

C Steel purlin and fireproofing with girder beyond.

D Heating and ventilating duct.

E Suspended ceiling with lights.

2 Richard Rogers, Lloyd's Building:

F Pedestal floor. A computer floor is used throughout and the horizontal plenum produced is used for distribution of air. This allows the concrete structure below to be exposed since it is not covered by a ceiling and ductwork.

G Supply ducts located in the raised floor. There are two zones reserved for ductwork, one above and one below the slab.

H Concrete on metal deck.

I Return ducts, which run in the layer between the waffle grid and slab above.

J Light fixture with slots for return air.

K Exposed concrete beam.

3 Norman Foster, Hong Kong and Shanghai Bank. The conventional system has been in effect turned upside down, but in addition certain of the strata have been combined.

L Computer access floor containing the communication and power wiring.

M Supply air ductwork. This layer is divided into three zones: the bottom for primary air distribution, the middle for secondary, and the upper for electrical outlets.

N Ceiling and lights. The ceiling follows the contours of the steel beams directly above. The system has the obvious advantage that the universal computer floor allows greater flexibility and the entire assembly takes up less vertical space than the conventional system.

O Steel structure and fireproofing. Unlike in the typical American office building, the systems are no longer independent, nor is the work of those who design and build them. *(AJ 9.84)*

Ultimately Foster was forced to make the same choice as Rogers: either exposed concrete or concealed steel for the structural system. He opted for the latter, so that structural expression at Hong Kong is through analogous rather than literal means. Foster exploits the possibilities of this system somewhat timidly. Note that there is considerable air space between the steel column and aluminum cover (figure 11.27). This allows for the provision of tolerance and the use of hierarchies of craftsmanship, which are atypical of High Tech buildings in general. The aluminum cover must be precisely erected but the column itself may be more crudely joined, and any inconsistencies between column and cover may be corrected when the cover is applied. Nor does the shape of the aluminum cover follow precisely the shape of the real steel column. Like many analogous structures, it closely parallels but does not duplicate the actual structure.

This desire to closely match cladding and structure accounts in part for the fact that, like Rogers, Foster inverts the floor-ceiling sandwich, placing the ductwork on top and the lighting inside the zone of the structure. This allows the ceiling to be configured into beam covers and coffers describing the beams they conceal.

Although the primary structural principle at work is steel in tension, there are few overt references to aircraft in the primary frame, nor could there easily be, given its clad nature. These references are confined to secondary structures, particularly the window mullions and sunshades, where the opportunity is rarely missed to carve out circular openings or taper beams to minimize the quantity of material.

But if the bank adheres closely to principles of aircraft design, its allegiance to the ideas of Viollet-le-Duc is no less rigid. There is an absolute clarity about what is structure and what is not, and (despite its concealment) an absolute hierarchy of structural elements. There is as a result an abundance of glass simply because, in the language of Gothic or International Style Modernism, glass represents the nonstructural. It should be noted that few such rigid principles are followed in the Mosquito or the Wellington, which have no external structural expression and which frequently depart from their primary structural principles where particular conditions make it advantageous to do so.

Foster made extensive use of off-site prefabrication not only for the bathrooms but for the mechanical system as well; due to a highly decentralized design, this could be designed as pods to be plugged in or unplugged from the building. Unlike at Lloyd's, the contract divisions follow a more conventional arrangement for the sake of unity and perhaps economy as well. The curtain wall is by a single supplier and uniformly wraps the building, including bathroom and mechanical units, which, although prefabricated, are delivered without skins.

Foster's analysis of the systems of building in the aircraft industry and his synthesis of these systems into real buildings demonstrate just how superficial Le Corbusier's analysis is by comparison. At the same time it must be asked whether this is a suitable application of these principles, particularly the idea of the minimum use of material. In the design of aircraft, where the weight of the finished product is of primary importance, the punching out of webs of structural members if commonplace. Quantity of material and weight are considerations in the design of buildings, but not of the same magnitude. Often simplicity of fabrication is more important than the minimum use of material, even if it requires substantially more material. It is doubtful that any of the methods Foster used to lighten the curtain wall made the building less expensive. It is more likely that they increased the amount of labor, as in the punched-out webs.

A comparison of the cost of Lloyd's and the Hong Kong bank with contemporary American office buildings is not entirely fair. If they cost more, this is to a large extent because they do more. In a cost comparison to an F-16, whose cost exceeds $30,000 per square foot of its footprint, they might appear to advantage. Still, one cannot ignore the fact that Hong Kong is one of the most expensive buildings ever built and that it took longer to complete than its conventional American counterparts. Obviously both Hong Kong and Lloyd's paid a heavy price in deliberately going against the pattern of contemporary building.

11.14

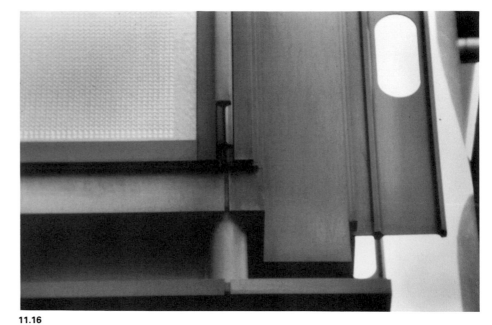

11.16

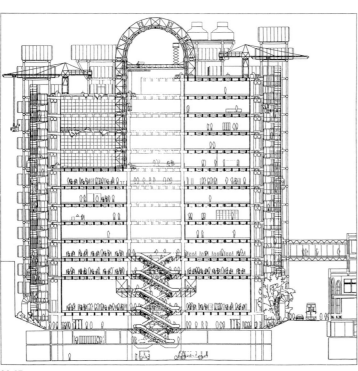

11.15

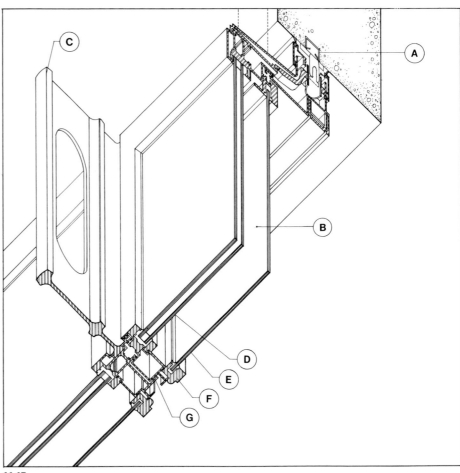

11.17

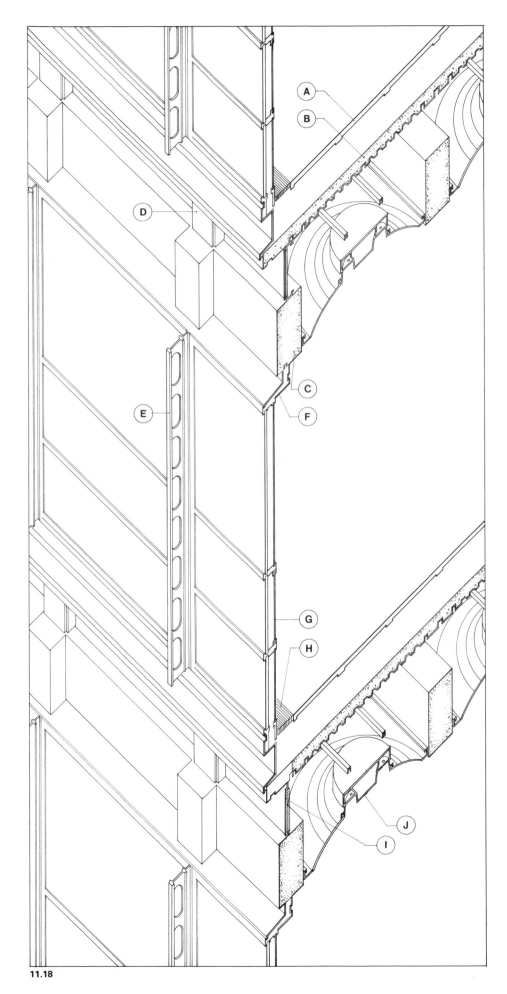

11.18

11.14 **Floor detail.** The columns and the waffle slab are cast in place. In order to achieve the square-edged precision, a form pan that could be disassembled was used, instead of the typical metal or fiberglass pan.

11.15 **Section.** The columns are located beside and not under the major beams, creating a column-free interior.
(RR)

11.16 **Mullion at corner.**

11.17 **Curtain wall details.**

A Insert cast in concrete beam with flexible connection to receive mullion.

B The air returned through the light fixtures is drawn under pressure between the glass panes to retard heat loss in winter and heat gain in summer.

C The web of this I-shaped extruded aluminum mullion is punched out to reduce the quantity of material. As with any beam, it is the edges, not the middle, that does the structural work.

D Outer layer of rolled pattern glass and solar control coated glass pane.

E Rolled glass inner pane.

F Aluminum frame to receive glass.

G The mullion is formed of two interlocking sections to permit thermal expansion.
(A+U 3.87, AJ 9.84, RR)

11.18 **Wall section.**

A Access floor. The conventional role of this system is to provide easy access to electronic services for the workstation. It is also used here to create a cavity for circulation of air as well, which is distributed through the floor and returned through the ceiling light fixtures.

B 100 mm concrete slab on modular steel permanent formwork trays.

C Beam of cast-in-place two-way concrete structure.

D Precast concrete pedestal. The slab is separated from the waffle below by the pedestal to allow services to run between slab and waffle.

E Anodized aluminum curtain wall mullion.

F Top transom. See figure 11.17. The separation of wall and glass is accentuated by the projection of the glass surface in front of the concrete.

G Triple glazing and ventilation cavity and with clear double-glazed operable window. Air is circulated through the cavity to minimize heat loss through the glass.

H Aluminum grating and diffuser.

I Fire-rated metal closure panel. Sometimes air is returned via a fishtail duct in this panel.

J Black-painted spun aluminum luminaire shield for lighting fixture. Air is returned through this fixture.
(AJ 9.84, RR)

11.19

11.20

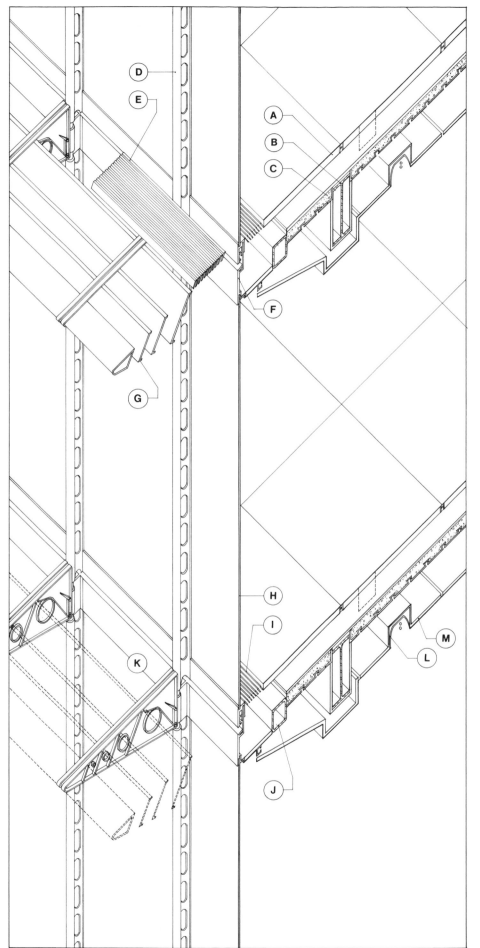

11.21

Hong Kong and Shanghai Bank

Norman Foster

Hong Kong, 1979–1984

11.19 View. Individual modules at each floor provide the heating and cooling for that floor alone. There is no central core with duct shafts and no mechanical floors. The elevators stop at sky lobbies marked by the trusses, not at each floor.
(Sir Norman Foster and Partners)

11.20 Steel framing under construction.
(Sir Norman Foster and Partners)

11.21 Wall section.
A Access floor on pedestals. This provides for rewiring of office machines and equipment as well as providing a space for air supply and return.
B Steel beam and fireproofing. The deep spandrel beam, which would normally be located at the building perimeter, is pulled well inboard so that it does not appear on the exterior. The section tapers toward the window, creating a minimal interruption in the glass plane as opposed to the deep spandrel that would result in conventional arrangement.
C Concrete topping on metal slab.
D Aluminum curtain wall. The webs of the typical mullion are punched out to minimize weight.
E Sunscreen grating and external access.
F Horizontal curtain wall member.
G Aluminum sunscreen blades.
H ½" tempered glass. The thin floor-ceiling sandwich maximizes the amount of exterior glass.
I Diffuser grating for supply air.
J 6" square steel tube to receive steel anchor T supporting curtain wall.
K Cast aluminum sunscreen bracket.
L Light fixture.
M Ceiling assembly.
(NF)

11.22 Hanger connection.
(Sir Norman Foster and Partners)

11.23 Hanger connection with fireproofing.
(Sir Norman Foster and Partners)

11.22

11.23

11.24

11.26

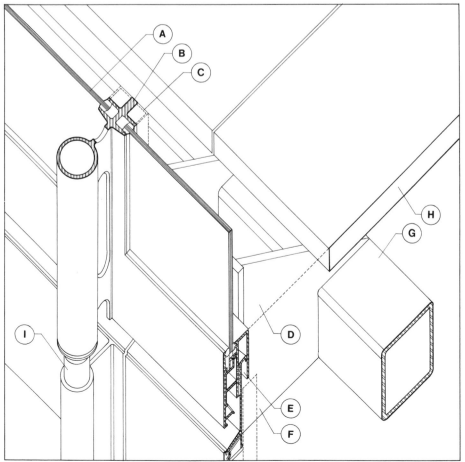

11.25

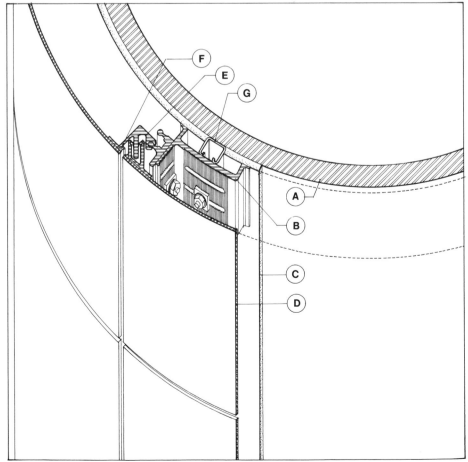

11.27

Hong Kong and Shanghai Bank

Norman Foster

Hong Kong, 1979–1984

11.24 Vertical mullion joint.

(Sir Norman Foster and Partners)

11.25 Curtain wall details.

A 12 mm tempered glass with glazing gaskets, neoprene setting block, and aluminum clip at the quarter points to hold the glass.

B Aluminum mullion with punched-out web to transfer the load on the glass to the floor structure.

C Closure for internal partition.

D Aluminum grille (not shown) for air.

E Aluminum extrusion to support glass, with sliding connection for assembly and to accommodate thermal movement and live load deflection. The mullion is hung from the floor above.

F Steel anchor T attached to stainless steel tube to carry load back to structure.

G Steel tube attached to steel structure.

H Access floor.

I Cast aluminum anchor assembly sleeved into mullion for thermal expansion and live load deflection.

(NF)

11.26 Typical column. Aluminum panel being installed on steel tube column with corrosion protection and fireproofing.

(Sir Norman Foster and Partners)

11.27 Column cladding details. Although numerous efforts were made to find a solution that would expose the structure, the final solution was to clad the steel in aluminum because of the need for fireproofing and insulation.

A 1200 mm round steel column with cementatious barrier coat corrosion protection layer. The actual structural section is a steel tube that varies in diameter.

B Adjustable extruded aluminum anchor 150 mm long, with neoprene water stops and stainless steel pins to interlock sections.

C Fireproofing and protective coating to prevent corrosion.

D ³⁄₁₆″ aluminum column cover of interlocking cylinder segments. The cover hides and protects the fireproofing, which is aesthetically unpresentable. The aluminum is less easily corroded than steel and can receive finishes that are more durable.

E Extruded aluminum trim, plug-welded to panel, with sliding connection to accommodate thermal movement and minimize "oil canning."

F Silicone seals.

G Anchor insert and bolt.

(NF)

Ultimately they delivered economy, but only in the sense of style and not of means, and that is perhaps the High Tech legacy, despite the strenuous efforts of its adherents. We can only justify these buildings as conforming to a future utopia in which economy of resources, economy of material, and economy of capital will be one. It is a utopia that Fuller thought existed in 1945 but that, by the measure of Hong Kong and Lloyd's, seems even farther away in 1995.

JEAN NOUVEL AND RENZO PIANO

Foster and Rogers were not the sole practitioners of High Tech in the late 1970s and early 1980s. Many of the others did not share all of their concerns and fascinations; two of the more conspicuous differences have to do with the length of spans and the prevalence of glass. The Pompidou Center, the PAT Center, and the Hong Kong and Shanghai Bank all have spans considerably greater than those of comparable buildings of the same type. The reasons given for this are of course flexibility of use and efficiency of material. But the spans are in excess of the requirements of many if not most users, and the economy of material was often achieved at considerable expense of resources. Like the late work of Mies van der Rohe, the approach seems to be a dead end, or perhaps the opposite—a direction to follow with no end in sight. Equally contradictory was the quantity of glass that the style seemed to require. The desire to express the primary structure and to suppress the secondary structure, while rendering both visible, often resulted in buildings in which all that was not structure was transparent. But clear, unprotected glazing was unlikely given the energy and comfort standards of the 1980s. The result is that High Tech curtain wall detailing has been a constant struggle to give glass those properties that it inherently lacks: shading and insulation.

Jean Nouvel's version of High Tech seems determined in part to avoid or resolve these contradictions. His spans are characteristically short and his interest is usually focused on technologically activating the environmental envelope of the building.

The Institut du Monde Arabe has structural spans that are fairly small by current standards; while subject to geometric regularity, it accommodates itself through changes and distortions of grids to unique conditions of the site or the program. Nouvel also seems less embarrassed than his English counterparts by the necessity of covering the steel frame with fireproofing and cladding, seeming to take delight in the seams and fasteners of the metal beam and column covers and not trying to hide the similarity of material and technique of the structural cladding to the rest of the curtain wall.

The building's best-known feature is the elaborate south facade, which is equipped with a series of operable lenses resembling camera irises which, when activated by the adjacent photocells, adjust to changes in solar radiation. Enclosing both is an elaborate triple-glazed curtain wall. The outer layer is insulating glass, the inner layer a single sheet that also functions to keep dust off the mechanism. Rather than the "stick" method, in which the wall is built up of individual linear members, it is fabricated in panels, which requires double mullions. Nouvel exploits this requirement by adding an expansion bellows to visually and technically isolate each panel. In a more questionable detail, he makes the inner panel mullions appear to be split when they are in fact joined. That the resulting wall pattern recalls a specific Arabic design is clearly to Nouvel a virtue, but at the same time seems a rather glib solution to the desire to give the building a symbolic character. If the building were occupied by South Americans, Asians, or Africans, what would the facade look like? Nor does it really escape from the frame and glass vocabulary of High Tech; it only takes more delight in the necessary modifications to the transparent envelope.

Renzo Piano's work after the dissolution of his partnership with Rogers and the completion of the Pompidou Center has adhered less rigidly to High Tech principles and been more inclusive of nonindustrial elements than that of his one-time partner. Piano has not disdained to use traditional materials such as brick and wood both as structure and as finish. He has used long spans and tension structures

11.28

11.29

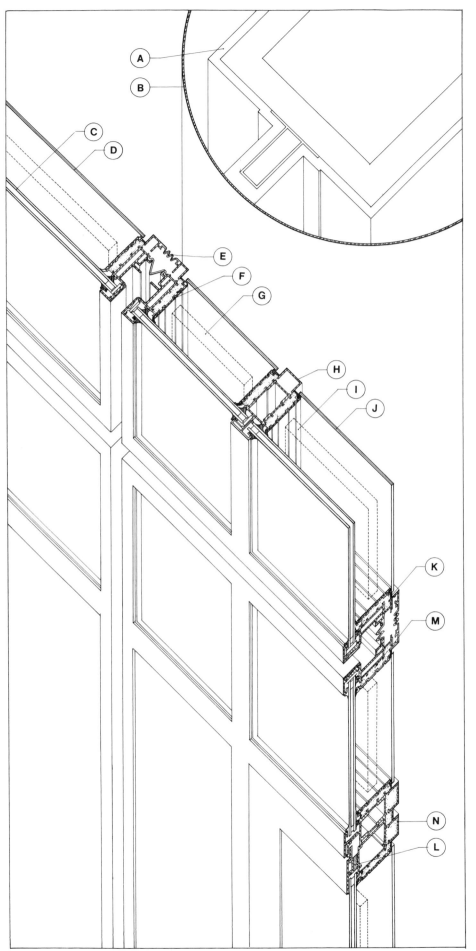

11.30

Institut du Monde Arabe

Jean Nouvel

Paris, 1981–1987

11.28 View.

11.29 Curtain wall detail.

11.30 Curtain wall section.
- A Column and fireproofing.
- B Metal column cover.
- C Insulating glass of two 4 mm layers with 12 mm air space.
- D 6 mm glass.
- E Neoprene bellows to accommodate thermal expansion of panels.
- F Split aluminum mullion to allow fabrication of the panels in separate frames.
- G Photovoltaic cell to activate lens.
- H Single aluminum mullion.
- I Lens that opens and closes to vary the quantity of heat and light penetrating the wall.
- J 8 mm glass. The glass at the larger opening is thicker.
- K Gasket to seal opening.
- L Polyurethane thermal break to minimize heat loss through the mullion.
- M The fins serve to reinforce the mullion or to receive fasteners or both.
- N Although it appears a split mullion, this particular section is one piece.

(Detail 1.88, JN)

where these seemed appropriate, but he seems less bound to structural expression and transparent envelopes.

In 1987 he completed an addition to the IRCAM portion of the Pompidou Center, in some ways a more typical example of late twentieth-century construction than its celebrated parent. It is a small-span steel-framed building in which the frame is clad and the exterior wall is for the most part masonry. Piano was determined to render this entire system expressive if not visible. The exterior wall is in principle a brick cavity wall, but it is a cavity wall like no other. The bricks have no mortar but are custom-made shapes set in aluminum racks so that all joints remain open. These are hung in front of an aluminum panel wall on the steel structure. The result is something like a typical brick cavity wall that has been dematerialized. In fact it functions as a kind of rain screen wall, equalizing the pressure between inside and out.

Piano, like Scarpa, thus attacked what is ultimately a more difficult question of Modernist technical expression than the structural frame. The most elaborate technical devices of modern buildings occur not in their frames but in their walls. Achieving an expression of this complexity is difficult at best. A great many contemporary "honest" buildings by Mario Botta, Tadao Ando, and others are content to portray the highly complex layered and specialized cavity wall as a solid mass. This is deceptive perhaps, but in many cases they have had little choice. Piano's IRCAM walls solve this problem but in so doing deprive the wall of most of the real economy it might have possessed, producing essentially one complex building inside another. It is as difficult to envision IRCAM as a prototype for future development as it is any of its High Tech predecessors.

However admirable the products of High Tech appear, one must admit that they are subject to some haphazard reasoning. How could buildings so concerned with economy take so long to build and be so expensive? Is the technological sophistication of the Concorde desirable in an office building? Like Modernist prototypes they are really utopian artifacts for a world in which values, economic values in particular, will be rearranged. Most of its protagonists are more reluctant than were their predecessors to describe their work as prototypes. Here they are, they seem to say, if you want them to be prototypes.

Less understandable and more frustrating is the reluctance of High Tech practitioners to acknowledge the amount of aesthetic manipulation going on, particularly in terms of composition. Is it really necessary for the PAT Center to be symmetrical? Is it really necessary that the Hong Kong and Shanghai Bank be so picturesquely carved away? It is not really a question that can be easily divorced from questions of structure. In Greek, Gothic, or Modern architecture a choice of structure is often a choice of compositional technique. But if the High Tech architects have been slow to acknowledge this relationship, their near relatives, the Deconstructivists, have accepted it with relish, and in some cases made it the foundation of their work.

DECONSTRUCTION: BERNARD TSCHUMI AND COOP HIMMELBLAU

Deconstruction, like Postmodernism or High Tech, is a term whose application often raises more questions than it answers, and like Postmodernism and High Tech it is a label usually resented by those to whom it is most often applied. However ambiguous the connection between deconstruction as a tool of critical analysis and as a style of design, its application in formal terms is fairly clear.

While many of its practitioners would disdain the obvious architectural implications of the word "deconstruct," Jacques Derrida, perhaps the movement's chief literary spokesman, sees such a connection in that, as a critical tool, deconstruction seems to seek out those elements that provide the "stability" in any work of art or literature. He wrote in a commentary on Hegel:

One first locates, in an architectonics, in the art of the system, the "neglected corners" and the "defective cornerstone," that which, from the outset, threatens the coherence and the internal order of the construction. But it is a cornerstone!

11.31

11.32

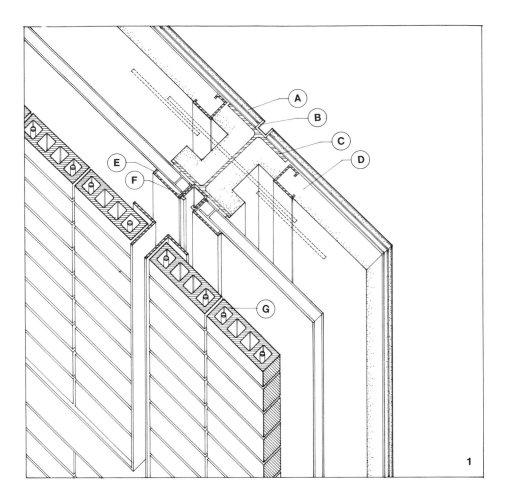

1

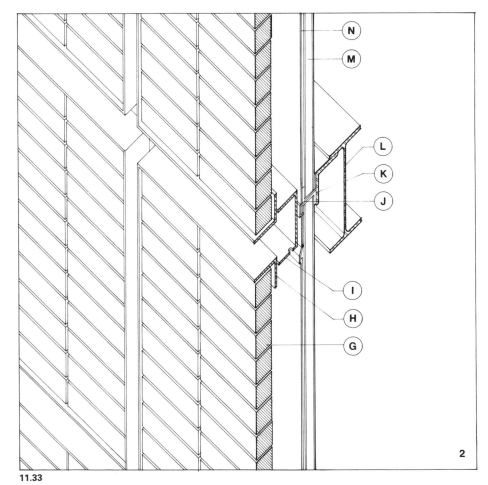

11.33

2

IRCAM extension

Renzo Piano

Paris, 1986–1987

11.31 View.

11.32 Detail.

(Jonathan Fabian)

11.33 Wall details.

1 Detail at column:
A Interior finish.
B Steel channel trim.
C Steel HEA 180 column.
D Insulation.
E Trim to secure wall panel.
F Channel strut.
G Brick panel in aluminum frame with
  open joints and air space behind.
  Brick sections are connected with
  stainless steel rods and separated
  by polyanide spacer.

2 Section at horizontal panel joint:
H 60 × 70 mm aluminum frame.
I 120 × 60 mm aluminum channel.
J Flashing.
K Steel angle to connect channel to
  beam.
L Steel section PE 120 structural
  frame of the building.
M Panel.
N Corrugated sheet cladding forming
  the actual waterproof barrier.
  (Detail 90, RP)

It is required by the architecture which it nevertheless, in advance, deconstructs from within. It assures its cohesion while situating in advance, in a way that is both visible and invisible (that is, corner), the site that lends itself to a deconstruction to come. The best spot for efficiently inserting a deconstructive lever is a cornerstone. There may be other analogous places but this one derives its privilege from the fact that it is indispensable to the completeness of the edifice. A condition of erection, holding up the walls of the established edifice, it can also be said to maintain it, to contain it, and to be tantamount to the generality of the architectonic system.[7]

The architectural implications of this type of thought have most frequently manifested themselves in the desire to build structures in which these "cornerstones" are called into question, which are on the edge or perhaps over the edge of instability.

Like High Tech theory, the roots of Deconstructivist theory are more firmly grounded in nineteenth- and early twentieth-century architectural thought than some of its adherents would like to acknowledge. Several critics have traced its origins to aspects of Russian Constructivism. Yet while it was certainly a tenet of Russian Constructivism that new materials, new technologies, and new conditions required new compositional devices, to one familiar with nineteenth-century admirers (or for that matter the critics) of Gothic architecture, there is something familiar in their line of thinking. It was a virtue of Gothic that elements were held in a delicate equilibrium that seemed barely sustainable. The parts were so interdependent that one could not be moved or altered without the destruction of the whole. The Deconstructivists might maintain that they have gone a step further and crossed a line into instability, but is this what they have done, and is it even possible? In fact, many of the aims of Deconstruction are antistructural. If the essential element of Deconstructivist architecture is instability, how is this instability to be achieved? Certainly not by building an unstable structure, but then how? By building a real structure that appears to be unstable but is not, or by the masking of a real, stable structure with an ornamental one that appears to be unstable? Would not both of these options dictate a return to the dishonesty of the past?

Bernard Tschumi's Parc de La Villette, being one of the first of these Deconstructivist buildings to be realized, was one of the first to face these questions. The two primary architectural elements designed by Tschumi for La Villette, the galleries and the folies, were always conceived as separate architectural entities, and although there were early attempts to unite the architectural language of the two, they had diverged considerably by the end of the second phase of construction. The competition design did not provide a clear image of the galleries but provided a clear function. One, the longest, was at grade, shading the north-south walk and bridging the canal; it stands free of the folies. The shorter gallery is elevated and runs east-west parallel to the canal, intersecting the folies. Early on Tschumi assigned to both a Deconstructivist role:

Architectural systems are always noted for the coherence they represent. From the Classical era to the Modern Movement, from Durand to the Constructivists and beyond, the notion of an incoherent structure is simply without consideration. The very function of architecture, as it is still understood, precludes the idea of a dis-structured structure. However, the process of superimposition, permutation and substitution which governed the Parc de la Villette plan could only lead to a radical questioning of the concept of structure—to its decentering—since the superimposition of three autonomous (and coherent) structures (points, lines, surfaces) does not necessarily lead to a new, more complex and verifiable structure. Instead, they open up a field of contradictory and conflictual events which deny the idea of a pre-established coherence.[8]

Early in the design process Tschumi brought in Peter Rice, who had engineered the Pompidou and PAT centers, to consult. Though many engineers might have found these notions of instability daunting at best, Rice took up the job with relish, and the final design bears his recognizable stamp. The final design of the north-south

11.34

11.35

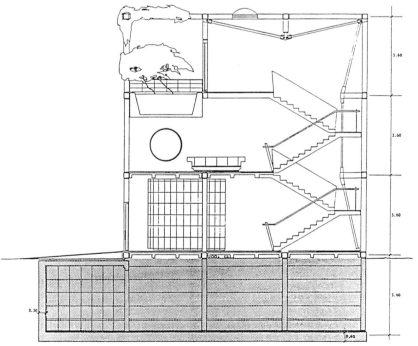

11.36

Parc de La Villette

Bernard Tschumi

Paris, 1984

11.34 Walkway.

11.35 Walkway detail.

11.36 Peter Rice design for folie. The structural system is a combination of precast columns and beams, square infill panels, and steel tension cables to give additional strength to the precast structural elements where necessary.
(BT)

gallery consists of an undulating canopy supported by a tubular box beam, in turn supported by a series of asymmetrical masts and cables. It contains many of Rice's (and Modernism's) favorite principles and techniques, cables in tension, masts in compression, exposed structure and connections, and high levels of craft. Its apparent complexity is due mostly to the fact that the spacing of the masts and the undulations of the canopy do not use the same module. (The spacing of the masts is drawn from the spacing of the folies while the spacing of the undulations is drawn from the column spacing of the adjacent nineteenth-century grand hall.)

Despite the fact that its structure is entirely exposed, the gallery does not tell us the complete story of its structure. The box truss that supports the canopy, for example, normally spans 65 feet between masts. At the point at which it crosses the canal, the truss spans nearly three times this distance with no visible changes to its cross section. This is accomplished by increasing the wall thickness of the tubes that make up the truss while keeping the outside diameter constant, adding additional material and additional strength without altering the exterior profile. This should not be construed as a criticism of the design, only an example of how subjective a view of reality any structure presents, even one that appears to hide virtually nothing.

If the galleries represent a manifestation of the Deconstructivist aesthetic in its literal form, the folies, in their final form, represent the opposite: Deconstructivist building in its representational form. The development of the folie designs were not as linear as was that of the galleries and the final result was a system of construction that seems to be the opposite of the galleries. This was not implicit in the original intent, although, like many aspects of the Parc de La Villette, it was an accident that proved acceptable and in some ways desirable. Nor was the final form solely the result of programmatic, legal, and economic constraints. Although these limitations must have seemed at times to be on the verge of destroying the entire conception, they also produced accidents that were not entirely objectionable. Ultimately the form was determined by a different set of "limits of representation" than that described by the Deconstructivists: the limited ability of literal structures to communicate ideas and the necessity for abstraction in the ability to communicate any architectural idea.

The folies, which contain a variety of programmatic elements—cafes, museums, education centers, etc.—were originally conceived in more philosophical terms. The word *folie* alludes not only to the familiar garden folly but to its French meaning, madness:

Although the Folies *proceeded from a simple construction principle, deviation alters the relationship to the structural grid. The grid then becomes a simple support around which a transgressive architecture can develop in relation to the original norm. The relationship between normality and deviation suggested a method for the elaboration for the* Folies. *First, requirements and constraints derived from the program are confronted with architectonic combination and transformation principles of the project. The confrontation results in a basic architectural state, the "norm." Then the norm is transgressed—without, however, disappearing. A distortion of the original norm results: deviation.*[9]

The mechanism for conveying these meanings was more geometric than structural, a 30-foot cube subdivided into 27 10-foot cubes. Other elements often containing program space were added onto the cube, and the cubes themselves were to be cut, hollowed out, fragmented, and otherwise interfered with to accommodate program and site, or in more purely Deconstructivist terms to establish and then violate a set of rules.

This posed a number of structural and constructional problems. Each member defining the cage of the cube was to be a square section of uniform size. This was in itself a simplification; beams and columns of identical lengths are not subject to identical forces. The short spans involved minimized this difficulty, but the distortions created others. The individual beam might span 10, 20, or 30 feet. Likewise beams or entire sections might be cantilevered. All of these structural demands

11.37

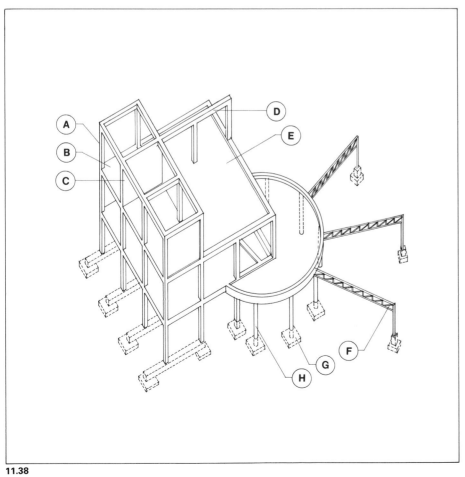

11.38

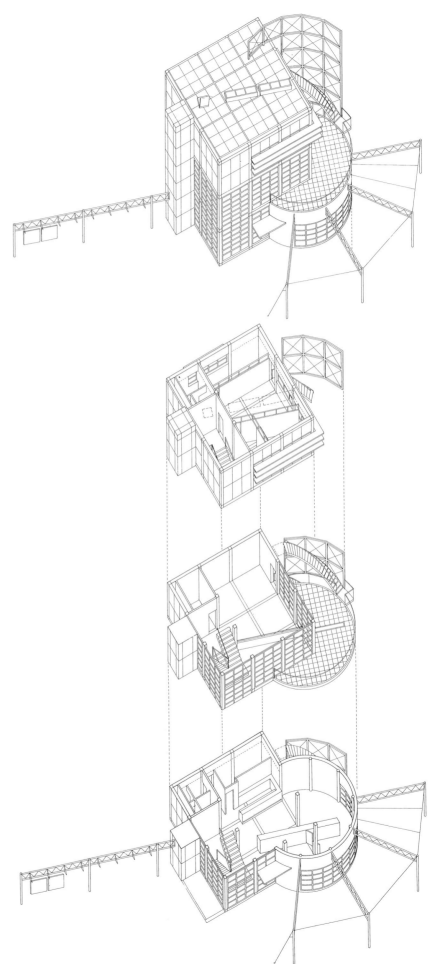

11.39

Parc de La Villette

Bernard Tschumi

Paris, 1984

11.37 Folie N-6.
(BT)

11.38 Folie N-6, framing.
- A 30 × 30 cm typical concrete column. Structural elements have the same cross section despite variations in load, to facilitate attachment of panels.
- B Concrete slab.
- C 15 cm concrete diaphragm wall for lateral bracing.
- D 30 × 30 cm typical concrete beam. The size is uniform to facilitate attachment of metal panels.
- E Recessed concrete slab to allow drainage under metal deck.
- F Steel truss with 80 × 80 cm steel column footing. The structural pieces visible on the exterior are steel.
- G 1.3 × 1.3 m concrete footing.
- H 30 cm round concrete column.
(BT)

11.39 Folie N-6, axonometric.
(BT)

had to be accomplished by structural members that appear identical on the exterior. There were programmatic complications as well. Some buildings were one story; some were three. Some contained sources of fire hazards such as kitchens while some had no occupiable space at all. From the point of view of the building inspector, each folie was a completely different type of building.

Tschumi's original structural concept called for a mixture of bearing walls and frames, but this proved inadequate to the complex set of programmatic and structural demands, and Peter Rice was asked to tackle this problem as well. His solution shows Rice at his most clever, keeping many of the formal characteristics that Tschumi desired while adding many of Rice's favorite structural devices (figure 11.36).

Each of the structural members of Rice's solution maintains a constant-dimensional cross section while accommodating as well as articulating its different structural conditions by the addition of tension cables. This gave greater depth to a beam with a greater span or greater stiffness to a column with a longer unbraced length, while maintaining the basic members with the same cross-sectional area. The lateral bracing and reinforcement required for cantilevers were also provided by tension cables. All elements were to be precast concrete, including floor planks, which are divided into nine smaller squares with ribs.

In the end Rice's solution was not used, in part because of cost, but perhaps because in structurally resolving these problems it visually resolved conditions that Tschumi wished to leave visually unresolved. For after all La Villette was not meant to be entirely or even primarily about structure. The final solution, if it lost something in structural explicitness and complexity, was more explicit as an abstract language. This solution of course demanded a very different constructional system, in which structural differences could be suppressed by a system of cladding that provided a unifying formal element. Hence the irony of La Villette. The power of the folies comes, in fact, out of an absence of structural expression, as they seem to defy the forces at work in a normal architectural structure.

The solution was to wrap columns, beams, and walls in a cladding of porcelain enamel steel panels, which hid any difference between structural elements or even materials. Thus liberated from the need for constructional unity, each structure took on its own character determined largely by pragmatic considerations. Columns or beams might be steel or concrete, might be precast or cast in place, depending on the particular condition. A cantilever might be steel to reduce weight. A column might be concrete if fireproofing was required. Concrete members are usually of uniform square cross section to facilitate attachment of the panels, which is easier if the dimension from the rear of the metal panel to concrete backup is constant.

In Tschumi's work after La Villette the ideas developed in the galleries have proved more important than the ideas of the folies, but while most employ exposed steel structures that, visually at least, verge on the unstable, these structures seldom make up the totality of the building. Most are in fact hybrids in which major structural elements framing a major space are coupled with a more conventionally built block in which structure is concealed using standard detail and layered construction.

Other Deconstructivists have more consistently applied the idea of exposed structure held in delicate equilibrium, often because the scale of the work involved makes this possible. But even these smaller projects cannot escape the kind of division in Tschumi's larger buildings between one structure that is exposed and representational and another that is concealed and merely functional.

A case in point is Coop Himmelblau's Open House, an important project with an unhappy history. The house was first designed in the architects' native Vienna in 1983, then commissioned to be built by a client in California. The work proceeded, but just as working drawings were completed the client died, and the project was put on temporary, and probably permanent, hold. Nevertheless, given the level of

11.40

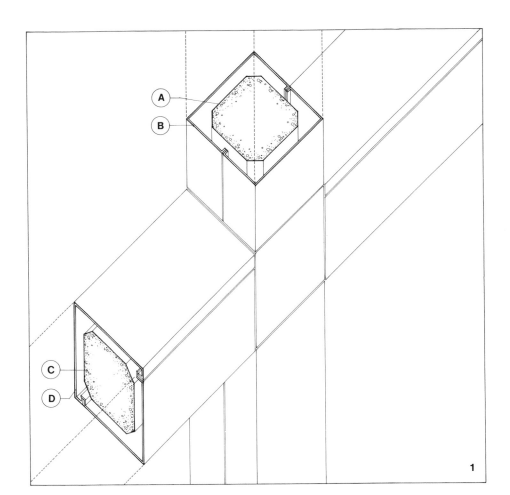

1

11.41

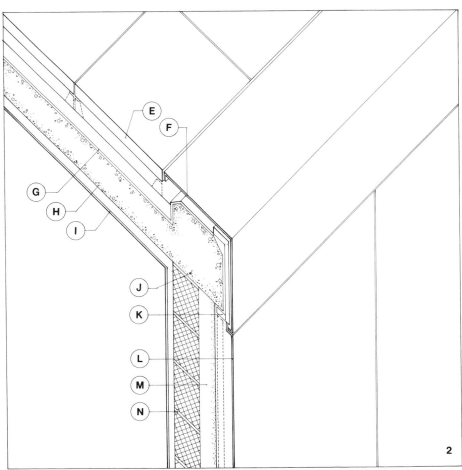

2

11.42

Parc de La Villette

Bernard Tschumi

Paris, 1984

11.40 Metal panel before installation.

11.41 Metal panel installed on column.

11.42 Folie P-6, wall details.
1 Detail at typical beam and column:
A Typical 30 × 30 cm concrete column.
B Two 20 × 40 cm U-shaped panels, porcelain enamel on steel.
C Typical 30 × 30 cm concrete beam.
D Two 40 × 40 cm and L-shaped panels, porcelain enamel on steel. The L-shaped panels place the joint on the side rather than on the horizontal surface.
2 Detail at junction of wall and deck:
E Paving slabs with open joints to allow water to penetrate to slab, sloped to drain. This allows the surface to appear flat.
F Porcelain enamel on steel beam cover.
G Waterproof membrane to intercept water that penetrates the joints.
H Concrete slab.
I Interior finish.
J 30 × 30 cm concrete edge beam.
K Panel lining.
L Porcelain enamel on steel wall panel.
M Insulation.
N Concrete masonry to sructually support metal panels and interior finish.
(BT)

development of the documentation it is possible to evaluate the probable constructional results.

The design process, according to the architects, was largely intuitive, although the intuition is informed to a degree by technology:

The first sketch was drawn eyes closed, with undistracted concentration on the feelings created by the imagined space, using the hand as a seismograph. . . .

The current of the energy in the sketch is translated into statics and construction. The building itself—resting on three points and taut—almost floats. The construction of the taut elements makes a double-glazed skin possible. Protection of the building is accomplished by double-shelled construction, suitable for a passive solar energy concept as well as ever possible alterations.[10]

The actual structure is a bit more complex but no less precariously balanced. There are five major elements, three of which—the box, the trusses, and the concrete wall—are in a structurally dependent relationship, while two, the pile-supported platform and catwalk, are semiautonomous.

The first of these, the triangular living space, is framed by five variously shaped trusses with pinned ends. One end of each is hinged to the platform; the other is attached to the second element, an oblong box. This box sits atop the third element, a concrete wall (figure 11.43). Both box and trusses are not only interdependent but appear to be on the edge, or at least near the edge, of collapse. The structure of the living room is largely exposed and built of industrial elements: steel trusses, aluminum skylight mullions, laminated glass. The structure of the box is largely concealed and is more of a hybrid. The basic frame is steel while the secondary framing is standard wood joists, studs, and plywood.

Standard is not the right word for the assembly of these components. While the inner floor is parallel to the ground and the walls are perpendicular to it, the outer walls, soffit, and roof are not. This necessitates two sets of joists and studs in some locations. The irregular corners of the steel frame were shop-welded for greater strength and accuracy, necessitating bolted field splices of the resulting L-shaped pieces (figure 11.45), and the wood framing is rarely at right angles to the steel, making a complex arrangement of blocking and double joists necessary.

Despite the intuitive nature of the design process, there is a great deal of environmental logic to the initial scheme. The triangular living room faces southeast and is provided with external horizontal shades. The entire room was to be a double shell with the layer in between as a space for air supply/return and heat removal. The double shell concept is sometimes overt and sometimes subdued. The slab is an airfloor similar to that used by Kahn and Le Corbusier, with small vaulted chambers, created by pouring concrete over half-cylinders of steel pipe, used for air supply. The rear and side walls are hollow, sometimes for plumbing and other utilities and sometimes for air return. The skylight was originally to be double-glazed to prevent heat loss and gain, but study proved that in the relatively mild winters of southern California this was not cost effective (the initial investment in a double skin was not offset by the savings in operating costs).

The exterior finish materials are a somewhat lower form of High Tech, corrugated metal on the lower walls, membrane roofing on the walls of the box. The use of these "vernacular" elements links this house with some of its California contemporaries that have exploited the vernacular side of industrialization through the use of everyday technological components. But Coop Himmelblau's primary technological interest is part of a general interest in opening up all architectural boundaries and rules, in pushing structural stability and instability to their limits. In a description of their more recent work they stated: "As we all know, architecture calls for at least three points of support in order to be stable. During the past few years we have started attempts at doing away with the third 'leg.'"[11]

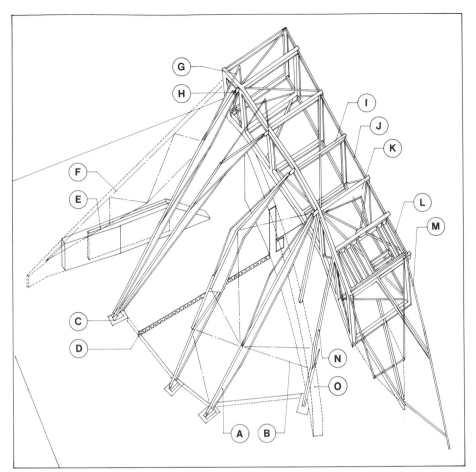

11.43

11.44

Open House (project)

Coop Himmelblau

Malibu, California, 1983, 1988

11.43 Framing.

A Truss I sections from steel plate, with top and bottom flanges typically ¾" × 8" and typical web of ⁵/₁₆" plate.

B Skylight framing (not shown).

C Pinned connection to pedestal at truss base.

D Airfloor concrete slab.

E Concrete wall with slot for air distribution.

F Wall framing to support sheet metal siding (not shown).

G Tubular frame for louvered sunshade.

H Pinned connection at truss. The box and truss are structurally codependent.

I Box framing from steel wide flanges, typically W 12 × 79's, with wood framing between.

J N 5 × 16 steel beam.

K Rigid L box frame.

L Box intermediate W 5 × 16 steel beam.

M Tubular balcony structure.

N Square steel tube support.

O Concrete wall.
(CH S.3.1, 3.2, 3.6)

11.44 Model.
(Tom Bonner)

FRANK GEHRY AND MORPHOSIS

Coop Himmelblau's fellow immigrant to California, Frank Gehry, shares with them an interest in the vernacular aspects of industrial products, but his use of instability is hardly systematic and any links in his work to the literary theory of deconstruction are tenuous. Gehry began his career as a sculptor and he brings to architecture a sculptor's sensibility; that is, he is often more interested in the tactile and visual qualities of materials than in their structural qualities, and he is not adverse to handling these materials in such a way as to evoke properties that they do not possess. The materials themselves are selected for their lack of value. Like his Modernist predecessors, Gehry derives his interest in vernacular material from Modern art:

I was trained early in my career by a Viennese master to make perfection, but in my first projects, I was not able to find the craft to achieve that perfection. My artist friends, people like Jasper Johns, Bob Rauschenberg, Ed Kienholz, Claes Oldenburg, were working with very inexpensive materials—broken wood and paper, and they were making beauty. These were not superficial details, they were direct, it raised the question of what was beautiful. I chose to use the craft available, and to work with the craftsman and to make a virtue out of the limitations.

Painting had an immediacy I craved for architecture. I explored the processes of raw construction materials to try giving feeling and spirit to form. In trying to find the essence of my own expression, I fantasized the artist standing before the white canvas deciding what was the first move. I called it the moment of truth.[12]

A typical type of Gehry design, at any scale, involves the division of the program into discrete elements that are then not so much reunited as configured in a way that allows them to maintain their own identities like so many objects of a still life on a table. Each element is typically given its own finish material and sometimes its own structural material as well. The resulting compositions are distorted, inflected, or simply warped, often giving the impression that surfaces have been peeled off, removed, or relocated. The fact that constructionally none of these things happen (finishes are not really peeled away, they are simply not provided in the first place) also gives his work a sculptural rather than a structural sensibility.

The Winton guest house in Wayzata, Minnesota, is a small example of this type, consisting of five discrete elements, each corresponding to a central program element and each given a different exterior finish: living room (lead-coated copper), bedroom (stone), kitchen/garage (Finn-ply plywood), study (galvanized metal), and inglenook (brick masonry). The last four of these are grouped loosely around the first, the elongated pyramid of the living room.

The house is hardly a structural experiment, but its diverse structure reinforces these elemental divisions, sometimes out of necessity, sometimes by choice. Two of the elements use simple platform framing (the kitchen/garage and the study) and differ only in finish materials. The brick walls of the inglenook, however, are load bearing and the roof exposed concrete. The stone-faced bedroom uses metal studs and joists rather than wood. The living room is a highly complex piece of wood framing using 12-inch studs resting on glued and laminated wood beams. The large studs may have been structurally necessary, but they also give the walls greater depth.

Gehry's great virtue as a detailer is the care he takes in the manner of joining the surface materials, always with an eye to revealing their thinness, their almost clothlike qualities in some cases. The plywood panels are joined with aluminum extrusions that reveal not just the joint but the depth of the plywood. The lead-coated copper and galvanized metal panels are joined like so many shingles rather than as panels, to emphasize their taut, thin sheet qualities.

The principal shortcoming of Gehry's work is the complexity of craftsmanship required to produce the appearance of straightforward simplicity. Examples are the valleys that occur where the living room joins the four other elements. Visually the rooms must appear as separate volumes; functionally they must be joined. Technically the water must be drained from the resulting valleys, and the result is

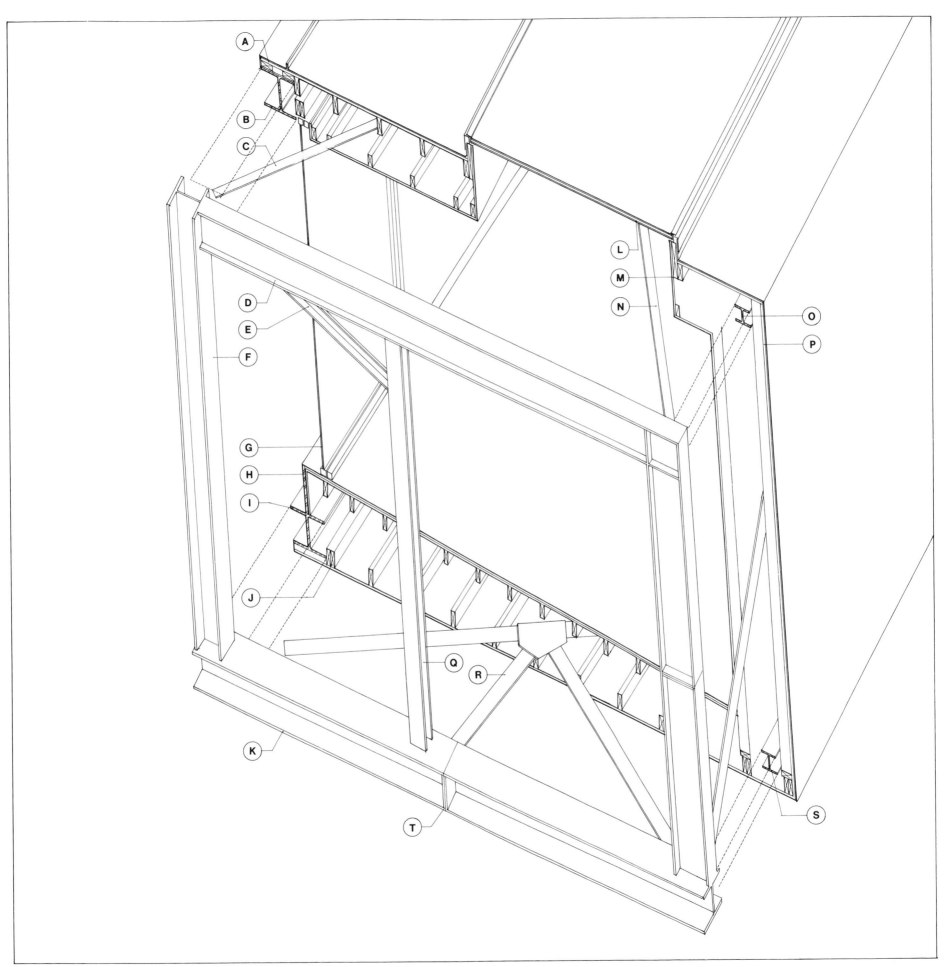

Open House (project)

Coop Himmelblau

Malibu, California 1983, 1988

11.45 Section.

A Roof coping.

B W 12 × 79 steel beam exposed on the interior of the house.

C 3 × 3" upper diagonal bracing.

D W 12 × 30 steel beam.

E Vertical lateral bracing.

F W 10 × 77 steel beam.

G Glass and window.

H Floor construction: $^{25}/_{32}$" tongue and groove maple flooring, ¾ plywood subflooring, and Douglas fir 2 × 6 floor joists 12" oc.

I W 12 × 79 exposed.

J Soffit construction: fluid-applied roofing membrane, ¾" marine grade plywood, R-19 glass batt insulation, and Douglas fir 2 × 6 floor joists 16" oc.

K W 12 × 30 steel beam.

L Double-glazed skylight.

M Inner wall of 2 × 4 studs 16" oc and ⅝" gypsum wall board.

N Horizontal diagonal bracing exposed at skylight.

O Small beam N 5 × 16.

P Wall construction: fluid-applied roofing membrane, ¾" marine grade plywood, R-19 glass batt insulation, and 2 × 4 studs 16" oc.

Q W 6 × 25 vertical steel section.

R 4 × 4 × ¼" steel angle diagonal bracing.

S W 5 × 16.

T Splice. Since the corners of the frame are not 90° angles, yet must be welded for structural reasons, these corners are shop-fabricated so that the splices are at midspan with bolted connections, so that the frame is delivered to the site as series of Ls.

(CH A.8.1)

11.46 Model interior.

(Tom Bonner)

11.46

11.47

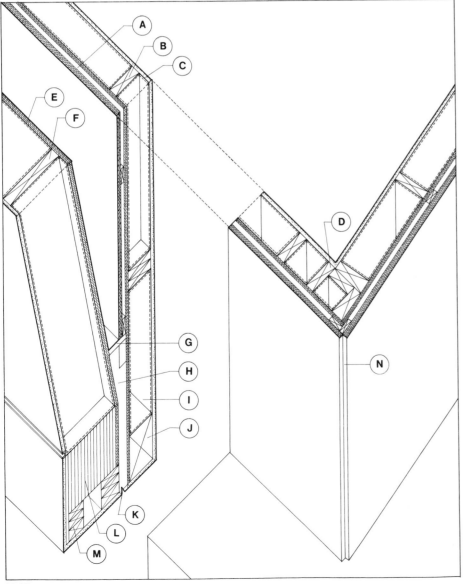

11.48

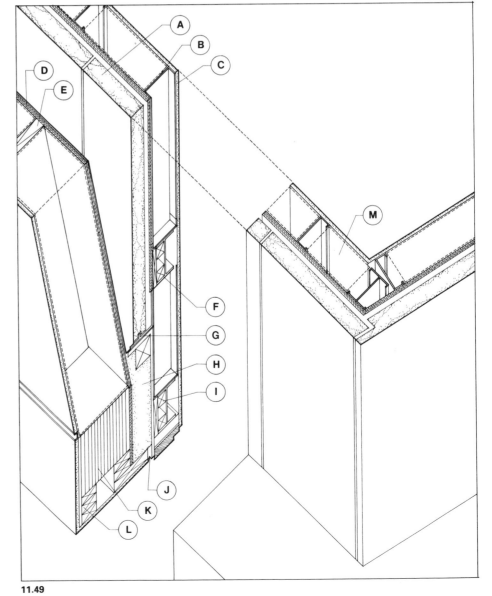

11.49

Winton Guest House
Frank Gehry
Wayzata, Minnesota, 1983–1987

11.47 View.
(Mark Darley © Esto)

11.48 Plywood wall detail at junction of living room wall (lead-coated copper) and kitchen wall (Finn-ply plywood).

A ¾" Finn-ply finish plywood over waterproof membrane on 1 × 3 wood nailers 24" oc and ½" structural plywood sheathing.

B Structural frame of 2 × 6 studs 16" oc.

C ½" gypsum board with plaster skim coat interior finish.

D Triple stud at corner to provide nailing surface.

E Outer layer of lead-coated copper sheet over waterproof membrane on ½" plywood sheathing.

F 2 × 12 rafters at 16" oc. The height of the living room wall requires a deeper structure.

G Cricket of lead-coated copper on ½" plywood and blocking, sloped to divert water out of valley.

H Formed-in-place insulation with waterproof membrane lapped over lead-coated copper.

I Batt insulation with 4 mm poly vapor barrier.

J Wood beam to support wall studs over door.

K Sheet metal joint cover to accommodate expansion of the different parts of the building.

L 8¾ × 11¼" glued and laminated beam to receive load of 2 × 12 rafters.

M Wood blocking to frame out finish surfaces.

N Aluminum extrusion at corner, with silicone sealant to protect edge.
(FG A-9, 10)

11.49 Stone wall detail at junction of living room wall (lead-coated copper) and bedroom wall (stone).

A 3" stone veneer with 1" air space on waterproof membrane and ½" plywood.

B 6" × 16 gauge galvanized metal studs at 12" oc.

C Insulation (shown dotted).

D Outer layer of lead-coated copper sheet over waterproof membrane on ½" plywood sheathing.

E 2 × 12 rafters at 16" oc.

F Steel beam to receive load of studs. The stone wall has a much greater dead load than the plywood wall in figure 11.48.

G 5 × 3½ × ⁵⁄₁₆" galvanized steel angle and lead-coated copper turned up under stone.

H Formed-in-place insulation with ½" plywood cricket on blocking, sloped to divert water out of valley.

I WF steel header.

J Sheet metal joint cover and wood door and frame.

K 6¾ × 11¼" glued and laminated beam.

L Wood blocking.

M Batt insulation and 4 mm poly vapor barrier.
(FG A-9, 11)

a complicated series of crickets, beams, and flashing, none of which is visible from the interior or exterior.

A Gehry trademark obviously missing from the Winton house is the exposed wood framing made famous in his own house of 1978. Partially exposed, partially modified standard wood framing became a device used by a number of Gehry's contemporaries and followers, perhaps because it was apparent by 1980 that steel framing was not about to replace the platform frame any time soon as the dominant single-family-house building system, perhaps because Gehry et al. were more interested in producing technically evocative objects than prototypes for some technological utopia.

The firm Morphosis has pursued a progressively more complex series of transformations to the platform frame. Early works were simple explorations in straightforward, even cheap materials: wood studs and joists, asphalt shingles, concrete masonry. The platform frame of the Seldak house is sliced through by a skewed strip window that renders the building a post and beam structure with wood curtain walls. This was done with large-scale timbers; larger buildings began to make use of steel frames integrated into and interrupting the basic platform frame.

One of the largest of these is the Crawford house. Dominated by a large curved retaining wall, it is composed of a series of complex interlocking grids. The architects see its framing devices as central to its spatial character:

These geometries together create a house made up of totemic pylons constructed of concrete, exposed steel T-frame structures, and walls of stucco and redwood. The progression of these solid elements is reversed in the character of the negative spaces. Ultimately, the relationship between center and periphery is inverted, forcing the life of the house to the periphery, where it comes into contact with those issues of site, context, and connection that form the underlying pattern of the project.[13]

The concrete pylons are on a 16-foot grid; the steel T elements made up of tubes are on a coincident 8-foot module (figure 11.50). The platform frame, largely covered, is on a much smaller 16-inch module, but one that is, at least in theory, coincident with the others.

The "negative" elements referred to are presumably the skylights and light monitors. In this sense the Crawford house is perhaps more Cubist than Deconstructivist, given the number of interruptions, both real and illusory, that occur in the building. Most of these have the result of informing us in some way about the construction of the building, although the details required to achieve this are not functional in the conventional sense.

The first of these interruptions is that of the steel T frame protruding through the platform frame walls. These T's sometimes form the support of the second-story stucco box, sometimes penetrate those stucco walls to form the head of a narrow window, and sometimes simply protrude through the wall to show where they are. Though structurally descriptive, this is a technical complication in that the steel beam must penetrate the environmental envelope of the building (insulation, waterproofing, etc.).

The wood joists and studs that the steel T's support are for the most part concealed beneath drywall, stucco, and redwood, except where the skylights occur. These are the negative interpenetrations. Each monitor occurs on an 8-foot structural grid and seems to cut away the finish materials of roofing, plywood, and drywall to reveal the structure below. The living room vault for example is at first glance a plywood vault supported by pairs of curved steel beams. At the monitor, however, the vault disappears to show the beams supporting the plywood vault, which are in turn supported by the curving steel beams.

This is another detail that, although it adds to the structural description of the house, creates another kind of illusion at the same time, a popular one with Gehry, Morphosis, Scarpa, and many others—the idea of finishes peeled away to reveal construction.

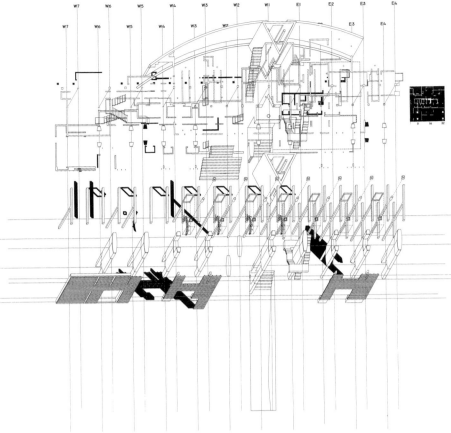

11.50

11.51

Crawford House

Morphosis

Montecito, California, 1987–1990

11.50 Drawing.

(Morphosis)

11.51 Model.

(Tom Bonner)

Finishes are of course rarely peeled away. More commonly, as at Crawford, they are not built. Building for the most part is an additive, not a subtractive process. Nevertheless the impression is that we are seeing the actual structure revealed, and the implication is that the part of the structure that is concealed is identical to the part that is exposed. This of course is a fiction; one can no more reveal construction without transforming it than one can reveal film without transforming it, and for a simple reason: craftsmanship. Any construction that is environmental in function requires the covering of one thing with another. In any construction where this occurs, it is inevitable that a higher level of craft and quality of materials should be established for the exposed parts, and it is foolish not to do so. The joint concealed need only be functional, not visually presentable. There can be a considerable difference in the wood beam that is structurally sound and the wood beam that is visually acceptable.

It can be argued of course that in the world of Gehry or Morphosis this is not the case, that we see every revealed joint, joist, and stud in its raw form; but neither is this the case. The crudest of the exposed wood joists is not so crude as the worst of the concealed joists. The roughest of the exposed wood is not so rough as the blocking and framing hidden deep under the finishes. This is not to criticize the Crawford house for dishonesty; it is simply a recognition that, like any building, ancient or Modern, it creates a structural narrative, but only by simultaneously creating a fiction.

One great virtue of the Crawford house is its acceptance and its revelation of the nature of the modern American single-family house. The majority of the houses examined in this book have been hybrids of wood platform framing and steel. Some have glorified the wood frame by suppressing if not concealing the steel; some have glorified the steel frame by suppressing and concealing the wood. The Crawford house gives both equal emphasis and in fact exploits the combination. The other great virtue is that, in the treatment of finishes in wall construction, fiction is presented as a necessity. One can create the fiction of a monolithic wall; or one can create the fiction of a layered wall in which the layers are cut back or peeled off to display what is below. The Crawford house opts for the latter, a fiction far closer to the truth than the former.

REGIONALISM

The similarity of intent between Gehry and Morphosis and their intellectual links with the architects of the Case Study houses raises the question of whether this is a regional phenomenon. The architects themselves would probably deny this, but the power of regionalism as an idea has not lost its appeal. It offers an escape from the monolith of industrialized processes and the whims of styles that change with increasing rapidity. Most of the advocates of this type of regionalism, notably Kenneth Frampton, have less faith in the possibility of a regionalism in the geographic sense (e.g., a California style) than in a site-specific or "critical" regionalism:

The term "Critical Regionalism" is not intended to denote the vernacular as this was once spontaneously produced by the combined interaction of climate, culture, myth and craft, but rather to identify those recent regional "schools" whose primary aim has been to reflect and serve those limited constituencies in which they are grounded. Among other factors contributing to the emergence of a regionalism of this order is not only a certain prosperity but some kind of anti-centerist consensus—an aspiration at least to some form of cultural, economic and political independence.[14]

Whether or not the practitioners of this regionalism adhere to Frampton's tenets, many seek a constructional parallel to tradition, intending through the use of vernacular, ordinary building components—concrete block, concrete walls, corrugated metal siding—to construct buildings that evoke the qualities if not the images of their vernacular, usually stone and timber, predecessors.

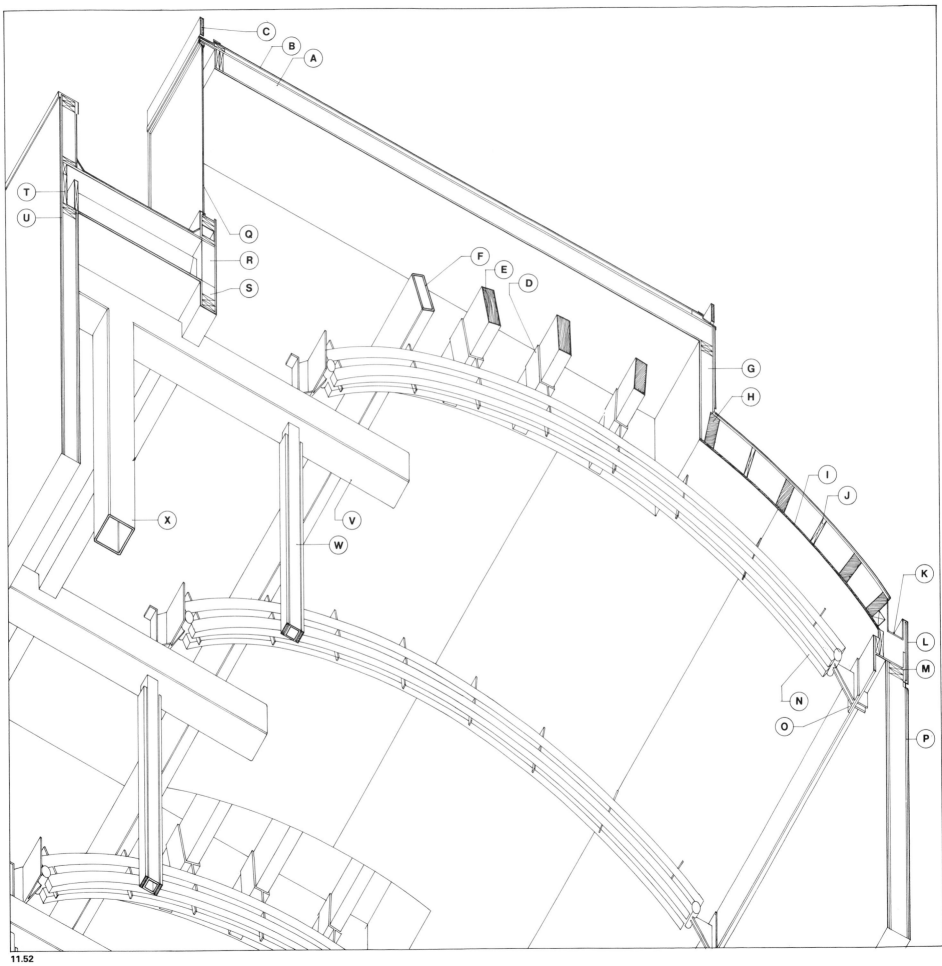

11.52

Crawford House

Morphosis

Montecito, California, 1987–1990

11.52 Section.

A Wood joist clerestory roof framing.

B Clerestory roof of 24 gauge galvanized iron hood with flashing and batt insulation.

C 2 × 8 redwood with 14 gauge galvanized steel gusset.

D Steel brackets to hold wood beam.

E 4 × 10 wood beam. These are exposed only where the monitors occur.

F 4″ × 10″ steel tube forming a continuous edge to the wood vault.

G Clerestory wall of 2 × 4s and plywood sheathing, R-14 rigid foil-backed insulation and two layers of 15 lb felt, and 1 × 6 redwood.

H 4 × 10 concealed wood beam.

I ¼″ plywood. This is interrupted by the monitor to allow light to enter.

J Roof of 16 ounce standing seam copper and two layers of 15 lb felt, and plywood on redwood beam and intermediate joists to support plywood and gypsum board between joists, with R-30 batt insulation in cavity.

K Copper gutter on steel plate and ⅜″ plywood.

L Copper flashing.

M Wide flange.

N Curved beam from four square steel tubes.

O Steel seat and mounting plate to connect circular beam to wall.

P Wall of ⅞″ cement plaster, two layers of 15 lb felt, 2 × 6 stud, ⅜″ plywood, and ⅝″ gypsum board interior finish with batt insulation.

Q Clerestory window.

R Wood beam.

S Interior wall.

T Small roof framing of plywood on wood joists, with gypsum board interior finish.

U Typical exterior wall.

V Steel tube beam serving as air supply in locations where there is a plenum behind the wall.

W 1″ finish birch plywood on 4 × 4″ steel column.

X Steel tube column.

(A-6, 41)

11.53 Interior.

(Kim Zwarts)

11.53

11.54

11.55

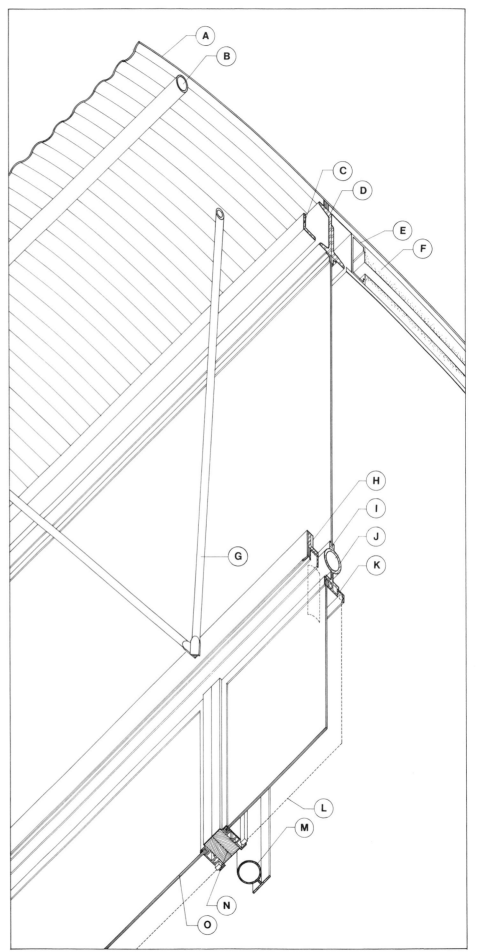

11.56

Magney house

Glenn Murcutt

Moruya, New South Wales, Australia, 1983–1984

11.54 View.

(Max Dupain)

11.55 View.

(Daniel Murcutt)

11.56 Wall details.

A   Corrugated zincalume roof, valley screwed to purlins, with 5 cm zinc or aluminum tube sleeved over roof sheathing.

B   6 cm galvanized hot-dip pipe purlin.

C   Angle.

D   Angle and channel.

E   Purlin. Although the roof surface is the same, the structural system supporting it changes dramatically from interior to exterior.

F   Roof construction: zone 75 insulwool on top, zone 50 on bottom, held in place by galvanized chicken wire mesh, with 50 mm space for air flow.

G   42 mm galvanized hot-dip pipe strut to support pipe above.

H   Natural anodized aluminum blinds in frame (not shown).

I   Frame for fixed glass.

J   Pipe frame.

K   Aluminum channel frame for glazing.

L   Insect screen.

M   114 mm pipe column.

N   Timber grounds.

O   Laminated or toughened glass.

(GMA 8226-3, 8226-4)

The difficulty is that the modern wall is subject to a different set of demands, particularly environmental ones, and the result is often another set of constructional fictions. The apparently monolithic walls of a Mario Botta building in fact involve two layers of masonry with an air space, insulation, and waterproofing between, not to mention a large number of concealed lintels. In his small-scale houses this hardly seems to matter, but eventually the layered bearing walls of his houses became the layered curtain walls of his brick buildings supported by concrete frames, which became his San Francisco Art Museum, a steel frame clad with the masonry cavity walls that have become his trademark.

Tadao Ando has avoided the cavity wall as successfully as any, using it only in concrete masonry and in concrete walls only in extreme climates. The danger of the universal application of uninsulated cast-in-place walls is the possibility of buildings that simply do not function particularly well, in which condensation and heat loss reach much higher levels than in comparable buildings built by more conventional methods. If this is where this ideology has led us, to a theory of good building that cannot function north of the 40th parallel without the expenditure of massive quantities of energy, perhaps it is time to leave the theory behind us. The counterargument is that we need to return to the more traditional methods of environmental control. This philosophy has provided some after-the-fact rationalizations of some oversimplistic designs, but also some original, if somewhat hybrid, results.

If there is such a thing as High Tech Regionalism, then Glenn Murcutt of Australia is its chief practitioner. The corrugated metal siding and tubular metal elements of his work seem to have an affinity with the work of Foster, Rogers, and others. Like them, he underlines the originality of the work by the conventional ideology of Modernism: material efficiency, inspiration of aircraft, exposed structure. But Murcutt sees his work as, if not regional, then certainly site specific and drawing on local precedents as a key to a problem's solution. His rather simple plans, usually a single-loaded corridor of rooms in enfilade or some combination of these elements, result from a desire to maximize cross ventilation, also evoking traditional Australian rural houses. His elaborate roof structures are designed to assist this aim, as well as to collect water. And while his buildings bristle with mechanical louvers, ventilators, etc., these are invariably passive and consume little or no energy.

The tube and corrugated skin structural system he favors is also not all it first appears. His biographer Philip Drew suggests that it simultaneously evokes traditional farm sheds, the construction of a Junkers W/34 (a plane Murcutt flew on in his youth), and in analogous fashion the wood pole and bark huts of Australian aborigines.[15] Murcutt probably would prefer the latter metaphor, although the visual results, particularly in the Magney house, are more suggestive of the airplane. The house has the elements of a typical Murcutt design: a long building one room thick to maximize cross ventilation, an airfoil-like corrugated roof that is given a complex configuration to assist air flow to the rooms and to collect water in the dry climate. Despite its imagery, drawn not so much from High Tech architecture as from High Tech's principal source, aircraft design, it is in Murcutt's view a specific response to the microclimate and culture of the region and the site.

This accounts in part for the fact that the imagery of the house is somewhat at odds with the structural reality. Murcutt wished to recall the structure of both vernacular metal farm buildings and aboriginal pole and bark huts, and to do so he had to elaborate certain aspects of the construction while suppressing others. The roof, for example, projects with the aid of a series of tubular brackets to provide shading of the glass below. The structure is exposed and the thinness and profile of the corrugated metal is visible at its edge. One might assume that this is the structure of the internal roof as well and that one is only seeing a small revealed portion of the whole. But the interior portion is far more complex, requiring purlins. Like many of his predecessors, Murcutt wraps the building with a kind of idealized representational structure.

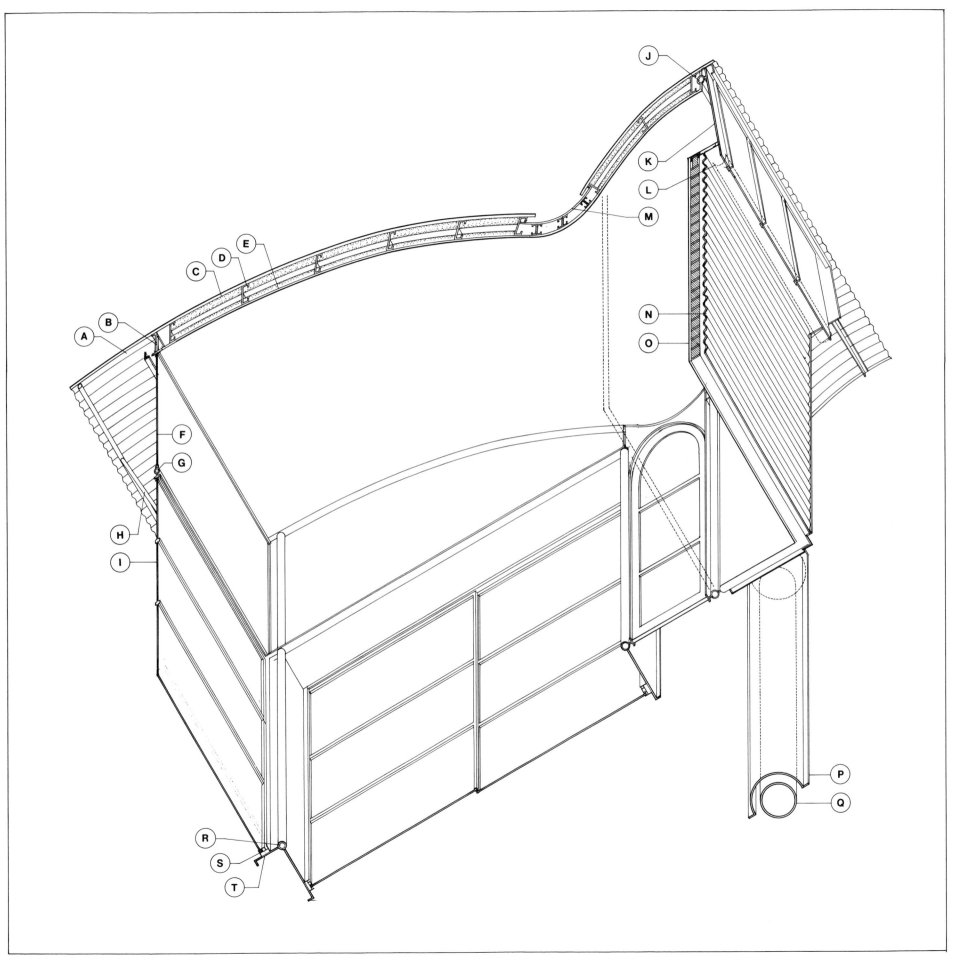

11.57

Magney house

Glenn Murcutt

Moruya, New South Wales, Australia, 1983–1984

11.57 Section.

A Corrugated zincalume ceiling valley screwed to purlins.

B Edge angle and channel.

C Zone 5 insulwood insulation.

D Purlin to support roof and ceiling panels.

E 5 cm insulation set on galvanized chicken wire mesh with gypsum board ceiling.

F Glass.

G Pipe frame to support windows.

H 6 cm galvanized hot-dip pipe purlin supported by 42 mm pipe strut.

I Sliding glass door.

J Pipe support.

K Sloped aluminum glazing with vent panel below.

L Gutter to collect water from window.

M Aluminum valley gutter to collect rainwater.

N Corrugated metal siding.

O Plaster on brick wall.

P Gutter extension.

Q Pipe to drain rainwater to cistern.

R Steel pipe column.

S Sliding door frame and wood ground.

T Metal plate.

(GMA 8226-3, 8226-4)

CONCLUSION

Despite the diversity of intention among the High Tech architects, the Deconstructivists, and their contemporaries, they all have found it necessary in most instances to construct a structural fiction, a narrative device to technically explain the construction of their buildings; and while these narratives used the actual constructional systems of the buildings as points of departure, and in many cases the actual raw materials of these systems, they all depart in some way from the reality.

Such narrative devices are in fact a reality of architectural construction in the late twentieth century. These architects should not be condemned as dishonest for their practices, any more than Tolstoy and Stendhal should be condemned for constructing a narrative that departs from the true history of the Napoleonic wars. It is a necessary feature of the act of architecture and in fact of the art of construction. One can criticize the architects to the extent that they have claimed their fictions to be realities, but for the most part this has not been the case.

This does not prevent these architects from claiming a moral and technical superiority to their Postmodern predecessors. They may argue that their narrative fictions are less naive, or better in line with the Zeitgeist, or closer to constructional reality, but they can rarely claim that they are that reality. As to which of these loosely defined doctrines presents the correct path for the future, technology cannot provide an answer, for it is not a technical question. Do we want buildings with the technical capacity of an F-15A, and are we willing to pay for them? Can we go on indefinitely designing buildings that break rules without pausing occasionally to establish rules? Is regionalism of any kind possible today?

The practitioners of regionalism and High Tech, like their predecessors Viollet-le-Duc and Buckminster Fuller, have produced buildings that are explicitly or implicitly critical of their societies, effectively challenging us to provide a world in which the constructional virtues of their work will be economical and commonplace. Deconstructivists and Postmodernists have contented themselves with ironic commentary on contemporary society, but this has not always enabled them to build more economically or with greater technical competence. Looking at the full range of examples presented in this book, however, one may legitimately ask if it is necessary or even desirable to choose among these alternatives. Those architects who were the most successful in this century, Aalto and Le Corbusier for example, were the most inclusive, saw the vernacular, the industrial, and the organic as exhibiting similar logic and incorporating similar principles, and thought that the combination of all three in one work was not only necessary but virtuous.

12 Conclusion

A self that has no possibility is in despair, and likewise a self that has no necessity.

If possibility outruns necessity so that the self runs away from itself in possibility, it has no necessity to which it is to return; this is possibility's despair.

The determinist, the fatalist, is in despair and as one in despair has lost his self, because for him everything has become necessity.

Søren Kierkegaard

Notre Dame, Chartres, Amiens, and Rheims have survived the twentieth century, although the latter two have just barely. The building Albert Kahn designed at Highland Park for Henry Ford, where 3,000 Model Ts were built in one day in 1913, was mostly demolished in the 1960s. The Rouge Plant is still a center of the Ford organization, but Kahn's Rotunda and Fuller's Dome burned in 1960. The Willow Run bomber plant designed in one night by Charles Sorensen, built in twenty months, where one B-24 was built every hour in 1944, was sold to Henry Kaiser to make automobiles, and then in turn sold to General Motors. At the time of this writing, it is scheduled to close within the year and not reopen. Its products have not done much better. Although 18,000 B-24s were built during World War II, 8,000 of them at Willow Run, there are today only thirteen B-24s left intact.

More happily, Beech Aircraft, which built Fuller's Dymaxion house prototype, is still in operation. The house itself, which sat forgotten for years on the Kansas prairie outside of Wichita, has found a home in Ford's museum in Dearborn. Henry Ford, having played a part in its inspiration in 1927, and who declined to become involved in any of Fuller's projects, finally came to its rescue after all.

The 1980s saw the end of many factories, some, like the Homestead Steel Mill, with far less glorious histories than Highland Park or Willow Run. Clearly an era of industrialization, certainly an era of American industrialization, is over. Those artifacts that perished did so perhaps because of those qualities that made them so admirable—their minimal, lithe, complex configurations of expensive material. Their legacy is far more likely to be ideological than physical. The cathedral, the suspension bridge, the airplane, the automobile, and the primitive dwelling remain architectural paradigms, and these objects, or at least our analyses of these objects, have supplied us with most of the tenets of good construction that we take for granted. These tenets center around three issues: economy of material, structural expression, and industrialization of building.

ECONOMY OF MATERIAL

When touring Norman Foster's Sainsbury center, Buckminster Fuller asked the question he would inevitably ask of any architect: "How much does the building weigh?" Foster did not know, but made the calculation and mailed Fuller the answer (5,619 tons, less per square foot than a Boeing 727). To Fuller, minimizing weight was the key to rational building. It may not be so for Foster, but it is certainly the key to style.[1] Nevertheless, there exist countless examples, in this book and elsewhere, of an economical use of material that does not produce an economic expenditure of capital. The continued popularity of masonry construction, even as a curtain wall material, is only one. (This leaving aside the obvious fact that while mass, weight, thickness, and density may be liabilities in aircraft and automobile design, they may be desirable assets in building.)

If you walk over the bridge that Bernard Tschumi and Peter Rice built across the La Villette Canal, you will experience the definite perception of movement; as you step on the deck it moves. It deflects, and you know that it deflects, and if you know anything about Peter Rice, you know that he wanted you to feel this. It is, however, a sensation that even the most dedicated believer in economy of material may find unsettling. The predictions of Fuller, Saarinen, and others, that in time we would become accustomed to this characteristic of modern construction, needless to say have not come about. While we all admire the style that economy produces, we all seek reassurance in buildings as well.

What gave those objects admired by the early Modernists—the airplane, the automobile, the bridge, and the ship—the style that made them so attractive was the unity of purpose in their design. Each subordinates all other functional considerations to an overriding goal. The airplane must lift the maximum weight by means of the minimum weight. Structure, weight, and aerodynamics are tightly interlocked, including such minute considerations as the aerodynamic effects of joining. Other considerations—passenger comfort, internal circulation, storage capacity—while important, are subordinate to the first criterion. If the results of this exercise are inordinately expensive, the design will simply go unrealized. Buildings, needless to say, lack this unity of purpose.

Nevertheless the bridge, the airplane, and the automobile (and perhaps the grain elevator and ocean liner) succeeded; they produced and continue to produce "style," something that solar energy, systems analysis, green architecture, computers, and fax machines have failed to do. The reasons for this are obvious: the importance of mass and weight to any conception of architecture. If architecture communicates pathos, tragedy, humor, or faith, it does so by the way in which it communicates gravity, stress, compression, tension, and craft—the way in which it communicates weight and the absence of weight, connection and the absence of connection.

STRUCTURAL EXPRESSION

To most contemporary rationalists, architectural construction remains a matter of structure; mechanical systems, cladding, and environmental shelter all have their place and dictate certain procedures, but the language of architecture remains the language of structure. It is an ideology not radically different from Viollet-le-Duc's.

This has no better illustration than the work of the High Tech architects, for however much they draw on the airplane and the automobile for formal inspiration, they are unwilling to cut the rope that binds them to the structural language of architecture, and their forms are inevitably configured to conform to this language. Of course the language's primary tenet is that structure should be expressed, hopefully in a literal way, but it has other corollaries:

The doctrine of skin and bones. Modernism has consistently divided buildings, new or old, into load-bearing-wall and frame-and-curtain-wall structures, and the frame structures themselves into the skeleton and the skin. It is easy to find examples that defy this classification; the Baths of Caracalla seem to be neither wall nor frame, as does the typical wood platform frame house. The frame-skin dichotomy itself is simply an abstraction imposed on a far more complex reality. Where in figure 10.5 does the structural frame end and the skin begin? Given that this frame is largely concealed in the finished building, the architect need not answer this question except to the building inspector, but for those dedicated to structural expression, there must be clarity. Most architects (and most building codes), for example, consider columns and beams supporting floors and roof to be structure, and mullions or girts supporting other wall surfaces to be nonstructure. As a result, primary frames are articulated with great clarity while secondary frames are either minimized or designed in a way that makes their subordinate role clear. Architects from Asplund to the younger Saarinen have meticulously celebrated the primary structural frame while going to great lengths to suppress the secondary, usually the glazed curtain wall, frames. In buildings like Saarinen's airports this can be difficult, given the curtain wall heights and spans involved. Foster, Rogers, and others have allowed the secondary frame to take on more character, but this is often possible only because the primary frames of their buildings are so dominating.

The doctrine of transparency. For many Modernists the frame and curtain wall concept (or skin and bones metaphor) dictates that the skin should be as light and thin as possible, usually of glass. Architects have done much to ameliorate the obvious environmental problems of this approach. Rogers's Lloyd's Building is clearly environmentally superior to Gropius's Bauhaus building, but its conception of structure and skin is the same.

The articulation of parts. That late Modernist architects have sought to articulate both primary and secondary frames is not surprising, given that such articulation is another tenet of the language of structural rationalism. A number of Modernists have made a point of polarizing functional differences that have otherwise been ignored: Kahn and Le Corbusier articulate the various functions of a window by devising vastly different mechanisms to fulfill each of the window's functions. Lewerentz and Asplund give each part of the program a structure, material, and level of detail unique to its functions. More common is the strategy of Mies van der Rohe, calling out and articulating each part of the curtain wall: the column that supports the floor, the mullion that supports the glass, and the frame that holds it. This seems a straightforward approach, but it is by no means universal. Eero Saarinen might combine two of these three functions in one element, column with mullion at GM, mullion with frame at Deere, and Ellwood or Prouvé might combine all three into one element. If a Deconstructivist is one who deliberately breaks the rules of a given language, then Ellwood and Prouvé have more right to the title than Frank Gehry or Coop Himmelblau. That the High Tech architects have rigidly adhered to this type of specificity of parts and functions, despite the fact that the models they choose to emulate (such as the Wellington bomber or the de Havilland Mosquito) have no such clarity of articulation of function, is an indication of their adherence to the "deep structure" of the traditional languages of architecture.

The doctrine of the nature of materials. As for those who sought form in the nature of materials, what they found there for the most part was whatever preconceptions they brought with them. Aalto found organic shapes; Kahn found the arches and vaults of Rome and Albi; Le Corbusier found the structure of tents and airplanes, as did Fuller. There is no doubt that the internal logic of this idea—of achieving the maximum structure with the minimum material—made sense, but only in relation to its own criteria. Too often the results were unnecessarily long spans and unnecessarily complex structures; structures that were entirely too self-referential and incapable of responding to site conditions, particularly urban ones, and structures more costly than more conventional but less minimal ones. Perhaps the ideological origins of some of this thinking created some of the problems. If a form was appropriate to one material could it be appropriate to another? Did the "character," what Louis Kahn called the "existence wall," dictate that forms be unique to certain materials? If a dome was in the nature of masonry, how could it be in the nature of concrete? If the skeleton was in the nature of steel, how could it be in the nature of wood?

Despite the inaccuracy of much of his architectural analysis, Viollet-le-Duc grasped the essential point of twelfth-century Gothic; it achieved style by pushing a material of relatively poor structural quality to its structural limits. The High Tech architects have in principle done the same with a material far superior, steel, but the structural limits of these materials are greatly in excess of all but a few of society's needs. Even if these types of structures are desirable, we face a problem unlike that of our twelfth-century counterparts, that our technological capacities are greatly in excess of our capital resources. If the technical knowledge to achieve a 200-foot span is readily at our disposal, the financial realities of most projects will drive us back to a 30-by-30-foot bay, resulting in less economy of material and certainly less "style" but a more truly economical result.

The modern translation of the principles of economy of material, minimum weight, and equilibrium has served us well for a small but significant portion of our building tasks—the one-story long-span shed, the gymnasium, the aircraft hanger, the exhibition hall. Applied to the small-scale commercial or institutional building, they often raise more questions than they answer. The most common criticism of long-span High Tech buildings is that they are too self-referential and self-absorbed to produce a city that has merit. The vision of Fuller's Dymaxion house standing alone on the Kansas prairie is exhilarating, but his prototypical suburb, in which an indefinite number of these same houses are placed in endless rows on quarter-acre lots, is equally deflating, and the larger giant urban domed megastructures of his late work are as claustrophobic as the Dymaxion house and car were liberating.

If one accepts the far more modest small-span steel and concrete structures characteristic of standard American building, the architectural role and the order that they dictate are far less clear. Frank Lloyd Wright said of the work of Mies van der Rohe: "He is trying to make the old box frame beautiful. He has come as near to it as anybody, but it can't be done."[2] Nevertheless, however superior the technologically minded architect may find the work of the High Tech architects to that of the Venturis, it is difficult not to recognize that the latter's definition of the problem is more inclusive than the former's; that an architect cannot always have the luxury of manipulating the basic structural and mechanical systems of a building to achieve "architectural" meaning, particularly a meaning that involves an expression of those systems. In fairness to the High Tech architects it should be pointed out that many examples of their work, particularly the early work of Foster and the later work of Piano, achieve a less dramatic result by manipulating a conventional arrangement of structure and systems rather than by drastically redefining them.

INDUSTRIALIZATION

In 1945 Lockheed, Consolidated Vultee, Beech, Kaiser, US Steel, and many other manufacturers assumed that the logical postwar market for their industrial capacity was the construction industry; that they would shift, with a few modifications, into housing production. Facing a similar situation in the early 1990s, current defense contractors have not, to my knowledge, heard any suggestion that they should turn their efforts to building construction. One might assume that we have seen the end of architecture's romance with industry. But if much of the old industrial plant is gone, its ideology remains, for we are still in large part bound by Ford's and Sloan's idea of what industrialization means.

Modernism's quick adaptation of the Ford ideal of standardization, and its stubborn refusal to give up the idea after it proved unrealistic, is curious. An idea that lasted no more than ten years in the automobile industry lasted five times as long in architecture, and is not without its adherents today. This is perhaps understandable if one considers the most prominent alternative to Ford's standards. Applying Sloan and Earl's vision of design based on marketing-styling, in which products would respond to whim and class prejudice and be arrived at more or less independent of technology, would have created a world in which architecture would be a subset of marketing. Ford's types represented the opposite, a world of products responding to concrete needs. If the products were all the same it was not because we were all the same but because we were all equal, that, having equal needs, we should be given equal amenities.

If there is a contemporary philosophy of what mass production ought to be, it is one that Ford or Sloan would not easily recognize, one that emphasizes minimum inventory and minimal defects; and if it has a prophet it is probably Taiichi Ono of Toyota. Michael Cusumano writes:

Ono became convinced that Ford's original system—producing a limited product line in massive quantities, and making each lot of components as large as possible to gain maximum economies of scale—contained two fundamental flaws. One was that only Ford's final assembly line achieved anything resembling continuous process flow, the ideal of all factory managers. Henry Ford developed a system to mass-produce one model, with no variations, which he sold in volumes reaching millions per year. His strategy was to attract customers with low prices and to earn a small profit in each vehicle. Ford offered no options or annual model changes because his manufacturing system relied on enormous dies and presses and specialized machine tools, which required a great deal of time, manpower, and money to change.

With this type of equipment, Ford naturally found it most economical to manufacture in lots as large as possible. Ford would stamp, for instance, 500,000 right-hand door panels in a single run and store them until the final assembly lines called for more right doors, rather than switch dies frequently to make different components as needed. But lots of this size created massive inventories and took up enormous amounts of warehousing space and operating capital, especially when sales fell below production or if equipment broke down and other problems developed to disrupt the process flow. Manufacturing components in such huge volumes also generated many defectives, since workers made mistakes or grew lax in quality control through shear monotony and the knowledge that there would always be spare parts and reject piles.

The second flaw Ono observed in the Ford system was its inability to accommodate consumer preferences for product diversity. . . . Ono did not believe General Motors abandoned mass-production techniques; in his view, the company merely adjusted to the market by establishing several body shops and allowing a variety of body shells on its final assembly lines. General Motors, like Ford, still tried to make as many standardized, interchangeable components as possible for its different car lines, and to produce components in lots as big as possible and then stock them rather than change equipment frequently. Managers were able to do this because annual model changes were largely cosmetic, involving a mere reshaping of sheet metal for the outer body shells.

Ono took General Motors' strategy one step further. He extended the ideal of small-lot production, which he found in the American company's body stamping shops and final assembly lines, throughout Toyota's entire production system. The "flexibility" of small lots eventually made it easier for Toyota to add more model lines and optional equipment during the 1950s and 1960s, to vary features such as emissions-control equipment or left-hand drive for different export markets, and to adjust production levels in times of slack demand or "oil shocks." [3]

The idea of standards and types died the strangest death of all. After the gradual erosion of the concept over the period of 1930–1950, it was revived in various forms by Kahn and by the urban typologists of the 1980s, and types became all but mandatory. Its unpopularity in the 1990s is not because it proved an incorrect interpretation of the process of mass production, or because it failed to produce maximum flexibility, or because it was technically unfeasible. It failed because it became philosophically unpopular. The idea of ideal types seems as remote to us as most of the other Platonic ideals of the Renaissance. Its influence today, such as it is, is due purely to the power of tradition, however abstract a tradition.

Standardization was in any case the most discussed and least practiced ideal of Modernism. It was a field with countless leaders and few followers. A large number of "prototypes" of standardization were constructed, but few were replicated by any other than their own creators. There was often no real economic advantage to doing so in any case, and the few standardized products that these architects developed were seldom produced in quantities or sizes to justify anything like an assembly line. Manufacturers who did mass-produce building components saw no reason to limit their market appeal by an overly rigid and limited set of components. The architectural results of a standardized approach were most often buildings with simple grids and repetitive elements, and the best designs that standardization inspired may have been those of the reactionaries, like Aalto or Asplund, who wished to provide an architectural alternative to the Model T ideal.

The situation today, eighty-six years after the opening of Highland Park, is something very like Aalto's elastic standardization, although Aalto would certainly deplore the architectural results. Windows, doors, cabinets, and other assemblies have standard sizes, but sizes that are comparatively small and numerous. The only real limitations are the maximum and minimum sizes. Most building products are highly standardized in some ways while enormously flexible in others. Steel sections must be of certain profiles, glass a certain thickness, pipe a certain diameter, but there are no rigidly adhered to standard lengths or areas of these components. There are construction modules in use; residential components are designed around a 16-inch/48-inch module, office components around a 5-foot module, but these modules are rapidly dispensed with the minute they become a hindrance to other goals.

The idea that mass production is inevitably linked with minimum weight would seem to have a logical validity, yet one of the most widely off-site-manufactured housing systems today is precast concrete, also without question the heaviest, and the most commonly mass-produced housing system—the modular home—violates another Modernist axiom in that it requires shipping large quantities of "air." Clearly these two systems have an economy of material that is unrelated to weight.

The idea that mass production is inexorably linked to precision is not borne out by these examples either; in fact their lack of precision is in some ways their chief virtue. Between July and December of 1993 the price of lumber rose dramatically, from $300 per 1,000 board feet to $500 per 1,000 board feet. This made the cost of wood-framed houses for the first time in recent memory competitive with that of steel residential framing, which had formerly been almost twice the cost of wood. The number of homes being built with steel framing tripled, bringing its total share of the market to a still meager 1 percent. Clearly if the former trend continues so will the latter, but ironically there is little real difference between the traditional wood home and this type of steel house, in which metal C studs and joists are substituted for their wood counterparts with the results architecturally indistinguishable from the interior and exterior. Industrialization is not just a matter of material; it implies precision planning and off-site assembly. The home-building industry, while perfectly willing to accept steel as a material, is unwilling to accept this type of industrialized procedure. Le Corbusier and Gropius proposed a system of building that would be preplanned, lightweight, dry, and high-tolerance. The American building industry has stubbornly adhered to a system that is heavy, wet, low-tolerance, and relatively spontaneous.[4]

There are surprisingly few architectural theoreticians (although there are certainly countless practitioners) who advocate some accommodation of the status quo. Those architects who wish to learn not from industrialization and its artifacts but from the opposite, the preindustrial vernacular, are more commonplace.

VERNACULAR BUILDING

The continued popularity of the vernacular ideal is easily, perhaps too easily, explained. If the physical products of the industrial age have lost much of their appeal, the social effects have lost none of their power to horrify. A less dramatic explanation is that a vernacular object produced in empirical innocence is much easier to admire and far more difficult to criticize than the most recent production of the avant-garde, the author of which, his protestations to the contrary, is all too familiar with the stylistic vicissitudes of history and his place in them.

Needless to say, this is not very good anthropology. Primitive man, if we must call him that, has no less cultural baggage than ourselves, perhaps more. The constructions of the Anasazi, the Dogan people, or the Australian aborigines are no less controlled by tradition, by custom, by religion, and by outside cultural influences, and ultimately no more or less inherently empirical than the constructions young architects in SoHo. Often "vernacular" buildings represent not so much empirical constructions without pretensions as naive reinterpretations of outside influences, and if we are to imitate them we can only do so by imitating their naiveté.

Nevertheless, the idea that traditional building techniques and vernacular forms represent a superior truth has been persistent in Modernism. Assuming that drawing on vernacular sources means drawing on vernacular building systems as well as forms—an assumption that is by no means universal—the vernacular model presents both problems and possibilities vis-à-vis the idea of monolithic building. For Glenn Murcutt the wooden farmhouses and aboriginal dwellings of Australia led to a conception of the wall that was layered, multifunctional, and environmentally responsive. To many, however, the vernacular ideal has meant the emulation of massive solid constructions, thick walls of stone or concrete, exposed beams of wood or steel.

I have written extensively on the naiveté of the idea that exposed construction is the only or even the best way to communicate the construction of a building. It is a rare system in modern building that does not require the covering of one thing with another. Architecture can never be the sum total of the technical minutiae of design. In concept or in execution, it requires a system in which some things are shown and in which some things are hidden. Despite the manifold difficulties in achieving a monolithic construction, it remains perhaps the most popular conception of good building among all young architects and not a few older ones, not least because it has been a tenet of Modernism almost from its inception. To Viollet-le-Duc the exposed iron ties of Italian Gothic were obviously superior to the concealed iron reinforcing of Soufflot's Pantheon, an analysis reinforced by the present state of the latter. The suspension bridge and the early aircraft seem to reinforce this analysis, though the automobile and post-1930 airplane seem to deny it. Contemporary architecture is divided into two groups who consider conventional contemporary building systems either too light or too heavy. On one side are those who feel that only the functionally excessive is adequate and who strive to achieve this goal through real mass—through massive, monolithic walls of masonry or concrete—or through the appearance of mass by artificially thick yet hollow walls or by stone veneers striving to retain the appearance of a traditional stone configuration. For their opponents, who must include the majority of the High Tech architects, no configuration is too complex, no quantity of labor too excessive, no quality of material too dear, if the result is the style that comes from economy of means.

Neither of these offers an easy direction to pursue. The pseudo-vernacular, which so conspicuously demonstrates the structural roles of a wall while so conspicuously concealing its role as insulator and vapor and pressure barrier—as an environmental envelope—is an odd choice indeed for a profession so naturally dedicated to environmental concerns. Those who have sought to achieve the appearance of the massive stone wall without the reality have perhaps fooled only themselves. Those like Scarpa or Piano who have sought to reconcile the layered nature of the modern wall with the character of traditional architecture are to be applauded, but few of their solutions lend themselves easily to universal application.

THE FUTURE AND THE PRESENT CONDITION

In 1960, on the last page of *Theory and Design in the First Machine Age,* Reyner Banham asked "whether architecture as we know it" could survive and compete with "what we are beginning to understand as technology."[5] This was essentially the same question asked by Le Corbusier and Sigfried Giedion: Can architecture compete with the products of technology? Today we are more likely to ask the opposite. Can the products of technology, considered as art, compete with the achievements of the past? For many, certainly most of the public, the answer is no. Nor is this only a symptom of late twentieth-century cynicism. It is a question asked by Amédée Ozenfant, Le Corbusier's collaborator in *L'Esprit Nouveau:*

Mechanisms often have a certain obvious beauty, because the substances employed by us happen to be governed by relatively simple laws, and, much in the manner of graphs, they exemplify those laws. . . .

There are beautiful objects . . . but there is no object, or factory, or mechanism, or piece of furniture, capable of inspiring in us emotions comparable with those evoked by Art. Has the most beautiful motor-car or the finest house an effect upon us equal to, parallel with, or equivalent to, some masterpiece of Art? When the Beethoven centenary was celebrated in Vienna, during the performance of Fidelio *there was not a dry eye in the audience. The Parthenon takes even the most insensitive by the throat. Has anyone ever seen a factory or piece of machinery that could move men to tears? The most elegant bicycle would be quite incapable of it.*

And besides, it is really very striking how lovers of machinery by preference collect ancient implements long out of date. Imagining they worship mechanism, in reality they offer sacrifice to a taste for antiques . . . and the aesthetic imperfections resulting from the primitive technic employed.

All that can be said is that a really efficient machine is more intriguing than one that is a failure, and a polished pebble more than a mere scrap of stone. For certain forms are pleasant, others painful, and everything that intellect produces must be of interest to us. But starting from this point, to place the machine on the pedestal of great sculpture, seems to me blindness, silly snobbishness, and ridiculous also.[6]

Although architects should no doubt continue to seek inspiration in vehicular design, it must be with the recognition of certain facts: that most of the technology will remain economically inaccessible, that real inspiration is likely to be more of spirit than of imitation, and that the only real economy achieved will likely be of a stylistic and not an economic character. And we should not be embarrassed if, as Ozenfant suggests, we find technological antiques more satisfying than state-of-the-art objects; and if we find a 1909 Antoinette VII more appealing than a Stealth F117, we are also likely to find the technology of the former more adaptable to the building processes to which we have access. Thus stripped of its ideological rationale, a language that draws on the products of industrialization for inspiration becomes simply another architectural language and can more easily accept the intrusion of other languages. Not an unappealing prospect when one realizes what this approach has enabled Asplund, Aalto, and others to achieve.

We might start by recognizing what Guadet and Viollet-le-Duc pointed out, that the front facade of Notre Dame conveys a different message from that of the rear. A building by Renzo Piano may be as moving as a building by Louis Kahn, but it will not be moving in the same way. It is not necessary, nor even possible, that we judge one of these responses to be superior to the other. If architecture is a language, must it not be capable of communicating sometimes solidity and sometimes lightness, sometimes permanence and sometimes temporality? The Modern architect, if he is to survive, must be able to do both, sometimes simultaneously.

The Modern architect must likewise recognize that a rigid adherence to one constructional language will not serve him. One must sometimes build exposed steel, sometimes concealed and clad, sometimes in raw concrete and sometimes with brick veneer. If one wishes to impose a hierarchy on these systems through a series of vaguely defined moral imperatives, one should first rethink the sequence of ideas that has led to these imperatives.

Whether the new language of architecture is to grow out of a transposition of the old, or from a wholesale disposal of tradition for a new beginning without formal preconceptions, is not ultimately an architectural question. At present the profession and public seem divided on the results of the cutting loose of form from technology that followed the Postmodernist interlude. The public seems happy to be free of Modernism's moral imperatives, which produced so few buildings they enjoyed and destroyed so many that they valued. The profession seems horrified at the results. What was to be a recognition that technology and imagery could enjoy a certain independence has resulted in a great deal of wretched excess and architectural packaging of the worst kind.

While the language of architecture and the nature of construction can never coincide, neither can they go their separate ways. Architecture may be an art, but it is an art whose subject matter is construction. What is it that makes a drawing an architectural drawing and not just a drawing if not a sense of scale and a sense of weight? In this regard Fuller, Saarinen, and Foster were right, just as Malevich, Albers, and Moholy-Nagy were right. Architecture is about weight and at the same time about its absence; it is not perhaps about minimum weight but it is about weight nonetheless.

Vladimir Mayakovsky, the Russian Constructivist poet, did not see America until 1925. By then, for him and for many, the gloss had worn off the bright technological future and he was, to an extent, disillusioned with what he found there. He wrote in "My Discovery of America":

The futurism of naked technology, of superficial impressionism of smoke and cables, whose great mission was to revolutionize the set, village ridden mentality— that great original futurism had been finally confirmed by America. . . . What is there in automobiles? . . . There are many cars, it is time to think how not to let them poison the cities' air. It is not a skyscraper—a place where it is impossible to live, and yet one lives. . . . Perhaps the technology of tomorrow, multiplying man's strength a millionfold, will find a way to abolish scaffoldings, booms and other technological surfaces.[7]

Perhaps this was a reflection of his disillusionment with the Soviet experiment, or the problems of his personal life, or perhaps the shock of confrontation with the reality of poetic images he had seen only in newspapers and magazines, but the disillusionment was not complete, and perhaps we should end where we began, with Mayakovsky standing on Brooklyn Bridge in 1925, and note that his thoughts there were the same as those of Montgomery Schuyler forty years earlier, that it is by work such as this that we will be judged by the future:

If
  the end of the world
                              befall—
and chaos
              smash our planet
                                    to bits,
and what remains
                      will be
                                  this
bridge, rearing above the dust of destruction;
then,
        as huge ancient lizards
                                    are rebuilt
from bones
              finer than needles,
                                        to tower in museums,
so
  from this bridge,
                    a geologist of the centuries
will succeed
              in recreating
                                our contemporary world.
He will say:
              —Yonder paw
                              of steel
once joined
              the seas and the prairies;
from this spot,
              Europe
                        rushed to the West,

scattering
        to the wind
                Indian feathers.

. . . .
For some,
       life
          here
             had no worries;
for others,
          it was a prolonged
                and hungry howl.
From this spot,
            jobless men
leapt
      headlong
           into the Hudson.
Now
      my canvas
            is unobstructed
as it stretches on cables of string
                   to the feet of the stars.
I see:
      here
         stood Mayakovsky,
stood,
       composing verse, syllable by syllable.
I stare
       as an Eskimo gapes at a train,
I seize on it
          as a tick fastens to an ear.
Brooklyn Bridge—
yes . . .
       That's quite a thing!

Notes

1 INTRODUCTION: THE ARTIFACTS OF INDUSTRIALIZATION

1. Frank Lloyd Wright, *An Autobiography* (New York: Longmans, Green and Co., 1932), p. 77. Wright gives a slightly different version in the Princeton lectures of 1930. While Wright consistently refers to this book as Viollet-le-Duc's *Dictionnaire*, several authors have shown that it could only have been the *Entretiens*.

2. Peter Collins, *Concrete: The Vision of a New Architecture* (New York: Horizon, 1959), p. 155.

3. Paul Turner, *The Education of Le Corbusier* (New York: Garland, 1977), p. 51.

4. Julien Guadet, *Eléments et théorie de l'architecture,* fourth edition, vol. 1 (Paris: Librairie de la Construction Moderne, 1901–1904), p. 214.

5. Eugène-Emmanuel Viollet-le-Duc, *Discourses on Architecture*, vol. 1, tr. B. Bucknall (New York: Dover, 1987), p. 300.

6. Eugène-Emmanuel Viollet-le-Duc, *The Foundations of Architecture: Selections from the Dictionnaire raisonné*, ed. Barry Bergdoll, trans. Kenneth Whitebead (New York: George Braziller, 1990), p. 176.

7. Ibid., pp. 178–179.

8. Guadet, *Eléments et théorie de l'architecture,* p. 117.

9. William Morris and Walter Pater, *Some Great Churches in France: Three Essays* (Portland, Maine: T. B. Mosher, 1912), p. 63.

10. Viollet-le-Duc, *Discourses on Architecture,* vol. 1, p. 270.

11. Ibid., vol. 2, p. 67.

12. Ibid., vol. 2, p. 129.

13. Ibid., vol. 2, p. 124.

14. Ibid., vol. 2, p. 120.

15. Montgomery Schuyler, "The Brooklyn Bridge as Monument," reprinted in *American Architecture and Other Writings*, ed. William Jordy and Ralph Coe (Cambridge: Harvard University Press, 1961), p. 335.

16. Ibid., p. 339.

17. Pamela Robertson, ed., *Charles Rennie Mackintosh: The Architectural Papers* (Cambridge: MIT Press, 1990), pp. 186–187.

18. Vladimir Mayakovsky, *The Bedbug and Selected Poetry* (New York: World Publishing Co., 1960), p. 177.

19. E. G. Asplund, "Art and Technology," *Byggmästaren* (1936), p. 168, trans. Lotta Löfgren; Le Corbusier, *When the Cathedrals Were White* (Paris: Plon, 1937; New York: McGraw-Hill, 1964), p. 77.

20. Horatio Greenough, *Form and Function* (Berkeley: University of California Press, 1947), pp. 60–61.

21. Morris and Pater, *Some Great Churches in France*, pp. 62–64.

22. William Lethaby, *Architecture: An Introduction to the History and Theory of the Art of Building* (New York: Oxford University Press, 1955), p. 158.

23. Ibid., pp. 159–160.

24. Le Corbusier, *Aircraft* (London: The Studio, 1935), p. 13.

25. Ibid., pp. 30, 56.

26. Henry Ford and Samuel Crowther, *My Life and Work* (Garden City, New York: Doubleday, Page & Co., 1922), p. 53.

27. Quoted in Allan Nevins and Frank Ernest Hill, *Ford: The Times, the Man, the Company,* vol. 1 (New York: Charles Scribner's Sons, 1954), p. 276.

28. Charles Sorensen, *My Forty Years with Ford* (New York: Norton, 1956), p. 115.

29. Walter Gropius, *The New Architecture and the Bauhaus* (London: Faber and Faber, 1935), p. 25.

30. Ibid., pp. 30–31.

31. Le Corbusier, *When the Cathedrals Were White*, pp. 167–168.

32. Alfred P. Sloan, Jr., quoted in Emma Rothschild, *Paradise Lost: The Decline of the Auto Industrial Age* (New York: Random House, 1973), pp. 38–39.

33. Frederick Gutheim, ed., *Frank Lloyd Wright on Architecture* (New York: Grosset & Dunlap, 1941), p. 110; E. G. Asplund, "Art and Technology," tr. Lotta Löfgren, p. 170.

34. Umberto Boccioni, "The Plastic Foundations of Futurist Sculpture and Painting," 1913, reprinted in *Futurist Manifestos*, ed. Umbro Apollonio (New York: Viking, 1970), p. 89.

35. Ibid.

36. Kazimir Malevich, *Essays on Art 1915–1933,* ed. Troels Anderson (Chester Springs, Pennsylvania: Dufour, 1968), pp. 173–174.

37. Ibid., pp. 200–201.

38. László Moholy-Nagy, "Abstract of an Artist," in Krisztina Passuth, *Moholy-Nagy* (New York: Thames and Hudson, 1985), p. 362.

39. László Moholy-Nagy, "The Dynamic Constructive System of Forces," reprinted in *Vision in Motion* (Chicago: Paul Theobald & Co., 1947), p. 238.

40. László Moholy-Nagy, *The New Vision [Von Material zu Architekur]* (New York: Wittenborn and Company, 1946), p. 62.

41. Le Corbusier, *Précisions* (Paris: G. Crès, 1930; Cambridge: MIT Press, 1991), p. 161.

42. Le Corbusier, *Une maison—un palais* (Paris: G. Crès, 1928), p. 48.

43. Mies van der Rohe, quoted in Fritz Neumeyer, *The Artless Word* (Cambridge: MIT Press, 1991), p. 245.

44. Alessandra Latour, ed., *Louis I. Kahn: Writings, Lectures, Interviews* (New York: Rizzoli, 1991), p. 131.

45. Asplund, "Art and Technology," p. 168, trans. Lotta Löfgren.

46. Marcel Duchamp, quoted in Phil Patton, *Made In U.S.A.* (New York: George Weidenfeld, 1992), p. 234.

47. Richard Neutra, *Life and Shape* (New York: Appleton-Century-Crofts, 1962), p. 189.

2   ELIEL SAARINEN IN DETROIT: 1926–1940

1. Albert Christ-Janer, *Eliel Saarinen* (Chicago: University of Chicago Press, 1979), p. 12.

2. *Eliel Saarinen: The Search for Form in Art and Architecture* (New York: Reinhold, 1948), p. 197.

3. Sigurd Frosterus, "Architecture: A Challenge" (1904), reprinted in *Abacus* 3, tr. The English Center (Helsinki: Finnish Museum of Architecture, 1983), p. 72.

4. Ibid., p. 75.

5. Ibid., p. 73.

6. Eliel Saarinen, *The Search for Form in Art and Architecture* (New York: Reinhold, 1948), p. 201.

7. Ibid., p. 119.

8. Ibid., pp. 200–201.

9. Ibid., pp. 222–223.

3   THE CONVERSION OF ERIK GUNNAR ASPLUND: 1930–1940

1. "Stockholmsutstalningen 1930," *Byggmästaren* (1930), p. 132.

2. Quoted in Colin St. John Wilson, *The Dilemma of Classicism: Erik Gunnar Asplund* (London: Architectural Association, 1988), p. 39.

3. E. G. Asplund, "Our Architectural Concept of Space," *Byggmästaren* (1931), p. 209, tr. in Stuart Wrede, *The Architecture of Erik Gunnar Asplund* (Cambridge: MIT Press, 1980), p. 236.

4. E. G. Asplund, "Our Architectural Concept of Space," p. 209, tr. Lotta Löfgren.

5. Hakon Ahlberg, Gustav Holmdahl, et al., *Gunnar Asplund Architect 1885–1940* (Stockholm: Byggmastaren, 1943, rev. 1950), p. 60.

6. E. G. Asplund, "Art and Technology," *Byggmästaren* (1936), p. 170, tr. Lotta Löfgren.

7. Ibid.

8. Christina Engfors, *E. G. Asplund Architect, Friend, and Colleague* (Stockholm: Arkitektur Förlag, 1990), p. 26.

9. Ibid., p. 39.

4   RICHARD NEUTRA AND THE ARCHITECTURE OF SURFACE: 1933–1952

1. H. H. Harris, *California State Polytechnic University Journal* 1, no. 28 (May 1992), p. 4.

2. Richard Neutra, *Survival through Design* (New York: Oxford University Press, 1954), p. 25.

3. Richard Neutra, "Problems of Prefabrication," *American Architect* 123 (December 1935).

4. Richard Neutra, *Life and Shape* (New York: Appleton-Century-Crofts, 1962), p. 265.

5. Quoted in Esther McCoy, *Vienna to Los Angeles: Two Journeys* (Santa Monica: Arts and Architecture Press, 1979), p. 12.

6. "Altadena House for William J. Beard," UCLA Special Collections (Box 778, F.7).

7. Peter Baxter, *Just Watch! Sternberg, Paramount and America* (London: British Film Institute, 1993), p. 95.

8. Josef von Sternberg, *Fun in a Chinese Laundry* (New York: Macmillan, 1965), p. 272.

9. Richard Neutra, "Prefabrication," *Arts and Architecture* 67 (June 1950), p. 39.

10. Richard Neutra, "Problems of Prefabrication," *The Architect and Engineer* 123 (December 1935), pp. 32–33.

11. UCLA Special Collections Kaufmann (Box 827, F.2).

12. UCLA Special Collections Kaufmann (Box 827, F.3).

13. Ibid.

14. Wallace Stegner, *Where the Bluebird Sings and the Lemonade Springs* (New York: Random House, 1992), p. 77. Although he does not mention him by name, it is clear from the context and description that the architect is Neutra.

15. UCLA Special Collections, Moore Box.

16. Thomas Hines, *Richard Neutra and the Search for Modern Architecture* (New York: Oxford University Press, 1982), p. 181.

5   ALVAR AALTO AND MARCEL BREUER: LIGHT, INDUSTRIALIZATION, AND THE VERNACULAR 1928–1963

1. Quoted in Göran Schildt, *Alvar Aalto: The Decisive Years* (New York: Rizzoli, 1986), p. 229.

2. Alvar Aalto, "The Influence of Construction and Materials on Modern Architecture," *ARK* 9 (1938), pp. 129–131, reprinted and translated in *Synopsis: Painting Architecture Sculpture* (Boston: Birkhäuser, 1980), p. 12.

3. Willem M. Dudok, *Willem M. Dudok* (Amsterdam: G. von Saane, 1954), p. 136.

4. Alvar Aalto, "European Reconstruction . . . ," *Abacus* 3 (Helsinki: Finnish Museum of Architecture, 1983), p. 129.

5. Aulis Blomstedt, quoted in Le Corbusier, *The Modulor*, vol. II (Cambridge: Harvard University Press, 1955), p. 167.

6. Aalto, "European Reconstruction," p. 132.

7. Alvar Aalto, "The Relationship between Architecture, Painting and Sculpture," 1969 in *Synopsis*, p. 26.

8. Marcel Breuer to Walter Gropius, May 23, 1941 (Harvard University, Houghton Library, File 518).

9. P. Morton Shand to Marcel Breuer (Special Collections, Syracuse University Library).

10. Cranston Jones, *Marcel Breuer: Buildings and Projects 1921–1961* (New York: Praeger, 1962), p. 232.

11. Breuer's First New Canaan house is discussed in Ford, *The Details of Modern Architecture*, volume 1, pp. 313, 315, and illustrated on pp. 318–319.

12. Paul Goldberger, "Rich Legacy of Innovative Furniture," *New York Times*, Friday, July 3, 1981, p. A11.

13. Pierre Reverdy quoted in André Breton, *Manifestoes of Surrealism* (Ann Arbor: University of Michigan Press, 1969), p. 20.

6   LE CORBUSIER AFTER 1928: 1928–1965

1. Le Corbusier, *Decorative Art of Today* (Paris: G. Crès, 1925; Cambridge: MIT Press, 1987), p. 109.

2. John Stroud, *European Transport Aircraft since 1910* (London: Aero, 1966), p. 104.

3. Laurent Aynac, *L'Exposition de démonstration et propagande du Sous Secrétariat d'État de l'Aéronautique 1921* (in the Fondation Le Corbusier).

4. Le Corbusier, *Vers une architecture* (Paris: G. Crès, 1925), p. 102.

5. Le Corbusier, "Maisons Voisin," *L'Esprit Nouveau* no. 2 (c. 1921), reprinted in *L'Esprit Nouveau* (New York: Da Capo, 1968), p. 214.

6. Gordon Crosby, "The Harmony of Outline," *The Autocar* 36 (July 2, 1921), p. 12.

7. Le Corbusier, *Aircraft* (London: The Studio, 1935), p. 12.

8. Le Corbusier, *The Marseilles Block* (London: Harvill Press, 1953), p. 42.

9. Le Corbusier, "Le Problème de la 'Maison Minimum,'" *L'Architecture Vivante* (Spring and Summer 1930), p. 7, reprinted in *L'Architecture Vivante* (New York: Da Capo, 1975).

10. "Les Maisons Métalliques en Allemagne," *L'Architecture Vivante* (Winter 1929), reprinted in ibid., p. 5.

11. Le Corbusier, "Villa aux Mathes," *Architecture d'Aujourd'hui* 7 (January 1936), p. 43.

12. H. Beran to Le Corbusier, 15 March 1935 (Mathes); Le Corbusier to H. Summer, 8 March 1935 (St.-Cloud) (Fondation Le Corbusier).

13. Salvador Dalí, preface to *Gaudí, the Visionary* by Robert Descharnes and Clovis Prévost (New York: Viking, 1969), p. 8; Le Corbusier, *Gaudí* (Barcelona: Ediciones Polígrafa, 1957), p. 22.

14. Le Corbusier, *Decorative Art of Today*, p. 47.

15. Le Corbusier, *Oeuvre complète: 1946–52* (Zurich: Editions Girsberger, 1955), p. 195.

16. Ibid., p. 190.

17. Le Corbusier, *The Marseilles Block*, p. 33.

18. Benedikt Huber and Jean-Claude Steinegger, *Jean Prouvé: Prefabrication, Structures and Elements* (New York: Praeger, 1971), p. 191.

19. A. E. J. Morris, *Precast Concrete in Architecture* (New York: Whitney Library of Design, 1978), p. 65.

20. Maxwell Fry, *Art in a Machine Age* (London: Methuen, 1969), p. 135.

21. Le Corbusier, *The Chapel at Ronchamp* (New York: Praeger, 1957), pp. 89–90.

22. James Stirling, "Ronchamp," *Architectural Review* 119 (March 1956), p. 161; Craig Ellwood, "The Machine and Architecture," *Arts and Architecture* 75 (June 1958), p. 19.

23. Allard to Le Corbusier, September 13, 1954 (Fondation Le Corbusier).

24. James Stirling, "From Garches to Jaoul," *Architectural Review* 118 (September 1955), p. 151.

25. John Winter, "Le Corbusier's Technological Dilemma," in *The Open Hand: Essays on Le Corbusier*, ed. Russell Walden (Cambridge: MIT Press, 1977), p. 322.

26. Reyner Banham, "On Trial: Jean Prouvé: The Thin Bent Detail," *Architectural Review* 131 (April 1952), p. 252.

7   SAARINEN, EAMES, FULLER, AND THE CASE STUDY HOUSES: 1940–1959

1. Charles Sorensen, *My Forty Years with Ford* (New York: Norton, 1956); Henry Ford and Samuel Crowther, *My Life and Work* (Garden City, New York: Doubleday, Page & Co., 1922); Allan Nevins and Frank Ernest Hill, *Ford: Decline and Rebirth, 1933–1962* (New York: Charles Scribner's Sons, 1963); Don Sherman, "Willow Run," *Smithsonian Air & Space* 7 (August/September 1992), pp. 74–85.

2. Eero Saarinen, "The Six Broad Currents of Modern Architecture," *Architectural Forum* 99 (July 1953), p. 113.

3. Eero Saarinen to R. B. Fuller, January 9, 1945 (Buckminster Fuller Institute).

4. Charles Eames and John Entenza, quoted in "What Is a House," *Arts and Architecture* 61 (July 1944), p. 24; R. Buckminster Fuller, quoted in "Comment on a Survey," *Arts and Architecture* 61 (July 1944), p. 39.

5. Esther McCoy, *Case Study Houses* (Los Angeles: Hennessey & Ingalls, 1977), p. 54.

6. Ibid., p. 57.

7. A set of shop drawings in the Library of Congress from the California Cornice Steel and Supply Corporation appears to show the new and modified structural members required for the revised design.

8. "Life in a Chinese Kite," *Architectural Forum* 93 (September 1950), p. 96.

9. Pat Kirkham, *Charles and Ray Eames: Designers of the Twentieth Century* (Cambridge: MIT Press, 1995), p. 116.

10. "Life in a Chinese Kite," p. 96.

11. McCoy, *Case Study Houses*, p. 105.

12. John Holusha, "Steel Gains in Home Building," *New York Times* (August 20, 1994), B37.

13. Unpublished manuscript in Buckminster Fuller Institute.

14. Robert Snyder, *R. Buckminster Fuller: An Autobiographical Monologue/Scenario* (New York: St. Martin's, 1980), p. 33.

15. Ibid., p. 53.

16. Speech by Starling Burgess on WICC Bridgeport, July 21, 1933 (Buckminster Fuller Institute).

17. Snyder, *R. Buckminster Fuller: An Autobiographical Monologue/Scenario*, p. 57.

18. R. B. Fuller, *The Artifacts of R. Buckminster Fuller*, ed. James Ward, vol. 2 (New York: Garland, 1985), p. 65.

19. "Hutments to Houses," *Architectural Forum* 80 (February 1944), pp. 91–94.

20. R. B. Fuller, *Designing for Industry* (Wichita, Kansas: Fuller Research Institute, 1945), p. 11.

21. R. B. Fuller, quoting Theodore Larsen, in *Arts and Architecture* 61 (July 1944), p. 39.

22. David Mondey, ed., *Encyclopedia of Aviation* (New York: Crown Publishing, 1977), p. 79.

23. R. B. Fuller to E. D. Stone, November 15, 1946 (Buckminster Fuller Institute).

8 EERO SAARINEN AFTER 1945: 1945–1962

1. Alfred P. Sloan, Jr., *My Years with General Motors* (Garden City, New York: Doubleday, 1964), pp. 301–305; S. Bayley, *Harley Earl and the Dream Machine* (New York: Alfred A. Knopf, 1983).

2. Eero Saarinen, *Eero Saarinen on His Work* (New Haven: Yale University Press, 1962), p. 30.

3. Ibid., p. 32.

4. Ibid., pp. 40–42.

5. Toshio Nakamura, ed., *Eero Saarinen* (Tokyo: A+U, 1984), p. 224.

6. In Leo Beranek, ed., *Music, Acoustics and Architecture* (New York: Wiley and Sons, 1962), p. 105.

7. Eero Saarinen, "Yale's Hockey Rink," *Architectural Record* 124 (October 1958), p. 152.

8. Vincent Scully, *American Architecture and Urbanism* (New York: Praeger, 1969), p. 198.

9. Eero Saarinen, "On TWA," *Architectural Record* 132 (July 1962), p. 133.

10. *Perspecta*, no. 7, Yale Architecture School Journal (1961), p. 29.

11. Saarinen, *Eero Saarinen on His Work*, p. 82.

12. Interview with Joseph Lacy.

9 LOUIS KAHN, SIGURD LEWERENTZ, AND THE NEW BRUTALISM: 1954–1974

1. Vincent Scully, *American Architecture and Urbanism* (New York: Praeger, 1969), p. 218.

2. Alessandra Latour, ed., *Louis I. Kahn: Writings, Lectures, Interviews* (New York: Rizzoli, 1991), p. 20.

3. Ibid.

4. Richard Saul Wurman, ed., *What Will Be Has Always Been: The Words of Louis I. Kahn* (New York: Access Press and Rizzoli, 1986), p. 236.

5. Ibid.

6. Latour, *Louis I. Kahn: Writings, Lectures, Interviews*, p. 119.

7. Louis I. Kahn, "How to Develop New Methods of Building," *Architectural Forum* 101 (November 1954), p. 157.

8. L. Kahn, "Exeter Library," *Architectural Forum* 137 (July/August 1972), p. 77.

9. Jay Wickersham, "The Making of Exeter Library," *Harvard Architectural Review* (1989), p. 138.

10. Quoted in "Museo d'Arte Kimbell," *Rassegna* 7 (March 1985), p. 67.

11. "Lighting Starts with Daylight," *Progressive Architecture* 54 (September 1973), pp. 82–85.

10 THE VENTURIS, GRAVES, SCARPA, AND THE LAYERS OF HISTORY: 1963–1984

1. Robert Venturi, *Complexity and Contradiction in Architecture* (New York: Museum of Modern Art, 1966), p. 72.

2. Ibid., p. 84.

3. Ibid., p. 120.

4. Robert Venturi, Denise Scott Brown, and Steven Izenour, *Learning from Las Vegas* (Cambridge: MIT Press, 1972), p. 76.

5. Colin Rowe and Robert Slutzky, "Transparency: Literal and Phenomenal," in Rowe, *The Mathematics of the Ideal Villa and Other Essays* (Cambridge: MIT Press, 1976), pp. 169–170.

6. Ibid., p. 175.

7. Kenneth Frampton in *Five Architects* (New York: Wittenborn & Co., 1972), p. 13.

8. Barbaralee Diamonstein, *American Architecture Now* (New York: Rizzoli, 1980), p. 61.

9. Sergio Polano, *The Other City* (Berlin: Ernst & Sohn, 1989), p. 16.

11 HIGH TECH, DECONSTRUCTION, AND THE PRESENT DAY: 1972–1988

1. Bryan Appleyard, *Richard Rogers, a Biography* (London: Faber and Faber, 1986), p. 13.

2. Daralice Boles, "Rogers' US Debut" (PA Technology Facility), *Progressive Architecture* 66 (August 1985), pp. 67–74.

3. Peter Rice, "Design for Better Assembly 5: Case Study: Rogers' and Arups'," *Architects Journal* 180 (September 5, 1984), p. 87.

4. John McKean, "Gold Standard," *Architects Journal* 177 (March 30, 1983), p. 14.

5. Norman Foster, lecture at Pompidou Center, February 1981, quoted in *Norman Foster: Buildings and Projects*, vol. 2 (Hong Kong: Watermark, 1989), p. 79.

6. Stephanie Williams, *The Hong Kong Bank* (Boston: Little, Brown, 1989), p. 126.

7. Jacques Derrida, "The Art of *Mémoires*," quoted in Mark Wigley, *The Architecture of Deconstruction* (Cambridge: MIT Press, 1993), p. 45.

8. Bernard Tschumi, *La Case Vide: La Villette* (London: Architectural Association, 1986), p. 3.

9. Bernard Tschumi, *Cinegramme Folie: La Parc de La Villette* (Sevessel, France: Champ Vallon, 1987), p. 27.

10. Wolf Prix and Helmut Swiczinsky, *Coop Himmelblau: 6 Projects for 4 Cities* (Frankfurt: Jürgen Häuser, 1990), p. 32.

11. Ibid., p. 38.

12. *The Pritzker Architecture Prize 1989: Presented to Frank Owen Gehry* (Los Angeles: Hyatt Foundation, 1990).

13. Peter Cook and George Rand, *Morphosis: Buildings and Projects* (New York: Rizzoli, 1989), p. 173.

14. Kenneth Frampton, *Modern Architecture: A Critical History* (New York: Thames and Hudson, 1992), p. 314.

15. Philip Drew, *Leaves of Iron: Glenn Murcutt: Pioneer of an Australian Architectural Form* (Pymble, Australia: Angus & Robertson, 1985), p. 13.

12 CONCLUSION

1. Ian Lambot, ed., *Norman Foster, Foster Associates: Buildings and Projects 1964–1989*, vol. 2 (London: Watermark, 1989–1990), p. 108.

2. Patrick Meehan, ed., *Frank Lloyd Wright Remembered* (Washington: The Preservation Press, 1991), p. 53.

3. Michael A. Cusumano, *The Japanese Automobile Industry: Technology and Management at Nissan and Toyota* (Cambridge: Harvard University Press, 1985), p. 270.

4. John Holusha, "Steel Gains in Home Building," *New York Times* (August 20, 1994), B37.

5. Reyner Banham, *Theory and Design in the First Machine Age* (London: Architectural Press, 1960), p. 32.

6. Amédée Ozenfant, *Foundations of Modern Art*, tr. John Rodker (1931; New York: Dover, 1952), pp. 154–155.

7. Vladimir Mayakovsky, "My Discovery of America," quoted in Wiktor Woroszylski, *The Life of Mayakovsky* (New York: The Orion Press, 1970), p. 380. For the poem that follows, see Mayakovsky's *The Bedbug and Selected Poetry* (New York: World Publishing Co., 1960), p. 177.

Bibliography

INTRODUCTION

Collins, Peter. *Concrete: The Vision of a New Architecture.* New York: Horizons, 1959.

Moholy-Nagy, László. *The New Vision (Von Material zu Architektur).* New York: Wittenborn, 1946.

Moholy-Nagy, László. *Painting, Photography, Film.* Cambridge: MIT Press, 1969.

Nevins, Alan, and Frank Ernest Hill. *Ford: Expansion and Challenge, 1915–1933.* New York: Charles Scribner's Sons, 1957.

Sloan, Alfred P., Jr. *My Years with General Motors.* Garden City, N.Y.: Doubleday, 1964.

Turner, Paul. *The Education of Le Corbusier.* New York: Garland, 1977.

Vriesen, Gustav, and Max Imdahl. *Robert Delaunay: Light and Color.* New York: Abrams, 1969.

Wright, Frank Lloyd. *An Autobiography.* New York: Longmans, Green and Co., 1932.

ELIEL SAARINEN IN DETROIT

Aldersey-Williams, Hugh. *Cranbrook Design: The New Discourse.* New York: Rizzoli, 1990.

Christ-Janer, Albert. *Eliel Saarinen.* 1948; rev. ed. Chicago: University of Chicago Press, 1979.

Komonen, Markku, and Kimmo Friman. *Saarinen Suomessa: Gesellius, Lindgren, Saarinen, 1896–1907.* Helsinki: Museum of Finnish Architecture, 1986.

Mikola, Kirmo, Marika Hausen, et al., *Eliel Saarinen: Projects 1896–1923.* Cambridge: MIT Press, 1990.

Saarinen, Eliel. *The City: Its Growth, Its Decay, Its Future.* New York: Reinhold, 1943.

Saarinen, Eliel. "The Royal Gold Medal, 1950; Address by Eliel Saarinen." *RIBA Journal* 57 (April 1950), pp. 216–217.

Saarinen, Eliel. *The Search for Form in Art and Architecture.* New York: Reinhold, 1948.

Archives: Cranbrook Archives.

Interview: Mark Coir.

ERIK GUNNAR ASPLUND

Ahlberg, Hakon, Gustav Holmdahl, et al. *Gunnar Asplund Architect 1885–1940.* Stockholm: Byggmästaren, 1943, rev. 1950

Asplund, E. G. "Ett Litet Special Varuhus" (Bredenberg). *Byggmästaren,* 1935, pp. 39–46.

Caldenby, Claes, and Olof Hultin, eds.; articles by Kenneth Frampton, Carl-Axel Acking, et al. *Asplund: A Book.* New York: Rizzoli, 1986.

Cornell, Elias. "The Sky as a Vault." In Christina Engfors, ed., *Lectures and Briefings from the International Symposium on the Work of E. G. Asplund.* Stockholm: Swedish Museum of Architecture, 1986.

Cruickshank, Dan, ed.; articles by Kirstin Neilson, Peter Blundell Jones, Martin Charles. *AJ Masters of Building: Erik Gunnar Asplund.* London: Architects Journal, 1988.

"Göteborg's Radhus" (Gothenburg). *Byggmästaren,* 1939, p. 168.

St. John Wilson, Colin. *Sigurd Lewerentz 1885–1975: The Dilemma of Classicism.* London: Architectural Association, 1988.

St. John Wilson, Colin. *Gunnar Asplund 1885–1940: The Dilemma of Classicism.* London: Architectural Association, 1989.

Schildt, Göran. *Alvar Aalto: The Decisive Years.* New York: Rizzoli, 1986.

"Specialty Shop Organized on Vertical Basis" (Bredenberg). *Architectural Record* 83 (June 1938), pp. 53–57.

Thening, Knut. "Stockholmsutstalningen" (1930 Stockholm Exhibition). *Byggmästaren,* 1930, pp. 121–128.

Wrede, Stuart. *The Architecture of Erik Gunnar Asplund.* Cambridge: MIT Press, 1980.

Archives: Swedish Architecture Museum; Getty Trust.

RICHARD NEUTRA

Boesiger, W., ed. *Richard Neutra 1923–50: Buildings and Projects.* New York: Praeger, 1966.

Boesiger, W., ed. *Richard Neutra 1950–60: Buildings and Projects.* New York: Praeger, 1959.

Arthur Drexler and Thomas Hines, *The Architecture of Richard Neutra: From International Style to California Modern.* New York: Museum of Modern Art, 1982.

"48 Systems of Prefabrication." *American Architect and Architecture* 149 (September 1936), pp. 28–40.

Freiman, Ziva. "Back to Neutra" (Kaufmann house restoration). *Progressive Architecture,* November 1995, pp. 73–79.

Hines, Thomas. *Richard Neutra and the Search for Modern Architecture.* New York: Oxford University Press, 1982.

Neutra, R. *Life and Shape.* New York: Appleton-Century-Crofts, 1962.

Neutra, R. *Survival through Design.* New York: Oxford University Press, 1954.

Neutra, Richard and Dione. *Richard Neutra, Promise and Fulfilment, 1919–1932.* Carbondale: Southern Illinois University Press, 1986.

Archives: Special Collections, UCLA; Special Collections, Syracuse University.

ALVAR AALTO AND MARCEL BREUER

Aalto, Alvar. *Alvar Aalto: The Complete Works.* 3 vols. Zurich: Editions d'Architecture Artremis, 1970–1978.

Aalto, A., *Alvar Aalto: Sketches and Essays.* Vienna: Akademie der Bildenden Kunst, 1985.

Bak, P., et al., *J. Duiker Bouwkundig Ingenieur.* Delft: Duikergroep, 1982.

Blake, Peter. *Sun and Shadow: The Work of Marcel Breuer.* New York: Dodd Mead, 1955.

Hoesli, Bernhard. *Alvar Aalto Synopsis: Painting Architecture Sculpture.* Basel and Stuttgart: Birkhäuser, 1970.

Jones, Cranston. *Marcel Breuer: Building and Projects 1921–1961.* New York: Praeger, 1962.

MacKeith, Peter. *The Finland Pavilions: Finland at the Universal Expositions, 1990–1992.* Helsinki: Kustannus, 1993.

Masello, David. *Architecture without Rules: The Houses of Marcel Breuer and Herbert Beckhard.* New York: W. W. Norton, 1993.

Neuenschwander, Edward and Claudia. *Finnish Architecture and Alvar Aalto.* New York: Praeger, 1954.

Pallasmaa, Juhani. "Image and Meaning in the Villa Mairea." Unpublished.

Pearson, Paul David. *Alvar Aalto and the International Style.* New York: Whitney, Library of Design, 1978.

Quantrill, Malcolm. *Alvar Aalto: A Critical Study.* London: Sakler & Warburg, 1983.

Schildt, Göran. *Alvar Aalto: The Complete Catalogue of Architecture, Design and Art.* New York: Rizzoli, 1994.

Schildt, Göran. *Alvar Aalto: The Early Years.* New York: Rizzoli, 1984.

Schildt, Göran. *Alvar Aalto: The Decisive Years.* New York: Rizzoli, 1986.

Schildt, Göran. *Alvar Aalto: The Mature Years.* New York: Rizzoli, 1991.

Spens, Michael. *Viipuri Library: Alvar Aalto.* London: Academy Editions, 1994.

Standertskjöld, Elina. "Alvar Aalto and Standardization." *Acanthus,* 1992. p. 74.

"Tuberculosis Sanitorium at Paimio." *The Modern Hospital* 72 (April 1949), p. 79.

Weston, Richard. *Säynätsalo Town Hall: Architecture in Detail Series.* London: Phaidon, 1993.

Weston, R. *Villa Mairea: Architecture in Detail Series.* London: Phaidon, 1992.

Archives: Special Collections, Syracuse University; Houghton Library, Harvard University; Alvar Aalto Archive.

Interview: Mikko Merckling.

LE CORBUSIER AFTER 1928

Aynac, Laurent. *L'Exposition de démonstration et propagande du Sous Secrétariat d'Etat de l'Aéronautique 1921.* Copy in the Fondation Le Corbusier.

Boesiger, W., and M. Bill, eds. *Le Corbusier and Pierre Jeanneret, Oeuvre complète.* 8 vols. Zurich: Editions Girsberger, 1930–1970.

Brooks, H. Allan, ed. *Le Corbusier, Buildings and Projects.* 32 vols. New York: Garland, 1987.

Curtis, William J. R. *Le Corbusier: Ideas and Forms.* New York: Rizzoli, 1986.

Ferro, Sergio, et al. *La couvent de la Tourette.* Marseilles: Éditions Parenthèses, 1987.

Huber, Benedikt, and Jean-Claude Steinegger. *Jean Prouvé: Prefabrication, Structures and Elements.* New York: Praeger, 1971.

Kultermann, Udo, ed. *Kenzo Tange 1946–69.* New York: Praeger, 1970.

Le Corbusier. *Aircraft.* London: The Studio, 1935; New York, 1988.

Le Corbusier. *Une maison—un palais.* Paris: G. Crès, 1928.

Le Corbusier. *The Marseilles Block.* London: Harvill, 1953.

Le Corbusier. *Précisions.* Paris: G. Crès, 1930. Trans. as *Precisions on the Present State of Architecture and City Planning.* Cambridge: MIT Press, 1991.

Le Corbusier. *Vers une architecture.* Paris: G. Crès, 1925.

Lucan, Jacques, ed. *Le Corbusier: une encyclopédie.* Paris: Éditions du Centre Pompidou, 1988.

Mondey, David, ed. *Encyclopedia of Aviation.* New York: Crown Publishing, 1977.

Morris, A.E.J. *Precast Concrete in Architecture.* New York: Whitney Library of Design, 1978.

Pawley, Martin. *Theory and Design in the Second Machine Age.* Oxford: Basil Blackwell, 1990.

Prelorenzo, Claude, et al. *La conservation de l'oeuvre construite de Le Corbusier.* Paris: Fondation Le Corbusier, 1990.

Raeburn, Michael, and Victoria Wilson, eds. *Le Corbusier: The Architect of the Century.* London: Arts Council of Great Britain, 1987.

Saddy, Pierre. *Le Corbusier: le passé à réaction poétique.* Paris: Ministère de la Culture, 1988.

Sbriglio, Jacques. *L'Unité d'habitation de Marseilles.* Marseilles: Éditions Parenthèses, 1992.

Sulzer, P. *Jean Prouvé: Das neue Blech.* Cologne: R. Müller, 1991.

Sumi, Christian. "The Immeuble Clarté." In Carlo Palazzolo and Riccardo Vio, eds., *In the Footsteps of Le Corbusier.* New York: Rizzoli, 1991.

"L'Unité d'habitation de Marseilles." *L'Homme et l'Architecture,* 11–12 (1947), entire issue.

Archives: Fondation Le Corbusier, Paris; Musée de l'Air et de l'Espace; Jean Prouvé-Archive, Stuttgart.

SAARINEN, EAMES, FULLER, AND THE CASE STUDY HOUSES

Albrecht, Donald, ed. *World War II and the American Dream.* Cambridge: MIT Press, 1995.

Bayley, S. *Harley Earl and the Dream Machine.* New York: Knopf, 1983.

Brownlee, David B., and David G. De Long. *Louis I. Kahn: In the Realm of Architecture.* New York: Rizzoli, 1991.

"Buildings for Defense . . . 1000 Houses a Day at $1200 Each" (Dymaxion Deployment Unit). *Architectural Forum* 74 (June 1941), pp. 425–429.

"Buildings for 194X." *Architectural Forum* 78 (May 1943).

"Case Study House No. 16." *Arts and Architecture* 70 (June 1953), pp. 20–32.

Clausen, Meredith. "Belluschi and the Equitable Building in History." *Journal of the Society of Architectural Historians* 50 (June 1991), pp. 109–129.

"Distinction from Exposed Framing" (Case Study House No. 16). *House + Home* 4 (September 1953), p. 140.

Fuller, R. Buckminster. *Designing for Industry.* Wichita: Fuller Research Institute, 1945.

"Houses for 194X." *Architectural Forum* 77 (September 1942).

Howland, Lewellen, III. "Starling Burgess." Manuscript in the Hart Nautical Collection, MIT Museums, 1985.

"Hutments to Houses." *Architectural Forum* 80 (February 1944), pp. 91–94.

Jackson, Neil. "Metal Framed Houses of the Modern Movement in Los Angeles, Parts 1 and 2." *Architectural History* 32 (1988), pp. 157–177; 33 (1990), pp. 167–187.

Marks, Robert W. *The Dymaxion World of Buckminster Fuller.* New York: Reinhold, 1960.

McCoy, Esther. *The Case Study Houses: 1945–1962.* Los Angeles: Hennessey & Ingalls, 1977.

Morpurgo, J. E. *Barnes Wallis: A Biography.* New York: St. Martin's, 1972.

Neuhart, John, Charles Eames, et al. *Eames Design: The Office of Charles and Ray Eames.* New York: Abrams, 1989.

Nevins, Allan, and Frank Ernest Hill. *Ford: Decline and Rebirth, 1933–1962.* New York: Charles Scribner's Sons, 1963.

Norway, Nevil Shute. *Slide Rule.* New York: William Morrow, 1954.

Pawley, Martin. *Buckminster Fuller.* London: Trefoil, 1990.

Smith, Elizabeth A. T. *Blueprints for Modern Living: History and Legacy of the Case Study Houses.* Cambridge: MIT Press, 1989.

Sorensen, Charles, with S. T. Williamson. *My Forty Years with Ford.* New York: W. W. Norton, 1956.

Underwood, Max. "Revealing Connections: The Techne of Charles and Ray Eames' Case Study House #8 and Rem Koolhaus–OMA's Villa dall'Ava." In *Community of Interests.* Washington, D.C.: AIA Press, 1994.

Ward, James, ed. *The Artifacts of R. Buckminster Fuller.* 4 vols. New York: Garland, 1985.

Archives: Buckminster Fuller Institute; Library of Congress (Eames Collection); Hart Nautical Collection, MIT Museums.

Interviews: Ray Eames, Pierre Koenig.

EERO SAARINEN AFTER 1945

Bayley, S. *Harley Earl and the Dream Machine.* New York: Knopf, 1983.

"80-Ton Keystone Completes St. Louis's Gateway Arch." *New York Times*, November 7, 1965, 8:45.

"Engineering of Saarinen's Arch." *Architectural Record* 133 (May 1963), pp. 188–191.

Fisher, Thomas, et al. "Landmarks" (TWA Terminal). *Progressive Architecture* 73 (May 1992), pp. 96–110.

"General Motors Technical Center." *Architectural Forum*, July 1949, November 1951, November 1954, November 1955.

Guise, David. *Design and Technology in Architecture.* New York: Van Nostrand Reinhold, 1991.

Mark, Robert. *Light, Wind, and Structure.* Cambridge: MIT Press, 1990.

"A New Airport for Jets" (Dulles Airport). *Architectural Record* 127 (March 1960), pp. 175–182.

Oishi, Masato. *Eero Saarinen.* Tokyo: A+U, 1984.

Papademetriou, Peter. "Coming of Age: Eero Saarinen and Modern Architecture." *Perspecta* no. 21 (1984).

Ramaswamy, G. G. *Design and Construction of Concrete Shell Roofs.* New York: McGraw-Hill, 1968.

Saarinen, Eero. *Eero Saarinen on His Work.* New Haven: Yale University Pres, 1962.

"St. Louis Finishes Gateway Arch." *New York Times*, October 29, 1965, p. 45.

Sloan, Alfred P., Jr. *My Years with General Motors.* Garden City, N.Y.: Doubleday, 1964.

Temko, Allan. *Eero Saarinen.* New York: George Braziller, 1962.

"Unique Architectural Elements of the GM Tech Center." *General Motors Engineering Journal* 3, no. 3 (May-June 1956).

Archives: Kevin Roche (Eero Saarinen); Smith, Hinchman and Grylls (GM).

Interviews: Kevin Roche, Peter Papademetriou, William Jarratt, George Moon, Joseph Lacy.

LOUIS KAHN, SIGURD LEWERENTZ, AND THE NEW BRUTALISM

Arnell, Peter, and Ted Bickford, eds. *James Stirling: Buildings and Projects.* New York: Rizzoli, 1984.

Banham, Reyner. *The New Brutalism.* New York: Reinhold, 1966.

Blundell Jones, Peter. "Intriguing Details: Lewerentz at Klippan." *Spazio e Società* 14, no. 53 (1991), pp. 88–97.

Boyarsky, Alvin. "Stirling Demonstrati" (Cambridge History Faculty). *Architectural Design* 38 (October 1968), pp. 454–478.

Brownlee, David B., and David G. De Long. *Louis I. Kahn: In the Realm of Architecture.* New York: Rizzoli, 1991.

Kahn, Louis I. *The Louis I. Kahn Archive.* 7 vols. New York: Garland, 1987.

Komendant, August E. *18 Years with Architect Louis I. Kahn.* Englewood, N.J.: Aloray, 1975.

Latour, Alessandra, ed. *Louis I. Kahn: Writings, Lectures, Interviews.* New York: Rizzoli, 1991.

"Logic in Precast Concrete" (Richards Medical Research Building). *Architectural Record* 126 (September 1959), pp. 233–238.

Loud, Patricia. *The Museums of Louis I. Kahn.* Durham: Duke University Press, 1989.

Prown, Jules David. *The Architecture of the Yale Center for British Art.* New Haven: Yale University, 1977.

St. John Wilson, Colin. *Sigurd Lewerentz 1885–1975: The Dilemma of Classicism.* London: Architectural Association, 1988.

Scully, Vincent. *Louis I. Kahn.* New York: George Braziller, 1962.

Seymour, A. T., III. "The Immeasurable Made Measurable: Building the Kimbell Art Museum." *VIA*, no. 7 (1984).

Stirling, James, and James Gowan. "Leicester Engineering Building." *Architectural Design* 34 (February 1964), pp. 62–81.

Wurman, Richard Saul, ed. *What Will Be Has Always Been: The Words of Louis I. Kahn.* New York: Access Press and Rizzoli, 1986.

Archives: Louis Kahn Archive, University of Pennsylvania and the Pennsylvania Historical and Museum Commission; Swedish Museum of Architecture.

Interviews: Carles Vallhonrat, Marshall Meyers.

VENTURI, GRAVES, SCARPA

"La 'Crosera de piazza' di Carlo Scarpa" (Olivetti Showroom). *Zodiac* 4 (1959), pp. 128–147.

Dal Co, Francesco, and Giuseppe Mazzariol. *Carlo Scarpa: The Complete Works.* New York: Rizzoli, 1984.

Five Architects. New York: Wittenborn, 1972.

Murphy, Richard. *Carlo Scarpa and Castelvecchio 1990.* Boston: Butterworth, 1990.

Murphy, R. *The Querini-Stampalia Foundation.* London: Phaidon, 1993.

Polano, Sergio. *Das andere Stadt.* Berlin: W. Ernst & Sohn, 1988.

Rowe, Colin. *The Mathematics of the Ideal Villa and Other Essays.* Cambridge: MIT Press, 1976.

Santini, Pier. "The New Shop of Carlo Scarpa in Bologna" (Gavina Showroom). *Zodiac* 10 (1962), pp. 169–181.

Schwartz, Frederic. *Mother's House.* New York: Rizzoli, 1992.

Tentori, Francesco. "Progetti di Carlo Scarpa" (Venezuelan Pavilion). *Casabella* 212 (1958), pp. 15–16.

Venturi, Robert. *Complexity and Contradiction in Architecture.* New York: Museum of Modern Art, 1966.

Venturi, Robert, Denise Scott Brown, and Steven Izenour. *Learning from Las Vegas.* Cambridge: MIT Press, 1972.

Wheeler, Karen, et al. *Michael Graves: Buildings and Projects 1966–81.* New York: Rizzoli, 1982.

Archives: Princeton University.

HIGH TECH, DECONSTRUCTION, AND THE PRESENT DAY

Appleyard, Bryan. *Richard Rogers: A Biography.* London: Faber and Faber, 1986.

The Arup Journal. London: Ove Arup Partnership.

Boles, Daralice. "Rogers' US Debut" (PA Technology Facility). *Progressive Architecture* 66 (August 1985), pp. 67–74.

Cook, Peter, and George Rand. *Morphosis: Buildings and Projects.* New York: Rizzoli, 1989.

Drew, Philip. *Leaves of Iron: Glenn Murcutt: Pioneer of an Australian Architectural Form.* Pymble, Australia: Angus & Robertson, 1985.

Farrelly, E. M. *Three Houses: Glenn Murcutt.* London: Phaidon, 1993.

Lambot, Ian, ed. *Norman Foster, Foster Associates: Buildings and Projects 1964–1989.* 4 vols. London: Watermark, 1989–1990.

"Lloyds and the Bank." *The Architects Journal* 184 (October 22, 1986), entire issue.

Matsuda, Naonori, ed. "Hong Kong Bank Technical Review." *Process Architecture* 70 (September 1986).

Nakamura, T., ed. *Renzo Piano Building Workshop 1964–1988.* Tokyo: A+U, 1989.

Nakamura, Toshio, ed. *Richard Rogers 1978–88.* Tokyo: A+U, 1988.

Nouvel, Jean. *Jean Nouvel.* Zurich: Artemis, 1992.

Powell, Kenneth. *The Lloyd's Building: Richard Rogers Partnership.* London: Phaidon, 1994.

Rice, Peter. *An Engineer Imagines.* London: Artemis, 1993.

Weinstein, Richard. *Morphosis: Buildings and Projects 1989–92.* New York: Rizzoli, 1994.

Williams, Stephanie. *The Hong Kong Bank.* Boston: Little, Brown, 1989.

Offices of Bernard Tschumi, Coop Himmelblau, Frank Gehry.

Interviews: Bernard Tschumi, Mark McVay, Frank Stepper, Glenn Murcutt.

GENERAL

Banham, Reyner. *Theory and Design in the First Machine Age.* London: Architectural Press, 1960.

Boyne, D. A., and Lance Wright, eds. *Architect's Working Details.* 15 vols. London: Architectural Press, 1969.

Frampton, Kenneth. *Modern Architecture: A Critical History.* 3d ed. New York: Thames & Hudson, 1992.

Mills, E. D., ed. *Architect's Detail Sheets.* London: Iliffe and Sons.

Mondey, David, ed. *Encyclopedia of Aviation.* New York: Crown Publishing, 1977.

Neville, Leslie. *Aircraft Designer's Data Book.* New York: McGraw-Hill, 1950.

Ogg, Alan. *Architecture in Steel: The Australian Context.* Red Hill, Australia: RAIA, 1987.

Pawley, Martin. *Theory and Design in the Second Machine Age.* Oxford: Basil Blackwell, 1990.

Roth, Alfred. *The New Architecture.* Zurich: Artemis, 1975.

Sands, Herman. *Wall Systems: Wall Systems by Detail.* New York: McGraw-Hill, 1986.

Trykare, Tre, ed. *The Lore of Flight.* Gothenburg: Cagner & Co., 1970.

Wilson, Richard, et al. *The Machine Age in America.* New York: Abrams, 1986.

Aalto, Alvar, xi, 101, 117–159, 221, 373, 419, 428.
 See also Otaniemi Institute of Technology;
 Paimio Sanitorium; Säynätsalo Town Hall;
 Viipuri Library; Villa Mairea
 and aircraft, 117, 119
 and Asplund, 53, 55, 61, 79, 81, 117, 119
 Baker House dormitory, 137
 and Breuer, 149, 151
 and Duiker, 121, 123
 Enso-Gutzeit building, 147
 experiments in wood, 125
 Finlandia Hall, 147
 Finnish Pavilion, World Exposition, Paris
  (1937), 127–129, 131, 133, 179
 Finnish Pensions Institute, 137, 147, 159
 furniture, 125, 131, 149
 handrail details, 63
 and industrialization, 119, 157
 and the International Style, 119–127, 145
 and Karelian architecture, 125, 127, 129
 and Le Corbusier, 117, 123
 and light and dematerialization, 121, 129, 143
 and Moholy-Nagy, 117, 119, 121, 123, 125, 127,
  129, 131, 133, 143
 Muurame church, 119
 and National Romanticism, 137
 on nature of materials, 23, 119, 125, 127, 129,
  423
 and Nordic Classicism, 119
 Riola church, 149
 and the Saarinens, 133, 137
 Seinäjoki Defense Corps building, 53, 119
 and standardization, 15, 61, 119, 145, 147, 149,
  426
 on Stockholm Exhibition (1930), 54, 57
 stone details, 147, 149, 159
 and structural expression, 127, 129
 and Surrealism, 127, 157
 Turun Sanomat building, 119, 121
 and vernacular and industrial juxtapositions,
  103, 127, 133
 and vernacular architecture, 119
 Villa Aalto, 129, 131
 Vouksenniska church, 149
 Wolfsburg Cultural Center, 147, 159
AF of L Medical Services Building, 307, 309, 311,
 313, 315, 317, 331
Agrigento, 75
Ahlberg, Hakon, 57
Ain, Gregory, 91
Aircraft design and construction, 9–11, 177, 421,
 422, 428
Airfloor system, 333, 335, 405
AIROH house, 255, 257
Albers, Josef, 19, 125, 429
 and Moholy-Nagy, 89
Aluminum accordion insulation, 105
American building, 239, 335, 413
 and steel, 426
Amiens cathedral, 5, 6, 421
Anderson, Marian, 253
Ando, Tadao, 397, 417
Aquinas, St. Thomas, 51
Archigram group, 381
Articulation of elements, 3, 423
Arts and Crafts movement, x, 26, 27, 29, 33, 43
Asplund, Erik Gunnar, x, xi, 51–83, 157, 373, 428.
 See also Bredenberg Department Store;
 Gothenburg Law Courts Annex; Stockholm
 Exhibition (1930); Woodland Crematorium
 and Aalto, 53, 55, 61, 79, 81, 117, 119
 articulation of elements, 423
 assistants on, 63, 73
 on Brooklyn Bridge, 6
 and Classicism, 51, 53, 61, 81
 as detailer, 59
 and economy of material, 53, 55, 57, 61, 63, 65

 and exposed construction, 55
 frame and skin construction, 423
 and Gothic construction, 55
 and Le Corbusier, 57, 59, 61, 63, 65, 79
 and Lewerentz, 335
 and light and dematerialization, 53, 55, 65
 Lister County Courthouse, 53
 and Modernism, 53, 55
 and Nordic Classicism, 51
 Skandia Cinema, 75
 and Spengler, 55
 and standardization, 15, 61. 426
 Stockholm Public Library, 51, 53, 65
 and structural expression, 57, 73
 and transparency, 55, 57
 and vernacular building, 79
 and vernacular objects, 20
 Villa Snellman, 53
Automobile construction, 11–15, 421, 422

Balloon frame, 89, 239
Banham, Reyner, 166, 211, 299, 349, 357, 427
 on Le Corbusier, 166, 211
 on Eero Saarinen, 299
 Theory and Design in the First Machine Age,
  427
Barnes, Edward Larrabee, 255
Baths of Caracalla, 422
Bauhaus, 89, 125
Baxter, Peter, 99
Beard house, 93–95, 97, 101, 113
 structure, 93
 windows, 93–94
Beech Aircraft Company, 251, 261, 421, 424. *See
 also* Dymaxion house
Belluschi, Pietro, 223, 227
 Equitable Building, 223, 227
Benton, Tim, 171
Beranek, Leo, 285
Bergson, Henri, 16, 17
Björkhagen. *See* St. Mark, Björkhagen
Black Mountain College, 257
Blomstedt, Aulis, 145
Bo, Jørgen, and Vilhelm Wohlert, Louisiana Mu-
 seum, 113, 115
Boccioni, Umberto, 17
 on material, 15–16
Bodiansky, Vladimir, 187
Booth, George, 27
Booth, Henry, 27, 29
Botta, Mario, 397, 417
Bredenberg Department Store, 57–61, 63, 79, 81
 curtain wall and stone details, 59, 61, 83
 stair, 59, 63
 structure, 57, 59, 73
Breuer, Marcel, 49, 113, 127, 151, 157, 160–163,
 221
 and Aalto, 149, 151
 Breuer house (first New Canaan house), 151,
  157
 Breuer house (second New Canaan house), 151
 Caesar cottage, 157, 160
 Cesca chair, 149
 and Gropius, 149
 on industrialization, 157
 and Moholy-Nagy, 151
 Robinson house, 151
 and structural expression, 157
 and Surrealism, 157
 and transparency, 157
 and vernacular and industrial elements, 149,
  157
 Wassily chair, 149
 Wolfson house, 151, 157, 163
Brooklyn Bridge, 5–7, 429–430
Buff, Straub and Hensman, Case Study House
 No. 20, 237

Bunshaft, Gordon, Lever House, 309, 311, 361
   curtain walls, x
Burgess, Starling, 241, 245, 247, 249
   Dymaxion car, 245, 249
   Enterprise, 241, 247, 249
   and Fuller, 241, 245, 249
Butler Company. *See* Fuller, R. Buckminster

Caldwell air conditioning system, 311
Candela, Felix, 291
Caproni hydroplane, 13, 166
Caproni triplane, 9
Case Study House program, 101, 217, 225, 228–
   233, 236–241, 259, 413
Catalan vaults, 201, 203
Chandigarh, 179, 189, 195–203, 291
   Assembly, 195, 197, 199, 201
   Governor's Palace, 195, 199, 203
   High Court, 195, 197, 201
   Secretariat, 195
Chareau, Pierre. *See* Maison de Verre
CIAM, 173
Concorde, 387, 397
Constructivism. *See* Russian Constructivism
Contini, Edgardo, 229
Coop Himmelblau, 397, 403, 405, 407, 409, 423
   Open House, 405, 407, 409
Cornell, Elias, 75
Cram, Ralph Adams, 355
Cranbrook Art Academy, 27, 39
   doors, 41
   Milles Studio, 45
   windows, 45
Cranbrook Educational Community, 13, 22, 27,
   219, 265, 267, 285. *See also* Cranbrook Art
   Academy; Cranbrook Museum and Library;
   Cranbrook School; Kingswood School
Cranbrook Museum and Library, 45, 47–49
   portico, 73, 75
   stone and column details, 47, 49
   structure, 47
   windows, 47
Cranbrook School, 33–39
   academic buildings, 29, 30, 39, 41
   dining hall, 29, 33, 37, 39, 41
   doors and paneling, 41, 43, 45
   main entry gate, 27, 33
   North Hall, 29, 30, 33
   Page Hall, 39
   study hall, 30, 35
   windows, 33, 35, 39
Critical regionalism, 413
Crosby, Gordon, 167
Curtain walls, modern, 57, 59. *See also under in-*
   dividual architects
Curtis, William, 197

Day and Kauder, 355
Deconstructivism, 375, 397–406, 411, 419
   and American construction, 413
   as critical analysis, 397
   and exposed construction, 413
   and Gothic rationalism, 399
   and instability, 399
   and Russian Constructivism, 399
   structural narratives in, 419
Deere, John, Headquarters, 293, 297, 299–303,
   423
   connections, 297, 303
   curtain wall, 297, 301, 303
   structure, 297, 301
De Havilland, Geoffrey. *See* Mosquito
Delaunay, Robert, 16, 17
   Équipe de Cardiff, 13, 16–17, 165
Dermée, Paul, 165
Derrida, Jacques, 397, 399
Dostoyevsky, Feodor, 379

Drew, Philip, 417
Dreyfuss, Henry, 255
Dry construction, 13, 271
Duchamp, Marcel, 20–21, 165
Dudok, Willem, Hilversum Town Hall, 137
Duiker, Johannes, Open Air School, 121
   Zonnestraal Sanitorium, 121
Dulles Airport, 195, 293, 296–299
   curtain wall, 297
   structure, 293, 297
Dymaxion house, second (Wichita). *See also* Ful-
   ler, R. Buckminster, 1927 Dymaxion house
   house, 241, 251–255, 421
   structure, 251, 253
   wall details, 253

Eames, Charles, 99, 217, 225, 228–233, 237, 239,
   241, 257
   and aircraft, 225, 237
   De Pree house (with Ray Eames), 237
   Entenza house (Case Study House no. 9), 225,
   229
   on industrialization, 225
   Kwikset house (with Ray Eames), 237
   and Museum of Modern Art Furniture Competition, 221
   and plywood, 221
   and Eero Saarinen, 219, 221, 225, 229
Eames, Ray, 219, 221, 225, 241
   involvement in Eames house, 237
Eames house, first design (Case Study House no.
   8), 225, 229
   prefabrication in, 229, 231
   redesign, 229
   structure, 229, 231
   wall details, 229
Eames house, second design, 231
   redesign, 434
   structure, 231, 233, 237
   wall details, 231, 233
Earl, Harley, 47, 265, 267, 277, 279, 291
Eco, Umberto, 373
Economy of material, ix, 2, 19, 21, 55, 57, 61, 63,
   65, 209, 211, 246, 249, 251, 255, 259, 261,
   307, 311, 335, 387, 389, 395, 422, 426, 427.
   See also under individual architects
   and automobiles, 11
   and economy of capital, 422
Eiffel Tower, 13
Eisenman, Peter, 357
Ekster, Alecsandra, 53
Ellwood, Craig, 99, 237–241
   articulation of elements, 423
   Case Study House No. 16, 237, 239, 241, 243
   Case Study House No. 17, 239, 241
   Case Study House No. 18, 239
   on industrialization, 239
   on Le Corbusier, 203
   on Ronchamp, 195
Entenza, John, 225, 241. *See also* Case Study
   House program
Esprit Nouveau, 165, 167, 427
Exeter. *See* Philips Exeter Academy library
Exposed construction, 427

Farman, Henri, 13, 165, 177, 241
Farman Goliath, 9, 11, 15, 21, 165, 166, 167, 171,
   177, 179. *See also* Le Corbusier
Fehn, Sverre, 81
First Unitarian Church, Rochester, 321–325, 327,
   329, 337, 341
   framing, 323
   wall details, 325
Five Architects, 357
Ford, Edsel, 217. *See also* Ford Motor Company
Ford, Henry, 15, 183, 257, 349, 375, 421. *See also*
   Ford Motor Company
   on minimum weight, 11
   on standardization, 11, 424
Ford, Henry, II, 257

Ford Motor Company, 11, 13–15, 257, 425
Ford Rotunda, 257, 259–263, 421
Foster, Norman, 259, 361, 379, 381, 387, 395, 417, 424, 429. *See also* Hong Kong and Shanghai Bank
  and aircraft design, 387, 389
  and economy of material, 387, 389, 395
  frame and skin construction, 423
  and Fuller, 421, 422
  Renault warehouse, Swindon, 387
  Sainsbury center, 421
Frame and skin construction, 11, 97, 269, 422–423
Frampton, Kenneth, 53, 359, 413
Freyssinet, Eugène, 175
Frosterus, Sigurd, 23, 25
Fry, Maxwell, 189
Fuller, R. Buckminster, 207, 217, 223, 225, 241–259, 387, 395, 419, 429. *See also* Dymaxion house; Ford Rotunda
  at Black Mountain College, 257, 259
  and Burgess, 241, 245, 249
  and Butler Company, 249
  on compression structures, 245
  and dry construction, 253
  Dymaxion bathroom, 101, 259
  Dymaxion car (with Burgess), 245, 249
  Dymaxion Deployment Unit, 249, 251
  on economy of material, 245, 249, 251, 255, 259, 261, 422
  and Foster, 421, 422
  4D Tower, 245
  geodesic dome, 257
  Grunch of Giants, 255
  and High Tech, 381
  on industrialization, 225, 249, 251, 261
  and Louis Kahn, 309
  and nature of materials, 423
  1927 Dymaxion house, 101, 223, 241, 245, 251, 255, 273

Gaudí, Antoni, 177
Geddes, Norman Bel, 219, 273
  Little Theater in the Round, 273
  and Eero Saarinen, 267
Gehry, Frank, 407, 410–411, 413, 423
  Gehry house, 411
  on materials, 407
  Winton house, 407, 411
General Motors Corporation, 13, 15, 47, 265. *See also* General Motors Technical Center; Kahn, Albert; Sloan, Alfred P., Jr.
General Motors Technical Center, 47, 49, 225, 265–281, 299, 303
  and automobile construction, 267
  curtain walls, 269, 271, 274–275, 277
  Dynamometer Building, 267, 269, 271, 274
  Engineering Complex, 267, 269, 273, 309, 311
  first design, 265–267
  glazed brick, 271
  stairs, 271, 273, 279
  Styling Administration Building, 277, 279
  Styling Auditorium, 269, 273, 277, 279, 281, 283
  Styling Studios and Shops, 271, 275
Geodetic construction, 257
Gesellius, Herman. *See* Gesellius, Lindgren, and Saarinen
Gesellius, Lindgren, and Saarinen, 23, 129. *See also* Saarinen, Eliel
  Finland Pavilion, Paris world's fair (1900), 27
  Pohjola building, 27
Giedion, Sigfried, 357, 427
  on Aalto, 127, 157
Goldberger, Paul, 157
Gothenburg Law Courts Annex, 57, 61–69, 71, 79, 81
  facades and curtain walls, 63, 65, 67
  railings, 69
  relation to old building, 63

structure, 63, 65, 67, 73
  wood paneling, 69
Gothic construction, 1–5, 6, 9, 55
  cathedrals, ix–x, 21
  equilibrium in, 2
Gothic rationalism, 167, 179, 197, 389, 423–424
  and High Tech, 379, 381
Gothic Revival, 11, 39, 273
Gowan, James. *See* Stirling and Gowan
Graves, Michael, 349, 356–365, 369, 375. *See also* Hanselmann house; Humana Building
  Fargo-Moorhead Cultural Center, 359
  Plocek house, 361
Great Pyramid, 3, 19
Greene and Greene, 365
Greenough, Horatio, 7
Gropius, Walter, 16, 99, 121, 127, 223, 423, 426
  and Breuer, 149
  and dry construction, 13, 271
  Fagus and Bauhaus building curtain walls, 93, 97
  General Panel system, 223
  and industrialization, 265
  and Moholy-Nagy, 17
  on standardization, 11, 15, 61, 89
  and vernacular building, 20
Guadet, Julien, 2–3, 6, 428
Guastavino tile, 177
Guimard, Hector, 189
Gwathmey, Charles, 357

Handley Page, Frederick, 177
Hanselmann house, 356–359, 361
  framing, 357, 359
  windows, 359, 361
Harris, Harwell Hamilton, 87, 91
Hawksmoor, Nicholas, 349
Hegel, Georg Wilhelm Friedrich, 397
Hejduk, John, 357
Highland Park Ford Plant, 11, 15, 22, 217, 421, 426
High Tech Modernism, 251, 343, 375, 379–397, 419, 422, 424
  and composition, 397
  and economy, 395, 397
  and Gothic rationalism, 379, 381
  and long spans, 395
  structural narratives in, 419
Hilberseimer, Ludwig, 121
Hines, Thomas, 113
Hoffmann, Josef, 367
Hong Kong and Shanghai Bank, 387–389, 392–395, 397
  cost, 389
  curtain wall, 393, 395
  structure, 387, 389, 393
  utilities, 389
Houses for 194X competition, 223, 225
Houses for Post War Living competition, 223, 225
Hugo, Victor, 27
  Notre-Dame de Paris, 1, 2
Humana Building, 360–365
  structure, 361
  wall details, 361, 363, 365

Industrialization, 26–27, 47, 87, 89, 93, 101, 113, 119, 157, 166–167, 171, 183, 203, 207, 211, 225, 239, 249, 251, 261, 265, 421, 424–425. *See also under individual architects*
  in Scandinavia, 55
  in World War II, 217, 219, 251, 265
Ingalls Hockey Rink, 285
  criticism of, 289
  structure, 289, 293
International Style Modernism, 17, 20, 53, 55, 89, 97, 117, 119, 127, 209, 341, 349, 359, 389
  and curtain walls, 57, 59
Iron construction in the nineteenth century, 3, 5
Izenour, George, 285
Izenour, Steven. *See* Venturi, Scott Brown and Associates

Jacobsen, Arne, 113
Jahn, Helmut, 361
Jeanneret, Charles. *See* Le Corbusier
Jeanneret, Pierre, 171, 187. *See also* Le Corbusier
Johnson, Clarence "Kelly," 265
Johnson, Philip, 363, 365, 369
Johnson and Burgee, AT&T Building, 363, 365
Junkers, Hugo, 9, 167, 181, 183, 195, 417

Kahn, Albert, 15, 257, 267, 421. *See also* Ford
    Rotunda; Highland Park Ford Plant; River
    Rouge Plant; Willow Run Bomber Plant
Kahn, Louis, 137, 219, 223, 259, 269, 305–335,
    385, 405. *See also* AF of L Medical Services
    Building; First Unitarian Church, Rochester;
    Kimbell Art Museum; Philips Exeter Acad-
    emy library; Richards Medical Research
    Building; Salk Institute for Biological Studies;
    Yale Center for British Art
  and American construction, 335
  articulation of elements, 423
  Bryn Mawr dormitory, 305, 331
  and economy of material, 307, 311, 335
  and General Motors Engineering Building, 309,
    311
  and hollow structures, 307, 309, 311, 337
  Indian Institute of Management, 323, 325
  Jefferson National Expansion Memorial compe-
    tition, 307
  and Komendant, 315, 317
  and Lewerentz, 335, 337, 341
  and metal structures, 307, 317
  on MIT chapel, 311
  and monolithic construction, 323, 331, 335
  and nature of materials, 423
  Parasol House, 307, 309, 313
  Philadelphia City Hall project, 309, 311
  and Eero Saarinen, 279, 285, 299, 305, 307, 309,
    311, 335
  spatial organization and structure, 65, 309, 317,
    319, 321, 327, 335
  and standardization, 335
  stone details, 331, 333
  and triangulated structures, 309
  Tribune Review Building, 321
  on vernacular building, 20
  and Wright, 311, 323
  Yale University Art Gallery, 307, 309, 311
Kaufmann house, Palm Springs, 103–107, 109
  door details, 107
  heating and cooling system, 103, 105
  Stegner on, 105
  structure, 103, 105, 113
  windows, 91
Kelly, Richard, 333
Kettering, Charles, 223, 265
Kierkegaard, Søren, 421
Kimbell Art Museum, 307, 327, 329–333, 335
  structure, 329
  ventilation, 329, 331
  wall details, 329, 331, 333
  windows, 331
Kingswood School (Cranbrook), 27, 39, 41–45
  column and stone details, 41, 43, 45
  dining hall, 43
  doors and paneling, 43, 47
  structure, 41
  windows, 43
Kirkham, Pat, 237
Kleihues, J. P., Sindelfingen Civic Gallery, 363,
    365, 367
Klippan. *See* St. Peter, Klippan
Klutis, Gustav, 53
Koenig, Pierre, 237, 239, 241–245
  Case Study House No. 21, 241, 243, 245
  Case Study House No. 22, 241, 245
Komendant, August, 315, 317
Kresge Auditorium, 283–285, 291
  critical reception, 285
  roof, 285

structure, 283
Kurokawa, Kisho, Nagakin Tower, 211

Larsen, Theodore, 255
Laugier, Marc-Antoine, 19
La Villette. *See* Parc de La Villette
Layered construction, ix, x, 21, 323, 331, 335, 428
Le Corbusier, 16, 22, 55, 57, 69, 101, 127, 165–
    207, 209–215, 269, 405, 419, 426–427. *See
    also* Chandigarh; Maekawa, Kunio; Maisons
    Loucheur; Ronchamp, Notre-Dame-du-Haut;
    Unité d'Habitation, Marseilles
  and Aalto, 117, 123
  aérateur, 181, 197, 199, 201, 211–212
  Aircraft, 9, 169, 177, 179
  and aircraft, 9, 11, 165–167, 169, 171, 177, 179,
    207, 211, 389
  and *L'Architecture Vivante*, 169, 171
  L'Art décoratif d'aujourd'hui, 166
  articulation of elements, 423
  and Asplund, 57, 59, 61, 63, 65, 79
  and automobiles, 13, 15, 167, 207
  on Brooklyn Bridge, 6
  Carpenter Center for the Visual Arts, 199
  and Catalan vaults, 177
  Centre Le Corbusier, 183, 197, 203, 207, 215
  curtain walls, 97
  and Dalí, 177
  and dry construction, 271
  Écoles Volantes, 207
  and economy of material, 211
  Errazuris house, 171
  L'Esprit Nouveau, 165, 167, 427
  Five Architects and, 359, 361
  free plan, 65, 321
  and Freyssinet, 175
  and Gaudí, 177
  and Gothic construction, 3
  Immeuble Clarté, 171, 183
  and industrialization, 81, 166–167, 169, 171,
    173, 183, 203, 207, 211, 265
  and Junkers, 167, 181, 183, 195
  La Celle-St.-Cloud, weekend house, 171, 175,
    177, 201, 203
  Lagny housing, 207, 209
  La Tourette, monastery, 201, 211, 212
  League of Nations project, 173, 357
  Liège pavilion, 179, 181, 203
  Maisons Jaoul, 201, 203, 215
  Ma Maison, 175
  Millowners' Building, 203, 323
  Monol houses, 175, 177
  and nature of materials, 23, 423
  object types, 20, 166, 183
  Oeuvre complète, 183
  Palace of the Soviets competition, 179, 221
  Pavillon des Temps Nouveaux, 179, 181, 189
  Pavillon Suisse à la Cité Universitaire, 59, 183
  and Perret, 2, 169, 175
  Philips Pavilion, 179
  Précisions, 20
  and primitive tent, 167, 169, 179
  and Prouvé, 183, 187, 207, 209, 211
  Roq and Rob housing, 181, 197, 203
  and Eero Saarinen, 283, 299
  stadium for 100,000 persons, 179
  and standardization, 13, 15, 87, 89, 121, 123,
    167, 173
  on structural expression, 166–167
  and Surrealism, 169
  Une maison—un palais, 171, 173
  Unités d'Habitation, 187, 189 (*see also* Unité
    d'Habitation, Marseilles)
  and vaults, 201, 203, 283
  and vernacular architecture, 20, 103, 169
  Vers une architecture, 9, 13, 166–167, 175, 177,
    179, 183, 197
  Villa at Carthage, 173
  Villa at Mathes, 171, 175
  Villa Cook, 166, 203
  Villa de Mandrot, 171, 173, 175

Villa Sarabhai, 177, 203
Villa Savoye, 169, 173
Villa Stein (Garches), 357, 173
and Viollet-le-Duc's *Dictionnaire raisonné*, 2
and Wanner, 171
Léger, Fernand, 165
and Aalto, 139, 151
Le Ricolais, Robert, 309
Lethaby, William, 9
Lévi-Strauss, Claude, 19
Lewerentz, Sigurd, 305, 335–345. *See also* St.
Mark, Björkhagen; St. Peter, Klippan
and articulation of elements, 423
and Asplund, 335
Chapel of St. Knut at Malmö, 73, 85, 335
Idesta, 335
and Kahn, 335, 337, 341
Woodland Crematorium, 51, 71, 335
Lindbergh, Anne Morrow, 23
Lindgren, Armas. *See* Gesellius, Lindgren, and
Saarinen
Lloyd's of London building, 381, 385, 387–391,
395, 423
cost, 389
curtain wall, 385, 391
prefabrication, 385
structure, 385
utilities, 385, 389
Loi Loucheur. *See* Maisons Loucheur
Loos, Adolf, 21, 99
Loud, Patricia, 333
Louisiana Museum. *See* Bo, Jørgen
Lustron house, 255, 257
Lutyens, Edwin, 349, 353, 357

Mackintosh, Charles Rennie, 6
Maekawa, Kunio, and Le Corbusier, National Museum of Western Art, 199, 209
Maison de Verre, x–xi, 121, 241
Maisons Loucheur, 169, 171, 173, 207, 209
structure, 169
wall details, 169
Malevich, Kazimir, 16–17, 429
and weightlessness, 16
Marseilles. *See* Unité d'Habitation, Marseilles
Mayakovsky, Vladimir, 429
"Brooklyn Bridge," 6–7, 429, 430
"My Discovery of America," 429
McCoy, Esther, 229
McKim, Mead and White, 177
Meier, Richard, 357
Mendelsohn, Erich, 87, 91
Meudon houses, 209
type 1, 209, 381, 383
type 2 ("coque"), 209, 381
Meyers, Marshall, 309, 333
Mies van der Rohe, Ludwig, 113, 127, 209, 223,
261, 365, 385, 395, 424
and the Bauhaus, 89
curtain walls, 97
Farnsworth house, 237, 239
IIT campus and buildings, 309
and Neutra, 105
reasons for not including, xi
and Eero Saarinen, 267, 269, 283, 297, 299
Seagram Building, 361
on standardization, 15
Toronto Dominion Center, 297, 299
and vaults, 283
and vernacular building, 20
Milles, Carl, 45
Milton, John, 117
Minimum material. *See* Economy of material
MIT chapel, 283, 285–287
structure, 287
wall details, 285, 287
Model T, 11, 13, 15, 21, 183, 217, 225
Modern painting and material, 15–19
Moholy-Nagy, László, 17, 55, 429

and Aalto, 117, 119, 121, 123, 125, 127, 129,
131, 133, 143
and the Bauhaus, 17, 19
and light, 17, 19
Light-Space Modulator, 19, 129, 133
and materials, 17, 19
and Neutra, 87, 89
Von Material zu Architektur, 19
Mondrian, Piet, 231
Monocoque construction, 177
Monolithic and layered construction, ix, x, 21,
323, 331, 335, 428
Moore house, 109–113
light and reflection, 109
structure, 109
wall and window details, 91, 109, 111, 113
water in, 109
Mopin system, 187, 189
Morphosis, 407, 411–415
Crawford house, 411, 413, 415
Seldak house, 411
Morris, A. E. J., 187
Morris, Bill, 265
Morris, William, 319
on Amiens, 3
on Gothic construction, 7
and vernacular building, 20
Mosquito, de Havilland, 177, 221, 235, 237, 389,
423, 427
Murcutt, Glenn, 417
Magney house, 417, 419
Murphy, Richard, 371

National Romanticism, 23, 119
Nature of materials, 5, 423. *See also under individual architects*
Nervi, Pierluigi, 291
Neutra, Richard, 87–113, 157, 225, 259, 273, 387.
See also Beard house; Kaufmann house;
Moore house; V.D.L. house; Von Sternberg
house
and the Bauhaus, 89
Brown house, 101
Case Study House program, 101
California Military Academy, 99
Diatom house, 101, 103
and Fuller, 101
GE Plywood house, 93, 101
and industrialization and prefabrication, 87, 89,
93, 101, 113, 265
and light, 87, 91, 97, 109
and Loos, 21
Lovell house, 89, 91, 93, 101, 113
McIntosh house, 101
Miller house, 91
Nesbitt house, 101
and radiant heating, 97
and reflective surfaces, 87, 99
and Schindler, 87, 113
standardized detailing, 89, 109
Strathmore Apartments, 91, 225
and vernacular architecture, 101
and Wright, 103, 105
New Brutalism, x, 305, 341, 343, 381
Nordic Classicism, 51, 119
Notre-Dame de Paris, 2, 428
Nouvel, Jean, 395
Institut du Monde Arabe, 395, 397
Nowicki, Matthew, Raleigh Livestock Pavilion,
285

Ödeen, Stig, 57
Ono, Taiichi, 425–426
Organic order, and Eliel Saarinen, 39, 41
Orvieto cathedral, 373
Östberg, Ragnar, Stockholm City Hall, 137
Otaniemi Institute of Technology, 137, 143, 145,
147
auditorium, 143, 145, 154, 157
stone, 143, 147
structure, 143

Ozenfant, Amédée, 427, 428

Paestum, Temple of Neptune, 63, 75
Paimio Sanitorium, 120–121, 123, 127
   structure, 121, 123
Palladio, Andrea, 367
Palmer, Vincent, 93
Palmer system, 93, 97, 99, 113. *See also* Neutra,
   Richard
Parc de La Villette, 399, 422
   and Deconstructivism, 399
   folies, 401, 403, 405
   galleries, 401
PA Technology (PAT) Center, 381, 389, 395, 397,
   399
   structure, 381, 389
Pawley, Martin, 166
Pei, I. M., 223, 225
Pellecchia, Anthony, 333
Perret, Auguste, 1–3, 119, 169, 175, 283
   Casablanca warehouses, 175
   and École des Beaux-Arts, 1
   and Gothic construction, 3
   and Guadet, 2
   and Le Corbusier, 169, 175
   and vaults, 283
   and Viollet-le-Duc, 1, 2
Philips Exeter Academy library, 321, 323, 325–
   329, 331, 333
   structure, 321, 327
   ventilation, 327
   wall and window details, 323, 325, 327, 329
Piano, Renzo, 379, 381, 424, 427, 428. *See also*
   Rogers, Richard
   and High Tech, 395
   IRCAM, 397, 399
   and layered construction, 397
Piazza San Marco, 27, 39, 267, 373
Poelzig, Hans, 33
Pompidou Center, 397. *See also* IRCAM; Rogers,
   Richard
Postmodernism, 343, 349, 361, 419, 428
   and construction, 349, 361, 365, 373, 375
Prouvé, Jean, 183, 187, 207, 209, 211. *See also*
   Meudon houses
   articulation of elements, 423
   CIMT building, 383
   Clichy, curtain wall, 211
   curtain walls, 209, 211, 383
   and economy of material, 209
   and Le Corbusier, 183, 187, 207, 209, 211
   and Pompidou Center, 379
   UNESCO, 385
   and Unité d'Habitation, Marseilles, 183, 207
   University of Nancy dormitories, 211
   Villejuif schools, 209, 383

Quantrill, Malcolm, 137
Queen Anne Revival, 39
Quonset hut, 249, 251

Rain screen principle, 363, 367, 397
Rapson, Ralph, 219, 257
Reverdy, Pierre, 157
Rice, Peter, 399, 401, 403, 422
   on tolerance, 381
Richards, J. M., 285
Richards Medical Research Building, 311–315,
   317, 329
   criticism of, 315
   framing, 313
   structure and utilities, 315
   window and wall details, 315
Rietveld, Gerrit, Schröder-Schräder house, 241
Rigid frame, 25
River Rouge Plant (Ford Motor Company), 13,
   217, 421
Roebling, John and Washington, Brooklyn Bridge,
   5, 6
Rogers, Richard, 379, 389, 395, 417. *See also*
   Lloyd's of London building

frame and skin construction, 423
   manifesto (1969), 379
   Pompidou Center (with Piano), 379, 381, 385,
   387, 395, 399
Rohrbach, Adolph, 177
Ronchamp, Notre-Dame-du-Haut, 179, 189–195,
   201, 203, 207
   preliminary design, 189, 191
   structure, 189, 191, 193
   wall details, 193
   window and door details, 193, 195
Rowe, Colin, 349, 357, 371
   "The Mathematics of the Ideal Villa," 349
   "Transparency: Literal and Phenomenal" (with
   Slutzky), 19, 349, 357
Rudi, A. *See* Scarpa, Carlo
Rudolph, Paul, 235, 237
   Hook house, 235
   Sanderling Beach Club, 235
Ruskin, John, 217, 255, 291, 335
   and vernacular building, 20
Russian Constructivism, 16, 53, 167
   propaganda kiosks, 53

Saarinen, Eero, 217, 219–225, 229, 257, 259, 261,
   265–304, 429. *See also* Deere, John, Headquarters; Dulles Airport; General Motors
   Technical Center; Ingalls Hockey Rink;
   Kresge Auditorium; MIT chapel; Saarinen,
   Swanson and Saarinen; TWA Terminal
   and Aalto, 133, 137
   articulation of elements, 423
   and Case Study House program, 225, 229
   Community Center for US Gypsum, 265, 267,
   271, 285
   and Eames, 219, 221, 225, 229
   frame and skin construction, 423
   Goethe festival tent, 285
   and industrialization, 47
   Irwin Union Bank and Trust, 41, 283
   Jefferson National Expansion Memorial, 279,
   283
   and Louis Kahn, 279, 285, 299, 305, 307, 309,
   311, 335
   and Le Corbusier, 283, 299
   London Embassy, 299
   and material minimalism, 299, 422
   and Mies van der Rohe, 267, 269, 283, 297, 299
   Oslo Embassy, 299
   on Richards Medical Research Building, 305
   on structural expression and sculptural manipulation of structure, 279, 289, 291, 293
   Tanglewood Opera house, 221, 223, 225, 273
   and tensile structures, 221, 271, 273, 289
   and thin-shelled vaults, 283
   unfolding house (PAC), 223, 225, 265, 267, 299
Saarinen, Eliel, x, 22–49, 219, 265, 279. *See also*
   Cranbrook Art Academy; Cranbrook Museum and Library; Cranbrook School; Gesellius, Lindgren, and Saarinen; Kingswood
   School; Saarinen, Swanson and Saarinen;
   Willow Run Town Plan
   and Arts and Crafts movement, 25, 27, 29, 33,
   43
   Centerline Housing, 225
   The City, 39
   on cladding, 23
   and correlation, 37, 41
   and falsehoods, 27, 45
   Helsinki Station, 23–25, 27
   and industrialization, 27, 47
   on material, 25
   and motifs, 29, 33, 43
   and organic order, 39, 41
   and Piazza San Marco, 27, 39, 267
   and structural expression, 29, 33, 39, 41, 45
   Venturi on, 351
   and Wright, 33, 39, 41, 43
Saarinen and Saarinen. *See* Saarinen, Eero
Saarinen, Swanson and Saarinen, 47, 133, 219

Safdie, Moshe, Habitat, 211
St. John Wilson, Colin, 335
St. Mark, Björkhagen, 335, 337, 339
    structure, 337
    wall details, 337
    windows, 337, 339
St. Peter, Klippan, 71, 335, 337, 343, 344
    structure, 337, 343, 344
    windows, 337, 341, 344
Salk, Jonas, 317
Salk Institute for Biological Studies, 311, 316–
        321, 329, 331
    concrete details, 319
    conference center, 319
    cost, 319
    stone details, 319
    windows, 319, 321, 327
Salon d'Automne, 165
Salon L'Aéronautique, 165
Sansovino, Jacopo, 367, 373
Säynätsalo Town Hall, 137, 139, 143, 146–153
    roof details, 143
    structure, 139, 149
    wall details, 139, 147
    window details, 139, 143, 151, 153
Scandinavia, detailing in, 125
    heat loss in, 63
Scarpa, Carlo, 349, 365, 367–375, 397, 411, 427
    Banca Popolare di Verona, 377
    Brion Cemetery, 367, 371, 373, 375
    Castelvecchio, 371
    as detailer, 365, 373
    5.5 cm module, 373, 375
    Gavina Showroom, 367, 371
    and layered construction, 367, 369
    and motifs, 367, 369
    Olivetti Showroom, 369, 371
    Querini-Stampalia foundation, 371, 373
    stone details, 369
    and Venetian construction, 367
    Venezuelan Pavilion for the Biennale, 369
    and Vienna, 367
    and Wright, 367
Schindler, Rudolph, 87, 99, 113
    and Neutra, 87, 113
    Translucent house, 87
Schütte-Lanz airship, 257
Schuyler, Montgomery, 5–6, 429
Scott Brown, Denise, 349–355, 357. See also Ven-
        turi, Scott Brown and Associates
Scully, Vincent, 289, 299, 305, 317
Semper, Gottfried, 19
Ship construction, 7–9
Shulman, Julius, 103, 241
Shute, Nevil, 257
Skidmore, Owings and Merrill, 219
Sloan, Alfred P., Jr., 265. See also General Motors
        Corporation
    on standardization, 13–15, 424
Slutzky, Robert, 349. See also Rowe, Colin
Sorensen, Charles, 11, 217, 421
Soriano, Raphael, 225, 237, 239, 257
Soufflot, J. G., Panthéon, 5, 427
Spengler, Oswald, 55
Spirit of St. Louis (Billy Wilder), 237
Stability and the automobile, 11
Stam, Mart, Van Nelle factory, 121
Standardization and types, 11, 13–15, 22, 61, 87,
        89, 119, 121, 123, 145, 147, 149, 167, 173,
        335, 424–426. See also Industrialization
    decline of, 425
Steel residential construction, 239, 426
Stegner, Wallace, 105
Stirling, James. See also Stirling and Gowan; Stir-
        ling and Wilford
    and Louis Kahn, 341
    on Maisons Jaoul, 203
    on Ronchamp, 195
Stirling and Gowan, Engineering Laboratory, Uni-
        versity of Leicester, 341

Stirling and Wilford
    Cambridge University History Faculty Build-
        ing, 341, 347
    Staatsgalerie, Stuttgart, 363, 365, 367
Stockholm Exhibition (1930), 54–57, 63
    bandstand, 55, 57
    Entry Pavilion, 55
    Transport Pavilion, 53, 55
Stone, Edward Durell, 261
Stone detailing, 363. See also under individual
        architects
    in Scandinavia, 59
Stonorov, Oscar, 219, 223
Street, G. E., 367
Stressed skin, 177
Surrealism, 127, 157
Suspension bridge, 5–9
Swanson, Robert, 27, 29, 221. See also Saarinen,
        Swanson and Saarinen

Tange, Kenzo, 199, 201
    Kagawa Prefecture Building, 199, 293
    Kurashiki City Hall, 201, 207
    National Olympic Gymnasium, 289, 291, 293
    Totsuka Golf Club, 199
Tatlin, Vladimir, 16
Team 4, 379
Temko, Alan, 267
Transparency, 21, 423
Tschumi, Bernard, 397, 403. See also Parc de La
        Villette
TVA house, 223
TWA Terminal, 291–295
    curtain wall, 291, 295
    structure, 291, 293

United Auto Workers, 13, 219, 223
Unité d'Habitation, Marseilles, 183–189, 199,
        201, 207, 211
    concrete details, 183, 187
    framing, 185, 187, 189
    steel version, 183
    wall details, 185, 189
U.S. Gypsum Company, 221
Utzon, Jørn, 113

Van der Leeuw, C. H. See V.D.L. house
V.D.L. house, 91, 93, 97, 99, 101, 113
    structure, 89, 91
    wall types, 89
    windows, 89, 91
Venturi, Robert, 349–355, 357, 371, 375. See also
        Venturi, Scott Brown and Associates
    Complexity and Contradiction in Architecture,
        351, 353
    and GM Technical Center, 351
    and Louis Kahn, 351
    and Eero Saarinen, 351
Venturi, Vanna, house, 351–352
    structure, 351
    trim, 353
    wall details, 353
Venturi, Scott Brown and Associates, 349–355,
        357, 359, 365. See also Wu, Gordon, Hall
    and layered space, 351, 353
    Learning from Las Vegas, 353
Vernacular building, 19–21, 103, 127, 133, 149,
        157, 417, 426–427
Vernacular objects, 22
Vesnin, Aleksandr, Pravda Tower, 53
Viipuri Library, 122–125
    light and heat, 123
    structure, 123, 125
    ventilation, 123
    wall and window details, 123, 125, 127
Villa Mairea, 129–145, 369
    column details, 131, 137, 139, 143
    integration of ventilation, 131, 133
    stair details, 133, 141, 143, 147
    structure, 131, 133, 135, 137

wall details, 129, 131, 133, 137
window details, 133, 145
Viollet-le-Duc, Eugène-Emmanuel, 3, 167, 189,
    245, 337, 389, 419, 422–423, 427–428
  Dictionnaire raisonné, 432
  Entretiens sur l'architecture, 1, 3, 5
  on Gothic construction, 5
  on iron, 5
  Wright and, 1
Voisin biplane, 16, 165
Von Sternberg, Josef, 99. *See also* Von Sternberg
    house
Von Sternberg house, 97–101, 113
  bathroom, 99, 101
  light details, 99, 101
  Palmer system design, 97
  walls and windows, 99
  wood design, 97
Vultee house, 255

Wachsmann, Konrad, 223
Wagner, Otto, 359, 365, 375
Wallis, Barnes, 257
  and geodetic construction, 257
  R–100 airship, 19, 257
  Wellesley bomber, 257, 259
  Wellington bomber, 257, 259, 389, 423
Wanner, Edmond, 171
Wickersham, Jay, 323
Wilford, Michael. *See* Stirling and Wilford
Williams, Stephanie, 387
Willow Run Bomber Plant, 47, 217, 219, 221, 265,
    421
Willow Run Town Plan, 305
Winter, John, 203
Wöhler Brothers building system, 171
Wohlert, Vilhelm. *See* Bo, Jørgen
Woodland Crematorium, 51–53, 57, 71–81, 83,
    335
  chapels of Faith and Hope, 71, 75, 81
  Classical elements in, 71
  columns, 71, 73, 81
  door and window details, 75, 77, 79, 83
  Holy Cross Chapel, 71, 75, 83
  portico, 47, 71
  stone details, 73, 77, 79, 83
  structure, 71, 75
  vestibule, 79
  Woodland Chapel, 51–53
Wood residential construction, 239, 426
Wrede, Stuart, 55
Wright, Frank Lloyd, 1, 3, 99, 424
  and Aalto, 137
  and Breuer, 157
  Fallingwater, 105
  and Gothic construction, 1, 3
  Guggenheim Museum, 291, 367
  Imperial Hotel, 91
  and Louis Kahn, 311, 323
  on Mies van der Rohe, 424
  and Neutra, 103, 105
  Ready-cut Homes, 91
  Robie house, 103
  and Eliel Saarinen, 33, 39, 41, 43
  on standardization, 15
  Usonian houses, 105
Wu, Gordon, Hall, 352–355, 357, 359, 422
  framing, 355
  in relation to Princeton campus, 355
  wall details, 353, 357
  window details, 355, 357

Yale Center for British Art, 333–335
  structure, 333
  ventilation, 333
  wall and window details, 333, 335

Zephrus, Bernard, 385
Zevi, Bruno, 285
Zonnestraal. *See* Duiker, Johannes